ABOUT THE AUTHOR

J. Gordon Melton is the director of the Institute for the Study of American Religion and a research specialist with the Department of Religious Studies at the University of California—Santa Barbara. He is a graduate of Garrett-Evangelical Theological Seminary and an ordained United Methodist minister. Over a long career, he has spent his waking hours traveling the world observing, ruminating upon, and writing about the broad spectrum of religions and the people who adhere to them. He has discovered that religion is not limited to people's beliefs, feelings, and solitary experiences, but that it also encompasses what people do, see, and create. These two aspects of religion mingle intimately in the phenomena described in this text.

Melton has authored more than 25 books on religious topics, including several encyclopedic works such as the *Encyclopedia of American Religions* and, most recently, the *Encyclopedia of Protestantism*. His scholarly texts include *A Will to Choose: The Origins of African American Methodism* and *American Religion: An Illustrated History*.

THE ENCYCLOPEDIA OF

RELIGIOUS
PHENOMENA

THE ENCYCLOPEDIA OF

RELIGIOUS PHENOMENA

J. Gordon Melton

VISIBLE
INK
PRESS

Detroit

The Encyclopedia of
Religious
Phenomena

Visible Ink Press®
43311 Joy Rd., #414
Canton, MI 48187-2075

Visible Ink Press is a registered trademark of Visible Ink Press LLC.

Most Visible Ink Press books are available at special quantity discounts when purchased in bulk by corporations, organizations, or groups. Customized printings, special imprints, messages, and excerpts can be produced to meet your needs. For more information, contact Special Market Director, Visible Ink Press, www.visibleink.com or (734) 667-3211.

Art Director: Mary Claire Krzewinski

Typesetting: The Graphix Group

ISBN 978-1-57859-209-8

Cover image of Stonehenge courtesy of Getty Images; cover image of the Hill of Crosses courtesy of AFP/Getty Images; cover image of statue of Kuan Yin courtesy of Time Life Pictures/Getty Images. Back cover image reprinted by permission of Getty Images.

Library of Congress Cataloging-in-Publication Data

The encyclopedia of religious phenomena / [edited by] J. Gordon Melton.
    p. cm.
 Includes bibliographical references and index.
 ISBN 978-1-57859-209-8 (alk. paper)
 1. Religion—Dictionaries. 2. Religions—Dictionaries. I. Melton, J.
Gordon.
 BL31.E467 2007
 200.3—dc22

                                                                    2007024001

Printed in the United States of America

10 9 8 7 6 5 4 3 2 1

CONTENTS

Introduction xi
Index 367

Making the Invisible Visible:
An Introduction

J. Gordon Melton

Among the many topics religious scholars ask themselves is "What is religion?" The answers are numerous, but among the most popular in recent years has been one offered by philosopher Alfred North Whitehead: "Religion is what an individual does with his solitariness." This definition points toward the important personal, invisible, and mystical aspects of religiosity, as well as to contemporary interest in spirituality. *The Encyclopedia of Religious Phenomena* focuses on the other half of the religious life—the communal, visible, and material part. It is not concerned so much with the broad aspects of religion—church, worship, organization, political activism—but rather with the phenomena out of which organized religious life is constructed and that inspire people to explore their spirituality.

Spirituality often comes to the fore in times of solitariness, during which the believer reflects and meditates. Experiencing religious phenomena can provide an impetus to such reflection. It is the extraordinary event, encounter, or experience that excites the religious imagination and motivates the spirit. But few people are so lucky as to have encountered a remarkable religious phenomenon in their lives. Many, therefore, seek ways to participate in the experiences of others. For example, they will make a pilgrimage to a holy site or try to visit someone who has had a profound religious experience.

The Encyclopedia of Religious Phenomena is about the intense religious experiences that a small minority of people have claimed to have had, the phenomena associated with those experiences, and the efforts made by the great majority of us to relate ourselves to those phenomena. Many of the entries here reflect a paranormal or otherwise spiritual element, while others concern objects, people, or places that are simply extraordinary in nature, yet still inspirational.

In this modern age, many are surprised to hear reports of extraordinary religious events and that there are people who take them seriously. After all, we seem to have passed beyond the age of miracles to enter a time when God does not communicate with humans. Especially in the modern West, people go about their daily business and only rarely hear about the spiritual side of existence. When we do hear of such reports, we typically strive for alternative explanations that affirm our skepticism and prove that the apparently dramatic is merely another example of the mundane.

Such an approach to religious phenomena is consistent with the tenor of our times. What were once thought to be "miracles" no longer survive close scrutiny. Increasingly over the last few centuries, skeptics, armed with scientific methodology, have uncovered the secrets behind claims of the supernatural. In the sixteenth century, for example, many Protestants discounted numerous Roman Catholic claims concerning miraculous relics and the spiritual benefit of many of the church's programs. More recently, the use of science to debunk claims of religious phenomena came into its own with the rise of Spiritualism in the nineteenth century. The claims of some Spiritualists about their ability to speak with the deceased, or that the dead are moving objects at a séance, for instance, have often been revealed as tricks. In this way, skeptics have provided a great service to the religious community in outing frauds who try to take advantage of people's hopes about life after death.

While useful for catching charlatans, scientific investigation can also provide clarity to some extraordinary claims about supernatural phenomena. Yet in other instances—usually from lack of material with which to work—scientists have been unable to offer mundane explanations. The divine is, by its very nature, not accessible to science, science being limited to what people can directly observe and measure. While science can occasionally point out the fraud of a religious con artist, it runs into a dead end when dealing with people who claim to have met God, talked with Kwan Yin, or seen a vision of the afterlife. Such firsthand reports are difficult to prove or debunk. Nevertheless, science has its role in the world of religious phenomena, so throughout this text the questions scientists have asked are raised and commented upon.

Most of us are aware, however slightly, of the more popular claims of religious encounters and the phenomena that flow from them. One example would be the many claims by people who have said they have seen the Virgin Mary, who often gives them messages to convey to the faithful. On occasion, however, some claims of religious phenomena seem outside the bounds of acceptability even to believers. One example appeared in the news during the writing of this book. Diana Duyser, a resident of one of the Caribbean Islands, claimed to possess a grilled cheese sandwich that bore an image of the Virgin Mary. She quietly kept the sandwich in her home for a decade. Word got out only after she sold it to a casino for a large sum of money.

In one sense, the grilled cheese sandwich story challenges our understanding of what is religious, while at the same time it fits into a long history of people seeing images in unexpected places—a pane of glass, a rock formation, a tree leaf. The grilled cheese sandwich teaches us yet again that in the area of religion we can expect the unexpected.

The Encyclopedia of Religious Phenomena is not an exhaustive listing of all the religious phenomena in the world, but it does offer a comprehensive spectrum of the primary ways people have experienced the divine and then sought to make that experience accessible to the larger public. Religious phenomena are an excellent tool for grasping the immense diversity of human behavior. They challenge us to replace ridicule and skepticism with open-mindedness and understanding.

AL-AQSA MOSQUE (JERUSALEM)

The Al-Aqsa Mosque is the most holy site for Muslims in Jerusalem and one of the most holy of places for all Islam. Its origin relates to a famous supernatural event in Muhammad's life, the so-called Night Journey or Al-Isra wa Al-Miraj. One evening he was visited by the angel Gabriel (from whom he was receiving the Qur'an). He led Muhammad to a spirit horse (*buraq*), which carried him to JERUSALEM. Here he met, among others, Abraham, Moses, and Jesus. In their presence, he offered a prayer to Allah.

While in the city, he had three dishes placed in front of him that contained, respectively, water, wine, and milk. Muhammad refused the water, knowing that if he chose it the Muslims would drown, and he declined the wine as it would mean Islam would leave the true path. He instead chose the milk, indicating the Muslim community would follow Allah's true religion. Gabriel confirmed his choice. Muhammad next visited heaven, where he met and talked with Allah before returning to Mecca.

The meeting with the prophets, the prayer, and the drinking of milk are all believed to have occurred on Temple Mount in Jerusalem at the spot currently occupied by the Al-Aqsa Mosque. Muhammad's presence in this place is further confirmed by the hoof print his horse left in a rock as it lifted Muhammad to heaven. Additionally, some believe the rock attempted to go to heaven with Muhammad and was pushed back into place by Gabriel, who left a handprint in it.

Following the capture of Jerusalem by the Caliph Omar in 638 CE, attention was immediately focused on the Temple Mount. The first spot marked by a building was the rock from which Muhammad was believed to have been lifted to heaven. That same rock, in the center of what is known as the Dome of the Rock, is also believed to be the axis of the world, the spot from which creation began and at which the final trumpet, ending history as we know it, will sound.

The original building on the site where Muhammad offered prayer was completed by Omar soon after the Dome of the Rock was dedicated. It was then rebuilt in the eighth century by the Caliph El-Walid.

Muslim presence in Jerusalem grew slowly, and in the eleventh century the Muslim rulers decided to Islamize the city by pushing the Christians out. In the process, a number of Christian churches were destroyed. Christian crusaders took the

Located in Jerusalem, the Al-Aqsa Mosque sits on land that is associated with miracles involving both Muhammad and Abraham. It is therefore regarded as holy land to both Muslims and Jews. *AFP/Getty Images.*

city in 1099, and those Muslims who survived the attacks were sold into slavery. Muslims were largely denied access to the Temple Mount until 1187, when Saladin (1138–1193) retook the city. Jerusalem then remained in Muslim hands (except for a few years in the thirteenth century) until 1917, when the British took control.

The Temple Mount is now surrounded by a wall that predates Muslim presence in the city but essentially marks its most sacred area. This area of the city is off-limits to non-Muslims on Fridays and major Muslim holidays. The major conflict is with Jewish believers who believe the rock in the center of the Dome of the Rock is the place where Abraham bound Isaac and prepared to sacrifice him (Genesis 22). The major Christian sites are close by, but outside the wall.

Sources:

Cragg, Kenneth.*The Dome and the Rock, Jerusalem Studies in Islam.* London: SPCK, 1964.

Graber, Oleg. *The Shape of the Holy: Early Islamic Jerusalem.* Princeton, NJ: Princeton University Press, 1996.

Landay, Jerry M., and the Editors of the Newsweek Book Division. *The Dome of the Rock.* New York: Newsweek, 1976.

Peters, F. E. *Jerusalem and Mecca: The Typology of the Holy City in the Near East.* New York: New York University Press, 1986.

ALCHEMY

Alchemy is a religious philosophical perspective that was popular during the medieval era. The exoteric quest of the alchemist was the transmutation of baser metals (those that were more common and hence of lesser value) into the more valued metals, gold and silver. Philosophically, this quest was seen as a symbol of personal transformation in which the individual self, with its base nature, was turned into the ideal moral and spiritual person. Alchemy was always the belief of a small number of people, and it lost even this small following as alchemists proved completely unable to manifest the object of their quest and as a contemporary understanding of subatomic structures emerged with the evolving of modern chemistry and physics.

Alchemy remains a fascinating subject for academics. Philosophically, it was a significant carrier of the dissenting Esoteric tradition, the major perspective challenging orthodox Christianity in Western society through the several centuries of the Christian era. It represents an enlightenment approach to the spiritual life: a counterpoint to the salvation offered by Christianity. Such approaches provide various spiritual disciplines or exercises (meditation, controlled breathing, psychic development) that produce altered states of consciousness and lead to a new spiritual awareness and an enlightened state of being.

While many alchemists possibly used their talk of chemical experiments to legitimize their own religious views (in a time when dissenting religiously could lead to torture and death), undoubtedly, some alchemists believed that they could build various contraptions, usually a furnace, in which a literal transformation of elements could occur. It is also the case that some alchemists, many probably con artists, talked wealthy people and rulers into financing their alchemical activity.

Today, medieval alchemy is dismissed as pseudoscience, although the study of alchemical philosophy flourishes. In that context, interest has shifted to modern claims of alchemical success. Through the nineteenth century, alchemy survived as a semi-secret fringe activity within the occult community, itself very much a fringe community at the time. The most famous alchemist of the era, known only as Monsieur L., remained in the background, but he allowed the writer Louis Figuier (1819–1894) to speak for him.

Through the twentieth century, a few alchemists emerged, most notably Armand Baubault in Europe and Frater Albertus in the United States. However, they remained reclusive figures, and only a few people took their claims of alchemical success with any seriousness.

Given the almost complete disappearance of alchemy as a scientific possibility, one can still approach it as an important historical philosophy that has left behind a set of texts, symbolic art work, and many pieces of apparatus used by those alchemists who seem to have actually attempted the transformation of base metals. These relics of alchemy can be found in libraries and museums in Europe, and to a lesser extent in the United States.

Sources:

Albertus, Frater. *The Alchemist of the Rocky Mountains.* Salt Lake City, UT: Paracelsus Research Society, 1976.

Barbault, Armand. *Gold of a Thousand Mornings.* London: Neville Spearman, 1975.

Fernando, Diana. *Alchemy: An Illustrated A to Z.* New York: Sterling Publishing Co., 1998.

Pritchard, Alan. *Alchemy: A Bibliography of English-language Writings.* London: Routledge & Kegan Paul, 1980.

AMRITSAR (INDIA)

The city of Amritsar in Punjab, India, is the center of the Sikh religion. Throughout the fifteenth century, where now a large urban complex is situated, there was only a small lake to which Guru Nanak (1469–1539), the founder of the Sikh faith, was known to retire and meditate. Through the decades following Nanak's death, his followers visited the site, which subsequently emerged as the religion's most holy place. The name of the city and the lake means "pool of nectar."

Nanak was succeeded in leadership of the small but growing Sikh community by designated gurus. The third guru, Amar Das (1479–1574), began to recognize the sacredness attributed to the lake, and he entrusted his successor, Ram Das (1534–1581), with the construction of an appropriate place for worship. He saw to the enlargement of the lake and laid the foundation of the temple, which was completed by the fifth guru, Arjun Dev (1563–1606). The temple was finished in 1601, and three years later the Adi Granth, the collection of the writings of the gurus that constitute the Sikh scriptures, was formally placed inside the temple. The Har Mandir Temple of God, as it was called, became the center of the relatively small Sikh community and a target by its enemies. In the eighteenth century it was destroyed on several occasions, the last time in 1767, only to be rebuilt.

The temple is entered via a causeway over the pool of nectar. Pilgrims may walk completely around the temple and find entrance doors on every side. Inside the temple, the space is dominated by the platform holding the Adi Granth. A tank within the temple contains water from the spring that feeds the lake. Here pilgrims may symbolically wash their soul with the holy water. On the shore of the lake at the other end of the causeway is a second, smaller temple, the Akal Takht. Each day begins with a priest bringing the Adi Granth to the Har Mandir. It is placed on its platform, and readings from it may be heard throughout the day. At the close of the day, the Adi Granth is wrapped in ritual cloths and returned to the Akal Takht. Next to the complex of temple buildings are dormitories and dining halls where all persons, regardless of religion, race, or gender, may find free room and board. The Har Mandir received its common name, the Golden Temple, after the upper exterior of the temple was covered with gold in 1830.

The Golden Temple made world headlines in 1984 when it became the site of a battle between Punjabis seeking a separate, autonomous Sikh nation (for which some Sikhs had argued throughout the twentieth century) and Indian prime minister Indira Gandhi (1917–1984). As he carried out this struggle, Sikh leader Jarnail

Singh Bhindranwale (1947–1984) made the Golden Temple his headquarters, and Gandhi vowed to capture him even if it meant storming the temple complex. In the end, the Indian Army stormed the complex, largely destroying the Akal Takht and killing a number of people, including many innocent pilgrims who were trapped in the temple when the army had originally set up a siege. Bhindranwale was also killed in the process. In retaliation for the violation of the Golden Temple, two of Indira Gandhi's bodyguards were assassinated.

Guru Nanak had been opposed to the very idea of pilgrimages, and to this day, Sikhs have shown some reluctance to identify visits to Amritsar as making a pilgrimage. However, the emergence of the Golden Temple as a sacred center of the faith prompted some of the faithful to view their visits as pilgrimages. Within a short distance of Amritsar, other sites sacred to the Sikhs may be found, including the gurudwara (worship center) at Tarn Taran built in honor of Guru Arjun Dev, the gurudwara at Gobindwal built by Guru Amar Das, and the memorial to Guru Angad Devji at Hazoor Sahib.

Sources:

Dogra, Ramesh Chander, and Gobind Singh Manusukani. *Encyclopedia of Sikh Religion and Culture*. New Delhi: Vikas, 1995.

Duggard, K. S. *The Sikh People Yesterday and Today*. New Delhi: UBS Publishers' Distributors, 1993.

Macauliffe, Max Arthur. *The Sikh Religion*. 6 vols. New Delhi: S. Chand & Company, 1978.

AMULETS

The use of amulets, objects believed to have magical or supernatural powers that will protect the wearer from some evil, have been common among people in all religious traditions since ancient times. They have generally been distinguished from talismans, objects designed to accomplish goals desired by the object's possessor, although in practice, amulets and talismans are difficult to distinguish. Amulets come in all shapes and sizes, indicative of the many cultures from which they derive and the spectrum of uses for which they are employed. They are often used in conjunction with specific magical formulas, prayers, or devotional activity.

In the premodern world, amulets were often associated with the spirit entities that were seen as freely populating the world. They were seen as the home to spirits, and often as a protection from the actions of evil or mischievous spirits (demons). Amulets could thus protect someone from illness, injury, impotence, or various mental disorders deemed to be caused by demonic possession or obsession. Relative to the social order, amulets were seen as providing protection from the wrath of neighbors, arrest, unfavorable decisions in court, and downturns in business.

In the West, a magical strain remained after Christianity came into dominance, especially at the popular level, and sacred objects were frequently viewed as having talismanic value. In some European cultures, concern with the protection from the veil has been strong, and amulet-like objects designed to protect one from the evil eye remain popular. However, Protestants attacked many of the magical elements remaining in Roman Catholicism (including the assigning of amulet-like efficacy to sacred objects, such as the relics of saints). Later, during the Enlightenment, amulets were largely relegated to the dustbins as superstitious objects and driven out of mainstream use.

With the revival of magic in the nineteenth century, amulets, shorn of much of their pre-scientific association with spirits and demons, began to make a comeback, at least within the magical community (admittedly a very small community relative to the total population). However, in the decades since World War II, not only has the Western Esoteric community expanded greatly, but cultural and religious practices from a variety of cultures where amulets remained popular have been disseminated by immigrants and the forces of globalization. Amulets of all varieties have become available from practitioners of Western Esotericism (especially Neo-paganism and ceremonial magic), practitioners of various Eastern and Middle Eastern religions, and commercial establishments supportive of both.

Today, amulets are generally seen as objects that contain or focus cosmic magical power, rather than the abode of spirits or demons. At the same time, ancient amulets have become popular items worn simply as jewelry or decoration.

Sources:

Andrews, Carol. *Amulets of Ancient Egypt*. Austin: University of Texas Press, 1994.

Budge, E. A. Wallis. *Amulets and Superstitions*. Oxford: Oxford University Press, 1930.

Elliot, Gabrielle. *The Creations of Talismans, Amulets, and Good Luck Charms*. Macclesfield, Cheshire, UK: New Wiccan Publications, 2000.

Pavitt, William T., and Kate Pavitt. *The Book of Talismans, Amulets, and Zodiacal Gems*. Detroit: Tower Books, 1914.

Vinci, Leo. *Talismans, Amulets, and Charms: A Work on Talismanic Magic*. New York: Regency Press, 1977.

AN NAJAF (IRAQ)

The town of An Najaf in central Iraq is the site of one of the holiest shrines for Shi'a Muslims, who constitute the largest segment of the country's population. The town is closely associated with Ali ibn Abi Talib (c. 602–661), the son-in-law of Muhammad and the fourth Caliph to lead the emerging Muslim Empire after the death of Muhammad. Ali came to his position of power following the assassination of Uthman in 656. Ali was himself assassinated in 661.

Ali's brief rule brought to the fore a strong disagreement within the Muslim leadership. Some championed the family of Muhammad as the most legitimate rulers in Islam, while the majority supported the historic evolution of the caliphate under the most capable leadership available. Following Ali's assassination, those who continued to support the leadership of his family, primarily through his son Husayn, would emerge as a minority community within Islam, known as the Shi'a.

The Tigris and Euphrates rivers, mentioned in the biblical book of Genesis 2:14 relative to the Garden of Eden, flow through Iraq. Many believed Iraq to be the cradle of humanity and An Najaf the burial place of both Adam and Noah. Ali's actual burial site was unknown, but a century after his death, Shi'a leaders announced An Najaf as the burial place and erected a shrine over the designated spot. As the Shi'a community matured, An Najaf became one of its most enduring pilgrimage sites. It attained new status in the twentieth century when the Iranian Shi'a leader Ayatollah Khomeini took up residence and directed his efforts against the Shah from there (1965–1978). During the first Gulf War, An Najaf became a center of resistance to Saddam Hussein, president of Iraq from 1979 to 2003, and the Shi'a sites suffered when government forces crushed resistance leaders in the town after the war.

Celebrations and pilgrimages have picked up considerably in the years following Hussein's capture by U.S. forces.

Sources:

Jafri, S. Husain M. *The Origins and Early Development of Shi'a Islam*. Oxford, UK: Oxford University Press, 2002.

Nasr, Seyyed Hossein, Hamid Dabashi, and Seyyed Vali Reza Nasr, eds. *Shi'ism: Doctrines, Thought and Spirituality*. Albany, NY: SUNY Press, 1988.

Tripp, Charles. *History of Iraq*. Cambridge: Cambridge University Press, 2002.

ANGEL OF MONS

In September 1915, noted British writer Arthur Machen published an article in the *London Evening News* about the World War I Battle of Mons, which had occurred in August of the previous year. The battle was the first significant engagement of the war between the British and Germans, and it resulted in a British retreat from the field.

In his article, actually a reprint of a story that had appeared in a book of his short stories published in the spring, Machen focused on the account of a British officer who reported that as the army moved west, he had seen shimmering lights in the sky from which emerged winged figures carrying bows and arrows. Thanks to the distraction provided by these figures, the British were able to make a successful disengagement from the Germans. He noted that two others had also seen and made note of the mysterious angelic forces. Machen later received letters verifying the event. The believability of the story was increased due to the semi-miraculous nature of the retreat against large odds of success.

The problem with the story, as Machen clearly stated in the original publication, was its complete fiction. Published many months after the battle, Machen wanted to provide a momentary distraction from a war that was not going well. Instead, he found people who wanted to believe the story was true. Most notable in this endeavor was one Phyllis Campbell, a nurse with the Red Cross. She claimed she had treated French soldiers who saw a Joan of Arc figure in the sky. Journalist Harold Begbie picked up the story and wrote a pamphlet about Mons, *On the Side of the Angels*, in which he included testimony of an officer who described watching the angels for more than 45 minutes around eight o'clock one evening. The story grew over the years. As late as 1930, a retired German espionage officer offered an explanation for the angels: They were a misinterpretation of motion pictures projected on the clouds by the Germans. As late as 1963, historian A. J. P. Taylor referred to the angelic event as fact in his history of the war. He cited Mons as the only battle where "supernatural intervention was observed, more or less reliably, on the British side."

In fact, the story is complete fiction, the events first recounted by Machen being a figment of his imagination that inadvertently played to the deeper hopes of his readers at a time of crisis. There is no verifiable evidence that any phenomena occurred during the retreat from Mons to have suggested the story.

Some powerful tales in history involve angels intervening in human events. Such is the case with the Angel of Mons story in which spirits from heaven helped save British soldiers during World War I. *Fortean Picture Library.*

Sources:

Begbie, Harold. *On the Side of the Angels.* London: Imperial War Museum, 1915.

Machen, Arthur. *The Angel of Mons: The Bowmen and Other Legends.* New York: G. P. Putnam's Sons, 1915.

Stein, Gordon. *The Encyclopedia of Hoaxes.* Detroit: Gale Research, 1993.

Taylor, A. J. P. *The First World War: An Illustrated History.* London: Penguin, 1963.

ANNE, SAINT

Saint Anne, the mother of the Virgin Mary, has had a secondary but important position in Western Christian thought and practice, especially since the declaration of the dogma of the Immaculate Conception (the idea that Mary was born without original sin) by Pope Pius IX in 1854. Among the first recognitions of devotion to Saint Anne is found in the church built for her by the Byzantine Emperor Justinian (d. 565). Her feast day (July 25th) recalls the dedication of the church as well as the reputed arrival of her relics in Constantinople in 710. Veneration of Saint Anne in the West was concentrated in France, although some of her relics made their way to Austria.

Among the churches dedicated to Saint Anne is Sainte-Anne-d'Auray in Morbihan, France. This seventeenth-century church originated in a vision of the Virgin Mary in 1623 to Yves Nicolazic, who was told to rebuild a chapel dedicated to Saint Anne that had reputedly existed at Auray from the

The mother of the Virgin Mary, Saint Anne, is associated with a number of miracles, including healing miracles emanating from her image. *Fortean Picture Library.*

fifth to the seventh century. As land was being cleared for the building, an old statue of Saint Anne was discovered. The coincidence of the apparition and the discovery of the statue quickly attracted pilgrims, and as word reached the ears of more pious rulers, they offered support. Most notably, Anne of Austria and Louis XIII of France presented a relic of Saint Anne to the new chapel.

The chapel at Auray suffered greatly during the French Revolution, when it was plundered and burned (although the statue survived). A new, large church adjacent to the chapel was constructed at the end of the 1860s. It is the site of an annual festival on July 25–26.

A second miraculous statue of Saint Anne was pulled from the sea by fishermen and now resides in the church of Sainte-Anne-de-la-Palue, also in Brittany. While carrying the statue to what would have been the nearest church, the men reached a spot where Saint Anne had requested the erection of a new church. The statue was said at this point to have become so heavy the men could not further move it.

French sailors took their veneration of Saint Anne to Quebec in the mid-seventeenth century. They built a chapel to her on the shore of the St. Lawrence River, where they had found safety in a storm. A healing miracle that occurred in 1658 while a second expanded chapel was being built set the church apart as a focus for divine healing. The church was rebuilt and expanded a number of times in the intervening years, and today the church of Sainte-Anne-de-Beaupré is part of a large complex of Catholic facilities that includes a hospital, monastery, and convent. It has become a favorite site among Native Americans and Canadians. In 1892, Pope Leo XIII sent a relic of Saint Anne to the shrine, and Pope John XXIII sent another in 1960.

Sources:

Cruz, Joan Carroll. *Relics*. Huntington, IN: Our Sunday Visitor, 1984.

Lefebvre, Eugene. *A Land of Miracles for Three Hundred Years*. Saint-Anne-de-Beaupré: Saint Anne's Bookshop, 1958.

Reames, Sherry, L. *Middle English Legends of Women Saints*. Kalamazoo, MI: Medieval Institute Publications, 2003.

APPARITIONS OF THE VIRGIN MARY

Apparitions of the Virgin Mary rank with healing miracles as one of the most reported religious phenomena. Since the appearance of Mary to Sister Catherine Labouré in a convent in Paris in 1830, the event from which the modern era of apparitions is usually dated, literally thousands of people have claimed to have seen (and/or received messages from) the Virgin Mary. These have occurred overwhelmingly in a Roman Catholic context, but occasional accounts by Protestants and Eastern Orthodox believers have also surfaced.

The most prominent apparitions, such as the ones at **LOURDES,** France, in 1854, and **FATIMA,** Portugal, in 1917, have received the approbation of the highest authorities in the Catholic Church and have become the subject of an international movement within the church to respond to and promote the approved apparitions. Contributing to the interest in apparitions have been claimed appearances that have attracted much attention but have yet to be approved (although they have not been disapproved officially). Such apparitions would include those at **MEDJUGORJE,** Bosnia-Herzegovina. The great majority of apparitions receive only local approval, if that. Some apparitions, especially a few of a spectacular nature that produce an immediate mass response among faithful Catholics, have been investigated and found to be wanting. In these cases, such as those that occurred for many years at Necedah, Wisconsin; Garabandal, Spain; and Bayside, New York (see **OUR LADY OF THE ROSES, MARY HELP OF MOTHERS**), have been officially disapproved. Both the Necedah and Bayside apparitions have become the focus of small schismatic movements.

A number of apparitions of the Virgin Mary attained significance by initiating new forms of Catholic piety, such as the **ROSARY,** or by becom-

At the grotto of Massabielle in Lourdes, France, an audience gathers to see whether Marie-Bernarde Soubirous will see a vision of the Virgin Mary. *Getty Images.*

ing the source of national cults of the Virgin. (See, for example, entries on **NUESTRA SEÑORA DE LA PRESENTACIÓN,** Virgen de la Purísima Concepción, **VIRGIN OF LAS LAJAS,** and Virgin of Urkupiña.) However, a new era of apparitions began in 1830 in Paris, this time against a backdrop of European skepticism that had begun undermining the role of the church in public life and would lead to the separation of the church from an official place in government hierarchies. The most dramatic changes would come in Italy, where the pope would be shorn of the territory over which he ruled as Italy became a modern secular state.

The apparitions of the Virgin throughout the nineteenth and twentieth centuries have been the foundation upon which a whole new emphasis on the role of the Virgin has been defined in the church. Mary became the subject of two proclamations that swelled the content of Catholic dogma (teachings necessary for the faithful to believe): In 1854 the doctrine of the Immaculate Conception (that Mary, like Jesus, was born without original sin) and in 1950 the doctrine of the Assumption of the Virgin (that Mary did not die but was taken directly into heaven at the end of her earthly existence) were proclaimed dogmas. In between these two events, the pope was declared to speak infallibly when acting as Pope Pius XII did in 1950 when he defined the new dogma. It has been noted that in recent years, popes often assert their power within the church through statements on the Virgin Mary.

Since the apparitions to Catherine Labouré in 1830, the main apparitions to which the worldwide Marian movement gives attention are:

La Salette, France (1846)
Lourdes, France (1858)
Pontmain, France (1870)
Knock, Ireland (1879)
Fatima, Portugal (1917)
Beauraing, Belgium (1932–1933)
Banneau, Belgium (1933)
Akita, Japan (1973)
Betania, Venezuela (1986)
San Nicolas, Argentina (1983–1990)

To these must be added the apparition at Guadalupe, Mexico. Although it occurred in the sixteenth century, only recently has significant attention been paid to this apparition and the miraculous picture of the Virgin that appeared as part of the occurrence. One unique case was a dramatic apparition in suburban Cairo, Egypt, in which thousands saw the Virgin walking on the roof of the Coptic Orthodox Cathedral. After many years, Roman Catholic authorities have given some approval to this incident. Other important apparitions that have attracted wide attention but have yet to receive more than local approval include:

Marienfried, Germany (1940)
Cuapa, Nicaragua (1980)
Kibèho, Rwanda (1981)
Achill, Ireland (1988)
Conyers, Georgia (1990–1998)

The approval of the Catholic Church of any particular apparition is a complicated process. After such an apparition occurs and people begin to respond to the occurrence and the messages received by those who see the Virgin, the local bishop may launch an investigation. In cases where there is no obvious fraud or teaching that is against orthodox faith, he may grant initial approval, which carries with it an encouragement for the piety that has emerged around the apparition. He may then move forward and offer an opinion on the supernatural element of the apparition. At this second level, investigation must rule out as sources of the apparition some problem with the visionaries, fraud, natural phenomenon, or demonic activity. Once the local bishop has offered an opinion, the case may be moved to a higher authority, most often the national council of bishops for the country, to a curial office in Rome, or even to the desk of the pope. Recent popes have played a dramatic role in approving various Marian apparitions by their statements, visits to the sites, and, as in the case of Fatima, canonization of the visionaries.

Once the bishop or higher authorities have ruled, two possibilities arise. First, the church may issue a negative ruling relative to a particular apparition. In that case, the faithful are not to believe in it nor participate in activities at the site. To the contrary, a positive ruling does not demand acceptance of the apparition. However, in that case, believers are asked to refrain from berating the messages received and the apparition. In the great majority of cases, devotional activity around an apparition remains purely a local matter, and the bishop chooses not to make any ruling. Such is the status of approximately 300 of the nearly 400 apparitions that have been reported in the twentieth century.

Scholars attempting to make sense of the Marian apparitions have approached them at many levels, and some important work has been done by historians and social scientists who have noted corollaries between the apparitions and significant social events. Those investigating the different apparitions have been careful in searching out mundane causations and cautious to report on events about which significant elements of doubt remain. Skeptics have been much more reticent to denounce the apparitions, at least those that have received support after investigations by the church, partly due to an insufficient number of researchers necessary to conduct the time-consuming and complex independent investigations. Thus, in large part, one is left with the opinions expressed by church authorities on the authenticity of such phenomena.

Those who believe in the apparitions have tended to take the messages spoken by Mary quite seriously. In most cases these messages have encouraged various forms of Catholic piety and an increase in the amount of time devoted to them. However, running through the messages have been a variety of dire predictions of an apocalyptic nature, warning the faithful about a fast-approaching end of the world. Students of the apparitions have attempted to correlate the messages of the different events to derive some comprehensive understanding of what they feel is the message that the Divine is attempting to communicate to humankind at this particular moment.

Sources:

Breen, Stephen. *Recent Apparitions of the Blessed Virgin Mary.* New York: Scapular Press, 1952.

Durham, Michael S. *Miracles of Mary: Apparitions, Legends, and Miraculous Works of the Blessed Virgin Mary.* San Francisco, CA: Harper, 1995.

Heintz, Peter. *A Guide to Apparitions of Our Blessed Virgin Mary.* Sacramento: Gabriel Press, 1995.

"The Mary Page (University of Dayton)." Posted at http://www.udayton.edu/mary/marypage21.html. Accessed April 1, 2007.

Zimdars-Swartz, Sandra. *Encountering Mary: From La Salette to Medjugorje.* Princeton, NJ: Princeton University Press, 1991.

APPORTS

Apports are objects that suddenly appear (materialize) in Spiritualist séances whose origin is attributed to the action of spirits. In some cases they are attributed to the spirits having materialized an object *de novo* and other times to their transporting the object from a remote location. In the later case, the object may actually belong to one of the sitters at the séance.

Through the early twentieth century, the appearance of apports was a popular feature of Spiritualist séances, and considerable energy was expended on theoretical speculations on the conditions that would support the reality of such objects. The theorizing became more complicated when living objects, flowers being among the most common, began to appear.

In the early twentieth century, as scrutiny of mediums by psychical researchers became common, many tried to understand the phenomenon of apports, but increasingly, as fraud rose to the top as the most likely explanation, observers tightened the conditions under which mediums operated. Initially, apport frauds were discovered inadvertently, as was the case with Australian Charles Bailey, who at Grenoble, France, in 1910, produced two live birds during a séance. He was unaware that the dealer from whom he obtained the birds would be among those present at the séance. Through the twentieth century, a number of Bailey's fellow mediums were found to be operating fraudulently, and the appearances of apports declined markedly.

Objects, both living and inanimate, that are caused to appear during séances are called "apports." The lilies in this photograph, for example, were said to have originated in the spirit world. *Fortean Picture Library.*

Today it is assumed that the production of apports by mediums would break a variety of natural laws, and that none have demonstrated their manifestation under test conditions. The production of apports in a séance would thus be a direct evidence of trickery. Among the most recent exposés of mediumistic fraud relative to apports was made by former medium Lamar Keene in the 1970s. He discussed the manner in which he produced apports by stage magic, often taking small objects from the homes of prospective sitters, only to return the objects during a séance.

Sources:

Keene, Lamar. *Psychic Mafia.* New York: St. Martin's Press, 1976.

Price, Harry. "The Mechanics of Spiritualism." Posted at http://www.survivalafterdeath.org/articles/price/spiritualism.htm#apports. Accessed April 1, 2007.

ARK OF THE COVENANT

In the sixteenth chapter of the book of Exodus in the Hebrew Bible (the Christian Old Testament), God orders the Hebrews to create a chest to hold, among other things, the stone tablets upon which the Ten Commandments were written. The Ark, also called the Ark of the Testimony and the Ark of the Testament, was to measure 2.5 cubits by 1.5 cubits by 1.5 cubits. It was to be made of wood of the shittah tree, a variety of acacia, and covered with gold. It had four gold rings through which poles were placed for carrying it. A gold rim with a crownlike appearance went around its upper edge. The top of the Ark was called the Mercy Seat, and it was the place of manifestation of God to his people.

Also made for the Ark were two angelic beings (cherubim), also of gold, all the more interesting as they seemed to contradict God's admonitions against making graven images. These cherubim were to be placed on the top of the Mercy Seat. After its construction, Moses was said to have entered the tabernacle where he heard God speak to him from above the Mercy Seat and between the two cherubim (Numbers 7:89).

The finished pattern of the Ark had probably been suggested by some similar chests the Hebrews had seen in Egypt, examples of which can now be seen in museums. The whole of the Ark, complete with poles, Mercy Seat, and cherubim, was to be placed in the holiest part of the tabernacle, the building that originally served as the center of worship for the ancient Hebrews. No one entered the Holy of Holies except the high priest, once a year, as part of the rites of the Day of Atonement. After the building of Solomon's temple, the Ark of the Covenant (and possibly other sacred objects) was placed within it. Prior to the Hebrews' permanent settlement in Palestine, the Ark was carried before the people as they moved from place to place, especially during the years in the Sinai wilderness.

Over the years, the Ark was used as an ensign in times of battle, and its miraculous effects became legendary. Its most famous use came at the city of Jericho. As part of their conquest of the Holy Land, the Israelites besieged Jericho. As God had commanded Joshua, the Ark led a procession conducted on each of seven successive days. At the end of the seventh procession, the walls of the city crumbled as trumpets blasted and the people shouted. The Israelite army then was free to enter and take the city. (Joshua 6:6–21).

The Ark remained in the temple built by Solomon for many years. However, in 586, in the days of Jeremiah, as a Babylonian army under Nebuchadnezzar that was destined to loot the temple approached, the Ark was removed from the temple and hidden. It has not been seen since.

The sudden disappearance of the Ark made it an object of speculation over the centuries, and in the twentieth century, in the wake of the successes of archeology in uncovering so many ancient sites, the search for the Ark of the Covenant or at least further information on its fate has arisen. Those who engage in the search have to contend with a spectrum of theories, including some claims by individuals that they have actually discovered the Ark.

It is said that an army that carries the Ark of the Covenant is invincible. The location of the Ark, however, has remained a mystery since the Jews hid it from the Babylonian army. *Getty Images*.

One prominent claimant to know about the Ark is the Ethiopian Orthodox Church. The church claims that Menelik, the son of Solomon and the Queen of Sheba, was given the Ark by his father as a means of protecting it. Menelik brought the Ark to a place called Tana Kirkos in Ethiopia, where it stayed for a period before being moved to the Church of Saint Mary of Zion in Axum. It is now in the care of a single monk, the Atang or the Keeper of the Ark. The job of Atang is for life. That monk never leaves the church grounds, and he is the only person permitted to see the Ark (or whatever is hidden at the chapel). Among those who give credence to this claim is Graham Hancock, a writer of alternative histories, especially of the ancient world.

Meanwhile, archaeologist Leen Ritmeyer, who has conducted research in Jerusalem on the Temple Mount, claims to have found the location of the Holy of Holies in Solomon's temple. The site has a place in the bedrock of approximately the same dimensions as the Ark, according to the biblical account. Ritmeyer has speculated that the Ark may be deep inside the Temple Mount.

However, many do not accept these claims. They search in the caves along the Dead Sea (where the Dead Sea Scrolls were found) or on Mount Nebo, located on the east side of the River Jordan, a site mentioned in the book of Maccabees, one of the books in the Apocrypha, a set of books that are accepted as part of the Bible by

Roman Catholics but not by Jews or Protestants. Some Mormons have claimed that the Hebrews discussed in the Book of Mormon brought the Ark with them to the Americas.

In 1981 the search for the Ark reached a new plateau with the release of *Raiders of the Lost Ark,* a popular motion picture directed by Steven Spielberg and written by George Lucas and Philip Kaufman. The movie picked up on another theory: that the Ark had been taken to Egypt. It also played upon beliefs that the Ark has paranormal powers that, in the movie, destroy the nefarious Nazis who try to gain possession of the Ark.

While never as popular a quest as searching for Noah's Ark, the drive to discover the location of the Ark of the Covenant has been the subject of a variety of archeological excavations, some conducted by serious archeological teams (usually as part of a broader archeological program) and others by amateurs, often relic hunters. To date, no substantial evidence has been produced to accept one claim over the others, and until hard evidence is produced, the location of the Ark of the Covenant and even the fact of its existence remain pure speculation.

Sources:

Boren, Kerry Ross, and Lisa Lee Boren. *Following the Ark of the Covenant: The Story of the Most Sought-after Artifact in the World.* Springville, UT: CFI Distribution, 2000.

Grierson, Roderick, and Stuart Munro-Hay. *The Ark of the Covenant.* London: Weidenfeld & Nicolson, 1999.

Hancock, Graham. *The Sign and the Seal: The Quest for the Lost Ark of the Covenant.* New York: Crown, 1992.

Ritmeyer, Leen. "The Ark of the Covenant: Where It Stood in Solomon's Temple." *Biblical Archaeology Review* 22/1 (1996): 46–55, 70–73.

ARUNACHALA (INDIA)

Arunachala (Sanskrit) or Tiruvanamalai (Tamil) is a sacred mountain in southern India approximately 100 miles southwest of Madras. At its base is a large temple dedicated to the god Shiva, whose complex ranges over 25 acres. Believers consider the mountain itself to be the largest Shiva linga in the world (the god's male sexual organ being a major representation of him). The temple dates to the early years of the Common Era, and its massive towers were erected in stages from the tenth to the sixteenth centuries. At the beginning of winter each year, for a ten-day period during the Hindu month of Kartikai, Arunachala hosts the Deepam festival to celebrate Shiva's light. The festival climaxes with a huge bonfire that is lit on top of the mountain.

Through the year, pilgrims engage in a practice called *Arunachala giri valam* (circling Arunachala), considered to be a simple and effective form of yoga. The walking is done barefoot, as wearing shoes on the mountain is considered a sacrilege.

Arunachala became well known in the West during the last half of the twentieth century as the popular guru Sri Ramana Maharshi (1879–1950) received visitors at his home on the mountain. Maharshi's first Western disciple was Frank Humphreys, who wrote articles about him in the *International Psychic Gazette.* These attracted Western teacher Paul Brunton (1898–1981), who visited Arunachala in 1931. He later authored two widely circulated books, *A Search in Secret India* and *A Message from Arunachala,* about his encounters. These helped to make Maharshi and the mountain globally famous, and through the last half of the twentieth century, visiting the mountain was the goal of numerous Western spiritual seekers. Among the most famous seekers who found their way to Arunchala was Abhishiktananda (Henri Le Saux; 1910–1973), a Roman Catholic priest who emerged as a leading voice in Christian-Hindu dialogue in the mid-twentieth century.

Sources:

Abhishiktananda. *The Secret of Arunachala: A Christian Hermit on Shiva's Holy Mountain.* New Delhi: Indian Society for Promoting Christian Knowledge, 1997.

Brunton, Paul. *A Message from Arunachala*. London: Rider and Company, 1936.

———. *A Search in Secret India*. London: Rider and Company, 1934.

Skandananda. *Arunachala: Holy Hill*. Madras, India: Weldun Press, 1980.

AURA

The aura is an emanation that surrounds all living things, especially human beings, which many believers in the Western Esoteric tradition, including the modern New Age community, claim to see and to be able to document. Many psychics, for example, claim to be able to see this emanation, completely invisible to the average person, and derive information from it, especially relative to the health of the person. Contemporary advocates of the existence of auras relate them historically to the lights said to shine around biblical and other holy figures, often pictured in Western art as halos. The aura is often said to be part of the invisible anatomy of the individual, which includes, among other invisible elements, the CHAKRAS.

Of particular interest have been the various attempts throughout the twentieth century to scientifically document the existence of the aura and create instruments that will make it visible to everyone. Such efforts began in earnest with the work of Walter J. Kilner (1847–1920), a British physician who in 1911 published an account of his research in *The Human Atmosphere*. He created a dicynin screen consisting of a layer of coal-tar dye sealed between two pieces of glass. He suggested that the aura became visible after looking through the screen in bright daylight and then immediately turning to look at a person in a dimly lit room. This process made three layers of emanation. The first, a dark layer, surrounded the body for about a half an inch. The next two layers extended from the body for about three inches and a foot, respectively. He related these layers to the invisible body doubles described in Esoteric literature. Kilner's research

built upon some nineteenth-century speculations and led some colleagues to attempt to substantiate his conclusions.

Kilner's research was largely dismissed by later researchers on light and perception, and the results he reported were seen as artifacts of the observer's own optic process rather than reflective of any emanation being produced by the subject being observed. These findings did not prevent the marketing of Kilner goggles, advertisements for which appeared in Esoteric periodicals as late as the 1970s.

Interest in the aura was revived in the last decades of the twentieth century by the development of a new photographic technique, kirlian photography. Discovered in the 1950s by two Russian scientists, Valentina and Semyon Davidovich Kirlian, this form of photography claimed to produce photographs of an energy field around and emanating from living objects. Kirlian photographs were made by placing the object directly on a photographic plate and using a small amount of electricity rather than light to imprint the image. Kirlian pictures produced on color film proved to be both intriguing and beautiful, and for a few decades a spectrum of scientists sought to find meaning in the pictures.

Kirlian photography ultimately proved a dead end. The most intriguing pictures, reputedly the very distinct images of people produced while they claimed to be in various altered states of consciousness, were determined to be artifacts of a badly controlled process. When the pressure placed on the film was controlled, the earlier produced differences disappeared. By the end of the 1980s, interest in the process had also disappeared.

Belief in auras continues within the Esoteric community, and many psychics still claim to be able to see them. No controlled experiments that would offer support to the meaningfulness of the aura as seen by psychics exist. Among recent claims largely based upon auras as seen by psychics are those related to the existence of INDIGO CHILDREN, special children born in the last generation whose aura has a prominent indigo component.

Sources:

Bagnall, Oscar. *The Origin and Properties of the Human Aura*. 1937. Reprint, New Hyde Park, NY: University Books, 1970.

Kilner, Walter J. *The Human Atmosphere*. London, 1911. Reprinted as *The Human Aura*. New Hyde Park, NY: University Books, 1965.

Krippner, Stanley, and Daniel Rubin. *Galaxies of Life: The Human Aura in Acupuncture and Kirlian Photography*. London: Gordon & Beach, 1973.

AUROVILLE (INDIA)

Auroville, an intentional community inspired by the teachings of Hindu guru Sri Aurobindo (1872–1950), is located in Pondicherry, the former French settlement on the eastern coast of India, south of Chennai (formerly Madras). Auroville was designed as a town where men and women from all of the world's countries would be able "to live in peace and progressive harmony above all creeds, all politics and all nationalities." Thus, Auroville was an experiment in realizing human unity. What has set Auroville apart from the many utopian experiments through the centuries has been the architecture that was created to embody the idealistic goals.

Although the concept of Auroville can be traced to the 1930s, it was not until the mid-1960s that a concrete proposal was generated by the Sri Aurobindo Society in Pondicherry and proposed to Aurobindo's longtime companion Mira Richard, affectionately called the Mother (1878–1973). After she gave her blessings, the idea was passed to the government of India and then to the United Nations. In 1966 UNESCO termed Auroville a "project of importance to the future of humanity."

Auroville was inaugurated on February 28, 1968, when about 5,000 people from some 125 nations gathered at a banyan tree in the center of the future city. Each person brought some soil from his or her homeland, which was placed in an urn that now rests in the city's amphitheater.

Auroville was originally designed as a giant spiral. At the center was an area dedicated to peace that included the Matrimandir and its associated gardens, a lake, the urn with the soil of the nations, and an amphitheater. The Matrimandir is a hundred-foot-high elliptical sphere whose interior is a place for quiet concentration and meditation. It was meant to be surrounded by a network of twelve gardens and a lake.

To the north is the industrial area that includes land for environmentally friendly industries, room for arts and crafts, and the city's administration. To the south is the residential zone, to the east a cultural zone, and to the west an international zone. Activity in the latter space centered on work that demonstrates human unity. Around the whole city is the green belt, approximately a mile wide, a zone for organic farms, wildlife sanctuaries, and forests.

As originally conceived, Auroville was to be home to 50,000 people. Unfortunately, the financial resources to realize the full dream have not been available, and the project remains very much an idea still in the process of being realized. Today, some 1,700 people from about 35 nations reside at Auroville. Only a small percentage of the buildings and landscaping proposed for the city have been created.

Sources:

Alain, G. *Auroville: A Dream Takes Shape*. Pondicherry, India: Auroville Press, 1995.

Auroville: The City the Earth Needs. Pondicherry: Sri Aurobindo Society, 1973.

Heehs, Peter. *Sri Aurobidno: A Brief Biography*. Oxford: Oxford University Press, 1989.

Minor, Robert Neal. *The Religious, the Spiritual, and the Secular: Auroville and Secular India* (SUNY Series in Religious Studies). Albany: SUNY Press, 1998.

Navajata, Sri. *Sri Aurobindo*. New Delhi: National Book Trust, India, 2000.

AUTOMATIC WRITING

Automatic writing is a form of **MEDIUMSHIP** (spirit contact) in which an individual allows an outside force or entity to take control of the motor functions in his or her arm to write messages reputedly from either a spirit being or from the individual's own higher consciousness. Through the nineteenth and twentieth centuries, automatic writing played an important role in the development of Spiritualism, and it continued to be an element in the New Age movement during the 1970s and 1980s.

At the very beginning of the Spiritualist movement, Andrew Jackson Davis (1826–1910) channeled many of his books by this method, as did his contemporary Thomas Lake Harris (1823–1906). Among the first generation of British mediums, William Stanton Moses (1939–1892) produced books channeled from a host of spirit entities under the collective title of *Spirit Teachings*. By the end of the nineteenth century, the majority of published communications from the spirit world were produced by automatic writing, a situation that would only change as means of recording verbal channeling improved through the twentieth century.

Among the more interesting products of automatic writings were the *Glastonbury Scripts*, produced by Frederick Bligh Bond (1864–1945). In 1908, Bond was placed in charge of the archeological excavations that were about to be undertaken at the ruins of Glastonbury Abbey, a medieval center of Catholic Church life that had been destroyed by Henry VIII. Though a competent amateur archeologist, Bond began to work with a medium, John Allan Bartlett, who worked under the pseudonym Alleyne, to produce maps of the site which Bond used to direct excavations. As excavations began, Bond quickly found the main buildings of the old monastic complex, much to everyone's astonishment.

Given the number of mediums engaged in automatic writing, it is not surprising that psychical researchers initiated investigations of the phenomenon. As with much spirit communication, it was difficult to assign the material to any independent spirit activity. This problem was attacked through some experiments in what was known as cross-correspondences. In these cases, several mediums at vast geographical distances received messages that were meaningless themselves, but when put together made sense. A large set of material generated by some of the more famous of the late nineteenth- and early twentieth-century mediums was assembled, only a small portion of which has been thoroughly analyzed and the subject of scholarly papers. Much of this material is stored in the archives of the Society for Psychical Research in England.

While many continue to use automatic writing as a technique to make contact with the realms of spirit beings, many others, both those skeptical of all paranormal claims and those open to many of them, have come to believe that automatic writing is largely the result of individuals tapping their own unconscious mind and is subject to purely mundane interpretations.

Sources:

Douglas, Nik. *The Book of Matan: Automatic Writing from the Brink of Eternity*. Suffolk, UK: Neville Spearman, 1977.

Muhl, Anita M. *Automatic Writing: An Approach to the Unconscious*. New York: Helix Press, 1963.

Wright, Theon. *The Open Door: A Case History of Automatic Writing*. New York: John Day Company, 1970.

Zmuda, Joseph. *Automatic Writing: Occult … or a Way to the Unconscious Mind?* San Francisco: Z-Graphic Publications, 1981.

AVEBURY (ENGLAND)

Avebury, one of England's most spectacular megalithic sites, has been inhabited for more than four millennia, its oldest part dating to approximately 2600 BCE. It is also one of the largest of such sites, being some 2,500 feet in diameter.

Avebury centers on two stone circles, both around 340 feet in diameter. At one time in the center of the southernmost circle rested a single stone surrounded by a rectangle of smaller stones. There was a cove of unknown purpose in the center of the northern circle. Surrounding the two inner circles is a large circular embankment, immediately inside of which was a ditch. On the inner edge of the ditch was a circle of some 100 stones, some of which remain in place. The site was constructed in stages, from the center outward. Among the later additions was a double line of stones (referred to as West Kennet Avenue) that led from Avebury to another site about a mile to the south. Avebury is older than Stonehenge, and most of its stones show little sign of having been reshaped before being put in place.

Given technology at the time, the construction of Avebury took many years and consumed a considerable percentage of the local inhabitants' resources above what was required simply to survive. The inner circles had 46 stones between them, some rising as much as 20 feet in the air and weighing upwards of 40 tons.

Over the centuries of the Common Era, the site fell into disuse, especially with the spread of Christianity. Beginning in the fourteenth century, records indicate efforts to remove the stones and use the land within the embankment for farming. The large stones were pulled down and used for houses and other structures. Study of the site began in the early eighteenth century by Dr. William Stukeley, who made the first detailed measurements along with a set of drawings. Unfortunately, Stukeley was not in the position to prevent further destruction of the site.

Since World War II, both amateur and professional study of Avebury, now a protected archeological site, has flourished. Some have picked up Stukeley's observation that the wider ground plan of Avebury represented a serpent passing through a circle (an alchemical symbol). A number of researchers integrated the data on Avebury into the growing acknowledgment that many of the megalithic sites were involved with the observation of the heavens by the ancient residents of England, and that the stone alignments marked cyclical movements of the sun and moon and possibly other planetary bodies. Alexander Thom's measurements indicate a sophisticated

knowledge of the moon's movements. These observations, of course, suggest that lunar activity played an important role in ancient British religion. Modern considerations also place emphasis on other nearby sites representative of the megalithic culture, such as **SILBURY HILL**, West Kennet Long Barrow, Windmill Hill, and the Sanctuary.

While much of the work on Avebury follows normal scientific methodology, a variety of more speculative methodologies have been used to overcome limits to understanding Avebury and other megalithic sites. Some have attempted to tease information from ancient folklore and popular legends, while a few used various psychic arts from clairvoyance to dowsing. One popular theory ties Avebury into a system of ley lines, a system of straight lines crisscrossing England and believed to connect various sacred sites. Conclusions drawn from these studies rest upon the evaluation of the methodology and the presence of independent verification. Such speculation has additional significance, however, as it attempts to tie the religion of ancient Britons into modern Pagan and alternative metaphysical religions. While many tourists visit Avebury out of historical interest, many Pagans and New Agers see their visit as a spiritual/religious experience.

Avebury is located in Wiltshire, some ninety miles west of London. Today, a village is located inside the embankment, and a modern road transverses the circle, entering and exiting through the breaks in the embankment. It has become one of England's top tourist stops.

Sources:

Brown, Peter Lancaster. *Megaliths and Masterminds.* New York: Charles Scribner's Sons, 1979.

Burl, Aubrey. *The Stone Circles of the British Isles.* New Haven, CT: Yale University Press, 1976.

Miller, Hamish, and Paul Broadhurst. *The Sun and the Serpent.* Hayle, Cornwall, UK: Pendragon Press, 1990.

Thom, Alexander. *Megalithic Sites in Britain.* Oxford: Oxford University Press, 1967.

Rivalling Stonehenge as one of the most archeologically interesing megalithic sites in England, Avebury may have similarly served as a tool for tracking the motion of stars and planets. *Getty Images*.

AVIGNON (FRANCE)

Avignon, a small city in southeastern France, found itself on the battle lines of various regional rulers through the first millennium of the Common Era. It acquired some additional importance in the thirteenth century. Opposing the entrance of French forces attempting to root the Albigensian heretics from the mountains of southeastern France, Avignon was forced to tear down its walls and fill up the moat, leaving it essentially defenseless. By the end of the century, the city had come under the hegemony of the king of Naples.

Early in the fourteenth century, a struggle arose between the king of France and claims of papal authority in temporal affairs. The popes lost. Boniface VIII (r. 1294–1303) was taken prisoner by King Philip the Fair (r. 1285–1314). In 1305 a Frenchman was elected pope, taking the name Clement V (r. 1305–1314). He reversed a number of papal pronouncements against Philip and then, in 1309, moved the seat of the papacy to Avignon. Although Avignon was not formally French territory, the move signaled to all the new role of France in directing papal decisions. In the few years left to the pair, Philip coerced Clement's participation in the destruction of the Order of Templars.

The papacy appeared to thrive in Avignon. In stages, successive popes built an impressive palace. The gothic, fortress-like building was dominated by a set of linked towers. Artists from Sienna were brought to decorate the palace with a number of frescos. The town prospered, and a university rose to prominence. In 1348, Clement VI (r. 1342–1352) formally purchased the city from Naples and incorporated it into the territory of the Papal States.

The struggle between church leaders in Rome and Avignon resulted at the end of the 1370s in the naming of two popes, one residing in Rome and one in Avignon. The different countries of Europe lined up behind their favorite. As each pope died and a successor was elected, the scandal of the division became unacceptable to all. A council was called to meet at Pisa in 1409. The council declared both popes deposed and elected a new, third pope. Neither of the two popes accepted their deposition, and Europe now lined up behind three popes. A new council met at Constance in 1414. It was able to heal the schism by deposing two of the papal claimants and allowing the third to resign. It then elected a new pope who took the name Martin V (r. 1417–1431). The resignation of Gregory XII, the pope residing in Rome, meant that his lineage would be remembered as the legitimate one, while the popes who resided in Avignon from 1378 onward were declared anti-popes.

The healing of the Great Schism of the papal office and its reestablishment in Rome led to the renewal of the struggle between the rulers of France and the pope. Although Avignon was formally considered papal territory, the French asserted their hegemony. Highlights of the struggle included Louis XIV's seizure and subsequent declaration of Avignon as an integral part of the Kingdom of France in 1663. An official and final determination of Avignon's status came in 1797, following the French Revolution, when the pope was forced to renounce all rights to the city. For a time, even the city's status as the seat of an archbishop was lost, but it was reestablished in 1822.

Today, the Palace of the Popes survives as the largest gothic palace in Europe and a major tourist site. After many years of use as a barracks, it was turned into a museum and a monument to an important era in French and Italian history.

Sources:

Calmann, Marianne. *Avignon*. London: Allison & Busby, 2000.

Housley, Norman. *The Avignon Papacy and the Crusades, 1305–1378*. Oxford: Oxford University Press, 1986.

Renouard, Yves. *The Avignon Papacy, 1305–1403*. London: Faber & Faber, 1970.

AYYAD, ALA (B. 2003)

In December 2003, a grandson was born to Aysha Ayyad. Not in itself an unusual event, the birth stood out by the presence of a birthmark spelling out an uncle's name in Arabic. Under normal circumstances, the child would have taken his own father's name. Because of the birthmark, however, and the fact that the uncle had been killed by Israeli soldiers operating in Palestine the previous March, it was decided to name him after his uncle instead. The uncle was a Hamas operative, and the child, who resides in Bethlehem, has been attracting pilgrims. The family has suggested the birthmark indicates Allah's favoritism of the Palestinian cause in the struggle with Israel.

According to the Islamic calendar, the child was born on the 27th of Ramadan, the day celebrated by Muslims as the day the Qur'an was revealed to Muhammad. Muslim clerics have deemed the birth a *karama*, a miracle of a lesser kind, as in Islamic thought true miracles only happen to the prophets. *Karama* is the term used to describe the many wonders worked by the many Muslim mystics and saints over the centuries. To have received a *karama* marks the child as very special.

Pilgrimages to the Ayyad home began just as preparation for Christmas celebrations by the Christian community were beginning, and the suggestion of a second miracle birth in Bethlehem was not lost upon them.

Sources:

"Bethlehem Baby Drawing Crowds: Palestinian Boy's Birthmark Seen as 'Miracle' and 'Mark of a Beast'." World Daily Net, December 3, 2003. Posted at http://www.worldnetdaily.com/news/article.asp?ARTICLE_ID=35935. Accessed April 1, 2007.

Babaji

In 1946, Swami **Paramahansa Yogananda** (1893–1952), founder of what today is known as the Self-Realization Fellowship (SRF), informed the world of his own guru lineage in his book, *Autobiography of a Yogi*. The practice of kriya yoga—the essence of the SRF's teachings—had originated around 1861 with Lahiri Mahasaya, who passed it to Sri Yukteswar (1855–1936), who in turn taught Yogananda. The interesting part of the story, however, was Yogananda's revelation that Lahiri Mahasaya had actually been taught by a mysterious figure known as Babaji. Babaji is said to have appeared to Yogananda early in the twentieth century, giving Yogananda his mission to teach in the West. Yogananda then demonstrated the power of the teachings by the incorruptibility of his body after death.

Since Yogananda's death, a variety of stories have emerged and now gather around Babaji. He has been identified as an incarnation of Lord Shiva, one of the primary Hindu deities. Various texts have been searched to find ancient accounts of his repeated appearances, and modern stories of more recent encounters have emerged. Babaji was identified, for example, with a person known as Haidakhan Baba who lived in the foothills of the Himalayas from around 1890 to 1922. He promised his followers in 1922 to return. That story was continued in the career of one Mahendra Baba (d. 1969), who through the 1950s and 1960s announced Babaji's return. By this time there were ashrams around India devoted to him. A person identified as Haidakhan Baba reappeared in 1970 and for fourteen years moved among the Babaji ashrams. Leonard Orr and Sondra Ray, the founders of the "rebirthing" movement, were among his American advocates, and Baba Hari Dass, an Indian guru residing in northern California, published a book about him. The Haidakhan Babaji movement is headquartered in Utter Predesh, India.

Quite apart from SRF or the Haidakhan Baba movement, another Indian teacher, S. A. A. Ramaiah, claimed that beginning in 1942, he and journalist V. T. Neelakantan became the direct students of Babaji and from him received the texts of three books, *The Voice of Babaji and Mysticism Unlocked*, *Babaji's Masterkey to All Ills*, and *Babaji's Death of Death*. He also revealed his actual beginning in human form. He was born in 203 CE in southern India (Tamil Nadu). His father was a priest of Shiva.

As a young man, Babaji traveled to the southern tip of Sri Lanka, where he studied with a guru and had a vision of Lord Muruga. He continued his studies in Tamil Naga and eventually went into the Himalayas to practice kriya yoga, into which he had been initiated. During this period he was transformed into a siddha and his body became free of the effects of disease and death. Since that time, Babaji has continued to exist, maintain a youthful appearance, and become the guide and inspiration of many of India's great spiritual teachers through the centuries.

Ramaiah later founded the International Babaji Kriya Yoga Sangam, which teaches all of the kriya yoga material that Yogananda did not feel the West was ready for during his decades in the United States. Ramaiah's work is carried on by Marshall Govindan, initiated by Ramaiah in 1971.

Among other persons who have claimed contact with Babaji is Swami Satyaswarananda, a guru who resides in San Diego, who has at Babaji's insistence republished the writings of Lahiri Mahasaya in a series called "Sanskrit Classics."

Sources:

Govindan, Marshall. *Babaji and the Siddha Kriya Yoga Tradition.* 2nd ed. Freiberg, Germany: Hans Nietsch Verlag, 1999.

Hari Dass, Baba. *Harikhan Baba Known, Unknown.* Davis, CA: Sri Rama Foundation, 1975.

Orr, Leonard, and Makham Singh. *Babaji.* San Francisco, CA: privately printed, 1979.

Satyaswarananda, Swami. *Babaji.* Vol. 1: *The Divine Himalayan Yogi.* 3rd ed. San Diego, CA: Sanskrit Classics, 1993.

Yogananda, Paramahansa. *The Autobiography of a Yogi.* Los Angeles: Self-Realization Fellowship, 1946.

BAHÁ'Í TEMPLES

The Bahá'í Faith is a relatively new world religion, growing out of the work of three Persian religious leaders: Siyyid Ali Mohammad, known as the Bab (1819–1850); Husayn Ali, who became known as Baha'u'llah (1817–1892); and Baha'u'llah's son, Abdu'l-Baha (1844–1921). Among its basic principles are affirmations of the one God who created a single humanity. The faith also believes that periodically (every 500 to 1,000 years), God sends a messenger to act as his spokesperson on Earth. Collectively, they have given God's one religion, the message of all the prophets being essentially the same. Bahá'ís recognize nine prophets: Abraham, Moses, Zoroaster, Buddha, Krishna, Jesus, Muhammad, Bahá'u'lláh, and his forerunner, the Bab (which means "the Gate" in Arabic). (Baha'u'llah's son, Abdu'l-Baha, and his nephew, Shoghi Effendi [1896–1957], led the movement after Baha'u'llah's death. After Shoghi Effendi passed away, a collective leadership emerged.)

The Bahá'í Faith now claims more than five million adherents scattered in more than 200 countries and worshiping in some 120,000 local centers worldwide. The movement grew steadily through the 1950s, but it made a large leap geographically in the 1960s when a concerted effort was made to open an initial Bahá'í center in every country.

The Bahá'í Faith does not build local centers. Instead, groups meet in homes or rented facilities, largely invisible on the religious landscape. However, the movement has placed on every continent a single house of worship or temple. No preaching or proselytizing occurs in the houses of worship. They are open daily for anyone to visit and engage in meditation or contemplation. The services that do take place at the temples consist entirely of recitations of the scriptures of the various religions.

The number nine holds great significance to Bahá'ís. As the highest single-digit number, nine symbolizes completeness. The Bahá'í Faith claims to fulfill the expectations of the prior religions and summarize the message of the nine prophets. The symbol of the faith is a nine-pointed star, and the symbolism is carried through in the Bahá'í temples, all of which are nine-sided with nine entrances. In each case, the nine sides reach upward to a single point.

An initial Bahá'í temple in Ishqabad, Turkmenistan, was completed in 1902. Shortly thereafter a second temple, in the Chicago suburb of

Wilmette, Illinois, was begun; the groundbreaking took place on May 1, 1912, occasioned by Abdu'l-Baha's visit to the United States. In the mid-1920s, Turkmenistan was incorporated into the Soviet Union. The U.S.S.R.'s anti-religion policies led authorities to expropriate the Turkmenistan temple in 1928, and a decade later it was converted into an art gallery. The building was damaged in an earthquake in 1948 and finally demolished in 1963. Meanwhile, work on the American temple proceeded at a very slow pace, and it was not ready for dedication until 1953.

Alongside the dramatic expansion of the faith in the 1960s, the program to construct a temple on every continent (except Antarctica) proceeded at a rapid pace. The additional temples followed a wide variety of styles within the basic requirement of having nine sides and doorways. The African temple opened in Uganda in 1961, followed by temples in Sydney, Australia (1961), Panama City, Panama (1972), Frankfurt, Germany (1974), western Samoa (1979), and Bahapour, India (1986). The foundation for the South American temple in Santiago, Chile, is scheduled to be laid in October 2008.

Sources:

Badiee, Julie. *An Earthly Paradise: Bahá'í Houses of Worship around the World.* Oxford: George Ronald, 1992.

"Fabrication Begins for Components on Bahá'í Temple in South America." Posted at http://news.bahai.org/story/505. Accessed March 24, 2007.

Leiker, Benjamin. "Sacred Bahá'í Architecture." Posted at http://bahai-library.com/?file=leiker_bahai_architecture.html. Accessed April 1, 2007.

Whitmore, Bruce W. *The Dawning Place: The Building of a Temple, the Forging of the North American Bahá'í Community.* Wilmette, IL: Bahá'í Publishing Trust, 1984.

BEAURAING/BANNEUX (BELGIUM)

In the 1930s, two sets of Marian apparitions occurred in Belgium. Because of their temporal and geographical proximity, they are generally linked, although in fact they were independent events.

The Virgin was seen in Beauraing, in French-speaking Belgium, beginning in November 1932. The visionaries were five children of two nominal Catholic families named Voisin and Degeimbre. On the evening of November 29, 1932, the three girls, Fernande Voisin (15 years old), Gilberte Degeimbre (9 years old), and Gilberte Voisin, and two boys, Andrée Degeimbre (14 years old), and Albert Voisin (11 years old), initially saw the Virgin walking in the air above a grotto that had been constructed to represent LOURDES at a convent school they attended. She was dressed in white with her feet obscured by a cloud.

On subsequent evenings, they again saw the Lady standing by a hawthorn tree adjacent to the grotto. At the time they stood on the street just outside the convent walls, and slowly a crowd gathered to watch them. She answered positively to a query concerning her identity as the Immaculate Virgin. Her message to the children was simple: "Always be good."

By December 8, traditionally celebrated as the feast day for the Immaculate Conception, some 15,000 people gathered at the convent. The children, lost in a state of ecstasy, were the only ones who saw the Virgin. Their ecstatic state was tested by observers who stuck pins into them and flashed lights in their eyes. The children returned each night, although the apparitions did not always occur.

On December 29, the Virgin appeared to Fernande with a heart of gold surrounded by rays. The next day, two more of the children saw the same heart. The next day the others also saw the heart. The message accompanying the heart vision was: "Pray always."

Mary announced January 3 as the day of her last appearance. Some 30,000 people gathered for the event, at which she said she would speak to each of the five children individually. When she initially appeared on January 3, only four of the children saw her. Speaking to the four individually, she identified herself as the Mother of God, the Queen of Heaven, and said her task was the conversion of sinners.

Fernande, the oldest of the children, seemingly left out of the last apparition, remained at the site after the other four departed. Then she and some of the gathered crowd heard a loud noise and saw a ball of fire on the hawthorn tree. The Lady reappeared and asked if Fernande loved her and her son. Given an affirmative reply, she said, "Then sacrifice yourself for me." She then disappeared for the last time.

The local bishop waited two years to appoint the standard commission to investigate the apparitions. It did not report for some time, and only in 1943 (in the midst of World War II and the German occupation of Belgium) were public devotions authorized. Further statements, including one on healing at the site, would await the end of the war.

Meanwhile, two weeks after the apparitions at Beauraing ceased, on January 15, 1933, a young girl named Mariette Beco, while looking out a window for her brother, saw a young lady in the yard. It was about seven o'clock in the evening. The Lady was wearing a white gown with a blue belt. An oval light surrounded her body. She had a rosary in her right hand, which was joined to the left in an attitude of prayer. A golden rose was on her right foot.

Two days later, for the first time in several months, Mariette attended mass and told the priest what had happened. She refuted the priest's suggestion that she had merely seen a statue of the Virgin at Lourdes by noting that the Lady she had seen was more beautiful. On several occasions as she followed the Lady, she fell abruptly to the ground. On the third occasion, she knelt near a ditch and was told that the water had been reserved for the Virgin. On the following evening, Mary identified herself as "the Virgin of the Poor" and reiterated her designation of the water at the ditch: "This spring is reserved for all the nations—to relieve the sick."

Over the next two months, Mary appeared on several occasions, during which she indicated her task of relieving suffering and called upon the faithful to pray. The last apparition occurred on March 2. An investigation of the apparitions to Mariette operated from 1935 to 1937. Devotion to Mary as the Virgin of the Poor was given preliminary approval in 1942.

The first healing related to the water from the spring (located some 300 feet from Mariette's home) came several months after the last apparition. A small chapel was built in 1933 to accommodate pilgrims, but it soon proved to be insufficient. A large church has subsequently been erected. Meanwhile, the hawthorn tree at Beauraing became the object of the pilgrims' attention, and here also many healings were reported. Today over one million people arrive each year.

The Belgian apparitions, while devoid of a startling theological revelation as at Lourdes or dramatic events as at Fatima, have become building blocks of contemporary Marian theological speculation. The visionaries remained out of the spotlight. As adults they married and tried to live normal lives.

Sources:

Beevers, John. *Virgin of the Poor: The Apparitions of Our Lady at Banneux.* Saint Meinrad, IN: Abbey Press, 1972.

Connor, Edward. *Recent Apparitions of Our Lady.* Fresno, CA: Academy Guild Press, 1960.

Piron, Paul. *Five Children: The Story of the Apparition of the Blessed Virgin at Beauraing.* New York: Benziger, 1938.

BENARES/VARANASI/KASHI (INDIA)

Benares, also known as Varanasi and Kashi, is thought by many to be the oldest continuously inhabited city in the world, and certainly all agree that the area has been inhabited for more than 2,000 years. The city is located southeast of Lucknow, on the banks of the sacred Ganges River.

Its name Varanasi derives from Varuna and Asi, the two tributaries of the Ganges between which it is located. Legendary tradition attributed the city's founding to Shiva, and it is believed that living there for a period of time and bathing in the Ganges, and/or dying there, in what is considered Shiva's hometown, releases one from the circle of rebirths (reincarnation). Death has come to be an integral part of the city's life. The last rites for the dead are a major religious activity repeated almost daily, and the cremation grounds lie in the heart of the city.

Buddhist beginnings are also connected to Benares. The city is quite close to **SARNATH**, where Gautama Buddha found enlightenment, after which he visited Benares (around 500 BCE) to deliver his first sermon.

Benares was deeply affected by the era of Muslim rule in the later Middle Ages. In the middle of the seventeenth century, the Mughal Emperor Aurangzeb (r. 1658–1707) attained the throne. His lengthy reign was marked by the wholesale destruction of Hindu temples and the general suppression of Hindu worship. Few of the present Hindu structures in Benares predate the eighteenth century, when Hindu control was reasserted in the region.

Since the return of Hindu rule, some 1,500 temples, palaces, and shrines have been constructed. Among the oldest is the Vishwanath Temple, rebuilt in 1777 by Ahilya Bai Holkar of Indore, on the same site of what had been the principal Shiva temple during the millennium prior to Aurangzeb. The temple roof and altar area are heavily decorated with gold. Among the modern structures is the Bharat Mandir, dedicated to "Mother India," a twentieth-century temple opened by Mahatma Gandhi. It contains a large, decorative marble map of India.

The real religious life of the city, however, is to be found along the ghats, the stairways that lead down to the river's edge. Here the holy men gather, the faithful come to take their symbolic baths, and the bodies of the deceased are cremated.

Sources:

Bhattacharya, B. *Varanasi Rediscovered*. New Delhi: Munshiram Manoharlal Publishers, 1999.

Eck, Diana. *Benares: City of Light*. Princeton, NJ: Princeton University Press, 1982.

Medhasananda, Swami. *Varanasi at the Crossroads: A Panoramic View of Early Modern Varanasi and the Story of Its Transition*. Calcutta: Ramakrishan Mission Institute of Culture, 2002.

Singh, Birendra Pratap. *Life in Ancient Varanasi: An Account Based on Archaeological Evidence*. New Delhi: Sundeep Prakashan, 1985.

Sinha, Kunal. *A Benarasi on Varanasi*. New Delhi: Bluejay Books, 2004.

BETANCUR, PEDRO DE SAN JOSÉ (C. 1626–1667)

On track to become the first Central American named as a Roman Catholic saint, Pedro Betancur was born in Vilaflor, the Canary Islands, on September 18, 1626. As a young man he worked as a shepherd, but he decided to migrate to Guatemala to make a new life for himself with the help of a relative in government service there. He moved to Cuba, but he stayed only long enough to replenish his depleted purse to cover his travel on to Central America. He had decided to become a priest and associated with the Jesuits, but he found himself unable to fulfill the educational requirements. Thus, in 1655, he joined the Franciscan order.

During his first three years as a Franciscan, Betancur organized a hospital, a homeless shelter, and a school, all aimed to serve the poor. Understanding that faith is for everyone, he became concerned for the wealthier elements of society and initiated walking tours through their neighborhood, during which time he would ring a bell and call for repentance. In the end, he organized a new order just to care for the several benevolent services he founded, the Order of Belén.

Besides his social service, Betancur became known for his severe acts of penance. He was known for self-**FLAGELLATION**, sleep deprivation, and lying with his hands outstretched on a full-size cross. These actions contributed greatly to his

Pope John Paul II declared Pedro de San José Betancur—portrayed in a picture above the seated pope—a saint in 2002. The Franciscan monk made his home in Antigua, which is now a popular pilgrimage site. *Getty Images*.

THE ENCYCLOPEDIA OF RELIGIOUS PHENOMENA

reputation for saintliness. He is also said to have thought up the idea of a procession on Christmas Eve in which participants assume the roles of Mary and Joseph and seek a night's lodging from their neighbors. Over the years, the practice spread throughout Central America and Mexico.

Betancur lived most of his life in Antigua, and he was buried there in the Church of San Francisco. There are now a set of related sites in Antigua that have become the focus of pilgrimage. First is a tree he is said to have planted. The sacristy of the Church of San Francisco houses many relics of the saint, including pieces of his clothing and a skull he used for meditating upon death. The original tomb inside the church still exists, though his body was put in a new tomb in 1990. There is also a display of crutches, canes, and other mementos left by people who were healed as a result of their visit to the church. Prayers to Saint Pedro are often made with candles that are rubbed on the tombs and then on the bodies of the afflicted. Those healed may leave messages of thanks, while those not immediately healed may leave behind their requests for Saint Pedro's intercession on their behalf.

Brother Pedro was nominated for sainthood as early as 1729, but his cause languished for more than two centuries. Meanwhile, in the mid-twentieth century, the church was heavily damaged in an earthquake. In the 1960s, the local Franciscans began to promote devotion to Pedro and began cataloguing the miracles claimed by pilgrims to Antigua. They also began to lobby for the reconstruction of the damaged church. Over the following decades, both concerns were answered. Betancur was beatified in 1980 and canonized by Pope John Paul II during a trip to Guatemala on July 31, 2002. The new church has become a leading pilgrimage site for Central American Catholics.

Sources:

Gaitán, Héctor. *El Hermano Pedro: El Santo de los Milagros.* Nueva Guatemala de la Asunción, Guatemala: Museo Fray Francisco Vázquez, 2002.

García Aragón, Leonardo. *Novena al Hermano Pedro de San José de Betancur.* Guatemala City, Guatemala: Tip. Nacional de Guatemala, 2002.

Pilon, Marta. *El Hermano Pedro, Santo de Guatemala.* Del Ejército, Guatemala: Edición Edit, 1974.

Samayoa, S. Otto, and Alma Serafica. *Vida Popular del Beato Pedro de san José Betancur.* 1962. 3rd ed. Guatemala City, Guatemala: Tip. Nacional, 1991.

BETHLEHEM

In 1 Samuel 16:1 Jesse, the father of the Jewish king David, is called a Bethlemite, and from the time of David's reign (tenth century BCE), Bethlehem had special recognition as the city of David's birth. It is so identified in Luke 2:4, where Jesus' birth in the city contributes to the Christian affirmation of Jesus' kingship.

No one actually knows where Jesus was born, but a small cave that at one time functioned as a stable became the spot most identified as the site. Following the acceptance of Christianity during the reign of Constantine (r. 306–337) in the fourth century, church leaders began to claim the site and initiated construction of a large basilica. By the end of the century, the town had become a major Christian pilgrimage destination.

The Church of the Nativity has survived many political changes, including the taking of Palestine by an expanding Islamic empire, several crusades, and the emergence of the modern state of Israel with the allocation of some land to the control of the Palestinian Authority. Bethlehem is in the land under the Palestinian Authority, although only a few miles outside of modern Jerusalem. As the twenty-first century began, Bethlehem was the site of an increased level of fighting between Palestinians and Israelis. In 2002, ongoing conflict led to a thirty-eight-day siege of the Church of the Nativity as Israeli troops attempted to capture Palestinian fighters who had taken refuge inside the church.

The courtyard in front of the church became the site of Christmas celebrations each year that extend for several weeks due to the differences in the liturgical calendar of the Eastern Orthodox and Roman Catholic/Protestant churches. Pilgrims who enter the church may stop at the

Chapel of the Kings (where tradition says the Three Wise Men worshiped the infant Jesus) before going downstairs to the Grotto of the Nativity, where a star marks the very spot where many believe Jesus was born. One interesting feature of the church is the so-called Door of Humility. The main door into the church was partially blocked in the sixteenth century to keep people from coming into the church riding their horses. Today, one has to lower one's head to enter.

Similar to several other sites in the Holy Land, the church represents a matter of conflict between older Christian groups. In this instance, the Franciscans (Roman Catholics) vie for control with the Greek Orthodox Patriarchate of Jerusalem. The church is also visited regularly by Muslims, who honor Jesus as a prophet as well as his mother, Mary, both of whom are mentioned in the Qur'an. Jews also visit the church, but many Orthodox Jews refuse to enter as lowering their head to go through the entrance is interpreted as bowing their head before a Christian holy site.

Close by the Church of the Nativity is a small cave formed in a deposit of chalk. The cave became an early focus of Marian devotion, and a legend survived that the white of the cave came from Mary having dropped some of her milk on the stone. To this day, local mothers will scrape small quantities of the chalk to mix in their babies' food. Though not as sacred as Jerusalem, the land in and around Bethlehem is remembered for its part in the life of Jesus, and nearby one may find locations that are believed by many to be places mentioned in the Bible. One may be shown the tomb of Rachel marked by the Dome of Rachel (cf. Matthew 2:18) just north of the city, the well from which David's warriors brought him water, and the field where the shepherds were visited by the angels announcing Jesus' birth.

Sources:

Crowfoot, J. W. *Early Churches in Palestine*. Oxford: Oxford University Press, 1941.

Hoppe, Leslie J. *The Synagogues and Churches of Ancient Palestine*. Princeton, NJ: Liturgical Press, 1994.

Raheb, Mitri, and Fred Strickert. *Bethlehem 2000: Past and Present*. Heidelberg: Palmyra, 1999.

BIBLE CODE

Throughout the 1990s a number of claims have been made that the text of the Hebrew Bible, what most Christians call the Old Testament, in particular the book of Genesis, contains references to a variety of contemporary events and persons completely unknown to those who wrote the biblical books. In 1997 a book entitled *The Bible Code*, authored by journalist Michael Drosnin, pushed the claims even further, suggesting the prediction of events prior to their occurrence, most notably the assassination of Israeli prime minister Yitzhak Rabin. Those who have subsequently supported the idea of a coded message in the Bible have also put forth a belief that the existence of such a code leads to the conclusion that God actually authored the text.

The more popularized presentation by Drosnin grew out of the research of a set of Israeli scholars, most notably Doron Witztum, Eliyahu Rips, and Yoav Rosenberg. In 1994 the trio published a rather unassuming article, "Equidistant Letter Sequences in the Book of Genesis," which detailed their discoveries from computer searches of the Hebrew text of the Bible. Choosing preselected words and dates, a computer can quickly search the text in a unique manner. The computer searches for words formed by looking at a preselected set of letters—every third letter or every twelfth letter, for example. The computer can also search the text both backward and forward. The distance between the selected letters is referred to as its step value. For this work, only the Hebrew text is used, the assumption being that the code disappears in translations and cannot be found in other books of equal length.

The suggestion to search for such a code came from the early twentieth-century writing of Rabbi Chaim Michael Dov Weissmandl (1903–1957), who without a computer did some searches of the text and made some preliminary findings. Though best known for his work to save Jews during the Holocaust, he was also an expert in deciphering ancient manuscripts. In 1983 Eliyahu Rips, a mathematician at Hebrew University in Jerusalem, initiated research on what became known as "equidistant letters sequences." Focusing on the book of Genesis, Rips and colleague Doron Witztum discovered an interesting phenomenon: the close appearance of pairs of conceptually related words. Using computer software prepared by Yoav Rosenberg, Witztum and Rips prepared a list of notable individuals and appellations appropriate to each from the *Encyclopedia of Great Men in Israel.*

In the wake of the publication of the Drosnin book, a variety of people became involved in the search for a Bible Code, and a controversy arose with two extremes represented. One proposed that the existence of the code was proof of the divine inspiration of the Bible; the other voiced skepticism of the existence of the code and concluded the work behind it was pseudoscience. The support of the code, based as it is in a knowledge of the Hebrew text, has been carried forward primarily by conservative Orthodox Jews. Criticism has come largely from liberal Protestant Christians and religious unbelievers.

That the convergence of seemingly significant terms occurs in the text has been established. The ongoing argument centers on divergent opinions concerning the meaning and relevance of the findings. The primary criticism has been that the findings are pure coincidence and that similar findings could be found in other books. For example, Australian mathematician Brendan McKay did searches of the Hebrew translation of *War and Peace,* in which he discovered a number of words related to the Jewish holiday Chanukah. He also responded to an off-the-cuff remark related to the assassination of Rabin, in which Drosnin challenged his critic to find references to assassination in a book like *Moby Dick.* McKay subsequently produced references to a spectrum of assassinated individuals, including Indira Gandhi, Martin Luther King Jr., and Robert F. Kennedy. The con-

troversy has continued with a number of books, pro and con, and a 2002 sequel to Drosnin's original book, *Bible Code II: The Count Down,* in which he claimed the Bible included information on the attacks in New York and Washington, D.C., on September 11, 2001.

Sources:

Drosnin, Michael. *The Bible Code.* New York: Simon & Schuster, 1997.
———. *The Bible Code II: The Count Down.* New York: Viking, 2002.
Ingermanson, Randall. *Who Wrote the Bible Code? A Physicist Probes the Current Controversy.* Colorado Springs, CO: Waterbrook Press, 1999.
Satinover, Jeffrey. *Cracking the Bible Code: The Real Story of the Stunning Discovery of Hidden Knowledge in the First Five Books of the Bible.* New York: William Morrow, 1997.
Stanton, Phil. *The Bible Code: Fact or Fake?* Wheaton, IL: Crossway Books, 1998.

BI-LOCATION

Bi-location, the ability to be in two locations simultaneously, also known as astral travel or out-of-the-body travel, is a rare event, even in the modern world where discussion of the possibility was heightened as Spiritualism and psychical research blossomed. Both Spiritualism and Theosophy assumed that humans possessed a body double made of a subtle substance usually invisible to the eye. In Theosophy, it was assumed that the spiritual self—the true essence of the individual—assumed several bodies, each more substantive than the last, during the process of moving into the gross physical body. As the person matured, the subtle bodies assumed an image like that of the physical body. Spiritualists usually assumed there existed an astral double, the reality of which accounted for a spectrum of phenomena such as ghosts.

Throughout the twentieth century, psychical researchers attempted to prove the existence of the astral double, most often in examining claims about hauntings and ghosts. However, a variety of living people claimed the ability to project their

Also known as astral projection, bi-location is the ability to project one's spiritual being to a separate location and, in essence, be in two places at the same time. *Fortean Picture Library.*

astral body, usually while their physical body was in a state of sleep or a trance. The first major exponent of astral travel was Sylvan J. Muldoon (c. 1903–1971), whose experiences became the basis of a series of books coauthored with psychical researcher Hereward Carrington (1880–1958), the first of which appeared in 1929. These books partially inspired the book *Astral Projection*, by Oliver Fox (pseudonym of Hugh G. Calloway; 1885–1949), which appeared in 1939. Interest continued throughout the century into the New Age movement with the emergence of Robert Monroe (1915–1995), who not only recounted his own *Journeys out of the Body* (1971), but offered to help other people experience what seemingly had become commonplace with him.

Contemporaneously with Monroe, psychic Ingo Swann became the subject of a set of tests by parapsychologists attempting to prove that Swann could astral project.

The problem with astral projection is that, although it is an often intense experience to the individual who reported a projection, there is little in the way of verifying the experience to another. Rare indeed are even anecdotal accounts of the projecting person being seen by another, though a few do exist.

The emphasis in psychical research on astral travel is in part an attempt to offer a basis for understanding tales of bi-location that appear in the lives of various saints. For example, Martin

De Porres (d. 1639), who spent his entire life in Peru, was seen to appear in various locations in Mexico or in far-off China or Japan. One popular story had him making repeated appearances to assist captives in northern Africa. De Porres also claimed to have been in other countries, and he often offered detailed descriptions of places he had visited overseas.

The tales of bi-locating saints and the modern studies of astral travel have left a less-than-convincing record of the possibility of such occurrences, and assessment of the reality of such events (though quite real to the ones who experience them) must remain for the future.

Sources:

Fox, Oliver. *Astral Projection: A Record of Out of the Body Experiences.* New York: Citadel Press, 1993.

Monroe, Robert A. *Journeys out of the Body.* Garden City, NY: Doubleday & Company, 1973.

Muldoon, Sylvan Joseph, and Hereward Carrington. *The Projection of the Astral Body.* New York: Samuel Weiser, 1972.

Rogo, D. Scott. *Leaving the Body: A Complete Guide to Astral Projection.* New York: Simon & Schuster, 1983.

Webster, Richard. *Astral Travel for Beginners.* St. Paul, MN: Llewellyn Publications, 1998.

BIORHYTHMS

In the 1970s, within the larger New Age movement, the notion of individual biorhythm charts was introduced. These charts purported to show the activity of three biological cycles that all humans beings experience from birth. According to the theory of biorhythms, these cycles have much to say about fluctuations in our energy levels and psychological states from day to day.

The idea of biorhythms in human life was initially proposed by German physician William Fliess (1859–1928). He claimed to have discovered two operative cycles, and from his work the contemporary theory evolved. In the 1920s an Austrian engineer, Alfred Teltscher, proposed a third cycle. Subsequently, Austrian psychologist Herman Swoboda (1873–1963) tied the three cycles to an individual's birth date. The discussion of biorhythms remained an activity of very few until the 1960s, when George S. Thommen authored a popular presentation of the idea and marketed it as a self-help tool for people seeking to improve the quality of their lives.

According to the theory, there are three significant rhythms to which one should pay attention. Each rhythm goes through a steady cycle, rising and falling. Because each cycle is of a different length, their highs and lows do not regularly coincide. The three cycles are: a 23-day cycle of physical strength and energy; a 28-day cycle of emotional and creative ability; and a 33-day cycle of mental activity. On any given day, one may feel (for example) physically energized, emotionally neutral, and mentally low. On rare days one can feel energized on all fronts or depleted on all fronts. By tracking one's cycles, one can, for example, schedule important events on days in which two or three cycles are peaking and avoid making key decisions when two or more cycles are at their low points. A biorhythm chart allows one to immediately know where they are in their cycles on any given day.

Attention to biorhythms peaked in the later 1970s after Bernard Gittelson authored a mass-market paperback book that affirmed Thommen's presentation, and a variety of devices appeared that greatly simplified the production of charts. The idea became a part of popular culture, and as charts of celebrities were calculated, famous events tied to highs and lows in their charts were publicized. At the same time, however, it also underwent closer scrutiny, its claim to quantify psychological states being highly verifiable. Unfortunately, the scientific texts of biorhythm cycles all yielded negative results. Anecdotal claims that tennis star Billy Jean King had scored her famous victory over Bobby Riggs when on a biorhythm high suggested that other outstanding performances would yield significant correlates. However, no such data was forthcoming. By the end of the 1980s, biorhythm charts had largely disappeared.

Sources:

Bainbridge, William Sims. "Biorhythms: Evaluating a Pseudoscience," *Skeptical Inquirer* (summer/spring 1978): 41–56.

Gittelson, Bernard. *Biorhythms: A Personal Science.* New York: Arco Publishing Company, 1975.

Hines, Terence M. "Comprehensive Review of Biorhythm Theory," *Psychological Reports* 83 (1998): 19–64.

Thommen, G. S. *Is This Your Day.* New York: Crown, 1973.

BLACK MADONNAS

The term "Black Madonnas" refers to representations of the Virgin Mary with black or dark-hued skin that appeared in Europe during the Middle Ages. In several cases, these representations have reputed miraculous elements in their origin. Several of these images can be accounted for by the relatively dark skin of the indigenous population among whom the image originated (such as Our Lady of Guadalupe in Mexico) or changes in an original image that turned black because of the degradation of the paint or the accumulation of additives from the many candles burned in close proximity to it over the centuries. There are several hundred Black Madonnas across Europe, many located in southern France.

Among the most important of the Black Madonnas that appear to have been painted as such is Our Lady of Czestochowa. The original painting resides at the monastery of Jasna Gora in Poland and has gained prominence in the later twentieth century because of the attention paid to it by Pope John Paul II. It is one of several paintings attributed to Saint Luke and discovered in the fourth century by Saint Helena (c. 248–c. 329), who is said to have brought it to Constantinople. However, its history is vague until the fifteenth century, when it arrived in Poland as the possession of Saint Ladislaus. As Poland was under constant threat by Tar

tars, Ladislaus decided to take the image to Opala. On the journey, he stopped in Czestochowa, and while there left the Virgin in the monastery in a chapel dedicated to her assumption. When Ladislaus prepared to continue his journey, his horses refused to move forward with the Virgin's image in his wagon. He took their reticence to move as a sign that the Virgin had found a home, and he left the painting in the brothers' care.

A famous black statue of the Virgin is located in southern Spain at Montserrat, near Barcelona. The documentation of this statue begins in the thirteenth century, when it seems to have been enthroned in the church at Montserrat, but legends attribute its origins to Jerusalem. It is said to have been moved to Spain in the eighth century to keep it from the invading Muslims. It disappeared for a century and a half until reputedly was found by shepherds in 890. While tending their sheep in the evening, in a setting reminiscent of the biblical shepherds in Luke 2, they saw lights in the sky and heard singing. They reported it to the local priest and he to the local bishop, both of whom also saw the phenomenon. Following the lights, they found the statue in a cave. Subsequently, a chapel was built to house the statue. Again, the history becomes somewhat vague until the statue's enthronement in its present location.

Meanwhile, a contemporary of the Spanish shepherds, Meinrad (d. 861), a holy man, lived in seclusion near Einsiedeln, Switzerland. He saw to the building of a small chapel near his residence in which he placed a small statue of the Virgin, which, like the Spanish statue, included a representation of the infant Jesus in her arms. A half century after Meinrad's death, a church replaced the chapel. In 948, just prior to the planned dedication of the new church, some people saw Jesus appear at the location and perform a mass. The Bishop of Constance subsequently arrived for the scheduled dedication service, but he was prevented from proceeding when he heard a voice tell him the church was already consecrated.

All three of these images of Mary have accumulated miracle stories around them. Healings

Images of the Black Madonna have existed in Europe since the Middle Ages. They may be the result of African influences, or the blending of Virgin Mary images with such Pagan gods as Isis and Artemis. *Fortean Picture Library.*

have been attributed to prayers addressed to Mary, and each has stories of being protected from damage to their surroundings. The church at Einsiedeln has suffered severe damage from fire on at least five occasions, but each time the chapel housing the Virgin was unaffected.

While more modern representations of the Virgin as black have been attributed to the enculturation of Catholicism, other explanations have been offered for the older, medieval images. Most commonly, they have been attributed to the continuity of images of the Virgin with that of pre-Christian Pagan deities, especially Isis and Artemis, both of whom were portrayed as dark-skinned. Anti-Catholics have used such reflections to support their belief that the Church supports idolatry, while Catholic apologists have suggested the connection was an attempt to introduce Christianity to a Pagan population. In addition, noting the preponderance of such images in France, it has also been suggested that they derive in part from the popular commentary of the Song of Solomon in the writings of Bernard of Clairvaux (c. 1090–1153). He interpreted the bride figure in this love poem as the Virgin, black and beautiful.

Sources:

Begg, Ean. *The Cult of the Black Virgin*. London: Penguin Books, 1985, 1996.

Benko, Stephen. *The Virgin Goddess: Studies in the Pagan and Christian Roots of Mariology*. Leiden: Brill, 1993.

Cruz, Joan Carroll. *Miraculous Images of Our Lady*. Rockford, IL: Tan Books and Publishers, 1993.

Preston, James, ed. *Mother Worship: Themes and Variations*. Chapel Hill, NC: University of North Carolina Press, 1982.

BLACK MASS

The Black Mass was the product of the creative imagination of medieval inquisitors. In the fifteenth century, the Spanish Inquisition turned its attention toward stamping out witchcraft (surviving remnants of pre-Christian Paganism), which was redefined as the worship of Satan (rather than the older Pagan pantheon). At the time, the Inquisition was limited in its task to the suppression of heresy (non-Orthodox forms of Christian belief) and apostasy (rejection of Christianity by former believers). Paganism, as another religion altogether, was outside its purview, hence the redefinition. Satanism, as the worship of the Christian anti-deity, clearly would qualify as apostasy.

Having created the image of an anti-Christianity, the inquisitors slowly built up a picture of what Satanists would do, centered upon the desecration and parody of Christian worship. The mass, the central act of Roman Catholic worship, would obviously be the target of Satanic abuse. Elements of the "black" or satanic mass might include the desecration of a stolen communion wafer, nudity, sexual acts, the sacrifice of an infant, the saying of the Lord's Prayer backward, and acknowledgment of Satan. The climax of the mass might be the invocation and appearance of Satan himself. Under torture, a variety of accused witches confessed to participation in such actions. The primary textbook offering a summary of Satanism was *The Witches Hammer* (*Malleus Maleficarum*) written by two Dominican inquisitors, Heinrich Kramer and Jacob Sprenger (1436–1495), and published in 1486.

It is to be noted that there is no acceptable evidence of an actual Black Mass being held until the seventeenth century. During the reign of Louis XIV (1638–1715), a fortune teller named Catherine Deshayes (d. 1680), popularly known as La Voisin, conspired with a libertine priest known as Abbé Guiborg to work magic on behalf of various people in the French court who wished to keep their place close to the king. In the process, Black Masses were conducted (some of which included one of the king's mistresses as an altar). When these were discovered, the inroads of La Voisin into the court threatened to bring down the government, and the affair was largely hushed up, with trials held in secret and key people being either executed or banished.

Black Masses reappeared at the end of the nineteenth century, again in France, where J. K.

Huysmans founded possibly the first of the modern Satanic groups. Huysmans authored a book, *La-Bas* (*Down There*), which included a detailed account of a Black Mass and would become a source book for future Satanic groups. However, few appeared to have picked up on the Satanic idea until the 1960s. In 1966, San Franciscan Anton LaVey (1930–1997) announced a new era of Satan and the formation of the Church of Satan. The church espoused LaVey's ideal of a set of anti-Christian values such as individualism, selfishness, and the expression of human drives suppressed by the church.

In 1969, LaVey published *The Satanic Bible*, the primary book guiding the Church of Satan. It included guidelines for holding a Black Mass. During the first decade of the church, Black Masses were held to the entertainment of the news media, some being attended by celebrities. LaVey's masses emphasized the sexual aspects, but given the church's teachings about being law-abiding, they eschewed any taking of life. The church and its several offshoots continue to practice a Black Mass.

Satanism, both of the LaVey variety or its more informal variety, has been an extremely rare phenomenon. The Church of Satan never had more than 2,000 active members and was largely gutted in the mid-1970s, when a number of leaders left and its groups (called grottos) largely dissolved. With the exception of the Temple of Set, which counts its membership in the hundreds, the groups that have come out of the Church of Satan have been very small and ephemeral.

On very rare occasions, informal Satanic groups have formed and, during their short life, committed one or more homicides. However, the threat from Satanism remains largely an imagined phenomenon propagated by a small number of conservative Christian church leaders. In 2004 an Italian heavy metal rock band called the Beasts of Satan were accused of killing two of its teenage members in an act of human sacrifice. In response, a prominent Roman Catholic University, the Regina Apostolorum, introduced a course on Satanism and the occult into its curriculum.

Sources:

Cavendish, Richard. *The Black Arts*. New York: G. P. Putnam's Sons, 1967.

Huysmans, J. K. *Down There (La-Bas): A Study in Satanism*. Trans. Keene Willis. New Hyde Park, NY: University Books, 1958.

LaVey, Anton. *The Satanic Bible*. New York: Avon Books, 1969.

Rhodes, H. T. F. *The Satanic Mass*. London: Rider, 1954.

BODHI TREE (INDIA)

The Bodhi Tree, a large fig tree located in Bodhgaya, India, is honored by Buddhists as the originating location of their faith. As the story goes, Gautama, the founder of Buddhism, had been engaged in various austerities in his search for enlightenment. After several years of such exercises, he realized their futility and changed his focus. He sat under a tree vowing not to rise until he attained his goal. Here he engaged in various mental disciplines and subdued his mind. He followed his enlightenment with seven days of sitting meditation, seven days of walking meditation, and then seven more days under the tree. In 623 BCE, Gautama emerged from this period as the Buddha, the Enlightened One, ready to deliver his teachings to his close disciples.

Over the next centuries, the most famous incident concerning the tree relates to the conversion of King Asoka (third century BCE) to Buddhism. He subsequently found his way to Bodhgaya to meditate by the tree. As the story goes, his angry wife had the tree cut down. Asoka responded by having the tree stump covered with dirt, over which he poured milk. The tree miraculously revived. He later had a stone wall built around the tree's trunk to protect it.

Sangamitta, Asoka's daughter and a Buddhist nun, took a cutting from a shoot of the tree to Sri Lanka, where the king, Devanampiyatissa, planted it at the Mahavihara monastery in the old capital of Anuradhapura. This tree, derived from the original tree, is now the oldest continually documented tree in the world.

Under this Bodhi Tree in India, Gautama Buddha is said to have meditated until he had fully realized the philosophy that is the foundation of Buddhism. *Getty Images*.

A century after Asoka, the original Bodhi Tree was destroyed by King Puspyamitra (second century BCE), although an offshoot of the tree was planted in its place. Then in 600 CE, King Sesanka, a zealous Hindu, destroyed the tree again. A new tree was planted in 620 by King Purnavarma. Little was heard of the tree for many centuries following Buddhism's destruction in India in the twelfth century. In the nineteenth century, British archeologist Alexander Cunningham visited Bodhgaya on several occasions and documented the destruction of the tree as it was then constituted. Already weakened by rot, in 1876 the last remnant of the tree was destroyed in a storm. Several people had collected the seeds, and in 1881 Cunningham planted a new Bodhi Tree

that stands today. That tree is the fourth in lineage from the original tree. With the support of the British colonial authorities, he began a restoration of Bodhgaya.

At the time Cunningham replanted the Bodhi Tree, Bodhgaya had fallen into highly partisan Hindu ownership. In the 1890s, Anagarika Dharmapala (1864–1933), a Sri Lankan Buddhist, founded the Maha Bodhi Society for the expressed purpose of raising the money to buy back the Bodhgaya and return it to Buddhist control. That campaign had a partial victory in 1949, when a new temple management committee took control of the site. It is still the case that a majority of the committee and its chairperson must be

Hindus, but Buddhists participate. In 2002, the temple at Bodhgaya was named a world heritage site by UNESCO.

Today, a number of Buddhist temples around the world have Bodhi Trees growing in or adjacent to them, all of which are believed to be offshoots of the one from Sri Lanka.

Sources:

Dharmapala, Anagarika. *The Arya Dharma of Sakya Muni, Gautama Buddha; or, The Ethics of Self Discipline*. 1917. Reprint, Calcutta: Maha Bodhi Book Agency, 1989.

Nissanka, H. S. S. *Maha Bodhi Tree in Anuradhapura, Sri Lanka: The Oldest Historical Tree in the World*. New Delhi: Vikas Publishing House, 1996.

BOROBUDUR (INDONESIA)

Although today it is buried in the jungle almost in the center of the island, Borobudur is the most interesting relic of the former Buddhist domination of Java. Today it survives as the largest Buddhist STUPA in the world.

A center for Vajrayana tantric Buddhist worship, Borobudur emerged on a site formerly used as a Hindu temple. The original site seems to have been chosen for its resemblance to Allahabad, India, where two rivers converge. These physical rivers are believed to converge with a spiritual river, thus creating a place where immortality is experienced.

Vajrayana is a form of Buddhism with practices that claim to speed up the process of attaining enlightenment. It is most often associated with Tibetan Buddhism, although it originated in India and spread to most of the main Buddhist countries. It spread through southeast Asia and to Indonesia in the eighth century. In Java it became associated with the powerful Sailendra dynasty. The several Sailendra who ruled in the late eighth and early ninth centuries expanded the Borobudur complex, which became the center of the faith on the island. By the end of the ninth century, however, the headquarters of the Sailendra kingdom shifted away from central Java, and religious hegemony in the area returned to Hinduism. Then in 1006, Java was shaken by a massive earthquake and an accompanying eruption of the Merapi Volcano. Ash from the volcano covered the site. It was abandoned and eventually lost in the jungle regrowth.

Borobudur remained lost to the larger world for the next 800 years. Sir Thomas Stanford Raffles rediscovered Borobudur in 1814. He led an original clearing of the site and an initial survey. A century later a massive restoration effort began, to be followed by a more recent effort in the 1980s by UNESCO. The archeological attention has led to the site being reclaimed from the jungle, if not returned to Buddhist worship.

The mound, which holds the temple above the jungle floor, has some 50,000 cubic feet of stone. The temple base is some 500 feet on each side. Above the base are eight terraces, each home to a number of relatively small stupas, memorials to enlightened individuals (or buddhas), and many statues of the Buddha. A pilgrim ascends the temple along a spiral pathway that features pictures of scenes from the major Buddhist scriptures depicting the path to nirvana. They lead to a central terrace upon which rests a large stupa surrounded by 72 small stupas. The central stupa is 105 feet high.

In its overall form, Borobudur is a picture of the cosmos similar to the pictures on some MANDALAS. Its shape is quite similar to Mount Meru, the home of the Buddhist deities. Its division into three basic levels—the base, the terraces, and the giant central stupa—represents the three divisions of the universe in Buddhist cosmology: the level of earthly entanglements, the terraces where one separates from the world and purifies desire, and the highest levels of emptiness and formlessness. The giant central stupa has two empty spaces into which a pilgrim may enter to experience the nothingness of nirvana.

It appears that Borobudur, as a Buddhist site, was constructed to house one of the relics of Gautama Buddha that were distributed through the Buddhist world as significant centers emerged. By its size and elaborateness, however, Borobudur became a sacred site in and of itself. Today, it resides in a land that is overwhelmingly Muslim, and only a few Buddhist pilgrims join the tourists who visit the site annually.

Sources:

Dumarçay, Jacques. *Borobudur*. Oxford: Oxford University Press, 1978.

Forman, Bedrich. *Borobudur: The Buddhist Legend in Stone*. New York: Dorset Press, 1992.

Marzuki, Yazir, Toeti Heraty. *Borobubur*. Jakarta: Djambatan, 1982.

Wickert, Jurgen. *Borobudur*. Jakarta: Pt. Intermasa, 1993.

BRANHAM, WILLIAM MARION (1909–1965)

William Marion Branham, a mid-twentieth-century healing evangelist, was a major force in the development of healing ministries in the Pentecostal movement worldwide. At the same time, his own doctrinal differences with many of his Pentecostal colleagues caused him to be alienated from the mainstream of Pentecostalism toward the end of his life, and he became an object of eschatological belief by his closest followers.

Branham was born April 6, 1909, in Burkesville, Kentucky. He dated his dedication to God, in the midst of a family soaked in poverty and alcoholism, to a mystical experience at the age of seven during which he heard a voice say to him, "Never drink, smoke or defile your body in any way for I have a work for you to do when you get older." As a young adult, he joined the emerging Pentecostal movement and experienced a call to the ministry that was tied directly to a healing. He was twenty-four years old when he launched an independent tent ministry that soon led to the establishment of the Branham Tabernacle in Jeffersonville, Indiana.

Because of their low social status, Branham left the Pentecostal community and identified himself as a Baptist. As he emphasized healing and miracles, however, he was soon alienated by his Baptist colleagues. He eventually found a home among the non-Trinitarian Pentecostals, who had an early center in Indianapolis.

It was not until after World War II that his ministry took off. While he had been preaching about God's healing, he had not himself received a healing gift. However, in an encounter with an angel, the gift was passed to him. The healing of the daughter of a fellow evangelist brought him a new set of contacts, and he began to travel the country speaking in Pentecostal churches. He did not emphasize his doctrinal differences and was widely heralded throughout the Pentecostal movement. In the early 1950s he toured Europe and Africa, and a future generation of healing evangelists associated with him, including A. A. Allen (1911–1970), Morris Cerullo (b. 1931), and ORAL ROBERTS (b. 1918).

In the 1960s Branham began to speak about his nonbelief in the trinity and his understanding that denominationalism was a basic evil. His stance alienated many of the people who had promoted him in the 1950s, such as Gordon Lindsey, who had edited Branham's magazine, not to mention the members of the various Pentecostal denominations, such as the Assemblies of God. Branham's following shrank to those independent churches whose members were oriented on his healing work. In 1963 he began to suggest that he was the end-time messenger spoken of in Malachi 4:5. This assignment of a biblical role served to identify his following as a distinct and very different subgroup within the Pentecostal community.

Those who believed in Branham as the end-time messenger founded The Voice of God Recordings and Spoken Word Publications to preserve and publish Branham's writings and sermons in both printed and audio formats. They continue to circulate Branham's material and await the end-time. Since Branham's death on December 24, 1965, the leadership of the movement that had grown around him continues to nurture the movement, and they have turned the land associated with him in Jeffersonville, Indiana, into a shrine to Branham's ministry. Visitors may see the original tabernacle, Branham's grave, and tour the offices where his work is perpetuated.

Sources:

Harrell, David Edwin. *All Things Are Possible: The Healing and Charismatic Revivals in Modern America.* Bloomington: Indiana University Press, 1975.

Lindsey, Gordon. *William Branham: A Man Sent from God.* Jeffersonville, IN: Spoken Word, 1950.

Stadsklev, Julius. *William Branham: A Prophet Visits South Africa.* Minneapolis, MN: privately printed, 1952.

Vayle, Lee. *Twentieth Century Prophet.* Jeffersonville, IN: Spoken Word, 1965.

Weaver, C. Douglas. *The Healer-Prophet, William Marion Branham: A Study of the Prophetic in American Pentecostalism.* Macon, GA: Mercer University Press, 1987.

BROWNE, SYLVIA (B. 1936)

Sylvia Browne emerged in the 1990s as one of the most prominent psychics in America and the author of a number of books promoting the reality of a paranormal dimension to life. Browne was born Sylvia Shoemaker in Kansas City, Missouri, on October 19, 1936. Her birth was auspicious, as she was born with a caul (membrane) over her face (an uncommon but by no means unknown phenomenon), which was interpreted as meaning she had inherited her grandmother's psychic abilities. These abilities began to show themselves during her childhood. Browne grew up as a Roman Catholic. She attended college in her hometown and began a career as a teacher in a parochial school. In the 1960s she moved to California and in 1972 married Dal Brown. (She later added the "e" to her name.)

In 1974 she and her husband opened the Nirvana Foundation and established its headquarters in Campbell, California. It became the vehicle for professionalizing Browne's psychic abilities. As she proved herself with a growing clientele, her career took off, and she became a popular guest on television talk shows and was invited to consult on various psychic situations such as clearing haunted houses. She also emerged as a trance medium with a spirit control named Francine, who claimed to be the spirit of an Aztec woman.

In 1986 Browne founded a new religion, which she called Norvus Spiritus, a form of metaphysical Christianity. It affirms a belief in the feminine aspect of God, reincarnation, and the essential spiritual nature of each individual.

Browne's career took off at the end of the 1990s, while she continued her national television appearances and published her 1998 autobiographical work, *Adventures of a Psychic: The Fascinating, Inspiring, True-Life Story of One of America's Most Successful Clairvoyants*, which she wrote with the assistance of Antoinette May. The book sold well, and a number of books appeared over the next five years. The new century has been marked by a public dispute with psychic skeptic James Randi, who has tried to goad Browne into accepting his offer of one million dollars if she can demonstrate her abilities in an acceptable scientific test.

Sources:

Browne, Sylvia, with Antoinette May. *Adventures of a Psychic: The Fascinating, Inspiring, True-Life Story of One of America's Most Successful Clairvoyants.* Carlsbad, CA: Hay House, 1998.

———. *Conversations with the Other Side.* Carlsbad, CA: Hay House, 2002.

———. *The Other Side and Back: A Psychic's Guide to Our World and Beyond.* New York: E. P. Dutton, 2000.

———. *Past Lives, Future Healing: A Psychic Reveals the Secrets to Good Health and Great Relationships.* New York: E. P. Dutton, 2001.

BUDDHA, RELICS OF THE

Gautama Buddha, the founder of Buddhism, died around 480 BCE at Kusinagara, a town in the northeast corner of Uttar Pradesh, India, near the border of Nepal. Various Buddhist scriptures tell the stories of his death and the events immediately following.

Relics such as the Sarira at Tanzhe temple, which includes remains of the Sakyamuni Buddha, are important in Buddhism, just as they are in Catholicism and some other beliefs. *AFP/Getty Images.*

According to the story, the Buddha's body was cremated. In the ashes were found a number of relics, including teeth and bones. Many of Buddha's followers of royal status expressed their desire to have the relics, and a Brahmin priest named Drona emerged to divide them equally. His initial decision was to create eight sets, one for each ruler desirous of having them. However, Drona was discovered to have hidden some relics, which were stolen.

By this process, the relics were distributed to eight cities in various parts of India, and those stolen to a ninth. Drona retained the vase that had previously held the relics. At each site to which the relics were dispersed, a STUPA was built to hold them. Drona also built a stupa to hold the

vase. A century later, King Asoka conquered all the lands where the relics had been sent, regathered the relics, and redistributed them to a variety of places throughout southern Asia, from Sri Lanka to China.

Buddhism, like Christianity, does not consider relics an essential part of its practice. Nonetheless, they do serve to humanize the often austere faith and provide a local focus for a faith that originated in a distant land many centuries ago. Relics have been seen as signs of the Enlightened One's constant presence. Also, like the Christian relics associated with Jesus (the TRUE CROSS, VERONICA'S VEIL, the SHROUD OF TURIN, etc.), there are usually significant gaps in the historical record tying those items presently claimed to be genuine relics of the Buddha to the events reputed to have occurred immediately following his death.

Places where some of the more important relics may be seen at Buddhist shrines worldwide include the following:

At Anuradhapura in Sri Lanka, the stupa Thuparama Dagaba houses what is said to be the Buddha's alms bowl and his right collarbone. In Kandy, at the center of the island nation, one may see the Buddha's tooth, now housed in a golden stupa known as Malagawa Vihara (or Dalada Maligawa).

In Myanmar, several strands of hair are to be found at the **SHWEDAGON PAGODA** in Ranyon. A tooth recovered from a collapsed pagoda in Mrauk-U, Myanmar, has been sent to the Golden Pagoda Buddhist Temple in Singapore.

China is home to two of the most famous relics of the Buddha. In Beijing, Ling Guang Si Monastery is home to one of the Buddha's teeth. The medieval capital, Xian, had been the home to the Buddha's finger bone, housed in Fa Men Si Monastery. That relic was lost, however, in the changes that occurred in China, including the rise and fall of various forms of Buddhism and then the rise of a secular government in the twentieth century. But in the 1980s, during archeological exploration in Xian, the subterranean crypt where the finger had been housed was rediscovered.

In 1994 the Kingdom of Thailand initiated a project at Kushinagar in northern India, where Buddha died, as part of a larger movement to reestablish Buddhism in the land of its origin. One part of the impressive monastic complex is the Maha Chetiya, a shrine designed by the Thai King Bhumibhol Adulyadej. Here Buddha's relics formerly kept in Thailand have been placed.

In 2005 and 2006, Lama Zopa Rinpoche, the spiritual leader of the Foundation for the Preservation of the Mahayana Tradition, an international Tibetan Buddhist organization based in Taos, New Mexico, organized a tour (including several stops in the United States) of a number set of Buddhist relics, including those of the Buddha. Some of these relics had been salvaged from statues in Tibet, where they had been enshrined for thousands of years before the Chinese occupation in 1951. With the **DALAI LAMA**'s urging, museums and monasteries that owned them donated the relics for the benefit of the Maitreya Project, an ambitious plan to build what would become the world's largest statue—a 500-foot-high bronze representation of a Maitreya Buddha in northern India. The statue would sit on a 17-story building designed as a throne that would include a prayer hall designed to accommodate 4,000 people.

Sources:

Fleet, J. F. "The Tradition about the Corporeal Relics of Buddha." *Journal of the Royal Asiatic Society* (1907): 341–363. Posted at http://www.lightwatcher.com/old_lightbytes/buddha_on_tour.html. Accessed April 1, 2007.

Maitreya Project. Posted at http://www.Maitreyaproject.org. Accessed March 23, 2007.

Rhys Davids, T. W. "Asoka and the Buddha-Relics." *Journal of the Royal Asiatic Society* (1901): 397–410.

Strong, John. *Relics of the Buddha*. Princeton, NJ: Princeton University Press, 2004.

CANTERBURY (ENGLAND)

The ancient town of Canterbury, in southeast England, was the center of the dissemination of Christianity throughout the British Isles. Christianity appears to have been introduced to the land in the fifth century, during the last years of the Roman occupation. Today, outside the wall to the east of the old town, is the church of Saint Thomas, the oldest parish church in England, which has been in continuous use since the sixth century. The local ruler, King Ethelbert, had married a Christian, and he allowed his new queen, Bertha, to include her personal chaplain, Bishop Luidhard, in her entourage. The bishop operated from Saint Thomas' Church.

In 596, Augustine (d. c. 604), a Catholic priest, arrived in England under orders from Pope Gregory I (c. 540–604) to convert the Anglos. Shortly after his arrival, he obtained control of a former Pagan temple, which he refurbished as a church that he named in honor of a Christian martyr, Saint Pancras. Only ruins of this church remain today.

A year after settling in England, Augustine traveled to France where he was consecrated as a bishop. Shortly after his return to his new home, the king accepted Christian baptism and gave

Augustine a building adjacent to the royal palace as the new seat of Episcopal office. Once refurbished, the building was consecrated, around 603, as the Church of Christ of Canterbury. Augustine would later be canonized and is today remembered as the first Archbishop of Canterbury.

In Augustine's later years, the king gave land adjacent to Saint Pancras for the erection of a monastic center. The project was completed by Archbishop Laurence, who followed Augustine. In later years, Saint Dunstan (d. 988) would name the abbey in honor of its founder. The monastery flourished as a major British educational center until the sixteenth century.

A new era for Canterbury followed the conquest of England by William the Conqueror (1027–1087). In 1070, Lanfranc, who came to England with William, became the first Norman Archbishop of Canterbury. He set about a thorough reorganization of the British church that included the appointment of Normans to many high clerical positions and the establishment of Canterbury as the chief center of the church in Britain (over against its primary rival, York). He also had the original church torn down and rebuilt the cathedral, beginning in 1067. He patterned the new building on a model favored in Italy at the time. He also used the subsequent dedication of the new cathedral to show his favoring of Pope Gregory VII (r. 1073–1085) over his rival for the papal office.

Over the years, Canterbury would become the site for numerous historical events. In the cathedral, Thomas à Becket (d. 1170) was murdered in response to his opposition to King Henry II's attempt to control the clergy. Becket's supporters quickly gathered his remains and treated them as they would a martyred saint. Those relics remain a treasured possession of the cathedral. The pope canonized Becket in 1173. Canterbury, already a site for pilgrimage, became more so in the next centuries, thus setting the stage for the famous set of stories about pilgrims on their way to Becket's tomb by Geoffrey Chaucer (c. 1343–1400), gathered in the *Canterbury Tales*.

In 1538 the monastery at Canterbury fell under Henry VIII's orders to dissolve all the British monasteries. Its destruction (only ruins remain) did not reach the cathedral, although it weakened its support community. As Archbishop of Canterbury, Thomas Cranmer (1489–1556) led the Protestant cause, only to be arrested in 1553 after Mary I (r. 1553–1558) came to the throne. After Cranmer was executed, Reginald Pole (1500–1558), who led the Catholic restoration in England, became Archbishop, but he died the next year. Succeeding Elizabethan Archbishops like Matthew Parker (1504–1575) and John Whitgift (c. 1530–1604) led the effort to establish a middle ground between continental Protestantism and Roman Catholicism.

With the overthrow of the Anglicans and the rise of the Puritans (Presbyterians), bishops were dismissed from their office. In 1642 Puritan forces despoiled the cathedral, and it was largely abandoned until the restoration of the monarchy in 1660. In the late seventeenth century, it reemerged as the headquarters of the Church of England and the center of the spread of the worldwide Anglican Communion. In the twentieth century, several of the archbishops of Canterbury have become world famous for their leadership in the international ecumenical movement and in redefining relationships between the Church of England, the Roman Catholic Church, and Eastern Orthodoxy.

Sources:

Brooks, Nicholas. *The Early History of the Church of Canterbury*. Leicester: Leicester University Press, 1984.

Gameson, Richard, ed. *St. Augustine of Canterbury and the Conversion of England*. Stroud: Sutton, 1999.

Knowles, David. *Thomas Becket*. London: A. &. C. Black, 1970.

Taylor, Martin I. *The Cradle of English Christianity: The Coming of St Augustine and St Martin's Church, Canterbury*. Canterbury: St Martin's and St Paul's PCC, 1997.

Woodman, Francis. *The Architectural History of Canterbury Cathedral*. London: Routledge, 1981.

CAREY, KEN

Through the 1980s and 1990s, Chicagoan Ken Carey was one of the most popular New Age channelers, sharing the material he had received through a set of books. His story begins with his quitting a job with the post office and moving to a rural setting in the Ozark Mountains of Missouri. Through the mid-1970s he and his wife lived without most of the major modern conveniences, such as electricity and plumbing, and he shut himself off from the larger society as manifest in newspapers, magazines, radio, and television. For a time he worked with an Amish carpenter.

He made the initial contact with a presence, whom he would later name Raphael, while lying in bed with a cold, and over the winter of 1978–1979 he channeled the material for what became his first book, *The Starseed Transmissions*, which was published under the channeled entity's name. Reflecting on the channeling process, Carey noted that the original communications were nonverbal. He received waves or pulsations that carried meta-conceptual information. Eventually, however, verbal material did come through, some of it originating with an entity who identified himself with Christ who had spoken in ancient time though Jesus.

The source of the channeled material varied from book to book, but some themes carried through the whole of the writings. He presented a very optimistic picture of transformation and progress that would often be punctuated by a period of uncomfortable change. In the 1980s his understanding of change was very much in line with the radical transformation anticipated by New Agers, but in the 1990s change was seen more as a constant part of human existence. He also believed that it was possible for humans to live in a better alignment with nature. He was against the gathering of so many people in urban complexes and saw an emphasis on rationality as blocking access to God.

In his more mature reflections on the channeling process, he has noted that he does not push his ego aside, as occurs with many trance mediums, but is a fully conscious participant in the process. He relaxes, and allows his ego to relax, thus allowing his awareness of the larger world to come to the fore.

Sources:

Carey, Ken. *Notes to My Children: A Simplified Metaphysics*. Kansas City, MO: Uni-Sun, 1984.

———. *Return of the Bird Tribes*. Kansas City, MO: Uni-Sun, 1988.

———. *Terra Christa: The Global Spiritual Awakening*. Kansas City, MO: Uni-Sun, 1985.

——— [as Raphael]. *The Starseed Transmissions: An Extraterrestrial Encounter*. Kansas City, MO: Uni-Sun, 1982.

———. *The Third Millennium: Living in the Posthistoric World*. San Francisco: HarperSanFrancisco, 1996.

CARGO CULTS

Early in the twentieth century, a new millennial religion developed in the islands of the South Pacific, primarily Melanesia. Believers looked for a new age of abundance that would come to them from out of the realm of the gods—the sky. The impetus for this new faith was the observation of the arrival of cargo destined for the British and French colonial authorities on airplanes. The early leaders of the movement saw the cargo as having originated from their own deities and ancestors, who intended it for the islands' native people, and as having been wrongly taken by the Europeans.

It appears that during World War II, when American soldiers arrived and the amount of cargo jumped exponentially, the origin of the cargo was ascribed to a new deity figure named John Frum. The exact origin of John Frum is not known, but some have speculated that it came from a misunderstanding derived from the interaction of the Americans with the native people. In introducing themselves, they would give their name and tell where in the United States they came from. Thus, for example, "I am John from …," became over time "John Frum." Also, an innovative businessman began a line of commonly used products (like soap) under the brand name John Frum.

The Americans also built new airfields upon which the airplanes that brought the cargo could land. When the war ended, the Americans abruptly departed, and suddenly the flow of cargo stopped. Many were convinced that Americans were closely tied to the cargo.

Since the end of World War II, the practice of the groups has centered on a version of what would be called sympathetic or imitative magic. Members engaged in activities that symbolized activities they had identified with the cargo's arrival: They made and dressed in clothes that resembled U.S. army uniforms. They put up American flags and marched under the flag in military formations. They cleared and leveled new airstrips and built large model airplanes.

The movement has appeared on a number of the South Pacific islands, but it thrives most where native religions remain strong, such as Vanuatu, where the movement has grown to the point that very distinct sectarian groupings have emerged.

Sources:

Inglis, Judy. "Cargo Cults: The Problem of Explanation." *Oceania* 28, 4 (June 1957): 249–263.

Rice, Edward. *John Frum He Come: Cargo Cults and Cargo Messiahs in the South Pacific*. Garden City, NY: Doubleday & Company, 1974.

Stanner, W. E. H. "On the Interpretation of Cargo Cults." *Oceania* 29, 1 (Sept. 1958): 1–25.

Worsley, Peter. *The Trumpet Shall Sound*. New York: Schocken Books, 1968.

CARTAGO (COSTA RICA)

The national shrine to the Virgin Mary in Costa Rica is not centered on an apparition of the Virgin, as is often the case, but on some unusual occurrences around a statue. In 1635 a young girl named Juana Pereira found a small stone statue of a woman with a child in her arms resting on a rock near a footpath. Thinking the statue would make a nice plaything, she took it home. The next day she found what appeared to be a similar statue at the same spot. She took it home only to discover that the first statue could not be found. This event repeated itself a third time, and she finally took the statue to the local priest. He recognized the statue as a representation of the Virgin and placed it in a chest at the church. It disappeared from the chest, and the priest and girl found it back at the rock.

The priest assumed at this point that the Virgin wished to be at the place where she was initially discovered, and shortly thereafter a small shrine was built to house the statue. Over the next generation veneration of the statue spread, and a chapel was built. In 1652 an association was created to care for the chapel.

The importance of the chapel was its location on the edge of Cartago, then the capital of Costa Rica, in an area where native people, Africans, and people of mixed blood resided, as opposed to the new Spanish ruling elite. In addition, the statue was made of a dark rock.

The status of the statue grew significantly in the eighteenth century when, on two occasions, it was the focus of prayer to protect the people of Cartago from volcanic eruptions (1723) and an epidemic (1737). In 1782 the statue, as the Virgen de los Angeles, was named the patron of Cartago. After the capital was moved to San José, it was named the patron saint of the country. A large church, the Basilica de Nuestra Señora de los Angeles, replaced the chapel in the early twentieth century.

August 2, the anniversary of the statue's discovery by Juana Pereira, is now a national holiday and a time of pilgrimage to the statue. On August 3, a procession takes the statue to the main church in Cartago, where it remains until the first Sunday in September, when it is returned to its permanent home.

The statue itself is only three inches tall. It is now richly clothed in gold, and only the face of the Virgin and the child are visible. It is displayed within a large, gold monstrance that enlarges its appearance. The small image was solemnly crowned in 1926. Nine years later, Pope Pius XI designated the shrine church as a basilica.

Of additional interest relative to the Virgen de los Angeles, the stone on which the statue was originally discovered is now in the basilica. The stone shows signs of being worn away as thousands of pilgrims pass by and touch it. A spring of water has appeared beneath the stone, and pilgrims may take the water home with them for use in anointing the ill.

Sources:

Fernandez Esquivel, Franco. *Nuestra Señora de los Angeles: Patrona de Costa Rica*. Cartago, Costa Rica: Editorial Cultureal, 1997.

Flores, Dra. "Nuestra Señora de Los Angeles, Patrona de Costa Rica." *María y sus siervos* 25 (1995): 4–12.

CAYCE, EDGAR (1877–1945)

More than half a century after his death, psychic Edgar Cayce continues to fascinate people due in large part to the efforts made to preserve the texts of all the readings that he gave the last two

Worshippers gather at the Basilica de la Virgen de los Angeles in Cartago, Costa Rica, the home of a miraculous statue of the Virgin Mary that is a mere three inches tall. *AFP/Getty Images*.

decades of his life and the support given to studies of those materials. The Association for Research and Enlightenment (ARE), based in Virginia Beach, Virginia, and the associated Edgar Cayce Foundation now maintain the source materials concerning Cayce and his work.

Cayce was born March 18, 1877, in Hopkinsville, Kentucky. He had rather mundane beginnings and as a young adult chose photography as a career. He attended the local congregation of the Disciples of Christ, a conservative Protestant group. His gradual rise from obscurity began in 1898, when Cayce came down with laryngitis. Absent the wide range of medicines available today, he allowed a friend to hypnotize him. Surprisingly, in the trance state, Cayce began to speak and prescribed a cure for his problem. The cure worked, and as word of what happened circulated through the community, others asked him to go to sleep and prescribe for them.

A decade after the original event, in 1909, he did a reading for Dr. Wesley Ketchum, a homeopathic physician, who subsequently arranged for Cayce to do similar readings for people on a regular basis. Cayce thus operated as an amateur psychic specializing in the problems of his neighbors for the next twenty years. He would probably have been forgotten had it not been for a man named Arthur Lammers, a theosophist who paid Cayce's expenses to come to Dayton, Ohio, in 1923 for a set of private readings. These readings significantly expanded Cayce's range; most importantly, Lammers, who believed in reincarnation, asked Cayce about the possible previous earthly lives he might have lived.

The Lammers readings became the origin of a whole new format for Cayce's activity, which came to be called "life readings." In future readings, he would commonly describe three or four past lives for those who came to him for a psychic session. The Lammers sessions also launched his career as a full-time psychic. Shortly after he returned to Hopkinsville, he closed his photography shop and moved first to Dayton, then in 1925 to Virginia Beach, where he lived the rest of his life.

With the financial assistance supplied by one of his followers, he was able to open a hospital and a school, although both had to be closed with the onset of the Depression, due to a loss of financial support. However, he rebounded in 1932 and founded the ARE. Those around Cayce kept detailed stenographic records of all his readings.

In the years following his death, Cayce's son, Hugh Lynn, and Cayce's closest supporters preserved the transcripts of the many readings and began to encourage their use to perpetuate the worldview that permeated them. A breakthrough in calling attention to Cayce came with the publication of a new biographical volume, *Edgar Cayce, the Sleeping Prophet*, by popular writer Jess Stern in 1967. Subsequently, a set of paperback books focusing on the material in the readings was published by the Paperback Library. In the wake of these publications, a new generation was drawn to Cayce, and ARE became a noted organization perpetuating the spirituality, medical views, and other ideas (Atlantis, prophecy, reincarnation, etc.) drawn from the Cayce texts.

The ARE has encouraged detailed studies of the Cayce texts that seek to expound upon the ideas and themes found there, or seek to verify various claims, such as the existence of remnants of the lost continent of Atlantis in the Bahamas. Critical scholarly studies of the materials have been less supported, especially those that have suggested more mundane sources for the material. For example, many of the remedies Cayce prescribed over the years come from nineteenth-century folk medicine. Remaining virtually ignored is the mass of astrological material in the readings.

Sources:

Bro, Harmon H. *A Seer Out of Season: The Life of Edgar Cayce*. New York: St Martins Press, 1996.

Cayce, Edgar Evans, and Hugh Lynn Cayce, *The Outer Limits of Edgar Cayce's Power*. New York: Harper & Row, 1971.

Cayce, Hugh Lynn. *Venture Inward*. New York: Harper & Row, 1967.

Johnson, K. Paul. *Edgar Cayce in Context: The Readings; Truth and Fiction*. Albany, NY: SUNY Press, 1998.

Melton, J. Gordon. "Edgar Cayce and Reincarnation: Past Life Readings as Religious Symbology." *Syzygy: Journal of Alternative Religion and Culture* 3, 1–2 (1994). Posted at http://www.ciis.edu/cayce/melton.html. Accessed April 1, 2007.

CHAKRAS

The Tantric tradition in Hinduism has proposed the existence of an invisible and subtle human anatomy that both parallels the human body and exists in its same space. That subtle anatomy consists of an energy system that flows through the human body much like the system of blood vessels or nerves. The primary channel runs along the spinal column, from its base to the top of the head. The primary channel is punctuated with seven essential psychic centers called chakras (also spelled *charkas*). It is believed that a storehouse of cosmic energy exists as latent potential in most individuals and that this energy, called kundalini, can be awakened in various ways, can travel up the spine awakening the various chakras as it moves, and upon reaching the crown chakra as the top of the head, can bring enlightenment. Belief in the Tantric anatomy, kundalini energy, and the chakras was brought into Theosophy in the late nineteenth century, and permeated the groups of the Western Esoteric tradition throughout the twentieth century.

As developed within Hindu and Esoteric thought, chakras have come to represent different attributes and activities associated with human life. For example, if a person's lower chakras are activated (apart from the higher ones), the individual is believed to operate from lower motives—the sex drive, gluttony, avarice, and selfishness. The fourth chakra, associated with the heart, is seen as the most active chakra among religious people, accounting for a variety of actions flowing from compassion and devotion. Spiritual healing is usually seen as an artifact of the heart chakra.

The sixth chakra, better known as the third eye, is said to be located in the center of the forehead and is associated with a range of psychic abilities. After closing one's eyes, one can usually see pictures at what appears to be a screen on the inside of the skull below the forehead. This phenomenon is commonly suggested to be a demonstration of the third eye. Attention to images that spontaneously appear on this inner screen while one is in a relaxed state (meditation) is an early step in most psychic development processes.

Some gurus (spiritual teachers) are credited with the ability to initially awaken the kundalini, a process called shaktipat. Those who teach kundalini yoga will also advise different activities, including various forms of controlled breathing that will further encourage the rise of the kundalini. Many practitioners of kundalini yoga claim to feel the rise of the energy during yoga exercises, and there are apocryphal reports of the sudden rise of kundalini doing physical damage to the body (though none of these stories have been verified). Among the prominent twentieth-century teachers of kundalini yoga was Padit Gopi Krishna (1903–1984), who claimed that kundalini was a biological force that could be studied scientifically. While this initially interested some people with scientific training, no research results have been published that offer to prove Gopi Krishna's claims about kundalini.

Sources:

Judith, Anodea. *Wheels of Life: A User's Guide to the Chakra System*. St. Paul, MN: Llewellyn Publications, 1987.

Krishna, Gopi. *Kundalini: The Evolutionary Energy in Man*. Boulder, CO: Shambhala, 1970.

Simpson, Liz. *The Book of Chakra Healing*. New York: Sterling Publishing Co., 1999.

Simpson, Savitri. *Chakras for Starters*. Nevada City, CA: Crystal Clarity Publishers, 2002.

CHARTRES CATHEDRAL (FRANCE)

The town of Chartres, southwest of Paris, is known internationally for its cathedral, considered an exemplar of thirteenth-century gothic architecture. That such a fine building should be erected in a relatively small town was the result of the town's having become a prominent center of the evolving devotion to the Virgin Mary in Western Catholicism.

Pilgrims make their way to Chartres, France, a holy place to Pagans and Christians alike. The cathedral at Chartres contains a shirt said to have been worn by Mary when she gave birth to Jesus. *Getty Images.*

Even prior to the arrival of Christianity in the area, the high ground upon which the cathedral was built had been the site of Pagan worship. For many centuries, Autricum, as Chartres was called in ancient times, was the center of a Gallic people, the Carnutes. On the high ground, a well was located where local priests, the Druids, practiced their divination. Christianity was present in France from the second century and permeated the region over the next centuries. Clovis I, the king, converted at the end of the fourth century. By the sixth century, Christian worship had pushed the Pagans from the high ground at Chartres.

Chartres became a pilgrimage site as the ninth century came to a close. At this time the city's church was given a piece of cloth that was purport-edly a shirt once belonging to the Virgin Mary. As stories gathered around the cloth, it was further asserted that the cloth was from the shirt worn by Mary when she was giving birth to Jesus. It is generally called the Veil of the Virgin. As the story goes, it was given by Mary to a widow and eventually found its way to Constantinople, the capital of the Byzantine Empire. The Byzantine emperor gave it to Charlemagne (768–814). Charlemagne's grandson, Charles the Bald (823–877), gave it to the church at Chartres in 876. The cloth was housed in an underground crypt, along with a statue of the Virgin to which couples hoping to bear children made their request known.

In the twelfth century, veneration of the Virgin Mary took a step forward with the likes of

Bernard of Clairvaux (1090–1153), who asserted Mary's role as an intercessor for Christians with her son. The enthusiasm for the Virgin provided the context in which the townspeople decided to build a cathedral. On June 10, 1194, after years of work and the outlay of their money, the new cathedral was destroyed in flames. Several people, including the guardians of the Veil, were trapped inside. Only when the fire was put out was it discovered that the people and the cloth had been safe in the underground crypt. The decision to rebuild came quickly.

The new cathedral took several generations to complete, even with the assistance of people across France and from other countries. Several different architects worked on the building, which reflects a variety of styles. The two spires at the front corners are completely different in appearance. Among the architectural features of the cathedral are its large rose windows, the one in the north carrying images from the Old Testament, and the one in the south depicting the apocalypse from the New Testament. Placed in the floor was an eleven-circuit labyrinth. The labyrinth was meant to be walked by those visiting the cathedral either as an act of penance (on one's knees) or as a symbolic pilgrimage. In the latter case, it could substitute for a pilgrimage to the Holy Land—a journey possible to only a small minority during the Middle Ages. The Chartres labyrinth is the only complete large labyrinth to survive from that era.

In addition to the Marian intentions of the pilgrims, the Druid well survived, and it maintained its fame as a source of healing. Many people, therefore, came to Chartres seeking a cure for their illnesses. Already a powerful sacred site in the eyes of believers, over the centuries after the new cathedral was completed, it sacredness was enhanced by the addition of more relics. Several martyrs were buried inside its walls. In the thirteenth century, the count of Blois donated a relic claimed to have belonged to Saint Anne, the Virgin Mary's mother.

Pilgrimages to Chartres were commonplace until the French Revolution. Among the many anti-religious acts of the Revolution, the church was vandalized, the statue of the Virgin in the crypt burned, and numerous relics destroyed. Most damaging was the removal of the lead that covered the roof, which was ripped off, melted, and taken away. It was not until 1836 that a restoration project was initiated, although it efforts were temporarily blocked by another fire, the worst since 1194. Fortunately, the cathedral was spared major damage during the two world wars.

Today, Chartres is once again a major religious pilgrimage site, although pilgrims must now compete with an equal number of tourists who visit the structure for architectural or other secular reasons. The building has also become the focus of significant occult speculation. Much of the art integrated into the building featured Pagan, magical, and astrological imagery, spurring speculation that Chartres was once home to Paganism (the veneration of the Virgin being a slightly disguised worship of the mother goddess) or that the building's architecture was an embodiment of medieval occult thinking.

While both Protestants and skeptics have withdrawn any belief in the relics housed at Chartres or in the veneration of the Virgin, millions of conservative Roman Catholics still look upon Chartres as an especially holy place. Among the modern activities sanctioned by the church is the walking pilgrimage from Notre Dame Cathedral to Chartres, a journey of some 70 miles.

Sources:

Adams, Henry *Mont-Saint-Michel and Chartres: A Study of Thirteenth-Century Unity*. New York: Doubleday Anchor, 1959.

Miller, Malcolm. *Chartres Cathedral*. London: Pitkin Pictorials, 1980.

Peguy, Charles. *Le Monde de Chartres*. Paris: Zodiaque, 1961.

CHIMAYO (NEW MEXICO)

Almost due north of Santa Fe, New Mexico, the village of Chimayo lies in the Sangre de Cristo Mountains. Far from a major highway, it is never-

Mud contained in a hole at the Nuestro Señor de Esquípulas church in Santa Fe, New Mexico, has healing powers, according to many Christians. *Getty Images.*

THE ENCYCLOPEDIA OF RELIGIOUS PHENOMENA

theless the destination of thousands of pilgrims annually, many of whom seek out a church named Nuestro Señor de Esquípulas. Inside the small chapel, they make their way to an even smaller room adjacent to the altar, where there is a hole filled with mud, the object of their pilgrimage. The mud is smeared on the body in the hope of bringing relief to the body, mind, and/or spirit of the devout believers. Elsewhere in the church are numerous objects, including crutches and braces, left behind by people as a record of their cure.

The petition to erect the chapel at Chimayo was granted in 1818. It is a modest adobe structure surrounded by an adobe wall. It was a privately owned chapel until the 1920s, when the owners ran into severe financial problems. The Roman Catholic Church purchased and currently maintains it.

The site has been related to a similar site in Esquipulas, Guatemala, where a parallel tradition of healing earth had led to the emergence of a church known locally for the healings that occur there. It appears that at the beginning of the nineteenth century, someone from Chimayo traveled to Guatemala, evidenced by the presence of a uniquely shaped wooden cross at both sites.

The healing earth of Chimayo had been known and venerated for centuries before Spaniards brought Christianity to the region in the sixteenth century. It is possible that the region was geologically active in relatively recent times and that the mud hole is the site of a former geyser. There are a variety of stories about the recognition of the mud as a healing substance, all the product of an oral culture, many contradictory in content.

Whatever the truth hidden in the various stories might be, today pilgrims come to gather small amounts of the mud. Some immediately apply it to their body or ingest it. Others carry it away for use back at home. Each evening, those who tend to the chapel refill the hole with dirt from nearby land, a fact not widely advertised. The largest number of pilgrims come during Holy Week when, besides visiting the chapel, they may also view a passion play recounting the life of Christ.

Sources:

de Borhegyi, Stephen F. "The Miraculous Shrines of Our Lord of Esquipulas in Guatemala and Chimayó, New Mexico." *El Palacio* 61, 12 (Dec. 1954): 387–401.

Trento, Salvatore. *Field Guide to Mysterious Places of the West*. Boulder, CO: Pruett Publishing Company, 1994.

CHROMOTHERAPY

Throughout the twentieth century, scientists (and especially psychologists) explored how color in the individual's environment affected behavior. Common knowledge now assumes that different colors can stimulate or depress the senses, arouse sexual feelings, attract attention, or even promote or retard healing. However, paralleling the scientific research on the effects of color has been scientific-like speculation on color as a healing power that has served as a foundation for different practices popularized within several New Age and Esoteric spiritual communities.

Such speculation has been traced to several men working in the mid- and late nineteenth century. Augustus James Pleasanton, in the 1870s, advocated what he termed "blue sunlight." He had, he claimed, been able to stimulate the growth of grape vine by using a blue filter over the sunlight shining on the plants. His claim led to the sale of panes of blue glass under which people could take sun baths. His work was seconded by a Dr. Seth Pancoast, who used blue and red lights to affect the nervous system, and E. D. Babbit, who made several claims about color's ability to effect various physical changes. Babbit is most remembered for his effort to "charge" water by putting colored glass containers in sunlight.

The work of these men and others was taken up by Dinshah Pestanji Ghadiali (1873–1966), an Asian Indian physician. As a young doctor, he began to treat patients with color and found measurable success. He moved to the United States prior to World War I and discovered the emerging naturopathic medical community. As the name implied, naturopaths sought natural forms of healing that avoided both the physical invasion of the body and the use of chemical drugs. Practitioners would prescribe different natural substances and vitamins—all of which could be seen as food supplements—and advocated a number of alternatives to surgery, from hatha yoga to massage. Color healing or chromotherapy fit the guidelines of naturopathy completely.

After attaining his citizenship in 1917, Ghadiali established his office in New Jersey. In the 1920s he developed a simple machine for projecting color on the body and proposed what he termed "spectro-chrome therapy." His new therapy made claims about the healing effects of light and of the different colors, and he found himself in conflict with the government for the rest of his life. However, his theories survived and underlie chromotherapy to the present.

Contemporaneous with Ghadiali, chromotherapy was taken into Theosophy by Ivah Bergh Whitten. Following a healing event in her life at the beginning of the century, she began to lecture on the occult properties of color that drew on a long history of teachings in Esoteric circles that integrated the colors of the light spectrum into a whole system of magical correspondences. These correspondences had been expanded in Theosophy, where colors were identified with the various theosophical ascended masters and the virtues associated with them. As her work spread, Whitten integrated insights from Ghadiali's teachings and introduced techniques using colored light for therapeutic ends.

Whitten passed her work—including her organization, the Amica Master Institute of Color Awareness (AMICA)—to Roland Hunt, who became a major exponent of chromotherapy through the middle of the century. In the decades after World War II, chromotherapy became one of a spectrum of alternative therapies that gained popularity in what emerged as the New Age and holistic healing movements of the 1970s and 1980s. Exponents included prominent personalities in the New Age community such as Corinne

Heline and Edgar Cayce, along with a variety of health writers such as Linda Clark. At the same time that chromotherapy was evolving in the English-speaking world, it was also finding support in continental Europe, where exponents includes the likes of German theosophist Rudolf Steiner and Swiss psychologist Max Luscher.

Ultimately, chromotherapy rests on the same ideological basis of much modern Esoteric teachings concerning a basic cosmic healing power. Light is identified with that primal healing energy and the different colors with useful forms of that light, which are relatively easily appropriated by the average person. Light may be applied to the body through sun baths under various color filters or through an artificial light source that directs a colored beam on the exposed skin. It may also be applied through different meditative techniques that begin with imagining a particular color and picturing it permeating the breath as one engages in regulated breathing.

As the new century began, chromotherapy continued to grow and expand. Practitioners have created (and trademarked) variations on the basic theory and practices, many integrating the most recent research in the physiological reactions to color uncovered by psychological research. In contemporary color therapy, the actual measured effect of color on the body and emotions are mixed in a complex manner with beliefs about the direct therapeutic effects of color on the body that have little or no empirical data to back them.

Sources:

Amber, Reuben B., and A. M. Babey-Brooke. *Color Therapy: Healing with Color.* New York: ASI Publishers, 1980.

Chiazzari, Suzy. *Nutritional Healing with Colour.* Shaftesbury, UK: Element, 1999.

Clark, Linda. *The Ancient Art of Colour Therapy.* New York: Simon & Schuster, 1974.

Gimbel, Theo. *The Colour Therapy Workbook.* Shaftesbury, UK: Element, 1993.

Whitten, Ivah B. *What Colour Means to You, and the Meaning of Your Aura.* Ashington, England: C. W. Daniel, 1933.

CITY OF REFUGE (HAWAII)

Scattered across the Hawaiian Islands are worship centers called *heiaus* that now manifest little of what made them places for religious gatherings, in spite of occasional signs that they are still minimally in use. Among the heiaus that operated on Hawaii prior to the nineteenth century, some were set aside as places of refuge. To understand their use, one must know a little about Hawaiian beliefs.

Hawaii was led by individuals who formed a royal caste—chiefs and kings—and priests. Those of royal personage were among the most notable manifestations of *mana* (spirit, divine power). As in other cultures, the priests were functionaries who carried out a range of religious duties. Built into the moral and religious codes was a set of rules (*kapu*) forbidding some activities (*taboos*), some serious and others fairly trivial. Violation of taboos often carried severe punishment, and even some seemingly trivial ones (such as a common person violating the space or prerogative of a royal personage) could result in death. It was also the case that many taboo violations could occur quite apart from any intentions.

Built into the Hawaiian system was a means of rectifying violations of a taboo: the places of refuge. Throughout the islands, each chief established and maintained a *pu'uhonua*—a place of refuge—where a person could find forgiveness, even for a violation that called for death. (The refuges also welcomed wounded warriors needing a place to heal and women and children trying to escape a battle nearby.) The sanctuary was endowed with supernatural protections. The chief saw to the building of a temple and an adjacent residence. Priests in residence carried out the specific duties assigned the sacred site. The royalty and priests together carved a number of *ki'is*, fierce-looking statues of deity-like creatures who enforced the sanctuaries' rules. To add to the mana of a sanctuary site, the bones of the successive chiefs would be buried in the temple.

In 1819 Kamehameha II (1797–1824) abolished the portion of the Hawaiian religion relative to taboos; as a result, the places of refugee had no remaining function. Ten years later Queen Ka'ahumanu (1768–1832), King Kamehameha I's (c. 1758–1819) widow, who had converted to Christianity, ordered the destruction of all of the sanctuary sites.

Today, the best place to see the history of the places of refuge is the City of Refuge (Pu'uhonua o Honaunau), located along the coast of the Big Island south of the city of Kona. This site dates at least to the beginning of the sixteenth century. Here, one may see a Hawaiian temple called the Hale o Keawe Heiau, a reconstruction of the original built around 1650. Emphasizing the seriousness of the activity that went on at the refuge, entrance for those seeking sanctuary was often by water—they swam across the bay to reach their destination. Once inside the place of refuge, the priest was charged with granting sanctuary and a form of absolution. Once the individual went through the sanctuary's ritual, it was as if the violation never occurred. The person could leave and pick up his or her life as before.

There were three temples at the City of Refuge, though only one has been rebuilt. The role of the additional sites have been lost to history, as has much of the Hawaiian religious system, destroyed largely before its beliefs and practices were recorded.

Sources:

Bennett, Wendell C. *Hawaiian Heiaus*. Chicago: The University of Chicago Libraries, 1932.

Emory, Kenneth P. "City of Refuge." *Paradise of the Pacific* 71 (July 1959): 66–67.

Mulholland, John F. *Hawaii's Religions*. Rutland, VT: Charles E. Tuttle Co., 1970.

Neasham, V. Aubrey. *Historic Sites Survey Report, Place of Refuge, Hawaii*. San Francisco: National Park Service, 1949.

COMETS

Since ancient times people have searched the heavens for information on the present and future. The primary product of such searching has been astrology and its cataloging of the regular movements of stars and planets. However, speculation has also flowed around less regular events—meteors, eclipses, and comets. Because they occurred less often and were spectacular displays when they did, they were seen as particularly important as signs of blessing and woe. Meteors were generally thought to presage happy events, as were stellar events such as super novas. There was some foreboding over eclipses and even dread with a brilliant comet.

Throughout the early years of Christendom, comets were seen as indicative of catastrophes, even the downfall of empires, a belief that gained the approbation of a number of leading thinkers throughout the centuries. Illustrative of this belief is one folktale that Pope Calixtus III (r. 1455–1458) excommunicated a comet as an instrument of the devil. He was possibly aware of the coincidental 1066 appearance of Halley's Comet with the Battle of Hastings, in which William the Conqueror seized the British throne from King Harold. The comet was said to portend war and the death of kings. As late as 1836, Halley's Comet was blamed for the deaths at the Alamo.

By the twentieth century, the science of astronomy began to assert itself. Although discovery of the poisonous nature of the gases in the tails of comets initially increased paranoia, astronomers eventually succeeded in reducing comets to the mundane in the eyes of most people. The public education was not altogether successful, however. In the late twentieth century, religious connotations associated with comets began to take shape with the appearance of Comet Kohoutek in 1973 (a comet notable as the first in several decades that would be seen by a majority of humankind). The comet proved less than spectacular, and the predictions that had been made about changes to the Earth did not come to pass.

In the spring of 1997, while most people were enjoying the show that Comet Hale-Bopp was putting on, a small group in Rancho Santa Fe, California, was watching it for quite different rea-sons. The Heaven's Gate group celebrated what was to be the occasion of transcending their human existence. When catastrophe did not overtake the Earth, in March of that year, thirty-nine members committed suicide.

Religious and apocalyptic speculation concerning comets has continued to the present, although it has been pushed to the fringe of popular culture.

Sources:

Chambers, G. F. *The Story of the Comets: Simply Told for General Readers*. Oxford: Clarendon Press, 1909.

Kronk, G. W. *Comets: A Descriptive Catalog*. Hillside, NJ: Enslow Publishing, 1984.

Moore, P., and J. Mason. *The Return of Halley's Comet*. New York: W. W. Norton & Company, 1984.

Schechner Genuth, Sara. *Comets, Popular Culture, and the Birth of Modern Cosmology*. Princeton, NJ: Princeton University Press, 1997.

White, Andrew D. *A History of the Warfare of Science with Theology in Christendom*. New York: Appleton and Co., 1897. Reprint, New York: Dover, 1960.

COMMITTEE FOR THE SCIENTIFIC INVESTIGATION OF THE CLAIMS OF THE PARANORMAL

The Committee for the Scientific Investigation of the Claims of the Paranormal (CSICOP) is one of two prominent organizations that devote a significant amount of time to the examination and debunking of various forms of religious phenomena that include claims of miraculous paranormal elements. CSICOP was founded by a diverse group within the American Humanist Association (AHA) whose members had become concerned about the marked revival of astrology in the West during the decades after World War II. In 1975, philosophy professor Paul Kurtz was a catalyst for gathering the signatures of a number of scientists denouncing astrology. The next year the AHA dedicated its annual meeting to an examination of what was termed the "new irrationalism," the popularity of interest in things psychic and occult. Out of that meeting, CSICOP emerged to counter the spread of what was termed pseudoscience. CSICOP saw itself as continuing earlier individual efforts to debunk the fraudulent phenomena that had become integrated into the Spiritualist movement.

CSICOP got off to a good start with the sponsoring of a periodical, the *Zetetic*, and a plan for public education on the scientific reason for rejecting many psychic claims. However, it soon ran into trouble when it set up a task force to examine the claims of French researchers Michel and Françoise Gauquelin, who claimed their statistical work was evidence that backed up basic astrological claims. The committee's research verified the Gauquelin claim's but, as later revealed by one of the committee's members, the research was altered so that negative findings could be reported. The scandal that followed tarnished the committee for a number of years.

Overcoming the problem with the Gauquelin research, CSICOP refocused on popular claims by psychics and by conservative religionists and assumed a role as a debunking organization eschewing further sponsoring of original research. In that regard, they have performed a valuable service in uncovering fraud, showing the mundane science behind some seemingly extraordinary events and providing popular education in the face of an ever-growing number of claims of paranormal phenomena and supernatural miracles. Among their notable successes was the exposure of several healing evangelists as fakes. The group's journal, *The Skeptical Inquirer*, has become a source-book for analysis of a wide range of paranormal claims. Much of this material has also been posted on the CSICOP Web site.

Along with a debunking of claims of occult and psychic phenomena, CSICOP has given considerable attention to traditional supernatural claims within the Roman Catholic Church. Coming under scrutiny, among others, have been APPARITIONS OF THE VIRGIN MARY, miraculous healings, weeping ICONS and bleeding statues,

and a range of relics like the SHROUD OF TURIN and pieces of the TRUE CROSS. In this endeavor, author and researcher Joe Nickell has come to the fore as a major voice countering the claims of Catholic scientists and spokespersons.

Sources:

Clark, Jerome, and J. Gordon Melton. "The Crusade Against the Paranormal." Parts 1 and 2. *FATE* 22, 9 (September 1979): 70–77; 32, 10 (October 1979): 87–94.

Kurtz, Paul. *The New Skepticism: Inquiry and Reliable Knowledge*. Amherst, NY: Prometheus Books, 1992.

Nickell, Joe. *Looking for a Miracle: Weeping Icons, Relics, Stigmata, Visions and Healing Cures*. Amherst, NY: Prometheus Books, 1993.

COMMUNES

One of the most popular forms of the religious life, adopted by small groups throughout human history, is communal living. It has been particularly related to Christianity due to the element of communal life evident in the first generation of the church in Jerusalem as described in the biblical book of Acts. It was said of the first church that its members had all things in common and that they sold their possessions and divided their resources among each other as they had need (Acts 2:44–45). While the communal life tended to disappear as the church grew, especially as it became the religion of the masses, there were always a few who attempted to live by this apostolic ideal. In the post-Constantinian era, this ideal would give birth to a new monastic movement that saw thousands of men and women withdraw from mainstream society to live a communal life.

Within the monastic movement, the essence to communal living included the individual's renunciation of private property (expressed in a vow of poverty) and the ownership of both the means of production and the fruits of work by the group as a whole. As monastic communities developed and different orders became owners of considerable real estate and other possessions, a philosophical distinction was posed between the ownership of property and its use. Thus individuals who did not own anything were able, as members of a wealthy order, within the rules of the order, to live in many ways quite luxuriously.

Ordered religious communities were often founded by individuals who claimed extreme religious experiences that placed them outside the ordinary and/or who had extreme ways of expressing their religious commitments. Many founders were people known to converse with various spiritual entities, especially the Virgin Mary, Jesus, angels, or different saints. The different orders also became the haven for other individuals who possessed various paranormal abilities, such as levitation, bi-location, conversation with spiritual entities, or manifesting the stigmata. Life within an order both prevented the general public from viewing some of the more extreme behavior associated with some individuals and protected the members from an often reactionary or phenomena-seeking population.

Many members of ordered religious communities, such as Roman Catholic or Eastern Orthodox churches, have proven themselves great assets to their churches by demonstrating fulfilling selfless devotion by dedicating themselves to teaching, missionary activity, and the manifestation of Christian ideals and possibilities.

Protestants have generally eschewed the monastic ideal in favor of placing an emphasis on each Christian living the devoted life previously seen as possible only for those in religious orders. The first generation of Protestants who had taken monastic vows often made a point of renouncing the vows and adopting a secular life that included marriage, the possession of property, and the managing of a household. In the nineteenth century, a reaction to the growing emphasis on the individual in Western Protestant countries, especially the United States, led to a reactionary movement that saw the founding of hundreds of communal societies. While most were short-lived, a few became quite successful

both in expressing a spectrum of communal ideals and surviving economically.

In the Protestant-dominated countries, the majority of communes have had a secular base. Reacting to forms of individualism that tended to destroy community and deny intimacy, communes practiced a lifestyle built around mutual work, shared meals, and attempts to bridge the gaps between the rich and poor. Those that lasted the longest have also adopted a common religious life, usually a form of free-church pietism without formal ties to any particular denomination. At the same time, some denominations experimented with the reintroduction of monasticism (Anglicans) and deaconess orders (Lutherans, Methodists).

Free from any denominational control, communes have been able to experiment with a variety of forms of organization (from the hierarchical to the ultra-democratic), patterns for religious living, and sexuality. The Shakers were among the most successful of the nineteenth-century communities. They chose to live a celibate life, developed distinct forms of architecture to embody that life (including, for example, separate doors for men and women), and put considerable energy in a variety of commercial enterprises. Other equally successful communal groups experimented with different forms of married life, including the complex marriage practiced by the Perfectionists at Oneida, New York, and the polygamy adopted by the Latter-day Saints. A few groups have tried forms of free love, but such communes have tended to be short-lived and rife with internal struggles. Most communes, however, such as the Hutterites, the most successful twentieth-century communal group, have continued traditional Christian teachings on sex and marriage, limiting sexual expression to monogamous married couples.

The number of communes expanded greatly in the twentieth century, especially during the 1960s, when they became one element in the hippie culture. Many communes were formed in the cities as a means of survival by street people, while at the same time, many more abandoned the city for the more "natural" idealistic life of the countryside. These communes were known for the new forms of spirituality they embodied. Many had come to find a new respect for religious experiences from their ingestion of various mood-altering drugs, especially LSD. Others had encountered one or more of the new Asian teachers who entered the country after the change of the immigration laws in 1965.

In the early 1970s, several years after the wave of commune-founding hit the hippie community, many members—wearied of drugs and tired of Eastern religions—turned to evangelical Christianity. The communes became the locus of a significant revival movement known as the Jesus People movement. From the Jesus People came a number of communally based new Christian groups, such as Jesus People USA, The Alamo Christian Foundation, and the controversial Children of God (now The Family International).

Scholars, even those who have studied communes extensively, have questioned the relevance of communes in the larger scheme of world events. Those who have followed a communal life have generally constituted a small minority of the religious community at any given moment. However, they have manifested an influence far beyond their numbers. As has been the case with the equally small peace churches, Christian communes have continually held the ideal of the unselfish life before the larger community, even while living separately from that community. Communes have also been a haven for those beset with strong religious experiences.

Communes exist almost invisibly in society. Most, like the very successful Hutterites, have chosen to live geographically apart. Most Hutterites live in North and South Dakota, and the great majority of Americans never see them apart from occasional television specials. Urban communes generally exist anonymously, its members choosing to assume a low profile among neighbors who might not understand the communal life.

Sources:

Kagan, Paul. *New World Utopias*. New York: Penguin Books, 1975.

McLaughlin, Corrine, and Gordon Davidson. *Builders of the Dawn: Community Lifestyle in a Changing World*. Scottsdale, AZ: Sirius Publishing, 1986.

Oved, Yaacov. *Two Hundred Years of American Communes*. New Brunswick, NJ: Transaction Publishers, 1993.

Pitzer, Donald E. *America's Communal Utopias*. Chapel Hill: University of North Carolina Press, 1997.

CONYERS, GEORGIA

In the 1990s, Conyers, a small town near Atlanta, Georgia, became the site of a series of claimed visitations by the Virgin Mary to a woman named Nancy Fowler. During these apparitions, Mary was generally referred to as Our Loving Mother.

Fowler's first encounter with Mary occurred in the 1980s when she was living in Atlanta, and included instructions to move to Conyers, where she purchased a farm. For a period of eleven years she experienced frequent visitations that began to attract large crowds. On August 15, 1991, a shrine was dedicated, and beginning on September 13, 1991, monthly gatherings for the regular apparitions of Mary were held. In all, she appeared forty-nine times, monthly for three and a half years and then annually (each October 13) through 1998. The apparitions call to memory the 1917 apparitions at Fatima, which also occurred on the thirteenth day of each month. The last Fatima apparition was on October 13, 1917. In addition to the more formal apparitions to Fowler, a number of the visitors to the site have also claimed to have had personal visitations.

The apparitions generally occurred at a spot behind the Fowler residence that came to be known as Holy Hill. The visible focus for pilgrims is a life-size statue of the Virgin as she appeared at Fatima. There was also a large crucifix and a well from which water, believed to have healing qualities, was drawn. The apparitions generally occurred within the shrine room that Fowler would enter at noon on the appointed day. She would describe what she was seeing and the content of any message she received. One of her assistants would relay the message to the gathered faithful.

The archbishop of Atlanta has assumed a neutral stance toward the apparitions. He has both noted the good that has come from them in strengthening the spiritual life of many, but at the same time he has ordered the priests of the archdiocese not to identify themselves with the farm or say mass there. He has also refused to start any formal investigation, although a large file on the apparitions is being accumulated at the Chancery offices. In 1998 the Ukrainian Catholic Church (an Eastern-rite church in full communion with Rome) established a parish on land adjacent to the Fowler farm. This parish is under a Ukrainian bishop, not the archbishop of Atlanta. It has opened a center on the property and announced plans to build a retreat center nearby.

In 1993 a team led by Dr. Riccardo Castanon, a professor of neuropsychophysiology at the Catholic University of Bolivia, conducted a series of tests on Fowler. He reported that she was entering various altered states of consciousness during the apparitions and did not show any signs of psychopathology. While not verifying the apparitions, Castanon's work did include criticisms of them.

Also in the early 1990s, a nonprofit corporation, Our Loving Mother's Children, was formed. It took charge of the program at the apparition site and has tried to ensure all that no individual is experiencing financial gain from the offerings of the many pilgrims. The corporation led the development of a welcoming environment for the tens of thousands who regularly visit. However, in 1999 Fowler had disagreements with the corporation and officially disassociated herself from it. Then in 2000, Our Loving Mother's Children turned over the management and operational responsibility for the site to the Ukrainian Catholic Church, though it remains active in promoting the site.

Sources:

Garvey, Mark. *Searching for Mary: An Exploration of Marian Apparitions across the U.S.* New York: Plume, 1998.

Teosorieto, Ron. *Mother of Great Love; Mother of Sorrow.* Godford, Aust.: privately printed, 1992.

COTTINGLEY FAIRIES

During the 1920s, British Spiritualists and theosophists endorsed a set of pictures taken, supposedly, of fairies by two young girls in the village of Cottingley. The pictures were taken by seventeen-year-old Elsie Wright and her cousin, Frances Griffiths. The first picture, taken in July 1917, showed Elsie with the fairies. A second picture was taken a few months later. The pictures were put aside for several years, then eventually fell into the hands of Arthur Conan Doyle (1859–1930), who in 1919 was gathering material to write an article on fairies. In 1920 he commissioned Edward J. Gardner (d. 1970) to investigate the pictures.

Finally convinced the pictures were what they purported to be, Doyle wrote an article for the December 1920 issue of *Strand* magazine, with a follow-up in the March 1921 issue. The article set off a storm of controversy, and Doyle was forced to defend himself and the pictures. The articles became the basis of his 1922 book, *The Coming of the Fairies,* in which Doyle wrote about his belief that fairies were a means of shaking up new secular worldviews. In this effort he was joined by theosophist and medium Geoffrey Hodson (d. 1983), who in 1925 published his own argument for the existence of fairies and defense of the photographs, *Fairies at Work and Play* (1925). In 1945 Gardner would write a book describing his involvement in the incident. He, like Doyle and Hodson, would die believing the photographs were real.

Skeptics attacked the photographs almost immediately. To most, the photographs appeared to picture flat figures rather than living, three-dimensional figures. Defense of the photographs depended on the integrity of the girls and their

This famous, but fraudulent, photo captures an image of the Cottingley Fairies reported by two English girls in the 1920s. The story of the fairies was supported by the writer Sir Arthur Conan Doyle, who believed in the hoax until the day he died. *Fortean Picture Library.*

families, and the inability of anyone to produce the actual mundane source of the fairies in the pictures. The pictures also passed the examination of photography experts of the day. Gardner's death in 1970 became the occasion of further attention to the Cottingley photographs, which—in spite of efforts by skeptics to destroy them—would not go away.

A breakthrough came in 1976 when *The British Journal of Photography* began to run a series of articles by Geoffrey Crawley, which thoroughly reviewed the pictures. The ninth installment of the series dropped the bomb: a letter from Elsie in which, for the first time, she admitted that the pictures were a hoax. She had perpetuated the hoax in part because she felt sorry for Doyle, who

had committed himself to defending the pictures. In the end, the representations of the fairies in the pictures could not be located as they had been drawn by Elsie, inspired in part from a book belonging to Frances, *Princess Mary's Gift Book.*

While the Cottingley fairy hoax is common knowledge today, thirty years after the exposure, the three books that backed the story remain in print and continue to be used in support of the existence of a fairy world within contemporary spiritualist and theosophical circles.

Sources:

Crawley, Geoffrey. "The Astonishing Affair of the Coming of the Fairies." *British Journal of Photography* 24 (December 1982–April 1983).

Doyle, Arthur Conan. *The Coming of the Fairies*. 1921. Reprint, New York: Samuel Weiser, 1972.

Gardner, Edward l. *Fairies: The Cottingley Photographs and Their Sequel*. London: Theosophical Society, 1945.

Hodson, Geoffrey. *Fairies at Work and Play*. London: Theosophical Society, 1925.

Princess Mary's Gift Book. London: Hodder & Stoughton, 1914.

CROP CIRCLES

Crop circles, large designs that have appeared in farm fields, have in the several generations of their existence moved from UFO enigma to object of New Age metaphysical speculation. The first modern crop circles appeared in Australia in 1965, but they were really called to the public's attention after they began to appear in England in 1972. By the end of the century, they had been found in some twenty-five countries.

The crop circles appeared as simple circles of flattened crops (usually wheat, corn, barley, or rye). They were enigmatic in that the method of flattening the grain stalks without breaking them was unknown and the creators of the circles did not reveal themselves. There were no obvious paths created from the nearest road to the circle, and as they multiplied in England, speculation abounded as to their extraterrestrial origin. The circles were considered by some to be maps or messages for UFOs.

Over time, the simple circles evolved into ever more complex patterns while skeptics sought to replicate the creation of the circles. Skeptics have been largely successful in showing how rather mundane equipment may be transported into a field after dark, used to make the circle in a few hours, and removed without leaving evidence of their means of entry to the site. Their success led most UFO researchers to turn away from crop circles as having any relevance to their endeavor.

By the time the UFO community withdrew interest in crop circles, New Age believers who professed to be in contact with extraterrestrials had begun to reflect upon the more complex designs as cryptic messages from their extraterrestrial friends.

Other New Agers, some not interested in extraterrestrials, have seen the crop circles as messages from Gaia—Mother Earth—and have interpreted them as reactions to the severe ecological damage affecting the planet. Crop circles, they believed, added strength to arguments against continued violations to nature. At the same time, some Christian ministers interpreted the crop circles as signs of the devil's activity on Earth.

It is of some interest that crop circles are short-term phenomena; they last at best only a few weeks since they were created, when crops near maturity and are destroyed during harvest. Thus, they have to be recreated each summer, and only pictures of them remain. Crop circles are rarely produced in the same field from one year to the next.

Sources:

Pringle, Lucy. *Crop Circles (The Pitkin Guide)*. London: Jarrold Publishing, 2004.

Schnabel, Jim. *Round in Circles*. Amherst, NY: Prometheus Books, 2003.

Silva, Freddy. *Secrets in the Fields: The Science and Mysticism of Crop Circles*. Charlottesville, VA: Hampton Roads Publishing Company, 2002.

CRYSTAL BALLS

Among the most popular forms of divination, crystallomancy, or scrying, involves the use of a clear sphere of crystalline material that may vary in size from three to seven inches in diameter. The size of the crystal ball greatly affects its price as the difficulty of locating a crystal larger than three or four inches without significant flaws increases significantly.

When used for divinatory purposes, the crystal ball assists the induction of an altered state of consciousness in the seer, who experiences visions by gazing into the crystal. Those who might also be present at the time that the visions are projected see nothing—it is entirely a subjective event for the seer. Crystallomancy has been practiced since ancient times, and over the years a set of prayers and invocations was developed for use prior to attempting any divination. Paracelsus (1493–1541) was among the first to openly declare the prayers of no importance, and most modern practitioners have dispensed with them. The primary preparation is inducing altered consciousness in order to access the subconscious. Other actions that might precede any reading are related to the particular understanding of divination held by the practitioner—divination being compatible with a variety of religious and philosophical perspectives.

Some users of the crystal also report that as they begin their scrying, they see a milky or smoky clouding in the crystal. This clouding may also be interpreted much as one reads tea leaves or other random arrangements of patterns.

Sources:

Achad, Frater. *Crystal Vision through Crystal Gazing; or, The Crystal as a Stepping-Stone to Clear Vision: A Practical Treatise on the Real Value of Crystal Gazing.* Chicago: Yogi Publication Society, 1923.

Besterman, Theodore. *Crystal-Gazing: A Study in the History, Distribution, Theory and Practice of Scrying.* London: Rider, 1924. Reprint, New Hyde Park, NY: University Books, Inc., 1965.

Pelton, Robert W. *Ancient Secrets of Fortune Telling.* South Brunswick, NJ: A. S. Barnes, 1976.

Sibley, Uma. *Crystal Ball Gazing: The Complete Guide to Choosing and Reading Your Crystal Ball.* New York: Fireside, 1999.

CRYSTAL SKULLS

The term *crystal skull* refers to a set of stone artifacts carved in the shape of a human skull. The oldest were carved in ancient Central America by the Aztecs and related peoples. However, these are of far less interest as religious phenomena than the small number of skulls, most of clear quartz, that have been proposed to originate in ancient Atlantis or outer space. Various paranormal phenomena are associated with these skulls

that have made them objects of veneration and awe by contemporary Esoteric believers.

The first of these latter skulls appeared in the 1940s. F. A. "Mike" Mitchell-Hedges (1882–1959) claimed that in 1923 he was in British Honduras (now Belize) with his seventeen-year-old daughter, Anna Mitchell-Hedges, excavating Lubaantun, an ancient Mayan city. He believed that Lubaantun held the secret of the ancient Atlantis. The skull, about five inches high and weighing about eleven pounds, resembled the earlier Aztec skulls but had a detachable jaw.

In describing the skull in later years, Mitchell-Hedges labeled it the "skull of doom" and suggested it was more than 3,500 years old and was produced by a lengthy process of rubbing down a large crystal. It took its name from its associations with the High Priest, who could will the death of others with its use. The sinister story attracted attention to the crystal over the years.

The crystal received attention in 1970, when Anna Mitchell-Hedges, who had inherited the skull, allowed art conservator and restorer Frank Dorland to examine it. He added to the legend with his declaration that it originated in Atlantis and accompanied the Knights TEMPLAR on their crusades in the Holy Land. More importantly, however, he claimed the skulls had been examined in a laboratory of Hewlett-Packard, where researchers found a number of unique attributes verifying its ancient production, including an absence of the kinds of microscopic scratches that would indicate it was carved. The entire story was recounted in a 1973 book by Richard Garvin. The book drew the attention of members of the then-emerging New Age movement to the crystal skull, which was seen as a very special case of the crystals that would become so important to New Agers in the next two decades. Subsequently, attention was called to the existence of other crystal skulls. Most of these skulls were put forward with accounts that traced them to Mexico or Central America, suggested their ancient origin, and tied them to various psychic phenomena. Most often

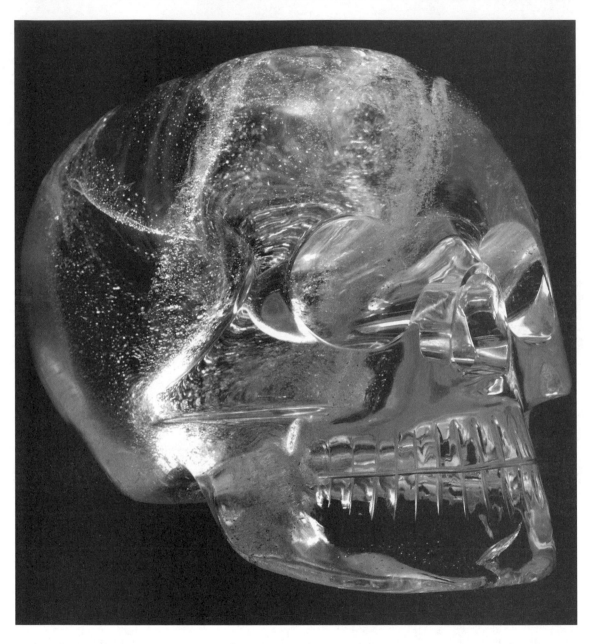

Speculations of the origins of crystal skulls run the range from outer space aliens to the advanced society of Atlantis. However, in the case of this pictured skull, once displayed at the British Museum, the supposed origin was not the ancient Aztec civilization but rather an attempted fraud. *AFP/Getty Images.*

they were touted as catalysts capable of producing various mental phenomena for the person owning or using them.

Unfortunately, the stories associated with the skulls have not been able to withstand critical scrutiny. The original Mitchell-Hedges skull, for example, appears to be the product of a hoax. Rather than collecting the skull in Belize in 1923, Mitchell-Hedges purchased the skull at an auction in 1943. There is no independent evidence to back up the claims of Frank Dorland, such as a crystal skull being with the Knights Templar during the Crusades. Other skulls that were examined during the 1990s were shown to be relatively modern productions, the close examination of their surfaces showing the marks of modern tools. In the mid-1990s, after receiving a crystal skull for the collection at the Smithsonian Institute, several scientists conducted an investigation of it and related skulls, all of which were tracked to rather mundane nineteenth-century origins.

While the crystal skulls attracted a modest amount of veneration, especially among people who had a prior interest in crystals in general, the negative connotations of the Mitchell-Hedges skull caused interest to wane. The primary exponent of the crystal skulls at present is New Age writer Joshua Shapiro.

If there was a claim about the skulls that was true, it was the assertion that they could be used for scrying, a form of clairvoyance generally associated with the use of crystal balls and magic mirrors. The skulls, in fact, resemble crystal balls, and it is this resemblance rather than any mysterious quality that accounts for their facilitation in scrying.

Sources:

Bowen, Sandra, et al. *Mysteries of the Crystal Skulls Revealed.* Pacifica, CA: J & S Aquarian Networking, 1988.

Galde, Phylis, and Frank Dorland. *Crystal Healing: The Next Step.* St. Paul, MN: Llewellyn Publications, 1988.

Garvin, Richard M. *The Crystal Skull: The Story of the Mystery, Myth and Magic of the Mitchell-Hedges Crystal Skull Discovered in a Lost Mayan City During a Search for Atlantis.* Garden City, NY: Doubleday & Company, 1973.

Nickell, Joe. *Secrets of the Supernatural: Investigating the World's Occult Mysteries.* Amherst, NY: Prometheus Books, 1991.

CRYSTALS

Few items were as popular or as controversial within the New Age movement of the 1980s as were crystals. New Age leaders championed the idea that crystalline substances were the bearers of great energies and, if used in the proper way, could transmit those energies for the miraculous **HEALING** of the body and spirit. This belief was a relatively minor part of Esoteric lore and entered popular culture via the practice of assigning birthstones for each month of the year, which in turn had grown from their origin as gemstones corresponding to astrological signs.

A new emphasis on crystals in the Esoteric community can be traced to **EDGAR CAYCE** (1877–1945), the American seer who regularly gave readings in trance for many years. Atlantis was a popular theme for Cayce, and crystals played a significant role in Atlantean culture. The Atlanteans had a large crystal stone that gathered energy from the stars, and that energy was used to power the culture. Its misuse led to the destruction of Atlantis. Cayce also advocated the use of crystals for assistance in healing and meditation and as protective amulets. In the late twentieth century, his ideas were furthered by Frank Alper, the founder of the Arizona Metaphysical Center in Phoenix.

Alper expanded upon the themes in Cayce's readings and was a leader in the emergence of the use of crystals as one of the major practices in the New Age movement of the 1970s and 1980s. Crystals were seen as great storehouses of universal energy (an energy described and popularized by **FRANZ ANTON MESMER** in the eighteenth century). Alper and other New Age leaders described the means of absorbing and otherwise using that energy in great detail. Different crystals of distinct color and cut were recommended for different purposes.

The fact that crystals are quite beautiful and have great value as jewelry and home decoration assisted their popularity among New Agers. However, their real attractiveness derived from claims of a scientific base relative to crystal power, called the piezoelectric effect. When crystals are compressed, they contract and give off a small light discharge. If electricity is run through a crystal, it will expand and vibrate. The fact that crystals vibrate at a set rate due to their thickness became important at one stage in the development of the radio; later, small silicon crystals became an important component in microcomputers.

Still, in spite of all the scientific use for crystals, science failed to provide any backup for the New Age claim that crystals stored energy. Scientific reviews of New Age crystal books forced the authors to withdraw their extravagant claims and revert to affirmations that crystals stored spiritual energy, undetectable by scientific instrumentation. The loss of a scientific base for understanding crystals did not destroy their use, but it has greatly inhibited their further promotion.

Sources:

Berkovitch, Sheril. *Crystal Workbook: The Spiritual, Healing, Transformational and Metaphysical Properties of Crystals and Healing Stones*. Victoria, Australia: Hihorse Publishing, 1995.

Chocron, Daya Sarai. *Healing with Crystals and Gemstones*. Weirs Beach, ME: Samuel Weiser, 1987.

Raphael, Katrina. *Crystal Enlightenment: The Transformational Properties of Crystals and Healing Stones*. Santa Fe, NM: Aurora Press, 1985.

Richardson, Wally, Jenny Richardson, and Lenora Huett. *Spiritual Value of Gem Stones*. Los Angeles: DeVorss and Co., 1980.

CUMAE (ITALY)

Dating to the ninth century BCE, Cumae is an ancient city in southern Italy not far from Naples. It was founded originally as a Greek colony, and it became the center of a Greek-speaking nation in the region. In the second century BCE, the area was absorbed by Rome.

On the Italian Peninsula, Cumae was most famous as the home of a priestess of Apollo known as the Cumaean Sibyl (prophetess). The Sibyl lived in a cave and wrote her prophecies down on leaves, which she placed at the mouth of the cave. Followers collected these, and many bound them together to form books.

The most famous story of the Sibyl comes from the sixth century BCE, during the reign of Tarquin II (r. 535–510 BCE) of Rome. The Sibyl left her cave and brought nine volumes of her prophecies to Tarquin. She offered these for sale at what seemed too high of a price. When Tarquin refused her offer, she burnt three of the volumes and offered the surviving six volumes at the same price. Tarquin again turned down her offer. She then burnt three more volumes and offered the surviving volumes at the same price. Tarquin's curiosity now got the best of him, and he bought the remaining Sibylline Prophecies.

These books became prized possessions of the Roman government to be consulted on important occasions, the somewhat enigmatic text being open to a variety of interpretations. The books were partially destroyed in a fire in 83 BCE, and the remainder survived until another fire claimed them in 405 CE.

Cumae continued to play a role on the Peninsula until it was destroyed and subsequently abandoned in 1205. The most prominent feature of the city was its Acropolis with its temple dedicated to Apollo, the remains of which were discovered in 1817. The Sibyl's cave, with its 60-foot-high ceiling and 375-foot entranceway, was one of several that transversed the city's Acropolis. Lost for many years, it was rediscovered in 1932. Today the Sibyl's cave is one of a set of ancient sites included in the Cumae Archeological Park.

Sources:

Fiego, G. Consoli. *Cumae and the Phlegraean Fields*. Naples: Mary E. Raiola, 1927.

Monteiro, Mariana. *As David and the Sybils Say: A Sketch of the Sibyls and the Sibylline Oracles*. Edinburgh/London: L. Sands & Co, 1905.

Temple, Robert K. G. *Conversations with Eternity: Ancient Man's Attempts to Know the Future*. London: Rider, 1984.

Toker, Cyril. *The Sibylline Books.* Ponte Vedra Beach, FL: Cumaean Press, 1989.

CUMORAH (NEW YORK)

Cumorah is a drumlin, a hill formed of drift from a receding glacier, located about four miles south of the village of Palmyra in western New York State. The hill has gained significance because of it role in the formative events of the Church of Jesus Christ of Latter-day Saints (LDS).

On the evening of September 21, 1823, an angelic messenger named Moroni visited the young Joseph Smith Jr. and showed him where a set of gold plates were buried that contained the history of the ancient inhabitants of the Americas. Four years later, Moroni returned and allowed Smith to dig up the plates and begin the translation of them. After working on the translation for the next few years, Smith published the text as the Book of Mormon. The Book of Mormon describes the story of a group of Hebrews who came to the Americas in the seventh century BCE. Their beliefs included an anticipation of the coming of Jesus Christ. They also had disagreements that led to their separation into two groups, the Nephites (led by a man named Mormon) and the Lamanites. After Christ appeared in America (following his resurrection), the two groups lived in harmony until the end of the second century CE but later fell into internecine warfare. At the end of the fourth century CE, the last of the Nephites were wiped out in a battle near the hill. After engraving the history of his people on golden plates, Mormon gave the plates to his son, Moroni, who buried them in 421 CE. As a resurrected angelic entity, Moroni returned in the 1820s to guide Smith to the plates.

Today the hill is a major sacred site of the LDS and several other churches that look to Joseph Smith Jr. as a prophet, such as the Community of Christ (formerly the Reorganized Church of Jesus Christ of Latter-day Saints). In 1928 the LDS purchased the Cumorah hill and in 1935 erected a monument atop it. Later a visitor's center was built near it, and since 1937, the LDS has staged an outdoor pageant at the hill that dramatizes the key events in the Book of Mormon.

In the last half of the twentieth century, Mormon scholars have raised a number of questions about the New York site, as the geography of the region does not fit the geography described in the Book of Mormon; some have proposed locations in Central America as more closely descriptive of those events. Meanwhile, non-Mormon scholars have found no historical or archeological evidence to independently verify the occurrence of the events that are described in the Book of Mormon.

Sources:

Clark, John. "A Key for Evaluating Nephite Geographies." *Review of Books on the Book of Mormon* 1 (1989): 20–70.

McGavin, E. Cecil, and Willard Bean. *Geography of the Book of Mormon.* Salt Lake City, UT: Bookcraft Inc., 1949.

Palmer, David A. *In Search of Cumorah: New Evidences for the Book of Mormon from Ancient Mexico.* Bountiful, UT: Horizon Publishers & Distributors, 1981.

CURÉ D'ARS

The man popularly known as the Curé d'Ars (the Curate of Ars), renowned for the healings that occurred around him, was born Jean-Baptiste-Marie Vianney at Dardilly, France, on May 8, 1786. He entered the priesthood as a young man, and he completed his studies at Ecully and the seminary at Verrieres. He was plagued by his inability to master Latin, but he finally completed his studies and was ordained in 1815. He was initially posted at Ecully. In 1818 he became the parish priest at Ars. Among his early accomplishments was the founding of an orphanage for girls.

Although of average intellectual accomplishment, as the Curé d'Ars, Vianney soon gained a reputation for his abilities in offering people spiritual counsel. Church members found him insightful and even supernatural in content. They began to come to him from neighboring parishes and

Jean-Baptiste-Marie Vianney, the Curé d'Ars, was not the most intellectual or wealthy of priests, but he was said to have remarkable powers of healing and clairvoyance, and was somehow able to financially support hundreds of needy people. *Fortean Picture Library.*

then from across France, and finally from other countries. Hearing confessions became the most time-consuming part of his days. His ability to have paranormal information about an individual's past or future became the matter of many testimonies. The number of healing stories, especially accounts of children, multiplied during and after his life.

It was said that he was plagued with a poltergeist, a noisy spirit that moves objects, for most of his adult life. He noticed that the manifestations were worse when a person was coming to him seeking consolation. He attributed the poltergeist to the devil.

Along with the clairvoyance and healings, people were amazed at the financial resources he was able to accumulate. He personally had no money, and his family was not wealthy. However, he regularly supported more than a hundred women and children, and he provided for the poor and destitute by overseeing the building of a number of institutional homes. With little publicity, the finances were regularly available to meet his commitments.

Vianney died at Ars on August 4, 1859. He was proclaimed venerable in 1874, beatified in 1905, and canonized in 1925. In 1929 he was declared the patron of parish priests.

Sources:

de la Varende, Jean. *The Curé d'Ars and His Cross.* Belgium: Desclee Company, 1959.

de Saint Pierre, Michel. *The Remarkable Cure of Ars: The Life and Achievement of Ars.* Garden City, NY: Doubleday & Company, 1963.

Ghéon, Henri. *The Secret of the Curé d'Ars.* Trans. F. J. Sheed. New York: Sheed & Ward, 1937.

Trochu, Francis. *The Curé D'Ars: St. Jean-Marie-Baptiste Vianney.* Rockford, IL: Tan Books and Publishers, 1927.

THE DA VINCI CODE

In 2003, a writer of popular thriller novels suddenly emerged from relative obscurity when his novel *The Da Vinci Code*, originally published as a paperback, became an international bestseller. Within two years Dan Brown's novel had been translated into more than forty languages and sold more than twenty-five million copies. It also became the center of an international controversy concerning the substance of the reputed factual material woven into the fabric of the plot, material that many saw as an attack upon Christianity in general and the Roman Catholic Church in particular. That controversy reached a new stage when the movie version of the book was released in May 2006.

The plot of *The Da Vinci Code* is fairly straightforward. Hero Robert Langdon, a Harvard professor introduced in Brown's earlier novel *Angels and Demons*, begins an investigation of the murder of the curator of the Louvre museum in France, whose body has been found next to an enigmatic cipher. Langdon, who specializes in art and symbology, attains the assistance of a cryptologist, and the pair begin a search through the symbols found in the art works of Leonardo da Vinci. Their search leads them into encounters with the very real Catholic organization Opus Dei and a somewhat fictionalized organization, the Priory of Sion, the protector of a historical secret that is threatened to be lost to humankind.

The Da Vinci Code is a novel, and it might have stayed on the bestseller charts for only a few weeks had it not been for the brief statement at the beginning that makes a number of assertions about the "facts" Brown used to structure the plot. The author writes:

> The Priory of Sion—a European secret society founded in 1099—is a real organization. In 1975 Paris' Bibliothèque Nationale discovered parchments known as Les Dossiers Secrets, identifying numerous members of the Priory of Sion, including Sir Isaac Newton, Botticelli, Victor Hugo, and Leonardo da Vinci.

> The Vatican prelature known as Opus Dei is a deeply devout Catholic sect that has been the topic of recent controversy due to reports of brain washing, coercion, and a dangerous practice known as "corporal mortification." Opus Dei has just completed construction of a $47 million National Headquarters at 243 Lexington Avenue in New York City.

All the descriptions of artwork, architecture, documents, and secret rituals in this novel are accurate.

As Langdon rushes across France and the United Kingdom in search of a murderer, he uncovers a set of secrets that revises both Christian and secular European history. In this new account, following Jesus' death, his wife Mary Magdalene, who was pregnant with Jesus' child, moved to France. There she bore a child named Sarah. The child continued Jesus' royal bloodline. Brown argues that Jesus charged Mary Magdalene with the task of building his church, not Simon Peter (as recounted in the Bible). Thus, while Jesus' male followers were building what became known as the Catholic Church, in France, the Jewish community protected Sarah and her descendants and honored Mary Magdalene. Eventually, in the fifth century, one of those descendants intermarried with French royalty, producing the Merovingian family. The Merovingians ruled until 751, when the Carolingians came to power. Although removed from the throne, the Merovingians did not disappear. The family continues to the present.

Among the descendants of the Merovingian kings was Godefroi de Bouillon (1060–1100), who led the first crusade and ordered the TEMPLARS into Jerusalem. He is less interested in taking the Holy Land from the Muslims than in locating a set of documents, the Sangreal documents, which tell the true story of Jesus and Mary Magdalene. Once he arrived in Jerusalem in 1099, he founded the Priory of Sion. It is the Priory's ongoing task to protect the Sangreal documents, guard the Tomb of Mary Magdalene (the real Holy Grail of legend), and nurture and protect the bloodline, i.e., those Merovingians who are still alive.

According to Brown, the Priory of Sion has continued to the present as a secret society and has included a number of notables in its lineage of Grand Masters. There are several alchemists, such as Nicholas Flamel and Robert Flood, as well as the reputed founder of the Rosicrucians, Valentin Andrea. From the artistic community,

the priory selected artists Botticelli and da Vinci, dramatist Charles Nodier, writer Victor Hugo, musician Claude Debussy, and poet Jean Cocteau. Scientists are represented by Robert Boyle and Isaac Newton.

Most of this history is pure fantasy. There are no records to indicate Mary Magdalene's bearing a child with Jesus or her journeying to France, and no records of her descendants surviving and marrying into the Merovingian family. Godefroi de Bouillon is a real person, though not a descendant of the Merovingians, who in 1099 did found an Abbey of Our Lady of Mount Zion in Jerusalem. This monastic community continued to exist until 1291 but was destroyed as Muslims retook the city. The surviving monks moved to Sicily and carried on for another century, but the order died out in the fourteenth century.

What is today known as the Priory of Sion is a very modern organization founded in 1956 in France by Pierre Plantard (1920–2000). It has no connection with the prior Abbey of Zion; rather, Plantard saw it operating within the relatively large Esoteric community of France. The priory never found its place, however, and remains a very small society. Between the demise of the Abbey of Zion and the founding of the modern Priory of Sion, there is no record of any secret organization with leaders such as da Vinci, Victor Hugo, and other such notables. It is, however, the practice of several modern Esoteric groups to claim a heritage that includes the historically notable. For example, the California-based Ancient and Mystical Order Rosae Crucis (AMORC, founded in 1915) includes in its pre-twentieth-century Rosicrucian lineage Leonardo da Vinci, Saint Teresa of Avila, Isaac Newton, Benjamin Franklin, Thomas Jefferson, and Claude Debussy, among others.

Although this story of Jesus, Mary Magdalene and the Priory of Sion did not originate with Dan Brown and *The Da Vinci Code*, it is a recently constructed myth. Plantard, with the assistance of two colleagues, Philippe de Chérisey (1925–1985) and Gérard de Sède (1921–2004), put together one part of the story, attempting to establish the claims of the Merovingians to the French throne and, incidentally, Plantard's place as a Merovingian descendant, which was published in a 1967 book, *L'Or de Rennes*. To document this story, Plantard and de Chérisey created a set of documents that they deposited at the French National Library. Plantard also claimed access to documents revealing the truth concerning the Priory of Sion that had been hidden in a church at **RENNES LE CHÂTEAU**, a small town in southern France. These documents had supposedly been discovered in 1897 by the parish priest Berenger Saunière, who used them to become wealthy. Plantard and his associates later admitted they had created the Priory of Sion story from whole cloth.

The story outlined in *L'Or de Rennes* was then taken up by three writers, Henry Soskin (aka Henry Lincoln), Michael Baigent, and Richard Leigh, in their pseudo-documentary book, *Holy Blood/Holy Grail*, published in 1982. To Plantard's story, the three authors added the account of Jesus, Mary Magdalene, and the royal bloodline. *Holy Blood/Holy Grail* became a bestseller in the Esoteric world, and it is the immediate source of the myth as presented by Brown. Brown also brings into the story some later accretions to the basic plot, including reflections on the Templar's Scottish outpost in Scotland, **ROSSLYN CHAPEL**.

In the wake of the success of Brown's book, a number of books have appeared that attempt to make Brown's readers aware that his "facts" are actually the outgrowth of an elaborate hoax and a pseudo-documentary and that no documents exist to offer any substantiation to his alternate history of Jesus and Christianity. As has been demonstrated with other modern hoaxes, however, it is unlikely that the myth will be laid to rest. In fact, in the wake of Brown's success, *Holy Blood/Holy Grail* has enjoyed a new spurt in sales, and at least two books supportive of Plantard's myth have appeared.

Sources:

Baigent, Michael, Richard Leigh, and Henry Lincoln. *Holy Blood/Holy Grail*. London: Jonathan Cape, 1982.

Beverley, James A. *Counterfeit Code: Answering the* Da Vinci Code *Heresies*. Pickering, ON: Bay Ridge Books, 2005.

Brown, Dan. *The Da Vinci Code*. New York: Doubleday & Company, 2003.

Introvigne, Massimo. "Beyond *The Da Vinci Code:* History and Myth of the Priory of Sion." Posted at http://www.cesnur.org/2005/pa_introvigne.htm. Accessed April 1, 2007.

Olson, Carl, and Sandra Meisel. *The Da Vinci Hoax: Exposing the Errors in* The Da Vinci Code. Ft. Collins, CO: Ignatius Press, 2004.

DALAI LAMA

The title Dalai Lama has, since the sixteenth century, designated the person who both headed the reformed or Gelugpa school of Tibetan Buddhism and was the temporal ruler of Tibet. The office can be traced to the fourteenth century and the creation of the Gelugpa school by Tsongkhapa (1357–1419). He founded a new monastery at Ganden that would become the major disseminating point for the new teachings. He was succeeded as abbot at Ganden by Gedun Drub (1391–1474), who went on to create the Tashilhumpo monastery near Shigatse, west of Lhasa, one of the centers that solidified the position of the Gelugpa tradition in Tibet. Gedun Drub was succeeded by Gedun Gyatso (1475–1542) and Sonam Gyatso (1543–1588), the latter destined to change the historical trajectory of Tibet.

Sonam Gyatso was invited by Altyn Khan, the ruler of Mongolia, to teach his form of Buddhism to the Mongolian people as a means of unifying them. Sonam Gyatso proved quite successful in his assigned task. As a first act before returning to Tibet, he proclaimed his patron as both the reincarnation of Kublai Khan and the embodiment of the bodhisattva of wisdom, thus assigning Altyn Khan both political and religious credentials. The khan returned the gesture by naming Sonam Gyatso "Dalai Lama," or "ocean of wisdom." He would subsequently be seen as an incarnation of Avalokitesvara (better known in the West as **KUAN YIN**), the bodhisattva of compassion. The

The Dalai Lama is the fourteenth incarnation of Avalokitesvara. As such, he is the spiritual and political leader of Tibet, though he now lives in exile in India while his country remains under Chinese rule. *Getty Images.*

title "Dalai Lama" was then retroactively applied to Sonam Gyatso's two predecessors.

The future Dalai Lamas would continue their relationship with the khan of the Mongols, and Lozang Gyatso (1617–1682), the fifth Dalai, with the assistance of Mongol troops, secured authority as the political leader of all Tibet. The Dalai Lamas retained power in Tibet until the 1950s.

The current Dalai Lama is the fourteenth. He was born Lhamo Dhondrub on July 6, 1935, in a small village in northeastern Tibet. Following the death of the thirteenth Dalai Lama, a search began for the child into which he would reincarnate. At two years old, Lhamo Dhondrub was put to the test and succeeded in recognizing the pos-

sessions belonging to the late Dalai Lama, and he was officially recognized as the successor. From that point he was seen as both the reincarnation of the Dalai Lama and an incarnation of the Buddha of Compassion. He was renamed Jetsun Jamphel Ngawang Lobsang Yeshe Tenzin Gyatso (meaning Holy Lord, Gentle Glory, Compassionate, Defender of the Faith, Ocean of Wisdom). He was enthroned at the **POTALA** Palace in Llasa on February 22, 1940, when he was four years old.

As he grew, a regency managed the affairs of Tibet. The crisis created by the Chinese Revolution and subsequent invasion of Tibet by the Chinese Army in 1950 led to the teenage Tenzin Gyatso assuming full powers as the Dalai Lama on November 17, 1950. During the next decade, he

THE ENCYCLOPEDIA OF RELIGIOUS PHENOMENA

completed his formal education and attempted to negotiate a settlement with the Chinese that would lead to the withdrawal of the army. Through the decade he operated from Llasa, but in 1959 there was a popular uprising against the Chinese that was brutally put down. The Dalai Lama joined the more than 100,000 Tibetans who had moved into exile. In 1960 he settled in Dharmadala, India, and created a government in exile, which he has headed ever since.

In the years since his exile, the Dalai Lama has worked to mobilize international support to reestablish an independent Tibet. That effort has not proved successful, and Tibet has been integrated into the Peoples Republic of China as the Tibet Autonomous Region. The government has been secularized, and, especially during the Cultural Revolution, efforts were made to destroy Tibetan Buddhism. That policy has more recently been replaced by one of accommodating a greatly weakened Tibetan Buddhist leadership.

From India, the Dalai Lama has operated as the political leader of all Tibetans in exile while also being the head of one group of Tibetan Buddhists. As a religious leader, he has promoted the spread of Tibetan Buddhism, including a project to preserve the literature of the faith, much of which was lost in the destruction of the monasteries in Tibet. He has worked to gain friends among influential Westerners to facilitate the movement of Buddhist leaders and the establishment of Buddhist centers globally. One unexpected consequence of his exile has been the dramatic spread of Tibetan Buddhism in the last decades of the twentieth century, the appearance of hundreds of books on Tibetan Buddhism in Western languages, and its acceptance by thousands of non-Tibetans.

In his effort to build support for Tibet, he has traveled widely and received a host of awards from those who support his efforts. Recognition culminated in 1989 when he was honored with the Nobel Peace Prize.

As the century came to an end, the Dalai Lama recognized that efforts to win the political independence of Tibet were not working, and he has subsequently redirected his efforts to the preservation of Tibetan nationhood and culture. He began to advocate what he termed "genuine self-rule" as part of China rather than independence from China.

In the meantime, in 1995 an issue arose over the designation of the new Panchen Lama, the previous one having died in Tibet. The Panchen Lama is the second-highest Tibetan religious authority. Two different people have been designated to carry on the office, one in China and one outside. Reflecting on the situation, on his sixty-fourth birthday, the Dalai Lama asserted that following his own death, reincarnation would not appear in Tibet or any area under Chinese control. He noted that the next incarnation would come to carry his work forward, not stifle it.

Sources:

Avedon, John F. *In Exile from the Land of Snows*. New York: Alfred A. Knopf, 1984.

Pilburn, Sidney, ed. *A Policy of Kindness: An Anthology of Writings by and about the Dalai Lama*. Ithaca, NY: Snow Lion Press, 1990.

Tenzin Gyatso, H. H. the Dalai Lama. *Freedom in Exile: The Autobiography of the Dalai Lama*. New York: Harper Collins, 1990.

———. *My Land and My People: Memoirs of the Dalai Lama of Tibet*. New York: McGraw-Hill, 1962.

———. *Ocean of Wisdom. Guidelines for Living*. Santa Fe, NM: Clear Light Publications., 1989.

DAMANHUR (ITALY)

Damanhur is a large communal group of some 800 members founded in 1975 by Oberto Airaudi (b. 1950). The community is located in the Valchiusella Valley, in the Alpine foothills north of Torino, Italy. Damanhur is organized as a Federation of Communities and Regions, and for many years its members considered the community a separate nation, signaled most visibly by the issuance of its own currency. Visitors exchanged their lira (or more recently, their euros) for the local currency while moving through the valley.

While Damanhur is interesting for a variety of reasons, from its life as a COMMUNE to church-state relations, it has added significantly to the manifestation of religious phenomena through its secretly constructed underground temple complex. Through the 1980s and 1990s, members of the temple carved a vast complex of rooms out of the Alpine rocks. Although several members had left the community prior to 1992, none had revealed the secret project. Its existence came to light that year only because of a lawsuit filed by a former leader.

The Temple of Mankind includes a number of rooms expressive of the group's own teachings, a form of Western Esotericism that draws on both ancient Pagan and modern theosophical beliefs and practices. Various halls in the temples are related to different aspects of the human psyche, and work within the temple is a visible representation of the journeys within and alchemical explorations of one's self.

When outsiders were admitted to the temple in the mid-1970s, they found it had seven large chambers connected by 150 meters of corridors. They were decorated with frescoes, mosaics, and stained glass. In one room was the largest Tiffany stained-glass dome in the world. The most important structures were the Earth Hall, symbolizing the male principle; the Water Hall, symbolizing the female principle; the Hall of Mirrors, which emphasizes the sky, air, and light; the Hall of Metals, symbolic of the struggle between mind and body; and the Hall of the Spheres, a place for Esoteric alchemical experimentation.

Integral to the temple's construction was its alignment to what are believed to be the currents of energy that flow around the planet. These "synchronic lines," similar to what elsewhere are called ley lines and to the flow of energy out of which FENG SHUI developed, create a global network that can be imposed on a world map, with nine lines flowing basically east-west, and nine flowing basically north-south. Four of these lines are believed to cross where the temple is located, and its various rooms were placed to coincide with the flow of the lines under the earth. Thus, work inside the temple not only includes work within one's self, but also connects individuals and the community with the larger cosmos.

Offended by the secret construction of such a large structure without reference to local building laws or even the knowledge of government officials, different authorities ordered the destruction of the temple, citing its violation of zoning regulations. However, academic and artistic voices were raised in its support and public opinion swung behind Damanhur. The move against the temple was blocked, and the planned construction to complete the project has been resumed. In the meantime, Damanhur has expanded its influence to the nearby City of Vidracco, where a majority of the city council is drawn from members of Damanhur.

Sources:

Introvigne, Massimo. "Damanhur: A Magical Community in Italy." In Bryan Wilson and Jamie Cresswell, eds., *New Religious Movements: Challenge and Response*. London: Routledge, 1999.

Merrifield, Jeff. *Damanhur: The Real Dream*. London: Thorsons, 1998.

DARK NIGHT OF THE SOUL

The "dark night of the soul" is a step in the mystic life in which, after experiencing some joy and success in the quest for mystic union, one enters a period of profound loss of any spiritual contact. The term entered the mystical vocabulary from the book of that name by Spanish mystic Saint John of the Cross (1542–1591), although the state had been described by mystics previously.

Mystics recognize that the development of the higher states of mystical consciousness includes a variety of obstacles and periods in which the joys and ecstasies that so motivate the mystic disappear for short periods as attachments to the things of the world are stripped away. However, the dark night refers to a state that happens only after one has made significant advancement toward the goal of mystical union. It seems to be a final obstacle prior to moving into a state of constant awareness of the divine presence. Essential to the dark night is a loss of the idea of the mystic's effort to engage in meditation and contemplation to an understanding of the ultimate impotence of human effort in spiritual affairs. In the end, the experience of the divine is a gift to the mystic. Saint John and others distinguish the dark night from other periods that negatively contrast with mystic highs by its length and the heightened sense of loss and despair.

In the profoundly secular experience of modernity, the idea of a dark night has been generalized to refer to the more common experience of disorientation that occurs during times of personal transition, such as occurs when one moves from adolescence to adulthood or when one experiences significant loss, perhaps through divorce or the death of a family member. In such cases, one often has to make a profound change in self-identity that can be accompanied by depression, anxiety, and even paranoia. Spiritually, it frequently includes a loss of any sense of relationship with higher spiritual realities (expressed differently according to the structures of one's religious life).

Knowledge of the commonness of the dark night experience allows a sense of hope, based on others' testimony as to its ephemeral nature, to permeate the time of depression and despair, after which a new self-image may emerge.

Sources:

Harkness, Georgia. *Dark Night of the Soul*. New York: Abingdon-Cokesbury Press, 1945.

John of the Cross. St. *Dark Night of the Soul*. Trans., abridged, and ed. by Kurt F. Reinhardt. New York: Frederick Ungar Publishing, 1957.

Underhill, Evelyn. *Mysticism*. New York: E. P. Dutton, 1930.

DARSHAN

Within the Hindu world, one of the most ubiquitous devotional activities is that of darshan. The term literally means gaining a glimpse of the divine. It refers to seeing in both the active sense of making an effort to view something considered sacred or divine and the passive sense of receiving into one's view the divine as presented. In the former sense, darshan can be understood as meritorious viewing; as such, engaging in darshan is advocated both as a duty of devotees and an act bringing great benefit through which the guru or a divinity shows grace.

Those of the Hindu faith will go out of their way to spend time in the presence of their teacher (guru) and/or travel great distances to see a particular holy person. The mere act of glimpsing the divine (which may be visibly presented in a person, a statue, or a sacred symbolic object, or invisibly as a vision of a supernatural being) is thought to convey the power, blessing, or merit of the object seen, quite apart from any verbal communication. Going to the large festivals held across India, where many holy people not otherwise accessible may be seen, provides the opportunity for darshan in a variety of situations.

The idea of darshan has passed to Sikhism, where the focus is upon the Adi Granth, the Sikh holy book that is seen as replacing gurus, and to Jainism, where images of the 24 ancient teacher/exemplars (the Tirthankaras) are the object of darshan.

Sources:

Davis, Roy Eugene. *Darshan: The Vision of Light*. Lakemont, GA: CSA Press, 1971.

Malhotra, Sharan. *Divine Darshan*. Columbia, MO: South Asia Books, 1994.

Meher, Baba. *Darshan Hours*. Berkeley, CA: The Beguine Library, 1973.

DAVENPORT BROTHERS

Little known today, the Davenport brothers were among the most heralded of Spiritualist mediums during the last half of the nineteenth century. With their spectacular demonstrations of spiritual presence, they did much to build the movement in both North America and England. Ira Eratus Davenport (b. September 17, 1839) and William Henry Davenport (b. February 1, 1841) were not even in their teens when the birth of Spiritualism was announced through the spirit rappings in the home of the Fox sisters in Hydesville, New York.

They would later claim similar spirit rappings had occurred in their home two years before the Hydesville occurrence, but in 1850 they began to experiment with table-tipping (using a table to get answers from the spirits). Soon after, Ira tried automatic writing. Having perfected their abilities to talk to the spirits, in 1854 the teenagers began their public career as performers, demonstrating their abilities to communicate with the spirit world. Ira had emerged as a direct voice medium, with the spirits reputedly using his vocal cords to articulate their messages.

The distinctive nature of the Davenports' demonstrations, however, were a number of physical manifestations of the spirits' presence. In a typical performance, for example, musical instruments would be placed on the floor. The brothers would be tied securely and left alone on stage. The lights would be turned out. People would see disconnected human hands floating around that would soon take up an instrument and play it. In the end, the lights would be turned on and the brothers would be found still securely tied to their chairs. Although some dismissed the show as stage trickery, many more were bewildered and could not find a reasonable explanation for what they had seen.

As the act was perfected, the brothers performed across the United States. In 1864 they made an initial tour of England and several countries on the continent. In 1876 they went to Australia, where William became ill the following year and, on July 1, 1877, died. Upon his return to America, Ira recruited another partner and continued to perform until a few years before his death on July 8, 1911.

For their appearances in England, they brought along the Rev. Jesse B. Ferguson (d. 1870). Ferguson's orations, which accompanied the brothers' act, were largely responsible for Sir Arthur Conan Doyle's conviction that they were genuine. Doyle would later become the brothers' dedicated champion.

The leading critic of the Davenports was magician Harry Houdini. He claimed he had visited with Ira toward the end of his life and that Ira shared with him the nature of the tricks that they had performed. Houdini was also able to demonstrate all of the phenomena the brothers had performed by simply slipping out of their bonds. Houdini's revelations did not deter Doyle, who never backed away from his view of the brothers as outstanding mediums.

Additional relevant material on the Davenports was brought forth in 1899 by skeptical author Joe Nickell, who examined the Davenports' scrapbook, which he found at the Spiritualist center at Lily Dale, New York. In the scrapbook were several revealing newspaper clippings supporting the nature of the brothers' act as stage magic. For example, the brothers generally allowed the stage and instruments they used to be examined ahead of time by members of the audience. A clipping from the May 23, 1863, issue of the Richmond, Indiana, newspaper told of a person applying an aromatic oil to the handle of the violin bow. After the performance, it was discovered that one of the brothers, who supposedly had been tied up the whole time, had the strong smell of the oil on it. Most of the audience then demanded their money back.

Today, the general consensus of those who study such phenomena is that the Davenports were simply stage magicians. At best they may have been dedicated Spiritualists who attempted to convince people of what they believed to be real by the use of their tricks, but their spectacular accomplishments were perpetrated by simple stage magic. They helped establish such trickery as a major element in Spiritualism through the mid-twentieth century and, as such trickery was exposed, largely deprived the movement of any credibility. Exposés of continued attempts to deceive believers with stage tricks have been published as late as the 1970s.

Sources:

Cooper, Robert. *Spiritual Experiences: Including Seven Months with the Brothers Davenport.* Heywood, 1867. London: 1967.

Houdini, Harry. *A Magician among the Spirits.* New York: Harper & Brothers, 1924.

Nichols, Thomas Low. *A Biography of the Brothers Davenport.* London, 1864. Reprint, New York: Arno Press, 1976.

Nickell, Joe. "The Davenport Brothers: Religious Practitioners, Entertainers, or Frauds?" *Skeptical Inquirer* 23, 4 (July–August, 1999). Posted at http://www.findarticles.com/p/articles/mi_m2843/is_4_23/ai_55208044. Accessed April 1, 2007.

DEE, JOHN (1527–1608)

John Dee, whose career was largely contemporaneous with that of Queen Elizabeth I, was an accomplished mathematician and astrologer, but he is best remembered as a CRYSTAL gazer. One of the crystal stones and the magical emblem upon which it rested have survived and may be seen on display at the British Museum in London.

Dee was living a quiet life when, during the reign of Mary I (1553–1558), he was arrested and accused of attempting to kill her through magic. After being released, he took the opportunity to travel abroad and only settled again in England after Elizabeth had established herself in power. He was able to reestablish his own position when called upon to speak on some new and interesting astronomical phenomena (including a new comet) in the 1570s.

His interest in scrying, or crystal gazing, emerged in the 1580s. Gazing into a crystal, he initially had a vision of angels in the spring of 1581. He claimed that the next year, the angel Uriel gave him a piece of crystal that could be used to communicate with the angels regularly. As he gazed into it, the angels would appear and grant information about the future. He found although he could work with the crystal, it was very difficult for him, so he was led to seek a colleague who could more easily converse with the angels. Dee

Astrologer and mathematician John Dee gained notoriety in Elizabethan England as a scryer who used a crystal ball to communicate with angels in a language he called Enochian. *Getty Images.*

then assumed the role of secretary, recording all that the angel said. He worked briefly with a person named Barnabas Saul, then was led to Edward Kelley (1555–1593), with whom he worked for five years, from 1582 to 1587.

The crystal used by Dee and Kelley was a globe that was fastened in a frame of gold with a cross on top. It sat on a magical emblem called the Sigillum Aemeth, an amulet that would protect any angelic contact from harmful side effects. The sigil was given to him in his earlier contacts, but it had actually appeared several decades earlier in a publication by German scholar Athanasius Kircher (1601–1680). On the table (made of sweetwood, according to angelic instruction) there was also a magical square and other magical emblems.

Among the gifts that came through the scrying was a new angelic language, Enochian. The magical square on Dee's table was written in Enochian. Today, books that explain and teach Enochian are readily available to practitioners of magic.

Dee and Kelley parted ways in 1587. They and their wives had spent the last several years of their collaboration in Europe. Dee returned to England, and Kelley went to Prague. There, Kelley was arrested as a fraud. Released, he traveled through Europe, but was again arrested in 1592 in Germany. He died from injuries he suffered trying to escape. Dee lived somewhat as a celebrity, periodically protesting the accusations that he was a wizard and conjuror of devils. He died in 1608.

Dee was largely forgotten over the years, but he was rediscovered in the early twentieth century by Spiritualists and has been adopted by modern ceremonial magicians as an important exponent of their work.

Sources:

Dee, John. *The Diaries of John Dee.* Ed. by Edward Fenbenton. Oxfordshire, UK: Day Books, 1998.

———. *A True and Faithful Relation of What Passed for Many Years between Dr. John Dee … and Some Spirits.* London, 1659. Reprint, 1974.

French, Peter. *John Dee: The World of an Elizabethan Magus.* London: Routledge & Kegan Paul, 1972.

Woolley, Benjamin. *The Queen's Conjurer: The Science and Magic of Dr. John Dee, Adviser to Queen Elizabeth I.* New York: Henry Holt, 2001.

DEGANAWIDAH
(FL. 1550–1600)

Deganawidah was the legendary founder, along with Hiawatha, of the Iroquois Confederacy, an association of five Native American peoples—the Senecas, Cayugas, Oneidas, Onondagas, and Mohawks—that brought them a political, cultural, and religious unity. His dates of birth and death are unknown, but he is believed to have worked on the Confederacy in the last half of the sixteenth century.

Various legends have surrounded Deganawidah, including one that attributed his birth to a virgin mother of the Huron people. According to the story, she'd had a dream that she would bear a son who was destined to plant the Tree of Peace. He is remembered as the one who was able to bring the different groups into a peaceful relationship and, among other things, end the practice of cannibalism. Deganawidah advocated the formation of a council of chiefs drawn from each of the participating groups to constitute the new government. Each of the five groups had an equal vote on matters that came before the Confederacy, although the attempt was made to make decisions by consensus.

Hiawatha, his disciple and assistant, was a Mohawk. Together, they performed several miracles that helped convince the Onondaga chief, Atotarho, of the truth of their message. The formation of the Confederacy was marked by the planting of a peace tree at a spot over which weapons had been symbolically buried in what is now Syracuse, New York.

The Confederacy became the most powerful organization of Native Americans in the American northeast woodlands. Their power was increased in 1722 when the Tuscaroras joined. The Iroquois were able to prevent European movement into their territory for many years and were still an active force as late as the American Revolution.

Sources:

Gibson, John Arthur. *Concerning the League: The Iroquois League Tradition as Dictated in Onondaga.* Winnipeg, MB: Algonquian and Iroquoian Linguistics, 1992.

Graymont, Barbara. *Indians of North America: The Iroquois.* New York: Chelsea House Publishers, 1988.

DELOS ISLAND (GREECE)

By the seventh century BCE the Greek island of Delos, in the Mirtoan Sea southwest of Athens and north of Crete, had become known as the birthplace of the god Apollo and his twin sister,

The seventh century BCE **Terrace of the Lions is one of many monuments on the Greek island of Delos, once an important center of Greek and Roman religions.** *Time Life Pictures/Getty Images.*

Artemis. The lake traditionally known as the site of the birth had now dried up. The island's role in the religious life of the region grew significantly after it came under Athenian control in 540 BCE and through its years of independence, beginning in 314 BCE. It functioned as the religious center for the islands of the Mirtoan Sea and, after 477 BCE, for the lands of the political coalition known as the Delian League, organized by the Athenians. When the Romans took over the island in 166 BCE, the islanders merely added places for the worship of the Roman gods and continued on as before.

Delos operated in tandem with Delphi for much of this time. The oracle of **DELPHI** would spend the six months of winter in Delos before returning to Delphi for the summer, and many would find their way to the island to consult the oracle. Every four years the island would host a festival featuring Olympic-like games.

Delos was covered in shrines to the many Greek (and Roman) deities. Today most are in ruins, and the island has become a gold mine for archeologists. Remnants of three Apollo temples, two Artemis temples and single temples to a spectrum of deities from Dionysius to Isis now dot the landscape.

Sources:

Barnard, Mary E. *The Myth of Apollo and Daphne from Ovid to Quevedo: Love, Agon and the Grotesque.* Durham: Duke University Press, 1987.

Fontenrose, Joseph. *The Delphic Oracle: Its Responses and Operations*. Berkeley: University of California Press, 1978.

Sackas, George, and Maria Sarla. *Delos Island: A Tourist Guide Book*. Athens, Greece: Artemis Publishing Co., 1972.

DELPHI (GREECE)

Delphi was the most important center for divination and the worship of Apollo in ancient Greece. The city of Delphi had been in existence for centuries when, in the seventh century BCE, it became the capital of the association of Greek states known as the Amphictyony. In the middle of the century, a temple to Apollo was erected at Delphi to celebrate the god's victory over a large snake, the python. At the end of the century, the Amphictyony engaged in a war against a neighboring city state and, following victory, dedicated the newly acquired territory to Apollo. Soon afterward, Delphi became the center of the Pythian (Apollonian) festival, celebrated every four years.

Over the years, as the sanctuary grew in importance and fame, it was a target for hostile neighbors and invading armies. It was periodically destroyed or plundered, but it continued to function. Oversight of the complex of temples that arose at Delphi was in the hands of the priestess of Apollo, the Pythia, who offered oracles (and who was also known as "the oracle"). Once a year she sat on a chair in the temple of Apollo adjacent to an open earth fissure from which fumes emerged. Some believe the fumes had an intoxicating property, allowing the priestess to enter an altered state of consciousness from which the oracles were pronounced. Originally, the priestess operated as an oracle once a year, but over a period of time she acceded to many requests and would perform on demand. During much of the oracle's existence, it was believed that in the fall Apollo departed the site for his winter quarters on DELOS ISLAND. The oracle of Apollo would reside in Delphi half the year and in Delos the other half.

Those requesting an oracle would first enact a ritual that included walking from the nearby community of Kirra (now known as Itea). Along the way they would pay a fee, take a ritual bath, and sacrifice an animal (usually a goat whose entrails would become an object of divination by the local priests). The visit culminated in their posing their question. The answer to the question would often be delivered in cryptic words that would require further interpretation by the priests.

Politicians, generals, and rulers consulted the oracle, often to obtain blessing on a decision that had already been made. Observers knowledgeable of Delphi were aware of the sensitive nature of any response to people in power and of the ambiguity that usually characterized the oracle's response, which could be interpreted in many possible ways.

The most famous of the priestess's pronouncements was given to King Croesus of Lydia (r. 560–546 BCE), who inquired about an upcoming battle. The oracle noted that the king would cross the river Halys and destroy a great army. He believed that victory was his, but when he lost the battle, those at Delphi pointed out that he had, in fact, destroyed a great army—his own.

The oracle remained active until the emergence of the Emperor Constantine (r. 306–337 CE). His rule launched Delphi's decline, which culminated in the prohibition of the worship of Apollo at Delphi and ordered the discontinuance of the Pythian games.

Today, tourists may visit Delphi, located on the side of Mount Parnassus across the Gulf of Corinth, north of the city of Corinth. Here, the ruins of a large complex of temples and related structures for the Pythian festival can be seen. After many years of abandonment, modern Neopagans have attempted to re-sacralize Delphi, but they have encountered a major problem in that Pagan worship is not allowed in Greece, where a strong establishment of the Orthodox Church exists. Several informal groups who wish to see a modern inauguration of the worship of the ancient Greek deities have begun a campaign to decriminalize such worship.

Sources:

Fontenrose, Joseph. *The Delphic Oracle.* Berkeley: University of California Press, 1978.

Parke, H. W. *The Delphi Oracle, Vol. 1: The History.* Oxford: Basil Blackwell, 1956.

Temple, Robert K. G. *Conversations with Eternity: Ancient Man's Attempts to Know the Future.* London: Rider, 1984.

DENTISTRY, PARANORMAL

Through the twentieth century, several Christian healer/evangelists claimed to be a catalyst for the filling of tooth decays and other dental work. Among the first was A. C. McCabe, a traveling evangelist, but more famous is Willard Fuller. Born in Louisiana, Fuller was raised a Southern Baptist and after college attended that church's New Orleans Baptist Theological Seminary. He pastored several Baptist congregations through the 1940s and 1950s before developing a debilitating disease that forced him away from his work. In 1959, he was healed of this disease and subsequently began a healing ministry in which the curing of dental problems became the most noticeable aspect. Through the 1970s he began to operate far beyond the Southern Baptist community, developed an independent Pentecostal theology, and became well known in New Age circles. He founded the Lively Stones Fellowship, the vehicle for his ministry. He also has trained and ordained hundreds of ministers.

Fuller's itinerant healing evangelism is directed to all who are ill, but he has emphasized a ministry of dental healing. He has noted that although dental needs may be somewhat less crucial than some other conditions, the sudden change in such hard and stony objects as teeth tend to bring about a transformation in those who witness it. Over the more than four decades of his work, people have given numerous anecdotal testimonies of healings experienced and of gold suddenly appearing in their mouth. In spite of the audacious nature of Fuller's claims, he appears to have had only minimal run-ins with skeptics or

the law. In 1968, for example, he was charged, while in Australia, with not operating in line with the Dentists Act of New South Wales—a formal matter that was, in fact, true—although he was not charged with having violated any law since he did not practice dentistry. Fuller, in his eighties, lives quietly in Florida, at the headquarters of his ministry.

In 1999, the miraculous filling of teeth manifested at the Toronto Airport Fellowship, a charismatic congregation that has been the source of an international movement popularly called the Toronto Blessing. The church had become well known as the launching point for what was termed "holy laughter." One evening in March, during a church conference, two female attendees from Capetown, South Africa, told a story of their father receiving a gold filling while watching a video of the church's pastor, John Arnott, and his wife, Carol. This testimony was followed by Arnott offering to pray for anyone who needed healing, especially those who wanted God to fill their teeth. Within a short time, some 20 people reported that new gold had appeared suddenly in their mouth. Reports mounted as the service continued, with stories of gold fillings, gold crowns, and gold replacing older metal fillings.

Attempts were made to gather written testimony from those who claimed a healing, pictures of the gold teeth were taken and posted on the Internet, and reports of similar occurrences began to come from associated congregations in other countries. The church urged the people to go back to their dentists to seek verification of what had occurred. In less than five percent of the cases were dentists willing to admit that any significant divergence from the person's previous dental records could be found. In some cases, individuals had forgotten they'd had gold fillings installed. In others, the change appeared to have been a mere polishing of previous fillings.

In May 1999, the situation at the Toronto church was complicated by the arrival of Silvania Machado, a Brazilian who claimed she had been healed of cancer and subsequently discovered that, during worship services, gold specks began to appear spontaneously on her face. After Machado spoke at the Airport Fellowship, Pastor Arnott collected some of the gold flecks and had them scientifically analyzed. Much to his disappointment, they turned out to be plastic glitter void of gold or other precious metal.

The reports of gold fillings led to significant criticism of the Toronto and associated groups from other Christians. Some saw the occurrences as unbiblical, while others criticized them as a trivial pursuit. Simultaneously, critics outside the church held the practice up for ridicule. The initial enthusiasm cooled as evidence of the Machado fraud surfaced and efforts to verify other incidents of supernatural gold proved difficult. Subsequently, emphasis on gold fillings faded quickly.

Sources:

Beverley, James. "Dental Miracle Report Draws Criticism," *Christianity Today* (May 24, 1999): 6.

Fuller, Willard. *"You Shall Know the Truth."* Palatka, FL: Lively Stones World Healing Fellowship, 1980.

St. Clair, David. *Psychic Healers*. New York: Bantam Books, 1979.

"They Go for the Gold: Gold Dust and Gold Teeth Filling Miracles Claimed in Charismatic Churches: Updates." Posted at http://www.cesnur.org/testi/go Xgold_updates.htm. Accessed April 1, 2007.

DIVINE MERCY

Divine Mercy, a standard subject in speaking of God in the Christian tradition, has become the focus of special devotional practice among Roman Catholics in the twentieth century. The new devotion is traced to Sister Josefa Menendez (1890–1923), a Spanish woman who in the year 1920 entered the Convent of Les Feuillants, Poitiers, France, a convent of the Order of the Sacred Heart of Jesus. During the four remaining years of her life, she had a number of visions that were dutifully recorded. Among her visions were those of Saint Madeleine Sophie Barat (1779–1865), the founder of the order, but by far the

most important were of Jesus. These visions built upon the devotion to the Sacred Heart of Jesus, a major practice of the order. In a series of visions beginning in 1920, Jesus told Josefa that he meant to use her to carry out a plan of enlightening the world concerning the mercy of his heart. She was to become an apostle of his love and mercy.

Menendez lived and died in obscurity, and only in 1838 was an account of her vision published, as *Un Appel à l'Amour*. The book found an immediate office and within a year had been reprinted several times and translated into a variety of languages, in English as *The Way of Divine Mercy*.

In the meantime, a similar set of visions had come to a Polish nun, Faustina Kowalska (1905–1939), who in 1925 had joined the Congregation of the Sisters of Our Lady of Mercy convent in Warsaw. Beginning in 1931, she had a repeated vision of Jesus with two rays of light coming from his heart, a pale ray signifying the water of baptism and a red ray the blood of atonement. At one point, Jesus spoke and asked that a picture be painted of what Faustina had seen, with the words, "Jesus, I trust in You." He promised blessings upon any who venerated this image. He told the young nun that Infinite Mercy was the most mysterious attribute of divinity, more so than either his infinite goodness or love. Through further revelations, numerous details for following the devotion were given to Faustina until her death on October 5, 1939.

After World War II, the devotion put forth by Menedez and Faustina hit a major obstacle. Faustina had recoded her vision in Polish, but being only semiliterate, she wrote phonetically. A hasty translation was sent to Rome in 1958. Based upon the translation, her ideas were declared heretical. In 1964, Karol Wojtyla, the new Archbishop of Krakow, ordered a better translation be made of Faustina's work. Based on that translation, the Vatican reversed its opinion. The text was later published as *Divine Mercy in My Soul*. Following Cardinal Wojtyla's election as Pope John Paul II, he began to manifest. His first official encyclical, *Dives Misercordiae* ("Rich in Mercy"), indicated his faith in the Divine Mercy

Ruins of Greek temples are all that remain of a once thriving religious site, where Zeus and his wife were worshipped. In one myth, too, an Egyptian priestess escaped the Phoenicians as a dove and landed on a tree that would become the location of an important oracle. *Fortean Picture Library.*

devotion. He subsequently oversaw Faustina's beatification in 1996 and canonization in 2000.

Sources:

Faustina, Blessed Sister. *Handbook of Devotion to the Divine Mercy.* Dublin: Divine Mercy, 1994.

Menendez, Josefa. *The Way of Divine Love; or, The Message of the Sacred Heart to the World and a Short Biography of His Messenger, Sister Josefa Menendez Coadjutrix, Sister of the Society of the Sacred Heart of Jesus, 1890–1923.* Brookings, SD: Our Blessed Lady of Victory Missions, 1981.

Michalenko, Seraphim. *The Divine Mercy Message and Devotion: With Selected Prayers from the Diary of Blessed Faustina.* Stockbridge, MA: Marian Helpers, 1995.

DODONA (GREECE)

The ancient center for the worship of Zeus at Dodona in northwest Greece became famous as a place to seek oracles concerning the future. It seems originally to have been a site for the worship of the mother goddess, who was replaced by Zeus around 1400 BCE. The mother goddess was reduced in standing, and at least locally became known as Zeus' wife, Diona.

The most important object at Dodona was a tree, variously noted to be beech or oak. The two deities were believed to reside in this sacred tree. Those who sought an oracle would approach the priests (or, in later times, the priestesses) and make their inquiry. The priests would then listen to the rustling of the leaves through which the Gods were believed to speak.

There are two famous stories about Dodona. Herodotus (c. 484–c. 425 BCE), the one who noted the transition of male to female personnel at the oracle, repeated a legend that the site originated in the plight of two Egyptian priestesses who had been abducted by the Phoenicians. They escaped their captors by turning themselves into doves and flying away. One flew to Dodona, landed on a tree, and demanded the founding of an oracle. The other flew to Libya where a similar event is said to have occurred (though no Libyan oracle existed to verify the report). It was also noted that the prow on the ship of Jason the Argonaut was believed to have been carved from wood from Dodona.

There were no buildings at Dodona for many centuries, but around the fourth century BCE a temple to Zeus was erected. In the next century, King Pyrrhus of Epirote became the oracle's patron and constructed a number of buildings as well as a wall around the main oracle tree for pro-

tection. Dodona subsequently became the center of life in that area of Greece.

Dodona was destroyed by an invading army in 219 BCE but rebuilt by King Philip V of Macedonia (238–178 BCE). It suffered from the Roman invasion of the region in 167 BCE. The oracle continued to function into the fourth century CE, during which time the sacred tree was cut down. Theodosius the Great (347–395), the Byzantine emperor, saw to the building of a Christian basilica at the site.

Today one may visit the site. Remnants of the temple to Zeus and the Prytaneum, a resting place for the priests of Zeus, are among the ancient buildings that may be seen.

Sources:

Delcor, Mathias. "The Selloi of the Oracle of Dodona and the Oracular Priests of the Semitic Religions." In J. Schreiner, ed. *Wort, Lied, und Gottesspruch: Beiträge zur Septuaginta. Festschrift für Joseph Ziegler.* Würzburg: Echter, 1972.

Parke, H. W. *The Oracles of Zeus: Dodona, Olympia, Ammon.* Cambridge, MA: Harvard University Press, 1967.

EASTER ISLAND

Easter Island is a single isolated volcanic island located some 2,000 miles off the coast of South America and an equal distance from the main clusters of inhabited islands of the South Pacific. It was given its Western name by Admiral Jacob Roggeveen, whose three ships visited the island on Easter Day in 1722. Locally it is known as Rapa Nui. Roggeveen informed the world of the giant statues that seemed to peer out to sea from the island, and they entered the catalog of the world's curiosities. In spite of the many interactions of the Easter Islanders with the outside world over the next two centuries, it was not until the eye-catching work of anthropologist/adventurer Thor Heyerdahl (1914–2002) in the 1940s that widespread public knowledge of the island arose, along with public involvement in the questions concerning its unique statuary.

Following initial contact by Westerners in 1772, additional ships occasionally visited through the end of the century. Early in the next century, venereal disease left by whalers took its toll. In the 1860s Peruvians raided the islands for slave labor. It is estimated that 90 percent of those taken into slavery died within a few years. The loss of the island's religious leadership to the slavers accounts for much of the loss of knowledge of the island's culture and the difficulty anthropologists and other scientists had in reconstructing it in twentieth century.

Ill treatment of the island's inhabitants reduced the native population to a mere 111 by the mid 1870s. The annexation of the island by Chile did little to improve the residents' lot, as the island was turned over to commercial interests who ran it much like a slave labor camp. The harsh conditions did not improve when the island was turned over to Chile's navy in 1953.

It was this harsh social context into which Thor Heyerdahl stepped with his idea of proving the Polynesians came from the Americas by boat, rather than from Asia. To prove his theory possible, he constructed a Polynesian raft, the *Kon Tiki*, and sailed it to Raratoa. The trip made him a celebrity and raised the issue of the origin of the culture that produced the large stone heads. In 1955 Heyerdahl, now an international celebrity, turned his attention to Easter Island. The team he assembled soon put together an initial story, which included the assertion that the island had been inhabited since the fourth century BCE. He also found in the oldest statuary on the island a resemblance to contemporaneous statuary from South America.

How and why the famous Easter Island statues were constructed remains the subject of speculation by archeologists today because the native inhabitants and their society was nearly wiped out by European invaders. *Roger Violett/Getty Images.*

Heyerdahl's work had a dramatic effect on the island. The Chilean government saw the possibility of attracting tourists. In 1966, the island's residents revolted and were able to completely reorder their life relative to Chile, including a constitution to structure their new freedoms.

Modern transportation opened the island to both tourists and scholars, and life steadily improved. By the end of the twentieth century, the population had risen to approximately two thousand.

Archeologists saw Heyerdahl's study as merely a first step in understanding Easter Island. Interest, of course, centered on the statues, locally called *moais*. These male figures stand some twenty-five feet high and weigh about fourteen tons. They had been carved out of the volcanic rock. Their mystery was accentuated by the lack of written records concerning them and the loss of much of the oral tradition. It was also the case that by the twentieth century, all of the statues, the existence of which had featured prominently in the early Western accounts of the island, had been toppled. It became the task of Heyerdahl and those who followed him to replace the figures in their earlier resting place. In the last generation, archaeologist Jo Anne Van Tilburg of the University of California at Los Angeles has emerged as the major scholar of Easter Island lore. She has concluded they represent stylized images of various chiefs. They seem to have been constructed in the years 1400 to 1600, and to have played a key role in the religious life of the Rapa Nui. They appear to have served as contact points for communication with divine entities. The lack of definitive records, however, will mean that variant opinions on the statues will probably arise as new studies are made.

Sources:

Heyerdahl, Thor. *Aku-Aku. The Secret of Easter Island.* London: George Allen Unwin, 1958.

———. *Easter Island: The Mystery Solved.* New York: Random House, 1989.

Orliac, Catherine, and Michel Orliac. *Easter Island: Mystery of the Stone Giants.* New York: Harry N. Abrams Inc., 1995.

Van Tiburg, Jo Anne, and John Mack. *Easter Island: Archaeology, Ecology, and Culture.* Washington, DC: Smithsonian Institution Press, 1995.

ECSTASY

Ecstasy is that higher state of consciousness common to all mystics in which the self is identified with God and, while different language is used, is seen as being united with God. During the state of ecstasy, the mystic is entranced and more or less oblivious to the external world, his or her attention being focused on the object of the original contemplation. Those who experience ecstasy find it a most enjoyable state. Ecstasy is the name given the psycho-physical state accompanying the mystical vision, and the quality of the vision will itself be relative to the spiritual state of the individual. Some people find moving into an ecstatic state relatively easy; others find it a rare occurrence.

Ecstasy is a trancelike state that may be more or less deep and last varying lengths of time. During the period of ecstasy, the body becomes somewhat rigid, retaining the position it was in when the ecstatic state was entered. Often, the body does not respond to outside stimuli, and sometimes observers will test mystics by sticking them with pins or attempting to burn them with a candle flame. Accounts of such tests are common in the biographies and reports on many mystics and visionaries. The ecstatic state usually includes a period of awareness of the object of contemplation, and even communication. It may also be followed by a state of unconsciousness not unlike a cataleptic state, in which the body remains rigid but the mystic feels great joy. The phenomenon of the rigid body is common not only to mystics, but to various people who might go into trance, such as Spiritualist mediums.

In evaluating the mystics, especially those who have later been canonized in the Roman Catholic tradition, ecstasy forms an interesting aspect of their spiritual life, but more concentration is placed upon the piety accompanying such states, the quality of any communications received from God, Jesus, or the Virgin Mary while entranced, and the life that flows from having experienced such states. It is noted that many people who have experienced multiple **APPARITIONS OF THE**

VIRGIN MARY have been seen to enter an ecstatic state, and their ecstasy (and the tests performed while in those states) have been put forth to credential them. While doubts about visionaries being in ecstasy have been used to discredit them, the substantiation of their ecstasy has been one of the lesser criteria in the church offering its approval of them. In the case of the apparitions of the Virgin Mary, the quality of the messages received from Mary and the evaluation of the life of the seer have been far more important.

It has been noted that ecstatic states have not been exclusive to the religious, or to the religious of just a few religious traditions. Besides being ubiquitous to all religions, it is also found among artists of various stripes (composers, singers, painters, etc.), suggesting that some people are born with a tendency to ecstasy or an ability to enter trance states that may be expressed in a variety of ways. Such approaches to the mystical life tend to judge it more a product of biology and social training than any particular spirituality. That is, entrance into an ecstatic state is much more a product of the body and psyche than of any particular supernatural or divine force in operation.

Those who experience ecstasy describe it in the most superlative terms. They also describe in a variety of languages their ultimate union with a Divine Transcendent Reality, and their attempts to relate to others the nature of their experience almost always falls into vague abstractions or the theology in which they have been trained. They may also make fine distinctions between stages of the whole ecstatic experience. The scientific study of ecstasy with the same instrumentation that has been used to study the many other states of consciousness is, by the very nature of ecstasy's appearances, still in a rudimentary state.

Sources:

Almond, Philip. *Mystical Experience and Religious Doctrine: An Investigation of the Study of Mysticism in World Religions*. Berlin and New York: Mouton, 1982.

Ellwood, Robert. *Mysticism and Religion*. New York: Seven Bridges Press, 1998.

Forman, Robert K. C., ed. *The Problem of Pure Consciousness: Mysticism and Philosophy*. Oxford: Oxford University Press, 1990.

McGinn, Bernard. *The Foundations of Mysticism*. New York: Crossroad Press, 1991.

Underhill, Evelyn. *Mysticism: A Study in the Nature and Development of Man's Spiritual Consciousness*. New York: E. P. Dutton & Co., 1961.

ECTOPLASM

Ectoplasm (literally, "exteriorized substance") refers to a phenomenon that began to appear in Spiritualist séances in the late-nineteenth century. Reports circulated that a mysterious vapor-like substance would on occasion flow out of the body of a medium while in trance. Increasingly, mediums claimed that the substance would resolve itself into the likeness of a person, a physical representation of an individual who resided in the spirit world. Often this person was identified as the spirit control who always worked with the medium and guided the séance from the spirit realm.

As early as the mid-eighteenth century, Swedish visionary Emanuel Swedenborg (1688–1772) claimed to have seen a vapor steaming from his body. Passing references to similar phenomena are found even earlier. However, it was not until the early twentieth century that any systematic attempt to study ectoplasm occurred. In 1908 Baron Albert von Schrenck-Notzing (1862–1929), a German psychical researcher, and Charles Richet (1850–1935), a French researcher, began close observation of Eva C. (public name of Marthe Béraud), a materialization medium. They and a later observer, Gustav Geley (1868–1924), published reports concerning the genuineness of the phenomena they had observed, in spite of stringent attempts to detect any fraud.

The early observations of ectoplasm were photographed, and these pictures show a variety of amorphous substances that seem to emanate or ooze from the several natural orifices of the medium's body, most frequently the mouth. Schrenck-Notzing summed up the early research in his 1920

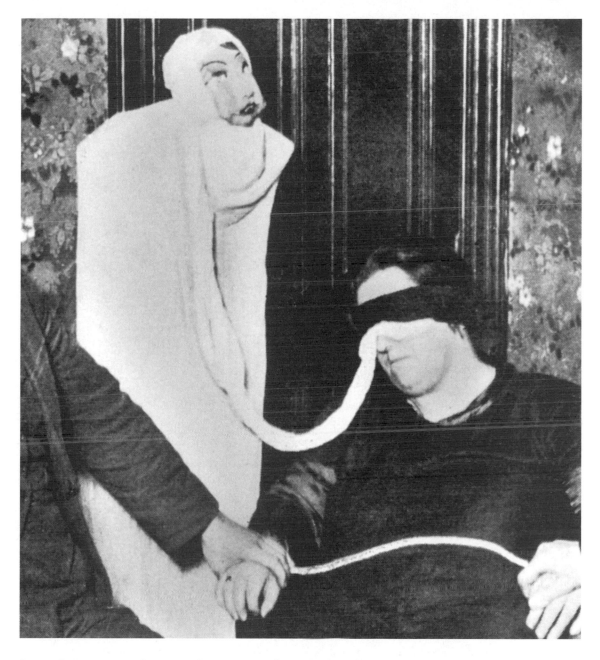

Spiritualists attempt to detect ectoplasm emerging from a medium during a trance at a séance. *Fortean Picture Library.*

classic, *The Phenomena of Materialization*, in which he asserted, "We have very often been able to establish that by an unknown process there comes from the body of the medium a material, at first semi-fluid, which possesses some of the properties of a living substance, notably that of the power of change, of movement and of the assumption of definite forms." Obviously, the existence of such a substance would have immense implications for our understanding of the world.

Over the next few decades a number of famous mediums, such as Mina S. Crandon (1889–1941), better known as Margery, and a variety of notable observers including Arthur Conan Doyle (1859–1930) offered their support to the idea of ectoplasm. Various psychic researchers speculated on the nature of ectoplasm and what its existence would mean for understanding the physical universe. However, beginning in the 1920s, one after another of the physical mediums was discovered in fraud, a result of the more sophisticated forms of detection. A significant event was the series of discoveries made following the death of Gustav Geley. Never-published photographs of Eva C. clearly showed fraudulent activity controlled by the medium's constant companion, Juliette Bisson. Wires running from Eva C.'s head were supporting the supposed ectoplasmic material.

A series of exposures of fraudulent activity led to the rapid decline of materialization séances and the claims to produce ectoplasm, though talk of the reputed substance remained a popular topic within Spiritualist circles, often accompanied by a bemoaning of the disappearance of the great materialization mediums.

Claims to produce ectoplasm and attempts to demonstrate its appearance did not disappear altogether, though the practice was banished to the fringes of the Spiritualist community. As late as 1960, parapsychologist Andrija Puharich (1918–1995) was allowed into materialization séances at Camp Chesterfield, in Indiana, and found the use of phosphor-covered cheesecloth being used to fake ectoplasm. These were published in a Spiritualist periodical, but similar false séances may still be viewed at Chesterfield and a few other Spiritualist centers to the present. Lamar Keene, a medium who operated in that subculture, left the movement in the mid-1970s and authored an exposé of it.

Recently, a new generation of both Spiritualists and psychic researchers have developed a fascination with the possibility that ectoplasm really does exist. In 1988 English professor John R. Crowley, a member of the Board of Trustees of the American Society for Psychical Research, wrote an article defending the reality of ectoplasm. Two years later, British Spiritualists founded the Noah's Ark Society, devoted to the revival of physical mediumship. Although small, it has become an international organization. Its periodical, the *Ark Review*, includes articles on ectoplasm, among other related subjects. In spite of this renewed interest, there is little evidence of the existence of ectoplasm, certainly not enough to indicate it was ever more than the center of an elaborate hoax worked by a small group of mediums operating as stage magicians. A heavy burden of proof rests on any who would advocate the existence of ectoplasm in the contemporary world.

The weakness of arguments for the existence of ectoplasm is one of the factors that has led to the decline of support for traditional Spiritualism, although other movements supportive of contact with spiritual entities thrive.

Sources:

Keene, Lamar. *The Psychic Mafia*. New York: St. Martin's Press, 1976.

Schrenck-Notzing, Baron Albert von. *The Phenomena of Materialization*. 1920. Reprint, New York: Arno Press, 1975.

EDWARD, JOHN (B. 1969)

John Edward, psychic and medium who attained national fame in the early years of the twenty-first century from his show on the Sci-Fi cable television network, was born and grew up in Long Island, New York. Eschewing the psychic abilities that emerged in his childhood, he attended college and later took a job in health management, in line with his college major. He married and has fathered two children.

While outwardly leading a mundane life, Edward pursued an avocational interest in things

Medium John Edward recieved considerable media attention and popularity during the broadcast of his television program, *Crossing Over with John Edward*, which ran from 2000 to 2003. *Getty Images.*

psychic. He read books and attended various psychically oriented events. Crucial to his development was his encounter with Florida psychic and medium Lydia Clar in the early 1990s. She is credited with making him aware of his abilities and directing him to use his talents. He became a psychic consultant and developed a large clientele.

His first book, *One Last Time*, which recounted many of his experiences with spirit contact and emphasized the basic Spiritualist claim that such contact was proof of life after death, appeared at the end of 1998 and the following year climbed to the top of the *Los Angeles Times* bestsellers list. About that same time, October 1999, he was featured in a special on the cable channel Home Box Office, *Life Afterlife*. Through this he established contact with the Human Energy Systems Labora-

tory, a parapsychology research facility in Tucson, Arizona, headed by Gary Schwartz and Linda Russek. Their work has focused on mediumship, and they have been enthusiastic in their support of Edward.

Edward's fame shot up radically in June 2000 when he began to host the television show *Crossing Over with John Edward* on the Sci-Fi network. Several years later, a book by Schwartz on his studies with Edward and others appeared. As Edward's fame spread, he became the target of skeptics who offered significant criticism of his work, including criticism of the television show, which was edited to show only his apparent success in reading for members of the audience. The show continued through 2003.

Sources:

Edward, John. *After Life: Answers from the Other Side.* New York: Princess Books, 2003.

————. *Crossing Over: The Stories behind the Stories.* New York: Princess Books, 2002.

————. *One Last Time: A Psychic Medium Speaks to Those We Have Loved and Lost.* New York: Berkley Publishing Group, 2000.

Schwartz, Gary. *The Afterlife Experiments: Breakthrough Scientific Evidence of Life after Death.* New York: Atria, 2003.

EDWARDS, HARRY (1893–1976)

Harry Edwards, the most outstanding Spiritualist healer of the twentieth century, was born in London on May 29, 1893. He grew up in Wood Green and at the age of fourteen completed his schooling and was apprenticed to a printer. His apprenticeship ended shortly before he joined the army in 1914. His unit was sent to India during World War I. While there he was promoted to captain and was sent to Iraq to build a railroad through the Middle East. He completed the war at the rank of major.

Upon his return to England, he married a childhood girlfriend, opened a printing business, and became involved in politics. A nominal member of the Church of England, in 1936 he visited a Spiritualist meeting looking for answers concerning the death of a nephew. He subsequently not only became deeply involved, but became a medium (a person believed able to directly contact the spirits of the deceased) himself. His fellow mediums, however, told him that he was more gifted as a healer and should concentrate his efforts in that direction. Their counsel was confirmed by his early experiences on behalf of several very ill people, some of whom he never met.

A healing ministry developed during the hours he could take from his printing business, weekends and evenings, and continued to grow until World War II broke out. He enlisted in the Home Guard and, during the war, healed as opportunity arose. One result of the war was the bombing of his home and the loss of his early healing records. He designated the front room of his new home as a healing room, and his healing work picked up and grew as the war came to a close. By 1946 it was obvious that his healing was taking precedence over his printing. He turned the business over to his brother and moved again, this time to Burrows Lea, where he had room to open what became known as the Healing Sanctuary.

The number of letters asking for healing grew to the thousands per week, and his public programs on healing were well attended. In 1953 he was included in an investigation by the leadership of the Church of England on "Divine Healing," which voiced its concern with healings that occurred outside of the services provided by physicians or priests. In spite of being basically ignored by the establishment, the work at the Sanctuary continued to expand.

In the 1960s Edwards wrote a number of books, including an autobiography. By this time, Edwards had become a major asset to the British Spiritualists movement, and he became an apologist for the cause. His book *Spirit Healing* especially emphasized the role of the spirits of the deceased in the healing process.

He continued to work until near the end of his life, going to South Africa on tour in 1976. He died on December 7, 1976, at Burrows Lea.

Sources:

Edwards, Harry. *A Guide to Spiritual Healing*. London: Spiritualist Press, 1965.

———. *A Guide to the Understanding and Practice of Spiritual Healing*. London: Healer Publishing Company, 1974.

———. *Spirit Healing*. London: Herbert Jenkins, 1963.

———. *Thirty Years a Spiritual Healer*. London: DE Cox & Wyman, 1968.

ESTABANY, OSKAR

Oskar Estabany, one of the most important psychic healers of the twentieth century, was a Hungarian army officer who migrated to Canada following the failed Hungarian Revolution in 1956. At some point around 1970, when Estabany was approaching his seventieth year, he contacted Bernard Grad (b. 1920), an associate professor of gerontology and noted cancer researcher, with claims about his healing abilities. Grad had become open to such alternative ideas earlier; he had researched the mysterious orgone energy and was a member of the Indonesian mystical group called Sabud.

With oversight of a large research laboratory and staff at McGill University, Grad decided to test Estabany's healing powers. He set up a series of experiments, which from the beginning improved on many previous experiments by focusing on life other than human life. The experiments concentrated first on increasing the rate of growth of barley plants and then of improving the healing rates in mice. The experiments were methodologically precise and carried out with double blinds. Among the many experiments were some in which Estabany was asked to concentrate on the water used to irrigate the barley, rather than seek directly to empower the seeds. The hypothesis of the experiment was that a healing power would have to be communicated to the

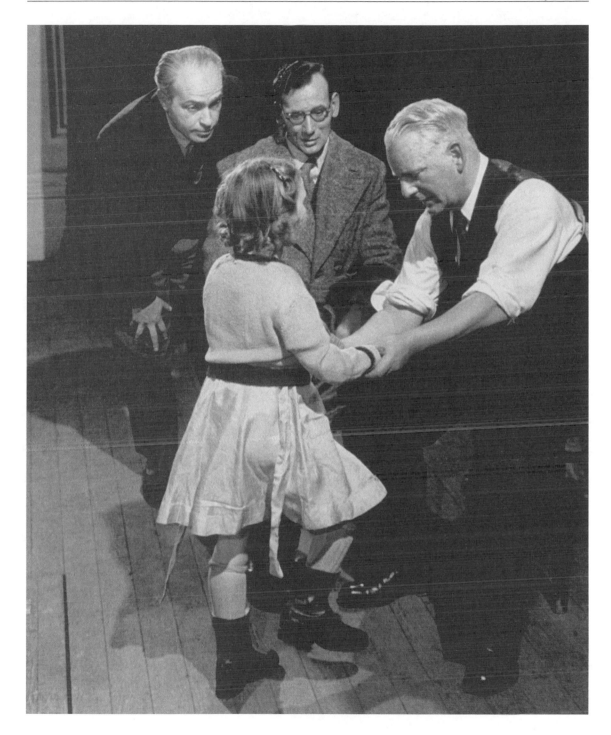

One of the most prominent Spiritualists of the twentieth century, Harry Edwards, shown here in 1952, led a ministry centered on his remarkable healing powers. *Time Life Pictures/Getty Images.*

water through the glass container and then conveyed to the plants. The spectacular results were presented in a set of papers in the early 1970s.

Estabany then moved to work with Justa Smith, a biochemist at Rosary Hill College in Buffalo, New York. Smith worked with enzymes and asked Estabany to increase the activity of enzymes previously damaged by ultrasound irradiation within a complex mixture. Again he was successful.

The aging Estabany finally went to work with theosophist and nursing instructor Dolores Krieger, who was seeking a nonreligious form of psychic healing that she could introduce into nurses' training. The technique they developed was given the name THERAPEUTIC TOUCH in 1972.

Estabany's work with Grad and Smith are among the most interesting experiments in psychic healing and to date stand unrefuted and little discussed in skeptical literature. They (and some additional experiments inspired by them) remain among the best evidence for the existence of a healing power as claimed by so many over the years.

Sources:

Grad, Bernard. "Some Biological Effects of the 'Laying on of Hands': A Review of Experiments with Animals and Plants." *Journal of the American Society for Psychical Research* 59 (1965).

———. "Telekinetic Effect on Plant Growth." *International Journal of Parapsychology* 3 (1961); 5 (1963).

Sayre-Adams, Jean, and Steve Wright. *The Theory and Practice of Therapeutic Touch.* New York: Churchill Livingstone Inc., 1995.

EXORCISM

Outside exorcism, few phenomena so vividly demonstrate the gap that exists between traditional religious believers and those attempting to express their faith in a modern context that assumes the validity of contemporary scientific worldviews. Religious beliefs in most traditions assume the existence of a variety of invisible entities—some good, others bad—that freely interact with humans in a variety of ways. As science and technology—especially the modern disciplines of the psychological sciences—have emerged, the idea of spirits or demons as an active part of human life has been all but abandoned. The idea of demon obsession/possession has been explained away in terms of different psychological disorders.

In spite of the dominance of psychological perspectives in the contemporary West, the belief that demons can afflict individuals and that exorcism can be used to drive away the demons and restore the person to normalcy continues to operate in some churches. The Deliverance movement in Pentecostalism is centered upon the effort to define demon activity today and to assist people in overcoming demonic influence in their lives.

Belief in demon possession and the emergence of exorcists as specialists in healing the possessed is documented liberally in ancient texts from around the world and probably predates writing. Jesus frequently exorcized individuals, and his apostles and followers continued that practice. As the hierarchy of the church developed over the first centuries of the Common Era, the office of exorcist was designated within the priestly orders and exorcism institutionalized as part of the process of joining the church. Thus, new Christians (including the church being confirmed) went through a rite in which God was asked to break the power of Satan in the individual's life and expel any demonic influence.

To the present, all priests in the Roman Catholic Church are ordained as exorcists as they pass through the minor orders, and in both the Roman Catholic and Anglican churches, confirmation still includes a ritualized exorcism. Most Protestant churches abandoned the practice after accepting the arguments put forth by theologian Martin Bucer (1491–1551) that exorcism of new believers was not a biblical practice and it should be reserved for people who were diagnosed as suffering from demon possession. The practice of exorcism declined steadily through subsequent centuries but experienced a revival in the late twentieth century.

The modern revival of exorcism can be traced to two quite independent sources. First, Christian missionaries throughout the twentieth century encountered cultures in Asia and Africa in which belief in demons remain high. While most missionaries have sought to eradicate the belief through education, others have adopted it and offered exorcism through the delivering power of God as a superior remedy. Some dramatic experiences of people being delivered from demons on the mission field fed a belief in demon possession among a small but growing number of Pentecostal ministers—all open to belief in the reality of demon possession because of their literal reading of the Bible. It is to be noted that across Africa, belief in demon possession and in malevolent magic worked by witches remains operative and occasionally makes the news when people are killed because of such beliefs.

Second, in the West, the rise of modern beliefs in demon possession cannot be separated from the cinema. A variety of movies, most notably the 1973 classic film *The Exorcist,* have presented vivid pictures of demon possession and attempts at exorcism. Although officially presented as fictional accounts, the movies have carried a subtle argument that they were based on real incidents.

The results of the modern reintroduction of belief in demon possession and the emergence of modern-day exorcists, both official and unofficial, have led to two phenomena. First, some ministers, usually from one of the many Pentecostal denominations, regularly attempt to exorcize church members and their families whenever dysfunctional behavior manifests. On rare occasions, such exorcisms taken to the extreme result in the death of the person being exorcized either due to neglect of a medical condition or physical harm directed toward the person diagnosed as possessed.

Second, Deliverance evangelists have attempted to introduce exorcisms as a regular part of congregational life to church members who do not experience the kind of dysfunctional or psychotic behavior normally associated with demon possession, and who exist in a culture that does not support belief in demons (with many contemporary

Christian leaders arguing that Christians are exempt from demon possession). In this context, demonic activity has been reinterpreted as the cause of a variety of negative and disapproved behavior patterns, from anxiety to obesity, in the lives of believers, and ritualized exorcism is offered as the remedy for individuals who seek to change their behavior.

The activity of the Deliverance ministries in the last decades of the twentieth century popularized engagement in what is termed "spiritual warfare." Assuming that Satan and his host of demons are constantly attempting to influence and win control over the lives of individuals, Christians are called upon to be in a constant state of vigilance and actively fight demonic attacks. Leaders in the spiritual warfare movement have also claimed the ability to discern and map the invisible dimensions where Satan, like a military general, strategically plans his attack on humanity. Satan is seen as launching campaigns by targeting specific geographical locations and undermining certain realms of human activity, such as music, recreational activities, and modern education.

Sources:

Cuneo, Michael. *American Exorcism: Expelling Demons in the Land of Plenty.* Garden City, NY: Doubleday & Company, 2001.

Hinn, Benny. *War in the Heavenlies.* Dallas: Heritage Printers and Publishers, 1984.

Macnutt, Francis. *Deliverance from Evil Spirits: A Practical Manual.* Grand Rapids, MI: Baker, 1995.

Wagner, C. Peter, ed. *Engaging the Enemy: How to Fight and Defeat Territorial Spirits.* Ventura, CA: Regal, 1991.

Whyte, H. A. Maxwell. *Demons and Deliverance.* Springdale, PA: Whitaker House, 1989.

EX-VOTOS

Ex-votos (literally, "according to the vow") are objects left at holy sites that document in some way a petition made by a pilgrim. Among the most simple of ex-votos (also called votives or, in Spanish, *milagros*) are simple published notices of

At holy sites around the world, it is traditional for many pilgrims, especially Roman Catholics, to leave behind various objects called "ex-votos." These symbolize their visit and their reason for their journey. *Fortean Picture Library.*

thanks to a patron saint for help received, which in Catholic countries may be published in the newspaper as a classified ad. More involved ex-votos, those of most interest to anthropologists, will include an illustration of the object of a prayer and some text describing what occurred or what the petitioner wishes to occur. These may be very simple or very elaborate and made out of a wide variety of materials. At healing shrines, ex-votos associated with an individual's illness (such as crutches, canes, or wheelchairs) or representations of body parts are often displayed to show the effectiveness of intercessions to the resident saint.

Today, ex-votos are most identified with Roman Catholicism, but they have been and continue to be used in a variety of religious traditions.

Found in ancient religious sites, ex-votos have been a significant means of discerning the exact purposes to which worship at the site was directed. The ex-voto is activated after its construction by leaving it at the holy site and/or close to a representation or relic of the saint/deity to whom one is making a request.

Among the most famous of ex-votos are those painted on pieces of tin that may be seen as shrines throughout Latin America. These usually picture events of a healing along with words of thanks.

Sources:

Ackerman, Jane. "The Theme of Mary's Power in the Milagros de Nuestra Senora." *Journal of Hispanic Philology* 8 (1983): 17–31.

Coulter, Lane, and Maurice Dixon, Jr. *New Mexican Tinwork: 1840–1940*. Albuquerque: University of New Mexico Press, 1990.

Egan, Martha. *Milagros: Votive Offerings from the Americas*. Albuquerque: University of New Mexico Press, 1991.

Mayes, Frances. *Ex Voto*. Barrington, RI: Lost Roads Publishers, 1995.

Salvatori, Mariolina. "Porque no puedo decir mi cuento: Mexican Ex-votos' Iconographic Literacy." In John Trimbur, ed. *Popular Literacy: Studies in Cultural Practices and Poetics*. Pittsburgh, PA: University of Pittsburgh, 2001, 17–42.

FACE CLOTH (OF JESUS)

Far less known than the SHROUD OF TURIN, which is the cloth or "napkin" many believe was used to wrap the body of Jesus following his crucifixion, the *sudarium* or face cloth that was reputedly used to cover and clean the face of Jesus after the crucifixion (cf. John 20:6–7) emerged in the last half of the twentieth century as an important element in establishing the authenticity of the shroud. The face cloth is approximately 32 inches by 20 inches. Unlike the shroud, there is no image on this cloth, only a few blood stains are visible to the naked eye.

According to the story that had developed about the cloth in the Middle Ages (prime sources being the *Book of Testaments*, a twelfth-century volume by Pelayo, the bishop of Oviedo, and the thirteenth-century *Chronicle of the World* by Lucus, the bishop of Tuy), the sudarium was kept in Jerusalem in an oak chest until the beginning of the seventh century. Around 614, when the Persians sacked Jerusalem, the box containing the cloth and several other relics was secreted out of the city by one Philip the Presbyter. He went first to Alexandria in northern Egypt, then on to Spain. In the seventh century, the box was received by Fulgentius, the bishop of Ecija (Spain), who passed it to Seville, where it was initially kept by Saint Isidore (c. 560–636). In 657 it was moved to Toledo, where it remained until 718, by which time the Muslim armies had entered and conquered most of Spain.

King Alfonso II (r. 791–842) was able to establish a Christian enclave in northwest Spain and brought the box to his capital at Oviedo after having kept it in a cave outside the city for some years. Alfonso built a chapel, the Camara Santa, to house the chest and its contents. The chapel was then incorporated to the new cathedral at Oviedo. Two centuries later, on March 14, 1075, the box was formally opened in the presence of King Alfonso VI (r. 1065–1109), his sister Doña Urraca, and Rodrigo Díaz de Vivar (aka El Cid, c.1043–1099). The items in the chest, including the face cloth, were catalogued. Then in 1113, King Alfonso I (r. 1104–1134) saw the chest covered with silver that had an inscription calling for veneration of the face cloth.

The face cloth has remained at Oviedo since the eighth century, and the cathedral became a favorite stopping place for pilgrims traveling to SANTIAGO DE COMPOSTELA. (The same Alfonso II who built the Camara Santa had also established the church at Santiago de Compostela and declared Saint James the patron of his kingdom).

In the controversy over the results of scientific testing of the Shroud of Turin, the face cloth at Oviedo was made available for testing. In the late 1980s, Msgr. Giulio Ricci, president of the Roman Center for Sindonology, called for a systematic study of the cloth. Early studies included the gathering of pollen from the cloth. Species from Palestine and North Africa were found, both consistent with the legends concerning the travel route the cloth took to Spain. These findings were discussed at the First International Congress on the Sudarium of Oviedo in 1994. Subsequent studies have found a variety of consistencies between the cloth and the shroud, including the same blood type being found on each. Ongoing testing of the sudarium is being largely handled by Guillermo Heras, who heads the Spanish Center for Sindonology.

The testing of the face cloth has thrust it into the midst of the shroud controversy, with champions on both sides of the issue. The cloth is relatively well documented from the eighth century, but there is still a seven-century gap between its surfacing in Spain and its reputed origin in the Holy Land. As the controversy emerged on the face cloth, in 1989 Pope John Paul II showed his favor with a visit to the sudarium in Oviedo.

It should also be noted that the cathedral at Oviedo also is home to a thirteenth-century statue of Jesus that attracted pilgrims for the healing associated with it and at one time displayed a vial of the Virgin Mary's blood (a relic also found in the chest housing the sudarium) and other relics associated with her.

Sources:

Bennett, Janice. *Sacred Blood, Sacred Image: The Sudarium of Oviedo; New Evidence for the Authenticity of the Shroud of Turin.* Littleton, CO: Libri de Hispania, 2001.

Guscin, Mark. *The Oviedo Cloth.* London: Lutterworth Press, 2000.

Heras Moreno, Guillermo, José-Delfin Villalain Blanco, and Jorge-Manuel Rodríguez Almenar. "Comparative Study of the Sudarium of Oviedo and the Shroud of Turin." Paper presented at the *III Congreso Internationale di Studí sulla Sindone* (Alencia: Centro Español de Sindonlogía, 1998), held at Turin, Italy. June 5–7, 1998.

FAKIRS

Fakirs are holy men in India and neighboring countries who have become known either from their performance of extraordinary feats accomplished from their years of practicing yoga, or their performance of miraculous events, often as part of a stage performance. In the nineteenth century, numerous accounts of the fakirs were recorded by Western visitors to India, perhaps the most well known being the so-called Indian rope trick, in which a rope is raised into the air without visible means of support and a young boy climbs it, only to disappear when he reaches the top. Among the most popular of books informing Westerners of the fakirs was Louis Jacolliot's *Occult Science in India and among the Ancients: With an Account of Their Mystic Initiations and the History of Spiritism,* published in the 1880s. Fakirs are mostly either itinerant Sufis (Muslim mystics) or Hindu SADHUS (those who have left the larger society to pursue a religious life). Fakir is an Arabic term meaning poor man.

A number of fakirs practice hatha yoga for many years and attain considerable control over their involuntary body functions. They are able, through moving into various trancelike states, to suppress different physical responses and even slow their rate of breathing. Notable among their abilities are reclining on a bed of nails without apparent pain or permanent scarring and being buried alive for extended periods of time.

Other fakirs perform a spectrum of magical tricks, from levitating assistants and walking on hot coals to eating fire, materializing objects out of thin air, or sticking their hands in boiling oil. Most of these tricks are done through various techniques of simple stage magic.

During the last half of the twentieth century, B. Premanand, the head of the Indian Committee for the Scientific Investigation of Claims of the Paranormal, has made the exposing of the fakirs a per-

A fakir in India sits on a bed of nails to demonstrate the power of his religious devotion. *Getty Images.*

Sources:

Chauvelot, Robert. *Mysterious India: Its Rajahs, Its Brahmans, Its Fakirs.* New York: The Century Co., 1921.

Jacolliot, Louis. *Occult Science in India and among the Ancients: With an Account of Their Mystic Initiations and the History of Spiritism.* Reprint, Whitefish, MT: Kessinger Publishing, 2004.

Ovette, Joseph. *Miraculous Hindu Feats.* Oakland CA: Lloyd E. Jones, 1947.

FATIMA (PORTUGAL)

In 1917 Fatima, Portugal, was the site of what became the most heralded apparition of the Virgin Mary in the twentieth century. The apparitions were initiated in 1916 by several visits by an angel to three shepherd children, Lucia Dos Santos, Francisco Marto, and Jacinta Marto. The children—aged nine, eight, and six, respectively—were illiterate at the time.

About a year after the angel's visits, on May 13, 1917, the children saw what they described as a beautiful young lady dressed in white and shining with light who appeared to them. At this initial encounter, she asked them if they wished to accept their calling, which would entail their suffering in reparation for the sin of people with the aim to convert them. They answered in the affirmative. She then told them to come to the same spot on the thirteenth of every month. At the October apparition, she would reveal her name and purpose.

The lady appeared twice, on June and July 13, and a crowd attended both visitations, word having spread far and wide of the children's claims. Hostility also grew against the children, and in August the local magistrate, a Freethinker, imprisoned the children so they could not attend. Some 18,000 people showed up at the spot of the promised apparition in their place. The virgin appeared to the children privately after their release.

The crucial events occurred on September and October 13. Some 30,000 joined the three children in September. Around noon the sky darkened, then a globe of light appeared in the east

sonal crusade throughout the country. While what they do might be quite acceptable as a magical performance, Premanand has been most insistent that it becomes illegitimate when used to convince people of the existence of the supernatural. Fakirs operate as a stage magicians' union, which passes the knowledge of how to produce the various phenomena from generation to generation. By his knowledge of stage magic, Premanand has been able to reproduce all of the tricks of fakirs, and he regularly travels the countryside showing people how it is done. Premanand has especially targeted the famous guru Satya Sai Baba, who is well known in India as a miracle worker and regularly "materializes" sacred ash for his followers.

Today, the actions performed by the fakirs are generally considered either accomplishment derived from disciplining the body with yoga and related techniques or simple stage magic.

Pope John Paul II visits Lucia Dos Santos in 1991. She was a Carmelite nun who was the last survivor of three children who saw visions of an angel and of the Virgin Mary in 1916 and 1917. *AFP/Getty Images.*

and headed toward a tree that had been the focal point of the apparitions. Some white flakes began to fall from the sky. The Lady, seen only by the children, said she would work a miracle on her last visit. The light receded into the eastern sky.

The crowd that gathered on the last day numbered between 70,000 and 100,000. It was a cloudy, rainy day. The Lady appeared to the children and delivered her message, then the children saw a ray of light go up from her to where the sun would have been in the sky. Lucia called for the crowd to look at the sun. As she spoke, the clouds parted and a bright, silver disk appeared in the sky. Everyone, believer and skeptic alike, saw it begin to twirl. The twirling sun shooting out lights was visible to people up to thirty miles away.

After about half an hour, the twirling sun was seen to plunge toward the earth, emitting a considerable amount of heat (enough to dry the clothing earlier soaked in the rain). Before the disc hit the ground, it stopped and flew away (a behavior that later prompted those interested in UFOs to compare it with a flying saucer). The next day, newspapers across the country carried the story of what occurred.

Several years after the events, two of the children passed away. They had been told that the Lady would come for them in a short time. The focus for many years was then on Lucia, who lived until 2005. She spent more than seventy years as a Carmelite nun, then passed away just a few weeks before Pope John Paul II, who had put full papal authority behind the apparitions with a series of activities. He initially visited Fatima (as had Pope Paul VI) and then, in response to the message of Fatima, consecrated Russia to the virgin. On May 13, 2000, he canonized the two deceased visionaries, Francisco and Jacinta.

Pope John Paul II's interest in Fatima was greatly stimulated by an event that occurred on the anniversary of the first apparition in 1981. In the middle of a crowd, he bent to kiss a picture of the virgin carried by a pious believer. As he did so, a bullet whizzed over his head. Had he not responded to the picture, he would have been killed.

The basic message at Fatima called for increased devotion to the rosary and the Immaculate Heart of Mary. However, during the July apparition, a longer secret message was given to the children. This secret message would become the focus of much interest in Fatima. The secret message was in three parts. Lucia committed the secret message to paper in the 1940s, but only the first two parts were revealed. These parts included a vision of hell and the need for further devotion to the sacred Heart.

The third part of the message was put in an envelope and sent to the Vatican. It was known that both Pope John XXIII and Paul VI were made privy to the Third Secret and decided not to reveal it. In 2000 John Paul II released the text of the third secret, seemingly doing so before Lucia died, so she could verify its authenticity. Part of the message dealt with an assassination attempt of a "Bishop in white." Many believed it to be a prophecy of the 1981 attempted assassination of John Paul. The revelation of the secret message noticeably slowed much of the wild speculation that had built up over the preceding years, especially in fringe Marian groups.

Sources:

Cirrincione, Joseph A., with Thomas Nelson. *The Forgotten Secret of Fatima and the Silent Apostolate.* Rockford, IL: Tan Books, 1988.

Kondor, Louis. *Fatima in Lucia's Own Words.* Fatima, Portugal: Postulation Centre, 1989.

Robertson, Timothy Tindal. *Fatima, Russia and Pope John Paul II.* Still River, MA: Ravengate Press, 1992.

Ryan, Finbar Patrick. *Our Lady of Fatima.* Dublin: Browne and Nolan, 1944.

Walsh, William Thomas. *Our Lady of Fatima.* New York: Image Books, 1954.

FENG SHUI

Feng shui (literally wind/water) is a form of geomancy (the art of divination utilizing geological and environmental features) developed in China. It studies both the natural and humanly constructed elements of any environment. A specialist in feng shui observes any given environment—for example, an office space in a high-rise building, the landscape of a mountain valley, a building as a whole—and the manner in which the people inhabiting that environment interact with it. Based upon that observation, the specialist makes recommendations on improving the relationship of the people with their surroundings.

Feng shui developed as an art and science in ancient China. The accumulated knowledge was passed through a set of elite lineage holders into the modern world, but like many ancient secrets, in the twentieth century it became the subject of numerous books and papers. While the basic principles of feng shui may be learned from a book, proficiency requires practice and the development of a certain level of intuition in applying the principles. Thus a role remains for master practitioners to ply their trade.

Basic to understanding feng shui is the foundational principle of yin and yang. This desire to balance opposites and thus bring harmony is a foundation of Chinese thought. Yin/yang calls to mind a variety of polarities: male/female, light/dark, cold/hot, etc. Each opposite implies the other, and each half of a polarity always contains the seed of the other half.

Feng shui also draws on an understanding of the five elemental energies—earth, metal, fire, water, and wood—each of which would be in interaction in any given environment. Feng shui assumes that a variety of energies not visible to the average person are operating in the environment, and the harmonious flow of these subtle energies affect the happiness, well-being, creativity, and even the health of the inhabitants of the environment.

Long the exclusive practice of the Chinese, in the twentieth century feng shui has become popular around the world. In Chinese society, buildings would be erected and internal space shaped with reference to providing the most harmonious situation. Architects and others responsible for putting up structures in the increasingly secularized societies dominated by Chinese in Asia will have their buildings and other structures criticized if deemed to be ignoring the analysis of feng shui. Furthermore, any veil that descends upon those who inhabit structures with "bad" feng shui will be blamed on the builders ignoring traditional wisdom.

Sources:

Carter, Karen Rauch. *Move Your Stuff, Change Your Life: How to Use Feng Shui to Get Love, Money, Respect and Happiness.* New York: Fireside, 2000.

Collins, Terah Kathryn. *The Western Guide to Feng Shui: Creating Balance, Harmony, and Prosperity in Your Environment.* Carlsbad, CA: Hay House, 1996.

Sang, Larry. *Principles of Feng Shui.* Monterey Park, CA: American Feng Shui Institute, 1995.

Wong, Eva. *A Master Course in Feng-Shui.* Boston: Shambhala, 2001.

FINDHORN (SCOTLAND)

Findhorn is a modern intentional community located north and east of Inverness, Scotland, on Moray Firth. Findhorn was one of the birth places of the New Age movement, and the channeled messages of some early residents, especially David Spangler, Eileen Caddy, and Dorothy McLean, helped structure the emerging movement. The center grew quite large as the New Age move-

ment peaked in the late 1980s, and it remains an important center perpetuating the Esoteric themes that came to the fore in the late twentieth century.

The rather isolated Findhorn rose out of obscurity due in large part to the extraordinary occurrences that accompanied its founding. Somewhat down on their luck, Peter Caddy (1917–1994), his wife, Eileen, and a friend, Dorothy McLean, had settled in a trailer court at the village of Findhorn. A necessary part of their survival through the winter of 1963–1964 was the garden they planted. In part to while away their time, Eileen began to channel messages from what were believed to be *devas*, or nature spirits. As they followed the advice of the messages, the garden prospered.

In 1965 Peter Caddy attended a meeting of other pioneering New Age leaders in Great Britain, and that gathering catalyzed the formal organization of the Findhorn community. By this time the garden had become famous, with claims that it was producing fruit and vegetables out of season (which in northern Scotland was very short) and that some of the vegetables were of an extraordinarily large size. These phenomenal natural products gave credence to the messages that were channeled through Eileen Caddy and, increasingly, through McLean. These messages were informally published and circulated through England's Esoteric community.

Early in the 1970s, an American named David Spangler came to Findhorn for a brief visit, then decided to join the community. While there, he began channeling and authored a book in which he advocated the idea that a New Age would be dawning in the next generation. That book, *Revelation: Birth of the New Age*, was published in 1976 and is credited with outlining the basic perspective around which the New Age Movement congealed. Spangler suggested that due to astrological realignments, new spiritual energies were now available to humanity and, if properly used, could bring a new era of people and light in the twenty-first century.

As the movement emerged, in 1975 Caddy purchased the nearby Clung Hotel, which became a center for conferences and workshops. By the early 1980s, some 250 persons had come to reside at the community, and a regular program for visitors developed and continues to provide its financial base. As the idea of a coming New Age faded in the 1990s, Findhorn adjusted to the changes of emphasis in the large Esoteric community that the movement had created, and the community has remained an important center as attention to Esotericism has grown.

Sources:

Caddy, Eileen. *The Spirit of Findhorn*. Forres, Scotland: Findhorn Press, 1997.

Pogacnik, Marko. *Nature Spirits and Elemental Beings*. Forres, Scotland: Findhorn Press, 1995.

Spangler, David. *Revelation: The Birth of a New Age*. San Francisco: The Rainbow Bridge, 1976.

FIREWALKING

A story is told of the miracle-working Saint Francis of Paola's (1415–1507) encounter with a papal representative sent to investigate him. The Monsignor critiqued his extreme lifestyle. In response, Francis walked over a bed of red-hot coals and then scooped up a few and presented them to his accuser, who retreated in his perplexity. The story illustrates the manner in which people of a wide variety of cultures discovered how to walk on fire apparently without being harmed, an event that would normally lead to extreme burns, if not death. Through the twentieth century, ethnologists have reported firewalking activity from such diverse places as Hawaii and Africa.

Saint Francis notwithstanding, firewalking was an extremely rare phenomenon in the West, and it became an object of fascination when found as a practice among the fakirs of India. It ranked with the Indian rope trick as the most intriguing feat of the fakirs, perhaps all the more interesting as the rope trick was rarely witnessed. Many Westerners got their first chance to actually see firewalking

when magician Kuda Bux (1906–1981) performed the trick in 1935 before an admiring audience from the University of London Council for Psychical Research and a host of news reporters. The council actually issued the first report pointing out that the ability to walk on fire was not due to any supernatural or paranormal ability, but a matter of simple physics: namely, the low thermal conductivity of burning wood and brevity of the contact between the burning coals and the walker's foot. In 1998 physics teacher David Willey organized a record-setting fire walk. He and fourteen others at the University of Pittsburgh walked a 165-foot coal bed, just for the fun of it.

Prior to the twentieth century, firewalking was most frequently integrated into a supernatural religious worldview, often a demonstration of some attribute of a deity. However, in the late twentieth century, it has been adapted by the Esoteric or New Age community as one of a spectrum of transformational tools. This new wave of firewalking appears to be traced to a 1977 article in *Scientific American* that explained firewalking in enough detail that many found it possible to duplicate the feat.

Among the people influenced by the article was Tolly Burkan, a teacher and author in the human potentials movement. In 1979 he began to teach his idea that firewalking could be used as a tool for personal growth, and by 1982 he was widely advertising his notion. The following year, he taught the technique to human potentials celebrity Tony Robbins, who put his organization behind the effort to spread firewalking internationally. Robbins agreed with Burkan that the practice was an excellent tool for expanding awareness, overcoming fears, and abandoning beliefs about one's personal limitations. Burkan took the practice to Europe and began to train other teacher/facilitators. Teachers were trained through the Firewalking Institute of Research and Education, which he founded, and then additionally through the Sundoor Foundation, founded by his former wife, Peg Burkan. The first book on firewalking appeared in 1989, Michael Sky's *Dancing with the Fire*.

While not as widespread as other New Age techniques such as, for example, the Tarot or crystals, firewalking has spread exponentially through the 1990s to the present and is no longer a magical secret held by a few professional firewalkers.

Sources:

Burkan, Tolly. *Extreme Spirituality: Radical Journeys for the Inward Bound*. Hillsboro, OR: Beyond Words Publishing, 2001.

Danforth, Loring M. *Firewalking and Religious Healing*. Princeton: Princeton University Press, 1989.

Nisbet, Matt. "The Physics Instructor Who Walks on Fire," October 25, 2000. Posted at http://www.csicop.org/genx/firewalk/. Accessed April 1, 2007.

Sky, Michael. *Dancing with the Fire: Transforming Limitation through Firewalking*. Santa Fe, NM: Bear & Co., 1989.

FLAGELLATION

Flagellation, the scourging of oneself or others, was a widespread form of punishment in the ancient world and as such has continued to the present day, though acquiring prominent critics. Religiously, flagellation acquired a place in the liturgical world of Western Christianity in the Middle Ages as increasingly more prominence was placed on the sufferings of Christ during the last week of his life. One expression of the contemplation of the sufferings of Christ was self-flagellation, a practice that took on added dimensions as a means for the expiation (doing penance) for one's sins. Christian self-flagellation as a popular practice can be traced to Italy and to the likes of Bishop Peter Damian (1007–1072), later named a doctor of the church. The practice entered the life of the Franciscans and Dominicans, and it was ultimately spread to several confraternities in the thirteenth century who made self-flagellation a keystone of their piety. By the high Middle Ages, it had become one of the most common forms of penance throughout Christendom. It was lauded as an expedient means of moving from a life oriented on desire to one focused on spiritual realities.

Groups that based their common life on flagellation began to see their role as doing not only self-penance but penance for all of Christendom. Such penance was understood as effective in averting disasters, especially those attributed to divine wrath. In the thirteenth century, penitential processions that included flagellants emerged, and various attempts by church authorities to curb the practice led in 1349 to a papal condemnation of such processions as heretical. While the condemnation (and the general abandonment of self-flagellation altogether by Protestants) limited the public demonstrations of self-flagellation, it did not greatly affect its use in private in religious orders. In the modern world it had become increasingly out of fashion, especially since Vatican II, when the more extreme forms of self-flagellation were mentioned disapprovingly.

Within the Roman Catholic tradition, self-flagellation (as well as more traditional portrayals of Christ's suffering during Passion week) is generally practiced among more conservative believers. It is, for example, reportedly a common practice used by members of the somewhat secretive Opus Dei organization. It is a regular part of the Easter celebration in several Catholic countries, the Philippines being the best documented. In the United States, large crowds gather annually for the reenactment of the Easter week events by the PENITENTES of New Mexico.

However, Christianity is not the only place where flagellation has taken on religious meanings. For example, self-flagellation is a central part of the Shi'a Muslim holiday Ashura. Ashura begins on the eve of the 10th day of the Islamic month Muharram to commemorate the martyrdom of Imam Hussein, the grandson of Prophet Mohammad, who was killed at KARBALA (Iraq) in 680 CE by those who opposed his claim to become the successor of Ali as caliph. The mourning ceremonies include self-flagellation and self-mutilation. Banned under the reign of Saddam Hussein, Ashura was celebrated in Karbala for the first time in forty years in 2003.

A practice that emerged in the European Dark Ages and still survives today is self-flagellation. In this photo, a penitent in Cutud, San Fernando, Philippines, follows the whipping ritual. *Getty Images*.

THE ENCYCLOPEDIA OF RELIGIOUS PHENOMENA

Flagellation, though of a more staid variety, was introduced into modern Witchcraft (or Wicca) by Gerald B. Gardner, its progenitor. According to Wiccan historian Aidan Kelly, Gardner was addicted to being whipped (a sexual practice often associated with British males). While other Wiccans have suggested that Kelly simply overstated the case, the use of scourging in Gardnerian rituals indicates a more positive approach to the practice. Here, it is tied not to penance and mourning, but put forward as one of a variety of means to develop one's magical skills. Other paths include the use of meditation or of trance states. In the Gardnerian rituals, the person being scourged is bound and the strokes delivered in a light, steady, monotonous, and slow fashion. Some have attempted to connect such flagellation with its use for erotic stimulation as part of various sexual practices.

Sources:

Cohn, Norman. *The Pursuit of the Millennium: Revolutionary Millenarians and Mystical Anarchists of the Middle Age.* Oxford: Oxford University Press, 1990.

Horka-Follick, Lorayne Ann. *Los Hermanos Penitentes.* Los Angeles: Westernlore Press, 1969.

Millado, Chris. "The Origins of Christian Self-Flagellation." Posted at http://www2.hawaii.edu/~millado/flagellationfolder/flagellation2.html. Accessed April 1, 2007.

ul-Amine, Hasan. *Shorter Islamic Shi'ite Encyclopedia.* Beirut, Lebanon: A Group of Muslim Brothers, 1969.

FORD, ARTHUR (1896–1971)

Arthur Augustus Ford, an American Spiritualist medium, became an important force in the attempt to integrate psychic phenomena into mainstream religion in the generation prior to the New Age movement. Ford was born in Titusville, Florida, and early began a religious pilgrimage that led him to Transylvania College in Lexington, Kentucky, and into the ministry of the Christian Church (Disciples of Christ). He served briefly as a pastor before joining the army during World War I.

During the war his psychic abilities came to the fore, and he was known as someone who "knew" the names of people who were going to die several days ahead of time. After the war he became a Spiritualist medium, and he traveled widely, offering trance sessions to people. He eventually settled in New York City as the minister of a congregation affiliated with the National Spiritualist Association of Churches. While there he attained his first and most enduring bit of fame when he claimed that he had broken the code that magician and Spiritualist critic Harry Houdini had left with his wife, through which he would communicate if he survived death. The announcement, in 1928, made Ford known far beyond the relatively small world of Spiritualism.

In the 1930s Ford came into conflict with the Spiritualists as he had come to believe in reincarnation, an idea traditionally rejected by the American Spiritualist movement. Belief in reincarnation was growing in America, and Ford's founding of the International General Assembly of Spiritualists in 1936 became just one of several schisms the movement faced as it splintered over attempts to accommodate reincarnationist perspectives.

In the 1940s Ford's circle of acquaintances grew to include a number of ministers in various Protestant churches. His séances with them led to the 1955 formation of Spiritualist Frontiers Fellowship (SFF), an American counterpart of the Churches' Fellowship for Psychical Research in England. SFF grew slowly through the 1960s, then rapidly after Ford's 1967 televised séance with Episcopal Bishop James A. Pike. Pike, one of the most prominent Protestant church leaders of the era, became a believer. Pike's subsequent book, *The Other Side* (1968), created a sensation at the time, although its long-term effect was blunted by the author's accidental death the next year. Ford died in 1971.

Spiritualist Frontiers Fellowship expanded significantly in the early 1970s and became an early legitimizing organization for church members who were exploring issues soon to be institutionalized in the New Age movement. It was particularly affected by two events. First, author Allen Spraggett, who worked with the Rev. William Rauscher, (Ford's literary executor), discovered that Ford had faked the 1967 séance with Pike. The evidence they produced not only called into question that event, but much of the evidential material produced by Ford in previous séances. Then in 1974, SFF went through a significant organizational shift. The new leadership made a series of disastrous decisions that cost the organization more than half its membership. It never recovered.

Ford's involvement in the Houdini affair and the Pike séance have kept his name alive, if only to be periodically denounced by the skeptical debunking movement that arose in the 1970s to oppose the growing popularity of uncritical belief in paranormal phenomena. However, a generation after his death, his legacy appears to lie in the effort he made to reach out beyond the Spiritualist community and network with those who believed but would not affiliate with Spiritualism. That effort was a significant precursor of the New Age.

Sources:

Ford, Arthur. *The Life Beyond Death*. New York: G. P. Putnam's Sons, 1971.

———. *Nothing So Strange*. New York: Harper, 1958.

———. *Unknown but Known*. New York: Harper, 1968.

Spraggett, Allen, with William V. Rauscher. *Arthur Ford, The Man Who Talked with the Dead*. New York: New American Library, 1973.

FORTUNE TELLING

Fortune telling is the task of discerning the future usually by what is perceived to be a supernatural or paranormal means, i.e., divination. The quest for knowledge of the future is as old as human history and appears to reach far earlier into prehistoric times. Some practices, such as astrology, were developed in the ancient world and have remained popular over the centuries while others, such as throwing molten lead into water to seek the initial of a future mate, came and went relatively quickly.

Historically, observers of human society have noted the many different forms that divinatory activity has taken. Popular ancient practices included the reading of the patterns formed by the intestines of a recently slaughtered animal, listening to the sounds made by a conch shell held to the ear, or discerning patterns in clouds of smoke. Divination is often closely related to perceptions about various spontaneous events (such as the appearance of comets, odd incidents accompanying a birth) believed to be an omen heralding the future.

In the West, the practice of fortune telling was popularly associated with the Roma people (the Gypsies). In centuries past, their practice of fortune telling was used to denigrate them as an outsider social group. In more recent years, the continued identification of the Roma with fortune telling has been used to discredit fortune telling and tie it to various fraudulent practices, such as the taking of large sums of money for a reputed knowledge of the future.

Divination may on occasion be an activity that anybody can practice, the reading of the future being based on folklore or well-known divinatory occurrences, such as the ground hog's shadow indicating the advent of spring, but most forms of divination require the work of a specialist. Some specialists can be trained, such as an astrologer, a palmist, or a reader of other divinatory devices such as the runes or tarot cards. However, divination often falls to people deemed to have special psychic or paranormal abilities. Such were the people who maintained the ancient oracle sites and the seers, soothsayer, and psychics of all ages. More often than not, the two roles mix in a complex fashion.

Attempts to predict the future of individuals or groups have been and continue to be made in all religious traditions, in spite of very active efforts in recent centuries to debunk the many different divinatory practices and efforts by many practitioners to redefine their practice and make it more "scientifically" acceptable. Astrology remains the most popular form of divination globally, while palmistry, tarot cards, the I Ching, and runes also have popular followings. Thousands of psychics (under a variety of labels) operate both professionally and as amateurs. In the West, many of these are attached to some extent to one of the Esoteric religions. Among Pentecostal Christians, a variety of leaders manifest the gifts of the Holy Spirit, including those with prophetic gifts.

As the New Age movement gained strength, an attempt was made to redefine various forms of fortune telling as transformative tools. The element of divining the future was thus often excised from practices such as astrology and Tarot card readings, which were used instead for self-understanding and discernment of deeply ingrained tendencies. However, fortune-telling tendencies always struggled to reassert themselves.

In spite of widespread condemnation of fortune telling as mere baseless superstition in Western (and increasingly Eastern) culture, fortune telling appears to be surviving and finding niches to operate in an increasingly tolerant and free society.

Sources:

Buckland, Raymond. *The Fortune-Telling Book: The Encyclopedia of Divination and Soothsaying*. Detroit: Visible Ink Press, 2003.

Easton, Cassandra. *The Complete Book of Divination: How to Use the Most Popular Methods of Fortune Telling*. London: Piatkus Books, 1999.

Kemp, Gillian. *The Fortune Telling Book: Reading Crystal Balls, Tea Leaves, Playing Cards, and Everyday Omens of Love and Luck*. Boston, MA: Little, Brown, 2000.

Pollack, Rachel. *Teach Yourself Fortune Telling: Palmistry, the Crystal Ball, Runes, Tea Leaves, the Tarot*. New York: Henry Holt & Company, 1986.

Shaw, Eva. *Divining the Future: Prognostication from Astrology to Zoomancy*. New York: Facts on File, 1995.

Smith, Richard J. *Fortune-tellers and Philosophers: Divination in Traditional Chinese Society*. San Francisco: Westview Press, 1991.

GARABANDAL (SPAIN)

The growing popularity of the devotion to the Virgin Mary as a result of the reported apparition at **FATIMA**, Portugal, in 1916 and 1917 had repercussions in neighboring Spain in 1961. On June 18, 1961, at San Sebastian de Garabandal, a small town in northwest Spain, four young girls—Mari Loli Mazon, Jacinta Gonzalez, Mari Cruz Gonzalez, and Conchita Gonzalez—saw an angel. This initial encounter was followed by others. On July 1, the angel announced that on the next day, the Virgin Mary would appear under the form of Our Lady of Mount Carmel.

Many were present the next day, though as is common in such cases, only the children saw the two angels and the Virgin, who made her first appearance to them. During the apparition, they seemed to carry on a conversation with the Virgin. Such apparitions became common over the next four years. Some 2,000 were recorded through 1965. During the apparitions, the girls appeared to be in a trancelike state, with their heads drawn back and the pupils of their eyes dilated. They were oblivious to their surroundings and on occasion were subjected to pin pricks or burns, to which they paid no attention.

As the apparitions continued, religious objects were handed to the girls, and they presented them

to the Virgin to be blessed with a kiss. The girls also received an invisible communion from the Virgin. This later aspect of the visions led to one of the more heralded events at Garabandal. At one point, the angel who had appeared to the children told Conchita Gonzalez that the invisible communion would become visible. On July 19, 1962, while in her ecstatic state, a white object appeared on her extended tongue. A picture, since widely circulated, captured the event.

The messages at Garabandal were somewhat mundane, calling for greater devotion and including only a few prophecies. Almost from the beginning, however, they became controversial and, along with devoted advocates, harsh critics arose. The local diocesan office made an initial evaluation in 1961. It concluded that the events in the isolated community offered no proof through which to understand the apparitions as true and authentic. In 1962 the local bishop ordered priests to refrain from saying mass relative to the apparitions. It was after this initial report that a number of tests were conducted on the girls by visiting scientists.

Finally, in 1986 the Bishop Juan Antonio del Val Gallo of Santander appointed a new commission to reevaluate the events at Garabandal. The results of the study were passed to Rome, and in 1987 the Bishop sanctioned priests celebrating mass

Children experience visions of angels and the Virgin Mary at San Sebastian de Garabandal, Spain. Invisible to adults, the visions were said to affect only children, who would go into a trance and receive holy kisses and communion. *Fortean Picture Library.*

in the local church. The story did not end there, as in October 1996 the Bishop Jose Vilaplana of Santander issued a letter denying that the events at Garabandal were of supernatural origin. Although primarily unsupportive in his statements, the local bishop has left room for supporters of Garabandal to call attention to the messages and organize devotional activities, especially pilgrimages.

Sources:

Albright, Judith M. *Our Lady at Garabandal.* Milford, OH: Faith Publishing Co., 1992.

Laffineur, Fr. Matiene and M. T. le Pelletier. *Star on the Mountain.* Lindenhurst, NY: Our Lady of Mt. Carmel de Garabandal, 1969.

Odell, Catherine M. *Those Who Saw Her: The Apparitions of Mary.* Huntington, IN: Our Sunday Visitor, 1986.

Pacual, F. Sanchez-Ventura Y. *The Apparitions of Garabandal.* Pasadena, CA: St. Michael's Garabandal Center for Our Lady of Carmel, 1966.

GELLER, URI (B. 1946)

Israeli-born Uri Geller emerged in the 1970s as one of the most controversial claimants of psychic abilities. He began his public demonstrations of psychokinetic powers in the 1960s but attained some international fame in 1971 after demonstrating his abilities to parapsychologist Andrija Puharich. Puharich brought him to America and introduced him to colleagues who were conducting psychical research.

In 1972 he demonstrated a spectrum of his abilities, most notably the seeming ability to bend metal spoons, at the Stanford Research Institute in California. The testing done there was monitored in part by retired astronaut Edgar Mitchell, who had thrown his prestige behind parapsychology. Subsequent televised demonstrations of his bending of metal objects, a phenomenon that became known as the Geller effect, brought Geller celebrity status. Puharich published a biography in 1974, and Geller's own autobiography appeared the next year. Various parapsychologists indicated their desire to test Geller.

At the same time, the growing skeptical/debunking movement, spearheaded by the Committee for the Scientific Investigation of the Claims of the Paranormal (CSICOP), denounced Geller as a clever stage magician. Two stage magicians, Melbourne Christopher and James Randi, asserted their expertise by demonstrating similar feats and loudly questioning the ability of parapsychologists to uncover fraudulent phenomena. Geller filed a lawsuit for defamation, but he failed to win the lengthy court battle against CSICOP and Randi. In the meantime, a number of people, especially a group of children in Japan, emerged with the ability to demonstrate the Geller effect.

After the lawsuit, Geller largely dropped out of the public eye. Nonetheless, many vied for his services, and for a time he worked with people hunting for oil and other valuable minerals. These efforts apparently proved quite successful, although the companies involved have been reluctant to confirm that their successes came from acting on information supplied by Geller. He made one attempt to return to the public spotlight in 1986 following the publication of a book, *The Geller Effect,* co-authored with Guy Lynn Playfair, a parapsychologist who believed in his powers. His efforts were largely ignored, however, and he returned to his more private career.

Geller has developed a presence on the Internet, and critics continue to document his activity. He has tried to ignore his critics and has written a number of books on paranormal themes, including (in 2001) an update on his post-1970s activities.

During the 1970s, Uri Geller drew media attention for his supposed psychokinetic abilities, such as the power to bend metal with his mind. His claims were later disproven, though Geller still asserts he has genuine paranormal skills. *AFP/Getty Images.*

Sources:

Geller, Uri. *My Story.* New York: Praeger, 1975.

———. *Unorthodox Encounters.* London: Robson Books, 2001.

———, and Guy Lyon Playfair. *The Geller Effect.* London: Jonathan Cape, 1986.

Panati, Charles, ed. *The Geller Papers.* Boston: Houghton Mifflin, 1976.

Randi, James. *The Truth about Uri Geller.* Buffalo, NY: Prometheus Books, 1982.

GIANT OF CERNE ABBAS (ENGLAND)

On a hillside in rural Dorset, England, a huge figure 180 feet tall has been cut deeply into the

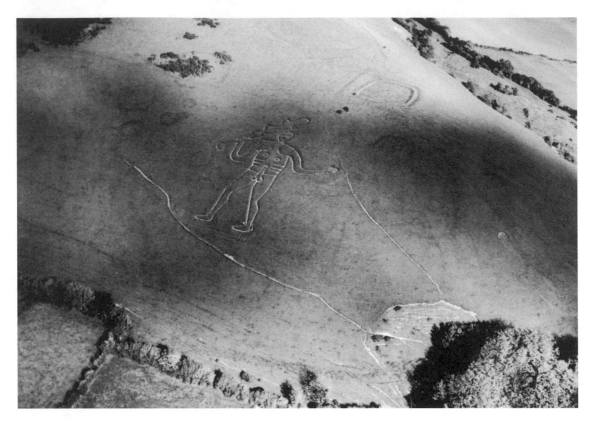

Just who carved this figure into an English hillside is an unsolved mystery, though the picture is clearly some sort of fertility symbol. Legend has it that women who sleep on the site are more likely to become pregnant. *Getty Images*.

underlying chalk. It is a nude male figure whose most prominent feature is an erect phallus and testicles. He holds a large club, and above his head on the hilltop is a place for maypole dancing.

The origin of the giant is obscure, but the best speculation is that it is a representation of the half-god Hercules. It was possibly cut during the reign of the Roman Emperor Commodus (r. 180–192 CE), who thought of himself as the reincarnation of Hercules. As emperor, Commodus dressed like Hercules, including the carrying of a club. Shortly before his death he officially assumed the title of Hercules. If this early origin of the Giant is assumed, it is easy to see the hill above the Giant as the site of fertility rites. It is

noteworthy that the people in the area took it upon themselves to keep the giant visible over the centuries, even after Christianity became dominant in the area. Local legends attribute fertility powers to the Giant, and tales circulate in Dorset of women who slept on the figure while seeking to become pregnant.

The Giant is first mentioned in writing in a 1694 note in the books of the local Church of England parish, the first published account being in 1751 in John Hutchins' *Guide to Dorset*. Some have suggested that the lack of an earlier mention of the figure means it was cut in the seventeenth century, a high possibility. When pictures began to be published of the Giant, on many occasions the phallus was blanked out.

Ronald Hutton, a historian of British Paganism, has identified the Giant with Denzil Holles, the first Baron Holles (1599–1680), the local lord of the manor. The figure could have been cut by his servants or even as a crude joke on His Lordship.

Sources:

Bettey, J. H. "The Cerne Abbas Giant: The Documentary Evidence." *Antiquity* 55 (1981): 118–121.

Castleden, R. *The Cerne Giant*. Wincanton: Dorset Publishing Company, 1996.

Clarke, Nigel. *The Rude Man of Cerne Abbas and Other Wessex Landscape Oddities*. Lyme Regis: Nigel J. Clarke Publications, 1998.

Fishwick, D. *The Imperial Cult in the Latin West*. Leiden: Brill, 1987.

GLASTONBURY (ENGLAND)

Glastonbury, a town in southwest England, arose out of prehistory in the middle of the seventh century when a Celtic church was established on top of one of the nearby hills—**GLASTONBURY TOR**. Three hundred years later, Saint Dunstan (924–988) refurbished and enlarged the church, which would evolve into a medieval monastic center. Glastonbury was one of the largest and wealthiest abbeys in the land, and its abbot's influence reached to the highest levels of the royal court in London. However, prior to the rise of the church in the area, layers of myths and legends may be unearthed.

Although far from the sea today, Glastonbury was surrounded by water a mere 2,000 years ago. The area is believed by many to have been a center for pre-Christian life and worship. The pre-Christian speculations meld into the identification of Glastonbury as the mythical Isle of Avalon, a word derived from the Celtic deity Avalloc (or Avallach), who ruled the underworld. Identifying Glastonbury with Avalon links the region with King Arthur and his Knights of the Round Table. Avalon was the final resting place of the good king.

Another popular legend is that, during the years of Jesus' life not covered in the Bible, Jesus accompanied Joseph of Arimathea, supposedly his great uncle, to Glastonbury. After Jesus' crucifixion, Joseph of Arimathea came into possession of the cup used at the Last Supper. He used the cup to catch some of the blood that flowed from Jesus' body as he was crucified. He returned to Glastonbury and buried the cup (which came to be known as the Holy Grail) just below Glastonbury Tor. Shortly thereafter, a spring, now called Chalice Well, began to flow. Its water was a source of health and youthfulness. If one accepts the story of Joseph and the cup, the real purpose behind the Knights of the Round Table becomes the discovery of the Holy Grail. On a more practical level, the story of Joseph served to bolster later British claims to have a Christian history that stood independently of Rome.

The legends that had grown up around Glastonbury were inextricably linked to the history of the old Celtic church/monastery in 1190, when the monks residing in Glastonbury Abbey claimed to have found the tomb of Arthur in the graveyard of Glastonbury Abbey south of the Lady Chapel. In the tomb was a lead cross about a foot long, with a Latin inscription: *Hic iacet sepultus inclitus rex arturius in insula avalonia*, "Here lies buried the renowned King Arthur in the Isle of Avalon." The artifact (now generally believed to be a hoax perpetrated by the monks) linked Avalon and Arthur to the town and Abbey. From that point, it became a popular pilgrimage site.

The bones in the tomb (reputedly of Arthur and Guinevere) were placed in caskets. King Edward I (r. 1270–1307) visited the abbey in 1278, at which time the remains were put in a black marble tomb that was placed before the high altar in the abbey church. Unfortunately, Glastonbury did not stand in the face of King Henry VIII's (r. 1509–1547) dissolution of the monasteries in 1536. Subsequently, the abbey was vandalized, and Arthur's remains disappeared.

After the destruction of the abbey, Glastonbury receded into history, but in recent centuries its legend has revived. The revival of interest in Glastonbury has been part of the growing popular and academic study of the Arthurian legends (some identifying nearby Cadbury Hill with Camelot) and of the ancient monolithic structures, especially Stonehenge, in neighboring Wiltshire. Through the twentieth century, Esoteric metaphysical believers and Christian mystics took up residence in and near Glastonbury to revel in its legendary past.

The legend of Glastonbury was considerably expanded in the 1920s by Katharine Maltwood. A student of the Arthurian legends, she began to study large-scale maps of the countryside surrounding Glastonbury Tor. She noticed in the patterns of the earthworks, field tracks, river banks, and other artifacts of the landscape what appeared to be a gigantic star map. As shown in the illustrations of her 1929 book, *A Guide to Glastonbury's Temple of the Stars*, the terrestrial features present the twelve signs of the zodiac in a giant circle, thirty miles in circumference, with Glastonbury Tor in the center. Some of the zodiacal figures are two to three miles in length and could be seen only from some miles in the air. If one accepted the idea of the Glastonbury zodiac, then one would also have to suggest that many centuries before the megalith builders, there was a community at Glastonbury that was able to shape the terrain to form the mystical and astrological patterns.

Contemporaneously with Maltwood, Frederick Bligh Bond (1864–1945), a local historian interested in Spiritualism, began to direct an excavation of the abbey that proved remarkable for the number of discoveries he made. In the wake of the discoveries, he disclosed that he had been directed by the spirit of a former monk who claimed to have lived at the abbey in its heyday.

In the decades since World War II, Glastonbury has come to life as one of Britain's foremost New Age centers. All of the sites associated with the old legends have been well marked, and the town now rivals Stonehenge as a magnet for tourists to western England. A variety of New Age and alternative groups have opened centers in Glastonbury, and a number of alternative religious events now occur there weekly. All of this activity has led to a veritable library of material about Glastonbury, ranging from tracts by true believers to the very skeptical volume by Robert Dunning, *Christianity in Somerset* (1970). Dunning claims that all of the stories about the region originated in the twelfth century as part of a deliberate attempt of the monks to raise money by promoting pilgrimage to the abbey.

Sources:

Fortune, Dion. *Avalon of the Heart*. London: Aquarian Press, 1971.

Greed, John A. *Glastonbury Tales*. Bristol, UK: St. Trillo Publications, 1975.

Lewis, Lionel Smithett. *St. Joseph of Arimathea at Glastonbury*. London: James Clarke, 1976.

Maltwood, Katharine. *A Guide to Glastonbury's Temple of the Stars*. London: James Clarke, 1964.

Roberts, Anthony. *Atlantean Traditions in Ancient Britain*. London: Rider and Company, 1977.

Wilcock, John. *A Guide to Occult Britain*. London: Sidgwick & Jackson, 1976.

Williams, Mary, ed. *Glastonbury: A Study in Patterns*. Hammersmith, UK: RILKO, 1969.

GLASTONBURY TOR (ENGLAND)

Glastonbury Tor, a teardrop-shaped hill, dominates the landscape around the town of Glastonbury, England, and the surrounding plain, the Summerland Meadows. In times past, at least part of the year it was an island. Today it is surrounded on three sides by the river Brue. Known through much of Britain's prehistory, it drew religious fervor and played a part in various popular legends. Modern New Age practitioners have added significantly to its spiritual lore.

Inhabited as early as 300 BCE, residents found it an easily defended position with a natural moat. Called *Ynis Witrin*, or Isle of Glass, the Tor was connected to the surrounding territory by a

A tower built by Celtic Christians in the seventh century CE stands atop Glastonbury Tor, a hill associated with many myths and legends from both Christian and Pagan traditions. *Fortean Picture Library.*

narrow strip of land, above water only at low tide. Several trade routes converged at Glastonbury, drawing Romans and other travelers. In the seventh century, a Celtic Christian monastic community settled on top of the Tor. The tower attached to their center is the only remaining structure on the Tor proper. (Some sources say the monastery was founded by the Welsh Saint David late in the sixth century.) The monastery was later relocated to the foot of the hill, and in the tenth century it became the home of the future saint, Dunstan (d. 988). Dunstan was one of the leaders of the monastic revival in England of the late tenth century, and he launched the history of Glastonbury as a center of British monastic life.

The thriving monastic community was able to level the top of the Tor and construct a large stone church on its height. This church was destroyed by an earthquake but was rebuilt in 1323. After Henry VIII closed and looted all of England's monasteries, the church on top of the Tor was destroyed a second time, this time by local residents who raided it for stone to be used in other structures.

During the Tor's monastic era, it also became associated with King Arthur. Arthur, probably a Celtic ruler who attained legendary status by defending his land against the movement of Saxons into the region, was supposedly buried at Glastonbury Abbey. Any use of the Tor would have been from its military strategic value. One of the more enduring stories concerns a local chieftain named Melwas who, it was later claimed, kidnapped Arthur's wife, Guinevere, and held her prisoner there until Arthur could negotiate her release.

In the modern world, the Tor has become the focus of a spectrum of mystical and esoteric lore. At the foot of the Tor is the Chalice Well, which some claim is the site where Joseph of Arimathea buried the chalice used at Jesus' Last Supper. Many ghost stories have accumulated around the Tor. The megaliths, medieval church buildings, and other notable sites around the Tor have been mapped and provide material for speculation about ley lines (straight lines connecting ancient sites believed to suggest that their placement was planned by the original builders). Among the more enduring legends, first recorded in medieval times, is that the Tor is hollow and the location of the entrance to the underworld. The hollow Tor stories connect the hill to fairy legends.

From a distance, the terraced pathway that wraps around the Tor is one of its most distinguishing features. Some have suggested the pathway was made as early as four or five thousand years ago, making it contemporaneous with Stonehenge. Noting that the pathway is similar to a labyrinth, some suggest it was the product of conscious human planning rather than simply a haphazard path up the mountain, possibly made originally by animals.

Today the Tor has been integrated into the New Age interest in Glastonbury and is an important site on the local tourist board's list of the community's sites. The revived and growing Neopagan community has pressed the case that Glastonbury be recognized as ancient Pagan territory. Some have claimed the top of the Tor was an ancient site for Pagan ceremonies, though convincing evidence is in short supply.

The many stories weaving in and out of the history of the Tor make it (along with the adjacent town) a tourist magnet and a popular goal for pilgrimages.

Sources:

Lewis, Lionel Smithett. *St. Joseph of Arimathea at Glastonbury*. London: James Clarke, 1976.

Roberts, Anthony. *Atlantean Traditions in Ancient Britain*. London: Rider and Company, 1977.

Wilcock, John. *A Guide to Occult Britain*. London: Sidgwick & Jackson, 1976.

Williams, Mary, ed. *Glastonbury: A Study in Patterns*. Hammersmith, UK: RILKO, 1969.

GOLDEN PALACE

As the International Society for Krishna Consciousness (ISKCON, the Hare Krishna Movement) grew, the founder, A. C. Bhaktivedanta Swami Prabhupada (1896–1977), appointed a set of leaders that began to function in the early 1970s as the governing body. Among these leaders was an early devotee known as Kirtananda Swami Bhaktipada, or simply Swami Kirtananda. In 1968 he led in the founding of the New Vrindaban Community outside Moundsville, West Virginia, as a place to demonstrate the possibility of an ideal society based on ISKCON's teachings. Vrindaban, India, is a sacred city, believed by many to be where the events in the life of Krishna and his consort occurred in the prehistoric past.

In 1973 Swami Kirtananda proposed the idea of building a home in the New Vrindaban Community for the aging founder of the Hare Krishna movement, where he could concentrate on completing the writing he had planned to do. As originally proposed, the house would have been a simple structure. As construction began, the plan became increasingly more elaborate. In 1977, as construction proceeded, Swami Prabhupada died. The building became even more elaborate as a monument to the deceased leader. The palatial finished product emerged in the 1980s as the state's most popular tourist attraction.

In the meantime, however, trouble developed at New Vrindaban, as the community had become known. First, Swami Kirtananda emerged on one end of a spectrum of opinion concerning how

ISKCON should proceed in the post-Prabhupada era. Kirtananda became the most conservative voice in the debates and eventually was expelled from ISKCON in 1987. New Vrindaban and the several temples under Kirtananda's control reorganized as a separate corporation.

Kirtananda's expulsion came in the wake of two then-unsolved murders associated with New Vrindaban, that of Charles St. Dennis in 1983 and of Kirtananda critic Steven Bryant in 1986. A decade of litigation followed the Bryant death that included the conviction of a member of the community, Thomas Dreshner, in connection with the St. Dennis murder. In 1996 Kirtananda pleaded guilty to a series of charges, including conspiracy to murder Bryant.

Through the years of litigation, an attempt was made to continue work on the vision that had developed to create at New Vrindaban an American equivalent of Vrindaban, India, and its seven main temples. The Golden Palace emerged as the first of the proposed seven structures around which the community would subsequently function. The negative results of the litigation brought the overall project to a halt.

Following Kirtananda's conviction, accompanied by widespread accusations that he was also a pedophile, many of Kirtananda's followers left New Vrindaban, and ISKCON moved to reintegrate the community into the larger organization, a process that took several years. Today New Vrindaban operates as an ISKCON community, and the Golden Palace has been maintained and is open to receive visitors. It remains a popular tourist attraction as an example of American Hindu devotion, although legal concerns, growing out of occurrences during Kirtananda's years of leadership, still hang over the community.

Sources:

Muster, Nori. *Betrayal of the Spirit.* Urbana, IL: University of Illinois Press, 1997.

Rochford, E. Burke, Jr. *Hare Krishna in America.* New Brunswick, NJ: Rutgers University Press, 1985.

Shinn, Larry D. *The Dark Lord: Cult Images and the Hare Krishnas in America.* Philadelphia: The Westminster Press, 1987.

GRAND TETONS (WYOMING)

The Grand Teton Mountains are a spectacular mountain range in northwest Wyoming, its highest peak reaching over 13,000 feet. They took on religious significance in 1934 when Guy W. Ballard (1878–1939) included accounts of his mystical experiences in the mountain in the first book for a movement that would become known as the "I AM" Religious Activity. According to Ballard, Ascended Master Saint Germain took him to the Tetons, where, at a point never specifically designated, "Saint Germain touched a great boulder. Instantly, the enormous mass tipped out perhaps four feet away from its original position. He motioned me to follow. We entered and, to my astonishment, stood before a large bronze door.... He stepped forward and pressed certain points on the door. The great mass of bronze weighing many tons swung slowly open, and admitted us into a spacious chamber from which a stairway, cut in the solid rock, led downward." They entered what is known as the Royal Teton Retreat, where they had a meeting with a group of Venusians.

The "I AM" and the several groups that have derived from it, such as the Church Universal and Triumphant, now understand the opening inside the Grand Tetons to be one of the two principal retreat centers in North America for the Great White Brotherhood, the groups of evolved individuals who are believed to guide the course of humanity from age to age. The other main retreat center is in **MOUNT SHASTA** in Northern California. The Grand Tetons center was established after the sinking of Atlantis.

Those in the "I AM" tradition believe that the Ascended Masters hold major conclaves at the Grand Tetons, especially in early January and July. These conclaves focus the Masters' work for the continued evolution of humanity. The ancient Chinese teacher Confucius is considered the primary leader of the Grand Teton center.

The Grand Teton Mountains in Wyoming took on new religious significance in 1934, when "I AM" leader Guy W. Ballard claimed to have religious experiences there. *Time Life Pictures/Getty Images.*

There are a number of anecdotal tales of believers in the "I AM" story spending time in Jackson Hole and Grand Teton National Park in hopes of making contact with the Masters and being invited into the retreat. However, none since Ballard have reported any significant contact.

Sources:

King, Gorfre Ray [pseudonym of Guy W. Ballard]. *Unveiled Mysteries*. Chicago: Saint Germain Press, 1934.

GREAT PYRAMID OF GIZA (EGYPT)

Of the seven wonders of the ancient world, the Great Pyramid built by the Egyptian pharaoh Khufu (also known as Cheops or Suphis) as his tomb is the only one left standing, although it has suffered greatly through time. It may be seen as one manifestation of ancient Egyptian religion's emphasis on death and the afterlife and the culmination of a tradition of creating elaborate tombs by Egypt's rulers and wealthy elite.

When completed around 2565 BCE, the Great Pyramid stood 481 feet high. Built between 2600 and 2500 BCE, it was the tallest human-made structure on earth until the nineteenth century. Carefully constructed, it was oriented to the cardinal points on the compass, and its blocks were laid with a high degree of precision.

Although the pyramid is mainly solid stone, it does have several rooms, corridors, and escape shafts. The primary room is the king's burial chamber, located at the center, which may be reached through the Great Gallery and an ascending corridor. This relatively large room measures 34 feet by 17 feet by 19 feet. The pharaoh was placed in a stone sarcophagus made of red granite, which was also used to line the room's interior walls.

The pyramid was originally covered with white limestone. However, after the Muslim conquest of the land, the limestone was stripped away and used for buildings being erected in nearby Cairo. The Arab conquerors actually attempted to destroy the structure, but they gave up after taking some thirty feet of stone from the top. Even before the attack on the outer surface, in 820 CE the Muslim caliph launched an exploration of the interior of the pyramid. His workmen burrowed through solid stone until they encountered one of the passageways that then led them to the King's Chamber and to the second, smaller room at some distance beneath it, popularly called the Queen's Chamber.

Besides its ancient religious significance, the Great Pyramid has additionally become an object of widespread religious speculation in the modern world. The first wave of speculation, coming on the heels of Napoleon's foray into Egypt in 1798, derived from the identification of the Great Pyramid with the altar to the Lord mentioned in the book of Isaiah 19:19–20:

> In that day shall there be an altar to the Lord in the midst of the land of Egypt, and a pillar at the border thereof … And it shall be for a sign and for a witness unto the Lord of hosts in the land of Egypt.

In the 1830s Col. Howard Vyse (1798–1853) made extensive measurements of the pyramid's interior. Based on those calculations, a British mathematician, John Taylor (1781–1864), and a Scottish astronomer, Charles Piazzi Smyth (1819–1900), claimed to have found prophecies embodied in the building's structure. Taylor claimed the architect was not an Egyptian, but an Israelite. Smyth's speculations were passed to the British

Israelites, who believed that the ancient Israelites continued to exist as the Anglo-Saxon nations of the world. A key to the speculations was the discovery of what Smyth called the pyramid inch, the unit of measurement he believed was used by the builders. His calculations led him to confirm the creation of the earth in 4004 BCE and to announce the coming of Christ in 1881.

Pyramidology, as the science of measuring and discerning the meaning of the Great Pyramid in Christian studies was termed, continued through the mid-twentieth century. It received a major boost by the interest of Charles Taze Russell (1852–1916), the founder of what today is known as the Jehovah's Witnesses. In 1940 a British researcher, Adam Rutherford, founded the Institute of Pyramidology and issued a multi-volume set of books that summarized the speculations. The institute's work is carried on by the American Institute of Pyramidology, located in the Chicago suburbs.

Christian pyramidology gave way to esoteric speculation on pyramids in general and the Great Pyramid in particular in the later twentieth century. Of course, as early as the 1880s, Ignatius Donnelly (1831–1901) had suggested that the pyramid was built by former residents of Atlantis, an idea carried on by Manly Palmer Hall (1901–1990) and **EDGAR CAYCE** (1877–1945).

In the 1970s speculation emerged that the pyramid structure itself concentrated a form of cosmic energy. The idea was initially broached by a Czech engineer, Karl Drbal, whose work was described in the best-selling book *Psychic Discoveries behind the Iron Curtain* (1970). This book, the source of a variety of activities pursued by people in the New Age movement, described Drbal's use of a pyramid to sharpen razors. Used razors could seemingly be regenerated by placing them under a properly aligned pyramid at the place of the King's Chamber in the Great Pyramid.

Several authors used the brief treatment of Drbal's pyramid to create a whole mythology of pyramids, including the notion that people could sit within large pyramid structures to receive heal-

The Great Pyramid of Giza is the most famous of Egypt's pyramids and serves as a spectacular testimony to ancient beliefs in the afterlife. *National Geographic/Getty Images.*

THE ENCYCLOPEDIA OF RELIGIOUS PHENOMENA

ing power or find stimulation for psychic development. Individuals experimented with using small pyramids to mummify food. The fad continued through the 1980s. By the 1990s, the lack of any real verification of the many anecdotal stories concerning the reality of a unique pyramid energy led to the demise of this latest form of pyramidology.

Sources:

Mendelsohn, Kurt. *The Riddle of the Pyramids*. London: Thames & Hudson, 1975.

Smyth, Charles Piazzi. *Our Inheritance in the Great Pyramid*. London: W. Isbister, 1880.

Tompkins, Peter. *Secrets of the Great Pyramid*. New York: Harper and Row, 1971.

Toth, Max, and Greg Nielsen. *Pyramid Power*. New York: Warner Books, 1974.

GREEN MAN

A decoration on many church buildings throughout Western Europe and the British Isles consists of a hominoid face surrounded by tree branches and leaves, as if someone were peering from the natural world on the human scene. Traced backward, the same form appears on early Christian gravestones and, as early as the second century CE, on pre-Christian monuments memorializing prominent citizens. The figures initially appeared on Christian buildings in the sixth century in TRIER, Germany, where the local bishop used some carvings from an abandoned Roman temple to decorate a new cathedral. Repetition of the motif spread gradually over the next century but became quite popular at the beginning of the second millennium CE. In Britain, the figure appears on such diverse buildings as Norwich Cathedral and Rosslyn Chapel, near Edinburgh.

Over the centuries, the meaning originally assigned the figure was forgotten, as was the case with much Pagan lore among the nonliterate peoples of Western Europe, and Christian thinkers began to suggest new Christian meanings for it. Some churchmen like Rabanus Maurus (c. 776–856), the Archbishop of Mainz, who himself

oversaw the building and decorating of a number of churches in his archdiocese, suggested the figure recalled the human sins of the flesh and served as a reminder that those perpetrating such sins were eternally doomed.

Today it is assumed that the Green Man, as the figure came to be called, is tied to Pagan reverence for and reliance upon the natural environment. As the motif dropped out of use in church buildings in the years since the Protestant Reformation, a variety of identities have been assigned to the Green Man from Sir Gawain, the green-clad knight in the Arthurian legends, to Robin Hood. Early in the twentieth century, the Green Man was integrated into the May pageants celebrating the beginning of spring. More recently, contemporary Pagans have recovered the Green Man, along with other fragments of ancient Pagan lore and art, as an expression of the male deity and a representation of the cycle of life, death, and rebirth. Pioneer Wiccans Doreen Valiente and E. J. Jones tied the Green Man and Robin Hood together as representations of leaders or practitioners of the Old Religion.

Sources:

Basford, Kathleen. *The Green Man*. Woodbridge: Boydell & Brewer, 2004.

Jones, Evan John, and Doreen Valiente, *Witchcraft: A Tradition Renewed*. London: Robert Hale, 1990.

GRILLED CHEESE SANDWICH (VIRGIN MARY)

Among the more unique and heralded religious phenomena early in the twenty-first century was a grilled cheese sandwich that, the owner claimed, bore an image of the Virgin Mary. The sandwich originated in 1994 when Diana Duyser of Saint Johns, Antigua, made the sandwich and, as she took her first bite, noticed an image of the Virgin Mary staring back at her. She stopped eating and, after examining the sandwich more closely, put it in a box that would remain by her bed for the next decade. She said it had brought

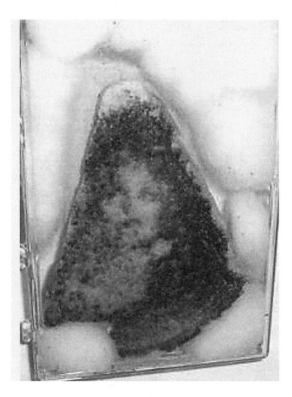

Looking closely and with a little imagination, the burn patterns on this grilled cheese sandwich convinced many that it was a miraculous image of the Virgin Mary. *AFP/Getty Images*.

her luck during these years, including some $70,000 in winnings from a local casino.

In 2004 she placed the sandwich for sale on the popular Internet auction site eBay. It was purchased for $28,000 by Golden Palace, an Internet gambling site. Golden Palace has a relationship with the Seminole Hard Rock Hotel and Casino in Hollywood, Florida, the site chosen to announce the purchase and the Golden Palace's plans to take the sandwich and other similar artifacts on a tour from Hollywood to Las Vegas. The sandwich traveled in a "virgin white Cadillac," and driving the car was *Miami Herald* reporter Jim Defede, who published a series of tongue-in-cheek articles about his trip.

Although Duyser had done nothing special to preserve the sandwich, it has remained fresh look-

ing and free of mold. It is one of an array of irregularly formed items that people have seen as depicting various personages apart from any human action to produce the representation. Similar objects have included rock surfaces, the swirls in glass, and the knots in trees.

In the wake of the interest shown in the unusual item, some industrious people jumped into the vacuum created by the sale to auction a "Virgin Mary in Grilled Cheese: Make Your Own" kit and a "Virgin Mary in Grilled Cheese Sandwich Replica." As publicity about the sandwich grew, various merchandizing items appeared, including T-shirts and decals. While the sandwich drew thousands of people to see it, it was, as might be expected, also the subject of much humor.

Sources:

Chang, Daniel, and Erika Bolstad. "Church Unlikely to Swallow Holy Toast." *Seattle Times* (November 28, 2004). Posted at http://seattletimes.nwsource.com/html/nationworld/2002102840_sandwich28.html. Accessed April 3, 2007.

GRIMOIRES

Grimoires are books containing descriptions of and instructions for performing magical rituals. The earliest were written as expressions of a Christianized Esotericism in the Middle Ages. As they were in essence heretical, grimoires existed as handwritten volumes carefully guarded by their owners. The information any grimoire contained would be passed only to a few highly trusted colleagues or students, hence the tradition that young magicians carefully copy the grimoire lent by their instructor in the magical arts.

Among the oldest of the medieval grimoires to survive was *The Key of Solomon*, the manuscript of which (written in Greek) has been tentatively dated to the thirteenth century. In the sixteenth century, in the wake of the relative freedom provided by the Protestant Reformation in Europe and the invention of moveable type, a very few grimoires (or portions thereof) were published, although the average person remained ignorant of their contents or even their existence.

These earliest grimoires were written with an understanding of a world inhabited by a variety of supernatural beings, most prominently angels and demons. The materials in the grimoires thus included a list of the names of the inhabitants of the supernatural world, how to contact them in relative safely, how to command them to carry out one's wishes (the essence of the magical act), and how to banish them from one's presence. There were also details of physical objects necessary and/or helpful in conducting a magical ritual, including various seals that protected the magician should things go wrong. Grimoires could be divided between those that centered on contact with angels and those professing contact with demonic forces.

The seventeenth and eighteenth century were marked by a changing worldview in which the ready ability to contact angels and demons by magical (or other) means was widely questioned, both by Protestants and by religious skeptics. As a result, the popularity and knowledge of magical operations and the materials needed to conduct them declined markedly. However, in the nineteenth century, a revival of magic took place. The fountainhead of that revival was the publication of the English text of a demonic grimoire, *The Magus*, by Francis Barrett in 1801. The book gave instructions in conjuring a variety of evil spirits.

A half-century later, Eliphas Levi (1810–1875), the most important magical writer of his generation, published a number of books explaining magic in a post-scientific world, ascribing the success of magic to a cosmic power not unlike that described in the writings of the mesmerists, rather than placing demons and supernatural beings at the center of the action. However, in his 1856 volume, *The Ritual of Transcendent Magic*, Levi discussed the several grimoires with which he had become familiar. In 1889 Samuel L. MacGregor Mathers (1854–1918) published *The Key of Solomon*, which became the basis for constructing a whole new set of magical rituals for a group led by Mathers, the Hermetic Order of the Golden Dawn, the most prominent of several ceremonial magic groups of the period.

The Golden Dawn's most eminent scholar-member, Arthur Edward Waite (1857–1942), surveyed a number of grimoires in his 1898 book, *The Book of Black Magic and of Pacts, Including the Mysteries of Goëtic Theurgy, Sorcery, and Infernal Necromancy*. Six years later, Aleister Crowley (1875–1947), the bad boy of the Golden Dawn, all but destroyed the organization by revealing many of its inner secrets when he published a copy of *The Lesser Key of Solomon* (also known as *The Lemegton*), which he had acquired from Mathers.

Crowley completed the psychologizing of magic, revamping it apart from the trappings of the medieval supernatural world and the Christian presuppositions assumed by the early grimoires. Through the twentieth century, the grimoires were replaced by the instruction books published for use within the several magical orders, most notably the Ordo Templi Orientis (OTO), that emerged as the Golden Dawn declined. A number of English editions of the medieval grimoires were published during that time, more as curiosities than as arcane texts sought by the slowly growing magical community.

In the last half of the twentieth century, another new generation of grimoires began to appear. A few attempted to fit within the continuing tradition of post-Crowley ritual magic, such as Nathan Elkana's *The Master Grimoire of Magickal Rites and Ceremonies* (1982), but most originated from a totally new branch of the Esoteric community, modern Neo-pagan Witchcraft, or Wicca.

Wicca emerged as a new religious movement in the 1950s, the brainchild of Gerald B. Gardner (1884–1964) and his early associates, including Doreen Valiente (1922–1999). It is an attempt to recreate ancient Pagan religion with a focus upon worship of the Great Mother deity, her consort the Horned God, and a number of lesser deities. The Goddess is evoked in a magical setting, and practitioners learn to make their way through life by utilizing magic to assist them in both their mundane and spiritual goals. Gardner and

Valiente put together a grimoire that contained ritual material for Wiccan covens, including instructions and rituals for the regular biweekly meetings (esbats) and the eight annual festivals (sabbats). Variations on the Gardnerian rituals (which were held in the nude) began to circulate in the nascent Wiccan community in the 1970s.

Very soon after the emergence of Gardnerian Witchcraft, in 1964, while information on the community was still a matter of intense interest by the tabloid press, a dissident member in England anonymously published the Wiccan rituals. Through the 1970s, several variations of the rituals were published by members of the growing community who felt that keeping them secret was no longer important, most notably American priestess Lady Sheba (1972). In recent years, a large number of new Wiccan grimoires have been issued, some as a means of attracting members to new Wiccan groups. The publication of such books has provided resources for the large number of solitary witches, those who practice apart from participation in any coven.

The effect of the publication of all the grimoires in the late twentieth century has been to make all of the secrets of the worlds of ritual magic and Witchcraft available to the general public. Those who continue to practice magic do so with an understanding that the true secrets of their craft are revealed not in the texts but in the practice, and thus the secrets of the esoteric realms remain just as hidden today as in centuries past.

Sources:

Barrett, Francis. *The Magus.* London: Lackington, Allen and Co., 1801.

Levi, Eliphas. *Transcendental Magic.* London: Redway, 1896.

Savedow, Steve. *The Magician's Workbook: A Modern Grimoire.* York Beach, ME: Red Wheel/Weiser, 1995.

Sheba, Lady. *The Grimoire of Lady Sheba.* St. Paul, MN: Llewellyn Publications, 1972.

Waite, Arthur Edward. *The Book of Black Magic and of Pacts, Including the Mysteries of Goëtic Theurgy, Sorcery, and Infernal Necromancy.* London: Redway, 1898.

GUADALUPE (SPAIN)

Guadalupe is a small village in rural Spain that has lent its name to two important sites relative to devotion to the Virgin Mary. Around 1300, a cowherd named Gil Cordero had a vision of what he described as a young lady radiating light who directed him to a cave near his home, where he found a statue of the Virgin. This statue was later identified as the same statue given by the pope to the Cathedral of Seville in the sixth century. That statue had been hidden and then lost following the Muslim invasion of Iberia.

Rather than return the statue to Seville, the Spanish king ordered the building of a church at the cave where the statue had been found, and the statue was renamed Our Lady of Guadalupe. A monastic community grew up at Guadalupe, which helped spread the veneration of the Virgin of Guadalupe throughout Spain and then to Spanish territories in the Americas. The occurrences at Guadalupe set the stage for what occurred in Mexico two centuries later.

By 1531 Spain had largely established itself in authority in Mexico and was attempting to establish Catholicism in place of the Aztec religion. One Aztec center was located at Tepeyac Hill, north of Tenochititlán (now Mexico City), where a shrine to an Aztec goddess had recently been destroyed by Spanish soldiers. As the story goes, on December 9, 1531, a young man had a vision of a woman surrounded by light and speaking to him in his native language. She asked that he carry a message to the local Catholic bishop that a church be built on the hill. The bishop put him off and demanded a sign by which he could be certain the young man spoke the truth.

The young man, Juan Diego, asked the Virgin's help. He then gathered some roses (not generally blooming in December), which he wrapped in his robe as a gift to the bishop. When he unwrapped the roses, on his robe was a picture of the Virgin as he had described her. Meanwhile, Diego's uncle reported that he, too, had seen the Virgin and received instructions that the image on the robe should be called the Virgin of Guadalupe.

The robe became a popular object of veneration very quickly. Many of the Spanish soldiers were familiar with the Spanish Guadalupe, and many of the Mexicans identified her with the former goddess of the hill. The new Mary cult that arose helped the Catholic Church receive the devotion previously directed toward the now-suppressed Aztec worship. As devotion to the Virgin of Guadalupe grew, she was credited with suppressing an outbreak of the plague in 1544 and stopping a flood two years later. The growing popularity of Our Lady of Guadalupe was marked by the building of a large basilica on the site in 1709 and by her being named the patroness of Mexico in 1754, patroness of Latin America in 1910, and Mother of the Americas in 1961.

Pope John Paul II, who became known for his devotion to the Virgin, was the first pope to visit the shrine, in 1979, three years after the dedication of the new cathedral church. He also beatified Juan Diego in 1990 and returned in 2000 to oversee the canonization ceremony. More than one million people a year travel to Guadalupe to view the picture of the Virgin that Juan Diego originally presented to the bishop in 1521. Especially important is December 12, the Feast of Our Lady of Guadalupe.

Almost every aspect of the story of Juan Diego has been called into question. There are no contemporaneous records of the apparitions and the miraculous cape. For example, Bishop Juan de Zumarraga, upon his return to Spain, presented a detailed account of his work in Mexico, but there is no mention of Juan Diego. It was not until 1648 that a written account of the apparition appeared. Skeptics have suggested that the image is merely a very good painting done by a native craftsman around which a legend later adhered.

In the 1980s the image underwent a variety of tests, which disclosed several unusual features and found nothing to discredit its unique nature. While far from conclusive, the scientists did bring the image and robe into the twentieth century and laid a basis for future discussion of the image from a scientific perspective. The most interesting studies of the cape were the taking of infrared photographs, which, when enhanced by computer, revealed a set of images in the eyes of the Virgin.

In the wake of the Pope's visits and the canonization of Juan Diego, devotion to Our Lady of Guadalupe has become more popular than ever. Copies of the image are ubiquitous throughout the Spanish-speaking community in the Americas and have now permeated even the English-speaking Catholic community. In the United States, shrines replicating the one in Mexico City have been erected in several locations, and similar shrines are now found in Italy and Japan.

Sources:

Callahan, Philip S. *The Tilma under Infra-Red Radiation*. Washington: CARA, 1981.

Demarest, Donald, and Coley Taylor. *The Dark Virgin: The Book of Our Lady of Guadalupe*. Freeport, ME: Coley Taylor, Inc., 1956.

Lee, George, C.S.S. *Our Lady of Guadalupe: Patroness of the Americas*. New York: Catholic Book Publishing Co., 1947.

Smith, Jody Brant. *The Image of Guadalupe*. New York: Doubleday & Company, 1983.

GUARDIAN ANGELS

Throughout the centuries, many have believed themselves the object of attention by a single benevolent supernatural being assigned the task of protecting and assisting the individual. Such a belief in guardian angels predates the founding of Christianity. It was evident in the life of different Mediterranean cultures and appears in a rudimentary form in ancient Judaism. Frequently cited to support belief in guardian angels is Psalms 90:11: "For he hath given his angels charge over thee; to keep thee in all thy ways."

Angels are messengers, divine beings sent to humans with words from God. Angels could appear in various forms, although they commonly

This undated Victorian era photo depicts a guardian angel. The concept of protective angels has remained popular from the days of ancient Judaism to modern times. *Time Life Pictures/Getty Images.*

resembled humans. The writer of the biblical book of Hebrews warned people to be kind to strangers as they might turn out to be angels.

It was but a small step for Christians to move from a general belief that angels exist and, on occasion, intrude into human situations to a pious belief in guardian angels, one attached to each human being that constantly acted for the welfare of that person. Among the first to give clear voice to the idea was Saint Jerome (c. 345–420), better known for his translation of the Bible into Latin. By the time of Thomas Aquinas (c. 1225–1274), the understanding of angels in the Western Christian tradition had undergone considerable refinement, and he asserted that guardian angels were drawn from the lowest order of angelic beings.

Liturgical recognition of guardian angels grew significantly in the seventeenth century after Pope Paul V (r. 1605–1621) added a feast focused on them to the annual calendar in 1608. Then Pope Clement X (r. 1670–1676) elevated the feast, now celebrated on October 2 as an obligatory observance for the church as a whole.

As belief in guardian angels spread, among the more interesting stories to emerge has been that of Augustine Dupré, a French nobleman who was reportedly commissioned by King Louis XVI (r. 1774–1793) to design a new currency for the nation. He incorporated a guardian angel on his design for one coin, only a few of which were minted before the French Revolution brought down the crown and landed Dupre in jail. Scheduled for the guillotine, Dupre was able to escape from his imprisonment and later attrib-uted his good fortune to the coin. Over the next years, the coin attained a reputation as a good luck charm. The design was later revived and used for the 20 franc pieces minted from 1871 through 1898.

Belief in guardian angels also passed into Spiritualism, where a belief in easy and frequent communication with the spirits of the deceased survived even though it was otherwise lost in the secularizing Western culture through the late nineteenth and early twentieth centuries. A few metaphysical teachers, such as California teacher Flower Newhouse (1909–1994), promoted belief in angels in the middle of the twentieth century. At the end of the century, a notable revival of belief in angels was noticeable within the New Age movement. This renewed interest manifested in the production of various objects picturing angels—figurines, candles, jewelry, and statuary—and of stores dedicated to marketing them.

Sources:

Lewis, James R. *Angels A to Z.* Detroit: Visible Ink Press, 1996.

Miller, C. Leslie. *All about Angels: The Other Side of the Spirit World.* Glendale, CA: Regal Books, 1973.

Newhouse, Flower A. *Natives of Eternity.* Vista, CA: privately printed, 1950.

HAGIA SOPHIA (TURKEY)

The Hagia Sophia (Holy Wisdom), now a mosque, was one of the early products of the success of Christianity in the Roman Empire. A persecuted religion for some four centuries, Christianity gained imperial favor during the reign of the Emperor Constantine (r. 306–337). In spite of the attempt of Julian the Apostate (r. 361–363) to return the empire to its pre-Christian religion, by the end of the century Christianity was securely established. Over the next several centuries it would, with imperial favor, become the religion of the people.

The Hagia Sophia was the brainchild of the Emperor Justinian I (r. 527–565), who conceived the idea of a "great church" for the Roman capital, then in Constantinople, the likes of which did not exist anywhere in the known world. An older church, which itself had replaced a temple to Apollo, possibly built by Constantine, was chosen to be replaced. This rested on a hill overlooking the Sea of Marmara. Construction began in 532 and lasted for the next five years. Patriarch Menas of Constantinople consecrated the new church on December 27, 537. It became the seat of the Archbishops of Constantinople, better known as the Ecumenical Patriarchs.

The new church is dominated by its dome, which rests atop four large piers. The dome, which rises some 200 feet above the floor of the cathedral, was constructed using the most advanced building ideas of its day. With imperial favor, the church was flowered with lavish gifts over the next centuries. It also came to house a variety of Christian relics, including many brought from the Holy Land by **HELENA**, the mother of Constantine.

The church suffered the first of many indignities in 1204 when the Crusaders, representing the Roman Catholic Church, captured and ransacked the city. They carried off much of the Hagia Sophia's wealth and holy treasures. On May 29, 1453, the Muslim army, under Sultan Mehmet II, captured Constantinople. Among the first sites he visited was the Hagia Sophia. He subsequently decided to transform the church into his imperial mosque. During this period, the many mosaics in the church were plastered over.

In 1934, following the fall of the Ottoman Empire, Kemal Ataturk, the new president of the new nation of Turkey, secularized the Hagia Sophia by turning it into a museum. However, he did little to restore the building. In 1993 representatives from the United Nations Educational, Scientific and Cultural Organization (UNESCO) surveyed the deterioration in the building and prompted some initial efforts to clean, repair, and restore the building. The uncovering of the mosaics remains a sensitive issue for the Turkish Muslim majority.

Sources:

Mainstone, Rowland J. *Hagia Sophia: Architecture, Structure, and Liturgy of Justinian's Great Church.* W. W. Norton & Co., 1997.

Mango, Cyril, and Ahmet Ertug. *Hagia Sophia. A Vision for Empires.* Istanbul: Ertug & Kocabiyik, 1998.

Swift, Emerson Howland. *Hagia Sophia.* New York: Columbia University Press, 1940.

HAJJ

One of the goals of any pious male Muslim is to make a pilgrimage to Mecca, Saudi Arabia, at least once in his life. That pilgrimage, called the Hajj, should be made in the second week of the last month of the Muslim year (which most commonly takes place in April or May of the common calendar). Women may make the Hajj, but to do so they must be accompanied by their husband, father, or other close male relative.

Muslims trace the history of the Hajj to Ibrahim (Abraham in the Jewish Bible), who was, with his son Ismail, entrusted with building the Kaaba ("House of God") at Mecca. It is believed that Ibrahim made an annual pilgrimage to Mecca, but that over the centuries Mecca degenerated into a pagan center. Undoubtedly, by the time of the prophet Muhammad, the Kaaba had become a site for the acknowledgment of the many deities of the people of Arabia. In founding Islam, Muhammad is credited with smashing the idols and establishing the Kaaba as a center for the worship of Allah alone. In announcing the Hajj, he saw himself as the instrument for reinstating the proper worship once followed by Ibrahim. Some of the rules of the Hajj developed from proscriptions of practices, such as walking naked around the site, that had accumulated around the site over the pre-Islamic centuries.

The immense growth of Islam and the spread of its adherents around the world had required a number of adjustments to the format of the Hajj. From the middle of the nineteenth century the number who annually make the journey has jumped from less than ten thousand to more than two million. A primary change has come in the improvement of transportation to Mecca proper. What used to take weeks or months can be done in a few hours. In recent decades, the Saudi government has moved to supervise the Hajj. It has seen to the erection of a number of service facilities for the pilgrims, many created in response to problems from previous pilgrimages.

The pilgrimage has several distinct phases. First, prospective pilgrims announce their intention to their home community. They then make the necessary arrangements to travel to Mecca and plan for the maintenance of those in their care during their absence. Future pilgrims should also ideally pay any debts and right any wrongs as part of the spiritual and moral preparation to participate in the sacred journey. Once the trip begins, the first goal is a spot just outside the sacred land where a station, called a *miqat,* is to be found. There, they again state their intention to make the pilgrimage. At this point, the males don a white robe, the *ihram,* a white seamless garment made up of two pieces of cloth. One piece covers the body from waist to ankle, while the other is thrown over the shoulder. For the duration of the pilgrimage, there are a number of rules that govern the individual, who will refrain from sexual intercourse, the wearing of jewelry, the cutting of hair or nails, or the shedding of blood, among others.

For most pilgrims, the next stage of their journey is the *umra,* or little pilgrimage. This part of the pilgrimage may or may not be done in connection with the Hajj proper. The *umra* begins with a visit to the great mosque, al-Masjid al-Haram. The Kaaba, a cube-like structure that is believed to lie directly beneath a similar heavenly structure, is located within the mosque. Upon arriving at the mosque, pilgrims march around the Kaaba in a counterclockwise direction seven times. Each time they pass the black stone that protrudes from the Kaaba, they recite a brief prayer, "In the name of Allah, and Allah is supreme." They also attempt to actually reach the Kaaba and kiss it, but this is impossible for most people given the contemporary crowds. Instead they make a gesture of kissing it. The next destination is a pair of hills not far from the mosque. Here they move seven times between the two hills, symbolically reenacting Hagar searching for water for Ismail after being abandoned by Ibrahim (at Allah's command). This activity, the *sa'y*, had sometimes been a dangerous activity, and many pilgrims have died here as the crowds move quickly between the two hills. After the *sa'y*, the pilgrims move to a well about a hundred yards from the mosque where Hagar was supposed to have finally found the water for Ismail. They drink the water and often take some home to share.

At this point, the Hajj proper begins and symbolically reenacts events from Muhammad's "Farewell Pilgrimage" of 632. On the first day, pilgrims move some five miles outside Mecca to the plain of Mina. After a night in a tent, they travel to the Plain of Arafat (often by bus), where they pray at the site where Muhammad delivered his farewell sermon. He spoke from Jabalal-Rahmah (Mount Mercy) and presented a program of reform in the religious, economic, social, and political realms. At the mount, pilgrims will stand for many hours reading the Qur'an and reciting (many times during the hours) a brief prayer. This standing, termed the *wuquf*, is considered by many the central occurrence of the Hajj, an act of complete surrender to Allah.

After sunset the pilgrims move as quickly as possible to Muzdalifah, where two more prayers are said. The quick movement is to reenact Muhammad's flight. Upon their arrival and after the prayer, the men and women separate. The men stay in Muzdalifah while the women return to Mina.

At the beginning of the next day (the third day of the pilgrimage), everyone gathers forty-nine small stones. Seven of these will be thrown

at three pillars located in Mina later that day. These pillars mark a spot where Satan appeared to Ibrahim. At the end of this third day, the Hajj is officially over.

Although the Hajj has officially ended, most pilgrims will extend their stay. The next days are a time of feasting that includes the sacrificing and consumption of animals, primarily goats and lambs. After eating, the men shave their heads, cut their nails, bathe, and put on fresh cloths. Women will cut three symbolic hairs and put on new clothes. During the next two days, the remaining stones will be thrown at the three pillars in Mina, seven at each stone on each day.

The pilgrims now return to Mecca and once again walk around the Kaaba. On their way home, pilgrims might visit other sites associated with Muhammad, especially Medina, where Muhammad was buried. After they complete the pilgrimage, they may add the word "Hajji" to their name.

Sources:

Husain, S. A. *A Guide to Hajj*. New Delhi: Kitab Bhavan, 1981.

Long, David Edwin. *The Hajj Today: A Survey of the Contemporary Makkah Pilgrimage*. New York: SUNY Press, 1979.

Peters, F. E. *The Hajj: The Muslim Pilgrimage to Mecca and the Holy Places*. Princeton, NJ: Princeton University Press, 1994.

HARDWAR (INDIA)

Hardwar, also known as Haridwar, is one of India's holiest sites, a city located on the sacred Ganges River at the point it exits from the mountains to flow across the plains. In ancient times it was called Kapilsthan, a reference to Kapil, an ancient sage credited with creating cosmology and psychology, who is said to have resided there.

The variant names of the city, Hardwar (Gate of Shiva) and Haridwar (Gate of Vishnu), call attention to two nearby shrines to these deities at Kedarnath and Badrinath respectively. Among the most holy objects in the city is a reputed footprint of Vishnu found on one of the steps leading into the Ganges, where pilgrims gather to bath.

Hardwar is the site of several of India's most well-attended festivals. Every spring, at the beginning of the Hindu year, there is a solar festival. Then every twelve years, Hardwar is one of four cities along the Ganges that host India's largest religious gathering, attended by millions, the KUMBH MELA. The Kumbh Mela is noted for the arrival of numerous holy men (called SADHUS and siddhis), many of whom have spent the previous years alone in the nearby mountains and forests. Halfway between the Kumbh Melas, a smaller celebration called the Ardh Kumbh is held. Hardwar is also a place where it is believed that spiritual liberation is assisted simply by being in its holy environs.

Hardwar is the home to many temples, ashrams, swamis, and gurus. The increase in the number of tourists and spiritual seekers in recent decades has led to the expansion of facilities dedicated to accommodating their needs.

Sources:

Dubey, D. P. *Prayaga: The Site of Kumbha Mela; In Temporal and Traditional Space*. New Delhi: Aryan Books, 2001.

Hebner, Jack. *Kumbha Mela: The World's Largest Act of Faith*. San Rafael: Mandala Publishing, 1991.

HARER (ETHIOPIA)

Harer, a small city in eastern-central Ethiopia, is the primary Islamic pilgrimage site on the continent of Africa. As a settlement, it appears to date to the seventh century CE. The entrance of Islam into Harer is attributed to Shaykh Abadir, who in the tenth century established Islam with the assistance of forty-four saints. In 1520 the city was captured by Ahmad Gran (1506–1543), a Somali empire builder, who made it the center of a large Muslim state. Somali rule ended after only half a century, but the new rulers from the Ethiopian Oromo people were also Muslims. Following Ahmad Gran's death, his widow built the distinc-

tive large walls around the city, which allowed it to maintain some independence until Egyptian forces invaded the region in 1875 and occupied Harer. In 1887 it was incorporated into Ethiopia by Menelik II (1844–1913).

The largest mosque in Harer is al-Jami, and part of the building dates to the eleventh century, making it possibly the oldest building in the city. However, possibly the most interesting site is the tomb of Abadir, which several times weekly is the scene of Sufi ceremonies.

Sources:

Munro-Hay, Stuart. *Historical Ethiopia: A Book of Sources and a Guide to Historical Sites*. Trenton, NJ: Red Sea Press, 2000.

Trimingham, John Spencer. *Islam in Ethiopia*. London: Oxford University Press, 1952.

HEALING, MIRACULOUS

No religious phenomena have proved as important as the many extraordinary healings that have occurred in various religious contexts from around the world. Such healings, due to their instantaneous nature, the nature of the disease that is cured, or the connection of the healing with specific religious events, are deemed to have occurred by means over and above ordinary healing efforts.

While such healings occur in all religious traditions, they have played a particular role in Christianity, which emerged from the healing ministry of Jesus and continued through the first century of the Common Era by his apostles. Within the Christian tradition, healings have been associated with particular saintly church members, and healing miracles, in fact, are a necessary part of the phenomena surrounding anyone whom the Roman Catholic Church would elevate to sainthood. Healing has also been associated with particular sites, frequently places where water is available, such as wells and springs. Increasingly in the modern ages, healings have been associated with sites where apparitions of the Virgin Mary have occurred. Healing sites have often been the destination of pilgrims, and sites of pilgrimages not originally associated with healings have often become healing sites over the centuries.

The Protestant movement was critical of much within Roman Catholicism that it saw as superstition and unbiblical accretions to the faith. In its disparagement of such phenomena as purgatory and the use of indulgences to grant souls relief from sufferings in this realm (nowhere mentioned in the Bible), Protestants also abandoned much of the Catholic Church's tradition concerning miraculous healing.

In the eighteenth century, secular skeptics added their voices to the initial Protestant critique of much of the naïve supernaturalism of medieval Catholicism. The children of the Enlightenment have attempted to explain all miracles in terms of mundane natural processes and have had faith that, where some mystery remains, science will eventually explain what has occurred. Relative to healing, science has begun to make progress in curing disease with the development of sanitation, the development of surgery, and, at the end of the nineteenth century, the discovery of germs followed by discoveries of various germ-destroying substances. In the twentieth century, the rise of the several psychological disciplines has further expanded the reach of secular healing arts.

Paralleling the development of modern medicine has been a succession of movements built around beliefs, practices and claims of extraordinary healings. A new era began with the activity of Austrian doctor **Franz Anton Mesmer** (1734–1815), who emerged to prominence in Paris, France, at the end of the eighteenth century. Mesmer proposed the existence of a universal cosmic energy that could be concentrated in various devices or in some human beings and could be passed to the sick, leading to their cure. A mesmerist could send this same energy into another person, causing him or her to go into a trancelike state. The belief in this underlying cosmic energy spawned a variety of movements in the next century. In the United States, through the 1840s mesmerists toured the country giving demonstrations of mesmerism (later to be called hypnotism). The thrust of the mesmerist movement was absorbed into Spiritualism at mid-century.

A wide variety of alternative healing movements emerged in Europe and America, from homeopathy to hydrotherapy (the water cure). Not unimportant was an advocacy of natural whole foods, especially associated with the Seventh-day Adventist Church. Most seekers and practitioners in these movements sought healing outside the practices of mainstream medicine and found their healing agents in rather mundane sources. Within Spiritualism, however, a number of healing mediums arose who claimed to facilitate the passing of healing energies from the spirit world. Such mediums might or might not be in direct contact with one or more spirit entities. Such healing became institutionalized in Spiritualism, though always taking second place to demonstrations of life after death in spirit contact.

Out of the chaos of healing practices, three new movements arose as the nineteenth century came to a close. First, in Massachusetts, a woman named Mary Baker Eddy (1821–1910) experienced a sudden healing following her realization that God was the only reality and that in God there was perfect health. Her healing in 1866 led to the founding of the Christian Science movement in 1875 and was eventually embodied in the Church of Christ, Scientist. One of Eddy's students was Emma Curtis Hopkins (1853–1925), whose own healing efforts, a variation on Eddy's work, led to the formation of the New Thought movement, which is now manifest through several metaphysical denominations such as the Unity School of Christianity, the United Church of Religious Science, Religious Science International, and the Divine Science Federation International.

Second, within the Holiness movement that emerged in Methodism in the years just prior to the Civil War, a new healing emphasis developed around several people who had themselves experienced a miraculous healing. Leading the way was former Presbyterian minister Albert Benjamin Simpson (1843–1919), who would create a new denomination, the Christian and Missionary Alliance, around what he termed the Four-fold Gospel that emphasized the work of Christ as Savior, Sanctifier, Healer, and coming King.

At the beginning of the twentieth century, the Holiness movement provided the context through which the Pentecostal movement emerged. That movement, based as it was on the gifts of the Spirit (1 Corinthians 12), not only continued the emphasis on healing but developed it far beyond anything imagined by Holiness leaders. Most of the well-known healing evangelists of the twentieth century—AIMEE SEMPLE MCPHERSON, JOHN GRAHAM LAKE, GORDON J. LINDSEY, WILLIAM MARION BRANHAM, ORAL ROBERTS, KATHRYN KUHLMAN, BENNY HINN—were or are all Pentecostals.

Third, also in Boston (where Mary Baker Eddy located her headquarters), Episcopal ministers Elwood Worcester and Samuel McComb launched a new spiritual healing within the larger Protestant churches that not only drew on a tradition of healing prayer but sought to be responsive to insights from the emerging discipline of psychology. The Emanuel Movement took its name from the Boston congregation that Worcester pastored. The movement spread an interest in healing through the Episcopal Church that, in 1955, found a new embodiment in the still-existent International Order of Saint Luke the Physician.

The different segments of the modern healing movement in the West have been divided by both terminology and their understanding of the extraordinary healing activity in which they are involved. Christian healers have generally been informed by a worldview that emphasized a world that runs according to a natural law established by God. Extraordinary healings are seen as the immediate activity of God who, for various reasons, including in response to someone's fervent prayer, chooses to set aside his own laws for the moment and heal someone. The essence of the idea of miracle is that God breaks in on his own creation to act in a supernatural manner.

Within Christian circles several names were used to describe such healings and the ministry that promoted them. *Divine healing* has been the most popular name, in which the emphasis is on the role of God through the Holy Spirit as the healer. As the movement developed through the twentieth century, the term *faith healing* was often used, with some emphasizing the role of the ill person's faith as an element in healing. That idea has largely been abandoned, however, following too many cases in which people of great faith remain ill while some people with no faith are healed. The movement recognizes the importance of healing evangelists and their ministry of prayer as catalysts, but affirms God's primary role in each individual healing.

Many across the spectrum of Christian and non-Christian healing ministries use the term *spiritual healing*. This ambiguous term can carry a variety of meanings, the essence being that the healing has a source in the invisible spiritual work rather than the mundane physical world. Christians can affirm the role of the Holy Spirit as God's healing agent, while Spiritualists can affirm the healing power from the realm of spirits. Others can affirm healing from a variety of invisible levels of existence.

Within the Christian Science/New Thought tradition, practitioners see healing in a somewhat different perspective. They affirm that God is the sum total of what is metaphysically real, and humans are created in the image of God. Illness, according to this thought, is the result of an erroneous view of our separation from God; it is metaphysically unreal. Healing comes from a change in perspective, a realization that God is All-in-All. Practitioners work to bring about the realization of Truth as a step in bringing about healing.

Most healers working in the Esoteric/Spiritualist/New Age tradition operate with a variation of mesmerist thought. They understand the cosmos to be infused with a universal energy that is intelligent and a source for healing. Healers are particularly capable of focusing that energy and directing it to where it is needed. In doing their healing work, they may or may not experience a flow of energy through and out of their own body. As part of their healing, they may also clairvoyantly come to an understanding of what is wrong with the person they are attempting to assist and how they are to direct the healing energy.

In the modern world, some Esoteric healers have also picked up much from Oriental methods of healing. For example, in Chinese medicine there is an understanding of a universal energy called *chi*, which many healers identify with the healing energy with which they work. In different Chinese healing arts, such as acupuncture, *chi* is seen as flowing through the body along a set of meridians. Illness comes from a blockage of the flow of *chi*, and healing comes from stimulating its normal movement. Movements such as REIKI combine insights from Eastern and Western understandings of spiritual healing.

In the 1960s many Westerners became interested in a form of healing that had developed in the Spiritualist churches of the Philippine Islands, PSYCHIC SURGERY. A variety of spectacular healings were reported from the ministrations of healers who reportedly opened people's bodies, removed pathological materials, and closed the bodies without leaving any sign that the bodies had ever been opened. Films of the healers at work seemed to confirm the early reports. Closer examinations of the healers, however, proved they were in fact engaging in an elaborate sleight of hand, usually involving the palming of chicken parts.

At the same time, healers with a theosophical background were bringing a more traditional form of Esoteric healing into hospitals under the label of therapeutic touch. Therapeutic touch was spiritual healing shorn of much of its metaphysical accretions but relying upon the affirmation of a form of healing power that could be transferred from a healer, usually a nurse, to a patient. Healing was seen as the result of a stimulation of the body's own healing potentials.

The practice of healing in the Esoteric community is based on a century of research that has attempted to document the existence of a healing energy, the key evidence coming from a set of experiments conducted by McGill University professor Bernard Grad in the 1960s and 1970s. His experiments showed dramatic changes in mice and plants produced by healer OSKAR ESTABANY. These experiments, which countered criticism that all spiritual healings are the result of the placebo effect, remain the bedrock of data on the efficacy of spiritual healing.

Critics have on occasion targeted spiritual healing. For many people, it constitutes a basic demonstration of a supernatural world. Critics have suggested that healings that do occur are due in large part to misdiagnosis of disease (that is, the patient was not ill in the first place) or the natural remission of a disease (noting that many people who claim healings will, in the future, die of the disease from which they had supposedly been healed).

Doctors have also done extensive results on the placebo effect. They have noted that people given a medicine with no healing properties will frequently respond as if they had received a potent medicine. Such results have often been noted in cases of pain relief, in which a sugar pill can produce the same result as popular pain killers.

Critics have also noted that many crippling conditions can be produced by the activity of a person's own psyche. Under the impact of emotional stress, the human body will assume conditions, hysterical paralysis being a well-known condition, that mimic the experience of severe trauma. Such conditions can on occasion be relieved by spiritual healing.

In the light of the many mundane explanations for some of the dramatic results claimed by healers, scientists have set a high threshold of evidence for verifying any incident of miraculous or extraordinary healing. They seek medical records of the existence of the diseased condition prior to the healing, a relatively quick change in the body's condition, post-event verification that the condition has disappeared, and later verification that it has not returned. Very few cases can provide such documentation, although some does exist, such as that acquired by the medical bureau at Lourdes. Most healers do not have the financial resources to conduct the kind of research necessary to verify the healings they see and are quite happy to continue their work as long as people profess being helped by it.

Skeptical attacks on the various forms of miraculous and extraordinary healing have done little to diminish the overall practice of spiritual healing, although the examination of several prominent healing evangelists in the 1980s revealed their engagement in significant fraud and led to their downfall. At the same time, merely questioning the efficacy of the healing work associated with the ministries of prominent healers such as Oral Roberts, Kathryn Kuhlman, or Benny Hinn has done little to diminish their popular support. In like measure, belief in the healing efficacy of the intercession of the Virgin Mary and pilgrimages to sites related to her remain a popular element in Roman Catholic piety.

The continuation of high levels of belief in the supernatural, including belief in miraculous healings, has been an enigma for many skeptics. At the beginning of the twentieth century, predictions were made of the demise of belief in religion and the enigmatic nature of the universe, but such beliefs have not wavered. There has been no manifest relationship between the rise of science and technology and any diminution of faith. In the field of medicine, successes have been countered by the vast redefinition of many social and psychological conditions that do not readily respond to traditional medical treatment as illnesses. At the same time, the spectrum of psychological practices fade into the various forms of spiritual healing. On a more practical level, the theoretical issues involved in questions of the relative efficacy of medicine or spiritual healing are somewhat distorted by the very real fact that many people are unable to access medical care due to the costs involved in its delivery.

Sources:

Cherry, Reginald B. *Healing Prayer: God's Divine Intervention in Medicine, Faith and Prayer*. Nashville, TN: T. Nelson, 1999.

Grad, Bernard R. "Some Biological Effects of Laying-on of Hands: A Review of Experiments with Animals and Plants." *Journal of the American Society for Psychical Research* 59 (1965): 95–127.

Krieger, Dolores. *The Therapeutic Touch: How to Use Your Hands to Help or Heal*. Englewood Cliffs, NJ: Prentice-Hall, 1979.

Nolen, William A. *Healing: A Doctor in Search of a Miracle*. New York: Random House, 1974.

Randi, James. *The Faith Healers*. Amherst, NY: Prometheus Books, 1987.

HEILIGENKREUZ (AUSTRIA)

Heiligenkreuz, a rural Cistercian abbey some 25 miles south of Vienna, Austria, claims to house one of the largest collections of fragments of the TRUE CROSS in existence. The abbey's founder, Otto, was the son of Leopold III (1075–1136), who would later be canonized for his founding and support of monasteries. Leopold V (1157–1194), who went on the Third Crusade, returned form the Holy Land with relics of the True Cross, which he gave to the Heiligenkreuz. As a result of the gift, the abbey became a destination for pilgrims. As the abbey's fame spread, Ludwig IX (1416–1478) donated a piece of Jesus' crown of thorns.

In spite of the plundering of the abbey by Turkish forces attempting to take Vienna in the sixteenth and seventeenth centuries and their final withdrawal from the region in 1683, the relics remained secure. In 1708 a reported miracle, a two-dimensional painting of a cross becoming three-dimensional, prompted a resurgence of interest in the abbey by pilgrims. A beautiful new church for the abbey was completed in 1744 and now houses the abbey's relics. The largest number of contemporary pilgrims find their way to Heiligenkreuz on September 14, the Feast of the Triumph of the Cross.

Sources:

Gaumannmuller, Franz. *Die Mittelalterliche Klosteranlage der Abtei Heiligenkreuz*. Heiligenkreuz-Wien, 1967.

Wright, Kevin J. *Catholic Shrines of Central and Eastern Europe: A Pilgrim's Travel Guide*. Liguori, MO: Liguori Publications, 1999.

HELENA, SAINT
(C. 248–C. 329)

Saint Helena (Flavia Iulia Helena) was the mother of the Roman Emperor Constantine (c. 272–337). She was born in the southern Balkans at Drepanum (later known as Helenopolis) on the Nicomedian Gulf, as the daughter of an innkeeper. She married Constantius Chlorus (250–306), the Roman emperor in the west during the last two years of his life. She was put aside by her husband around 292 as he wished to marry up. Nonetheless, Helena's son Constantine would succeed his father in the emperor's chair. He favored Christianity, and his mother converted. She became not only a devout but an enthusiastic Christian who used her position as the beloved mother of the emperor to assist the spread of Christianity. A variety of churches in different locations cite her as the force behind their founding.

Saint Helena is most remembered, however, for her visit to Palestine late in her life. She visited both Bethlehem and Jerusalem, and she is said to have been responsible for the construction of the Church of the Nativity and a basilica on the rocky outcropping then believed to be the site of Jesus' crucifixion. In moving around Jerusalem, she had workers clear the debris that had accumulated in previous centuries. It was in cleaning the debris at the reputed site of Jesus' burial that she discovered what she believed was the true cross upon which Jesus had been crucified. Actually, she discovered three crosses, those of Christ and the two thieves who were crucified with him. To discern which was the TRUE CROSS, she brought them to a woman ill with an incurable disease. The woman touched each cross. After touching one of them, she was immediately cured. That cross was designated the True Cross. Subsequently, Helena divided the cross into three pieces. One was taken to Constantinople, one sent to Rome, and one remained in Jerusalem.

While the wood of the True Cross may have been the most notable item recovered by Helena, she also was said to have located numerous other items, such as an ICON drawn by Saint Luke and the relics of the THREE MAGI who had visited the infant Jesus. She also traveled into the Sinai Desert and designated the mountain where God gave the law to Moses. There she erected a tower, which subsequently became the site of SAINT CATHERINE'S MONASTERY, home to the burning bush.

There is much doubt as to the veracity of the story of Helena in the Holy Land. Her contemporary, Christian historian Eusebius (d. 342), wrote of her journey, mentioning a variety of occurrences and describing her hope of finding something that would be a direct link to Jesus Christ. But he does not mention any success in that quest. The first mention of her finding the cross was in 395, when Saint Ambrose of Milan referred to it in a sermon preached on the sixty-fifth anniversary of Helena's death. It is then described in the edited copy of Eusebius' *Church History* in the material added by Rufinus (c. 345–410), who included the story of the miraculous resurrection.

The Helena story was accepted by many in the Middle Ages. The growing legend, especially as it expanded during the medieval era when so many "relics" were brought to Europe, became one of the most potent forces in the revamping of Catholic piety in the centuries prior to the Protestant Reformation. It is also to be noted that the Atlantic island upon which Napoleon was exiled is named for her.

Sources:

Borgehammar, Stephen. *How the Holy Cross Was Found: From Event to Medieval Legend*. Stockholm: Almqvist & Wiksell, 1991.

Pohlsander, Hans A. *Helena: Empress and Saint*. Chicago: Ares Publishers, 1995.

Thiede, Carsten Peter, and Matthew d'Ancona. *The Quest for the True Cross*. New York: Palgrave, 2002.

Whatley, Gordon. "Constantine the Great, the Empress Helena, and the Relics of the Holy Cross." In Thomas Head, ed. *Medieval Hagiography: An Anthology*, Garland Reference Library of the Humanities, vol. 1942: 77–95. New York: Garland, 2000.

A tradition in Lithuania of erecting crosses for various personal and even political reasons has resulted in this unique display of Christian faith known as the Hill of Crosses, visited in this photo by Pope John Paul II. *AFP/Getty Images.*

HILL OF CROSSES (LITHUANIA)

One of the most unique shrines in all of Christendom, the Hill of Crosses (Kryziu Kalnas) is a small hill upon which tens of thousands of Lithuanians have placed crosses, some as memorials to the dead, others as acts of political defiance, still others as celebrations of personal and national independence. Today the hill is a dense forest of crosses of all shapes and sizes.

The Hill of Crosses is located some ten miles north of Siauliai, Lithuania, almost to the Latvian border. It appears that the hill was originally a Pagan holy site, and that the tradition of placing crosses on the hill dates to the fourteenth century when Teutonic Knights controlled the region.

The modern development of the site as a place for individuals to make symbolic statements can be dated to the nineteenth century. In 1795 Russia took control of the area, which was not returned to Lithuania until 1918. In 1831–1832, the peasants attempted an unsuccessful revolt, and the first cluster of crosses was placed on the hill in their memory. By the end of the century there were some 150 large crosses, which grew to around 400 large crosses joined by thousands of smaller ones as World War II began.

After World War II, when the area was reincorporated into the Soviet Union, the hill became a symbol of Lithuanian nationalism. The small act of adding a cross to the hill became a way of opposing what was seen as Soviet occupation. Three times, the Soviet authorities leveled the hill (1961, 1973, and 1975) and destroyed the crosses. They converted the site into a waste and sewage dump. Pilgrims returned and rebuilt the site. Lithuania gained its independence with the fall of the Soviet Union, and in September 1993 Pope John Paul II visited the site to pay homage to the people who had maintained the hill over the years.

Historians have traced the phenomenon of the hill to a tradition of making wooden crosses that is an integral part of village piety and culture in Lithuania. The craft seems to have developed after the Christianization of the country in the fifteenth century, and today there are some 200 cross-crafting masters residing in Lithuania. Crosses are typically decorated with floral and geometric designs and statues of Christ or saints.

The typical Lithuanian crosses that originally decorated the hill have been joined by a spectrum of crosses from around the world, brought by pilgrims from many countries who have made the journey to Siauliai in recent decades.

Sources:

Dailadre, Ricardar. *Kriziu Kalnas/The Mount of Crosses.* Vilnius, Lithuania: Zurnales "Veidas," 1993.

HILLULA

Persons of Jewish faith have an analogous celebration to the Christian devotion to the saints and the Muslim veneration of deceased Sufi leaders. They will gather, frequently at the grave, to honor and remember the life and work of a holy person on the anniversary of his or her death. These communal events are most common among Hassidic Jews who gather to honor their deceased rebbes (holy men). If the death date is unknown, they will gather on Lag Ba'Omer (the 33rd day of Omer, the period between Passover and Shavuot), the day to remember the lives of two great sages, Rabbi Akiva (second century CE) and Rabbi Shimon bar Yochai. The latter was the spiritual leader of the Bar Kochba Revolt against Rome in 135 CE. Modern Hassidic Jews believe that during the twelve-year period when Rabbi Shimon hid from

Roman authorities, he experienced many miracles and the prophet Elijah came to him and taught him the secret mysteries of the Torah (known today as the Kabbalah).

The celebration of hillula includes many familiar elements, including chanting and singing, prayer, holy conversation, and the attempt to ritually obtain the blessing of the deceased person. As they near the tomb, men and women will move to separate sides. As they come close to the tomb, they may reach out to touch it or even lie down on it. They may place objects believed capable of absorbing the holy person's power on the tomb. Women may wait to give a male child his first haircut at the tomb.

The idea of celebrating the anniversary of a holy person's death with festive activity, rather than mourning, comes from the belief that a saint's life reaches the pinnacle of its development on the last day of the holy person's life, and is thus a time to be remembered with joy. The word *hillula* also relates the celebration to marriages, as the return of a holy person's soul to its origin was understood to be analogous to a wedding. Sephardic Jews believe that at the hillula celebration, all of the accomplishments of a holy person are presented again to the world, but on a higher level.

Today large hillula celebrations, held at his burial place in Meron in northern Israel, mark the date assigned to the death of Rabbi Shimon Bar Yochai on Lag Ba'Omer. As many as one hundred thousand people make the annual pilgrimage, and large bonfires burn throughout the night. The hillula for Meir Ba'al Ha-nes (twenty-first century CE) is held annually in Tiberias, while Israeli Jews of North African background hold festivals in Netivot at the grave of Israel Abu-Hatsira ("Babi Sali"), a twentieth-century holy man from Morocco. Around the world, most Hassidic groups gather on the anniversaries of the deaths of their former leaders.

Sources:

"Celebration of Lag BaOmer." Posted at http://www.ou.org/chagim/lagbaomer/. Accessed April 1, 2007.

Cerena, Ruth Fredman. "Flaming Prayers: Hillula in a New Home." In Jack Kugelmass, *Between Two Worlds: Ethnographic Essays on American Jewry* (Ithaca: Cornell University Press, 1988): 162–191.

HINN, BENNY (B. 1952)

By the beginning of the twenty-first century, Benny Hinn had overcome a number of critics to emerge as the major exemplar of the Pentecostal healing tradition. Hinn was born in Jaffa, Israel, the son of the former mayor of the city. He was raised in an Eastern Orthodox environment.

At the age of eleven, Hinn had a vision of Jesus. Shortly thereafter, his family moved to Toronto, Canada. The initial vision did not seem to change the normal trajectory of his life, but a second vision in 1972 led to his personal conversion to Christianity, and he entertained the option of entering the ministry. He soon joined a charismatic group that met in a local Anglican church. In 1973 he attended services conducted by Pentecostal healer **KATHRYN KUHLMAN** (1907–1976). This visit to her church in Pittsburgh catalyzed his decision to become a minister. The following year he was healed of a stuttering dysfunction that had been an obstacle to his preaching, and he soon was regularly delivering sermons around Toronto.

Although not closely associated with Kuhlman, Hinn discovered that healings were spontaneously occurring at the services he led. As his reputation as a healer spread, he was invited to speak across the continent, and he began to appear on a weekly television show. Following Kuhlman's death in 1976, he began to identify himself as carrying on a similar ministry. As was true of Kuhlman, he rarely laid his hands on people to pray for healing. Rather, in his services he waits for people to experience healing and then invites them forward to testify to their healing and receive a confirming blessing from him. Often in this encounter, the healed will be filled with the Holy Spirit, manifest by their falling backward as if pushed. This experience is termed **SLAYING IN THE SPIRIT**.

In 1983 Hinn relocated to Orlando, Florida, and became the pastor of the Orlando Christian Center (now the World Christian Center). During the next two decades he was attacked on a number of fronts. Like Kuhlman, he was charged with claiming many healings that never occurred. His orthodoxy was questioned by some countercult spokespersons. Others charged him with living an extravagant lifestyle inappropriate to his calling. In response, Hinn made several changes in his theology and specifically repudiated some ideas that others had read into his writings, although some conservative critics have not been satisfied.

Today, Hinn continues to lead what has become a global endeavor. Benny Hinn Ministries has opened offices in fifteen countries in Europe, Asia, and Latin America.

In 2004 he announced the formation of the World Healing Fellowship, a denomination-like association of ministers and congregations. A short time before, Hinn had moved his headquarters from Florida to suburban Dallas, Texas. *This Is Your Day!*, Hinn's television show, airs daily on cable across North America and in some 60 other countries. Hinn resides in Orange County, Florida, where his television show is taped.

Sources:

Fisher, G. Richard, and M. Kurt Goedelman. *The Confusing World of Benny Hinn*. 9th ed. St. Louis, MO: Person Freedom Outreach, 2004.

Hinn, Benny, *The Anointing*. Nashville, TN: Thomas Nelson, 1997.

———. *Good Morning, Holy Spirit*. Rev. ed. Nashville, TN: Thomas Nelson, 2002.

———. *He Touched Me: An Autobiography*. Nashville, TN: Thomas Nelson, 2000.

———. *Kathryn Kuhlman: Her Spiritual Legacy and Its Imact on My Life*. Nashville, TN: Thomas Nelson, 1999.

HOLY BLOOD (BRUGES, BELGIUM)

On Ascension Day each May, visitors to and citizens of the city of Bruges, Belgium, participate in the Procession of the Holy Blood, an annual pag-

A bottle containing what many believe to be the blood of Jesus is kept in a chapel at Bruges, Belgium. Once a year, on Ascension Day, the bottle is carried through the city during the Procession of the Holy Blood. *Fortean Picture Library.*

eant in which a bottle believed to contain the blood of Jesus Christ is carried through the city. The activities include a reenactment of the arrival of the Count of Flanders, who brought the bottle to Bruges originally in the thirteenth century.

Throughout the year, the vial of blood is kept in the chapel of the Holy Blood on the central square in Bruges. The church was originally built in the twelfth century, with a second story added in the fifteenth. It has subsequently gone through several extensive renovations. The blood, originally kept on what is now the ground level, rests on a silver altar in the church's upper level. It is on public view each Friday and every day from May 3 through May 17. Adjacent to the church is a museum that details the story of the Holy

Blood and contains other items of value owned by the church.

The bottle that contains the substance, which is believed to be blood, is made of crystal and seems to date to the eleventh or twelfth century. It was probably made in Constantinople (modern-day Istanbul) as a container for perfume. The occasion for the bottle and its blood being brought to Belgium was the Sixth Crusade in the 1220s. Jerusalem fell to the Muslims in 1244. The earliest mention of the annual procession is from a charter of the Unloaders' Guild from 1291.

Although the procession is part of the annual May festivities, the tradition that Diederik van den Elzas, Count of Flanders, brought drops of the Holy Blood from Jerusalem in 1149 and the belief that said blood was preserved by Joseph of Arimathea, the person mentioned in the Bible as facilitating the burial of Jesus after the crucifixion, are generally discounted today.

Sources:

"The Holy Blood." http://www.holyblood.com/EN/0. asp. Accessed April 1, 2007.

HOLY COAT OF TRIER

The Holy Coat of Trier (or Treves), Germany, a plain brown piece of cloth without visible seams, is a relic housed in the Roman Catholic cathedral at Trier. It has traditionally been identified as the coat Christ wore the last days of his life when he was arrested, beaten, and crucified. The earliest account of the coat dates from the twelfth century. The *Gesta Trevirorum* notes that the coat was presented to Bishop Agritius (314–334) by the Empress **HELENA** (c. 248–c. 329). Helena was the mother of the Roman Emperor Constantine, and she used her position to promote Christianity after her son legalized it in 312. She traveled to the Holy Land and reputedly recovered several relics associated with Christ, most notably the cross upon which he was executed. While more famous for her promotion of the **TRUE CROSS**, she also recovered the seamless coat for which the Roman soldiers gambled as Jesus suffered on the cross.

The relic stayed in Trier through the next centuries and was placed on display on several occasions during the sixteenth century, when its religious future was called into question upon the rise of Protestantism. (Several prominent Protestant leaders had denounced the coat, noting that several rivals for the Trier relic were on exhibition at other European churches, most notably at Argenteuil, France.) During the continued unrest and wars of the seventeenth and eighteenth century, the coat was hidden away. Following Napoleon's conquest of the region, in 1810 the local bishop felt confident enough to bring the relic from its then hiding place in Augsburg. It has since remained in Trier.

In the modern world, the Holy Coat has been the subject of a variety of critiques, many due to the audacious claim made about its origin. For many centuries, the case for authenticity was based on a document that lay in the archives of Trier, called the "Sylvester Diploma." However, this document, once believed to have been sent by Pope Sylvester I (r. 314–335), has not survived critical scrutiny and is no longer considered genuine. The fact of the coat's being tied to Helena also ties it to other equally questionable Christian relics, not to mention the absence of contemporary fourth-century records concerning Helena and the Holy Land.

In the mid-1840s a piece of ivory, depicting the empress seated before the church and a procession bringing a chest into the church, became the focus of a reexamination of the legendary depositing of the coat at Trier. The ivory, lost for many years, was found in 1844. In 1846 it was made available to the Archeological Society of Frankfort, which issued a statement fixing the ivory as originating in the fourth or fifth century. Noted Catholic historian Guido Görres defended the relic in his pamphlet "The Pilgrimage of Treves," published in 1845.

To date, the coat has not been subject to the kinds of tests that other relics, such as the SHROUD OF TURIN, have undergone. To complicate matters, in the nineteenth century, to better preserve the coat, it was immersed in a rubber solution. It is doubtful that such tests as carbon dating, which might have helped date the item, could now yield satisfying results.

Since 1810 the coat has been placed on display at various times, and on each occasion hundreds of thousands of pilgrims have made the trek to Trier. The most recent showing was in 1996.

Sources:

Clarke, Richard F. *A Pilgrimage to the Holy Coat of Treves*. London: Longmans, Green and Co., 1892.

Plater, Edward A. *The Holy Coat of Treves*. London: Washbourne, 1891.

HOLY GRAIL

The Holy Grail is the name given the cup used by Christ during his Last Supper with his disciples. As Luke described it in his Gospel, "And he took the cup, and gave thanks, and said, 'Take this, and divide it among yourselves'" (Luke 22:17). Most Christians assume the cup there mentioned no longer exists. In the Middle Ages that assumption was challenged.

Between 1180 and 1240, several pieces of historical fiction, composed in Western Europe, told the reputed story of the Grail, the quest to find it (since it had been lost or hidden), and the quest of the hero, a man named Percival, to find the Grail. The most important pieces from this era are the *Conte del Graal* by Chrestien de Troyes, an epic poem to which others added numerous verses; *Parzival*, an epic poem written in German by Wolfram von Eschenbach (d. c. 1216); and the anonymously written folk tales collected as the *Mabinogion*. To these may be added the poetic writings of Robert de Boron, one element of which included the story of Joseph of Arimathea. One thirteenth-century novel, *Queste del St. Graal*, became the most famous of these early literary pieces as its content was taken almost entirely by Robert Malory (fifteenth century) for his *Morte d'Arthur* (1485), the most widely read volume on King Arthur, his knights, and the Grail over the centuries.

As the various stories were conflated, the accounts began with the cup of the Last Supper coming into the possession of Joseph of Arimathea. There is a certain logic to this initial connection, as in the Bible, Joseph is the one who asks Pontius Pilate for permission to take Jesus' corpse to prepare it for a proper Jewish burial (Matthew 27:57–60). The story elaborates on this, however, by saying Joseph stands under the cross and catches Jesus' blood in the cup—the event that gives the cup its reputed magical properties. With the cup, he travels to the British Isles, where he founds the Christian movement (which means British Christianity predates the later evangelism of the islands by representatives sent from Rome).

During the years of the good King Arthur, various knights undertook the quest for the lost Grail, of which Percival is the most noteworthy. A few, like Sir Galahad, were also successful in their quest, but most failed due to their various character flaws. Though some knights found it, they did not bring it back with them to the larger society or Christian community. Various groups were subsequently believed to have become the possessors of the Grail, the most famous being the mysterious Knights **TEMPLAR**. If the Templars had the Grail, it was lost again when the order was suppressed by the French King Philip the Fair (1268–1314) at the beginning of the fourteenth century.

Several churches claim to possess the Grail. For example, there is an ancient cup with an Arabic inscription on its base that the cathedral at Valencia, Spain, prizes as the original Grail. Crusaders brought a green cup to Genoa, Italy, and for many years it was claimed to be the Grail and to be made of emerald stone. Napoleon took possession of it after conquering northern Italy. When it was being returned to Genoa after Napoleon's defeat at Waterloo, it was proved to be made of mere glass, a fact that greatly weakened Genoa's claims concerning it origin. Additional stories have tied the Grail to such varied

locations as **ROSSLYN CHAPEL**, the spring at **GLASTONBURY TORY, OAK ISLAND**, Nova Scotia, and Accokeek, Maryland.

Among the most interesting new twists on the Grail legend was supplied by Michael Baigent, Richard Leigh, and Henry Lincoln in their best-selling book, *Holy Blood, Holy Grail*, originally published in France in 1982. In this volume, the Grail legend was integrated into an alternative secret history that asserts Jesus survived the crucifixion and, with Mary Magdalene, founded a bloodline (the holy blood) that later emerged as the Merovingian royal family in France. The protection of the bloodline was the great secret of the Knights Templar, a task later passed to the Freemasons.

Sources:

Ashley, Mike, ed. *The Chronicles of the Holy Grail*. New York: Carroll & Graf, 1996.

Baigent, Michael, Richard Leigh, and Henry Lincoln. *Holy Blood, Holy Grail*. New York: Bantam Books, 1983.

Bryant, Nigel. *The Legend of the Grail*. Woodbridge, Suffolk: D. S. Brewer, 2004.

Marino, John B. *The Grail Legend in Modern Literature*. Woodbridge, Suffolk: D. S. Brewer, 2004.

Matthews, John. *The Grail, Quest for the Eternal*. London: Thames and Hudson, 1981.

HOLY INFANT CHILD OF PRAGUE

One of the most popular representations of Jesus within Roman Catholicism is the original of the popular statue of Jesus as a child. This is found in a church dedicated to the Virgin Mary, the Church of Our Lady Victorious, in Prague, the Czech Republic. The origin of this statue is somewhat obscure, but the idea for it can be traced to traditional representations of the Virgin Mary holding the baby Jesus in her arms and independent representations of the infant child by medieval artists. This particular statue seems to have been made in Spain and came to Prague as a wedding gift to a Spanish woman Maria Manriquez de Lara when she married the Czech noble-man Vratislav of Pernstynwho. The family later passed it to Carmelite monks in Prague.

The statue suffered damage during the Thirty Years War when Swedish and Protestant soldiers overran the city. However, a Father Cyril later found the statue and put it on display for public veneration. One day, as he prayed, the infant Jesus spoke to him: "Have pity on Me and I will have pity on you. Give Me My hands and I will give you peace. The more you honor Me, the more I will bless you." Afterward, even in its dam-aged state, it became the catalyst for several heal-ings. Some of those who were healed provided the funds to refurbish the statue and provide the rich clothes in which it is adorned.

Eventually, a separate chapel was built for the statue. It now rests on a marble altar surrounded by a host of gold angels. The statue itself, made of wax, is encased in a silver frame. More than 50 outfits of the most expensive materials have been presented to the infant Jesus.

Pilgrimages to the chapel occur annually, but they swell around May 27, the day the statue is paraded through the streets of the city. An effort to make the Holy Infant Child of Prague well known has undergirded its popularity. It gained significant support in 1924, after Pope Pius XI sent a representative to officially crown the sacred image. Not only are many copies of the statue now present in Catholic churches globally, but related shrines focused on the Holy Infant have arisen in several countries. Such shrines exist in the United States at Prague, Oklahoma; New Haven, Con-necticut; and Traverse City, Michigan.

Sources:

Cruz, Joan. *Prayers and Heavenly Promises*. Rockford, IL: Tan Books, 1990.

Devotion to the Infant Jesus of Prague. Rockford, IL: Tan Books, 1975.

Forbelsky, Royt. *Horyna: Holy Infant of Prague*. Prague: Arentinum, 1992.

Infant of Prague Devotions. Boston: St. Paul Books & Media, 1992.

HOLYWELL (WALES)

Holywell, or Saint Winefride's Well, the most prominent healing site in Great Britain, dates to the seventh century. Around 660 CE, a young woman named Winefride refused the advances of a local prince named Caradoc. Refusing to take "no" for an answer, he drove the woman to seek sanctuary in the local parish church. Before she could reach the church, however, he overtook and beheaded her.

At this point legend takes over. As the story proceeds, a spring of water emerged at the spot where her head lay on the ground. The water's healing powers were initially put to use by Wine-fride's uncle, who reunited the head to the body. After he offered a prayer, Winefride was resurrect-ed and lived another 15 years as a nun. The area around the spring grew into the present-day city of Holywell, Wales.

She was buried at Guetherin, Wales, but in the twelfth century her body was exhumed and taken to Shrewsbury in England. The church at Shrews-bury became a new pilgrimage site without nega-tively affecting the number of pilgrims traveling to Holywell, where the waters were gathered in a pool and a chapel erected over it. Steps were cre-ated for easy access to the water for those who wished to immerse themselves. It joined a num-ber of other holy water sites across Great Britain.

In the fifteenth century, the mother of Henry VII saw to the construction of a larger stone building over the pool. The internal walls were decorated with pictures of Winefride's life. It appears the shrine to Saint Winefride was partic-ularly favored by Lady Margaret, the grandmother of Henry VIII, which may be why Henry skipped the destruction of the site when he moved against other Catholic sites in the 1530s. Still, the body and relics of Saint Winefride were taken from Shrewsbury and lost. As Great Britain became predominantly Protestant, the well remained a popular pilgrimage spot. Today the walls are cov-ered with graffiti written by people who have been healed over the centuries.

The faithful regularly flock to the site where Saint Winefride was healed after being beheaded in the seventh century by the cruel prince Caradoc. Holywell, as the name implies, is a well said to contain miraculous healing waters. *Getty Images.*

Since Catholics again attained legal status in Great Britain in the nineteenth century, the Jesuits have managed the site. In 1851 and 1887, Rome assisted in a new emergence of the well into prominence by issuing indulgences for pilgrims. Saint Winefride's feast day is July 22, and the following Sunday each year is a national day for pilgrimage to Holywell. The pilgrimage includes a procession during which a reliquary containing the only surviving relic (Saint Winefride's finger) is marched from the town to the well.

Sources:

Charles-Edwards, T. *Saint Winefride and Her Well: The Historical Background.* Holywell: W. Williams and Son, n.d.

David, Christopher. *St. Winefride's Well: A History and Guide.* London: Kenion Press, 1971.

HOME, DANIEL DUNGLAS (1833–1886)

Largely forgotten today outside of students of paranormal phenomena, Daniel Dunglas Home was one of the most famous mediums of the nineteenth century. He demonstrated a variety of feats, most notably levitation, and unlike a number of his colleagues, Home was not caught performing stage magic. To this day those who do not accept the reality of psychic phenomena remain hard-pressed to explain and/or duplicate Home's feats. He also performed his feats in normal lighting, rather than the darkness preferred by the fake mediums.

Home was born March 20, 1833, in Currie, Scotland. At the age of nine he moved with his aunt, who had adopted him, to the United States, and he spent the rest of his youth in Greenville, Connecticut, and Troy, New York. He was said to have experienced his first paranormal events during his teen years. Among his talents was the prediction of people's death. His aunt came to believe he was possessed of the devil and around 1850 turned him out of her home. He soon emerged in the context of the developing Spiritualist movement, and some of the prominent people of the day—author William Cullen Bryant, chemist Robert Hare, and Judge John Edmonds—saw his early feats and were mystified.

Harvard professor David Wells, accompanied by three other investigators, saw Home cause a table to move about off the ground, though Home was not near it. Two of the witnesses, only with great difficulty, were able to stop the movement. They released it, and it again lifted off the floor. Home was seen to self-levitate in 1852.

Homes moved to England in 1855 and soon became the center of attention as Spiritualism started to take hold. Among those who saw Home was poet Robert Browning, who penned a vicious attack on him, "Mr. Sludge, the Medium," even though Browning had himself been stumped for an explanation to Home's feats.

The single most famous incident in Home's life occurred in December 1868. At a séance in his

Nineteenth-century medium Daniel Dunglas Home purportedly had the ability to levitate himself, among other feats. Even today, debunkers of paranormal activities have found it hard to disprove eyewitness accounts of his skills. *Fortean Picture Library.*

London apartment, those in attendance saw his body elongate. Then he rose from the ground. Upon his descent, he walked into the next room and walked out the window. The attendees saw him apparently floating outside the window, three stories in the air. Home subsequently floated into the room, feet foremost. On other occasions he demonstrated his ability to handle fire.

Harry Houdini, who had exposed a number of fraudulent mediums, claimed he could duplicate Home's feats, but never proved able. That fact sums up the problem of evaluating Home. He did things that seemed to contradict the laws of physics but was never caught attempting to accomplish his feats with the techniques of stage magic. During the last years of his life, many who observed his séances wanted to expose him but were unsuccessful. They were even unable to suggest how he might have done them. Home died on June 21, 1886, following a number of years of declining health.

Sources:

Burton, Jean. *Heyday of a Wizard: Daniel Home the Medium*. London: George G. Harrap, 1930.

Home, D. D. *Incidents in My Life*. London: Longman, Green, 1863.

Jenkins, Elizabeth. *The Shadow and the Light: A Defense of Daniel Dunglas Home*. London: Hamish Hamilton, 1982.

Stein, Gordon. *Encyclopedia of Hoaxes*. Detroit: Gale, 1993.

ICONS

Sacred icons are a form of Christian art especially identified with Eastern Orthodoxy, the form of Christianity that emerged in the Eastern half of the Mediterranean Basin and then spread into Eastern Europe and Russia. The two-dimensional representations of Christ, the Virgin Mary, and the saints developed from the earliest forms of Christian art scrawled on the walls of the catacombs in the centuries prior to the legalization of Christianity under Constantine in the fourth century CE. As the church became a public and even privileged institution, the use of iconic representations accompanied the improvement in their quality and their development in a stylized format.

Not everyone approved of the use of icons, of course. An extremely iconoclastic movement (opposing icons) arose in the lands immediately east of the Orthodox strongholds in Constantinople, Antioch, and Jerusalem. Iconoclastic strength peaked in 754 when the Council of Constantinople moved to abolish icons. However, church leaders faced an immediate negative reaction, leading to a reversal of its position in 787 at the second Council of Nicea (the seventh Ecumenical Council), which authorized the veneration of icons. The battle continued over the next seventy years

as critics of icons found support from the Byzantine Emperor. Theophilus (r. 829–842) was decidedly anti-icon, but following his death, the rulings of 787 were reaffirmed, and the iconoclasts steadily lost support from that point.

To Eastern Christians, icons are not just pictures but "windows to Heaven," a doorway through which the believer can see truths beyond what is revealed by mere words. One particular truth demonstrated by icons is that of the incarnation, God becoming flesh in Jesus Christ. When Christ incarnated, he demonstrated that God's creation—the world and humanity—is good, and that even flesh is not inherently evil.

Iconic art developed in several stages. The Russian icon came to the fore in the tenth century. The fourteenth century is considered the "Golden Age of Icons." By this time, the painting of icons was governed by a strict code of rules concerning design, symbols, style, and colors, and these rules, in turn, were governed by a set of theological principles. Uppermost, the representations of Jesus, the Virgin Mary, and the saints were meant to capture spiritual realities. Far from being mere realistic portraits of their earthly appearance, they were meant to be visible pictures of their embodied spirit, now seen by the eye of faith.

In developing the symbology of the icon, each element was assigned a definite meaning. For example, eyes were slightly enlarged to remind the believer of the need for eyes of faith. Hands were often depicted giving a blessing. Color was placed appropriately relative to the figure to show, for example, gold as representing the divine light, blue as faith, or purple as royalty. The process of producing an icon is termed "writing" rather than drawing or painting, and the process of understanding its truth is called "reading" it.

Some images on icons became very popular and gave their names to different types or styles of icons. The most popular pictures of Christ portray him as Pantocrator, the Ruler of All. Here he is pictured with a book, his right hand raised in a blessing with two fingers uplifted signaling his two natures. Mary, possibly even a more popular subject than Jesus of iconographers, comes in a variety of styles—holding the baby Jesus and pointing to him (Hodegetria), touching her cheek to the baby Jesus (Eleousa), and sitting on a throne with the Baby Jesus on her lap (Panakranta), among others.

Many icons have become known because of miracles associated with them, including some known to exude blood or tears. Others are famous for the healings that have been experienced by devotees. The oldest known icon is known for its association with a miraculous snowfall. The icon known as Salus Populi Romani ("Protector of the Roman People") is attributed to Saint Luke, author of the biblical gospel, and is one of the many items discovered in the Holy Land by Saint Helena, the mother of Constantine. It is currently housed at Saint Mary Major Basilica in Rome. That church was the result of an **APPARITION OF THE VIRGIN MARY** to Pope Liberius and two other people, whom she told to build a church on Esquiline Hill. She would mark the spot with a snowfall, which would be quite apparent as it was August. At celebrations marking the anniversary of the church, white rose petals are dropped on worshipers.

Another famous icon attributed to Saint Helena is Our Lady of Czestochowa, one of the so-called **BLACK MADONNAS**. This icon eventually found its way to Poland. In the 1380s Ladislaus, the Prince of Opole and regent for King Louis of Poland, offered a prayer to the Virgin asking where her image should be placed, and in a dream she pointed to a hill at Czestochowa. Ladislaus endowed a monastery and left the image with the monks. In the 1430s the monastery was attacked. A soldier attempting to steal the icon slashed the cheek of the image three times, and he died as he made the third cut. Since that time, attempts to repair the image have remained unsuccessful. Two hundred years later, Swedes invaded the land. That the army was unable to capture the monastery led King John Casmir to name Mary the Queen of Poland.

Sources:

Ivanov, V. *Russian Icons*. New York: Rizzoli International Publications, 1988.

Onasch Konrad, Schnieper. *Icons: The Fascination and The Reality*. New York: Riverside Book Company, 1997.

Pasierb, Janusz. *The Shrine of the Black Madonna of Czestochowa*. Warsaw: Interpress Publishers, 1980.

IFE (NIGERIA)

Ife (aka Ilé Ife), an ancient city in southwest Nigeria, is believed by the Yoruba people of Nigeria as the place where creation occurred. The orisha Olodumare, the Supreme God (the one who has the fullness of everything), gave certain materials to his emissary (or perhaps son), the orisha Oduduwa. He brought these to the place known now as Ife and used them to create the earth, separating the land from the water. Archeologists have suggested the city is at least a thousand years old, and the region inhabited for another thousand years.

The Yoruba were divided into various groups, each with royal leadership. The royal families believe they have descended from the first king of Ife, Oduduwa. After Oduduwa's death, his children left the city to found their own kingdoms. Oduduwa is believed to have had sixteen sons, who later became powerful traditional rulers of Yoruba land.

Through the centuries, Ife existed as a city state whose paramount importance was its role as the original sacred city and the dispenser of basic religious thought, including the divining technique known as Ifa, an indispensable tool in defining the course of one's life. At Ife one finds the acknowledgment of a basic pantheon of Yoruba gods, or orisha, estimated variously to number 201, 401, 601, or more. Some divinities are said to have existed when Oduduwa created the earth, while others are outstanding individuals who have been deified. Among the more popular deities are Shango (god of thunder and lightning), Ifa (or Orunmila, god of divination), and Ogun (god of iron and of war). These deities have been brought to the Americas by the practitioners of Santeria.

The old Yoruba kingdoms have been superseded by modern Nigeria, but the royal leadership persists at a less formal level. The kings of the Oni people of Ife and the Alafin people of Oyo, further to the north, are still the most highly respected Yoruba kings and religious leaders in Nigeria. Ife is home to the palace of the Oni.

Ife was destroyed in 1849 and rebuilt in 1882. Today, approximately 300,000 people live in Ife.

Sources:

Abimbola, Wande, ed. *Yoruba Oral Tradition*. With a contribution by Rowland Abiodun. Ile-Ife, Nigeria: Department of African Languages and Literature, University of Ile-Ife, 1975.

Bascom, William. *Ifa Divination: Communication between Gods and Men in West Africa* Bloomington and London: Indiana University Press. 1969.

Dennett, Richard Edward. *Nigerian Studies; or, The Religious and Political System of the Yoruba*. London: Cass, 1968.

Forde, Cyril Daryll. *The Yoruba-speaking Peoples of Southwestern Nigeria*. London, International African Institute, 1962.

IMAGE OF EDESSA

Edessa, known today as Urfa, is located in southeastern Turkey, not far from the Syrian border. The Christian historian Eusebius, writing around the year 324 CE, claimed he came into possession of two letters, one reputedly written by King Abgar of Edessa to Jesus Christ, and the other Jesus' reply. In the former, Abgar notes that he had learned of Jesus' healings and, as he was ill, he requested Jesus to come and heal him. In the reply, Jesus says that he will commission a disciple to come to Abgar after he completes his early mission. The letters are obviously later documents, reflecting not only an anti-Semitic theme in the third century church, but the tradition of doubting Thomas.

According to the developing tradition, Jesus designated Thomas to go to Edessa, but Thomas passed that task to one of his disciples, Addai. In a document written at the beginning of the fourth century CE, *The Doctrine of Addai*, Thomas's colleague became the instrument of bringing Christianity to the city. Soon after his arrival, the king sent for Addai and was healed. Unfortunately, Addai's mission was undone by Abgar's son, who was not a believer. In the give and take between Addai and Abgar, *The Doctrine of Addai* mentions the painting of a cloth with Jesus' face on it and the giving of that cloth to Abgar. That act is not connected to his healing.

The story of the cloth underwent a significant enrichment in later centuries. Written around 596 CE, Evagrius Scholasticus' (c. 536–c. 600) *Ecclesiastical History* tells the story of a piece of cloth discovered in 544 in Edessa, which the author describes as "created by God, and not produced by the hands of man." Then in the eighth century, John of Damascus (d. 749), in his work *On Holy Images*, recounts that Abgar had, in fact, requested an image of Jesus. In response, Jesus had placed a piece of cloth to his face, and his image miraculously was transferred to the cloth.

By the time that John was writing, the Image of Edessa had disappeared. In 609, the Persians overran Edessa. At this point, a variety of stories emerged about the image's fate. The most promising account suggests it was exchanged for some Muslim prisoners in 944, taken to Constantinople, then captured by Crusaders when they sacked the city in 1204. They would have taken it to the West, but no account of its deposition has been found.

Any further telling of the story must make mention of a variety of cloths that existed in the Eastern Christian world that were said to have an image not made with hands, but supernaturally imprinted. These would later become known as *vera inconas,* or true icons, the most famous being VERONICA'S VEIL. In each case, the cloth showed the portrait of Christ's head and face in a reddish pigment.

The particular *vera icona* called the Image of Edessa would not be very important were it not that contemporary writers have suggested it was the icon now known as the SHROUD OF TURIN. The Shroud, whose supporters claim to be the burial shroud in which Jesus' body was wrapped following the crucifixion, first appears in the fourteenth century, more than one hundred years after the disappearance of the Image of Edessa. Some equate the Shroud with the Image of Edessa, which is recovered after its disappearance, thereby pressing the Shroud's credentials backward by almost a millennium.

Ian Wilson is the leading spokesperson suggesting the Image of Edessa, known as simply a cloth bearing the face of Jesus, was in fact the Shroud folded so as to present only the face. This argument has been accepted by only a few Shroud apologists.

Sources:

Nickell, Joe. *Inquest on the Shroud of Turin: Latest Scientific Findings.* Amherst, NY: Prometheus Books, 1998.

Tribbe, Frank C. *Portrait of Jesus: The Illustrated Story of the Shroud of Turin.* New York: Stein and Day, 1983.

Wilson, Ian. *The Mysterious Shroud.* Garden City, NY: Doubleday & Company, 1986.

INDIGO CHILDREN

In the early 1980s a psychic named Nancy Ann Tappe, who specialized in the seeing and reading of the AURA (a color energy field which many psychics claim to see around living objects), publicized what she discerned as a significant change in the auras of children. In her 1982 book, *Understanding Your Life through Color,* she claimed many of the children then being born had a new color in their aura, indigo. This color distinguished them as a special new group of beings taking incarnation and explained why the children were both a sign of significant coming shifts in the culture and were being misunderstood. The concept was then picked up and widely publicized in two books by Lee Carroll and Jan Tober, *The Indigo Children* and *Indigo Celebration.* Lee Carroll is a channeler who delivers the messages from an entity named Kyron, and Jan Tabor is Carroll's wife.

The concept of indigo children cannot be understood apart from the situation concerning the medical community's defining two new diseases, attention deficit disorder (ADD) and attention deficit hyperactivity disorder (ADHD), and the widespread diagnosis of numerous children with one or both of these diseases. By 1990 approximately a half-million children had been diagnosed as having ADD or ADHD. By 1998 that number jumped to four million, or 10 percent of the school-age population. ADD and ADHD are frequently associated with patterns of classroom disruption and misbehavior by children at school. The primary treatment for ADD and ADHD has been a drug called Ritalin, which suppresses the symptoms, and has placed teachers whose classes have been disrupted by overactive children, who seemingly were unable to concentrate on their lessons, among those often favoring the use of Ritalin. Parents and various public awareness groups have complained of the side-effects that have manifested from the use of the drug.

According to Tappe, Carroll, and Tober, many of the children diagnosed with ADD or ADHD are indigo children. These are special children, they say, who are very sensitive, have a spectrum of psychic abilities, and come into life with a high level of wisdom. They act as if they are old souls in young bodies. Proponents of the indigo children hypothesis have cited cases of children remembering their past incarnations as evidence of their current status.

Indigo children are distinguished by characteristics often valued in adults, but rarely valued in children. They act as individuals with entitlements, have problems with authority, and do not like to engage in various repetitive activities. They are creative and thus reject situations, such as elementary schools, where rote learning is often valued more than creative talents.

The discussion of indigo children, largely limited to New Age circles, has added a religious dimension into the popular controversy concerning ADD, ADHD, and Ritalin. Because of its basis in the unique ability of one woman to see the aura of the special children and its being tied to equally controversial channeling work of Carroll, the idea of indigo children has done little other than become a salve for parents who reject the implication of their children being diagnosed with a somewhat permanent disorder, and one that carries with it a significant social stigma. Meanwhile, a variety of means for treating ADD and ADHD without Ritalin and other strong mood-altering drugs have been proposed.

Sources:

Carroll, Lee, and Jan Tober. *An Indigo Celebration: More Messages, Stories, and Insights from the Indigo Children.* Carlsbad, CA: Hay House, 2001.

———. *The Indigo Children. The New Kids Have Arrived.* Sedona, AZ: Light Technology Publishing, 1999.

Shaya, James, James Windell, and Holly Shreve Gilbert. *What You Need to Know about Ritalin.* New York: Bantam, 1999.

Virtue, Doreen. *The Care and Feeding of Indigo Children.* Carlsbad, CA: Hay House, 2001.

Iona (Scotland)

Iona emerged out of obscurity in 563 CE, when a prominent Irish church leader named Columba (c. 521–597) suddenly left his former career and began a new one on a small, isolated island off the western coast of Scotland. Columba was born in Donegal in northern Ireland and received the best education available at the time. Raised in the church, he was ordained to the priesthood at the age of twenty-four and became a monk. After an epidemic struck his monastery he returned to Donegal, but he spent most of his time wandering across Ireland, founding new churches and monasteries. His education, oratorical skills, and forceful personality had placed him on an upward trajectory, but suddenly in 563, for reasons not altogether understood, he dropped everything and moved into a self-selected exile.

Iona became the disseminating point for the evangelizing of Scotland. Columba gained the permission of King Brude, a Pagan, to preach to the Picts, the people who inhabited Scotland. Columba would establish more than a hundred churches through the rest of his life. In the years that followed, he established more than one hundred churches there in Alba, as Scotland was then called. Columba was most successful among the Western Isles, where today there exist the ruins of many churches dedicated to him. To the northeast, farther removed from Iona, it was more difficult to make inroads among the heathen. But in later years Columba's followers reaped the fruit of the seeds he had sown with his preaching.

Iona continued to flourish as a missionary and monastic center through the seventh century. From its community, a group of monks led by Saint Aidan (d. 651) moved to establish the community on the island of Lindesfarne. It lost some of its leadership role through the eighth century as papal authority was asserted over the British Isles. In the ninth century, however, Vikings destroyed the community. It would never regain its ecclesiastical prominence. A monastery was again established on the island in the thirteenth century but was dissolved by Henry VIII in the 1530s.

The monastic buildings on Iona fell into ruin over the centuries after the Reformation. Then in 1938, George MacLeod (1895–1991), a prominent Scottish Presbyterian minister from Glasgow, launched a new ecumenical Christian community committed to seeking new ways of living the Gospel in the contemporary world. Moving with some colleagues to Iona, the community initiated its effort by rebuilding the abbey on the island as a base of operation. The community was to be radically ecumenical, multinational, and racially inclusive, and to work for the renewal of the church in every aspect of its life. Through the last half of the twentieth century, the community became an influential organization. Besides a residential community that maintains the rebuilt monastic complex, the Iona community has a number of nonresidential members throughout the British Isles and associate members around the world.

The existence of the Iona Community has brought the island back to life as a destination for Christian pilgrims. Adding to the community's impact has been the more recent rise of Celtic Christianity. Modern devotees of the Celtic Christian movement see a unique form of Christianity as having developed in the British Isles, beginning in the second century and continuing through the early Middle Ages when Latin Christianity, as represented by the Roman Catholic Church, was imposed on the land. Modern Celtic Christians see the original Iona center established by Columba as an integral part of their historical foundation.

Sources:

Clancy, T., and G. Markus. *Iona: The Earliest Poetry of a Celtic Monastery*. Edinburgh: Edinburgh University Press, 1995.

Ferguson, Ronald. *George MacLeod: Founder of the Iona Community*. London: Harper Collins, 1990.

Herbert, Maire. *Iona, Kells and Derry: The History and Hagiography of the Monastic Family of Columba*. Oxford: Oxford University Press, 1988.

MacLeod, George F. *Only One Way Left*. Glasgow/Edinburgh: Iona, 1964.

Ross, David. *The Story of Saint Columba*. Lanark, UK: Waverley Books, 1999.

ISTANBUL (TURKEY)

Istanbul, formerly known as Constantinople, was once a great center of Christianity and rivaled Jerusalem as a destination of Christian pilgrims. However, in the fifteenth century it was overrun by a Muslim army and subsequently became the center of the Ottoman Empire and an Islamic focal point.

Long inhabited, the site that became Istanbul was chosen by Rome as a new administrative center from which the eastern part of its empire could be more effectively administered. The town of Byzantium was chosen as the new administrative center in 146 BCE, and the city of New Rome emerged. The city thrived for five centuries, then began a new era under the Emperor Constantine (c. 272–337). In 330 CE, in his honor, the city was renamed Constantinople.

Constantine converted to Christianity, and during the later years of his reign the city emerged as a great Christian center. In the 320s, Constantine's mother HELENA (c. 248–c. 329) made her famous trip to Palestine where she located a number of reputed Christian relics, many of which were brought back to Constantinople. The city, along with the nearby communities of Nicea and Chalcedon, became the site of most of the important church councils at which the orthodox doctrine of the Christian church was hammered out and the creedal statements embodying the council decisions were promulgated. The council of 381 was, for example, held at Saint Irene's Church, at the time the main cathedral church in Constantinople.

Two hundred years after Constantine, the Emperor Justinian I greatly enhanced the status of the Christian community with the construction of the HAGIA SOPHIA, which remains impressive for its size and opulence. When completed, it was the largest building in the world and an appropriate monument to Roman power and the new role of Christianity in the Mediterranean Basin.

During the more than a thousand years of Christian rule in the city, the Hagia Sophia suffered damage on two occasions. Much of the artwork was damaged during the period of the iconoclastic controversy (726–843). The iconoclasts believed images in the churches were equivalent to idolatry. Much more damage was done in 1204, when frustrated Crusaders from Western Europe sacked the city and took charge for the next half century. Though reconstructed after 1261, much of the church's former glory never returned.

In 1453 the army of Sultan Mehmet II overran the city and brought the Christian Era to an end. He and his successors rebuilt the city as an Islamic one. The Hagia Sophia was turned into a mosque and appropriately redecorated. Saint Irene's Cathedral was turned into an armory for the sultan's troops. The primary Muslim holy site became the **TOPKAPI PALACE**, adjacent to Saint Irene's Church, where a set of the relics of Muhammad were assembled.

The Ottoman Empire continued through World War I and came to an end with the Turkish revolution in the 1920s, which brought a secular government. The new era brought a variety of changes to both Christian and Muslim sites. The Hagia Sophia was turned into a museum. Saint Irene's Church, restored in the 1970s, now serves as a concert hall. Topkapi Palace is the city's primary tourist site today and retains some sanctity because of the relics housed there in two rooms called the Chamber of the Sacred Relics. Included are some of Muhammad's teeth, a letter written by him, and a mold of his footprint.

The oldest surviving Christian site in Istanbul is the Monastery of Saint John the Baptist of Studius. It dates to the fifth century CE and was at one time both a great center of intellectual endeavor and home to a variety of relics of Eastern Christian saints. It was also converted to a mosque after the Ottoman conquest and remained such until it was severely damaged by an 1843 earthquake. Today it is a museum.

Sources:

Edmunds, Anna C. *Turkey's Religious Sites*. Istanbul: Damko, 1997.

Kuban, Dogan. *Istanbul: An Urban History*. Istanbul: History Foundation, 1996.

Ousterhout, Robert. *Master Builders of Byzantium*. Princeton, NJ: Princeton University Press, 2000.

JAGANNATH

Jagannath is the name of a Hindu deity (an incarnation of Vishnu); a prominent Hindu temple located in Puri, a coastal city in the state of Orissa in eastern India; and a festival celebrated by Vaishnava Hindus worldwide. Vaishnavas, Hindus who primarily honor Vishnu as the major Hindu deity, believe that Lord Jagannath was responsible for the creation of the whole universe. In the temple in Puri, Jagannath is closely associated with his sister Subhadra and his brother Balabhadra.

The Puri Temple was built by Raja Ananta Varman Chodaganga Dev in the twelfth century CE, then maintained by successive Hindu rulers through the next four centuries. In 1558 Orissa was conquered by Afghan Muslims already in power in neighboring Bengal. The Afghans held Orissa until 1592, during which time worship at the Puri Temple was suppressed. After they were driven out, even though Muslim influence continued to dominate in the region, the statues were reinstalled and worship of Lord Jagannath resumed.

Lord Jagannath and his siblings are installed in the sanctuary in the rear of the temple. A daily ritual begins at 5 a.m. and consists of several meals (the presentation of food offerings, called **PRASADAM**), several dressings (costume changes)

of the statues, and the distribution of food to the people.

The Puri Temple is part of the Hindu attempt to mark the subcontinent as holy space. At the same time, the area is to some extent a religious and cultural enigma. Jagannath and the associated deities at the Puri Temple are seen as officially related to the local tribal people, who are considered to exist outside of the traditional tribal or caste system. Generally, members of the higher castes would not consider eating with such outsiders. However, at Puri, the tribal groups prepare all the prasadam (holy food), and pilgrims eat it without regard to the caste rules. Some have suggested that what occurs at the temple may be derived from an earlier effort to reform the caste system.

The major attraction at Puri is the annual Jagannath festival that occurs in midsummer. The deities are placed in three large carts and carried from the temple to their "summer temple," the Gundicha Mandir, a little over a mile from the main Jagannath temple. The cart upon which Lord Jagannath rides is a massive wooden structure constructed from hundreds of logs cut from the sacred *phasi* trees, a forest of which is kept in cultivation just for this annual event. Two slightly smaller carts carry Subhadra and Balabhadra. Lord Jagannath's cart requires four thousand men to it pull it, and

Jagannath Rath Yatra Festival attendees in Calcutta, India, honor Jagannath, one of the many incarnations of the Hindu god Vishnu. *AFP/Getty Images.*

THE ENCYCLOPEDIA OF RELIGIOUS PHENOMENA

once it is moving it is extremely difficult to stop (this fact being the origin of the popular war term *juggernaut*). Devotees in the tens of thousands gather to watch Lord Jagannath take the short trip. He will stay in the summer temple only seven days and is then returned to the main temple.

The Jagannath festival, though held in smaller versions in several other Indian cities, was largely unknown in the West until the advent of the International Society for Krishna Consciousness (ISKCON), the Hare Krishna movement, in the United States in the 1960s. Very soon after organizing, ISKCON began to hold Jagannath festivals in different American cities, and their annual reenactment of the trip to the summer temple has become a popular attraction. It is currently held each summer in the major cities throughout the West where the movement has established temples.

Sources:

das Goswami, Satsvarupa. *A Visit to Jagannath Puri*. La Crosse, FL: Gita-nagari Press, 1987.

Deo, Jitamitra Prasad Singh. *Origin of Jagannath Deity*. New Delhi: Gyan, 2003.

Eschmann, Ann, Hermann Kulke, and Gaya C. Tripathi, eds. *The Cult of Jagannath and the Regional Tradition of Orissa*. New Delhi: Manohar Press, 1978.

Schnepal, Burkhard, and Herman Kulke. *Jagannath Revisited: Studying Society, Religion and the State in Orissa*. New Delhi: Manohar, 2001.

JAMA MASJID (INDIA)

Jama Masjid, in Delhi, India, is one of the largest mosques in India and all the more impressive for housing several RELICS of Muhammad the Prophet. It was erected by order of the Mughal emperor Shah Jahan (1592–1666), better known for building the Taj Mahal. He completed the mosque in 1644. Architects chose red sandstone and white marble as their main building materials.

While the mosque is valued by students of architecture as a culminating example of the Muslim presence in northern India, the primary attraction is the small, white shrine in the north-

west corner of the courtyard, where the relics of the Prophet are kept. In the northeast corner of the shrine is a red hair from the beard of Muhammad. Other items include Muhammad's sandal, a chapter of the Qur'an written on deerskin (one portion reportedly written by Muhammad's grandson), the canopy from Muhammad's tombstone, and Muhammad's footprint on a stone.

Many local worshipers believe the mosque will be the site where Muhammad will eventually return to earth to announce the final judgment.

Sources:

Berinstain, Valerie. *India and the Mughal Dynasty*. New York: Harry N. Abrams, 1998.

Rothfarb, Ed. *The Land of the Taj Mahal*. New York: Henry Holt and Co., 1998.

JAMES OSSUARY

On October 21, 2002, the popular scientific journal *Biblical Archaeological Review* announced the existence of an ancient limestone box described as an ossuary, or burial box, some 50 centimeters by 25 centimeters by 30 centimeters. The ossuary shows an inscription carved on its side in Aramaic that reads: "Ya'akov bar Yosef akhui di Yeshua," which in translation becomes "James, son of Joseph, brother of Jesus." If genuine, this box would be the earliest tangible evidence of the existence of Jesus of Nazareth, outside of the biblical narrative. The box also reiterated the questionable nature of the many relics that now exist throughout Christendom which claim to come from the time of Jesus' ministry, from the SHROUD OF TURIN and VERONICA'S VEIL to icons supposedly tied to the apostle Luke.

The authenticity of the ossuary was immediately called into question, and as far as possible, preliminary tests were run to support the claims of its proponents. Among the first to pronounce on it, Israeli geologists confirmed that the limestone is from the Jerusalem area and was probably quarried in the first or second century CE. Also, an analysis of the surface of the box suggested the

Thousands pray at the Eid al-Adha festival at the Jama Masjid mosque in New Delhi. One of the most important Muslim mosques in India, Jama Masjid is home to a number of relics from the Prophet Muhammad. *AFP/Getty Images.*

inscription was made soon after the ossuary was fashioned from the rock. The language and style of the inscription are consistent with that of the first century (20 BCE–70 CE). Critics have noted the same scholarship that authenticated it could possibly have faked it.

Primary doubts about the ossuary begin with its checkered modern history. Reputedly it was found in a cave near Silwan by an Arab laborer who subsequently sold it to an antique dealer, who in turn sold it to the present owner. There is little information on the site where the ossuary was found, which could ideally be examined independently.

Adding its voice to doubts about the ossuary, on June 18, 2003, the Israeli Antiquities Authority formally announced its opinion that the box was a forgery. Their report emphasized both the findings from their careful examination of the box and the problems of its modern discovery. Rochelle Altman, one scholar who had examined the box, concluded that the part of the key inscription that reads "Jacob (James) son of Joseph" was likely carved in the first century, but that the later part of the inscription, which reads "brother of Joshua (Jesus)," was a later addition, probably from the third or fourth century. Altman noted significant stylistic changes between the two parts of the inscription.

Sources:

Eshe, Esther, Tal Ilan, Dr. Avner Ayalon, and Orna Cohen. *Final Report of the Examining Committees for the*

The discovery of the James ossuary in 2002, seen here on display at the Royal Ontario Museum, has sparked considerable debate. Is the inscription on the limestone box genuine, and does it mean that it contains the bones of Jesus Christ's brother? *AFP/Getty Images.*

Yehoash Inscription and James Ossuary. May 18, 2003. Posted at http://www.bibleinterp.com/articles/Com mittees_report.htm. Accessed April 1, 2007.

Lemaire, André. "Burial Box of James the Brother of Jesus." *Biblical Archaeology Review* 28, 6 (November/December 2002): 24–33, 70.

Witherington, Ben. "Bones of Contention: Why I Still Think the James Bone Box Is Likely to Be Authentic." *Christianity Today* 47, 10 (October 2003): 42. Posted at http://www.christianitytoday.com/ct/2003/010/2.42.html. Accessed April 1, 2007.

JANUARIUS, SAINT

Twice a year in the Cappella del Tesoro (Chapel of the Treasure) at the main cathedral in Naples, a small vial containing a dark substance is put on public display. More often than not, within a few minutes, the substance begins to liquefy and even foam, a process often described as boiling. After a while, the substance inside the vial returns to its solid state and is returned to its permanent resting place elsewhere in the church. Records of this reputed miracle date to the fourteenth century. The substance inside the vial is claimed to be the blood of the martyred saint, Bishop Januarius of Ben Vento.

According to legend, Saint Januarius was a victim of the persecution of Christians that occurred under the reign of Roman Emperor Diocletian toward the end of the third century. He was initially cast into a fiery furnace, but he emerged unharmed. He was then tossed to the lions, but they refused to approach him. He and his companions were, however, finally killed by beheading at Pozzuoli. At the time of his death, supposedly, two vials of his blood were collected and taken with the body to the catacombs. The body and the vials were moved several times over the next years, but they were finally given a permanent resting place in the Neapolitan cathedral in the thirteenth century. Today one of the vials is essentially empty, its contents having been given in small quantities to several prominent people in the eighteenth century.

Since the fourteenth century, for eight days in May (commemorating the entrance of the saint's body into Naples) and again in September (beginning on the legendary day of martyrdom, September 19), the vials have been placed on view. Over the centuries the vials have been brought out at different times to respond to the visits of prominent individuals or to ward off threatened disasters, such as an eruption of Mount Vesuvius. For many years, the vial was also displayed for several days in December.

The vial containing the blood is housed in a silver case, which has a clear glass window for viewing and a handle by which it may be carried. When placed on display, the vial is placed close to a silver container said to contain parts of the skull of Saint Januarius. The ritual begins with prayers that are repeated by the congregants requesting that the "miracle" take place. Also present are a group of poor women, the "zie di San Gennaro" (aunts of Saint Januarius), who have become known for the enthusiasm with which they join in the supplication for the miracle—which may become even more exuberant if there is a delay in the liquefaction of the substance in the vial.

Those who support the miraculous nature of the Miracle of Saint Januarius have bolstered their belief with several arguments. First, they have noted that none have come forward in all the 600-plus years of the miracle to claim it is a hoax or attempt to expose the nature of any fraud. At the same time, the idea of a simple trick being worked on the public would necessarily involve many leading figures in the church over a number of centuries. They also point to an instance in 1902 in which a physicist was allowed to pass light through the vial during the liquefaction process and review the results on a spectroscope. The distinctive lines of the spectrum of blood appeared, suggesting there are at least traces of blood in the contents of the vial.

Critics have, however, proposed no simple trickery. Rather, they suggest a fraud occurred in the fourteenth century and does not involve anyone who lives today or in recent centuries. Herbert Thurston, a Roman Catholic apologist who wrote widely on the issue of miracles within the church, called attention to the existence of other, similar instances of the blood of saints. He noted that almost all of these were in and around Naples, suggesting that whatever change occurs in the vial is related to a secret discovered locally and fostered on posterity.

Contemporary critics suggest that at some point prior to the first recorded viewing of the miracle in 1389, the vials were filled with a substance that changes from solid to liquid at the normal temperature of the Cappella del Tesoro (somewhere between 66 to 80 degrees Fahrenheit). As to the contents of the vial, several suggestions have come forward, though until the vials are opened and a sample obtained for chemical analysis, no definitive answer can be given.

A team of Italian researchers, Luigi Garlaschelli, Franco Ramaccini, and Sergio Della Sala, have suggested a mixture of salt water, chalk, and iron chloride. American skeptical researcher Joe Nickell and John Fischer have suggested a mixture of a nondrying oil, such as olive oil, and a substance such as beeswax. Such a mixture is congealed in a cool space but quickly liquefies with a rise in temperature of just a few degrees. A small amount of pigment produces the appearance of blood.

Meanwhile, until more definitive tests are run on the contents of the vial itself, the twice-annual displays of the blood of Saint Januarius continue in the Cappella del Tesoro in Naples.

Sources:

Cruz, Joan Carroll. *Relic: Shroud of Turin, True Cross, Blood of Januarius, History Mysticism and the Catholic Church.* Huntington, IN: Our Sunday Visitor Press, 1984.

Nickell, Joe. *Looking for a Miracle.* Amherst, NY: Prometheus Books, 1998.

Thurston, Herbert. *The Physical Phenomena of Mysticism.* London: Burns & Oates, 1952.

———, and Donald Attwater, eds. *Butler's Lives of the Saints.* 4 vols. New York: P. J. Kennedy & Sons, 1956.

JERUSALEM (ISRAEL)

Jerusalem and the surrounding territory is possibly the most sacred place on Earth, land revered by the followers of three of the world's most prominent faiths—Judaism, Christianity, and Islam. Its place in Judaism was established when King David made it his capital and brought to the city the ARK OF THE COVENANT, in which God focused his presence to the children of Israel. King Solomon, David's successor, then built the temple to house the Ark. Destroyed by the conquering forces in 587 BCE, the temple was rebuilt following the Jews' return from exile in 538 BCE. However, many Jews also believe Jerusalem is the site at which, long before David, Abraham prepared to sacrifice his son Isaac in the famous incident recorded in the biblical book of Genesis 22:2–19.

Centuries later, Jerusalem became the center for the ministry of Jesus and the site of his passion, death, and resurrection. In Jerusalem, on the day of Pentecost, Christians believe God's Holy Spirit descended upon Jesus' disciples, and the Christian Church was founded.

For Muslims, Jerusalem is second in importance only to Mecca and Medina, where Muhammad (570–632) lived. While Muhammad never traveled to Palestine, he is believed to have visited Jerusalem during what is termed the Night Journey. From Mecca, Muhammad was supernaturally transported to the Temple Mount in Jerusalem, from which he ascended into heaven and conversed with Allah.

Jerusalem is also integral to traditional views on the culmination of human history for believers of the three faiths. For Jews, Jerusalem was their traditional homeland, control of which has been at several points in history denied them. Thus, a return to Jerusalem from their global dispersal has been a major theme in Jewish thought. This additionally interacts with a belief that from Jerusalem, the end-time events of human history will be initiated, culminating in the resurrection of the dead.

Christianity, a movement suppressed through its early centuries, immediately voiced its claims on Jerusalem as soon as it attained some favor in the Roman Empire during the reign of the emperor Constantine (r. 306–337). The city became metaphorically an earthly image of the coming kingdom of God and the literal site from which the end-time events described in the book of Revelation would emanate.

For a segment of the Muslim community, Jerusalem has come to be seen as the place where the End of Days, including the return to life of the dead, will begin. That belief, by no means a consensus, has led many Muslims to seek burial close to the Temple Mount.

The broad claims of the three religions to hegemony over specific locations, and the particular claims of individual subgroups within the three large faith communities, accumulated as successive rule came to the city and the surrounding territory. A significant challenge to Jewish hegemony in the city began in 63 BCE with the conquest of the city by the Romans. That rule would be marked by the execution of Jesus and then, in 70 CE, the siege of the city and destruction of the Second Temple by Roman forces. In 135, the Romans destroyed much of the remaining city and barred both Jews and Christians access to their most holy sites.

In the fourth century Constantine opened Jerusalem to Christians, and Christian leadership dominated the land for the next three centuries. Jews received very limited rights to visit their sites, although access was gradually increased over

The holy city of Jerusalem contains many historical sites that are of immense importance to Jewish, Christian, and Islamic traditions. It has thus been a hotspot for wars ranging from the medieval Crusades to modern-day terrorism. *Fortean Picture Library.*

succeeding centuries. In 638 the initiation of Muslim rule led to the destruction of many Christian facilities while initiating the construction of many Muslim sites. The most important site was, of course, the Dome of the Rock, marking the site of Muhammad's journey to heaven. The Dome occupies the site of the former Second Temple, and its existence thus blocks any desires of Jews to rebuild their temple.

The reestablishment of Christian rule in Jerusalem became the object of the medieval crusades, but except for a brief period (1099–1187), the city remained in Muslim hands until the fall of the Ottoman Empire after World War I. The arrival of the British, who established a protectorate over the city in 1917, led to three decades of

Christian efforts to reclaim parts of the city. In 1947 Jewish residents of Palestine initiated a successful war whose goal was the establishment of Israel as an independent state. Despite succeeding in their basic objective, they were unable of include most of Jerusalem in the new nation. Most importantly, the Old City, including the Temple Mount, came under the control of Jordan, a Muslim nation. While Jordan allowed Christians access to their sites, Jews were not granted the same privileges. Two decades later, during the 1967 war, Israeli forces took control of the Old City, and it remains under Israeli authority to the present.

In 1947, when Jordanian forces took control of the Old City, they denied Jews access to the WAILING WALL, now generally called the Western

Wall, the remnant foundation of the Jewish temple, which had over the centuries become a focus of Jewish aspirations for their traditional homeland. That wall fell into the hands of Jewish forces on June 7, 1967, and Jewish leaders immediately found their way to it. It subsequently became the single most important Jewish site in the city.

Muslim attention to the city is concentrated on the Temple Mount, now defined by the surrounding wall built by Herod the Great in the first century BCE. It is the site of the Dome of the Rock, the AL-AQSA MOSQUE (erected over the site where Muhammad originally landed in Jerusalem), and more than one hundred other Muslim structures. Although the Israeli government now controls the Temple Mount, it has respected the Muslim establishment that has been created, and to this day Jews are forbidden to venture within the Mount's walls.

Beginning with the visit of HELENA (c. 248–c. 329), the aging mother of Constantine, Christian leaders began to identify and mark the sites where the major events in the life of Jesus and his apostles occurred. No site was more important than that of Jesus' crucifixion and burial. Once it was identified by Helena, Constantine launched the building of the Church of the Holy Sepulcher. That church became the culminating point of the interrelated sites marking the last events of Jesus' life, beginning with his condemnation to death, torture, and the carrying of the cross to his place of execution. The path that Jesus walked is now called the Via Dolorosa (Sorrowful Way), and the symbolic reenactment of the Via Dolorosa has become a significant devotional practice in the Roman Catholic Church, whose members are encouraged to pray through the Stations of the Cross. The Via Dolorosa begins at the Lion's Gate and passes the Church of the Condemnation, a variety of small chapels, an Armenian Catholic Church, and an Ethiopian church before culminating at the Church of the Holy Sepulcher. The importance of Jesus' treading of the Via Dolorosa was underscored in the response to the 2004 blockbuster movie *The Passion of the Christ*, directed by Mel Gibson.

Besides Jesus' last days, the locations of a variety of occurrences from Jesus' ministry have been designated and today remain pilgrimage sites. They would include the pool at Bethesda where Jesus healed a lame man, the pool of Siloam where he cured a blind man, the Garden of Gethsemane where he went to pray, and the Mount of Olives where he spoke the Lord's Prayer. Several churches now commemorate the site of Jesus' ascension into heaven. The Church of the Assumption is the traditional site of the grave of the Virgin Mary; however, Roman Catholics have come to believe that Mary was taken bodily into heaven at the end of her earthly existence—a belief that was declared dogma in 1950.

Modern Jerusalem is one of the most religiously diverse cities in the world, with many of the sectarian divisions of the three major faiths represented in its residents. In addition to the older sites relative to the founding and major historical events of Islam, Judaism, and Christianity, the modern leadership of the various elements of their communities have centers in Jerusalem. At the center of the religious communities are organizations that seek to represent the larger Christian, Jewish, and Muslim groups in the city and others that seek to provide dialogue between them.

Sources:

Bahat, Dan. *Carta's Historical Atlas of Jerusalem*. Jerusalem: Carta, 1995.

Gonen, Rivka. *Biblical Holy Places: An Illustrated History*. New York: Macmillan, 1987.

Grabar, Oleg. *The Shape of the Holy: Early Islamic Jerusalem*. Princeton, NJ: Princeton University Press, 1996.

Hollis, Christopher, and Ronald Brownrigg. *Holy Places: Jewish, Christian, and Moslem Monuments in the Holy Land*. New York: Praeger, 1969.

JOHREI

Simply put, Johrei is a method of channeling divine light to an individual through the hands of a practitioner, and as such shares much with many other forms of spiritual healing. However, the particular practice known as Johrei was initially propounded by Mokichi Okada (1882–1955), a Japanese businessman, art collector, mystic, and teacher. A former member of Omoto, one of the early Japanese new religions, Okada had a vision of the Buddhist bodhisattva Kannon (Kuan Yin) in 1925. She gave him the Divine Light (Johrei) and told him to step out as a prophet. Several years later he founded the Great Japan Association for the Veneration of the Bodhisattva Kannon. Divine healing was a major purpose of the association. The organization made several transformations over the next decades and eventually emerged as Sekai Kyuseikyo (the Church of World Messianity).

Okada called members to work for an accelerated coming of paradise on Earth through an outpouring of Divine Light. This outpouring will be accomplished primarily through the giving of Johrei by the members trained within the church and a parallel practice of *shizen noho*, a form of natural agriculture.

Johrei understands the human condition as one in which individuals accumulate impurities that lead to illness. Thus, as part of the regular worship services and at other times throughout the week, Johrei is shared to create purification. Those channeling the Johrei wear a symbol, called an *ohikari*, around their neck. It is considered to be a sacred focal point. As the healers begin healing, they hold the palm of their hand a few inches from the body of the person receiving the healing. They believe a ray of healing light moves from their palm, and they often experience this ray. The ray ultimately is traced to Okada, who is regarded as a bodhisattva, or enlightened one. The healing may be done in silence or accompanied with prayers and chanting. Besides healing physical conditions, Johrei is believed to remove bad karma, deal with stressful life situations, and bring spiritual purification.

Sekai Kyuseikyo began to expand beyond Japan in the 1950s, and the practice of Johrei was introduced to America in 1953. It generally operates in North America as the Church of World Messianity or the Johrei Fellowship. Centers may be found around the Pacific basin and in Europe.

Sources:

Okada, Mokichi. *Johrei: Divine Light of Salvation*. Kyoto: Society of Johrei, 1984.

———. *Teachings of Meishu-sama*, Vols. I and II. Atami, Japan: Church of World Messianity, 1967–1968.

Spickard, J. V. "Spiritual Healing among Followers of a Japanese New Religion: Experience as a Factor in Religious Motivation." *Research in the Social Scientific Study of Religion* 3:135–156, 1991.

JOSEPH OF CUPERTINO (1603–1663)

Among the most frequently cited individuals capable of producing paranormal phenomena, by both secular parapsychologists and believers in religious miracles, is Joseph of Cupertino. A variety of contemporary accounts of his levitations by highly reputable people became the bedrock of his reputation and eventually carried him to canonization as a saint by the Roman Catholic Church.

The future saint was born Joseph Desa on June 17, 1603, at Cupertino, near Brindisi in what was then the kingdom of Naples, now part of Italy. He was raised in poverty. As a child he began to experience ecstatic visions, and as a young adult he determined he wished to become a monk. However, his unusual experiences proved an initial obstacle. Although apprenticed to a shoemaker, Joseph applied for admittance to the Franciscans, but he did not meet their educational requirements. However, in 1620 he was accepted as a Capuchin lay brother. His sporadic and spontaneous movement into ecstatic states of consciousness intruded upon his assigned duties, and the order dismissed him. He was finally accepted into a Franciscan monastery near his hometown. Although not formally educated, he was ordained to the priesthood in 1628. His monastic brothers saw him as a person of extreme spirituality and possessed of wisdom derived from his visionary experiences.

Nonetheless, his activity did cause considerable problems of monastic routine. Over the next decades he was largely confined to his room and an adjacent chapel. He did not attend most of the daily communal devotional exercises and did not say mass in the monastery's main church. As knowledge of the unusual occurrences attributed to him spread, efforts were made to keep him from becoming a public spectacle. At one point he was questioned by the inquisition, and on several occasions he was made to change locations as his brothers wearied of his unique life.

The ecstasies were frequent, but he also experienced still more spectacular events, in particular those involving levitation. One incident occurred in 1645 when the High Admiral of Castile, who served as the ambassador of Spain at the papal court, interviewed Joseph and then accompanied him to the chapel at Assisi, where Joseph then resided. Upon entering the chapel, Joseph looked upon the statue of the Virgin Mary and began to levitate above the heads of those present. After a short period in the air, he floated to the floor and returned to his cell without speaking to the admiral's wife or others who had been waiting for him in the chapel.

There was contemporary interest in the events around Joseph. Those who witnessed his ecstasies noted that he was oblivious to outside noises save the voice of the monastery's superior. He was on occasion hit, pinched, stuck with a needle, and even burned, but no such action disturbed his trancelike state.

Joseph died at Ossimo on September 18, 1663, and was buried in the church. Following his death an inquiry was started concerning his sainthood, which, due to the nature of some of the reported occurrences, took many years of scrutiny. He was finally beatified, receiving one step toward canonization, in 1753 by Pope Benedict XIV. The pope had obviously been deeply affected by his reading of the many eyewitness accounts of Joseph's levitations. He argued that if such evidence was rejected, no historical evidence could ever be accepted. In 1767 Pope Clement XIII named Joseph a saint.

Today, parapsychologists point to Joseph as possibly the best instance of repeated levitations, while skeptics have grounded their arguments on the seeming inability of reproducing Joseph's feats in a contemporary setting. While levitations of a number of saints have been reported, none approach the number (some 70 occasions) and the credible eyewitnesses of Joseph's. The only person who nears his feats of levitation is Spiritualist **DANIEL DUNGLAS HOME** (1833–1886).

In 1962 a movie called *The Reluctant Saint*, starring Maximilian Schell, portrayed Joseph of Cupertino's life.

Sources:

Betz, Eva K. *Another Man Named Joseph: The Life of Saint Joseph of Cupertino*. Greymoor, NY: Franciscan Friars of the Atonement, 1965.

Cendrars, Blaise. *Saint Joseph de Cupertino*. Villiers le Bel: Le Club du Livre Chrétien, 1960.

Leroy, Olivier. *Levitation: An Examination of the Evidence and Explanations*. London: Burns Oates & Washbourne, 1928.

KABBALAH

The term Kabbalah means "doctrine received from tradition." At one time it referred to the entire corpus of Hebrew writings apart from the Pentateuch (the first five books of the Bible), but over the centuries it has come to designate a particular mystical system that came to the fore in the Middle Ages and was later adapted for use by non-Jewish Esotericists.

The Kabbalah describes the cosmos as having emanated from the utterly transcendent and unknowable God (the *Ein Soph*). The emanations appear as ten realms, the sephiroth, each emerging from the realm immediately above it. The tenth sephiroth includes the visible, manifest world. The ten sephiroth have been pictured in an intricate diagram called the Tree of Life, with the sephiroth shown as circles. In the diagram, the circles are connected to each other by lines, termed paths. The Tree of Life serves as a map of the spiritual realms one may traverse during meditative and magical states.

During the sixteenth century, following the banishment of the Jewish community in Spain and Portugal, kabbalistic wisdom was dispersed across Europe and found its way into Christian hands, the Old Testament scholar Johann Reuchlin (1455–1522) being a major force in the development and dissemination of a Christianized Cabala.

In subsequent centuries, the Hassidic Jewish movement, the major exponents of the Kabbalah, spread across Eastern Europe, where a variety of Hassidic dynasties were created around lineages of holy men, rebbes, who perpetuated this mystical form of Judaism. These communities assumed the brunt of the Nazi Holocaust and were largely wiped out, although remnants escaped to either Palestine or North America. In the decades since World War II, the Lubavitcher community has emerged as the single largest Hassidic group and now includes more than half of all Hassidic believers. Another Hassidic group, the Satmar, possibly the second largest, has become well known for its opposition to the Zionist vision that led to the creation of the modern state of Israel.

The Cabala was also integrated in the revival of magical religion in Western Europe in the nineteenth century. French magician Eliphas Levi (1810–1875) utilized the Cabala as a major building block of the system of ceremonial magic he developed. Magical activity, especially the development of the individual magician, was related to the Tree of Life. Levi advocated **TAROT** cards as magical tools and pushed the development of the Tarot decks so they correlated with the Cabala. While few contemporary ritual magicians follow the Cabala exclusively, almost all use it to some degree.

Bringing the two traditions of Kabbalah and Cabala together are the works of Philip Berg, the leader of the Kabbalah Centre, a controversial movement that has attempted to popularize the teachings of Jewish mysticism quite apart from the traditional Hassidic communities. It has attracted a number of celebrities—among them Madonna, Demi Moore, Roseanne Barr, Britney Spears, Sarah Bernhardt—while being heavily criticized by some Jewish leaders for distorting and diluting the tradition.

Sources:

Berg, Philip S. *Kabbalah for the Layman: A Guide to Cosmic Consciousness; an Opening to the Portals of Jewish Mysticism.* Richmond Hill, NY: Research Centre Of Kabbalah, 1982.

Greer, John Michael, *Paths of Wisdom: The Magical Cabala in the Western Tradition.* St. Paul, MN: Llewellyn Publications, 1996.

Reuchlin, Johann. *On the Art of the Kabbalah.* New York: Abaris Books, 1983.

Scholem, Gershom. *On the Kabbalah and Its Symbolism.* New York: Schocken Books, 1960.

KAMAKURA (JAPAN)

Today but a small town, Kamakura does not immediately reveal itself as once the capital of Japan or a key site in the development of Japanese religious life. However, the many temples and shrines in the town and its immediate environs speak to its designation as one of Japan's holiest sites. Kamakura is home to some sixty-five Buddhist temples, nineteen Shinto shrines, and one of the most famous statues of the Buddha in the world.

The sleepy village of Kamakura emerged out of obscurity at the end of the twelfth century, when the Minamoto family took control of Japan and established their government in the city. Although power was centered in Kamakura, the emperor continued to reside in Kyoto, and the Minamoto shogun paid him due respect. What

little power remained in Kyoto was lost in 1221, when the shogun's army defeated the imperial forces, although the emperor and his court remained in place. The shogunate ruled until 1333, when the imperial rule was reestablished.

A number of the most famous Japanese Buddhist leaders lived during the Kamakura Era: Honen (1133–1212), Shinran (1173–1262), Eisai (1141–1215), Dogen (1200–1253), Ippen (1239–1289), and Nichiren (1222–1282). Honen founded, and Sinran and Ippen expounded upon, Japanese Pure Land Buddhism. In an age in which Buddhism was seemingly in decline, the trio offered the public the opportunity to end the cycle of rebirth for a new home in the Pure Land (Heaven) by the regular recitation of the *nimbutsu*, the name of Amida Buddha. Pure Land Buddhism went on to become the largest Buddhist community in Japan.

Although Zen arose early in the seventh century, it did not gain a real foothold until the early Kamakura period (1185–1333). Eisai became the instrument of introducing Zen Buddhism into Japan, and today he is considered its founder. Turned out by the Buddhist leadership ensconced in power in Kyoto, the emergence of the Kamakura shogunate provided a fortunate opportunity. In 1200 Eisai established Jufuju-ki, the first Zen center in Kamakura, and found strong support among the warriors (the samurai) that were the basis of the shogunate's power. In 1214 he also wrote a treatise on tea and its healthful qualities that would become the source of later Japanese adoption of the beverage and its practice of the tea ceremony.

Eisai's later contemporary, Dogen (1200–1253), established the Soto school of Zen in Japan. Soto placed more faith in long periods of meditation and is best known for its practice of *zazen*, or sitting meditation. Dogen's stay at Kamakura was very brief. He moved there in 1247, but he found Rinzain practice so firmly established that he moved on to more fertile territory. Today, Engaku-ji and the four other Rinzai temples in Kamakura maintain the Zen base in the region.

The Giant Buddha in Kamakura is an enduring legacy to the history of this Japanese city that was the center of Zen Buddhism from the late-twelfth through early fourteenth centuries. *Fortean Picture Library.*

Engaku-ji has even greater importance to Western Zen students. Soyen Shaku (1859–1919), the Zen teacher who attended the World Parliament of Religions in 1893, was from Engaku-ji, and this center was among the first to open its doors to Westerners.

Eisai followed a form of Zen called Rinzai, whose practitioners believed they would find enlightenment through spontaneous flashes. They became best known for their use of the *koan*, questions whose answers seem to defy logic. In the realization of the answer, one is pushed toward enlightenment.

In Kamakura, Pure Land Buddhism would become visible in the Giant Buddha. Weighing approximately 121 tons, it is 43 feet in height and about 30 feet wide from knee to knee. Originally constructed of wood, it was significantly damaged in a storm and in 1252 was reconstructed in bronze. It was cast in several pieces and assembled in its present resting place. Several hills built over the statue were destroyed, and since 1495 it has remained in the open. Although it is a statue of an enlightened one, it is not of Gautama Buddha (the founder of Buddhism) but of the bodhisattva Amida Buddha, around which Pure Land Buddhism is focused.

As Pure Land Buddhism spread across Japan, the youthful Nichiren, ordained as a priest at age fifteen, began his quest for spiritual truth. He asked why people who put their faith in the *nembutsu* still experienced the spectrum of painful conditions. This and other equally puzzling problems motivated his studies after he settled in Kamakura in 1238. Four years in Kamakura and eleven years roaming the countryside visiting the different Buddhist groups led him to one firm conclusion: that in the writing known as the Lotus Sutra, the essential teachings of the Buddha were summarized.

In 1253 Nichiren announced his conclusions to his fellow Buddhists. He attacked faith in the *nembutsu* and in its stead he called for the chanting of the "Great Title" of the Lotus Sutra—"Namu Myoho Renge Kyo"—as the practical way

by which everyone could realize the deepest truths of Buddhism. The reaction was intense and negative. Feeling his life threatened, Nichiren fled to Kamakura and lived in a hut. He worked the streets preaching to whoever would listen. His anti-elitist message took hold among common people.

Nichiren's efforts aroused active opposition from both Buddhist leaders and government authorities. His house was burned down in 1260, and the following year he was arrested and exiled. He returned to Kamakura in 1263. After years of the government more or less tolerating him, in 1271 he was again formally exiled. Returning to Kamakura in 1274, he again tried to gain government backing. When he failed, he moved permanently to Mount Minobu. Today the several Nichiren-shu temples at Kamakura recall Nichiren's adventures there.

Apart from the spread of the several new forms of Buddhism during the Kamakura period, several of the temples have some individual characteristics that continue to attract special constituencies. Tokeiji, for example, is famous for attracting women. Since the thirteenth century it has served as a refuge for battered wives who could get a divorce by serving as nuns at the temple for a few years. The Hase Kannon Temple boasts the tallest wooden statue in Japan, an eleven-headed carving of the bodhisattva Kannon (aka Kuan Yin), the bodhisattva of mercy.

While Buddhism dominated the Kamakura period, the presence of Shinto should not be forgotten. Among the oldest temples in Kamakura is the Amanawa Jinja, dating to the eighth century. This shrine was protected by the shogun, though otherwise distinctly favoring Buddhism, as one of the shogun's relatives' wives believed she received help in bearing a son from her activity at the jinja.

When the shogunate fell in 1333, the power once again shifted to Kyoto, and Kamakura lost its place on history's stage. The once-bustling city again became a quiet town. Rediscovered after World War II, today Kamakura draws visitors from around the world—pilgrims and tourists, believers, students of religion, and those who merely appreciate the artistry of the buildings and gardens.

Sources:

Kasahara, Zazuo, ed. *A History of Japanese Religion.* Tokyo: Kosei Publishing Co., 2001.

Saunders, E. Dale. *Buddhism in Japan with an Outline of Its Origins in India.* Philadelphia: University of Pennsylvania Press, 1964.

KARBALA (IRAQ)

The town of Karbala in present-day Iraq is one of the most holy sites of Shi'a Muslims. Shi'a is one of the two larger divisions of Islam, although the main Sunni community is almost ten times larger in size. The Shi'a minority traces its origin to the squabbles over control of the emergent Islamic Empire in the decades after the Prophet Muhammad's death. Muhammad's death in 632 CE was followed by the reign of the four caliphs. Following the assassination of the caliph Uthman in 656, Ali ibn-Abi-Talib, Muhammad's son-in-law, the husband of Fatima, was chosen to succeed him by the powers that existed in Medina, Arabia. Ali was challenged by Mu'awiya, and when Ali was assassinated in 1661, Mu'awiya was acknowledged as the new caliph by most of Ali's supporters. Thus began the Umayyad dynasty that would rule Islam for the next century.

Ali's two sons, Hasan (d. 669) and Husayn, accepted Mu'awiya, but in 680, Husayn refused to accept Mu'awiya's son Yazid as the new caliph. He eventually decided to moved to Mesopotamia (Iraq), where he believed he had strong support. However, as he journeyed to his goal, he encountered the caliph's supporters at Karbala. When he refused to surrender, he and all his 86 companions were killed. He was seen as a martyr by many, and the site of the deaths and the burial site of Husayn quickly became a pilgrimage destination. As the Shi'a Muslims emerged as a distinctive group, disagreeing with the Sunni on a variety of lesser points of belief and practice, Karbala emerged as one of their most holy sites. A key of divergence between the two groups is the acknowledgment that Islamic leadership properly passed to Ali and Husayn rather than the caliphs of the Umayyad dynasty.

The martyrdom of Husayn was memorialized in a shrine that was built at his burial site and commemorated in an annual pageant that reenacted his death. The mosque shrine, Masjid al-Husayn, has had a checkered existence. It has been destroyed and rebuilt on a number of occasions, most recently in 1801. At that time it was targeted by the ultraconservative Arabian Sunni group, the Wahhabis, who would eventually come to dominate neighboring Saudi Arabia. When rebuilt, the walls of the new courtyard were decorated with the entire text of the Qur'an. It was again damaged in the 1991 Gulf War, was restored, and became an object of considerable attention in the Second Gulf War, with American troops making a self-conscious effort to spare it further damage.

Over the years, Shi'a Muslims have made numerous pilgrimages annually, but two dates drew the greatest number. Ashura, the tenth day of the month of Muharram on the Muslim calendar, marks the day of Husayn's death. A pilgrimage also occurs forty day later, the twelfth day of the month of Safar. At these times, pilgrims participate in various activities reenacting the battle and deaths. Men march through the street flagellating themselves and allow cuts to be made on their head. They are often pictured with blood freely flowing from their various wounds. Others, less interactive in their commemoration of the battle and deaths, may purchase tablets made from the clay of the battlefield.

Among the martyrs of 680 was Abbas, Husayn's half-brother. His tomb, some 1,500 feet from that of Masjid al-Husayn, is also visited by pilgrims, and Abbas is seen as a source of miracle healings. Healing powers have also been ascribed to the clay tablets, which may be consumed by those seeking a restoration of health.

Iraqi ruler Saddam Hussein had his power base in the Sunni areas of Iraq and for many years forbade public Shi'a celebrations at Karbala. They were held for the first time in more than a quarter century in 2003 following his deposition from power.

Sources:

Aghaie, Kamran Scot. *The Martyrs of Karbala: Shi'a Symbols and Rituals in Modern Iran.* Seattle: University of Washington Press, 2004.

Nakash, Yitzhak. *The Shi'is of Iraq.* Princeton, NJ: Princeton University Press, 2003.

KHAJURAHO TEMPLES (INDIA)

Famous for their many sculptures depicting left-hand Tantrism and the erotic arts, the temples of Khajuraho are unique both to India and the world. They also have a fascinating story behind them. At the beginning of the tenth century CE, the daughter of a Brahmin priest, Hemavati, claimed to have become pregnant by the moon god. The child of the union, named Chandravarman, was seen as part mortal and part divine. In spite of the lofty claims as to the child's father, Hemavati was seen as an unwed mother and eventually left her home to live in the forest, where she raised the child. He emerged as a great leader and founded a dynasty in central India. He championed his mother's claim that he was descended from the moon god.

By the time Chandravarman became king, his mother was deceased. However, she came to him in a dream and told him to build a temple that would show human passions and lead those who viewed them to understand the emptiness of human desires.

Temple construction began in 950 CE by Chandravarman and was continued through the next two centuries by the successive rulers of the dynasty. In the end, eighty-five temples were constructed. The design of the temples was in some discontinuity with other Hindu temples, even those dedicated to Shakta and open to left-hand Tantrism. Thus as the dynasty waned in the later twelfth century, political power shifted away from Khajuraho and the temples were neglected, abandoned, and forgotten. They were rediscovered during the years of British rule, but the explicit nature of the many sculptures slowed the spread of knowledge of them until the late twentieth century. Only in the last generation have the twenty-two surviving temples been restored. They now stand as major Indian tourist attractions, and enough people have traveled to Khajuraho that a new airport has been constructed to handle their needs.

Aside from their content, the temples are also unique architecturally. They rest on high platforms and point upward in a distinctive manner, not unlike twentieth-century skyscrapers. They are among the most blatant celebrations of human sexuality in a religious context ever constructed.

Sources:

Lal, Kanwar. *Immortal Khajuraho.* New York: Castle Books, 1967.

Mishra, P. K. *Khajuraho: With Latest Discoveries.* New Delhi: Sundeep Prakashan, 2001.

Vidya, Prakash. *Khajuraho: A Study in the Cultural Conditions of Chandella Society.* Bombay (Mumbai), India: D. B. Taraporevala Sons & Co., 1967.

Zannas, Eliky. *Khajuraho: Description of the Candella Temple Complex at Khajuraho; Life in the Time of the Candellas.* Den Haag, Netherlands: Mouton, 1960.

KHOMEINI, AYATOLLAH (1902–1989)

The role of the ayatollah, a title that designates a high-ranking religious leader, in Shi'a Islam became widely known following the Iranian revolution of 1979 and was again widely publicized during the Iraqi War that toppled Saddam Hussein, Iraq's leader from 1979 to 2003. Ayatollah Seyyed Ruhollah Khomeini, leader of Iran from 1979 to 1989, was born Ruhollah ibn Mustafa Musawi Khomeini Hindi on September 24, 1902, in Khomein, a town some one hundred miles southwest of Qom, Iran.

Khomeini's grandfather, Seyyed Ahmad, moved from his home in Lucknow, India (hence the word Hindi added to Khomeini's name) and settled in Khomein. As a young man, Ruhollah Khomeini began to move toward life as a Shi'a clergyman, and he received his higher education at Arak and Qom. Through the 1920s and 1930s he served as a junior clergy in Qom. He advanced in the Shi'a system as he became known as an accomplished scholar/teacher, and he gained the support of many who did their studies with him.

In 1961 the senior clergyman in Qom died. Khomeini emerged as a successor to the late Ayatollah Boroujerdi. He quickly emerged as a voice against the secularizing of the government proposed by the Shah of Iran, Mohammad Reza Pahlavi. He organized opposition to the so-called "White Revolution" proposed by the Shah in 1963.

On June 3, 1963, Khomeini delivered a speech in which he attacked the Shah directly. Two days later he was arrested. He was not released from house arrest until April 7, 1964. Several months later Khomeini again denounced the Shah, this time for his pro-American policies, and he questioned the legitimacy of the government. He was again arrested on November 4, 1964, and he was ordered into exile in Turkey. He stayed in Turkey for a year and then moved to the Shi'a center at al-Najaf in Iraq. While there he authored a book on his understanding of government and leadership in the Islamic community.

Facing unrest from the Ayatollah's supporters in Iran, the Shah acted to have him removed from Iraq. In 1978 Khomeini moved to Paris, which had the effect of making him much more accessible to the world's media. His following in Iran continued to grow, and by January of 1979 the Shah's position had become untenable. He withdrew, and on January 31 Khomeini returned to Iran. Over the next ten days he organized opposition to the token government that the Shah had left in place. That government fell on February 12.

A referendum held at the end of March indicated massive support for an Islamic republic. Thus, April 1, 1979, was proclaimed by Khomeini as the first day of the government of God. He was named Imam as the highest cleric in Shi'a Islam. When the Islamic republic was established short-

The Ayatollah Khomeini led the Iranian Revolution of 1979 that overthrew the U.S.-supported shah and brought about a new era of Shi'a religious conservatism to the country. *Getty Images.*

ly after that, he was named the Supreme Leader. Though in poor health, he ruled the country for the next decade, until his death on June 3, 1989.

Several observers have noted the manner in which Khomeini's exile and return followed the pattern of the Shi'as' twelfth Imam of the tenth century. According to Shi'a belief, this Imam, a descendant of Muhammad, disappeared in 941 CE. While many thought he had been assassinated, the faithful believed that he was alive, and has remained alive, and will at some point reappear to rule the world.

Sources:

Khomeini, Ayatollah. *Sayings of the Ayatollah Khomeini; Political, Philosophical, Social and Religious.* New York: Bantam Books, 1980.

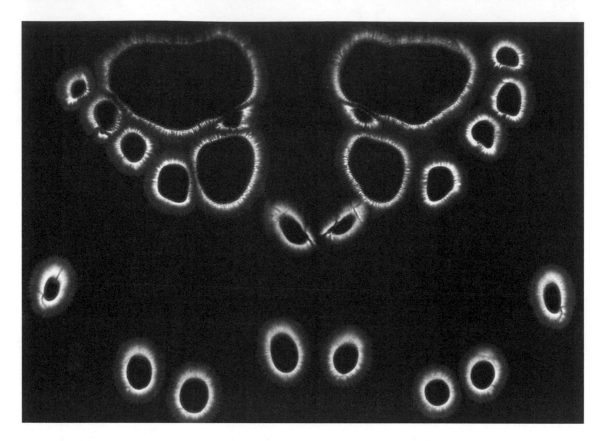

Seymon Davidovich Kirlian invented a method of photography that supposedly can capture images of people's auras. *Fortean Picture Library.*

Martin, Vanessa. *Creating an Islamic State: Khomeini and the Making of a New Iran.* London: I. B. Tauris & Co., 2000.

Montazam, Mir Ali Asghar. *The Life and Times of Ayatollah Khomeini.* London: Anglo-European Publications, 1994.

KIRLIAN PHOTOGRAPHY

In the 1970s people in the West became aware of a new photographic technique that utilized a high-frequency, high-voltage, low-amperage electrical field to produce pictures of what was described as a biofield. Objects thus photographed, especially living objects, showed a glowing discharge surrounding the object, which was especially beautiful when color film was used.

The process of Kirlian photography is named after Seymon Davidovich Kirlian, an amateur inventor and electrician of Krasnodar, Russia, and his wife and research associate, Valentina Kirlian. Together they began initial research in electrical photography in the early 1940s.

The nature of the effects produced by Kirlian photography has offered hope of producing information useful to medicine and biology, but in the 1960s it caught the attention of people interested in psychic phenomena. The discharge around objects was identified with the AURA around living objects that many psychics claimed to see. Possibly the photographs would offer a general verification of their psychic vision.

In the 1970s in the West, a number of parapsychologists obtained the equipment necessary to reproduce Kirlian photographs and began to look for effects that correlated with findings concerning psychokinesis, especially psychic healing. Taking pictures of people's hands, especially fingertips, became a popular activity wherever psychically inclined people gathered. In some cases very interesting pictures could be taken of people in a normal state of consciousness as opposed to when they were preparing to heal someone.

After several years of initial experimentation, increasingly more rigid controls were applied to the pictures, especially controls for the pressure between the film and the object being photographed. When such controls were enforced, all of the interesting effects previously seen disappeared. By the beginning of the 1980s, Kirlian photography had largely been discarded as a technique capable of making visible hidden psychic energies. Meanwhile, little relevance was found for Kirlian pictures in other fields.

Sources:

Krippner, Staley, and Daniel Rubin. *Galaxies of Life: The Human Aura in Acupuncture and Kirlian Photography*. London: Gordon & Beach, 1973.

Moss, Thelma. *The Body Electric: A Personal Journey into the Mysteries of Parapsychological Research, Bioenergy and Kirlian Photography*. Los Angeles: J. P. Tarcher, 1979.

Snellgrove, Brian. *The Unseen Self: Kirlian Photography Explained*. London: C. W. Daniel Company, 1996.

KNOCK (IRELAND)

In 1879 Knock, a relatively small community in County Mayo, Ireland, became the scene of an apparition of the Virgin Mary that occurred on the evening of August 21, 1879. It began as two women, Mary McLoughlin and Mary Beirne, strolled by a local church in the late afternoon. At the gable end of the building, they saw three luminous figures, one of whom they identified as the Virgin and the others as Joseph and John the Evangelist. They watched for some time, but as darkness approached Mary Beirne left to inform her family of what was happening, and soon various neighbors came to the church, even though it was raining. Some of the neighbors discerned an altar with a young lamb on it and a cross in the moving scene, and one boy claimed to see angels over the altar. There was no sound, and none of the figures spoke. The luminous scene continued for several hours, and it was later noted that a farmer a half-mile away had also seen the light at the back of the church.

The experiences of the people who gathered at the church were broadcast around the village and subsequently became the subject of a lengthy investigation by the Archbishop of Tuam, who initially refused to make any statements for or against the event. Two commissions, one soon after the apparition and a second in 1936, concluded that the witnesses were basically trustworthy. Over the years, Knock became a place of pilgrimage, and Irish nationalists adopted the site as part of their struggle for an independent country. They had Our Lady of Knock declared the Queen of Ireland.

Knock took a major upward step as an important pilgrimage site in the last half of the twentieth century. Knock's parish priest, Monsignor James Horan, led an effort to expand the site and oversaw the building of a new, large church. In 1979 Pope John Paul II gave his blessing to the site with a personal visit.

Horan's efforts stirred a major controversy when he secured government funds to have an airport built near Knock, seen by many as a boondoggle created to serve pilgrims. The controversy died when the airport became a commercial success. Knock has now become one of the building blocks of Marian theology in the Roman Catholic Church. It is often compared to the apparition at Pontmain, France, which occurred in 1871, as both occurred in the evening with no words being spoken.

Sources:

Curtayne, Alice. *The Story of Knock*. New York: Scapular Press, 1956.

McShane, John. *Our Lady of Knock*. Indianapolis, IN: Brigittine Press, 1948.

Neary, Tom. *The Shrine of Our Lady of Knock Guide Book*. Knock, Ireland: Custodians of Knock Shrine, 1979.

Smith, William. *The Mystery of Knock*. New York: The Paulist Press, 1954.

Walsh, Rev. Michael. *The Apparition at Knock: A Survey of Facts and Evidence*. 2nd ed. Tuam, Ireland: St. Jarlath's College, 1959.

KUAN YIN

Few divine entities, even Gautama Buddha himself, can compete in popularity with Kuan Yin or Avalokitesvara, the goddess/god of compassion in the Mahayana Buddhist world. Kuan Yin represents the female aspect, and Avalokitesvara represents the male. Statues of Kuan Yin/Avalokitesvara can be found in the great majority of Buddhist temples in China and Japan, and images of the goddess/god permeate the culture. Kuan Yin's role is often compared to that of the Virgin Mary in Roman Catholicism. Kuan Yin is a bodhisattva, an enlightened being who has given up her own attainment of heaven/nirvana to assist others on their pilgrimage through life. In Japan she is known as Kannon.

The worship of Avalokitesvara found its way to China in the third century, where it became especially identified with the Pure Land sect, which offered members the goal of rebirth in the heavenly Western Paradise. Three bodhisattvas—Ameda Buddha, Mahasthamaprapta, and Avalokitesvara—are central to Pure Land practice. As the lord of compassion, Avalokitesvara is seen as an emanation of Amita Buddha (the leader of Pure Land) and as the guard of the world in the time between the departure of the historical Buddha and the future appearance of the coming Buddha, Maitreya.

The Lotus Sutra, a Buddhist writing that appeared in 406 CE, introduced Kuan Yin. In the next centuries, Kuan Yin would be reconceptualized as a female and identified with Avalokitesvara. Vajrayana Buddhists (most identified with Tibet but widely diffused in China in the eighth and ninth centuries) popularized Kuan Yin as a beautiful, white-robed goddess, and by the ninth century a statue of Kuan Yin graced most Chinese Buddhist monasteries.

The transformation of the male Avalokitesvara into the female Kuan Yin was aided by the story of Miao Shan, an eighth-century Chinese princess. She seems to be the source of the feminine representation of Kuan Yin (aka Quan Shi Yin or Kwan Yin). Beginning in the twelfth century, Buddhist monks settled on Putuo Shan, an island off the coast of Zhejiang and south of Shanghai, where Miao Shan lived and devoted her life to healing and to saving sailors from shipwrecks. They spearheaded the spread of the veneration of Kuan Yin through northern China. As her worship spread, her attributes multiplied, though most were extensions of her perceived compassion and attention to the most helpless in society. She has, for example, been seen as helping barren women and is often, like the Virgin Mary, pictured with a child in her arms.

The many images of Kuan Yin vary according to which attribute is being emphasized. As the omnipresent divine Mother, she is seen with multiple eyes and a thousand arms. She may be pictured, for example, with a white lotus (a symbol of purity), a dove (fertility), a vase (to pour out mercy), or a rosary (to call upon the many Buddhas for assistance). From China, veneration has spread to Japan, Korea, Taiwan, and since the nineteenth century, the West, where her name has become synonymous with miraculous occurrences and the expressions of compassion by Buddhists toward their neighbors.

The primary Kuan Yin center remains at Putuo Shan. It has been identified with Potalaka, the mythical island cited as Kuan Yin's home in various Buddhist writings of the eighth and ninth centuries CE. The pilgrim to contemporary Putuo Shan will find a number of monasteries and temples dedicated to her veneration. Those who visit the island, in the relatively tolerant atmosphere

The Mahayana Buddhist goddess Kuan Yin is depicted in statues and other artworks throughout Asia and around the world. Kuan Yin has come to represent the female side of Avalokitesvara and is one of three bodhisattvas associated with the Pure Land sect. *Time Life Pictures/Getty Images.*

that has arisen in China since the end of the Cultural Revolution, often hope to be granted a vision of the goddess. Specific locations on the island have been identified as especially auspicious sites for having such visions.

Kuan Yin temples may now be found around the world. Prominent examples include the Kannon temples in northern Tokyo and in Kamakura; the temple on Waterloo Street in Singapore; Kek Lok Si Temple in Penang, Malaysia; and the Kuan Yin Temple in Honolulu, Hawaii, one of the oldest functioning Buddhist temples in the United States.

Sources:

Blofeld, John. *Bodhisattva of Compassion: The Mystical Tradition of Kuan Yin*. Boulder, CO: Shambhala, 1978.

Karcher, Stephen. *Kuan Yin*. London: Time Warner, 2003.

Palmer, Martin, Jay Ramsey, and Man-Ho Kwok. *Kuan Yin: Myths and Prophecies of the Chinese Goddess of Compassion*. San Francisco, CA: Thorsons, 1995.

Yu, Chun-Fang. *Kuan Yin*. New York: Columbia University Press, 2000.

KUHLMAN, KATHRYN (1907–1976)

In the early 1970s, as the Charismatic movement emerged in North America, few in the new Charismatic community could draw a crowd like Kathryn Kuhlman. Her own rising career as a healing evangelist merged with that of the movement in which she found a home. Kuhlman had been born in Concordia, a suburb of St. Louis, Missouri, on May 7, 1907. Even in her childhood years she expressed a desire to become a minister, and at the age of fifteen she dropped out of school and began preaching. Prejudice against female preachers was almost universal, and she could not find a church to ordain her or license her evangelical work. She preached in those churches that would hear her. After more than twenty years as an independent minister, Kuhlman was preaching in Franklin, Pennsylvania in 1946 when a woman stood up in the service and claimed that she had been healed. In the next years, Kuhlman centered her work in Pittsburgh, where she preached regularly at the Carnegie Auditorium.

As the number of healings increased, Kuhlman and her audiences began to experience two very different realities. Those who attended her services would listen to her sermons and then sit through a time in which Kuhlman would call out people seemingly at random in the audience and pronounce them cured of various ailments. Kuhlman herself would, as her sermon proceeded, experience a radical shift of consciousness that would separate from her body and seem to float above the audience. Meanwhile, another consciousness would take over her body and direct the healing service. She did little study of what was happening to her, feeling that if she came to understand it, the healings would go away.

Kuhlman's rise from obscurity began in 1962 after her first book, *I Believe in Miracles*, appeared. Journalist Allen Spraggett then penned a very sympathetic biography in 1971. Through the 1970s she regularly spoke to large audiences around the United States, and through the mid-1970s she had a television show that featured people who had been healed in her meetings.

At the height of her fame, a physician named William Nolen included Kuhlman in his study of contemporary healers, and he attacked the validity of many of their claims. Among cases he investigated, he discovered people whose condition before their healing could not be documented and others who had subsequently passed away from the disease from which they had supposedly been cured. Nolen's book came out in 1975. Unfortunately, Kuhlman herself died the next year of heart disease. She continued to be remembered kindly in Charismatic circles. One of her associates, **BENNY HINN**, has continued her healing ministry.

Sources:

Kuhlman, Kathryn. *God Can Do It Again*. Englewood Cliffs, NJ: Prentice-Hall, 1969.

———. *I Believe in Miracles*. Englewood Cliffs, NJ: Prentice-Hall, 1962.

The Kumbh Mela festival recalls the Hindu story of a battle between gods and demons for the nectar of immortality known as *amrita*. Part of the festival involves taking ceremonial baths at one of the four cities in India where drops of *amrita* fell to earth. *AFP/Getty Images*.

———. *Nothing Is Impossible with God.* Englewood Cliffs, NJ: Prentice-Hall, 1974.

Nolen, William. *Healing: A Doctor in Search of a Miracle.* New York: Random House, 1975.

Spraggett, Allen. *Kathryn Kuhlman: The Woman Who Believes in Miracles.* New York: Thomas Y. Crowell, 1970.

Warner, Wayne. *Kathryn Kuhlman: The Woman Behind the Miracles.* Ann Arbor, MI: Servant Publications, 1993.

KUMBH MELA

In India, a story is told of ancient times in which the various supernatural beings agreed to contribute to a common task of obtaining the nectar of immortality (called *amrita*). They gathered a pot of the sacred substance, but some demons decided to keep the amrita for themselves and tried to run away with it. The gods pursued the demons, and a battle ensued that lasted twelve days. During this battle, drops of amrita fell on four locations, now the sites of four cities: Prayag (near the city of Allahabad, in the state of Uttar Pradesh), **HARDWAR** (in Uttar Pradesh), Ujjain (in Madhya Pradesh), and Nasik (in Maharashtra).

Each of these four sites, located on the bank of a major river, now hosts the Kumbh Mela festival that celebrates the battle of the gods for the pots of amrita. At different times during the twelve-year cycle (symbolic of the twelve days of battle), the festival convenes in one of the four cities, the exact site and date being determined by the movement of the planet Jupiter astrologically. These gatherings, which occur approximately every three years, are the largest pilgrimage gatherings in the world, with as many as thirty million pilgrims in attendance.

The festival is marked by the presence of thousands of Hindu holy men and women designated by different names, such as monks, saints, and SADHUS. The holy people are also called *tirthas*, which means they are seen as contact points between earthly and divine realities. They will pick a spot from which to teach and conduct DARSHAN, in which disciples gather to sit in their teacher's presence, during the early days of the festival.

The time of the Kumbh Mela includes a mélange of religious activities, although the primary activity in which most people participate is a ritual bath that is to be taken on one specific day. At the specified day at the most auspicious hour, thousands of holy men from many different Hindu sectarian groups take their ceremonial bath. Immediately thereafter, millions of festival attendees will attempt also to take their bath. The most negative aspect of the festival has been the periodic deaths of people who are trampled in the rush to the river.

The festival at Prayag is identified with the ninth-century philosopher Sankaracharaya (788–820 CE). He had encouraged a gathering of holy men at the four monasteries he had established, but these were located at sites significantly remote from each other. Hence a more central location, Prawag, was chosen. During the next centuries similar riverside gatherings were originated and maintained by various lesser-known holy men. One goal of these gatherings was the creation of mutual respect and understanding of the different segments of Hinduism.

Sources:

Ghosh, Ashim. *Kumbh Mela.* Calcutta: Rupa & Company, 2001.

Govind, Swarup. *Nashik Kumbh Mela: A Spiritual Sojourn.* Mumbai: India Book House, 2003.

Tully, Mark. *Kumbh Mela.* Varanasi: Indica Books, 2001.

KUSINAGARA (INDIA)

Gautama Buddha (c. 563–c. 483 BCE), after a long and successful life in laying the foundations of Buddhism, spent his last days at Kusinagara, a town in eastern Uttar Pradesh, where he delivered a number of important discourses, including the Mahaparinirvana Sutra, on the subject of diligence, and admitted the last followers to be received as Buddhists by him personally. Following the Buddha's death, his body was cremated and the remains divided among eight Buddhist kings from different parts of India. Some of his ashes were enshrined at Kusinagara.

The importance of Kusinagara was expanded during the reign of the Buddhist King Asoka in the third century BCE. He initiated a period during which most of the religious structures in the community were constructed. It remained an active Buddhist center for many centuries, until the Buddhist community was destroyed during the years of Muslim rule beginning in the ninth century. For almost a thousand years Kusinagara was lost in the jungles. It was relocated in 1880 by British explorers. Extensive excavations have uncovered the remains of a large monastic community that survived into the eleventh century.

Today, two important ancient remains are the focus of believers' attention. The Chankhandi Stupa marks the spot where many believe that Buddha was cremated. In the midst of the ruins is a large pillar originally erected by King Asoka. None of the Buddha's relics that had been placed in the STUPA are known to exist. Close by is the Mahaparinirvana Temple, in the midst of which was found a large statue of a reclining Buddha. In 1927 Burmese Buddhists rebuilt the temple.

Indian, Japanese, and Sri Lankan Buddhists have jointly built a modern Buddhist center to welcome pilgrims and facilitate their visit. In 1994, to commemorate the fiftieth anniversary of the enthronement of King Bhumibhol Adulyadej of Thailand and to contribute to the effort to reestablish Buddhism in India, Thai Buddhists constructed Wat Thai Kusinara Chalermraj, one of several contemporary Buddhist temples now in Kusinagara.

Sources:

Majupuria, Trilok Chandra. *Holy Places of Buddhism in Nepal and India: A Guide to Sacred Places in Buddha's Lands*. Columbia, MO: South Asia Books, 1987.

Panabokke, Gunaratne. *History of the Buddhist Sangha in India and Sri Lanka*. Dalugama, Kelaniya, Sri Lanka: Postgraduate Institute of Pali and Buddhist Studies, University of Kelaniya, 1993.

Tulku, Tarthang, ed. *Holy Places of the Buddha*. Vol. 9: *Crystal Mirror*. Berkeley, CA: Dharma Publishing, 1994.

LABYRINTH

A labyrinth is an intricate structure that may include chambers and passageways and is often constructed to perplex and confuse anyone within it. The classical labyrinth is circular, with an entrance and passageways that carry the person along paths parallel to the circumference but ever closer to the center. The idea of a labyrinth as a maze comes from the fact that throughout the maze, the person will find a number of blind alleys. In the modern world, labyrinth-like mazes have been adapted as games, with many shapes and many levels of complexity.

In adapting the labyrinth as a religious tool, most modern exponents draw a distinction between the labyrinth and the maze. While the two are similar at first glance, the maze is seen as a puzzle to be solved with numerous twists and turns, and most importantly, choices between junctions, the wrong choice being a blind alley. Mazes are multicursal; there are many paths. Labyrinths, on the other hand, are unicursal. While possessing a more or less elaborate pattern, they have only one path that leads to the center and bring one out again. As such, the labyrinth becomes a metaphor for pilgrimage. In walking the labyrinth's path, one is making a spiritual journey to the deepest levels of the self or a spiritual reality. The return path brings one back to mundane reality with a new understanding of the self in the world.

Modern proponents look to the labyrinth at CHARTRES CATHEDRAL as a particularly important example of a religious labyrinth. The builders of Chartres integrated a labyrinth in the blue and white stones used for the Cathedral's floor, near the entrance at the west end of the nave and adjacent to the baptismal font. This labyrinth (like similar labyrinths in other gothic church buildings) was created in the context of a medieval emphasis on pilgrimage. Many who might want to go on pilgrimage were prevented by various reasons. The labyrinth could be walked, sometimes the path being covered on one's knees, as a substitute for an actual pilgrimage. The labyrinth at Chartres was used as a substitute for a trip to Jerusalem, a most dangerous pilgrimage site at various times during the centuries of and following the Crusades. The Chartres labyrinth consists of twelve rings. The path slowly takes the pilgrim to a rosette in the middle. Along the path one makes twenty-eight loops, taking on along a complex pattern that moves back and forth across the labyrinth from close to the center and back toward the outside and finally to the center.

Similar to mazes, except they only have one path to the center and out again, labyrinths serve as religious symbols for holy pilgrimages. *Fortean Picture Library.*

Use of labyrinths fell to a low point in the eighteenth century, but they have been revived in the last half of the twentieth century by both Christians and students of the Esoteric realms who share an interest in inner spiritual explorations. For example, Esoteric believers frequently look to what is known as the classical Cretan labyrinth, associated with the ancient Greek story of the Minotaur. According to the stories, King Minos of Crete had a labyrinth constructed to house the half-bull, half-human offspring of his wife Pasiphae and a bull. He then confined Daedalus (who designed the labyrinth) and his son Icarus in the Labyrinth. The two made wings of feathers and wax and flew to freedom, but Icarus then flew too close to the sun

and died when the sun melted the wax that held his wings together. At a later date, Theseus, the son of the king of Athens, joined the human tribute paid by Athens to Crete. Put in the labyrinth, he killed the Minotaur and used a ball of string to find his way out.

The labyrinth described in the Minotaur stories is obviously a maze. What is put forth today as the classical Cretan labyrinth is a unicursal labyrinth that takes one around the center seven times before midpoint is reached. It is a mathematically abstract representation of the labyrinth from the myth that was displayed embossed on Cretan pottery and coins. The seven circuits thus become easily associated with a variety of eso-

THE ENCYCLOPEDIA OF RELIGIOUS PHENOMENA

teric realities: the seven colors of the rainbow, the seven chakras, and numerous magical correspondences.

Christian proponents of the labyrinth see it primarily as a tool for meditating on one's presence with God. The most notable contemporary labyrinths are to be found in Anglican churches such as the Cathedral of Saint Philip in Atlanta, Georgia, and Grace Cathedral in San Francisco. Grace Cathedral has two full-size replicas of the Charters labyrinth, one outside and one inside the cathedral, and is home to Veriditas, an association of people who actively use the labyrinth and train people to facilitate it as a spiritual tool.

Sources:

Artress, Lauren. *Walking a Sacred Path: Rediscovering the Labyrinth as a Spiritual Tool.* New York: Riverhead Books, 1996.

Geoffrion, Jill Kimberly Hartwell. *Praying the Labyrinth: A Journal for Spiritual Exploration.* Cleveland, OH: United Church Press, 1999.

West, Melissa Gayle. *Exploring the Labyrinth: A Guide for Healing and Spiritual Growth.* New York: Broadway, 2000.

Westbury, Virginia. *Labyrinths: Ancient Paths of Wisdom and Peace.* Philadelphia: Da Capo Press, 2003.

LAKE, JOHN GRAHAM (1870–1935)

Pioneer Pentecostal healer John Graham Lake was born on March 18, 1870, in Ontario, Canada, but grew up in Michigan, were his family relocated during his childhood. He experienced Christian salvation through the Salvation Army. He trained for the ministry but decided to become a businessman, first with a newspaper and then in real estate.

Happiness eluded him during this period of his life. Eight of his fifteen brothers and sisters died of various childhood illnesses. And as he began married life, a brother was an invalid, and two of his sisters had been diagnosed with serious problems. A short time later, he learned his wife had tuberculosis. Then in 1899, his brother was healed after a visit to John Alexander Dowie (1847–1907), a Chicago preacher with a healing ministry. In subsequent visits, his two sisters were healed. Finally, his wife was healed, although tuberculosis was still an incurable disease at the time.

As a result of these healings and his own study of the scripture, Lake joined the staff of Dowie's Church and then began a branch in Sault Ste. Marie, Michigan. In 1904 he moved to Chicago. Four years later, having experienced a Pentecostal baptism of the Holy Spirit in 1907, he went to Africa, where over the next five years he had a spectacular ministry in starting congregations (more than six hundred) and training local ministers (1,250) to serve the millions of converts. Out of his work came a spectrum of churches known in southern Africa as the Apostolic and Zionists church, through which Pentecostalism was introduced to the continent.

Lake's wife died in 1908, having given birth to seven children. In 1913, Lake saw the need to devote more time to his family, and he retired from his African work to return to the United States. He remarried and settled in Spokane, Washington. It is estimated that over one hundred thousand people traveled to Spokane to participate in his healing services.

In 1920 he moved to Portland, Oregon, where for a time he experienced the same success he'd had in Spokane. He eventually retired to Spokane, where he lived his final years, dying there on September 15, 1935.

Sources:

Lake, John G. *John G. Lake: The Complete Collection of His Life Teachings.* Comp. by Roberts Liardon. Tulsa, OK: Albury Publishing, 1998.

———. *John G. Lake: His Life, His Sermons, His Boldness of Faith.* Ed. by Kenneth Copeland. Fort Worth: TX: Kenneth Copeland Publications, 1994.

Reidt, Wilford H. *John G. Lake: A Man without Compromise.* Tulsa, OK: Harrison House, 1989.

LALIBELA (ETHIOPIA)

Among the most spectacular holy sites in the world are a group of eleven churches that have been carved out of rock of the Lasta Mountains some 250 miles north of Addis Ababa, Ethiopia. The origin of these buildings is ascribed to King Lalibela (c. 1185–1225), a ruler of the Zagwe dynasty, which had come to power a century before his reign. Popular legends assert that the rulers of the Zagwe dynasty were the descendants of the handmaid of the Queen of Sheba, though there is no evident to support the claim.

During his reign, Lalibela made a pilgrimage to Jerusalem, a trip that deeply affected his psyche. One of his first actions subsequently was to rename the stream that flowed through the city of Roha (a name reflecting the red volcanic rock that underlies the town), from which he ruled the land, after the Jordan River. He renamed a local hill after the Mount of Olives. His efforts to create a second Jerusalem culminated in the carving of the eleven churches. Seven of the churches were carved straight into the cliffs of the mountain. Their sanctuaries weave deep into the hillside. Four of the churches were carved from blocks of the volcanic rock that were isolated by excavating downward. The churches are connected to each other by small passages and tunnels. The entire project took twenty-four years.

While the trip to Jerusalem was the occasion of the church building, Lalibela hagiography looks to a vision the king had early in his life. His older brother, the previous king, tried to poison Lalibela. Instead of dying, Lalibela was carried by an angel to heaven, where he was shown the work he would later accomplish.

Following the completion of the churches, Lalibela abdicated his throne and assumed the role of a hermit. He spent the rest of his life in the holy space he had created. The Ethiopian Orthodox Church later canonized Lalibela and renamed the city in his honor. When the Zagwe Dynasty came to an end in the thirteenth century, political power moved southward, but Lalibela remained the spiritual heart of Ethiopian Orthodoxy.

Thousands of pilgrims visit Lalibela the year round, but especially in the two weeks following Christmas. Most of the churches remain in good condition, and much of the original decoration of the interiors has survived. The United Nations Educational, Scientific, and Cultural Organization (UNESCO) has ranked the churches the eighth most unique historical site in the world. A select set of pilgrims, young women, make their way to the pool outside of the Church of Saint Mary, where many will spend the night immersed in the pool in hopes of ending their barrenness. All the churches are still active centers of worship.

Sources:

Findlay, L. *The Monolithic Churches of Lalibela in Ethiopia.* Cairo, 1943.

Gerster, Georg. *Churches in Rock: Early Christian Art in Ethiopia.* London: Phaidon, 1970.

Irmgard, Bidder. *Lalibela: The Monolithic Churches of Ethiopia.* Cologne: M. DuMont Schauberg, 1958.

LA SALETTE (FRANCE)

On September 19, 1846, the mountain of La Salette in southeastern France became the site of an important and still controversial apparition of the Virgin Mary. The visionaries were two young shepherds, Melanie Calvat (d. 1904), then fourteen years old, and Maximin Giraud (d. 1875), then eleven. The Virgin appeared out of a globe of light, seated with her head in her hands. She was dressed in a white, pearl-studded dress with a tiara on her head. She wore a crucifix around her neck.

The Virgin delivered a simple message aimed at the growing practice of people working on Sunday and the rise of public blasphemy, which would be met with punishments in the form of famine and damage to crops. The children were told to spread this brief public message. However, the Virgin also gave each of them a secret message of greater length. They did not initially divulge these messages, but would tell them to Pope Pius

This statue in La Salette, France, commemorates the apparition of the Virgin Mary, who visited two young girls in 1846. The incident inspired the founding of the Missionaries of La Salette. *Roger Violett/Getty Images.*

IX in 1851. As has been common, the local bishop established a commission to investigate the apparitions, and in the face of opposition to his investigation, he later established a second commission to reexamine the event. In 1846 he approved the development of devotion to Our Lady of La Salette, and in spite of critics in both the secular and church community, the building of a church on the site commenced in 1852.

While devotion to the Virgin at La Salette developed, much interest focused on the secrets and their content. Maximin's secret predicted France's fall into apostasy and unbelief and the coming of the Antichrist. The more lengthy secret given to Melanie saw evil times approaching for Europe, especially France and Italy, and bemoaned the loss of piety and zeal by the priests of the church. There were a variety of specific prophecies. The continuing controversy concerning the apparition led Melanie to move to Italy, where she published what purported to be the text of the secret in 1879.

The 1879 publication lifted the controversy to a new stage. Immediately, critics attacked the text by claiming it varied significantly from the 1851 text sent to Pius IX, having been heavily influenced by Melanie's reading of apocalyptic literature and other questionable materials. Many bishops in France took action against the 1879 publication and those who believed it. After Melanie's death in Italy in 1904, the controversy eventually died out, the secret moved into oblivion, and the veneration of the Virgin of La Salette continued based upon the public message.

The church at the site of the apparition became the base of a new religious order, Missionaries of La Salette, although during the controversy over the secret the order was driven out of the land and its personnel replaced by secular priests. The Missionaries of La Salette continues today as an international religious organization.

Sources:

Bloy, Leon. *She Who Weeps: Our Lady of Salette*. Fresno, CA: Academy Library Guild, 1956.

Dion, Henri. *Maximin Giraud, berger de La Salette, ou La fidelité dans l'épreuve*. Montsura, France: Editions Resiac, 1988.

LATIHAN

Latihan is the name given to the major spiritual exercise practiced by the Subud religion. Subud emerged early in the twentieth century as one of a number of new spiritual movements in Indonesia. It was founded by R. M. Muhammad Subuh Sumohadiwidjojo (1901–1987), generally called simply Pak Subuh. It was brought to the West at the end of the 1950s through the efforts of English linguist Husein Rofé and John G. Bennett, a student of George I. Gurdjieff. Bennett took seriously Gurdjieff's admonition to watch for a teacher to come from Indonesia, then known as the Dutch East Indies.

The latihan follows the impulse of Pak Subuh's original experience of the power of God and is described as releasing the primordial power that is latent in everyone. When the power manifests, the body will react. It might cause any one of hundreds of different body movements, from the graceful to the grotesque. The manifesting power might also lead to various vocalizations or emotional expressions. Initially, the manifestations may be cathartic and assume their more unpleasant forms. However, over time the movements become a manifestation of tranquility, joy, and oneness with the divine.

The latihan is seen as completely spontaneous. It cannot be taught or learned, but it can be transmitted from one person to another. Any person wishing to receive it (termed "being opened") will stand in the presence of someone who has been opened previously. The new person assumes a receptive state and allows whatever occurs to occur.

Adherents of Subud generally gather twice a week to experience the latihan with fellow believers. Generally, men and women meet separately.

Sources:

Bennett, J.G. *Concerning Subud*. New York: Hodder & Stoughton, 1959.

Crouse, Roseanna. *The Flowering of the Latihan of Subud*. Palm Springs, CA: Undiscovered Worlds Press, 1990.

Geels, Antoon. *Subud and the Javanese Mystical Tradition*. Richmond, UK: Curzon Press, 1997.

Rofé, Husein. *The Path of Subud*. London: Rider & Co., 1988.

LAYING ON OF HANDS

The laying on of hands is a ritual symbolic activity used primarily in the Christian tradition for a variety of purposes that are tied together by a belief that the Holy Spirit is active in the process. Two purposes are foremost: that of commissioning a church member for service in the church or world, and the healing of an individual's body, mind, or soul. The practice of the laying on of hands derives from the Bible. For example, the ordination of church leaders is derived from passages such as Numbers 27:18–23, in which God commands Moses to lay his hands on Joshua in a ceremony before the priest, and Acts 6:6, where the church's first deacons are set apart for service.

Over the centuries, as the sacramental system developed, the church's ministerial leadership defined Holy Orders as one of the seven sacraments. Future priests passed through a set of minor and two major orders (deacon and priest). Ordination to each level of the priesthood was accompanied by the laying on of hands, which also was integral to the consecration of a bishop (considered a third major order of ministry). The practice in the Roman Catholic Church was passed to the several Protestant churches. Although the Protestant churches went about the task of reexamining all aspects of the tradition as developed within Roman Catholicism, the many biblical references to laying on of hands made the practice quite acceptable. The laying on of hands for ordaining leadership remains one of the most ubiquitous practices throughout the many denominations of Christian churches.

It was also noted that the laying on of hands frequently accompanied prayer for healing. Jesus laid his hands on those brought to him for healing (Luke 4:40), and in the days of the early church, Ananias was sent to lay his hands on Paul, who had been struck blind following his vision of Christ on the road to Damascus (Acts 9:17). This practice became common in the church, though often done in a perfunctory manner.

An emphasis on prayer and healing had a marked revival at the end of the nineteenth century. Early exponents included Episcopal layman Charles Cullis (1833–1892); German pastor Johan Christoph Blumhardt (1805–1880); A. B. Simpson (1843–1919), founder of the Christian and Missionary Alliance; British Holiness minister William Boardman; and Australian evangelist John Alexander Dowie (1847–1907), the founder of ZION, ILLINOIS. At the beginning of the twentieth century, Rev. Elwood Worcester launched the Emmanuel movement from his parish in Boston, which gave birth to a continuing interest in spiritual healing in the Episcopal Church.

In the twentieth century, the laying on of hands as a practice accompanying prayer for healing has been most noticeable within Pentecostalism. The Pentecostal movement was centered upon the life in the Spirit as pictured in the biblical book of Acts. Members were expected to manifest one or more of the gifts of the Spirit mentioned in 1 Corinthians 12, among which healing was most prominent. The exercise of the healing gift has usually been accompanied with the laying

on of hands, a practice with which the general public had become familiar through its widespread presentation on television, beginning with the healing services of evangelist ORAL ROBERTS in the 1950s.

Pentecostals also use the laying on of hands in prayers for individuals to receive the baptism of the Holy Spirit. The biblical support for this practice is found in many passages in Acts, such as Acts 8:17, which mentions Peter and John placing their hands on some Samaritans who subsequently received the Holy Spirit.

The laying on of hands, especially in healing situations, is frequently accompanied by physical sensations of heat and the passing of energy from one person to the other. The sensations are experienced more often by the one praying for healing than the one for whom prayer is offered. Such experiences are not limited to Christians but are common to most people who practice healing by the laying on of hands, notably in the modern Western Esoteric tradition. This had led some to search for a more mundane explanation for both the experiences of the laying on of hands and the subsequent experiences of healing. Parapsychologists, for example, have run experiments that seek to discover a healing power common to humankind.

The most authoritative experiments in healing were conducted by Bernard Grad, a professor at McGill University in Montreal, who conducted a series of experiments with OSKAR ESTABANY, a Hungarian immigrant who professed to have healing powers. In an effort to take the effects of human psychological responses out of the picture, Grad had Estabany attempt to affect the growth rate of plants and the healing rate of laboratory mice that had been wounded by the removal of a patch of skin. In these double-blind experiments Estabany produced spectacular results. Estabany was later able to produce similar results in experiments with biochemist Justa Smith.

Contemporaneous with Bernard Grad's work, Dolores Krieger, a nurse and member of the Theosophical Society, conducted studies in what she termed therapeutic touch. THERAPEUTIC TOUCH is a form of laying on of hands, but practiced in a very different environment than that of most Christian churches. Krieger offered it in a scientific setting, and the method has subsequently been taught in courses for the training of nurses.

The healing done by people such as Estabany and the nurses trained by Krieger does not appear vastly different from that done in Christian circles, although some Christian healers take great effort to separate themselves from any spiritual healing done in any context other than Christian.

Sources:

Blomgren, David K. *Prophetic Gatherings in the Church: The Laying on of Hands and Prophecy.* Portland, OR: Bible Press, 1979.

Krieger, Dolores. *Accepting Your Power to Heal: The Personal Practice of Therapeutic Touch.* Santa Fe, NM: Bear & Co., 1993.

O'Connor, Edward D. *The Laying on of Hands.* Pecos, NM: Dove Publications, 1969.

Prince, Derek. *Laying on of Hands.* Seattle, WA: The Study Hour, n.d.

Shepherd, M. II., Jr., "Hands: Laying on of Hands." *The Interpreter's Dictionary of the Bible,* Vol. 2. Nashville, TN: Cokesbury, 1962.

LEVITATION

Levitation is the act of ascending into the air and floating in apparent defiance of gravity. While by no means common, it was an effect attributed to many Catholic saints. In most cases, the levitation reported was of a few inches to a few feet and lasted for only a short period of time. In stark contrast were the levitation experiences of Joseph of Cupertino (1603–1663), who on a number of occasions would rise while praying before the altar in his monastery or before the statue of the Virgin Mary. Cupertino was seen to rise above the heads of those witnessing it.

The levitation of objects became one of the phenomena reported to occur in Spiritualist séances, although there was always the explanation that the phenomenon was more closely related to stage magic than anything paranormal. Such explanations did not work as effectively for the occasional report of human levitation. The most spectacular incidents involved DANIEL DUNGLAS HOME (1833–1886), whose most memorable levitation occurred on December 13, 1868, when he was seen to rise and float out of one window on the third floor and around the wall to another, through which he reentered the house. Although frequently analyzed by skeptics, no satisfactory explanation of the event has been put forth. Moreover, it has not be duplicated in the years since.

Alexandra David-Neel visited the Tibetan masters who practiced an exercise known as *lung-gom-pa*, which was mastered during one of the famous three-years seclusions in which many Tibetans engage. Those who engage in this practice, it is noted, grow very light and seem to have no weight. Among the specific exercise that is done in lung-gom-pa involves sitting cross-legged on a cushion. After slowly filling the lungs with air and holding his or her breath, the practitioner jumps up using the crossed legs but not the hands, then returns to the cushion in the same position. That exercise is then repeated multiple times. Practiced Tibetans could jump quite high off the ground. After a long period of practice, the accomplished practitioner was said to be able to travel great distances using the technique, never touching the ground and seeming to float in the air. David-Neel said she observed some accomplished lumg-gom-pa practitioners who operated in a trance state with their attention focused on a distant object toward which they moved.

In the mid-1970s, something like the lumg-gom-pa technique was introduced into the West by Maharishi Mehesh Yogi, the founder of the transcendental meditation (TM) movement. He seemed to be offering those who had first mastered TM a program by which they could learn to levitate. This became one of the most controversial aspects of TM. While informally, the Sidhi program seemed to offer to teach levitation, its promotional material was much more circumspect: "During the first stage of Yogic Flying, the

Whether of a person or an object, levitation is the act of elevating something through paranormal means. It is often an art reportedly practiced at Spiritualist séances. *Fortean Picture Library.*

body lifts up and moves forward in short hops. Subjectively one experiences exhilaration, lightness, and bliss."

The achievement of levitation remains elusive, although the feats of stage magicians continually offer the hope that it is possible. The accounts of those who seem to have levitated in the past remain, but they remain in the past. No one in the present generation has demonstrated the power, a fact that calls into question even the best accounts of the past.

Sources:

Gardner, Martin. *On the Wild Side: The Big Bang, ESP, the Beast 666, Levitation, Rainmaking, Trance-Channeling, Séances and Ghosts, and More.* Amherst, NY: Prometheus Books, 1992.

Leroy, Oliver. *Levitation.* London: Oates & Washbourne, 1928.

Orme-Johnson, D.W., and P. Gelderloos. "Topographic EEG Brain Mapping during Yogic Flying." *International Journal of Neuroscience* 38 (1988): 427–434.

Richards, Steve. *Levitation: What It Is, How It Works, How to Do It.* London: Aquarian Press, 1983.

LINDSEY, GORDON J.

Pentecostal minister Gordon J. Lindsey emerged in the 1950s as one of the most important proponents of miraculous healing, though his work was largely in the background and thus not as well known as that of his contemporaries, such as William Marion Branham or **ORAL ROBERTS**. Lindsey was born at Zion, Illinois, the community founded by pioneer healer John Alexander Dowie. His family moved during his childhood years and for a time stayed in southern California as members of the Pisgah Grande Christian commune.

Lindsey was fourteen when he first heard **JOHN GRAHAM LAKE**, an early Pentecostal healer from the West Coast. Soon afterward, he received the baptism of the Holy Spirit and spoke in tongues. Within a few years he had become a full-time Pentecostal evangelist. He eventually married a woman who was a member of the church founded by **AIMEE SEMPLE MCPHERSON**, another prominent West Coast healer.

Lindsey began to move out of obscurity in the years after World War II. He was pastoring a small church in Ashland, Oregon, when he met William Branham. Impressed, he left the pas-

torate and became Branham's manager and the editor of a new periodical, *Leaves of Healing*, heralding the emergence of a new wave of spiritual healing activity in the larger Pentecostal movement. The following year he founded the Voice of Healing Fellowship and began organizing annual conventions. The fellowship's headquarters, established in Dallas in 1952, became the publishing center advocating not only Branham, but a host of new healing evangelists that soon came on the scene, such as Oral Roberts, Morris Cerullo, and Velmer Gardner.

In 1962 the Voice of Healing Fellowship was superseded by the Full Gospel Fellowship of ministers and churches, a new Pentecostal denomination. In 1966 the many far-flung ministries that Lindsey had initiated were brought together under a new umbrella organization, Christ for the Nations. Lindsey died in 1973, but his work was carried on by his very capable spouse. Over the next decades, Freda Lindsey emerged as a leader in her own right and built the ministries initiated by her husband into a major force in the Pentecostal world.

Sources:

Harrell, David Edwin, Jr. *All Things Are Possible.* Bloomington, IN: Indiana University Press, 1975.

Lindsey, Freda. *My Diary Secrets.* Dallas: Christ for the Nations, 1976.

Lindsey, Gordon. *The Gordon Lindsey Story.* Dallas: Christ for the Nations, 1983.

LOCUTIONS

Locutions are messages heard by an individual and believed to be from a supernatural or divine source (as opposed to apparitions, which are seen). Such locutions may be heard as external sounds, perceived as words imprinted on the imaginative faculty, or concepts or truths that a person realizes but must then formulate into words. Of these three, the second is the most common. It is often a component of a total encounter with an angelic or divine being, such as the Virgin Mary, that also includes an apparition. For example, Bernadette Soubirous, who saw the Virgin at Lourdes, was said to have received the message accompanying the apparition as words received in her heart. Among the many people who had locutions and also described and commented on the process was Saint Teresa of Avila (1515–1582).

One modern example of locutions can be seen in the experience of Fr. Stefano Gobbi. A priest in Milan, Italy, Gobbi heard his first locution in 1972 during a moment of concern for some former priests who were organizing against the Catholic Church. The Virgin Mary told him to take refuge in the Immaculate Heart of Mary. Similar locutions continued, and the next year he began to keep a record of the messages. The messages motivated him to form an association of priests ready to consecrate themselves to her Immaculate Heart and encourage the laity to be so consecrated and to strengthen their bond to the pope and the church. The association's first meeting took place in September 1973, and the movement spread worldwide as the Marian Movement of Priests.

In sharp contrast to Gobbi is William Kamm (b. 1950), an Australian Roman Catholic layperson and founder of the Order of Saint Charbel. Kamm was born in Germany and claims to have begun having mystical experiences as a teenager in 1968. Having moved to Australia, a few years later he founded a program called the Marian Work of Atonement. Over the years, the Virgin Mary appeared to him and on numerous occasions spoke to him. By the end of the 1990s, he had received more than six hundred locutions covering a wide range of issues about personal piety and behavior, but most notably on the future of the Catholic Church. In 1982 he was given the designation Little Pebble, which has been understood as a reference to Saint Peter (believed by Roman Catholics to be the first pope), whom Jesus called the Rock. Messages also suggested that Kamm was to be the next pope after John Paul II.

Kamm's messages increasingly placed him in tension with Roman Catholic authorities. Adding to the issues raised by the publishing of various messages that challenged the church's authority and even orthodox teachings, in the mid-1990s he was caught in an adulterous relationship that led to his divorce and public statements justifying his adultery.

In 2000 the Most Rev. Philip Wilson, the Bishop of Wollongong, established a commission to examine Kamm and his writings. As a result of their negative conclusions, the Bishop ordered him to cease his work, close the religious order he had founded, and refrain from making any statements implying that the Catholic Church approved of what he was or had done. Wilson went on to state that after examinations going back to 1984 and reaching offices in Rome, the church had concluded that Kamm's locutions were not supernatural, the content was false, and his work was harmful to the church's membership.

Kamm, of course, is only one of a number of people around the world who claim to receive private revelation from Mary, Jesus, one of the saints, or an angelic being. As a whole, the church makes no appraisal of these revelations as long as they remain largely unpublicized and no obvious teachings that contradict Catholic teachings are evident.

Sources:

Gobbi, Stefano. *To the Priests Our Lady's Beloved Sons.* 17th edition. St. Francis, ME: National Headquarters of the Marian Movement of Priests in the United States, 1996.

The "Last Pebble": The Official Publication of Petrus Romanus, the Last Pope. 2 vols. Australia: William Kamm, 1999.

Teresa of Avila. *The Life of St. Teresa of Avila, including the Relations of Her Spiritual State.* London: Burns & Oates, 1962.

LORETO (ITALY)

Loreto is a small town south of Ancona on the Adriatic coast of Italy that many believe received the house in which Mary was told of the future birth of Jesus. The miracle transportation of the house is said to have occurred in 1294, and since the fifteenth century, when Pope Julius II gave his approval, the town has become a growing site of pilgrimages.

The story of Mary's house begins in 330 CE, when **HELENA**, the mother of the Emperor Constantine and a recent convert to Christianity, traveled to the Holy Land. Among the many relics of the life of Jesus she reportedly uncovered was the home in which Jesus grew up at Nazareth. She then saw to the construction of a church to protect the site. While not as important as other Holy Land sites, it would remain a pilgrimage site into the thirteenth century. In 1187 Nazareth was taken by Muslims. Pilgrimages were not allowed for a generation, but they resumed for a period in the next century. In 1263 the church that had been built by the Crusaders at the beginning of the twelfth century was destroyed.

Then, on May 10, 1291, the house at Nazareth is said to have suddenly disappeared. Writing in 1472, Pietro di Giorgio Tolomei of Teramo recounted the travel of a group of men from Loreto traveling to the Holy Land and discovering a sign at the Nazareth location saying the house had disappeared. It was said to have suddenly reappeared in the town of Tersatto (now in Croatia), where it remained for three years. On December 10, 1294, the house disappeared again, only to reappear in Recanati, where it would stay only a matter of days before moving again to Loreto. Supposedly, in 1296 Mary appeared to a man in Loreto in a dream and revealed the origin of the house to him. His story led to the pilgrimage of the men from Loreto to Nazareth to look for the site and measure the size of the foundations of the building that had disappeared from there. The retelling of this story in 1472 served to establish the Loreto location as the new location of the home.

Since Pope Julius' approval, pilgrimages have grown, and Loreto has been integrated into Marian piety. A sixteenth-century litany, the Litany of Loreto, was adopted for use at the shrine, and it, too, became integral to Marian piety in many locations. The building at Loreto also took up the slack caused by the loss of the replica of **MARY'S HOUSE** that had been constructed in Walsingham, England, but destroyed when Henry VIII despoiled the monasteries in 1538. In 1938 Loreto was again elevated, and pilgrims may now receive the same indulgences for their trek there as if they had gone to the Holy Land or to **LOURDES**.

The house at Loreto is made of limestone and cedar. The cedar does not grow in that area of Italy, but was common in the Holy Land. The one-room house now contains a statue of the Virgin. It is completely enclosed in a church building. Some four million pilgrims visit annually.

Sources:

Hutchinson, William Aubrey. *Loreto and Nazareth*. London: F. Dillion, 1863.

Monelli, Nanni. *La Santa Casa a Loreto, La Santa casa a Nazareth*. Loreto: Congregazione Universale della Santa Casa, 1997.

Thornton, Francis B., ed. *Our Lady of Loreto: Shrines of the World*. St. Paul, MN: Catholic Digest, 1958.

LOURDES (FRANCE)

Possibly the most well-known apparition of the Virgin Mary occurred at Lourdes, a small town in southern France near the Spanish border. Here a young girl, Bernadette Soubirous (1844–1879), had visions of the Virgin over a period of six months in 1858. The initial vision occurred on February 11, within days of her receiving her first communion. As she searched for wood near a grotto, a moving rosebush caught her attention, and shortly thereafter a young and beautiful woman appeared above the rosebush. Bernadette dropped to her knees and began to pray, the woman joining in. The woman then disappeared.

Over the next six months, the Lady appeared on eighteen occasions. She began to speak to Bernadette during the third apparition. During her ninth appearance, the Lady told Bernadette to dig in the ground, then drink from and bathe in the water that would emerge. The spring that subsequently emerged was designated as a healing spring of water for all, and a chapel was to be built at the site.

When the naïve and somewhat ignorant Bernadette asked the local priest to build the chapel requested by the unknown woman, the priest instructed Bernadette to inquire as to the identity of the Lady. In the last apparition the Lady identified herself as the Immaculate Conception. The concept of immaculate conception, that the Virgin Mary had been born without original sin, was then being debated by Catholic theologians. (Among non-Catholics, immaculate conception is often confused with Jesus' birth from a virgin, rather than Mary's birth without sin.) This notion coming from Bernadette helped convince the parish priest that she had, in fact, seen the Virgin.

Bernadette's claims to having seen the Virgin met with mixed responses from an increasingly secularized French public and government. While Lourdes became famous as a healing shrine, the government occasionally moved against it and at one point closed it for several years.

Bernadette suffered from various illnesses in the years after the visions, and they delayed her entrance into a religious order. Finally, at the request of the local bishop, the Sisters of Nevers accepted her into the Convent of Saint-Gildard. Her illnesses only increased, and on April 16, 1879, she died at the convent's infirmary. Her body was allowed to remain on view for three days, and many came to venerate it. On April 19 it was placed in a coffin and sealed in the presence of a number of witnesses. With permissions secured, May 30, 1879, Bernadette's coffin was transferred to the chapel of Saint Joseph, at the convent. In September 1909 her coffin was opened, and her body was discovered to have remained uncorrupted. This phenomenon, of course, added to her reputation. Her body can be seen today in the Nevers chapel.

The spring at the grotto became the site of a growing number of cures and continues to flow to the present day. Thousands of cures have been claimed, although only a minuscule number have passed the very strict standards of the medical

A statue of Saint Bernadette commemorates the famous appearance of the Virgin Mary at Lourdes, France, where she visited the young Bernadette Soubirous on several occasions in 1858. *Getty Images.*

bureau that was established to examine the more spectacular cases and pronounce them medically unexplainable. The small chapel originally built at the grotto eventually had a basilica erected over it. A nearby church, the Basilica of Saint Pius X, was dedicated by Angelo Cardinal Roncalli (later known as Pope John XXIII) during his years as Papal Nuncio to France. It can accommodate a crowd of thirty thousand. Bernadette was canonized in 1933 by Pope Pius XI.

Sources:

Carrel, Alexis. *The Voyage to Lourdes*. New York: Harper, 1950.

Cranston, Ruth. *The Miracle of Lourdes*. New York: Image Books, 1988.

Laurentin, René. *Meaning of Lourdes*. Dublin: Clonmore and Reynolds, 1959.

Neame, Alan. *The Happening at Lourdes: The Sociology of the Grotto*. New York: Simon and Schuster, 1967.

Taylor, Therese. *Bernadette of Lourdes: Her Life, Death and Visions*. London: Burns & Oates, 2003.

LUMBINI (NEPAL)

Although most of the biographical facts concerning Gautama Buddha are matters of scholarly dispute, tradition locates his birthplace as Lumbini, in present-day Nepal. It is now considered one of four major holy places of international Buddhism. Many accept the story that Maya Devi, Buddha's mother, gave birth while traveling to her parent's home in Devadaha. She took a rest in Lumbini under a sal tree. The event is dated as early as 642 BCE, and as late as 566. The infant is said to have spoken immediately after separating from his mother: "This is my final rebirth." He then took seven steps to the four cardinal points of the compass, and a lotus flower sprang forth with each step.

King Asoka visited the area seven centuries later, in 249 BCE, and erected a stele commemorating the event. He also ordered the building of a wall around the village and erected a stone pillar and four STUPAS to mark the spot, and he reduced the taxes the village would have to pay in the future.

Lumbini remained a Buddhist center until the ninth century CE. During the next millennium, when Muslims and then Hindus controlled the region, the Buddhist structures were destroyed and even the memory of the location lost. Then in 1895, Alois A. Feuhrer, a German archeologist, discovered the Asoka stele. Further probing led to the uncovering of a temple whose interior showed scenes of the Buddha's life. This temple was probably constructed over one of the stupas originally erected by Asoka. Further excavations throughout the twentieth century have led to rediscoveries of many of the Buddhist sites. Japanese Buddhists raised money to have the area restored, and in recent decades it reemerged as a destination for Buddhist pilgrims in spite of its relative inaccessibility.

Today, Lumbini is home to a Tibetan Buddhist monastery, a Nepalese temple (which the former United Nations secretary general U Thant, of Burma, helped finance), the Maya Devi Temple, and the pillar with the Asoka stele. The garden where the birth actually occurred is now well kept, and visitors may also go to the nearby Puskarmi pond in which the infant Buddha got his first bath.

Sources:

Majupuria, Trilok Chandra. *Holy Places of Buddhism in Nepal and India: A Guide to Sacred Places in Buddha's Lands*. Columbia, MO: South Asia Books, 1987.

Panabokke, Gunaratne. *History of the Buddhist Sangha in India and Sri Lanka*. Dalugama, Kelaniya, Sri Lanka: Postgraduate Institute of Pali and Buddhist Studies, University of Kelaniya, 1993.

Tulku, Tarthang, ed. *Holy Places of the Buddha*. Vol. 9: *Crystal Mirror*. Berkeley, CA: Dharma Publishing, 1994.

MACHU PICCHU (PERU)

Machu Picchu is a medieval Inca site, most likely a royal religious retreat center used around 1460 CE, located high in the Andes some fifty miles northwest of Cuzco, Peru. It is off the beaten track and lacks any governmental, economic, or military value—hence the belief that it primarily served as a religious center. Adding to its mystique is that it remained unknown to the larger world until the beginning of the twentieth century. It was missed by Spanish forces who overran the territory in the 1530s and by subsequent Peruvian governments, which had little reason to extend their hegemony into sparsely populated areas. It was discovered in 1911 when an archeologist working the area was invited to the site by the local residents. Hiram Bingham (1875–1956) was shown an abandoned site that was largely intact.

The site includes a central plaza and an adjacent temple surrounded by a variety of buildings, apparently living quarters for religious leaders, royalty, and other important persons. A large altar stone is located in the temple. The whole complex sits on a ridge between two high peaks. It appears to have been seen as the home of a powerful mountain spirit whose acknowledgment was integrated into the worship of the sun. It also appears that it was a special place for a group of virginal females (the Chosen Women) who were specialists in the Inca religion.

The exact nature of what occurred at Machu Picchu remains a matter of speculation. However, students of archeoastronomy have claimed the site was used for astronomical observations. Protruding from the altar in the temple is the Intihuatana stone (called the "Hitching Post of the Sun"), which some assert to be an indicator of various notable stellar occurrences, especially the summer and winter equinoxes. At midday on the equinoxes (March 21 and September 21), the sun is directly above the pillar, erasing its shadow. Thus the sun can be viewed as sitting upon the pillar and at that moment "tied" to the altar.

During the last generation, exponents of contemporary Esotericism (the New Age movement) have seen Machu Picchu as a site possessing particular spiritual power. They have spearheaded pilgrimages to the remote location and have invested the region with a variety of religious values. It is seen as a place of transformation or openings to spiritual awareness, and a land of not only geological but spiritual highs. Harking to Chinese ideas of FENG SHUI, tour leaders see the region as the focus of natural energies that flow

These remains of the city of Machu Picchu date back to the Inca Empire in the fifteenth century. The site is believed to have been an important religious center. Today, it has also come to be a spiritual place in the eyes of modern New Agers. *Aurora/Getty Images*.

around the high peaks, through underground openings, and suffusing the nearby valleys.

Sources:

Bingham, Hiram. *Lost City of the Incas*. New York: Duell, Sloan, and Pearce, 1948.

Cumes, Carol, and Romulo Lizarraga Valencia. *Journey to Machu Picchu: Spiritual Wisdom from the Andes*. St. Paul, MN: Llewellyn Publications, 1998.

Reinhard, Johan. *Machu Picchu: The Sacred Center*. Lima, Perú: Nuevas Imágenes, 1991.

Waisbard, Simone. *The Mysteries of Machu Picchu*. New York: Avon Books, 1979.

Wright, Ruth M., and Alfredo Valencia Zegarra. *The Machu Picchu Guidebook: A Self-guided Tour*. Boulder, CO: Johnson Books, 2001.

MacLaine, Shirley
(b. 1934)

Shirley MacLaine, dancer, actress, author, and outspoken leader in the New Age movement, was born April 24, 1934, in Richmond, Virginia. She is the sister of actor Warren Beatty. Her entertainment career began with ballet classes, which she began to help strengthen her weak ankles.

Following her junior year in high school, MacLaine went to New York and won a part in the chorus of the Broadway musical *Oklahoma*. The several months in the show cemented her desire to go into show business. After completing high school she returned to New York. Her big

THE ENCYCLOPEDIA OF RELIGIOUS PHENOMENA

break came when, as understudy to Carol Haney, she played the lead in *The Pajama Game*. In 1955 she received her first role in a film, *The Trouble with Harry*, directed by Alfred Hitchcock.

From that point MacLaine's career was on an upward trajectory. A mere five years later she received her first Academy Award nomination for *Some Came Running*. She was subsequently nominated for *The Apartment* (1961), *Irma la Douce* (1964), and *The Turning Point* (1978). She finally won for *Terms of Endearment* in 1984.

In the 1960s MacLaine also emerged as a political activist. She opposed American involvement in Vietnam and supported efforts for women's rights and civil rights. As an active Democrat she supported the nomination of George McGovern. She has continued to be attentive to various social and political concerns.

In the late 1970s she made a move further away from her Southern Baptist childhood and began an active exploration of psychic phenomena and Spiritualism in the emerging New Age movement. She had written two autobiographical books, *Don't Fall off the Mountain* (1970) and *You Can Get There from Here* (1975), and in her third book, *Out on a Limb* (1983), she began to reveal her new spirituality. The New Age media reviewed the book favorably, and her celebrity status rose significantly.

The made-for-television movie version of *Out on a Limb*, aired in the fall of 1987, marked MacLaine's transition from New Age aficionado to leadership. The movie showed her encounters with several mediums and reviewed some of the events, such as an out-of-body trip from a hot tub in Peru, that solidified her faith in the New Age. That same year she held the first of what she called Higher Life Seminars, in which she presented what she had learned through her years of exploration. She also wrote several sequels to *Out on a Limb* and produced a video tape, *Shirley MacLaine's Inner Workout* (1989).

With money from her seminars, MacLaine purchased 180 acres in Baca, a subdivision south of

Crestone, Colorado, where a large number of New Age and Eastern religious centers are located. MacLaine announced her intention to build a large alternative-healing center on her land, but local citizens blocked her plans, fearing the town would become even more overrun with tourists.

Through the 1990s to the present, MacLaine has continued her acting career, her political involvement, and her New Age life. She currently has an Internet site, http://www.shirley-maclaine.com/, that focuses on her spiritual concerns. Those who are attached to her spiritual vision have been organized into Independent Expression (IE), an Internet community described as an "ever-expanding circle of friends that gather on line to share experiences and explore ideas with the goal of finding our own truth." MacLaine writes a monthly *ShirleyGram* for the IE community. In May 2004 she accepted the invitation of the New York College of Health Professionals, a holistic health educational facility, to address the graduating class on the subject of alternative medicine, at which time she was given an honorary doctorate.

Sources:

MacLaine, Shirley. *The Camino: A Journey of the Spirit*. New York: Pocket Books, 2000.
———. *Going Within: A Guide for Inner Transformation*. New York: Bantam Press, 1990.
———. *Out on a Limb*. Toronto: Bantam Press, 1984.
———. *You Can Get There from Here*. New York: Bantam Press, 1976.

MAGIC MIRRORS

In a popular children's story, the wicked and vain queen satisfies herself of her own status by gazing into a mirror each morning and saying the words of incantation, "Mirror, mirror on the wall, who's the fairest one of all?" As the story progresses, the mirror alters its normal affirmation of the queen by both affirming Snow White's beauty and telling the queen her location. The story reflects a common mundane understanding of magic mirrors.

In fact, neither magic nor mirrors ever operated as portrayed in the story, with people asking questions of a mirror with the expectation that a voice would come forth from it offering information, as though from the mouth of a knowledgeable person. Rather, mirrors were shiny objects that were one type among many used by mediums and others to place themselves in a trancelike state that allowed them to contact the spirit world or other levels of consciousness.

In ancient times catoptromancy, or scrying, was a designated way of divining (obtaining divine knowledge not commonly available to mere mortals) by focusing attention on a shiny object that reflects light, such as the surface of a lake, a polished metal surface, or crystal. Concentrating on such reflective surfaces often produces images and visions that may then be interpreted. The use of a magic mirror was thus analogous to the use of a crystal ball, another popular object used when scrying.

Relevant to understanding scrying was the relatively late discovery of the use of the metallic coating applied to the backs of sheets of glass produce the modern mirror. Such mirrors only came into common usage in the twelfth century and remained quite expensive until the nineteenth century. Thus, over the centuries, those who practiced magic and divination by the use of "mirrors" designated a host of different items as forms of the magical mirror—various glass objects filled with water, polished stones, etc. Those who practiced Cabalistic (Kabbalistic) magic developed a set of seven "mirrors" that fit a complicated system of astrological correspondences and were appropriate for use on the seven days of the week. The mirrors for each day were Sunday (gold), Monday (silver), Tuesday (iron), Wednesday (mercury), Thursday (tin), Friday (copper), and Saturday (lead). Wednesday's mirror had to be made of glass filled with liquid mercury.

Sources:

Clogh, Nigel R. *How to Make and Use Magic Mirrors.* London: Aquarian Press, 1977.

Neale, Robert E. *The Magic Mirror: Reflections on the Nature and Relevance of Magic.* Seattle, WA: Hermetic Press, 2002.

Reed, Uma. *Developing Your Intuition with Magic Mirrors.* Carlsbad, CA: Hay House, 1998.

Tyson, Donald. *How to Make and Use a Magic Mirror: Psychic Windows into New Worlds.* St. Paul, MN: Llewellyn Publications, 1990.

MAHATMA LETTERS

One of the most important books for members of the Theosophical Society, but little known outside the membership, *The Mahatma Letters* were a set of some 120 pieces of correspondence reputedly written by two of the Ascended Masters who had been corresponding with cofounder Helena P. Blavatsky (1831–1891). Originally written between 1880 and 1884 by Masters Morya and Koot Hoomi, the letters were directed to A. P. Sinnett (1840–1921), the editor of the newspaper *The Pioneer,* published in Allahabad, and to A. O. Hume (1829–1912), a British government official and founder of the Indian National Congress. A few excerpts of the letters had been published shortly after they had been received, but the whole set of correspondence was not issued until 1923. (Two years later, a companion volume, *Letters of H. P. Blavatsky to A. P. Sinnett,* was published. This volume included correspondence to both Sinnett and his wife, Patience Sinnett.)

Sinnett preserved the documents through the almost four decades of his life after receiving the correspondence, and he left them to Maud Hoffman. Shortly after receiving the letters, she allowed Trevor Barker to transcribe them for publication. (The originals were deposited with the British Museum in 1939 for safekeeping.)

Sinnett, a convert to Buddhism, was attracted to Blavatsky and the Theosophical Society soon after she moved to India in 1878, and he wrote several articles about the miraculous events occurring at the Theosophical headquarters in Madres. These attracted the attention of the leadership of the Society for Psychical Research in London, who dispatched Richard Hodgson (1855–1905) to India to investigate what was occurring. Among the items he looked into was the seemingly miraculous appearance of the letters from the Mahatmas. These letters had appeared sporadically over a four-year period in the cabinet in the Shrine Room in the headquarters building. The letters had great importance for the fledgling movement, as they reflected on basic ideas of the theosophical cosmos, not the least being the organization of the spiritual hierarchy whom the several Masters represented. The seemingly extraordinary origin of the letters supplied additional evidence of their authority.

Hodgson wrote a devastating report in which he concluded that the letters had been written by Blavatsky, who then deposited them in the cabinet from an opening in her bedroom, located behind the Shrine Room. He also discovered indications that additional miraculous occurrences upon which Sinnett had reported had been fraudulently produced. Awareness of these events had largely started during his meeting with Emma Coulomb, a former close associate who claimed to be Blavatsky's co-conspirator in producing the fraud. The letters ceased to appear after Hodgson's exposé was published. Through the rest of the decade, Blavatsky wrote a series of letters attempting to defend herself and the society from the charges leveled by Hodgson.

Interestingly enough, by the time of the publication of the letters in 1923, the society had largely put the Hodgson report behind it and had moved into a new phase under Annie Besant (1847–1933), who was engaged in the promotion of Jiddu Krishnamurti (1895–1986) as the world savior and the clairvoyant writings of Charles W. Leadbeater (1854–1934). Although welcomed by many as a return to the original teachings put forth by the society in the pre-Besant era, the publication of *The Mahatma Letters* also highlighted the situation that allowed their production.

In recent decades, a new generation of theosophical apologists have returned to the era of *The Mahatma Letters* and have attempted to rehabilitate Blavatsky's reputation, with mixed results.

Sources:

Blavatsky, Helena P. *Letters of H. P. Blavatsky to A. P. Sinnett.* Edited by A. Trevor Barker. London: Theosophical Publishing House, 1924.

Conger, Margaret M. *Combined Chronology: For Use With the Mahatma and Blavatsky Letters.* Pasadena, CA: Theosophical University Press, 1973.

Harrison, Vernon. *H. P. Blavatsky and the SPR: An Examination of the Hodgson Report of 1885.* Pasadena, CA: Theosophical University Press, 1997.

Mahatma Letters to A. P. Sinnett from the Mahatmas M. and K. H. Transcribed, compiled, and with an introduction by A. Trevor Barker. New York: Frederick A. Stokes Co., 1924.

Waterman, Adlai E. [pseudonym of Walter A. Carrithers, Jr.]. *Obituary: The "Hodgson Report" on Madame Blavatsky.* Adyar, Madras, India: Theosophical Publishing House, 1963.

MALACHY, SAINT (1094–1148)

Saint Malachy, best known for his prophecies concerning the lineage of popes and their end in the present time, was a Roman Catholic bishop. He was born in Armagh and ordained to the priesthood in 1119. Five years later he was named bishop of Connor. He became head of the Irish church as archbishop of Armagh in 1132. He had an interesting and historical episcopate, quite apart from his prophecies, though these need not concern us here. Early in 1139 he visited Rome, during which time he asked for special favors for the dioceses of Armagh and Cashel. He again headed for Rome in 1148, but he became ill on the journey and died before reaching his goal.

It was during his first visit to Rome that he reputedly compiled his most famous prophecies concerning the popes. Reportedly, the prophecies came in a vision of the future in which a long list of the pontiffs from the twelfth century to the end of time were presented to him. The list included some 112 individuals, beginning with Celestine II (elected in 1130). Each individual is designated by a short phrase or mystical title that must be interpreted. Those who follow the prophecies explain these titles as referring to trait, historical fact, or other reference to the particular pope so designated. For example, the title assigned to the person who became Urban VIII was *Lilium et Rosa* ("the lily and the rose"). Some have suggested the title refers to the coat of arms of Florence, which includes a *fleur-de-lis,* and his escutcheon, which has three bees (insects who gather honey from lilies and roses).

Of particular interest in the twenty-first century, Pope John Paul II would be the pope #110 on Malachy's list. Thus, following him would be one more pope and then the last pope, of whom it is said, "In the final persecution of the Holy Roman Church there will reign Peter the Roman, who will feed his flock amid many tribulations, after which the seven-hilled city will be destroyed and the dreadful Judge will judge the people. The End."

Reputedly, Malachy gave his manuscript to Innocent II, the pope who reigned at the time of his visit, and that the document containing the prophecies passed to the church's archives where they were lost for four centuries. They were rediscovered in 1590 and published a few years later by Benedictine monk Arnold de Wyon.

Apart from the prophecies, a number of miracles were reported of Malachy. He was canonized a half-century after his death 1199. But what of his prophecies? Soon after their publication, critics questioned their authenticity. The basis of the critique has been the 400 years between their supposed origin and the time of their revelation. There is no mention during Malachy's lifetime that such a document existed. There has been some hint that their publication was an attempt to affect the upcoming election of a new pope. More recent critiques have centered on the often torturous process to find some fact about each pope to make them fit Malachy's list. That being said, Malachy's prophecies have retained considerable support both outside and inside the Catholic Church.

Sources:

Bander, Peter. *The Prophecies of St. Malachy.* Rockford, IL: Tan Books, 1973.

Hogue, John. *Last Pope: Prophesies of St. Malachy for the New Millennium.* Boston: Element Books, Incorporated, 2000.

Luddy, Ailbe J. *Life of St. Malachy.* Dublin: M. H. Gill & Son, 1930.

MANDALAS

The mandala (Sanskrit for "circle") is a complex geometric design found in Tantric Hindu and Vajrayana Buddhist practice. It may be painted on a wall or on cloth or paper, and on occasion it is created as a sand painting. It may be seen as a more complex evolutionary form of the YANTRA, used to symbolize the cosmos, or in turn the yantra may be seen as a more specialized version of the mandala. The mandala is often understood as a symbolic palace. Such a palace may contain four gates oriented to the four corners of the earth, and it may be located within circles that form protective barriers by way of elements (such as purity, devotion, or resolve) that one must attain to enter the palace.

Inside the palace may be a selection of the many symbols of the deities and/or the faith. Buddhists may find, for example, a diamond, symbol of a clear mind; the *ghanta* or bell, symbol of the female; the *yantra* or thunderbolt, symbol of the male; the wheel of the Dharma, a symbol of the Buddhist eightfold path; or the lotus, a symbol of the Buddha's teachings.

The mandala is made in a precise fashion and its construction integrated with a ritual that includes the chanting of mantras, words of power. The ritual accompanies the empowerment of the mandala, which, when completed, is seen as a power object of cosmic energy. Concentration upon or visualization of a mandala enables the believer to access the energy it embodies. In their most grandiose form, temples may be constructed as giant mandalas. In the twentieth century, the use of the mandala has moved into Western Eso-

Complex circular artworks known as mandalas are replete with symbols relevant to Tantric Hindu and Vajrayana Buddhist beliefs. The marks have specific meanings, and when they are created during a religious ceremony the results contain powerful cosmic energies. *Fortean Picture Library.*

teric thought after being brought to the West by the Theosophical Society. It has often attracted people initially as simply an object of aesthetics.

Sources:

Arguelles, José, and Miriam Arguelles. *Mandala.* Boston: Shambhala Publications, 1995.

Brauen, Martin. *The Mandala: Sacred Circle in Tibetan Buddhism.* Trans. Martin Wilson. Boston: Shambhala Publications, 1997.

Hall, Manley Palmer. *Meditation Symbols in Eastern and Western Mysticism: Mysteries of the Mandala.* Los Angeles: Philosophical Research Society, 1988.

McLean, Adam. *The Alchemical Mandala: A Survey of the Mandala in the Western Esoteric Traditions.* Grand Rapids, MI: Phanes Press, 1989.

MARY'S HOUSE (ENGLAND)

In 1061 Lady Richeldis de Faverches, the widow of a Norman nobleman, experienced several visions of the Virgin Mary in which the Virgin spiritually took the Lady on a visit to the home in Nazareth where the angel Gabriel announced the coming birth of Jesus. In the vision, the Lady took measurements of the house so a replica of it could be built in Walsingham, England, where Lady Richeldis resided. At the replicated residence, visitors could acknowledge the Annunciation as the root of their redemption and seek help for a variety of needs. Once the plans for the house and the site were established, Lady Richeldis paid for its construction and for the erection of a stone chapel around the building. (Interestingly, the Walsingham church resembled a British residence of the period rather than a Palestinian house. A building that is claimed to be the original home of the virgin is found in **LORETO**, Italy.)

In the twelfth century a soldier returning from the Holy Land brought with him a vial of what he claimed was the Virgin Mary's milk. He donated the vial of this miraculously surviving substance to the shrine, and it served to further make Walsingham one of the most notable pilgrimage sites in the land—possibly the earliest of the great sites devoted to the Virgin that proliferated through the medieval period in Europe. At the height of the shrine's popularity, a song about Walsingham was published that called attention to the healings that had occurred there, including the cure of leprosy.

Eventually, the house and chapel fell into the hands of the Augustinian order, which erected a monastery around it. Pilgrims found their way to the chapel regularly until Henry VIII began despoiling the British monasteries. In 1538 the Virgin's house was torn down and the remains burned, as was a statue of the Virgin that graced the chapel. Further pilgrimages to the site were banned.

In the 1890s Charlotte Pearson Boyd purchased a chapel that had been constructed along the road from London to Walsingham. It was termed the Slipper Chapel because here many pilgrims left their shoes and walked the last mile to the Virgin's house barefoot. She donated the chapel to the Catholic Church, which refurbished it and installed a new statue of the Virgin. She received little support from most British Catholics of the time, for whom pilgrimages had lost their popularity. Then in 1931, in front of the well at the old monastic site in what is now the village of Little Walsingham, an Anglican priest named Alfred Hope-Patten built a replica of Mary's house inside a new stone chapel. Hope-Patten's action jogged the attention of the Catholic community, which moved a few years later to proclaimed the Slipper Chapel a national Catholic shrine. Subsequently, a large new church has been erected adjacent to it.

In the decades since the opening of the Anglican chapel at Walsingham, efforts have been made to promote pilgrimages, and at times the Church of England, the Roman Catholic Church, and even the Orthodox Churches have cooperated on activities at the two sites. However, to this day, the acknowledgment of one site by the other is minimal.

There is also little discussion today of the lost vial of the Virgin's milk or the finger claimed to have been from Saint Peter's hand, which had attracted pre-Reformation pilgrims. However, the water from the well, believed to have curative powers, remains, and daily a priest sprinkles pilgrims with it. Others carry small vials of the water home with them. Hundreds of testimonies of healings have been received by those currently managing the site. Pilgrims visit the site year round, but certain activities, in particular those associated with Mary (such as the feast of the Annunciation, March 25), are times for special religious services.

Sources:

Gilbert, H. M. *Walsingham and Its Shrine*. London: Oates & Washbourne, 1934.

Guardians of the Shrine of Our Lady of Walsingham. *The Shrine of Our Lady of Walsingham: England's Nazareth*. Norwich: Jarold Publishing, 1991.

Obbard, Elizabeth Ruth. *The History and Spirituality of Walsingham*. Norwich: The Canterbury Press, 1995.

Stephenson, Collin. *The Walsingham Way*. London: Dartman, Longman. and Todd, 1970.

MASADA (ISRAEL)

Masada, initially built by Israeli King Herod the Great (37–4 BCE) as a summer resort, became a site of Jewish martyrdom in the first century CE and, in the post-Holocaust world, a site celebrated by Jews worldwide. The site sits on a hill with steep sides overlooking the Dead Sea, and while it was built in the luxury befitting a king, the location was also chosen with its possible role as a defensive fort and a place of haven from enemies. At one point, when Parthians invaded his land, Herod sent the females of his family to Masada, where they were protected until the danger passed.

Masada is not remembered today because of Herod, however, but because of events three-quarters of a century after he passed from the scene. In 66 CE, Jewish rebels opposed to the Roman rule of Palestine captured Masada and turned it into a mountain stronghold. These Zealots awaited a Messiah who, unlike the Christian messiah, would assume rule over Israel and thus replace the contemporary Roman authorities. Capturing Masada was but one step in a war to drive the Romans out. The war failed, and in the end, Masada became the last bit of land controlled by the rebel forces.

Given its isolated location and the problem of actually laying siege to it, the Romans waited until 74 CE to remove this final challenge to their authority. The rebels did not give up easily, and only after an effort that lasted more than a year did the mountain fall. However, when the Romans finally entered the fortress, they discovered that all of the rebels had committed suicide. Prior to their death, they also destroyed anything of value, leaving nothing for the soldiers to loot. The 960 defenders of the fort had held off an army of 10,000; only two women and five children survived the final attack.

Masada has become a symbol of courage for Israelis, and one eagerly grasped after the founding of the nation of Israel. In recent decades, the Israeli army has regularly brought new recruits to Masada as part of their swearing-in ceremony.

Visitors to the site today may see Herod's palace, with its notable mosaics, the baths reminiscent of the conquering Romans, and a synagogue. After the fall of the fort, the site was uninhabited for many centuries, until a group of Benedictines erected a small monastery. They are no longer there.

Of more than passing note: The only contemporaneous source of information about the events at Masada are found in *The Jewish War*, written by historian Flavius Josephus (37–c. 100 CE).

Sources:

Pearlman, Moshe. *The Zealots of Masada. Story of a Dig*. New York: Charles Scribner's Sons 1967.

Wasserstein, Abraham, ed. *Flavius Josephus: Selections from His Works*. New York: The Viking Press, 1974.

Yadin, Yigael, and Gerald Gottlieb. *The Story of Masada*. New York: Random House, 1969

MATERIALIZATION

As Spiritualism spread in the late nineteenth century, it was built around the messages received

Built by King Herod, Masada became best known as a stronghold for Jewish rebels against the Roman Empire in the first century CE. Today it remains a powerful historic symbol for the Israeli people. *Getty Images*.

from the spirit world through mediums. These messages were offered as demonstrations that individual life after death was a reality. The messages were generally communicated as a small group of people gathered in a darkened room where the medium would enter a trance state—at meetings called séances. However, as early as 1860, people began to report that during the séances they began to see things, such as luminous streaks of light, the face of a loved one, hands otherwise disconnected from a body, shadowy forms. Over time, these vague items became full-fledged human figures.

As séances evolved, the medium would often be placed in a special cabinet. His or her hands and feet would be tied to the chair, and the door closed. As visible manifestations began to occur, it was felt that tying the medium would prevent any hoaxing. In an attempt to understand the phenomenon, a mysterious substance called ectoplasm was posited as the material from which the ghostly figures were produced.

After the foundation of the Society for Psychical Research in England and its American equivalent in the 1880s, researchers quickly found their way to various mediums who claimed to be the instrument around which materializations of various kinds occurred. Among the earliest investigations was that of Richard Hodgson (1855–1905), who traveled to India to investigate the unusual claims being produced by Helena P. Blavatsky (1831–1891), one of the founders of the Theosophical Society. His lengthy 1885 report describing the phenomena and his conclusion that they were produced by various fraudulent methods did much to discredit the society and call fellow researchers to be more skeptical when examining mediums. Hodgson later investigated and reported on several materialization mediums.

In spite of his warnings, Hodgson's fellow researchers enthusiastically investigated the materialization mediums, often allowing their final reports to be skewed by a hope that the phenomena were real and an unwillingness to believe the mediums fraudulent. Among the most important

cases was that of William Crookes (1832–1919), who investigated the young and beautiful Florence Cook (1856–1904) and put his own reputation behind the genuineness of the rather spectacular materializations produced in her séances. The early years of psychical research juxtaposed positive reports on unexplained phenomena with accounts of mediums exposed as hoaxers.

Over time, however, all of the phenomena encountered were explained away as stage magic, and few of the more famous of the materialization mediums escaped incidents in which their attempts to work stage magic were plainly revealed to all concerned. Through the early twentieth century, belief in the impossibility of materializations in Spiritualist séances became the consensus among psychical researchers, and the phenomenon was largely discontinued within the Spiritualist movement.

In spite of the inability of mediums to verify their claims of materialization, pockets of belief have continued and debunkers have arisen to expose the activity of fraudulent mediums. In each generation, a few researchers have hoped that at least some materializations were real and that new technology could provide the instrumental data to prove such claims. For example, in 1960 Andrija Puharich (1918–1995), an enthusiastic psychical researcher, used infrared film to photograph materialization séances at Camp Chesterfield, an independent Spiritualist center in Indiana. Once the film was developed, the fraud was quite evident, although the resulting scandal did not end the practice. In like measure, Lamar Keene, a medium who had made a career of fraudulent practices, left the movement and wrote a book exposing not only the techniques he had used but the small circle of mediums who continued to bilk believers, many of whom found their way to their churches amid grief over the recent death of a loved one.

Except for these small remaining pockets of fraudulent mediums and their followings, little belief in the possibility of the materialization of spirits remain. Occasionally, a Spiritualist will attempt to hold out the possibility of materialization and bemoan the lack of great phenomena-producing mediums like those in the heyday of the movement, but even these voices have become rare.

Sources:

Carrington, Hereward. *The Physical Phenomena of Spiritualism*. New York: Dodd, Mad, 1932.

Hall, Trevor H. *The Spiritualist: The Story of Florence Cook and William Crookes*. London: Duckworth, 1962.

Keen, Lamar, as told to Allen Spraggett. *Psychic Mafia*. New York: St. Martin's Press, 1976.

Stein, Gordon. *Encyclopedia of Hoaxes*. Detroit: Gale, 1993.

McPherson, Aimee Semple (1890–1944)

Aimee Semple McPherson, a famous Pentecostal healer and early female preacher, was born on October 9, 1890, in Ingersoll, Ontario, Canada. During her formative years, her mother was a member of the Salvation Army, which promoted females in the ministry, but when Aimee found doubts arising on her Christian belief, she turned to a Pentecostal minister, Robert Semple. She married him in 1908 and the two left for a missionary life in China. Shortly after their arrival in Hong Kong, however, he died and left her the mother of a newborn child.

Back in the United States, with the assistance of her mother, Aimee began the life of an independent traveling evangelist. Toward the end of World War I, she moved to California. She was becoming famous for her preaching, and healing became an important part of her services. Her reputation was greatly enhanced in 1921 when a woman confined to a wheelchair stood up and began to walk.

In 1923 she dedicated the Angelus Temple in Los Angeles. It remained her base of operations for the rest of her life. The largest church along the West Coast at the time, it seated 5,000 and was dominated by a cross that was visible from many miles away. In 1924 she bought a radio station and began one of the pioneering broadcast ministries. The temple also became home to a number of crutches and other implements left behind by those who were healed by Sister Aimee.

In 1925 she opened LIFE Bible College for the training of future ministers and missionaries. She launched her own "Salvation Navy," the Church of the Foursquare Gospel. Ministers she trained moved out to found lighthouses, as local congregations were called.

While she was already a celebrity, McPherson's fame (or infamy) was greatly increased by an event in the spring of 1926. On May 18, 1926, she went swimming in the Pacific Ocean and disappeared. After unsuccessful searches, many concluded that she had been swept out to sea and was dead. Thirty-two days later, she reappeared in Agua Prieta, Mexico. She claimed she had been kidnapped and taken out of the country. Many believed her, but others doubted the story. Some noted that the engineer at the radio station, Kenneth G. Ormiston, had also disappeared during this time. Some speculated the two were having an affair. However, 50,000 believers gathered on June 23 to welcome her back to the Angelus Temple. Evidence of the reputed affair was never conclusive, and a formal investigation of the whole matter finally dwindled away.

She continued to hold forth at the Angelus Temple through the 1930s. As the Depression rolled through the state, she organized various relief efforts. She continued to travel, frequently overseas. When she died September 27, 1944, she left behind a thriving denomination with a growing global presence.

Sources:

Bahr, Robert. *Least of All Saints*. Englewood Cliffs, NJ: Prentice-Hall, 1979.

Blumhofer, Edith L. *Aimee Semple McPherson: Everybody's Sister*. Grand Rapids, MI: Eerdmans Publishing Company, 1993.

Epstein, Daniel Mark. *Sister Aimee*. New York: Harcourt Brace Jovanovich, 1993.

Pentecostal healer Aimee Semple McPherson, shown here in 1928, was a dynamic public speaker who built a large following of believers in the 1920s and 1930s. *Getty Images*.

McPherson, Aimee Semple. *This Is That*. Los Angeles: Bridal Call Publishing House, 1919.

Thomas, Lately. *Storming Heaven*. New York: William Morrow and Company, 1970.

MECCA (SAUDI ARABIA)

Mecca, a city in western Saudi Arabia, was the birthplace of the Prophet Muhammad and the site of the Kaaba ("House of God"), the most holy place in the world for Muslims. Muslims around the world face Mecca when they pray and are obliged to make a pilgrimage to the city at least once in their lives, if at all possible.

Islam had its beginning in Mecca. It was in a cave outside the city that Muhammad began to receive the revelations that became the Qur'an, Islam's holy book, and it was in Mecca that Muhammad first preached the truths that Allah (God) had confided in him. Muhammad's eviction from Mecca in 622 is the event from which the Muslim calendar begins. He returned in 630 to establish monotheism, destroy the many deity statues and shrines that surrounded the Kaaba, and institute the Islamic practices relative to the Kaaba that give structure to Muslim prayer and worship to this day. Muhammad by then resided in Medina, but toward the end of his life he made a final trip to visit Mecca, one that is commemorated in the HAJJ, the annual pilgrimage to Mecca.

Mecca was a holy site for centuries prior to Muhammad's career. The Kaaba, an ancient stone building measuring 45 feet by 33 feet by 50 feet, is located within a *masjid* (mosque). The present building, not the original one, is made of granite. It has a single door and no windows. Inside are several gold and silver lamps suspended from the ceiling and three wooden pillars that support the ceiling. According to tradition, the Kaaba was originally built by Adam but was destroyed in the Noahic flood. It was rebuilt by Abraham and his son Ishmael (at this point the Qur'an builds on the Jewish Bible). Muslims trace their lineage to Ishmael rather than Isaac, Abraham's other son.

Also located at the Kaaba is the large Black Stone. Arriving inside the mosque that contains the Kaaba, pilgrims are known to kiss the Black Stone, thought by many to have been a meteorite. Mythic accounts suggest that it fell from heaven or was brought to Earth by angels. Some stories suggest it was originally white, but turned black by taking in the impurities of the many human touches over the centuries. In the tenth century, it was carried away by some Islamic dissidents and held for ransom for some twenty years. Today the stone is built into the eastern wall of the Kaaba. It has broken into three large pieces and some smaller fragments and is now kept together with a silver band encased in a stone ring.

Control of the Kaaba was originally in the hands of Muhammad's physical family, but it eventually fell under the hegemony of outsiders, including the ruler of Egypt and, beginning in 1517, the Ottomans. Modern Saudi Arabia was created in the 1920s and assumed control of Mecca as the Ottoman Empire was dissolved. In 1932 the government began to self-consciously support the Hajj and has steadily created structures to assist the annual pilgrimages. The number of pilgrims has grown exponentially through the last half of the twentieth century. During the Hajj, the population of Mecca increases from 200,000 to as much as two million.

Sources:

Peters, F. E. *The Hajj: The Muslim Pilgrimage to Mecca and the Holy Places.* Princeton, NJ: Princeton University Press, 1994.

———. *Mecca: A Literary History of the Muslim Holy Land.* Princeton, NJ: Princeton University Press, 1994.

Stewart, Desmond. *Mecca.* New York: Newsweek, 1980.

MEDIUMS AND MEDIUMSHIP

The Spiritualist movement has traditionally been built around mediums, special people believed to be particularly sensitive to the subtler realities of the cosmos and hence particularly capable of communicating with spirit entities. The National Spiritualist Association of Churches asserts in its Declaration of Principles: "A Spiritualist is one who believes, as the basis of his or her religion, in the communication between this and the spirit world by means of mediumship, and who endeavors to mould his or her character and conduct in accordance with the highest teachings devised from such communion."

Mediumship has largely been understood by analogy to the radio, which works by receiving waves of energy that vibrate at distinct rates. Thus a medium was defined as a person who was sensitive to the higher vibration of the spirit world. Mediums could thus serve as the voice box of spirits who spoke to or through them. Some mediums operated while in only a slightly altered state of consciousness and relayed material they perceived from their contact with the spirit world. Others operated in a full trance and allowed what were believed to be spirit entities to take control of the medium's body and speak using the medium's vocal cords. It was a common phenomenon for trance mediums to have one or more control spirits who would emerge first when the medium went into trance, then act as master of ceremonies for other spirits to appear and speak. One variation on mediumship was supplied by AUTOMATIC WRITING, in which the medium allowed his or her motor function to be controlled by the spirit entity to write messages with pen and paper.

Spiritualism emerged around the rather primitive mediumship demonstrated by the youthful

Fox sisters, Kate and Margaret, who heard rappings in their house, but the movement took a quick step forward with the full-trance mediumship of Andrew Jackson Davis. He not only operated as an instrument through which individuals could receive brief communications from deceased loved ones, but he also delivered lengthy treatises of spiritual teachings from reputedly evolved spirit entities, a practice more recently called channeling.

One especially controversial phenomenon attributed to mediums was materialization. Through the last decades of the nineteenth century, dozens of mediums emerged who claimed not only to communicate with the dead, but also to allow them to briefly manifest in a ghostly state. The materialization of spirit entities during the small gatherings for spirit communication called séances was but one of a variety of visible manifestations of spirits that mediums facilitated. For example, some mediums used cameras to take pictures of those who came to them. Mediums would also cause a variety of "impossible" physical phenomena, such as the levitation of objects placed in the center of the room during a séance, or the teleportation of small objects from other locations to the séance room. Overwhelmingly, the physical phenomena associated with mediumship has been shown to have been produced by fraud, a fact that has called appropriate reprobation on the movement as a whole. Today, with few exceptions, Spiritualism has been content to fall back on the basic verbal communications from the spirit world that gave the movement birth.

Mediumship is a phenomenon by no means limited to the Spiritualist movement. Analogous religious functionaries, special people who have access to information and contact with different spirit entities, operate in a variety of religious traditions and include shamans from indigenous religions and those who speak with angels in modern Christian churches. Mediumship itself expanded in the last generation as a result of the New Age movement. As a whole, Spiritualists did not positively relate to the New Age movement, but integral to the New Age were channelers. Through the 1980s literally thousands of channelers emerged, offering New Age believers the information they received from a variety of spiritual beings. That Spiritualism tended to distance itself from the New Age accounts in large part for its lack of growth while related movements were rapidly expanding during the 1980s and 1990s.

The investigation of mediums took center stage in the early decades of psychical research, beginning in the 1880s. It produced very mixed results, and interest in mediums waned significantly in the 1930s, with the emergence of parapsychology as a laboratory science and its emphasis on documenting the basic phenomena of extrasensory perception. New interest in channeling emerged in the 1980s, but no significant progress was made in advancing knowledge of the phenomena. While some mediums were shown to demonstrate extraordinary powers, the attempt to document the reputed source of such powers in paranormal entities or spirit beings proved beyond the methodologies and instruments available to researchers.

Sources:

Christopher, Milbourne. *Mediums, Mystics and the Occult.* New York: Crowell, 1975.

Garrett, Eileen. *My Life as a Search for the Meaning of Mediumship.* London: Rider, 1939.

Gauld, Alan. *Mediumship and Survival: A Century of Investigation.* London: Heinemann, 1982.

Hastings, Arthur. *With the Tongues of Men and Angels: A Study of Channeling.* Fort Worth, TX: Holt, Rinehart, & Winston, 1991.

Van Praagh, James. *Talking to Heaven: A Medium's Message of Life after Death.* New York: Penguin, 1999.

MEDJUGORJE (BOSNIA-HERZEGOVINA)

Medjugorje is a village in present-day Bosnia-Herzegovina, an area that has experienced significant religious and political conflict throughout the twentieth century. In a largely Muslim region, the village was a haven for Roman Catholics. Through the centuries, the faithful had been primarily under the guidance of priests of the Franciscan order, but in 1878 Pope Leo XIII ordered secular clergy into the area. In the midst of this contested space, in 1981 five teenagers and one ten-year-old began experiencing visions of the Virgin Mary. From the beginning the beautiful lady with a starry crown and a child in her arms was identified as the Virgin, a fact confirmed when she initially spoke to them. Apparitions occurred daily, and within a few days large crowds began to gather. These gatherings created an immediate problem, as they constituted unauthorized meetings for worship in what was then the irreligious state of Yugoslavia. However, the local priest was soon convinced that the visions were legitimate and moved to protect the children from the police. He eventually was arrested and sent to prison on charges of opposing the state system of socialism.

The children were subjected to a variety of tests, and most concluded they were not faking the apparitions and were in a genuine altered state of consciousness. The faithful began to report miracles, especially healings. The local bishop appointed a commission to initially decide on the validity of the occurrences, but he found himself restrained by considerations of government opposition. Meanwhile, a large number of pilgrims from neighboring countries, especially Italy, began to flock to Medjugorje.

As the study commission pursued its work, the bishop replaced two of the remaining Franciscan priests in the diocese with secular priests. The priests appealed to the Virgin at Medjugorje, and she supported their cause over the bishop's. This action appears to have occasioned the bishop's turning against the apparitions and denouncing them as a collective hallucination. However, large crowds were now coming, and the government saw them as beneficial in projecting an image of Yugoslavia as an open country. Even during the days of the fighting following the breakup of Yugoslavia in the 1990s, the apparitions and pilgrimages to Medjugorje continued.

The basic message of Medjugorje has been a call for a return to traditional Catholic piety focused on the five weapons than can be used against Satan in spiritual warfare: daily prayer of the Rosary; fasting on Wednesdays and Fridays; daily reading of the Bible; monthly confession; and frequent attendance at the Eucharist. However, much of the interest in the apparitions has been generated by the so-called ten secrets that the Virgin has been imparting to the six visionaries. The secret messages each concern happenings predicted to occur in the future. Only one of the secrets has been made public, a promise by Mary to mark the hillside site of the apparitions with a visible and indestructible sign.

The ten secrets have been revealed individually to each of the visionaries. As each receives all ten, the Virgin stops appearing to that person on a daily basis. As of 2005, three had received all ten secrets, and the Virgin now appears to them once annually. Three others have received nine of the secrets and continue to experience apparitions daily at 6:40 p.m.

Medjugorje remains one of the most controversial Marian sites in the world. It has engendered significant support, and Medjugorje organizations now sponsor regular pilgrimages to the site from around the world. At the same time, official statements have been far from supportive. Local bishops have stated their own inability to find anything supernatural, although church authorities have not moved to stop the pilgrimages except in cases where a bishop or diocese appears to be an official sponsor. It does not seem that further official action will be forthcoming in the near future.

Sources:

Connell, Janice T. *The Visions of the Children: The Apparitions of the Blessed Mother at Medjugorje.* New York: St. Martin's Press, 1992.

Hebert, Albert J. *Medjugorje: An Affirmation and Defense.* Paulina, LA: A. J. Hebert, 1990.

Manuel, David. *Medjugorje under Siege.* Orleans, MA: Paraclete Press, 1992.

Six children purportedly had visions of the Virgin Mary in 1981 in the Roman Catholic enclave of Medjugorje in Bosnia-Herzegovina. Occuring in a largely Muslim area, the apparitions reportedly continue today and are the subject of ongoing controversy. *Fortean Picture Library.*

Sivric, Ivo. *The Hidden Side of Medjugorje: A New Look at the "Apparitions" of the Virgin Mary in Yugoslavia.* Saint-Francois-du-lac, PQ: Psilog, 1989.

Weible, Wayne. *The Final Harvest: Medjugorje at the End of the Century.* Orleans, MA: Paraclete Press, 1999.

MEIJI JINGU (JAPAN)

The Meiji Jingu, a shrine located in Tokyo and the leading center of national Shinto in Japan, is one of the newest of the world's major pilgrimage sites. It was built in 1920 to honor the life and accomplishments of the Emperor Meiji (1852–1912) and his wife, the Empress Shoken (1850–1914). Emperor Meiji, born on November 3, 1852, oversaw a prosperous era generally seen as the transition period during which Japan moved into the modern world. He ruled Japan for more than a half century (1867–1912) and had been responsible for establishing the state religion of Shinto and promoting it as an integral element in the identity of the Japanese people. He was buried in Kyoto, his birthplace, and the shrine was built to house his soul. Empress Shoken was born on May 28, 1850, in Kyoto. Best known for her promotion of the Japanese Red Cross, she was also buried in Kyoto.

The construction of the shrine culminated the series of regulations that had guided the rise of Shintoism over Buddhism. The Japanese military officially sponsored the site, which became a visible focus for the belief in the divinity of the Emperor. State Shintoism was promoted as something above and beyond religion, leaving individuals free to choose a religious faith (although religious organizations were forced into a select few groups recognized by the government). Members of the population were expected to give their assent and behave appropriately relative to State Shinto regardless of their religious commitments otherwise. The fact that the emperor was seen as divine created numerous problems for religious people across the Buddhist and Christian spectrum.

The shrine rests in the midst of a large park in Tokyo. The entrance is through Japan's largest *tori* (gate). The three main buildings are the Outer Shrine, the Inner Shrine, and the Main Shrine. Shinto believers who visit will initially engage in a brief purification ceremony that includes rinsing their hands and gurgling water. Once they enter the shrine, there is the opportunity to make an offering, acknowledge the deity spirits (*kami*), and engage in an act seeking one's fortune. The nearby Treasure Museum houses articles that belonged to the imperial couple and a photo display that facilitates memories of their life.

The shrine was destroyed during World War II. Following the war, the United States insisted on the transformation of the emperor's office from absolute monarch to merely a symbol of the unity of the Japanese people (similar to the British monarch). In 1946 the emperor made a formal declaration that he was not a divine spirit (*kami*). Shintoism was also disestablished as the state religion. After a decade under the new system, the shrine was rebuilt in 1958. It continues to be the site of a site of eleven annual Shinto festivals. In addition, it serves as a major recreational park. The surrounding garden, some 33,000 square meters in size, includes an art museum and a variety of sports facilities for baseball, tennis, golf, swimming, and others. The park includes more than three hundred species of trees that were brought from across the country.

Beyond its religious role, the Meiji Jingu has become a major tourist attraction that draws several million visitors annually.

Sources:

Kasahara, Kazuo. *A History of Japanese Religion.* Tokyo: Kosei Publishing, 2001.

Reader, Ian, Esben Andreasen, and Finn Stefansson, eds. *Japanese Religions: Past and Present.* Honolulu: University of Hawaii Press, 1933.

MENAS, SAINT (D. C. 296 CE)

Saint Menas (a.k.a. Mar Mina) is one of the most honored saints in the Egyptian Coptic

Orthodox Church, and many reports have come forth of healings at his tomb. Menas had a miraculous beginning, as his previously barren mother attributed her pregnancy to her prayers before an icon of the Virgin Mary. Menas served in the Roman army. During the reign of the emperor Diocletian (r. 284–305), Menas protested the anti-Christian stance being promulgated through the empire by deserting. He spent five years in hiding before deciding to announce his Christian faith publicly as persecution against the Christian community grew. For his act, he was tortured and executed. His body was returned to Egypt for burial.

Menas' body was laid to rest at Mareotis, in the desert not far from Alexandria. His tomb became a focus of attention following the changes in Christianity's status throughout the Roman Empire under Constantine (c. 272–337) and Justinian I (527–565). Accounts of miracles associated with Menas' tomb significantly increased the number of pilgrims, and a monastery and town began to arise close by, as there was a spring to supply water. The emperor Arcadius (r. 383–408) erected a large church. Also, in the sixth century, a church was erected in honor of Menas in Cairo (later destroyed by the Muslims and rebuilt).

Karm Abum, the desert town and monastery where Menas was buried, was completely wiped out in the middle of the ninth century. Abandoned, it was forgotten over the centuries. Early in the twentieth century, the site was uncovered by a German archeologist, C. M. Kaufmann. Among his findings were numerous small flasks bearing the phrase "Remembrance of St. Menas." Similar flasks, believed to have once contained water from the nearby spring, have been found at locations throughout the sixth-century Christian world.

There the matter stood until 1943. The Coptic patriarch to Alexandria prayed for the city as opposing armies approached. When the city escaped destruction, he attributed the good fortune to Saint Menas. He then ordered the rebuilding of the shrine at Karm Abum.

Sources:

Budge, E. A. W. *Texts Relating to Saint Mêna of Egypt and Canons of Nicaea in a Nubian Dialect.* London: British Museum, 1909.

Meinardus, Otto F. A. *2000 Years of Coptic Christianity.* Cairo: American University in Cairo Press, 1999.

Salih, Abu. *The Armenian: The Churches and Monasteries of Egypt and Some Neighboring Countries.* Ed. and trans. by B. T. A. Evetts. Piscataway, NJ: Gorgias Press, 2001.

MESMER, FRANZ ANTON (1733–1815)

Franz Anton Mesmer, primarily remembered today for the term mesmerism, a somewhat archaic name for hypnotism, stands at the fountainhead of the contemporary movements that emphasize extraordinary and miraculous HEALING. Mesmer was born in Austria and studied medicine at Vienna. During his student days he developed the ideas with which he would later be identified, all based around the notion of a universal magnetic fluid that permeated the cosmos. This fluid accounted for the truth of astrology (the influence of the planets on human life), and it could be manipulated by a knowledgeable person to place others in a trance or cause their healing. Mesmer apparently developed this idea after watching a healer who applied magnets to his patients' bodies. Based on his ideas, he developed a medical practice.

Eventually, Mesmer moved to Paris, where he became a successful physician with an increasingly wealthy and influential clientele. By 1784 his activities had become controversial, and his influence had grown to such a point that a commission of doctors and scientists was appointed to examine his work. The commission concluded that there was no evidence of any universal fluid, then termed animal magnetism, and that Mesmer's healing work was due to mere suggestion and the imagination of the patients.

The commission report did much to blunt Mesmer's success, but by no means did it suppress

In this eighteenth-century depiction, Franz Anton Mesmer "mesmerizes" people using his ability to manipulate a universal magnetic fluid that could put subjects into a trance. Today, this is more commonly known as hypnotism. *Fortean Picture Library.*

an allegiance to his ideas. In the early decades of the nineteenth century, people dedicated to Mesmer's understanding of animal magnetism created a popular movement in both Europe and North America. The understanding of animal magnetism became the basis of a revived Esoteric community that would build on Mesmer's scientific approach rather than on supernatural ideas of spirits and demons.

Mesmer himself retired some time after the commission report and lived quietly in Switzerland, where he died in 1815. The movement he started is considered the impetus for the modern practice of hypnotism, a term used when the practice of assisting others into a trancelike state was shorn of the idea of animal magnetism. Some understanding of animal magnetism, although now known by alternative names such as "universal force," undergirds the practice of spiritual healing in the Esoteric community.

Sources:

Darnton, Robert. *Mesmerism and the End of the Enlightenment in France.* Cambridge, MA: Harvard University Press, 1968.

Gauld, Alan. *A History of Hypnotism.* Cambridge: Cambridge University Press, 1992.

Mesmer, F. A. *Mesmerism: A Translation of the Original Medical and Scientific Writings of F. A. Mesmer, M.D.* Compiled and translated by George J. Bloch. Los Altos, CA: William Kaufmann, Inc., 1980.

MILK-DRINKING STATUES

While reports of bleeding and crying statues are plentiful in the West, similar reports, shaped by local religious perspectives, occur in the East. Among these are reports from India of statues that drink milk. It is to be noted that within Hinduism the cow has a special place due to its connection in Hindu holy books with the deity Krishna. Respect for the cow is seen as a visible symbol of one's respect for all life and as a step toward a vegetarian lifestyle. Thus, cow's milk has a certain sacred quality and is often presented to deities in the temples as offerings.

Thus, in the fall of 1995 it was more surprising to Westerners than Indians that a statue of Genesha in a temple in New Delhi was drinking milk. (Genesha is the deity who, in the form of an elephant, is often found at the doorway of Hindu temples.) The story began on September 21, when a priest had a dream in which Genesha asked for a drink of milk. Upon waking, the priest offered a spoonful of milk and was startled when the statue actually drank it. An account of the occurrence quickly moved across the city, and not only did people begin showing up at the temple to see the drinking statue, but reports emerged of other statues that were drinking such offerings. Within twenty-four hours of the first news broadcasts, statues in other countries were reported as also drinking milk.

Scientists sent to investigate soon concluded that the milk was not being drunk, but was being absorbed by the porous stone out of which the statues had been carved. Their conclusions were soon confirmed as puddles of milk began to form around the drinking statues. Within a few days, efforts to feed the statues ceased, and the enthusiasm surrounding the events died out. However, many Hindus now consider the event to have been a miraculous occurrence, some suggesting that it signaled the birth of a great soul. Others saw it as a great worldwide event, the first ever for the now far-flung Hindu global community.

Sources:

"Hindu Milk Miracle." Posted at http://www.mcn.org/1/ Miracles/mmiracle.html. Accessed April 1, 2007.

MIRACULOUS MEDAL

The Miraculous Medal is a small medallion that pictures the Blessed Virgin Mary that began to appear in France in the early 1830s. It was one product of the series of apparitions of the Virgin to Catherine Labouré (1806–1876), a nun with the Sisters of Charity in Paris. According to the story, she was awakened one evening in July 1830 for the first of three conversations with the Virgin. In this initial apparition, Mary told Catherine that she had a mission for her. In a second conversation in November, she filled out the nature of the mission: the asking of God's graces for a troubled world. In a third apparition, Catherine saw Mary standing on a globe with rays of light coming from her outstretched arms. She also stood on a serpent (a symbol of Satan in Christianity) and appeared to be crushing it. Around Mary were the words: "Mary, conceived without sin, pray for us who have recourse to thee." She told Catherine to have medals struck with Mary pictured as she now saw her. Mary promised graces on all who would wear it.

Catherine explained the visions to her confessor, who assisted her in attaining the approval of church authorities to have the medals struck. The first were made and distributed in 1832. Subsequently, an official inquiry was made into the apparitions, and approval of them was given in 1836. From that time, the wearing of the medals spread exponentially.

Saint Catherine persuaded the Daughters of Charity and the priests of the Congregation of the Mission to assist with her mission of spreading Miraculous Medal devotion. The priests then founded the Association of the Miraculous Medal with national affiliates in other countries. Pope Pius X approved the association's charter in 1909, and the American affiliate was opened in 1918. It now has more than a million members.

The apparitions given to Catherine Labouré are now seen as the first of a number of apparitions that have been the focus of a greatly revived veneration of the Virgin Mary in the Catholic

Church. Subsequent apparitions at **LOURDES**, France, and **FATIMA**, Portugal, would have far-reaching consequences for Catholic devotional life. Meanwhile, the wearing of the Miraculous Medal took its place as an important building block of modern Catholic Marian devotion.

Sources:

Breen, Stephen. *Recent Apparitions of the Blessed Virgin Mary.* New York: Scapular Press, 1952.

Dirvan, Joseph I. *Saint Catherine Labouré of the Miraculous Medal.* New York: Farrar, Straus & Cudahy, 1958. Reprint, Rockford, IL: Tan Books and Publishers, 1994.

Englebert, Omer. *Catherine Labouré and the Modern Apparitions of Our Lady.* New York: Kennedy, 1959.

Windeatt, Mary F. *The Miraculous Medal: The Story of Our Lady's Appearances to Saint Catherine of Labouré.* Rockford, IL: Tan Books & Publishers, 1991.

MOODABIDRI (INDIA)

Moodabidri, in the Indian State of Karnataka, about twenty miles from Mangalore, is a sacred pilgrimage site for Jains. Jainism is one of the smaller religions that developed on the Indian subcontinent. It dates to the sixth century BCE and the career of Vardhamana Mahavira (599–527 BCE), a contemporary of Buddha, although there is no evidence they knew one another. Jainism is distinguished as a nontheistic religion with an emphasis on the reverence of life. *Ahimsa*, the nonviolence to life, finds its most extreme expression among those Jains who wear a cloth over their mouth to keep from breathing in insects and carry a brush to sweep any small life forms from their path as they walk.

Moodabidri is home to some eighteen Jain temples, called *basadis* (literally, "abodes of gods"). One of the temples, called variously the Saaveerakambha or the Chandranatha Basadi, is renowned for its one thousand granite pillars, no two of which are identical. The temple also has a collection of carved images of Jain tirthankaras, exemplars of the Jain faith who are deemed to

have reached a state in which both attachment and aversion to things have disappeared.

The Moodabidri temples were built during the height of Jainism in the region in the fourteenth to sixteenth centuries. The oldest temple, the Guru basadi, is home to the Dhavala texts, a set of twelfth-century manuscripts written on palm leaves.

Moodabidri is home to one of the largest Jain communities in India, although they constitute only a minority of the town's residents.

Sources:

Dhaky M. A. *The Indian Temple Forms in Karnataka Inscriptions and Architecture.* New Delhi: Abhinav, 1977.

West, E. W. *History of the Bombay, Karnataka; Musalman and Maratha: 1300–1818.* Delhi: Asian Educational, 1989.

MOTHER OF THE WORLD (RWANDA)

In the African country of Rwanda, in the town of Kibeho, seven young people experienced a set of **APPARITIONS OF THE VIRGIN MARY** in which she called herself the Mother of the World. The apparitions began in November 1981 in three separate locations. Three of the visionaries, Alphonsine Mumureke, Anathalie Mukamazimpaka, and Marie Claire Mukangango, lived at a Catholic boarding school. Three were Catholics who lived in the countryside. The seventh, named Sagstashe, was not a Christian. He began to receive visits from the Virgin, converted, and took the name Emmanuel. Among the early messages given to him was a warning to prepare for final judgment.

The first apparition was initiated over the noon lunch hour in the school's dining hall on November 28. Alphonsine heard a voice calling to her. Going into the corridor outside the dining hall, she saw a beautiful woman in a white dress with her hands clasped together over her breast and her fingers pointing upward. She described herself as the Mother of the World. The two other girls began to see the Virgin early in 1982. As they were joined by the four visionaries who did not live at the school, people began to gather in support of their visions.

For six of the seven visionaries, the messages continued to be received through 1983. Alphonsine, however, continued to receive messages each November 28 through 1989. After an examination by the local bishop, initial approval to them was given in 1988.

Rwanda was, of course, shaken by the genocidal war of 1994–1995, which many survivors saw as proof of the accuracy of the apocalyptic aspect of the messages. During this period, Alphonsine and Emmanuel were both killed, though the remaining five visionaries are still alive. To date, no shrine has developed at the site in Kibeho where most of the apparitions were seen and the messages received. In 1997 the Vatican gave an initial assessment that the visions were authentic.

In keeping with many apparitions, those at Kibeho also advocated a particular form of devotion, in this case the use of a chaplet, a string of fifty prayer beads (similar to the ROSARY, which has 150 beads). In particular, the apparitions called attention to the Chaplet of the Seven Sorrows of Our Lady, a medieval prayer cycle that emphasized the experiences that brought Mary sadness in her earthly sojourn.

Sources:

Brown, Michael H. *The Day Will Come.* Ann Arbor, MI: Servant Publications, 1996.

Connell, Janice T. *Meetings with Mary.* New York: Ballantine Books, 1995.

Lindsey, David Michael. *The Woman and the Dragon: Apparitions of Mary.* Gretna, LA: Pelican Publishing Company Inc., 2000.

MOUNT ATHOS (GREECE)

Mount Athos, the most famous Greek orthodox monastic center in the world, is located on Halkidiki Peninsula, south and east of Thessaloniki. Prior to the emergence of Christianity, the area was considered the home of the gods; however, Christian tradition suggested the area was visited by the Virgin Mary in the company of the Apostle John. Christian ascetics (in the sixth century) and monks (in the tenth century) eventually established themselves there. In 1060, the Byzantine emperor decreed that the peninsula would be a male-only area, and in succeeding centuries it emerged as a primary center of Christian monasticism. Monasteries serving monks of a number of nationalities were built, and its continuing status as a male-only domain was set. By 1500 the population of monks had reached around 20,000.

Mount Athos became a center of Hesychasm, a system of prayer advocated by Saint Gregory Palamas (1296–1359). Hesychasts believe it is possible—through an exacting format of activity that includes asceticism, detachment, submission to a spiritual guide, and constant prayer—to see the very uncreated Light of God. Contemplation of the Light is the true purpose of humanity. They tie the experience of seeing the Light to the Transfiguration (Matthew 17:1-6). Dedicated Hesychasts were known to sit all day in a chosen spot while repeating silently the prayer, "Lord Jesus Christ have mercy on me." Gregory Palamas was a monk at Athos before becoming bishop of Thessalonica in 1349. The teachings set off a considerable controversy in the Greek Church, with opponents accusing the Hesychasts of a variety of heresies from pantheism to the dividing of God (which could not be seen) from His Light (which could be seen).

Throughout the fourteenth century, the practice was argued throughout the Greek Church and became the focus of several councils. In the end, opposition was identified with the Roman Catholics (with whom the Greek Church had split), and the Hesychasts won the day. The theological presupposition upon which the practice at Athos was built was accepted as orthodox, even though the practice itself remained primarily a practice of monks. Hesychast practice remains alive and well at Athos.

An important site in both ancient Greek and modern Christian religions, Mount Athos has been the center of the Hesychasm sect of Christianity since the fourteenth century. *Fortean Picture Library.*

Today, male visitors are allowed on the peninsula and number in the tens of thousands annually. Some come merely as tourists, others to visit the different monasteries, a few of which possess items known for their miracle-working powers, or to visit with a particular monk who serves as a spiritual counselor. At least three of the monasteries claim a fragment of the TRUE CROSS.

Athos is now home to around three thousand monks. There are some hermits, but most of the monks reside in one of twenty monastic communities.

Sources:

Bryer, Anthony, and Mary Cunningham. *Mount Athos and Byzantine Monasticism*. Aldershot, UK: Ashgate Publishing, Very Fine/Fine, 1998.

Kadas, Sotiris. *Mount Athos: An Illustrated Guide to the Monasteries and Their History*. Athens: Ekdotike Athenon, 1989.

Valentin, Jacques. *The Monks of Mount Athos*. London: Andre Deutsch, 1960.

MOUNT FUJI (JAPAN)

One of the most recognizable sites in Japan, Mount Fuji is Japan's highest peak at 12,389 feet, and it is a major reminder of the island's volcanic past. The near-perfect volcanic cone became a sacred site in prehistoric time, and its natural appeal was integrated into both Shinto and Buddhism. Early activity relative to the mountain included dances performed by young women dressed in white robes reminiscent of the puffs of smoke periodically emitted from the volcanic peak. The women were identified with two mythic females known for their beauty and heroism. The mountain also became the home to a number of female shamans/mediums, many of whom resided in the caves near its foot.

Mount Fuji also became a major site for the development of Shugendo, a mountain-based religion that reacted to the attempt to impose Buddhism on Japan in the seventh century CE. Shugendo drew teachings and practices from a wide variety of religions then available in Japan (including tantric Buddhism). Shugendo emerged as a method for developing psychic or spiritual powers. Its practitioners, the Yamabushi (literally, "those who sleep in the mountains"), chose mountains like Fuji as their training grounds. The Yamabushi, who constituted a male fraternity, withdrew from ordinary society, adopted a special diet, and underwent a variety of physical trials. They believed that in the mountains they could be in direct contact with the divine entities who resided there. The Shugendo remained an active religious tradition until the Meiji reforms in the late nineteenth century.

Climbing Mount Fuji became a popular activity over the years. An old path up the mountain, originating in the village of Murayama, was created and dominated through the centuries by the Shugendo. Today, there are four other popular routes to the summit.

In the thirteenth century, legends began to build around Hitoana, a large cave located near Fujinomiya. It was seen as the home of the Bodhisattva Sengen, a female being who was discovered by Nitta Shiro Tadsune (d. 1203), a representative of the shogun. Nitta's adventures would later be embellished by Japanese fiction writers.

Religious reverence focused on Mount Fuji was significantly elevated in the seventeenth century by the activity of Hasegawa Kakugyo (1541–1646), who settled in Hitoana, lived an ascetic life, and claimed a variety of revelations. These revelations, which included the production of a set of undecipherable symbols, became the focus of Fuji Ko, the

cult of Fuji, that exists to the present day. It was perpetuated by Kakugyo's successors, who brought veneration of the bodhisattva Maitreya, the future Buddha, together with Fuji Ko.

Much to the consternation of Japanese authorities, Fuji Ko spread across Japan and spawned several offshoots, such as the Millennial Fuji Ko. These have survived to the present and even received a boost from the post–World War II secularization of Japanese culture and the promotion of pictures and replicas of the mountain for tourist consumption.

Today, late summer is the most popular time for visiting the mountain. Many people, from mountaineers to religious pilgrims, attempt the climb to the summit. Each of the old routes is now marked by the presence of rest stops. Pilgrims carry a staff, and the station's name is burned onto the staff as they reach each successive rest point. Paths up the mountain are such that those not otherwise trained in mountain climbing can reach the top.

Sources:

Kasahara, Kazuo. *A History of Japanese Religion*. Tokyo: Kosei Publishing, 2001.

Uhlenbeck, Chris, and Merel Molenaar. *Mount Fuji: Sacred Mountain of Japan*. Leiden: Hotei Publishing, 2000.

MOUNT HOREB

One of the puzzles to which biblical scholars have periodically turned their attention is the location of Mount Sinai, where God gave Moses the Ten Commandments. In the Bible, Mount Horeb appears to be another name for Sinai. Those scholars who accept the documentary hypothesis of the first books of the Bible, the majority of contemporary Bible scholars, have offered an explanation. The documentary hypothesis suggests that the first five books of the Bible were composed by editing together manuscripts from four traditions (named J, E, P, and D) rather than being originally written as a single text basically as they appear today. That being the case, Sinai is the name used for the mountain of God in the J and P documents (for example, Exodus 19:11 or Leviticus 7:38) and Horeb in the E and D documents (Exodus 17:6 and 33:6).

However, whether one accepts the documentary hypothesis or not, the problem of locating Horeb/Sinai remains. Over the centuries, the location of the site of the giving of the law was lost, and the exact date of the Exodus has been a matter of considerable debate. The search for Sinai appears to have been a Christian concern; by the time the kingdom of Judah emerged, memory of the location of Sinai had been lost and was apparently of little concern. However, as early as the second century CE, Christians appear to have gone into the Sinai desert looking for it.

According to biblical accounts, the mountain was located some eleven days' journey from Kadesh-barnea, and was located adjacent to a flat area large enough for the Hebrews to camp at its base. There is no agreement on the location of Kadesh-barnea and other sites mentioned in the biblical narrative relative to the Exodus. However, a variety of locations were examined, and during the fourth century, during the reign of the emperor Constantine (r. 306–337), the peak known as Jebel Musa was selected as the site. Its selection was not altogether based on its close conformity to biblical descriptions, however, but due to the visit of Constantine's mother **HELENA** (c. 248–c. 329) on her famous trip to the Holy Land. Along with Jerusalem and Bethlehem, she visited Jebel Musa and erected a tower and small church. The fixing of the site seems to have been confirmed to Helena in a dream. During the reign of the Emperor Justinian I (483–565), it is said, a monastery was constructed at the site of the tower. It appears that, in fact, Justinian was responsible for building a castle-like structure, **SAINT CATHERINE'S MONASTERY**, to protect the monks who had previously come to reside in the area.

Others have identified Sinai as the place near Midian (in the Arabian desert across the Gulf of Aqaba from the Sinai Peninsula) where Moses had

the experience of encountering God in a burning bush as recorded in Exodus 3. Paul identifies Arabia as the location of Sinai (Galatians 4:25). Some support to this idea was offered by the historian Josephus (c. 37–100 CE). Additional evidence is cited from the apparently volcanic nature of the mountain, which spewed forth fire and smoke while the Hebrews camped near it. Those who support the Midian location of Sinai/Horeb have identified it with the peak known as Jabel el Lawz, noting its similarity with the mountain and adjacent land described in the Bible.

Amateur archeologist Ron Wyatt, famous for his search for **NOAH'S ARK**, has championed the Midian site. He claims to have found parts from Egyptian chariots in the nearby Gulf of Aqaba, which would have been the place the Israelites crossed the Red Sea. He has also suggested the valley largely surrounded by Jabel el Lawz's volcanic rim is the place they camped when Moses received the Ten Commandments. Though the evidence is by no means conclusive, the Arabian desert site is certainly one possibility for the place described in the Book of Exodus.

Sources:

Cornuke, Robert, and David Halbrook. *In Search of the Mountain of God: The Discovery of the Real Mount Sinai*. Nashville, TN: Broadman and Holman, 2000.

Har-El, Menashe. *Sinai Journeys: The Route of the Exodus*. San Diego, CA: Ridgefield Publishing Company, 1983.

Kitchen, Kenneth A. *On the Reliability of the Old Testament*. Grand Rapids, MI: William B. Eerdmans. 2003.

Robertson, C. C. *On the Track of the Exodus*. Thousand Oaks, CA: Artisan Sales, 1990.

Wyatt, Ronald E. *Discovered: Noah's Ark*. Costa Mesa, CA: World Bible Society, 1989.

MOUNT KAILAS/LAKE MANASAROVAR (TIBET)

The spectacular Mount Kailas in Tibet and the equally beautiful Lake Manasarovar, which lies at its base, are sacred to both the Buddhists and followers of the Bon religion in Tibet, as well as the Hindus in India. The waters that flow from the glaciers on Mount Kailas feed the lake (the highest freshwater lake of any size in the world) and four rivers: the Indus, Brahmaputra, Sutlej, and, most importantly, the Ganges.

Tibetan Buddhists identify Mount Kailas with Mount Meru, the mythological center of the universe and symbolic of the single-pointedness of mind sought by practitioners. It embodies the principle of fatherhood. Bathing in Lake Manasarovar is said to assist one's entrance into paradise, and drinking the water can lead to healing. Pilgrims walk around the lake, occasionally stopping to bathe in its waters and quench their thirst. The lake embodies the mother principle. The completed trek around the lake, which takes three days or more, leads to instant Buddhahood.

Among the important mythological events to occur at the mountain and lake was the encounter of Buddhist pioneer Milarepa and a representative of the traditional Tibetan Bon religion. They held a competition demonstrating their spiritual powers. At one crucial point, the Bon leader flew to the top of the mountain on his drum. When he arrived, Milarepa was waiting for him. As pilgrims make their journey around the mountain, they pass by a set of what are believed to be Milarepa's footprints and a shrine that houses a silver-covered conch shell that belonged to him.

Over the centuries, the Buddhists built thirteen monasteries near the mountain and lake and along the path the pilgrims travel to them. During the Cultural Revolution (1966–1976), the monasteries fell victim to the Red Guards. Their artworks were taken and their building destroyed. Pilgrimages began again in 1981, and subsequently most of the monasteries have been rebuilt, though resident to only a token number of monks. They now serve the pilgrims and mark the progress of their trek around the mountain. Among the best descriptions of the region come from the accounts of modern pilgrims.

Many Hindus consider the mountain the axis of the world, and its sacredness interacts with the sacred quality of the rivers that have it as their source. Among the many stories told of the mountain is that it was the site of the god Shiva meeting one of his consorts, Meenakshi. Meenakshi was a king's daughter born with three breasts. It was said that she would lose one of them when she met her future husband. When she met Shiva, the third breast disappeared. Their wedding took place at Madurai, Tamil Nada, now the sight of a temple built in 1560 in Meenakshi's honor. Each evening the temple is closed, and the main statue of Shiva is taken from its daytime spot to a room designated as Meenakshi's bedroom as music is played. It is returned at six o'clock the next morning. Three festivals annually mark the lovers' life together.

Jains believe that Rishaba, the first of their tirthankaras (teachers), received enlightenment at Mount Kailas.

Sources:

Johnson, Russell, and Kerry Moran. *The Sacred Mountain of Tibet: On Pilgrimage to Kailas.* Rochester, VT: Park Street Press, 1989.

Pranavananda, Swami. *Kailas-Manasarovar.* Calcutta: S. P. League, 1949.

Thurman, Robert A. F. *Circling the Sacred Mountain: A Spiritual Adventure through the Himalayas.* New York: Bantam, 1999.

MOUNT SHASTA (CALIFORNIA)

To the Native Americans of northern California and southern Oregon, Mount Shasta was a dominating presence. A volcanic cone visible for almost a hundred miles, it was the most prominent geological feature in the region and often the locus of some unique meteorological phenomena, such as reticular clouds that would circle the peak. The mountain became the subject of many mythological stories and the site of various religious practices.

California's Mount Shasta is an important location in Native American creation myths. Since its discovery by white settlers, the mountain has also become a key locale for Lemuria, "I AM," and even UFO believers. *National Geographic/Getty Images*.

An oft-recounted story concerned the grizzly bear and the origin of human life. It seems the Chief of the Great Sky Spirits made a hole in the sky through which he dropped snow and ice. The resulting mound created on Earth is Mount Shasta. He then stepped on the mountain's top to begin a tour of the world. Where his hands touched, trees sprang up. Where he stepped, the snow melted and became rivers. From his walking sticks he created the animals, the biggest being Grizzly Bear. The Chief made his home inside the mountain, and fires from his lodge could sometimes cause smoke to rise from the mountain's peak. Humans were the result of the Chief's daughter marrying Grizzly Bear's son. From Shasta, Grizzly Bear's grandchildren scattered across

the earth. Because of their kinship, the Native Americans refused to kill grizzlies.

When Europeans discovered Mount Shasta in the nineteenth century, they were equally impressed with it, and by the end of the century a new set of stories began to accumulate around it. In 1899 *An Earth Dweller Returns*, a channeled book through Phylos the Tibetan (the pseudonym of Frederick William Oliver), integrated Mount Shasta into an emerging occult myth of the lost continent of Lemuria, which is the Pacific Ocean's equivalent of Atlantis. Writing under the pen name of Wishar Spenie Cerve, H. Spencer Lewis, the founder of the Ancient and Mystical Order Rosae Crucis (AMORC), furthered the

Lemuria–Mount Shasta connection in his Rosicrucian text, *Lemuria, the Lost Continent of the Pacific* (1931).

The significance of Mount Shasta took on a heightened significance in the mid-1930s when Guy Ballard (1878–1939), founder of the "I AM" Religious Activity, published the story of his adventures on the mountain's slope. Ballard claimed that, while walking around the mountain, he met the Ascended Master Saint Germain. During their encounters, Saint Germain gave Ballard the basic teaching of the "I AM" movement and initiated regular communications from the Masters that would continue through Ballard's life.

Mount Shasta became a sacred site for the "I AM," and in the 1950s the members purchased land near its slope. Here they began to have regular summer gatherings and organized an annual outdoor pageant in which they portrayed their understanding of the life of Jesus, with an emphasis on his ascension, rather than his death and resurrection.

More than any other group, the "I AM" put Mount Shasta into the consciousness of Spiritualists and New Agers in North America, and although the UFO era began to the north near Mount Rainier, Shasta soon was integrated into popular flying-saucer lore. Various New Age groups established headquarters in Mount Shasta, the small community at the base of the mountain, including the Radiant School of Seekers and Servers, the Association of Sananda and Sanat Kumara, the Essene New Life Church, and the Ascended Master Teaching Foundation. Between them, a vast literature of modern Shasta lore has been published.

Sources:

King, Godfré Ray [pseudonym of Guy Ballard]. *Unveiled Mysteries.* Mount Shasta, CA: Ascended Master Teaching Foundation, 1986.

Phylos the Tibetan [pseudonym of Frederick William Oliver]. *An Earth Dweller Returns.* Los Angeles: Borden Publishing Co., 1899.

Sananda, as recorded by Sister Thedra. *I, the Lord God Say unto Them.* Mount Shasta, CA: Association of Sananda and Sanat Kumara, 1954.

Schroeder, Werner. *Man: His Origin, History and Destiny.* Mount Shasta, CA: Ascended Master fellowship, 1984.

Van Valer, Nola. *My Meeting with the Masters on Mt. Shasta.* Mount Shasta, CA: Radiant School, 1982.

MOVING STATUES

While not the most frequent of miracles associated with the Virgin Mary, periodically reports appear of people seeing statues of the Virgin move in ways that would appear to defy the natural order. For example, in 1998 a three-foot-high statue of Mary sitting in the yard of Raquel Fernandez of Corpus Christi, Texas, was seen by a passerby to have moved. The passerby told Fernandez what she had seen. The two then watched the statue for a moment and saw it turn its head, open its eyes, and take several steps. Word of the occurrence spread quickly, and suddenly people began to arrive to pray before the statue, and a number of them also reported seeing the statue move. Adding to the lore were reports of healing from those who came to pray. The statue hit the news when next-door neighbors began to complain about the crowds and asked that the statue be removed to a church.

Among the most famous of the moving statues is one of the Virgin at Ballinspittle in County Cork. It was first reported to have moved in 1985, after which it drew crowds of believers for several years. Over the years the crowds slowly dwindled. Then in 1997, new reports of the statue moving emerged and the crowds returned. According to the new reports, only the Virgin's head has moved, and it moves only on those feast days dedicated to her. Interestingly enough, another moving statue can be found at the nearby Mount Melleray Cistercian Abbey and Shrine in County Waterford.

Church authorities have been most reluctant to back stories of moving statues and generally do not acknowledge such reports to the point of

A group gathers at a site in Ireland where a statue of the Virgin Mary is believed to periodically move. *Fortean Picture Library.*

THE ENCYCLOPEDIA OF RELIGIOUS PHENOMENA

appointing a formal investigation committee. Many church leaders openly question the veracity of such reports.

Sources:

"Ballinspittle Statue Reported Moving." *Irish Times* (August 11, 1997). Posted at http://www.ireland.com/cgi-bin/dialogserver?DB=all. Accessed April 1, 2007.

Howard, Heather. "Neighbor Wants Virgin Mary Statue Moved." *Corpus Christi Caller Times* (March 6, 1999). Posted at http://www.caller2.com/autoconv/newslocal99/newslocal570.html. Accessed April 1, 2007.

MUDRAS

Mudras are the symbolic hand gestures found primarily in statues of Buddhist deities and bodhisattvas. Mudras consist of hand gestures and finger positions and derive from a system of nonverbal communication between students of yoga. To one who understands the intention behind the various mudras, they evoke both meaning and power. Throughout the East, from Tibet to Korea and Japan, mudras will manifest in rituals, dance, and the performance of spiritual exercises.

There are a large number of mudras, but five have become central to the presentation of images of the Buddha. The Dharmachakra mudra, for example, recalls the Buddha's first sermon at SAR-NATH. Both hands are pictured with the thumb and forefinger touching to form a circle (the Wheel of the Dharma), and the three remaining fingers extended, to which additional meaning is ascribed. The Bhumisparsha mudra recalls the Buddha's enlightenment, with the right hand touching the earth and the left hand placed flat in the lap. The Varada mudra, emphasizing the Buddha's charity and compassion, shows the left hand, palm up and fingers extended. The Dhyana mudra is made with the left hand placed in the lap, a symbol of wisdom (a feminine virtue). Various symbolic objects may then be placed in the open palm. The Abhaya mudra, usually pictured with a standing figure, shows the right hand raised and the palm facing outward. The left hand is at the side of the body, often with the palm also facing outward.

Throughout the Buddhist world, one will find statues of **KUAN YIN**/Avalokitesvara showing one of the five mudras or variations thereon. There is even one figure, the thousand-armed Kuan Yin, in which each hand is arranged to show a different mudra.

Mudras may be very complicated, among the most intricate being the Yonilingum mudra, which is one of a set of mudras symbolic of the human generative organs and used in Tantric practice.

Sources:

Chandra, Lokesh. *Mudras in Japan*. Vedam eBooks, 2001.

de Kleen, Tyra. *Mudras: The Ritual Hand-Poses of the Buddha Priests and the Shiva Priests of Bali*. London: Kegan Paul, Trench, Trubner & Co., 1924.

Hirschi, Gertrud. *Mudras: Yoga in Your Hands*. Weirs Bach, ME: Weiser Books, 2000.

Premakumar. *The Language of Kathakali: A Guide to Mudras*. Allahabad, India: Kitabistan, 1948.

MYSTERY HILL (NEW HAMPSHIRE)

Mystery Hill is an American megalithic site, often compared to British sites such as **AVEBURY** or **STONEHENGE**, located in New Hampshire some forty miles north of Boston, Massachusetts. The site is a somewhat chaotic collection of structures: walls, cave-like enclosures, and oddly arranged stones, the largest weighing some eleven tons. Lacking the symmetry of most of the European sites, Mystery Hill does possess what are believed to be astronomically significant stone placements such that the site could have been used to measure the major solar movements (solstices and equinoxes). The most interesting structure is the so-called Sacrificial Stone. The flat stone has a channel carved around its perimeter and a possible blood drain at one corner. The opening under the stone would allow a religious functionary to operate during any religious ceremonies.

What has kept Mystery Hill from the kind of recognition given the European sites is its questionable origin. It does not have a history of existence dating to the movement of Europeans in the area (1730s) nor a Native American folklore attached to it. Modern records begin in the early nineteenth century when a man named Jonathan Pattee owned the site. Many assumed he and his family built the site, although at least one structure is known to predate Pattee. In any case, during the nineteenth century and early twentieth century, the area was compromised before any archeologist could document it. In the 1930s William B. Goodwin, the owner at the time, did much irreparable harm to the site.

Apart from Pattee, people have suggested the structure, which is about twenty-five miles from the Atlantic shore, is Viking in origin, a pre-Colombian Irish structure (a theory favored by Goodwin), or an ancient Native American site.

Items found at Mystery Hill have been dated to between 1,000 and 3,000 years old, but the Native Americans of the region are not known to have worked in stone; there is no evidence of a megalithic culture in New England.

The cause of Mystery Hill as an ancient site of archeological significance is kept alive by the New England Antiquities Research Association, an amateur archeological association founded in 1964 that seeks to document New England's prehistory. Most current writing about Mystery Hill seems to favor its pre-Columbian European origin.

Sources:

Cahill, Robert Ellis. *New England's Ancient Mysteries*. Salem, MA: Old Saltbox Publishing House, 1993.

Fell, Barry. *America, B.C.: Ancient Settlers in the New World*. New York: Simon and Schuster, 1989.

Lambert, Joanne Dondero. *America's Stonehenge: An Interpretive Guide*. Kingston, NH: Sunrise Publications, 1996.

NOAH'S ARK

Chapters 6–8 of the biblical book of Genesis tell the story of Noah and his family surviving a catastrophic flood inside of a great ship, the Ark, built and designed according to God's instruction. For centuries this story was accepted as literal truth by most believers, but like other stories, modern biblical interpreters have called it into question. Among the objections are the seeming contradictions in the text itself, which many see as two different accounts of Noah that had been placed rather naively side by side. The stories differ on a number of points, including the number of animals taken into the Ark prior to the flood.

One response to these objections has been to explore Mount Ararat, the mountain upon which the Ark ultimately came to rest when the floodwater receded. If the flood had actually happened, remnants of the Ark could be found buried in the ice high above the tree line on the mountain's slope. Such a possibility was suggested by several people who attempted to launch expeditions to the top of Ararat in the mid-twentieth century.

The location of Mount Ararat has presented a continuing problem. It is located in northeast Turkey, just ten miles west of the Iranian border and twenty miles south of Armenia. Prior to the fall of the Soviet Union, Armenia was one of the Soviet states. Expeditions to Ararat have tended to bring harassment by sensitivities of Turkish authorities to outsiders working so close to its borders. However, in spite of the mountain's location, rumors of the Ark's continued existence periodically surfaced.

In 1955 a Frenchman named Fernand Navarra, who had previously visited the mountain on two occasions, announced the finding of a piece of wood showing human workmanship, discovered 13,750 feet up the side of the mountain. He brought a small piece of the wood when he returned from his expedition. In 1969 he and others found additional pieces of old wood at two different Ararat sites. He also subsequently wrote a book, *Noah's Ark: I Touched It*, that was translated into a number of languages and further stimulated interest in the Ark. Unfortunately, when subjected to scientific testing, the samples of wood proved to be of relatively recent origin. It was even suggested that Navarra had planted wood on his earlier expeditions, then retrieved them at a later date.

Meanwhile, in 1959 a Turkish pilot taking pictures to map the region photographed a ship-shaped object on another mountain some fifteen miles from Ararat. Various people who examined

One of the great modern debates stemming from the Old Testament concerns the fate of Noah's Ark, which many believe to be located near the top of Turkey's Mount Ararat. *Time Life Pictures/Getty Images*.

the photographs made increasingly interesting statements about the possibilities of the object, especially after *Life* magazine published the pictures in 1960.

An organization called the Archaeological Research Foundation (ARF) mounted an expedition in the summer of 1960, concluding that the object was simply a natural anomaly—namely, a clay formation in the midst of a lava field. The ARF personnel found no manmade artifacts or wood. That seemed to put an end to any interest in the site.

However, one person, Ron Wyatt, a Seventh-day Adventist from Madison, Tennessee, felt the ARF had been hasty in its conclusions. In 1977 he visited Turkey to investigate the abandoned

site. Following his visit he wrote a thirty-six-page booklet with the confident title *Noah's Ark Found*. Though possessed of no particular linguistic skills and unable to reach the disputed site on his first visit, he nevertheless claimed to have turned up a set of items that justified some rather startling conclusions. His purported findings included some stone sea anchors, petrified timbers from the Ark (discovered in an Armenian graveyard), a house built by Noah that included stones with inscriptions describing the flood, and Noah's burial site.

Over the next few years, the personable Wyatt convinced several notable people to take a second look at the site, including *Apollo XV* astronaut Col. Jim Irwin, Dr. John Morris, head of the Institute for

Creation Research, and Marvin Steffins, president of International Expeditions. Amid hopeful claims of having found the true Ark, Wyatt went on to found Wyatt Archaeological Research and expand his searches for other biblical sites. He would later claim that he had discovered the location of Sodom and Gomorrah (two cities destroyed by God for their wickedness), the exact spot where the Hebrews crossed the Red Sea out of Egypt, and the burial place of the lost ARK OF THE COVE-NANT below the spot where Jesus was crucified. Details concerning these claims now appear on the Wyatt Archaeological Research website. Along the way, he has lost the support of most of the scholars who had given early, tentative support, and few today take his claims seriously. Nonetheless, he continues to circulate several books and videos, especially items touting the ship-shaped structure he claims to be the true Ark.

Meanwhile, a variety of efforts to locate the Ark continue at Mount Ararat and other nearby locations in the mountainous region. They have all been inconclusive to date. The discovery of an object that could verify the biblical story of Noah and the flood face considerable obstacles. Given both the dominant opinions concerning the story of the Ark and the importance of debates over biblical authority, any object bearing claims to date to Noah's time would have to pass a battery of tests verifying its ancient status. At present, no object has met even preliminary qualifications.

Sources:

Amirault. "A Great Christian Scam." Posted at http://www.tentmaker.org/Dew/Dew7/D7-AGreatChristianScam.html. Accessed April 1, 2007.

Bailey, Lloyd R. *Noah: The Person and the Story in History and Tradition*. Columbia: University of South Carolina Press, 1989.

LaHaye, Tim, and John Morris. *The Ark on Ararat*. Nashville, TN: Thomas Nelson Inc. and Creation Life Publishers, 1976.

Navarra, Fernand. *Noah's Ark: I Touched It*. Gainesville, FL: Bridge-Logos Publishers, 1974.

Wyatt Archeological Research. http://www.wyattmuseum.com/. Accessed April 1, 2007.

NUESTRA SEÑORA DE LA PRESENTACIÓN

One of the earliest apparitions of the Virgin Mary reported in the Americas occurred in the 1580s at Quinché, Ecuador, to some of the native Oyacachi people. They saw a woman in a cave who promised to assist them with the threat posed to their children by a bear. This event occurred during a time when many Quinché people were being converted to Catholicism.

About this same time, a sculptor named Diego de Robles had carved an image of the Virgin, with the baby Jesus in her left arm and a scepter in her right hand, for a client who in the end did not pay the price earlier agreed upon. In 1585 de Robles traded the statue to the Quinché people in return for some wood. When the statue arrived, the people were surprised to find it to be an image of the beautiful lady they had seen in the cave.

In 1604 the local bishop ordered the statue to be moved from the site near the cave to the village of Quinché. It has subsequently been covered in gold-laden finery. The Virgin stands on a half moon of silver, and both Mary and Jesus have crowns of gold that were added in 1943.

The annual festival for the Virgin in Ecuador is November 21. The present shrine was declared a National Sanctuary in 1985. The Nuestra Señora de la Presentación is considered the national patron of Ecuador.

Sources:

Salazar Medina, Richard. *El Santuario de la Virgen de el Quinche: Peregrinación en un espacio sagrado milenario*. Quito: Ediciones ABYA-YALA, 2000.

Sono, Carlos. *Nuestra Señora del Quinche*. Quito: Tip. "La Rápida," 1903.

OAK ISLAND (NOVA SCOTIA)

Oak Island, a small island in Malone Bay southwest of Halifax, Nova Scotia, is the site of Canada's most fabled mystery site, the so-called Money Pit. Here, a fabled treasure was reputedly buried by pirates in the seventeenth century. Since the 1790s people have searched the area around the Money Pit, but with no success. In recent decades, however, interest in the island has been renewed as this obscure, out-of-the-way location has been mentioned as part of the contemporary development of an alternative history of the Knights Templar and the search for the **HOLY GRAIL**.

According to this alternative history, following the attempt by King Philip the Fair (1268–1314) of France to destroy the **TEMPLARS**, some of the knights made their way to Scotland. During their stay they made friends with Lord Henry Sinclair (d. c. 1400), who had previous ties to the Templars and whose lands included Rosslyn.

Sinclair controlled a fleet of ships commanded by Carlo Zeno (1334–1418). The pair conquered the Faeroe and Shetland Islands, and it appears Sinclair sent Zeno in search of new lands to conquer. Subsequently, Zeno traveled west and, almost a century before Christopher Columbus, traversed the Atlantic Ocean, finally dropping anchor off the shores of Nova Scotia. When Zeno reported his discovery, Sinclair decided to visit this new land. The voyage occurred over the spring and summer of 1397. Arriving toward the beginning of June, they made their headquarters on the peninsula between the Gold and Gapreau rivers, from which they explored south as far as Massachusetts. Left behind when Sinclair returned to Scotland were several Templars, possibly the seed of a future colony. Also carried to Nova Scotia were some of the Templar treasures, including the Holy Grail.

The connection between Oak Island and the grail legends was made by Canadian writer Michael Bradley in his 1988 best-selling volume, *Holy Grail across the Atlantic*. Bradley argued that the Knights left in Nova Scotia went on to help settle and develop New France and even the United States. Following his initial book, Bradley began to search for further evidence of Templar presence in North America.

In a second book, *Grail Knights of North America*, he presented what he had found, which was enough to excite Grail believers, but not enough to lead historians to rewrite history. The most important evidence that the Templars found their way to North America is the papers and maps left by Carlo Zeno, the Venetian explorer who spent a number of years in the North Atlantic exploring the lands from the Faeroe and Shetland Islands to Greenland. Bradley has since continued to develop his views concerning the presence of the Templars in North America and the nature of the Holy Grail. In a third book, *Swords at Sunset: Last Stand of North America's Grail Knights* (Manor House, 2005), he ties the Templars to the story told in the Book of Mormon.

Sources:

Bradley, Michael. Michael Bradley homepage. http://www.michaelbradley.info/. Accessed April 1, 2007.

———. *Grail Knights of North America*. Toronto: Hounslow Press, 1998.

———. *Holy Grail Across the Atlantic*. Toronto: Hounslow Press, 1988.

———. *Swords at Sunset: Last Stand of North America's Grail Knights*, Wellington, NZ: Manor House Press, 2005.

OMENS

Omens are phenomena or occurrences that are believed to foretell the future. A popular element of ancient worldviews, they have largely dropped out of favor in the post-scientific West, and the concerted effort to banish "magical thinking" has led to a considerable demise in a belief in omens in all but the most isolated parts of the world.

Omens imply a real connection between seemingly unconnected events. For example, the fact that a groundhog has or does not have a shadow on a specific day is tied to the weather in the months ahead. The connection between a sign and future reality (which lacks any logical relationship) was explained as being a message from the gods (the omen being a supernatural means of communication), and/or the sign and future event were tied together magically.

Traditionally, there were two kinds of omens. Some were phenomena that were sought out (or even manufactured) as a means of answering a specific question. Thus, in ancient Rome a sheep could have been opened up so that the intestines could be read as a means of ascertaining the future. However, omens were generally thought of as events that occurred quite apart from human effort, especially when they involved events in the sky, the unusual flight of birds, an eclipse or comet, or the arrangement of the stars and planets. Any unusual event could be interpreted as a sign portending the future.

There are various speculations as to the origin of omens, but by the time written records appear, omens are very much a part of human thinking. They survived most recently in the various observations of farmers who have sought predictors of good and bad crops.

Omens might be interpreted as having a socially broad reference or merely of individual application. In the days in which omens were seen as being related to the larger community, government officials not only took an omen seriously, but would strive to outwit the predictions so as to avoid disasters. For example, should signs generally believed to negatively affect the ruler be seen, the ruler might change places with a commoner in the belief that any negative fate would fall upon the substitute ruler. There have been modern day political leaders who have been influenced by what they considered to be omens, as well. In one famous example, during World War II, Germany's Adolf Hitler believed that the death of American President Franklin Roosevelt was an omen suggesting that the war would soon reverse itself and Germany would win.

Many omens have an impact that is limited to an individual, such as a broken mirror that portends seven years bad luck. These are of the essence of what is generally thought of as the realm of superstition. Such omens, often referred to as old wives tales, can maintain a subliminal hold on the human imagination. It is not uncommon to see a person who professes to not be super-

stitious avoid a path recently crossed by a black cat, refuse to walk under a ladder, or avoid stepping on a crack in the pavement.

Possibly the most persistent consideration of omens is found in the search for the signs of the time, the events believed by many conservative Christians to signal the end-time events foreseen in the Bible. Many conservative thinkers believe in a literal historical reading of millennial passages in the Bible and assume that the promised return of Jesus will be preceded by a specific set of events vaguely described in the New Testament. For example, many Evangelical Christians once believed that the founding of the state of Israel (1948) signaled that the last generation before the return of Christ had begun.

Sources:

Bluestone, Sarvananda. *How to Read Signs and Omens in Everyday Life.* Rochester, VT: Destiny Books, 2001.

Dunwich, Gerina. *The Wiccan's Dictionary of Prophecy and Omens.* New York: Citadel Press, 2000.

Waring, Philippa. *Dictionary of Omens and Superstitions.* London: Souvenir Press, 1998.

OUIJA BOARD

The ouija board, introduced to the public in the late nineteenth century, is a popular instrument of spirit communication. This toy harks back to a similar instrument used in ancient Greece by the followers of the philosopher Pythagoras. In the years after the American Civil War, Spiritualism fostered a public interest in contacting what were believed to be spirits of the deceased. Given the relatively small number of mediums, various other means were tried to allow anyone to make contact, including several different simple devices.

Then in the mid 1880s, a new idea circulated in the Spiritualist community. They created a board about 20 inches square upon which the letters of the alphabet, the ten numbers (0–9), and the words "yes" and "no" were displayed. On this board, one places a small device with three legs and a hole in the middle through which one can

People seeking spiritual guidance use a ouija board to contact spirits who they believe can answer their questions. *Fortean Picture Library.*

read a character, number, or yes/no response. To use the ouija board, two people sit facing each other and place their fingertips lightly on the small reading device. They allow it to move about the larger board, spelling out messages in answer to their questions. The most interesting aspect of this apparatus is the frequency with which it seems to work.

In 1890, Elijah J. Bond filed a patent for a form of the new message board. The next year, with partners Charles W. Kennard and William H. A. Maupin, he began marketing his board as a novelty game. They called it a ouija (pronounced wee'-ja) board, claiming that the word was Egyptian for good luck. Since ouija is not an Egyptian word, others have suggested various origins of the name. After a decade of manufacturing the ouija board,

in 1900 the Ouija Novelty Company hired William Fuld (d. 1927) as its president. Fuld set about reinventing the ouija board, and with a capable marketing effort he sold hundreds of thousands of them. He publicly claimed to have invented the board, naming it for the French (*oui*) and German (*ja*) words for yes. The company continued to manufacture the ouija board until 1966, when rights were sold to Parker Brothers, which continues to market it today. Through the years, a variety of competing message boards have been manufactured and sold, but none have attained the popularity of the ouija board.

Though marketed as a novelty toy, those who use it often see it as a more serious device, and so a variety of books exist about messages received by people using the ouija board. In many cases, people who initiated spirit contact through the ouija board moved on to more efficient forms of communication, usually direct voice mediumship. Among the more important Spiritualist volumes related to ouija board use is the literature of Patience Worth, who wrote a set of books channeled through St. Louis housewife Pearl Curran.

Due to interest in other forms of mediumship, little research has been done on the ouija board and how it operates. Many skeptics have assumed that it operates through the subconscious activity of the people who have their hands on the board. Some have attributed its apparent operation to the "ideomotor effect." The mind, without reference to the consciousness, can stimulate subtle muscular movements that cause the reading device to move and spell out intelligible messages. As with many mediumistic communications, these results can appear startling. Since they originate from the ouija board users, the predictions can have more relevance than the readings from a professional medium. Observers have noted that in most cases, if the users are blindfolded, the messages spelled out on the board tend to become gibberish.

Sources:

Covina, Gina. *The Ouija Book*. New York: Simon & Schuster, 1979.

Litvag, Irving. *Singer in the Shadows: The Strange Story of Patience Worth*. New York: Macmillan Company, 1972.

St. Christopher, Michael. *How to Use a Ouija Board*. Los Angeles: International Imports, 1995.

OUR LADY MEDIATRIX OF ALL GRACE (PHILIPPINES)

In August 1948, the Virgin Mary appeared to Teresita Castillo, a Carmelite novice, while she was in her assigned cell. Then in September of that year, she appeared again while Sister Teresita was in the convent's garden. She asked the novice to return to the same spot daily for the next fifteen days. During these sightings, the messages stressed some common themes, especially the

need for humility and penance. The Virgin Mary also requested the faithful to remember the clergy and the pope in their prayers, to pray the ROSARY, and attend a special mass on the twelfth day of each month. She further asked for a statue to be placed where she appeared.

The Virgin's initial appearance in the garden was signaled by a shaking of a vine; she requested that the vine be blessed. When Sister Teresita saw the Virgin, she was standing on a cloud and was clothed all in white with a belt around her waist; she carried a golden rosary. She called herself the Mediatrix of All Grace.

The garden in which the apparition appeared has since become the site of numerous other reports of miraculous occurrences. People have seen the sun spin (as it did at FATIMA), and some have reported being showered in rose petals that had images of Mary or Jesus on them. These rose petals have been catalysts for healings. Sister Teresita was also the subject of other paranormal experiences, including visitations by various angels and deceased saints. On one occasion, while lying in her bed ill, she received communion from an angel.

These apparition sightings and miraculous occurrences were not well received initially. Because of the controversy caused by them, both the convent's mother superior and the local bishop were replaced, and Sister Teresita was forced to leave the convent. There were a number of articles in Philippine newspapers ridiculing the miracles, and the church's investigation yielded a negative report. Church authorities ordered the destruction of the statue, but the nuns at the convent secreted it away. Church authorities also ordered the nuns not to talk about the apparition. There the matter rested for several decades. Then, in 1990, there was a new series of spiritual visions—this time they were not at the convent but at another location in Lipa City.

On January 24, 1991, rose petals began to fall straight from the sky again at the Carmelite convent in Lipa City. A few days later, six children playing in the garden at the convent saw the statue of the Virgin Mary come to life. In light of these more recent apparitions, the church has established a committee to conduct a new investigation. As of 2005, that committee has yet to report. Meanwhile, the statue remains in the chapel at Lipa and the pictures of the rose petals have been widely circulated.

Sources:

Keithley, June. *Lipa*. Manila: Cacho Publishing House, 1992.

Swain, Ingo. *The Great Apparitions of Mary: An Examination of 22 Supranormal Appearances*. New York: Crossroad Classic, 1996.

OUR LADY OF KEVELAER (GERMANY)

The Marian shrine at Kevelaer, which is about 35 miles northwest of Düsseldorf, Germany, dates to 1641. It marks the site of an extraordinary encounter involving a Dutch peddler named Hendrik Busman, who was traveling through the area (then a part of Holland). He had stopped to pray at a roadside shrine when he heard a woman's voice say to him, "Build me a chapel on this place." He initially ignored the voice and went on his way, but on three different occasions, the voice returned. Finally, he gave in and started to build a small chapel. On Easter the next year, his wife saw an APPARITION OF THE VIRGIN MARY. As a result of the vision, Busman came to believe that a small portrait of the Virgin known as "Our Lady of Luxembourg," which had been offered for sale to his wife, was meant to be placed in the chapel. He purchased it and saw it placed inside the chapel when it was finished in June.

The story of the chapel spread, and pilgrims began to arrive soon after its dedication. The first spectacular miracle occurred in September: the healing of a lame boy named Peter van Volbroek. In 1654 the original chapel was taken down and replaced with a larger church, and in 1864 a massive church, the 5,000-seat Basilica of Mary, was dedicated.

In 1888 a mission station was founded in South Africa by Abbot Francis Pfanner and named for the German Marian site. In 1932 Fr. Vitalis Fux, who served the South African mission, was in Germany and learned that a second picture of "Our Lady of Luxembourg" existed and was still in the hands of the family of the man from whom Busman had purchased the miraculous picture that graced the Kevelaer shrine. He contacted the family and eventually negotiated the purchase of the picture for the new church being built at Kevelaer in South Africa. Before returning home, he visited the visionary Therese Neumann in Konnersreuth, Germany, who touched the picture and authenticated it.

Fr. Vitalis was only able to return to South Africa after World War II, in 1947. Once installed, the South African shrine became a pilgrimage site and was given official status by the local bishop in 1953. The German and South African sites have subsequently developed a close working relationship.

Sources:

Grittern, Astrid. *Die Marienbasilika zu Kevelaer*. Köln: Rheinland-Verlag 1999.

Schwering, Burkhard. *Gelobt seist Du, Maria: Volkstümliche Darstellungen des Wallfahrtsbildes von Kevelaer*. Freiburg: Herder, 1987.

Wright, Kevin J. *Catholic Shrines of Central and Eastern Europe*. Liguori, MO: Liguori Publications, 1999.

OUR LADY OF PEACE CATHEDRAL (IVORY COAST)

The basilica of Our Lady of Peace located in Yamoussoukro, Ivory Coast, is the largest Christian church in the world. It was planned and bankrolled by Felix Houphouet-Boigny (1906–1993), the first president of the country, as part of an effort by Roman Catholics to build a following in the former French colony. By the 1980s, the country was approximately 30 percent Christian (equally split between Catholic and Protestant), 30 percent Muslim, 30 percent following traditional African religions, and 10 percent following other beliefs.

The Ivory Coast officially became a French colony in 1893, and it remained under French control until 1960. Following its independence, Houphouet-Boigny, leader of the Parti Democratique de la Cote d'Ivoire (PDCI), became president, a post he retained until his death on December 7, 1993. The early years of his presidency were marked by relative prosperity, but through the 1980s the country fell increasingly into poverty.

In 1983, Houphouet-Boigny oversaw the movement of the capital from coastal Abidjan to Yamoussoukro. He also announced plans to build the cathedral, and on August 10, 1985, Pope John Paul II blessed the building's cornerstone. Construction was completed in 1989, but the pope refused to participate in its final consecration on September 10, 1990, reputedly because of the contradiction implied by the erection of such an expensive building in such a poverty-ridden land.

Objections aside, the completed basilica emerged as the tallest religious structure in the world. The cross on the dome reaches to 158 meters (518 feet), the dome itself being 60 meters (197 feet) high. The church has some 368 columns of various styles, and there are 36 surfaces of stained glass. It seats 7,000 people, and allows standing room for an additional 11,000 in the nave. Built in post-Renaissance style somewhat reminiscent of Saint Peter's in Rome, Our Lady of Peace has two long wings attached to the porch that include 128 Doric columns. The wings encompass a seven-acre plaza that can accommodate 30,000 people.

The new cathedral, which seemed to be consuming so much of the country's gross national product to serve less than twenty percent of the population, became a matter of intense controversy. To placate the other religious communities who were not Christian, the president also saw that a temple and an impressive mosque were erected in Yamoussoukro.

Sources:

Fuchs, Regina. *Ivory Coast*. Edison, NJ: Hunter Publishing, 1991.

Hebblewaite, Peter. "Ivory Coast's Basilica May Turn into White Elephant." *National Catholic Reporter* (March 30, 1990).

OUR LADY OF THE ROSES, MARY HELP OF MOTHERS

One of the most controversial claims concerning an apparition of the Virgin Mary in the contemporary world center on Veronica Lueken (1923–1995). Lueken's unusual experience began in 1968 when Saint Therese of Lisieux (1873–1897) appeared to her and began to dictate poems and other spiritual writings to her. Then, in 1970, the Virgin Mary appeared to Lueken and told her that she would reappear on June 18, 1970, at the nearby Saint Robert Bellarmine Church in Bayside, Queens, New York. She then left instructions that the church's priest prepare for the visitation and erect a shrine and basilica on the same site. The new church would be dedicated to "Our Lady of the Roses, Mary Help of Mothers".

Lueken became Mary's voice, and Mary appeared to her quite frequently. The messages arrived as the Roman Catholic Church was going through changes instituted by Vatican II, the all-church assemblage of Roman Catholic bishops that gathered in the early 1960s. The messages to Lueken spoke against many of these changes, as well as the general social and moral disintegration she perceived around her. As the messages continued and the crowds grew, the church moved against Lueken and her following. She was denied use of the church grounds, and so meetings were moved to the nearby Flushing Meadows Park in Queens.

Through the mid-1970s, the messages became more and more critical of the Catholic Church. In 1975 they endorsed a popular conspiratorial idea that Pope Paul VI (1897–1978) had been replaced with an imposter. Several Catholic bishops in the area, whose members attended the meetings at which Lueken spoke to the Virgin, issued statements denouncing the meetings. The groups, under the name Our Lady of the Roses,

Mary Help of Mothers, gradually aligned with some other independent Marian centers with which they shared a similar conservative perspective. Lueken continued to receive messages until her death in 1995. Since that time the meetings have continued, with prayers using the ROSARY the central practice.

Among the unusual occurrences attending the apparitions are a set of unique photographs. Beginning in the 1970s, photographs taken by people attending the apparition sessions reported strange objects showing up in their pictures. One included a luminous cross, another the words "1972 Jacinto" (a reference to the Fatima apparitions). Many had a variety of strange lines of light. These "miraculous" photographs became so important that the Virgin gave instructions on taking them with a camera that allowed instant development and thus little opportunity to fake the pictures. Lueken's followers have interpreted the pictures as added evidence that God is trying to communicate with humanity in preparation for the imminent end of the world.

In 1986, the Roman Catholic Bishop of Brooklyn issued a statement reiterating earlier statements declaring that the Church did not consider Lueken's revelation credible. He also emphasized that the revelations contradicted Catholic teachings and were sowing seeds of doubt among the faithful relative to the Church's leadership, especially regarding the claims about the pope being replaced by an imposter.

Sources:

Incredible Bayside Prophecies on the United States and Canada! Lowell, MI: These Last Days Ministries, 1991.

Our Lady of the Roses, Mary Help of Mothers. Lansing, MI: Apostles of Our Lady, 1990.

OYOTUNJI (SOUTH CAROLINA)

Oyotunji Village, a traditional West African Yoruba village, was founded in Beaufort County, South Carolina, in 1970 by Adefunmi I, who leads it as both king and priest. Since its existence became public knowledge in the early 1970s, it has become one of the major pilgrimage sites for African Americans seeking to learn about their heritage.

The man now known as Oba Ofuntola Oseijeman Adelabu Adefunmi was born in 1928 as Walter Eugene King. Raised a Baptist, he abandoned the faith of his childhood in 1950 and went on a quest for his African roots. An early step in his spiritual quest was a trip to Haiti, where he discovered voudou first hand. In 1955, in Brooklyn, New York, he founded the Order of Damballah Hwedo Ancestor Priests. Damballah is one of the primary deities acknowledged in voudou, and veneration of one's ancestors is a major practice. In 1959 the world of Santeria, a version of the magical religion brought from West Africa by slaves in previous centuries, was opened to him in Cuba, and the Order of Damballah subsequently evolved into the Shango Temple. The members aspired to a recovery of what they saw as their Nigerian ancestral ways. As the temple continued to evolve, including the founding of an educational arm and the African Theological Archministry, the group aspired to a new lineage of Orisa (deity) worship that placed Nigeria at its core, but was still relevant to modern African Americans. In the mid-1960s, word reach Nigeria of what Adefunmi was attempting, and Ooni Adesoji Aderemi, a Yoruban priest, traveled from Africa to see what was occurring. This eventually led, in 1972, to Adefunmi's ordination into the Yoruban priesthood by the Oluwa (King) of Ijeun at Abeokuta, Nigeria.

Meanwhile, back in South Carolina, the members of the African Theological Archministry built a replica of a Nigerian village. It included a central house for King Adefunmi and his wives. It also housed a staging area for the rites appropriate to the various African deities. Before noon each day, only Yoruban is spoken, so most tourists arrive in the afternoon for their visit. They are welcomed as if they were entering another country and introduced to the behavior proper to the foreign environment.

The number of full-time residents at Oyotunji remains small at about 50 people (one must learn Yoruban to function), but it has become the center of a revival of African religion within the African American community. There are some 10,000 affiliated members across the United States.

Sources:

Brown, David H. *Santeria Enthroned: Art, Ritual, and Innovation in an Afro-Cuban Religion*. Chicago: University of Chicago Press, 2003.

Eason, Djisovi Ikukomi. *"A Time of Destiny": Ifa Culture and Festivals in Ile-Ife, Nigeria and Oyotunji African Village in Sheldon, South Carolina*. Bowling Green, OH: Bowling Green University, Ph.D. dissertation, 1997.

Hunt, Carl M. *Oyotunji Village*. Washington, DC: University Press of America, 1979.

Padre Pio (1887–1968)

Padre Pio, a modern saint and miracle worker, was born Francesco Forgione on May 25, 1887, at Pietrelcina, Benevento, in southern Italy. Raised in relative poverty, he had a mystical bent. He was only fifteen when he became affiliated with the Capuchin Order, and he was made a full member four years later. He was ordained on August 10, 1910.

That he was truly an unusual person first became evident to his monastic brothers in 1918, when on September 20 Padre Pio had a vision of Jesus and received the STIGMATA on his hands and feet. Word spread through the order and in the surrounding community over the next months, and it was picked up in newspapers the following year. As a following developed across the country, in 1923 the Catholic Church made an initial assessment that the stigmata were not of supernatural origin. That ruling did little to stop the development of a following. Pio organized several social service projects, and people began to form prayer groups that supported the charitable efforts. The groups drawn to Padre Pio were pushed to the fringe of the Catholic Church, which officially denied the veracity of any of the unusual events reported in the monk's life. At various times he was forbidden to hold public masses.

Knowledge of Padre Pio remained somewhat confined until World War II, when American soldiers discovered him. It was also in the 1940s that a young Polish priest, Karol Wojtyla (the future Pope John Paul II), first visited him. However, after the war, Padre Pio turned his attention not to his increasing following, but to his several social projects, especially a hospital that was built near the monastery where he resided, San Giovanni Rotundo. Through the rest of his life he would manage the hospital, the House for the Relief of Suffering, spending much of his free time listening to confessions from the growing number of pilgrims. Stories circulated of a spectrum of paranormal occurrences, ranging from BI-LOCATIONS to miraculous HEALINGS. Among the better documented cases of the latter involved seven-year-old Matteo Pio Colella, the son of one of the hospital's physicians. He was cured of meningitis in 2000 after being abandoned by his doctors, who concluded that he would soon die. He recovered quickly following a prayer vigil on his behalf. Matteo later said that he had seen an elderly man with a white beard wearing a brown monastic habit.

Padre Pio died on September 23, 1968, and immediately a popular demand for his canonization arose. The effort on his behalf succeeded in

Many miracles are associated with the Capuchin monk Padre Pio, who was said to have experienced the stigmata (seen here in this photo) after having a vision of Jesus. He later managed a hospital in Italy for many years, where healing miracles were attributed to him. *Getty Images*.

the 1990s, when Pope John Paul II oversaw the ceremonies at which Padre Pio was named venerable (1997), was beatified (1999), and finally canonized (2002). In recent years, the amount of popular literature on Pio has grown exponentially. The places associated with him at San Giobnani Rotundo have become pilgrimage sites, and he is honored globally through organizations such as the Padre Pio Foundation.

Sources:

McCaffery, John. *Blessed Padre Pio: The Friar of San Giovanni*. Ridgefield, CT: Roman Catholic Books, 1999.

Ruffin, Bernard C. *Padre Pio: The True Story*. Huntington, IN: Our Sunday Visitor, 1982.

Schug, John A. *A Padre Pio Profile*. Petersham, MA: Saint Bede's Publications, 1987.

PENDULUMS

Simply put, a pendulum is an object hanging by a cord attached to a fixed point that may be released to swing freely in space as gravity and inertia allow. The pendulum consists of a weight on the end of the string or cord which swings back and forth with a high degree of regularity. Pendulums are most commonly seen through their use in clocks.

The pendulum became a religious device when it was adopted for various **FORTUNE TELLING** purposes. Of course, its most popular use as a divinatory device is largely secular—namely, as a means of dowsing for water or other substances found in the earth. Pendulums often replace the forked sticks used by many dowsers. They have also been used for medical diagnoses (radiesthesia).

The theory behind the use of the pendulum assumes that the person using it is already sensitive to the object of the divination, and that the pendulum amplifies that sensitivity and that its movements make visible what would otherwise be invisible. In the nineteenth century, the pendulum was introduced into Spiritualism. It was believed that the spirits moved the pendulum in response to questions put to them and caused the pendulum to move in certain prearranged ways to give the answer. Commonly, answers will be limited to yes or no answers.

In the twentieth century, some people have emerged who claim that they can read the pendulum in sophisticated ways and draw from it more complicated answers than simple yes-or-no responses. It may be used for map dowsing, for instance. Pendulums, maintain some, can also point the way to desired objects by swinging them over a map, or they can provide medical data by swinging them over the picture of a person, or offer information useful in solving crimes.

Pendulums used for divination are among the items most vehemently attacked by skeptics who emphasize the lack of controlled experiments backing up the claims of those who use them in psychic contexts. In this case, the simplicity and verifiable nature of the pendulum make them ideal for experiments, while the same characteristics make them appealing to treasure hunters and those favoring alternative medical treatments.

Sources:

Bentov, Itzhak, *Stalking the Wild Pendulum: On the Mechanics of Consciousness*. Rochester, VT: Destiny Books, 1988.

Hitchings, Francis. *Pendulum: The Psi Connection*. London: Fontana, 1977.

Olson, Dale W. *Pendulum Bridge to Infinite Knowing: Beginning through Advanced Instructions*. Eugene, OR: Crystalline Pub., 1996.

Webster, Richard. *Pendulum Magic for Beginners: Power to Achieve All Goals*. St. Paul, MN: Llewellyn Publications, 2002.

PENITENTES

The Penitentes, or Los Hermanos Penitentes, is a semi-secret association of Roman Catholics in the American Southwest who have become well known for their extreme practice of penance in an effort to make reparation for their sins. Their practice centers on various forms of bodily mortification, especially FLAGELLATION, and culminates annually in a ritual reenactment of the crucifixion of Jesus. Almost all members of the group reside in northern New Mexico and southern Colorado.

The practices of the Penitentes have been traced back to the medieval flagellants, specifically to the Third Order of Franciscans founded by Saint Francis of Assisi in the thirteenth century. Unlike the brothers and sisters of the first and second orders of Franciscans, the Third Order were lay believers who continued to live a secular life but showed their commitments to Christ through a set of strict disciplines. That the group was early on called the Order of Penitents indicates the priority assigned to various penitential actions as vital elements in the discipline.

The Franciscans entered New Mexico in the sixteenth century, and for the next 300 years they remained a powerful force in the expansion and maintenance of the Catholic Church's presence in the New World. However, through the early nineteenth century, as the territory passed from Spanish to Mexican and then American hands, the Franciscan leadership was stripped of its power and eventually disappeared. The Penitentes appear to have arisen partially to fill the vacuum of leadership in areas with little of no pastoral care.

As the movement emerged, it came to exist as a decentralized association of locally autonomous groups. The local fraternities select their own officers, with the *hermano mayor* or elder brother given extensive authority. The elder brother usually holds office until his death. Though a few women have been admitted to a female auxiliary, the group is basically a male association.

The year-round practices of penitence become focused during holy week. It is during this time, for example, that new members are admitted to the group. The initiation ceremony occurs in the *morada* or council house. After satisfactorily answering a set of questions, the candidate proceeds to wash the feet of the other members, receives lashes from any members whom he may have offended in the past, and finally receives an incision in the shape of the cross on his lower back.

As the movement grew, it became known for its actions on Good Friday (the day commemorating Christ's death in the Christian calendar), during which members conducted a public procession and most would flagellate themselves. Leading the procession would be one or more people carrying a heavy cross. The procession would culminate in the planting of the cross in the ground and the lashing of one of the members to it. Though this part of the ceremonies was conducted in private, at various times non-members have photographed or otherwise observed it.

The Catholic Church has officially distanced itself from the Penitentes, and on several occasions attempted to suppress it. As early as 1886, the archbishop of Santa Fe, for example, ordered the groups to stop flagellation and the carrying of the crosses. He distributed copies of the rules of the Franciscan Third Order and asked them to reformulate their activity in accordance with it. He was largely ignored, however. In spite of subsequent attempts to disband or reform the movement, it has persisted to the present day, and in recent years large crowds have been drawn to the sites of the processions.

Sources:

Ahlborn, Richard E. *The Penitente Moradas of Abiquiú.* Washington, DC: Smithsonian Institution Press, 1986.

Carroll, Michael P. *The Penitente Brotherhood: Patriarchy and Hispano-Catholicism in New Mexico.* Baltimore: Johns Hopkins University Press, 2002.

Henderson, Alice Corbin. *Brothers of Light: The Penitentes of the Southwest.* New York: Harcourt, Brace & Company, 1937.

Weigle, Marta. *Brothers of Light, Brothers of Blood: The Penitentes of the Southwest.* Albuquerque: University of New Mexico Press, 1976.

———. *A Penitente Bibliography.* Albuquerque: University of New Mexico Press, 1976.

PHILIP

The fictional ghost Philip Aylesford, created in 1972, has become one of the most important characters in evaluating claims of paranormal contacts by Spiritualists, New Agers, and others. Philip made his appearance in a group assembled by parapsychologists who had assembled eight people to participate in a series of séances. The group began their work by creating a fictional character and composing a biography for him.

Philip was supposedly a British aristocrat who lived in the middle of the seventeenth century. He was a royalist during the period of the Commonwealth and a Catholic at a time England was controlled by Protestant Puritans. His wife, Dorothea, was a beautiful woman, but somewhat distant and sexually unexciting. Philip found some diversion in the arms of a gypsy woman whom he installed in a house on his estate, Diddington Manor. His wife discovered his tryst and accused the gypsy of witchcraft, leading to her trial and execution. In remorse, Philip committed suicide.

Once his life was sketched out, the group began to attempt to contact Philip. After some time at which they built a group consciousness of Philip, the group began to hold séances as they imagined a Spiritualist might do. Within a short time, Philip began to manifest, initially responding with table raps. Whoever made the rapping sounds claimed to be Philip Aylesford. Among other things, he began to fill in details of his life. He also moved the table around. While the information from Philip was rather mundane, the psy-

In a highly unusual experiment, a group of parapsychologists was able to create a fictional person named Philip and have him appear in séances. The story was related in the 1976 book *Conjuring Up Philip: An Adventure in Psychokinesis* by Iris M. Owen. *Fortean Picture Library.*

chokinetic effects with the table were extraordinary. The experiment was concluded with a public séance that was filmed. Philip rapped on the table, moved it about, changed the lighting in the room, and levitated the table.

The results of the Philip séances and the activity of the fictional spirit remains one of the most important references in evaluating the source of other extraordinary phenomena, especially those assigned to nonhuman entities. The experiment suggested that a small group of people can produce among themselves (quite apart from fraud or stage magic) some unique and unusual phenomena of the type that has on a number of occasions been ascribed to supernatural forces.

Sources:

Owen, Iris M. *Conjuring Up Philip: An Adventure in Psychokinesis.* Toronto: Fitzhenry & Whiteside, 1976.

PILGRIMAGE

A pilgrimage is a journey to a sacred place for the purpose of receiving some spiritual value. The nature of that value varies widely and might include increasing one's sense of identification with a particular faith, gaining a sense of mystical contact with supernatural reality, cultivating spiritual merit or understanding, or receiving a particular benefit, such as the forgiveness of sin. Certainly in the first sense, all religions have sites that are particularly associated with their beginning and/or serve as the current earthly center(s) for worship and sacred activity. Even for religions such as Judaism or Sikhism that do not place a great deal of value on pilgrimages, a journey to the **WAILING WALL** in Jerusalem or to the Golden Temple in Amritsar, India, can give the faithful a deeper tie to their faith community.

The greatest emphases on pilgrimages in the contemporary world are found in Islam and Roman Catholicism. Among the five pillars of Islam, making the pilgrimage to Mecca, the **HAJJ**, is demanded of physically capable believers at least once in their lifetime. The Hajj occurs each year on five days during Dhu al-Hijjah, the twelfth month of the Muslim lunar calendar. On the Common Era (CE) calendar, the Hajj takes place at a different month each year. In the modern world, the pilgrimage has become highly ritualized. It begins in **MECCA**, Saudi Arabia, and over several days visits nearby locations before arriving at the Kaaba, the most sacred site acknowledged by Muslims.

Pilgrimages within Christianity began around the sites associated with Christ's death and resurrection in Jerusalem, but also extended to the various places he was said to have visited during his life. With the geographical spread of Christianity, the sites associated with the 12 Apostles, especially their martyrdom, attained sacred status. Persecuted during its first three centuries, Christians paid considerable attention to the acts of martyrs. Popular piety began to ascribe to martyrs the power of granting the remission of canonical penances (requirements laid out in the confessional for a believer to make restitution for sin). Gradually, the tombs of martyrs and the sites of their martyrdom became places to be visited, as well. There, pilgrims could offer prayer and veneration of the martyr and know that the taint and penalty of sin was being removed. In the early Middle Ages, as the sacrament system of the Church developed and a penitential system erected, pilgrimages were designated as one of a spectrum of adequate actions which could make restitution for a variety of sins, a singular serious sin, or a lifetimes' accumulation of sin.

Within Catholicism, the number of pilgrimage sites multiplied over the centuries, but pilgrimages to ROME were seen as the epitome of the pilgrim's quest. Over the years such pilgrimages have been organized and ritualized, as has the Hajj. The clothing to be worn, the attention to personal hygiene, and (for the rich) the mode of travel, walking being preferred, are traditionalized. As targets of pilgrimages were identified, services emerged to provide for the pilgrim's needs, including the stationing of soldiers along the most popular routes to protect pilgrims from robbers.

Pilgrimages were also tied to the system of indulgences. In Roman Catholic belief, God forgives even the most heinous sin for the sinner who repents. However, some recompense for the sin must also be made. At the same time, the Church is seen as possessing a treasury of merits bequeathed it by Christ and the saints. Thus, the Church may intervene on behalf of individual Christians and use that storehouse of mercy to relieve the temporal punishment due for their sins. In issuing indulgences, the Church seeks not only to assist individuals, but also to promote acts of devotion and charity. Indulgences, usually seen as remitting one's time in purgatory, may be given for specific acts of pilgrimages.

India is covered with holy sites associated with the exploits of the gods, the waters of a sacred river, and/or the presence of holy men. Sacred texts, the *Puranas*, detail different sacred sites and the merit to individuals who travel to them with a proper consciousness. Once on site, bathing at such sites is an especially meritorious act. The improvement in transportation in recent decades underlies a significant increase in the numbers of pilgrims, and the tourist industry has made a noticeable shift in its programs to service pilgrims. As with devotees of other religions, many Hindus have conflated pilgrimages with vacations.

A list of the more prominent pilgrimage sites in India would include BENARES (also known as Varanasi or Kashi); Uttar Pradesh, which is also sacred to Buddhists and Jains; RISHIKESH; Vrindaban, associated with the deity Krishna; Puri, site of the annual Jagannath festival; and the four cities that host the large KUMBH MELA festivals (HARDWAR, Allahabad, Ujjain, and Nasik).

Unlike Hindus, Sikhs do not engage in pilgrimage to gain spiritual merit. Guru Nanak, for example, offered a spiritualized perspective on pilgrimage, equating it with inner exploration and the improvement of one's moral resolve. However, Sikhs do venerate their founding gurus and find inspiration in visiting sites like the Golden Temple in AMRITSAR associated with them. Visits to such shrines help focus the group's teachings and remind people of the moral uprightness to which they are called. Still, the emphasis is as Guru Nanak said, "My places of pilgrimage are to study 'The Word,' and contemplating its divine knowledge within me."

Buddhism, while attempting to reform Hinduism, developed a vast role for pilgrimage, but then it died out in its land of origin. The reestablishment of Buddhism in India in the twentieth century has led to a recovery of the sites most associated with Gautama Buddha's life: LUMBINI, where he was born; SARNATH, where he gave his first public sermon; and KUSINAGARA, where he died. A particular effort was made through the twentieth century to obtain the spot where he attained Buddhahood (enlightenment), Bodhgaya, under the BODHI TREE. According to the

Mahapirinibbana Sutra, Buddha told Ananda, his chief disciple, that the pious should visit these four places and any who happen to die while on pilgrimage will be reborn in a "realm of heavenly happiness."

Over the centuries, as Buddhism spread, a number of additional sites have been designated, not the least being places where Gautama Buddha's RELICS have been preserved and are on display. In different countries, sacred sites exist. In Tibet, for example, Mount Kailas and the adjacent Lake Mamsa attract not only Buddhist but also Hindu and Jain pilgrims, who identify it with the mythical Mount Meru, the axis of the world. Borobudur, a temple in the middle of Java, was built when the island was home to a large Buddhist community.

Sources:

Cousineau, Phil. *The Art of Pilgrimage: The Seeker's Guide to Making Travel Sacred*. Newburyport, MA: Conari Press, 2000.

Gitlitz, David, and Linda Davidson. *Pilgrimage: An Encyclopedia*. Santa Barbra, CA: ABC-Clio, 2002.

POTALA (TIBET)

In Buddhist thought, Mount Potala is the mythical home of Bodhisattva Chenresi (better known in the West by her Chinese name, Kuan Yin). On a hill overlooking the Llasa Valley in Tibet was a cave, which in the years after Buddhism entered the country was considered to be a location favored by Chenresi with her presence. Seventh-century Tibetan ruler Songtsen Gampo built a palace on the hill in 637. That palace would eventually become the residence of the Dalai Lamas.

Seventeenth-century Tibet was dominated by Lozang Gyatso (1617–1682), the fifth Dalai Lama whose life is pictured in a mural on the Great West Hall within the Potala. He is credited with allying himself with the Mongols and then unifying Tibet under the Gelugpa Buddhists whom he led. He also began the massive construction project that created the Potala as it is today. The so-called red palace was completed in the decade after Gyatso's death, during which time the country's regent attempted to rule in place of the Dalai Lama's designated successor. The completed palace is some 384 feet in height and 360 feet wide; it has over a thousand rooms that cover an area of some five square miles. It underwent its last major renovation in the 1920s during the time of the thirteenth Dalai Lama.

From the seventeenth century until 1959, the Potala served as both the seat of the Tibetan government and the home of the Dalai Lama. Following the Chinese invasion of Tibet and its annexation by the Peoples Republic, the Dalai Lama moved into exile in neighboring Tibet. As the Chinese took control of the country, most of its holy sites (especially the monasteries) were looted and/or razed to the ground. However, the Potala, including the Buddhist chapels within it, were exempted from the destruction experienced by the Buddhist community. Today it has once again become a pilgrimage site for Buddhists and is a key tourist stop for foreigners visiting Tibet.

The palace remains one of the most sacred of sites to Tibetan Buddhists, though today it is essentially a museum without any official status. The oldest surviving temples in the country are contained within the walls of the White Palace. They date to the seventh century. One of these temples, known as Phakpa Lhakhang, houses possibly the most holy object recognized by Tibetan Buddhists: a statue of Bodhisattva Chenresi. The bodies of eight of the previous Dalai Lamas are housed there, preserved in STUPAS in the palace's several chapels. The stupa of the fifth Dalai Lama is the largest. It is made of sandalwood and decorated with gold and precious stones.

Sources:

Phuntsok, Namgyal. *Splendor of Tibet: The Potala Palace, Jewel of the Himalayas*. Dumont, NJ: Homa & Sekey Books, 2002.

Potala Palace. Llasa, Tibet: Managing Bureau of Cultural Relics, Tibetan Autonomous Region, 1988.

PRAMBANAN (INDONESIA)

Prambanan, or Lorojonggrang, the largest Hindu temple complex in Indonesia, was a direct result of the change of political control when the Hindu Sanjaya Dynasty replaced the Buddhist Sailendra Dynasty in the southern half of the island of Java. Buddhists had constructed a large STUPA complex at BOROBUDUR north of Yogyakarta. The Prambanan temple complex was only 25 miles from Yogykarta and about 12 miles from Borobudur.

Intensive construction on Prambanan appears to have been commenced by Rakai Pikatan (who had a Buddhist wife) about 850 CE. He built the main temple, and various groups of believers added additional buildings. The main temple had a wall separating it from the other temples, and the nearby river was diverted to flow past it.

The Sanjaya Dynasty identified itself with Shiva, and Javanese Hinduism was intensely Shavite in form. In addition, worship at Prambanan mixed veneration of the deities with obeisance to the king. Some of the lesser temples represented the attempts of lesser royalty to assert their position in both the heavenly and political hierarchy.

The fate of Prambanan followed closely that of its rival Borobudur. Java was conquered by Islam, and Hinduism was suppressed. The acknowledgment of previous rulers as Prambanan was especially attacked. In time, the complex was abandoned, the site overrun by jungle, and its very existence forgotten. It was only rediscovered in 1733 when a Dutch explorer, C. A. Lons, reported having come across it. The first efforts at clearing the site, however, did not begin until 1885. Real restoration, begun in the 1930s, was stopped by the advent of World War II. Restoration of what were literally hundreds of temples at the complex continues today, though believers again began to utilize the site after the Shiva temple was rededicated in 1953.

The complex centers on the Main Shiva temple and fifteen additional, slightly smaller temples, including temples dedicated to Vishnu and

Brahma. Outside the wall that separates the center square are 224 small temples arranged in four rows. The farther the temple is from the center, the smaller in height it is. A second wall surrounds these smaller temples. Gates admit people to the various areas of the complex. While reconstruction continues, the complex has become a favorite site of the Hindu minority on Java, as well as other Indonesian islands.

Sources:

Bunce, Frederick W. *The Iconography of Architectural Plans: A Study of the Influence of Buddhism and Hinduism on Plans of South and Southeast Asia.* New Delhi: D.K. Printworld, 2002.

Iyer, Alessandra. *Prambanan: Sculpture and Dance in Ancient Java. A Study in Dance Iconography.* Bangkok: White Lotus Press, 1998.

Jipto, Moert, and Bambang Prasetyo. *The Siwa Temple of Prambanan.* Yogyakarta, Indonesia: Penerbit Kanisius, 1992.

Jordaan, Roy E. *In Praise of Prambanan: Dutch Essays on the Lord Jonggrang Temple Complex.* Leiden: KITLV Press, 1996.

PRASADAM

In the Hindu tradition, prasadam (literally, "the grace or mercy of God") is food blessed by a deity and then shared with devotees and others as a temple or shrine. During various forms of worship, Hindu believers may offer items of food to the deity (or deities) who have been enshrined. As other acts of worship proceed (chanting, kirtans, etc.) the food is offered and it is believed that the deity partakes of the essential aspect of the food. The food is thus considered blessed. The officiating priest(s) may then take a portion of the offered food, the rest being returned to those who offered it. It will subsequently be shared with others and consumed. The sharing of prasadam is a popular act at any Hindu celebration, as well as regular gatherings at temples for festivals and holidays. It is especially appropriate at PILGRIMAGE sites.

In the modern West, prasadam has become widely known in non-Hindu circles from the

A young boy shares *prasadam* during the Rath Yatra Festival in Kolkata, India. Once the food is blessed by a deity, it becomes holy and may be shared with the faithful. *AFP/Getty Images.*

activity of the International Society for Krishna Consciousness (the Hare Krishna movement). This devotional association makes the production of prasadam part of its daily activity and oversees the sharing of prasadam as part of devotional and evangelical activities. The blessing of Krishna on the food carries to those who partake in it and facilitates their return to the godhead. Members of the Society are urged to offer all the food they prepare to Krishna and to eat only food that has been so offered.

The belief in prasadam underlies the Krishna Food for Life program, which is centered on the preparation and distribution of prasadam (defined as "sanctified vegetarian food"). The movement's founder, A. C. Bhaktivedanta Swami (1896–1977), left his followers with the admonition that

no one within ten miles of a Hare Krishna facility should go hungry.

Sources:

Mahatma Dasa. *Krishna Consciousness at Home: A Practical Guide.* Los Angeles: Bhaktivedanta Book Trust, n.d.

Rajan, Nalini. *Prasadam: Food of the Hindu Gods.* Mumbai, Vakils, Feffer & Simons, 2003.

PSYCHIC SURGERY

Within the Spiritualist community, psychic surgery refers to two very different phenomena. Many Spiritualists believe that each person possesses an astral double, an invisible, subtle body that reproduces the physical body. Some medium healers can see this body, and while in a trance they believe that they are able to make surgical-like changes in that body that will then be reproduced in the physical body. When watching such a psychic surgeon, the entranced medium will assume the posture of a surgeon and make motions in space as if conducting an invisible operation.

However, the term psychic surgery is more commonly used to refer to a form of psychic healing that became popular in the Philippines in the years after World War II. In this form of healing, the medium appears to open the body (blood will often flow), remove tissue from it and close it up without leaving a scar. Such operations are usually performed without any antiseptic and no cases of later infection have been reported.

The most famous of the Philippine healers was Tony Agapoa. After accounts of his healings began to circulate in the West in the 1960s, a number of Americans traveled to the islands and made films of him and others who performed similar operations. Through the 1970s and 1980s considerable enthusiasm was generated because the films showed what appeared to be the healers making incisions, placing their bare hands inside the body (primarily the stomach region), removing tissues, and closing the body as if no incision had been there.

By the end of the 1970s, a variety of observers of the Philippine operations began to claim that psychic surgery was simply a form of slight-of-hand stage magic. Several professional paranormal debunkers with stage magic credentials were able to reproduce every effect that appeared in the movies of the Philippine healers. Once pointed out to Westerners who traveled to the Philippines, the fraud became evident to all. Hearings were held in Washington in 1974 and 1984 calling attention to the fraud, and accounts of the tricks performed by the healers circulated widely in the 1980s that virtually stopped the market of foreigners.

Philippine healers caught performing their tricks, including the use of chicken parts that were palmed and made to appear as if they had been taken from the body, defended their practice as a means of establishing belief in the more traditional psychic healing they were actually performing.

That defense did little to rehabilitate their reputation, however. Several healers who came to the United States in the early 1980s were arrested and escaped prosecution only by fleeing back to their homeland. In spite of the exposure, psychic surgeons continue to operate in the Philippines, and supporters in the West continue to try to argue for the genuineness of the phenomenon.

Sources:

Christopher, Melbourne. *Mediums, Mystics and the Occult*. New York: Thomas Y. Crowell, 1975.

Licauco, Jaime T. *The Truth behind Faith Healing in the Philippines*. Manila: National Bookstore, 1981.

Sherman, Harold. *Wonder Healers of the Philippines*. London: Psychic Press, 1967.

Sladek, Marti. *Two Weeks with the Psychic Surgeons*. Lisle, IL: Spiritual Pathways Institute 1976.

Valentine, Tom. *Psychic Surgery*. New York: Pocket Books, 1975.

Q, R

Qigong

The term qigong refers to a set of practices integrated into traditional Chinese exercise, meditation, and healing practices. The practices are tied together by the belief in *qi* (also known as chi or *ki*), the universal energy existing throughout the cosmos. In psychic circles, *qi* is usually identified with prana, spirit, and other names for cosmic energy. In traditional Chinese healing practices, such as acupuncture, *qi* is pictured as flowing through the body along a number of invisible channels called meridians. Disease is the result of blockages of the normal energy flow through the body.

Qigong has both its esoteric side, known only to a few master practitioner-teachers, and a practical side, as demonstrated in the popular practices in which the public engaged. Qigong masters traditionally horded their knowledge and passed it on orally to a few successors. The role of qigong radically changed after the Chinese revolution. The Maoist government suppressed the Taoist and Buddhist centers and monasteries from which most qigong teachings were generated and oversaw the destruction of numerous qigong texts. As a result, some teachers fled to southeast Asia and the west, and some of the texts began to be published.

The height of suppression of traditional practices in China, viewed by many as superstitious practices, occurred during the decade of the cultural revolution that began in 1966. In the aftermath, Chinese leadership began a reevaluation of traditional culture, one result of which was the encouragement of qigong. A national association of qigong groups emerged and the practice flourished. At the same time, several teachers established themselves in the west.

Qigong reemerged as a secular practice, though some connection to Taoism and Buddhism, which were also reemerging at the same time, continued. The teachings about qi as the underlying cause of qigong's value helped the practice retain some of its religious connections. It also led to the appearance of parapsychologists in China who carried out a number of experiments attempting to scientifically verify the existence of qi.

One effect of the reemergence of qigong was the founding of a number of new groups, which were more or less attached with the national qigong association, to perpetuate its practice. One such group, called Falun Gong, was founded in the 1990s by Master Li Hongzhi. It ties the practice to a variety of traditional Buddhist ideas, but as a total set of teachings it was a new religious movement in which qigong practice was an essen-

Various exercises are associated with the practice of qigong. Such religious groups as the Falun Gong in China use qigong to manipulate *qi* energy for physical and spiritual benefits. *Getty Images*.

THE ENCYCLOPEDIA OF RELIGIOUS PHENOMENA

tial tool leading to enlightenment. Li left China in 1996 and now resides in the United States.

Falun Gong claimed millions of practitioners inside China by the end of the 1990s. It also came under attack. It was independent of the national association and was advocating a new religious teaching independent of the state-approved China Buddhist Association at its temples. After a newspaper criticized Falun Gong on April 25, 1999, some 10,000 members engaged in a silent protest at Tiananmen Square in front of the government buildings in Beijing. This demonstration, which came as a surprise to government security forces, had a completely opposite effect than that desired by the organization. Rather than stopping the actions against it, Falun Gong became a major target of government suppression. The Chinese government moved to destroy the organization, and inside China it has largely succeeded in suppressing it. Numerous adherents were jailed and all public activity outlawed. The organization was declared an evil cult.

By 1999 Falun Gong had nevertheless spread to a number of countries outside China, and adherents have organized an international campaign to call attention to the suppression of the movement inside China. It has negatively branded the government for violating human and religious rights, as well as for engaging in the torture and killing of its members. The Chinese government has retaliated by charging the movement with denying members proper medical care and thus causing the death of many people. While justifying its actions within China, the government's charges have found little support outside the country.

Sources:

Hon, Sat Chuen. *Taoist Qigong for Health and Vitality. A Complete Program of Movement, Meditation, and Healing Sounds.* Boston: Shambhala, 2003.

Hongzhi, Li. *Zhuan Falun (Revolving the Law Wheel).* Hong Kong: Falun Fo Fa Publishing Co., 1994.

Jahnke, Roger. *The Healing Promise of Qi: Creating Extraordinary Wellness through Qigong and Tai Chi.* Chicago: Contemporary Books, 2002.

Lee, Richard E. *Scientific Investigations in Chinese Qigong.* San Clemente, CA: China Healthways Institute, 1999.

Wong, John, and William T. Liu. *The Mystery of China's Falun Gong: Its Rise and Its Sociological Implications.* Singapore: World Scientific Publishing Co. and Singapore University Press, 1999.

RAJGIR (INDIA)

Rajgir, the ancient capital city of the Magadha kingdom, was among the first spots visited by Gautama Buddha as he began to spread the teachings of his new religion. It is only some 20 miles from Bodhgaya, where he attained enlightenment. Among the converts during the Buddha's 12-year stay was King Bimbisara, who attended his talks on Gridhakuta Hill (Vulture Peak). Here Buddha would deliver what are termed the Wisdom Sutras (some of his first words recorded in writing). Buddha also frequently spent periods of meditation at the Jivkamaravana monastery, which was then located in a beautiful orchard. The nearby Saptaparni Caves is the site of the first Buddhist council that was called by his leading followers after the Buddha's death. Ajatsatni, one of the Buddha's leading disciples, received some of his ashes and built a STUPA to hold them and an adjacent monastery. That site is now a mound used as a graveyard.

Like most Buddhist centers, Rajgir suffered from the changing political and religious forces in China. The once flourishing city is today just a small town. However, as part of the global Buddhist effort to revive Buddhism in the land of its birth, Japanese Buddhists have constructed a contemporary stupa on top of Gridhakuta Hill that is known as the Shanti Stupa or Peace Pagoda.

Only ruins remain of Venuvana Vihar, the monastery constructed by King Bimbisara as a residence for Buddha.

Sources:

Majupuria, Trilok Chandra. *Holy Places of Buddhism in Nepal and India: A Guide to Sacred Places in Buddha's Lands.* Columbia, MO: South Asia Books, 1987.

The 2,000-year-old Buddhist university of Nalanda lies near the ancient Indian city of Rajgir, one of the first places Gautama Buddha taught after his enlightenment in Bodhgaya. *Getty Images*.

Panabokke, Gunaratne. *History of the Buddhist Sangha in India and Sri Lanka*. Dalugama, Kelaniya, Sri Lanka: Postgraduate Institute of Pali and Buddhist Studies, University of Kelaniya, 1993.

Tulku, Tarthang, ed. *Holy Places of the Buddha*. Vol. 9. *Crystal Mirror*. Berkeley, CA: Dharma Publishing, 1994.

RAPPINGS

The modern Spiritualist movement began rather unceremoniously in the home of a family named Fox in the town of Hydesville, New York, in 1848. The family, especially two of the children, Kate (1836–1892) and Margaret (1833–1893), found their routine disturbed with rapping noises that could be heard throughout the house. The children assumed that someone was making the noises and gave the name Mr. Splitfoot to him. At one point, in a somewhat playful mood, Kate called aloud, "Mr. Splitfoot, do as I do," and she then clapped her hands twice. She then heard two rappings as if in response. From this incident, over a period of time, the family devised a code in order to turn the rappings into an intelligible form of communication.

The rappings continued through the rest of the year, and many people came to hear and participate in the communications. Eventually, the girls were sent away, but the rappings followed them to their new homes. Margaret went to live with her older sister Leah in Rochester, New York, and here the rappings not only continued but were combined with poltergeist phenomena that included objects being thrown at people by the spirits.

In Rochester, Kate was investigated by two committees, neither of which could come up with a mundane explanation for the rappings. Both she and her sister Leah would go on to become professional mediums. At their séances, in addition to the rapping sounds, objects would move about. As the movement spread, the occurrence of the rapping, and the movement of the table around which the people trying to contact spirits would sit, were common.

Over the next generation, rappings and table tipping would be replaced by trance mediumship in which the person leading the group of people gathered to contact the spirit world would go into a trance and allow spirits to speak through him or her. To this vocal means of communication would also be added various physical phenomena, especially materializations. Much of the physical phenomena would later be proven fraudulent.

One reason that rappings died out was the ease with which they could be produced fraudulently, and from the beginning a number of critics denounced the phenomena as the product of trickery. For example, as early as 1869 British medium William Ferguson testified how he produced and sold simple magnetic devises that could be used to produce the rapping sounds.

Sources:

Brownson, Orestes. *The Spirit-Rapper*. Boston: Little Brown, 1854.

Carrington, Hereward. *The Physical Phenomena of Spiritualism*. London: L. T. Werner Laurie, 1907.

Jackson, Herbert G., Jr. *The Spirit Rappers*. Garden City, NY: Doubleday & Company, 1972.

Pearsall, Ronald. *Table-Rappers*. London: Joseph, 1972.

REIKI

Reiki is a system of spiritual healing that emerged in the west in the 1970s. It has since grown to become one of the most successful movements associated with what was known as the New Age.

Reiki is a healing system utilizing what is variously called *chi, qi,* or *prana,* that same universal magnetic energy described in the eighteenth century by FRANZ ANTON MESMER.

Reiki practitioners are taught to attune to the flow of energy by meditating upon various symbols; they then attempt to facilitate the flow of that energy to their patients in the most efficacious manner. Instruction in Reiki is carried out in levels from beginning to master. At each level students learn to attune more effectively with an additional set of symbols. (Knowledge of the actual symbols is part of the confidential aspect of the Reiki system, though most have been revealed in various Reiki publications.) Reiki is largely based on Chinese medicine, which postulates the existence of a set of energy meridians running through the body. Illness occurs when the free flow of energy through these meridians is inhibited. In Reiki, the student is taught to interact with the client's energy system; the hand placements are also related to stimulating the downward flow of energy in the body, especially along what is termed the gall bladder meridian, which runs vertically from the head to the toe.

Reiki was created by Japanese teacher Mikao Usui (1865–1926). He was affiliated with a Japanese Spiritualist group, Rei Jyutsu Kai, whose headquarters was near the holy mountain of Kurama Kai. He seems to have developed his new healing system by 1914. In 1921 he moved to Tokyo, and over the next five years taught his system to some 2,000 people. He also published a small book with a brief description of Reiki, the answers to some frequently asked questions, and some poems composed by the Japanese emperor designed to advise people on a worthy life. Following Usui's death in 1926, his successor built Reiki into a national movement.

Among Usui's students was Chujiro Hayashi (1878–1941), the last person Usui trained as a master. A former naval officer, after becoming a Reiki master he opened a clinic. Among those who found their way to Hayashi was Hawayo Takata (1900–), a Japanese woman born in Hawaii. When her health failed in the 1930s she went to Japan and eventually found her way to Hayashi's clinic. She was healed under his care and with some persistence she convinced him to train her as a healer. She was named a master in 1937.

Takata operated quietly as a Reiki healer in Hawaii for several decades. The combination of being without a successor and the emergence of the New Age movement led her to teaching in 1973. She designated her first student as a master in 1975. Over the next five years she would train 22 people as masters. In 1979, she took an additional step and named two of the masters as grand masters: her daughter Phyliss Furumoto, who resided in Hawaii, and Barbara Ray of Atlanta, Georgia. Through the 1980s, most new masters were students of either Furumoto or Ray. Shortly after Takata's death, Ray formed the American Reiki Association (later renamed the American International Reiki Association) and authored the first book on Takata's system, *The Reiki Factor* (1983). In 1983, Furumoto founded the Reiki Alliance. Today, most Reiki healers receive credentials through one of these two major Reiki lineages.

A significant change in the Reiki community occurred in 1989, when Reiki master William Rand challenged the practice of charging $10,000 for Reiki master training. From the Center for Reiki Training in suburban Detroit, Michigan, he began master training programs for a mere $600. He also authored a textbook that revealed many of the heretofore confidential Reiki teachings.

Meanwhile, the growing number of practitioners began to mix Reiki with the wide variety of spiritual options now available in the west. By integrating Reiki with another spiritual tradition/practice, they have created new variant forms of Reiki that are usually identified with modifying names. Among these are Tera-Mai Reiki, Karuna Reiki, and Shambhala Reiki, to name just a few examples.

In the 1990s, Reiki spread globally, and it is now available in most urban centers around the world. There are thousands of professional Reiki healers who work full time at their profession, and many more who practice Reiki along with other esoteric disciplines.

Sources:

Haberly, Helen L. *Reiki: Hawayo Takata's Story*. Olney, MD: Archedigm Publications, 1997.

Petter, Frank Arjava. *Reiki: The Legacy of Dr. Usui*. Twin Lakes, WI: Lotus Light Publications, 1998.

———. *Reiki Fire*. Twin Lakes, WI: Lotus Light Publications, 1997.

Rand, William. *Reiki for a New Millennium*. Southfield, MI: Vision Publications, 1998.

RELICS

Among the more controversial issues engaging the Roman Catholic Church in the modern world is its continued use of relics. The critique of some relics in the Middle Ages led to a rejection of their use by Protestants and a complete denunciation of relics by modern skeptics. Officially, a relic is something belonging to or connected with Jesus or one of the saints. Typically, relics are bodies of these holy people, or parts thereof, or pieces of clothing they wore. The church also distinguishes between first-class relics (a body part or an instrument used in their penance or torture) and a second-class relic (an object such as clothing that had been in close contact with them).

The most widespread use of relics was in the altars of local churches. It is a rule not to dedicate the altar of a Catholic church until after the relics of a saint or martyr have been formally entombed therein. The relics may be sealed in the sepulcher, a symbolic tomb.

The church insists that relics are not objects of worship or adoration, but are venerated as signs of God and Christ. The saints now rest in the presence of God and their remains thus become appropriate symbols of the deity whom they served. This distinction in Catholic teachings is often lost in practice. The canonization process includes consideration of miracles (especially healings) that have been associated with the person considered to be designated a saint. Some

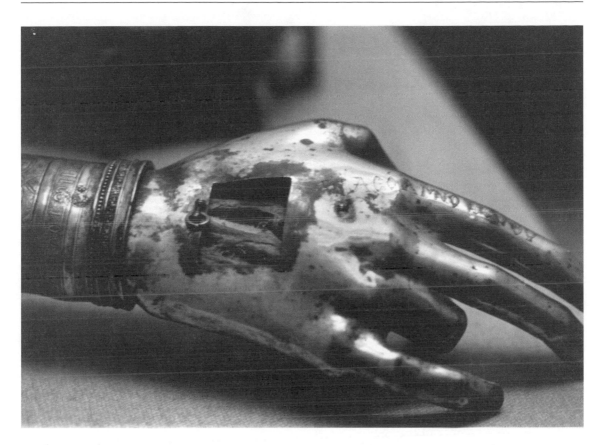

Relics, usually bones or articles of clothing from Jesus or important Roman Catholic saints, are often kept at church altars. Sometimes they may be stored in unique ways, such as these bones preserved inside a metallic hand. *Fortean Picture Library.*

saints such as **PADRE PIO** are famous for miracles, and the devotion and expectancy for extraordinary events directed to such saints is often difficult to distinguish from worship.

The most prized relics are those connected directly to Jesus and the events in his life, death, and resurrection. Such relics would include any articles of clothing he wore, pieces of the true cross on which he was crucified, the crown of thorns he wore, the spear used to pierce his side, the cup from which he drank at the Last Supper, and other objects related to the biblical story. Beginning in the fourth century, when the church became a legal entity under Roman Emperor Constantine, one can notice a heightened inter-

est in relics. Much of that interest was generated by **HELENA** (c. 248–c. 329), the mother of Constantine, who converted to Christianity and toward the end of her life traveled to Palestine, explored Jerusalem and Bethlehem, and reportedly found Jesus' cross and other important relics.

During the era of the crusades, interest in relics grew immensely as returning crusaders brought a variety of items home from Palestine that they claimed were true relics (for example, the blood of Jesus, milk from the Virgin Mary). At the same time, stories of miraculous occurrences around saintly individuals, including the unusual preservation of their bodies, multiplied. Wealthy individuals, prominent church leaders, and powerful rulers attempted to collect and endow local churches with prominent relics. Many were gathered for inclusion in Saint Peter's Cathedral through its construction in the sixteenth century. Among the many treasures claimed to be found there are various relics of the Apostle Peter, **VERONICA'S VEIL**, the **SPEAR OF LONGINUS** used at the crucifixion, and a piece of the **TRUE CROSS**.

Even as relics were promoted in the Middle Ages, questions as to their authenticity were raised. For relics related to Jesus and other people who appear in the New Testament narrative, there was frequently a significant gap between the apparent ages of these items and the time period from which they supposedly came. In the modern world, historians and scientists have joined forces to study relics and analyze their true age. The critique of the historicity of many prominent relics, such as the **SHROUD OF TURIN** or the crown of thorns (now housed in Paris, France), has been supplemented by scientific studies of the many extraordinary occurrences associated with them, such as the noncorruptibility of the body of different saints.

The Roman Catholic Church does not commonly attempt to authenticate relics, especially those used in the altars of local churches. It does, however, offer its seeming approbation of some relics by its allowance and/or approval of the veneration of some, or by, for example, its inclusion of prominent relics in equally prominent locations such as Saint Peter's Cathedral. The Church, too, makes the acceptance or rejection of a particular relic a matter of compulsion, and it allows for the continuing critique of individual relics by the Church's scholars.

In a broader sense, the term "relics" may be used for items connected to religious objects from other than the Roman Catholic tradition, or even the Christian tradition. For example, the Armenian Orthodox Church claims to possess the spear of Longinus. In the last half of the twentieth century, there have been a variety of claims that relics of **NOAH'S ARK** have been discovered, and amateur archeologist Ron Wyatt claimed to have discovered a number of items mentioned in the Jewish

Bible (Christian Old Testament) such as the **ARK OF THE COVENANT** and the tablets upon which God inscribed the Ten Commandments. Claims about Noah's Ark, which became caught up in debates over the authenticity of the Bible, attracted many Protestants, and they have become as controversial as any of the Roman Catholic relics.

Sources:

Bentley, James. *Restless Bones: The Story of Relics*. London: Constable, 1985.

Gauthier, Marie-Madeleine. *Highways of the Faith: Relics and Reliquaries from Jerusalem to Compostela*. Trans. J. A. Underwood. London: Alpine Fine Arts, 1983.

Landes, Richard. *Relics, Apocalypse, and the Deceits of History: Ademar of Chabannes, 989–1034*. Cambridge: Harvard University Press, 1995.

Nickell, Joe. *Looking for a Miracle*. Amherst, NY: Prometheus Books, 1998.

Standish, Russell R., and Colin D. Standish. *Holy Relics or Revelation: Recent Astounding Archaeological Claims Evaluated*. Rapidan, VA: Hartland Publications, 1999.

Wilson, Steven, ed. *Saints and Their Cults*. Cambridge: Cambridge University Press, 1983.

RENNES LE CHÂTEAU (FRANCE)

Rennes le Château is a very small town in southern France whose former parish priest Berenger Saunière (1852–1917) has become the subject of a number of rumors in the twentieth century. Reputedly, in 1897 he discovered a hidden treasure that made him a wealthy man. Later tales would suggest that his treasure was not gold or some other material valuables, but a set of secret documents that led Saunière to various people in the Esoteric community who became the source of his wealth.

The story of Saunière is in fact much more mundane. It appears that he began trafficking in masses; that is, he advertised himself as a poor priest who would say masses for a fee. At the height of his career, he was receiving income from across Europe for saying some 5,000 to 6,000 masses. Many of these were never said, and eventually he was the subject of action against him by the local bishop. Though never wealthy, he did acquire property and subsequently erected some buildings in Rennes le Château.

The story of a treasure was initially floated by Saunière as his defense in the face of accusations against him. The story was later embellished and overheard by Pierre Plantard (1920–2000), a minor figure in France's Esoteric community, who claimed that he was the last surviving descendant of the Merovingians, the family that had ruled France for several centuries until it was replaced by the Carolingians in 751 CE. Plantard was also the founder of a small Esoteric society, the Priory of Sion, through which he asserted his claim to be a Merovingian descendant and thus the rightful claimant to the French throne.

In constructing this modern myth, Plantard claimed that the treasure found by Saunière in 1897 was in fact a set of documents that revealed the truth concerning the Priory of Sion and the Merovingians. Saunière supposedly used the information in the documents to confront the Bourbon royal family of France, the pretenders to the French throne. His money was thus the result of this blackmail.

The story of Rennes le Château was included in the 1982 Esoteric bestselling volume *Holy Blood/Holy Grail*, which expanded upon Plantard's story of the Merovingians by further asserting that Mary Magdalene had been pregnant with Jesus' child at the time of Jesus' execution and that she subsequently traveled to France, where a daughter was born. The descendents of her child later married into the Merovingian family. Thus the Merovingians are not only the rightful rulers of France but also the physical descendants of Jesus.

The publicizing of Rennes le Château in *Holy Blood/Holy Grail* made the town and the church the subject of interest of a number of amateur researchers, all in hopes of verifying the various claims about it. During the last two decades of the twentieth century, speculation on Rennes le Château became a veritable cottage industry with

more than two-dozen books being produced in French and English. These books expanded upon the basic story, though adding little substance. Interest peaked again after novelist Dan Brown included an account of Rennes le Château in his 2003 international best-selling thriller, THE DA VINCI CODE.

Sources:

Baigent, Michael, Richard Leigh, and Henry Lincoln. *Holy Blood/Holy Grail*. London: Jonathan Cape, 1982.

Brown, Dan. *The Da Vinci Code*. New York: Doubleday & Company, 2003.

Fanthrope, Lionel, and Patricia Fanthrope. *Secrets of Rennes le Château*. York Beach, ME: Samuel Weiser, 1992.

Introvigne, Massimo. "Beyond *The Da Vinci Code*: History and Myth of the Priory of Sion." Posted at http://www.cesnur.org/2005/pa_introvigne.htm. Accessed April 1, 2007.

RICHMOND, CORA SCOTT (1840–1923)

Cora Scott Richmond, a Spiritualist medium, speaker of renown, and co-founder of the National Spiritualist Association, was born Cora Lodencia Veronica Scott on April 21, 1840, near Cuba, New York. She was born with a veil or caul, a membrane that covers the face in some babies that has been the subject of many folk beliefs. The attending physician therefore suggested her name, Cora, which designated a person with special powers. Richmond grew to womanhood during the first generation of the Spiritualist movement, which was centered in her home state. In 1851, the family moved to the Hopedale colony at Milford, Massachusetts, a communal establishment that drew on both Universalist and Spiritualist teachings. They stayed only a short time and then moved to Waterloo, Wisconsin, to establish a branch of the Hopedale community. At Waterloo, the still youthful Richmond began to show her spiritual talents, the first manifestation being her falling asleep and writing spirit messages on a school slate. She quickly evolved into a trance medium.

As she evolved, other members of her family began to manifest various mediumistic powers, as well. She also acquired a spirit control, a single spirit who would assume the role of guiding her to contact the spirit realm. In this case, the control was said to be Adin Augustus Ballou, the deceased son of Adin Ballou, the founder of the Hopedale colony. Most mediums have a control who will manifest and serve as a kind of master of ceremonies when the medium goes into trance. After the spirit control manifested for Richmond, other spirits developed a close relationship with her and frequently appeared at séances. At the age of fifteen, Richmond began to offer teaching (channeling) sessions, and it was announced that 12 different spirits were speaking through her.

In 1854 she was invited to move to Buffalo, New York, to share the state with Thomas Gales Foster, an advocate of Spiritualism, which at the time was still a decentralized movement. On occasion, she accepted tests of her abilities, including the holding of spontaneous lectures on subjects about which she had no previous knowledge. After two years in Buffalo, she moved on to New York City for a period. While becoming a successful trance lecturer, she also met and married Dr. Benjamin Hatch, a man who proved to be both a con artist and wife beater. When her situation was brought to the attention of the Spiritualist leadership in New York, they stepped in and assisted her in obtaining a swift divorce. She was soon able to resume her career. Over the next years she traveled widely, including a first trip across the Atlantic in 1873. She stayed in Great Britain for two years. When she returned from England, she became the pastor of a Spiritualist church in Chicago, a position she would hold for the remaining fifty years of her life. In 1878 she married William Richmond, a union that proved to be all the earlier marriage had not been. Rather than exploit her, he became her helpful assistant. He learned shorthand and began to take down and transcribe her lectures for publication.

Cora Richmond had previously published works such as a 250-page epic poem, "Hesperia," on the theme of brotherhood accomplished by Hesperia, the spirit of liberty. Among her later major works are two on Spiritualist philosophy, *Psychosophy* and *The Soul in Human Embodiments*. She also wrote a fictional work, *Zulieka*. She developed an introductory presentation concerning Spiritualism, which was delivered at the Parliament of the World's Religions that gathered in Chicago in the summer of 1893. That same year she participated in the founding of the National Spiritualist Association and was elected the association's first vice president. Her lectures were a regular part of the association's annual meeting for the next 20 years. She passed away on January 3, 1923, in Chicago.

The church she served continues today as the Church of the Spirit located on Chicago's north side. The National Spiritualist Association evolved into the National Spiritualist Association of Churches, which remains as the largest Spiritualist body in the United States.

Sources:

Barrett, Harrison Delivan. *Life Work of Mrs. Cora L. V. Richmond*. Chicago: Hack & Anderson, 1895.

Cutlip, Audra. *Pioneers of Modern Spiritualism*. 4 vols. Milwaukee, WI: National Spiritualist Association of Churches, n.d.

Richmond, Cora L. V. *Psychosophy*. Chicago: privately printed, 1888.

———. *The Soul: Its Nature, Relations, and Expressions in Human Embodiments*. Chicago: The Spiritual Publishing Co., 1887.

RILA (BULGARIA)

Not long after Bulgaria converted to Eastern Orthodoxy, a hermit named Ivan Rilski (tenth century) began a monastery in the Rila mountains in the south-central region of the country. He soon became known as a healer and miracle worker, a wise counselor, and teacher. He attracted others to his monastic practice, and they joined him in creating one of the most prominent religious building complexes in the country. He would later be canonized by the Bulgarian Ortho-

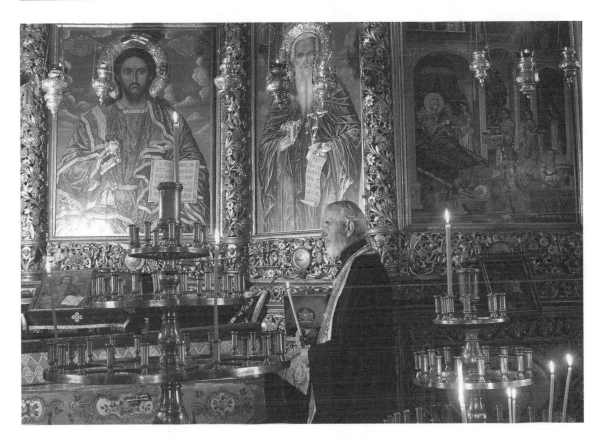

A priest lights candles at the Church of the Birth of Holy Mother at the monastery in Rila, Bulgaria, which was founded by a tenth-century hermit and is home to unique relics and artifacts, such as Raphael's Cross. *AFP/Getty Images*.

dox Church, and his mummified relics are on exhibit in the monastery's church.

The monastery thrived through the fourteenth century with the support of the Bulgarian monarchy, but suffered greatly after the invasion of the Ottoman Turks in the fifteenth century. With Russian support, it revived somewhat at the beginning of the sixteenth century, but it was only with the complete overthrow of Muslim rule in the nineteenth century that a real revival was possible. The main church was erected in the mid 1840s. The monastery is home to a set of valuable icons painted in the fourteenth to nineteenth centuries, and a unique creation called Raphael's Cross. The cross was made of a whole piece of wood. The monk Raphael used simple tools to carve hundreds of figures and religious scenes on the cross. He finished his work in 1802 after twelve years of work.

Sources:

Chavrukov, Georgi. *Bulgarian Monasteries*. Sofia: Naouka I Izkoustvo, 1974.

Stamov, S., Angelova, R., et al. *The Architectural Heritage of Bulgaria*. Sofia: State Publishing House "Telnika," 1972.

Thomas, John, and Angela Constantinides Hero. *Byzantine Monastic Foundation Documents: A Complete Translation of the Surviving Founder's Typika and Testaments*. Washington, DC: Dumbarton Oaks Research Library and Collection, 2000.

RISHIKESH (INDIA)

Rishikesh, one of the holiest of Hinduism's religious sites, is located in the northern Indian state of Uttaranchal, along the Ganges River as it flows through the Himalayan Mountains. Among the many stories about the origin of Rishikish is one centered on Lord Shiva, one of the three most important deities in Hinduism. As told in the *Shrimad Bhaagvad*, during the timeless past, the mythic inhabitants of the universe were attempting to search the ocean of consciousness in the hopes of causing the emergence of the nectar of immortality, *amrit*. However, before the amrita would come forth they encountered a wave of deadly venom. None wanted to drink the venom, but this was part of the necessary process to obtain amrita. At this point Shiva stepped forward and drank the venom. It stuck in his throat, turning it blue. The spot where Shiva stood while consuming the venom is located about eight miles from Rishikesh, where the Nilkanth Mahadeo temple is now found.

Today, Rishikesh is where a number of old temples are located. It is a place for the gathering of a number of SADHUS, many of whom spend most of their lives alone in the nearby forests. It is also the home of several prominent centers founded by twentieth-century gurus, and the beginning point for a pilgrimage for other holy sites even farther up in the mountains.

Built in the twelfth century, the Bharat Mandir is Rishikesh's oldest temple. It is named after Bharat, the brother of Rama, an incarnation of Lord Vishnu, to whom the temple is dedicated. The original temple was destroyed by Tamerlane (1336–1405), the Turkish conqueror who invaded the region in 1398. It was later rebuilt. Over the centuries, a number of famous sages lingered here to venerate Vishnu, some claiming to have been granted a vision of him.

Swami Sivananda (1887–1963) created Shiva Nanda Ashram, which is home to one of the most famous yoga schools in the world and the headquarters of the Divine Life Society. Sivananda, who had wanted to be a physician in his younger years, recreated the image of Hundu monks (*sannyasins*) by advocating their being of service to the community. The original clinic founded by Sivananda grew into one of India's largest charitable hospitals.

Equal in fame to Sivananda is Maharishi Mehesh Yogi, who brought transcendental meditation to the west. Ved Niketan has been his main Indian center, though it is not as important as it was in the 1960s, when, for example, the British musical group the Beatles came to Rishikesh to meet their guru. The ashram also sponsors a large Ayurveda medical center. These and the other active ashrams participate in the annual celebration of international yoga week, which occurs the first week of February.

When the sadhus come to town, one of their destinations is the Triveni Ghat, a place along the river where pilgrims gather to gain the blessings available from bathing in the river. Each evening a ceremony called the Maha Aarti is performed. It is marked by the floating of flames on the river.

The entire region (Rishikesh is only 15 miles from the equally holy city of HARDWAR) is filled with temples and sacred sites. Rishikesh, though, serves as a special starting point for pilgrims wishing to make the access point of the Char Dham, the four holy centers of Badrinath, Kedarnath, Gangotri, and Yamunotri. Pilgrims to these four remote temples seek to achieve peace and harmony, and hope to rid themselves of their worldly pain and sorrows.

Across the river from Rishikesh is Tapovan, which also houses temples worthy of the pilgrims' attentions, including one dedicated to Lakshmana, who purportedly carried out penances there.

Sources:

Keemattam, Augusthy. *The Hermits of Rishikesh: A Sociological Study*. New Delhi: Intercultural Publications, 1997.

Khullar, Reeta, and Rupinder Khullar. *Gateway to the Gods: Haridwar Rishikesh; Yamunotri Gangotri Kedarnath Badrinath*. New Delhi: UBS, 2004.

Saltzman, Paul. *The Beatles in Rishikesh*. New York: Viking, 2000.

Venkatesananda, Swami. *Sivananda: Biography of a Modern Sage*. Sivanandanagar: Divine Life Society, 1985.

ROBERTS, ORAL (B. 1918)

Oral Roberts, the most prominent Pentecostal healing minister of the twentieth century, was born January 24, 1918, in Pontotoc County, Oklahoma. He was the son of an independent Pentecostal minister. In 1935, he became ill with tuberculosis, but he was healed at a Pentecostal revival meeting. He later attended Oklahoma Baptist College and Phillips University, which is affiliated with the Pentecostal Holiness Church.

In 1947 he left the pastorate to become a full-time evangelist with a ministry center on prayer for healing. He settled in Tulsa, Oklahoma, founded the magazine *Healing Waters*, and wrote one of his most popular books, *If You Need Healing—Do These Things*. As early as 1952 he penned an autobiographical book, and he has periodically expanded and updated it since then.

Roberts became one of the pioneers of religious broadcasting when in 1954 he began what became one of the most successful television ministries. He began to film his own revival tent meetings and featured his prayers for healing, along with a sermon, on his weekly show. His crusades, writing, and television work consumed the next decade.

In the mid 1960s his ministry underwent a variety of changes. In 1963, Oral Roberts College (now University) was chartered, and the first students arrived two years later (he passed the presidency of the university to his son Richard Roberts in 1993). Then, in 1964, he left the Pentecostal Holiness Church, joined the newly formed United Methodist Church, underwent its course of study for the ministry, and was eventually ordained a Methodist minister. He discontinued the tent ministry that had formed the core of his work. In 1970, Roberts published his book, *The Miracle of Seed Faith*, which signaled a new direction in his ministry. Along with healing, Roberts began to suggest that God's plan included prosperity for believers.

The 1980s and 1990s were years of triumph for the long-lived Roberts as the Charismatic revival greatly enlarged the Pentecostal community and Oral Roberts University became the revival's leading educational institution. Roberts's television ministry evolved through the years and continues under his son Richard, who has gradually assumed leadership of the many structures created by his father.

Roberts's career has not been without controversy. Almost from the beginning of his healing ministry, he has had to deal with critics of healing ministries in general. In spite of critics who charge that many reported healings never occurred (charging the people healed were not really sick or that the healing did not really occur), enough people were helped in his ministry to overwhelm the critics. Roberts was also beset by family problems, including the suicide of his homosexual eldest son and Richard's messy divorce in 1979. These problems were largely behind him when in 1988 he celebrated his fiftieth wedding anniversary with his wife, Evelyn.

Continuing to be active into the twenty-first century, though at a much reduced pace, Roberts has written more than 120 books. His original periodical continues under the title *Miracles Now*.

Sources:

Harrell, David E. *Oral Roberts: An American Life*. Bloomington, IN: Indiana University Press, 1985.

Lippy, Charles H. *Twentieth-Century Shapers of American Popular Religion*. New York: Greenwood Press, 1989.

Roberts, Oral. *Expect a Miracle: My Life and Ministry*. Nashville, TN: Thomas Nelson, 1995.

———. *If You Need Healing—Do These Things*. Tulsa, OK: Standard Printing, 1947.

———. *The Miracle of Seed Faith*. Charlotte, NC: Commission Press, 1970.

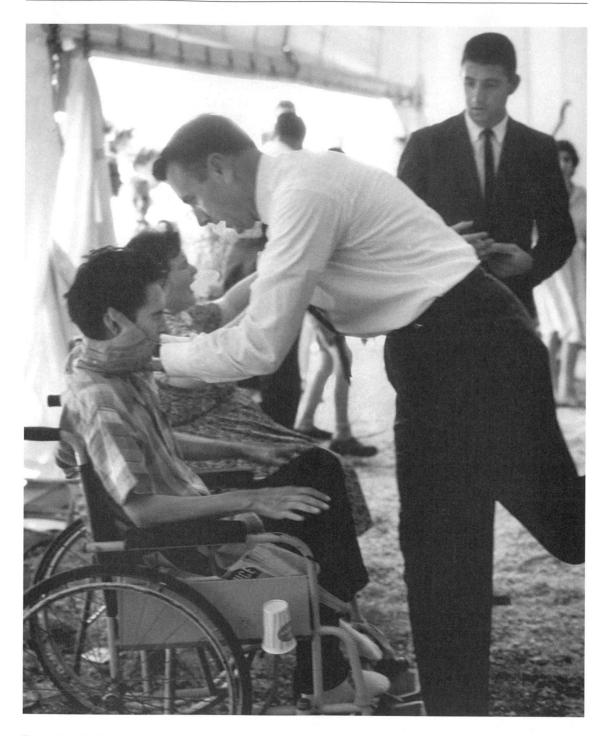

Evangelist Oral Roberts, shown here in 1962, has long been famous for his practice of spiritual healings through the power of Christ. *Time Life Pictures/Getty Images*.

THE ENCYCLOPEDIA OF RELIGIOUS PHENOMENA

ROME/VATICAN CITY (ITALY)

In the spring of 2005, following the death of Pope John Paul II (1920–2005), millions of television viewers watched a broadcast of Rome and the tiny Vatican City that serves as the center of the billion-member Roman Catholic Church, the largest religious organization in the world. Several million pilgrims joined the television audience as the church went through the process of burying their leader and went through the arduous process of electing his successor. The major public ceremonies were conducted in the single most important religious site in the city: Saint Peter's Basilica.

Even before it became the center of the Catholic Church, however, Rome was the center of a great empire, and hence home to numerous pagan temples. Rome's origins date back to at least to the fifth century BCE and the lengthy rule of Servius Tullius (r. 578 to 534 BCE), who included religion among the many aspects of the Roman civilization he helped establish. He is particularly associated with the development of the cult to the goddess Diana on Aventine Hill, where the temple dedicated to her still stands. Today, scattered about the city in various states of ruin, are temples to many pagan deities.

By far the most impressive of the surviving pagan temples is the Pantheon, which is dedicated to the twelve Olympian gods, the main deities of the official Roman religion. The impressive building is covered with a dome that has a span of 142 feet. From its erection around the year 125 CE until the fifteenth century, it was the largest dome in the world. Two previous buildings had existed on the site, too, but both had been destroyed by fire.

The major transition of Rome from a primarily pagan to a primarily Christian city can be traced to the fourth century CE and the reign of the Emperor Constantine (c. 272–337). He built the Church of Saint John Lateran, the first large basilica in the Christian world. This church emerged as the center of Roman Catholic and papal authority for many centuries. In the Middle Ages, it would be the site of some of the most important councils held by the Catholic Church. Over the course of its history, it has been destroyed and rebuilt several times, the last time being in the seventeenth century.

Surviving through the centuries are a number of relics. Among the more significant items to be seen today at the Church of Saint John Lateran is a staircase believed to have been brought to Rome by Constantine's mother, Helena (c. 248–c. 329). Tradition suggests that the staircase and its 29 steps originated in Jerusalem and was walked upon by Jesus during his Passion. In former years, the stairs functioned to connect the church with what was then the papal residence. The church also contains a private chapel for the popes, the Sancta Sanctorium, which houses some of the key relics connecting Rome with the site of Christian origins in the Holy Land. Among these relics are what are believed to be the True Cross, a lock of hair from the Virgin Mary, a fragment of bread from the Last Supper, and some bones from the two Johns (John the Baptist and John the Evangelist) for whom the church is named. Finally, the church also houses a number of Jewish artifacts brought to Rome by Vespasian, who sacked Jerusalem in 70 CE.

The Church of Saint Mary Major, the first major church in Christendom dedicated to the Virgin Mary, dates back to a vision of the Virgin in the middle of one of Rome's very hot summers. The following story recounts events from the mid-fourth century CE, but the story itelf seems to have first appeared in the eleventh century.

A wealthy Roman resident was told in the vision to build a church where he found snow falling the next morning. His vision coincided with the pope's receiving of a similar message in a dream. The next morning snow covered the Esquiline Hill. The original building was replaced with a large basilica in the fifth century, following the proclamation of Mary as the Mother of God by the church council at Ephesus. An image of Mary in the church is thus named Our Lady of the Snows.

The Church of Saint Mary Major was connected to the Church of Saint John Lateran during the medieval era by the relic of a full-length image of Jesus ascribed to the Apostle Luke. It was periodically carried in procession from the Lateran to Saint Mary's. The arrival of the image at Saint Mary's was seen as symbolically reuniting Jesus with his mother.

These two early churches in Rome were preceded by sites inhabited by the Christian community through the centuries. Primary among these are the catacombs into which it is believed the persecuted often took refuge. The catacombs are the places for the burial of many Christians, including many saints. Over 500,000 bodies are to be found in the more than 60 miles of the underground catacomb networks.

Christian life in Rome is tied to the arrival of two of the most famous of Jesus' apostles: Peter and Paul. Paul came to Rome around 65 CE and was eventually executed there. He was buried outside the city walls in a cemetery belonging to a Roman lady named Lucina. On this site in the fourth century, Constantine would oversee the erection of a large basilica that came to be known as the Church of Saint Paul Outside the Walls. Peter, regarded by Roman Catholics as the first bishop of Rome, was also executed in the city. He was buried on the site of the present Vatican City, and here Constantine also built another large basilica. The basilica was demolished in the early sixteenth century, however, and replaced by the present Saint Peter's Basilica.

The Constantinian basilica had fallen into disrepair during the years when the popes resided in France. Thus it was that Pope Nicholas V (r. 1447–1455) suggested the building be replaced by a new church. The building process would cover the next century and a half and be caught up in the larger ongoing demands for reform within the church. Efforts to raise money to support the construction of Saint Peter's became an important element leading to the emergence of Protestantism and the splitting off of much of the northern and western European countries from the

Catholic fold. The present building was finally dedicated in 1626.

Saint Peter's dome is slightly larger than that of the Pantheon. The overall surface area of the interior is impressive at more than 160,000 square feet (compared to the 90,000 square feet covered by the cathedral in Milan, Italy, and the 84,000 square feet of Saint Paul's in London). The church houses a number of relics, many tracing their history to **Saint Helena**'s search of the Holy Land in the fourth century, and has become the place where many of the church's most impressive services occur including the canonization of saints and the coronation of successive popes.

As Christianity spread throughout Europe, Rome became a focus of pilgrimage. To the churches of Saint John Lateran, Saint Mary Major, Saint Paul Outside the Walls, and Saint Peter's, three additional churches emerged as primary objects for visitation: Saint Lawrence Outside the Walls, the Holy Cross, and Saint Sebastian. To these have been added other churches dedicated to various saints.

Radiating outward from Vatican City, one can now find the offices of the Curia, the international administrative offices of the Catholic Church, numerous colleges and seminaries, the international headquarters of many ordered communities, and the offices of an uncounted number of official and unofficial Catholic organizations. Twelve buildings within Rome but not in the city, including, for example, the churches of Saint John Lateran, Saint Mary Major, and Saint Paul Outside the Walls, have extra territorial rights that exempt them from either expropriation or taxes by the Italian government.

Vatican City is considered to be a separate country, though some of the affairs generally conducted by a sovereign state are handled by Italy's government. It issues its own currency and stamps, has its own flag, and its own police force. The complex political relationship between the governments of Vatican City and Italy, and the Roman Catholic Church, has led to an equally complex set of relationships between the Vatican and other governments and ecclesiastical entities worldwide.

Sources:

Barrett, David. *The Encyclopedia of World Christianity.* 2nd ed. New York: Oxford University Press, 2001.

Hager, June. *Pilgrimage: A Chronicle of Christianity through the Churches of Rome.* London: Weidenfeld & Nicolson, 1999.

Hebblethwaite, P. *In the Vatican.* Oxford: Oxford University Press, 1987.

Introvigne, Massimo, PierLuigi Zoccatelli, Nelly Ippolito Macrina, and Verónica Roldán. *Enciclopedia delle Religioni in Italia.* Leumann (Torino): Elledici, 2001.

Tylenda, Joseph N. *The Pilgrim's Guide to Rome's Principal Churches.* Collegeville, MN: Liturgical Press, 1993.

ROSARY

The Rosary is both a form of repeated prayer very popular in the Roman Catholic Church and a designation of the string of prayer beads used to assist the counting of the prayers. The use of such prayer beads is by no means confined to Catholicism or Christianity. Their origin predates Christianity in the Middle East, and Muslims, Buddhists, and various Esoteric groups also use them. The Catholic Rosary generally consists of 50 beads, with a marker bead dividing them into groups of ten.

In Catholicism, the Rosary derived from devotional practices relative to the reciting of the biblical Psalms, of which there are 150. The saying of a brief prayer thrice around the Rosary models the repeating of the Psalms. In actual practice, the Rosary is generally said using the prayer known as the Hail Mary. After saying it ten times, the Lord's Prayer (the "Our Father") is repeated. In the modern world, a large number of variations on the Rosary have appeared.

The present practice of saying the Rosary derives from events attributed to Saint Dominic (c. 1170–1221). At that time, the Dominican Order had been placed in charge of the Inquisi-

tion, whose first task was the suppression of the Albigensians, a Christian Esoteric group that had grown in strength to challenge the Catholic hegemony in southeastern France. In the initial stages of the reconversion campaign, Dominic is said (there being no contemporary accounts) to have entered into a period of intense prayer and penance. At one point he became unconscious and was visited by the Blessed Virgin Mary, who told him to preach the Psalter (i.e., the Rosary). His subsequent opening sermon in the Cathedral at Toulouse was marked by a variety of "supernatural" signs, including the movement of the arms of the Virgin on a painting that hung in a prominent place in the church.

The Rosary was popularized on a wider scale by Alain de la Roche (1428–1475), who in 1470 founded the Rosary Confraternity. Pope Leo X gave his official commendation to the Rosary in 1520, and its spread over the next centuries followed the establishment of the Dominicans around the world. It subsequently became the most popular form of expression of Catholic piety—apart from attendance at mass—and is widely used in connection with other forms, such as the wearing of SCAPULARS.

Sources:

Beebe, Catherine. *Saint Dominic and the Rosary.* New York: Farrar, Straus & Cudahy, 1956.

Gaffney, J. Patrick. *The Rosary: A Gospel Prayer.* Bay Shore, NY: Montfort Publications, 1990.

Gribble, Richard. *The History and Devotion of the Rosary.* Huntington, IN: Our Sunday Visitor, 1992.

Winston-Allen, Anne. *Stories of the Rose: The Making of the Rosary in the Middle Ages.* University Park, PA: Pennsylvania State University, 1997.

ROSSLYN CHAPEL (SCOTLAND)

Rosslyn Chapel, more properly called the Collegiate Chapel of Saint Matthew, is a worship center now affiliated with the Scottish Episcopal Church. It is located in the Esk Valley a few miles south of Edinburgh. It is the completed part of

Rosslyn Chapel near Edinburgh, Scotland, is a sixteenth-century church that has become famous for the symbols adorning its interior. Some believe that these symbols hold clues to the location of the Holy Grail or the Ark of the Covenant. *Getty Images*.

what was originally planned to be a much larger church. The church was begun at the insistence of Sir William Sinclair (1410–1484). He left an endowment to continue the work, which continued until 1571, when secular authorities, influenced by the Protestant Reformation, claimed the moneys meant to build an obviously Roman Catholic Church.

For the next century, the Catholic Sinclairs and Protestant authorities argued about the chapel. Along the way, in 1650, Oliver Cromwell attacked Rosslyn Castle and desecrated the chapel by using it as a stable. In 1688, a riotous mob further vandalized the building. It lay abandoned until 1736, when it was restored. Services now related to the Episcopal Church (the Scottish equivalent to the Church of England) began, and in the last-half of the twentieth century recognition of the historical importance of the chapel has undergirded its restoration.

In recent years, Rosslyn Chapel has assumed a prominent role in the alternative history focused upon the Knights Templar. The Templars had become quite wealthy, and some speculate that those knights who came to Scotland brought a significant amount of their treasure with them. Some of that treasure had been accumulated when the original members of the order were in Jerusalem on a Crusade. According to this story, King Philip the Fair of France (1268–1314) tried to suppress the Templars, but some of the group escaped and found refuge in Scotland. Here they came into contact with Sir Henry Sinclair (d. c 1400), whose lands included Rosslyn. Sinclair, working with Italian sailor and explorer Carlo Zeno (1334–1418), had actually discovered North America in the 1390s, having landed at Oak Island, Nova Scotia, in 1396.

Rosslyn Chapel was begun by Sir Henry's grandson, Sinclair, a half century after Sinclair's reputed voyage to Canada. His grandson assumed a significant role in directing the architects to include a variety of oddities into the design and decoration of the building. Much of its value today relates to the symbolism adorning the interior. For example, the ceiling includes a number of obscure symbols about which many have speculated. A prize of £5,000 has been offered to anyone who can decipher their meaning. The chapel also boasts the largest number of **GREEN MAN** carvings of any European medieval chapel.

However, the primary speculations about the chapel concern the possibility that treasure lies in its crypt—possibly even the **ARK OF THE COVENANT** or the **HOLY GRAIL**. Among the evidence cited to support these claims is the resemblance of the chapel's floor plan to that of Herod's Temple in Jerusalem. If the Templars brought items plundered from under the temple in Jerusalem, a chapel modeled on the temple would be an appropriate resting place. The speculation about Rosslyn became another element of Templar history integrated into the best-selling novel, *THE DA VINCI CODE* (2003).

Sources:

Knight, Christopher, and Robert Lomas. *The Hiram Key: Pharaohs, Freemasons and the Discovery of the Secret Scrolls of Jesus.* Rockport, MA: Element Books, 1997.

Laidler, Keith. *The Head of God: The Lost Treasure of the Templars.* London: Weidenfeld & Nicolson, 1998.

Ralls, Karen. *The Templars & the Grail: Knights of the Quest.* Chicago: Quest Books, 2003.

Wallace-Murphy, Tim. *The Templar Legacy & The Masonic Inheritance within Rosslyn Chapel.* Rosslyn, Scotland: "The Friends of Rosslyn," n.d.

RYDÉN, VASULA (B. 1942)

Vasula Rydén, a Greek Orthodox laywoman, reputedly began receiving messages from God in 1985. In the intervening years, as the messages were publicized, a movement known as the True Life in God Movement has developed around her. At the time she began receiving messages, she resided in Bangladesh. She initially resisted the messages because she was confused about what she was experiencing, but she slowly became comfortable with these communications.

In 1988 she began to accept invitations to speak publicly about the messages. As the messages were transcribed, they were translated into a variety of languages for publication. In her travels she has been especially attuned to invitations that offer the opportunity to speak to religious leaders about the unity of Christian churches and peace between peoples. A number of invitations have come from non-Christian groups, as well. The messages are described as an outpouring of the ineffable love of Christ, coupled with a call to personal repentance, reconciliation, peace, and cooperation. Rydén has called for an intimacy with God that never loses sight of God's holiness.

Rydén has also conveyed a set of related messages to Christians. For example, she emphasizes the need to reconcile the date on which Easter is celebrated (the western and eastern churches calculate the date for setting Easter using different calendars). She has prophesied that the Russian church will be reborn and become the spiritual head of many nations.

Rydén's messages have been received by a process generally called AUTOMATIC WRITING (though that is a term she does not like), the handwriting of the messages being quite distinct from that of her normal handwriting. She has noted that when the messages first started coming she received them in silence. Later, she began to hear the words that were being written. She now writes while kneeling before a set of ICONS.

In 1998, as the result of one of her visions, Rydén began a project to feed the poor in the Holy Land. The vision was of the Virgin Mary holding the baby Jesus. A short time later, she was given an icon painted by a Romanian woman that was a replica of the vision. The icon was one of several confirmations of the vision and led her to open several centers known as Beth Myriams. These centers are now located not only in the Holy Land but also in additional countries such as Kenya, Bangladesh, India, and the Philippines.

A global movement, drawing Orthodox, Catholic, and Protestant believers, has grown up around Rydén's messages, and groups around the world have organized to facilitate her travels and listen to her messages. The messages have been translated into more than 25 languages.

Sources:

Neirynck, Jacques. *The Vassula Enigma: In Direct Communication with God?*, Wantage, Oxon, UK: English Association of True Life in God, 2001.

Rydén, Vasula. *True Life in God.* 12 vols. Independence, MO: Trinitas, 1986–2003.

SACRED HEARTS OF JESUS AND MARY

Devotion to the Sacred Heart (of Jesus or of Mary) is a popular form of Roman Catholic piety. Catholic iconography frequently pictures Jesus and Mary with stylized hearts imposed on their chests. In the case of Jesus, a crown of thorns symbolic of His sufferings generally encircles the heart; above the heart is a cross and flame. The Sacred Heart of Mary is pictured variously, sometimes in a fashion resembling the heart symbol on Jesus, while sometimes it is pierced by a blade or simply shown as a heart.

Devotion to the Sacred Heart began as contemplation on the suffering of Jesus relative to His crucifixion. While on the cross, He was stabbed in the side with a spear. Through the Middle Ages, contemplation of the wound in Jesus' side shifted to a veneration of His heart. It drew content from all of the traditional associations of the human heart, with a spectrum of compassionate emotions, and found resonance in various scriptural passages. However, the symbolism reached a new height in the seventeenth century. This was especially due to the efforts of two people: Margaret Mary Alacoque (1647 1690) and Jean Eudes (d. 1681).

Sister Margaret Mary had seen apparitions of Jesus since childhood, and they continued after she joined the Visitation Order in 1671. Two years later, on December 27, she had a new vision of Jesus. He revealed the secrets of his Sacred Heart, which, she noted, he had concealed up until then. He also told her that she would be the one to spread the message of the Sacred Heart and save people from the abyss of perdition. Two subsequent visions in 1674 and 1675 provided further direction.

With the help of her fellow nuns, Sister Margaret Mary began the efforts to establish the devotion to the Sacred Heart, which began with a special altar at the convent. She then commissioned a painting of the Sacred Heart and copies were printed for widespread distribution. Soon, several booklets were written to provide basic information on the devotional practice. The practice first spread through the Visitation Order, and each Visitation Chapel erected a Sacred Heart altar.

At the same time, Eudes launched an effort to propagate the devotion to the Heart of Mary. His campaign began in Autun, France, in 1648, and then spread across the country. Eudes's message eventually made it to Rome, where it failed to gain papal approval. However, through the next century, unofficial devotion continued. By the mid-1850s, approval was granted to the Office and Mass of the Most Pure Heart of Mary. In 1856, with special urging from the French bishops, a feast of the Sacred Heart of Jesus was approved for the whole Church.

The Basilica of the Sacred Heart on Montmartre in Paris emerged as one of the great centers promoting the Sacred Heart. Erected between 1876 and 1912 with the help of public subscriptions, it marked the fulfillment of the supplication to the Sacred Heart for France made during the Franco-Prussian War (1870–1871). The interior of the basilica is dominated by a mosaic of the Sacred Heart showing Jesus with His arms open wide. In 1899 Pope Leo III consecrated the human race to the Sacred Heart of Jesus. Devotion to the Heart of Mary received support in the twentieth century after many apparitions of the Virgin Mary were seen. Meanwhile, Sacred Heart of Jesus devotion was championed in the parallel devotion to the **DIVINE MERCY** initiated by Sister Josefa Menendez (1890–1923), a young Spanish woman who had joined a French religious order.

Devotion to the Heart of Mary is often intertwined with that of Jesus. The practice was heavily criticized in the mid-twentieth century for its over-sentimentality and the tendency of Jesus to be pictured as somewhat effeminate. However, the practice was revived during the pontificate of John Paul II. It has also been supported by stigmatist **PADRE PIO**.

Sources:

Arnoudt, Peter J. *The Imitation of the Sacred Heart of Jesus.* Rockford, IL: Tan Books, 1974.

Fos, Robert. *The Immaculate Heart of Mary.* Huntington, IN: Our Sunday Visitor, 1986.

Haring, Bernard. *The Sacred Heart of Jesus: Yesterday, Today, Forever.* Liguori, MO: Liguori Publications, 1999.

Hume, Ruth Fox. *St. Margaret Mary, Apostle of the Sacred Heart.* New York: Farrar, Straus & Cudahy, 1960.

Menendez, Josefa. *The Way of Divine Love; or, The Message of the Sacred Heart to the World and a Short Biography of His Messenger Sister Josefa Menendez Coadjutrix Sister of the Society of the Sacred Heart of Jesus 1890–1923.* Brookings, SD: Our Blessed Lady of Victory Missions, 1981.

SADHUS

A sadhu (literally, "forest dweller") is a Hindu ascetic who leaves worldly pursuits to concentrate on religious goals. There are an estimated four to five million residing in India, and they represent an aspect of Hinduism that has not been exported to the West. Sadhus renounce "the world" in order to focus entirely on enlightenment and the life beyond death. They cut family ties, possessions, and home from their lives. They wear little or no clothing and eat what little food they are given or can scrounge from the countryside. Sadhus tend to live by themselves, spending their days in devotion to their chosen deity, though they will often show up in great numbers for large traditional festivals such as the **KUMBH MELA**.

Sadhus represent the more extreme forms from the entire spectrum of the Hindu religion with its numerous deities and multitude of techniques to reach the desired religious goals. Different sadhus will spend most of their waking hours in the practice of austerities, forms of yoga, or techniques of meditation that an average believer might practice for a short time daily or weekly. The most extreme behaviors involve the adoption of a posture that will be maintained day and night for many years—this often leads to the degeneration of parts of the body. Some sadhus go naked and rub their bodies with ashes (a symbol of death and rebirth). Others refuse to cut their hair, and like the Biblical Samson, think of their hair as the basis of supernatural power. The extreme practices usually have their basis in the activities of the deities as described in the Hindu holy books. The appearance of the sadhu—marks on the forehead, the color of any clothing, etc.—gives clues as to the deity that is being honored.

Most sadhus are celibate, having renounced sex along with other aspects of ordinary life. However, some from the tantric traditions do engage

Hindu ascetics known as sadhus, such as this man in Kathmandu, Nepal, dedicate themselves to the pursuit of enlightenment through a life of isolation, self-deprivation, and feats of physical endurance. *AFP/Getty Images*.

in sex as a means of enlightenment. Also, many are known for their injections of various mind-altering drugs, such as marijuana, which, like sex, can become a tool to speed enlightenment. The god Shiva is especially identified with *charrus* (hash). The sadhu should be distinguished from the *sanyassin* (renouncers), who take a formal vow to renounce everything, including sex, family, and even their names.

There are a few female sadhus, known as *sadhvis*, too. Most of these are older women, usually widows. Being a sadhvi is one of the few possible pursuits for widows in traditional Hindu society. Sadhus are overwhelmingly male, however, and many of the groups to which they belong do not allow women to associate with them. In recent decades, a few non-Indians have adopted the sadhu life, as well.

Included among the sadhus are some who are referred to as FAKIRS, who make their living by demonstrating various unusual yogic feats or stage shows of magic. These are often passed off as demonstrations of miraculous feats.

Sources:

Ghurye, G. S. *Indian Sadhus*. Bombay (Mumbai), India: Popular Prakashan, 1964.

Gross, R. L. *The Sadhus of India: A Study of Hindu Asceticism*. New Delhi: Rawat Publications, 2002.

Hartsuiker, Dolf. *Sadhus, the Holy Men of India*. Rochester, VT: Inner Traditions, 1993.

Oman, J. C. *The Mystics, Ascetics and Saints of India*. London: T. Fisher Unwin, 1905.

Tripathi, B. D. *Sadhus of India*. Bombay (Mumbai), India: Popular Prakashan, 1978.

SAI BABA (B. 1926)

Sai Baba is one of the most popular (and controversial) of contemporary Indian spiritual teachers (gurus). He heads what is claimed to be the largest ashram in the country. Sai Baba was born Satyanarayan Raju in the small village of Puttaparthi, Andra Pradesh. Biographical details of his early life are scant (and even his birth date is in

doubt), but according to official sources, when he was 14 he began to behave in such a way as to make his family and fellow villagers believe he was possessed by a demon. Satyanarayan countered the accusation by saying that he had in fact been visited by the spirit of Sai Baba of Shirdi (1856–1918), the much-admired miracle-working guru of Maharashtra. The previous Sai Baba had been revered as a perfect master and a *bhagwan* (blessed one), a common title given to the most honored of teachers signifying that their level of wisdom is like that of a deity (a concept often difficult for westerners to grasp) and *avatar* (incarnation of divinity).

Sai Baba emerged as a popular teacher, and he soon out-performed his contemporaries with his miracles. His common miracles included materializing small objects for his followers, most often some *vibhuti* (sacred ash), and on occasion he caused valuable objects such as gold jewelry to appear. Numerous healings are attributed to him, too, as well as at least two resurrections of dead people.

Sai Baba established his ashram, Prasanthi Nilayam, at Anantapur, Andra Pradesh. It is currently managed by the Sri Sathya Sai Central Trust, which was formally organized in 1972. Through the trust, Sai Baba has led the Sri Sathya Sai Institute of Higher Learning, which became a university in 1981. More recently, he founded the Sri Sathya Sai Institute of Music, located in his hometown of Puttaparthy. He has inspired the opening of several hospitals, while also establishing a wide spectrum of services to minister to the poor. Evidence of the size of his following was clearly indicated when a modern airport had to be constructed near the ashram in order to facilitate the transportation needs of the millions coming to Prasanthi Nilayam.

Though the recipient of many honors and the support of government officials, Sai Baba has become the target of numerous critics. The most extreme critics charge that his miracles are merely stage magic. The Indian Committee for the Scientific Investigation of the Claims of the Paranormal, headed by the now-famous "Anti-Guru,"

Indian guru Sai Baba is the controversial leader of the Prasanthi Nilayam ashram. His claims to performing miracles have been attacked by numerous critics, and in 1993 an attempt was reportedly made on his life. *AFP/Getty Images.*

B. Premanand, have continually attempted to expose Sai Baba's often crude attempts to "materialize" objects by using sleight of hand. Though the evidence for trickery on Sai Baba's part is substantial, it has done little to lessen his support, at least in India.

Sai Baba has also been attacked by some close former devotees, young men who claim that he abused them sexually. Then on June 6, 1993, six residents of Prashanti Nilayam, including Radha Krishna Menon (one of the people implicated in assisting Sai Baba with his fake miracles), were killed in Sai Baba's bedroom. Police later claimed that four were assailants attempting to assassinate Sai Baba, and two were killed protecting their guru.

The critiques of Sai Baba have helped make way for a would-be rival. A young guru, Bala Wsai Baba, has established himself in the Kurnool district of Andhra Pradesh. He also claims to perform miracles and has attracted a substantial following, though nothing like the more famous Sai Baba.

Sources:

Baskin, Diana. *Divine Memories of Sathya Sai Baba.* San Diego: Birth Day, 1990.

Brooke, Tal. *Avatar of Night. Special Millennial Edition.* Berkeley, CA: End Run Publishing, 2000.

Hislop, John S. *Seeking Divinity.* Tustin, CA: Sathya Sai Society of America, 1997.

Murphet, Howard. *Sai Baba Avatar.* India: Macmillan Company of India, Ltd., 1978.

SAINT CATHERINE'S MONASTERY (EGYPT)

Among the holiest of sites for both Christians and Jews is the mountain where God is said to have given His laws to Moses. Many identify that spot, variously called Mount Sinai or **MOUNT HOREB**, with a mountain peak otherwise named Jebel Musa. Mount Sinai also has religious significance for Muslims, who identify it as the place where Mohammad's horse ascended into heaven. This mountain was visited in the fourth century by Constantine's mother, **HELENA** (c. 248–c. 329), on her famous trip to the Holy Land, during which she identified a number of holy sites and gathered a number of reputed relics of Jesus and those closest to him. While at Jebel Musa, she erected a tower and small church. During the reign of the Emperor Justinian I (483–565), a monastery was purportedly constructed at the site of the tower. It appears that, in fact, Justinian was responsible for building the castle-like structure, Saint Catherine's Monastery, to protect the monks who had come to reside in the area, possibly since the time of Helena's visit.

Saint Catherine's Monastery has changed little since the sixth century. Its main entrance is still marked by the large wooden door that is now

1,400 years old. Inside are inscriptions in honor of the Emperor Justinian and his "late Empress" Theodora. They appear to have been created sometime between Theodora's death in 548 and Justinian's in 565.

A path behind the monastery leads up the mountain to the spot where, it is alleged, God inscribed the law on a rock tablet. On that spot there is now a small chapel. Inside the chapel is the rock that is said to be the source from which the tablets were made; on the western wall is a crevice where Moses hid when God's glory passed by (Exodus 33:22). Of equal importance to the mountain behind the monastery is another treasure—the burning bush. Visitors to Saint Catherine's will today be taken to see the bush that some believe was the same one Moses saw burning without being consumed (Exodus 3).

At a later date, Sinai was said to have been visited by the prophet Elijah, who had an encounter with God after his devastating dealings with Queen Jezebel. The spot he heard God speak is marked by a spot halfway up the mountain called Elijah's Basin (1 Kings 19).

Also among the monastery's treasures is a library of ancient manuscripts and icons that is often compared to the Vatican library in its importance. The collection includes thousands of volumes written in a spectrum of ancient languages—Greek, Coptic, Arabic, Armenian, Hebrew, Slavic, Syriac, etc. The most well-known item found in the library is the fourth century Codex Sinaiticus (now in the British Museum in London). This is one of the most ancient complete texts of the New Testament. It was discovered in the 1850s by Constantin von Tischendorf (1815–1874), a German biblical scholar.

Saint Catherine's was named after the legendary Saint Catherine of Alexandria. She was a young girl who converted to Christianity after experiencing a vision. She was subsequently martyred by beheading, and angels took her body to Mount Sinai, where it was found and identified by one of the monks. The Saint Catherine story is now considered largely spurious.

Sources:

Forsyth, William H., and Kurt Weitzmann. *The Monastery of Saint Catherine at Mount Sinai: The Church and Fortress of Justinian.* Ann Arbor, MI: University of Michigan Press, 1973.

Galey, John. *Sinai and the Monastery of St. Catherine.* Givatayim, Israel: Massada, 1980.

SAINT JOSEPH'S ORATORY (MONTRÉAL)

Saint Joseph's Oratory, a prominent structure in the middle of the city of Montréal, Quebec, has become a major center for Roman Catholics because of the many healings that have been attributed to pilgrimages there. The oratory had an inauspicious beginning in the hands of its unexpected founder. Brother André (1845–1937) was an uneducated brother assigned to a humble position in his order, the Congregation of the Holy Cross. He had been a sickly child, his frail body hindering both his school attendance and his search for a vocation. As a young man, he encountered some Holy Cross brothers, and in 1870 he joined their order. During his novitiate he learned to read in order to go through the basic program of spiritual formation required of all new brothers. Following his admission to holy orders in 1872, he was assigned as the porter at the College of Notre-Dame-du-Sacré-Coeur in Côte-des-Neiges, a position he would retain for the next forty years.

Soon after he assumed his duties, members of his order began to experience healings as a result of Brother André's prayers. Rumors began to spread, and guests who visited the college soon made similar testimonies about miraculous healings. Brother André ascribed these powers to Saint Joseph (the human father of Jesus) toward whom he had developed an early devotion. He also began to nurture the idea of developing a shrine to Saint Joseph and soon associated his idea with Mount Royal in Montréal.

Brother André began work on the original small chapel in 1904. He was assisted by people who had come to know of him. Once the chapel was opened, word spread quickly that it was a place where healings occurred. During the next 15 years, the church had to be rebuilt three times to accommodate the swelling crowds. The present church, which was first completed in 1918, seats 4,000. Construction work continued through the century, however. The dome, which stands about 200 feet high, rests on Mount Royal. It is the highest structure in Montréal and may be seen from almost anywhere in the city.

The Oratory is itself an imposing building. However, it is its continued association with healings that has cause hundreds of thousands of pilgrims to visit it annually. On the lower level of the church is the shrine to Saint Joseph, Brother André's crypt, and a display of crutches and other artifacts left behind by the many who have found their health during their visit. Brother André died in 1937, and a million people viewed his casket. His name was blessed (a step toward canonization) in 1982.

Sources:

Bergeron, Henri-Paul. *Brother André, C.S.C.: The Wonder Man of Mount Royal.* Montréal: Fides, 1969.

Hatch, Alden. *The Miracle of the Mountain: The Story of Brother André and the Shrine on Mount Royal.* New York: Hawthorn Books, 1959.

Lafrenière, Bernard. *Brother André According to Witnesses.* Montréal: St. Joseph's Oratory, 1990.

SAINT NECTAN'S GLEN (ENGLAND)

Saint Nectan (c. 458–510) was a legendary saint from the west of England. Little is known of his life, though the stories associated with him appear to derive from memories of his life as a hermit who dedicated himself to assisting those in his neighborhood. He is believed to have been the eldest son of the Welsh king Brychan. As a young man he left home, crossing the Bristol Channel to arrive at Hartland Point in Devon. There he settled in a valley with a pleasant spring. Following the example set by the Egyptian hermit Anthony,

he lived by himself and built a small church near the spring. He became well known throughout Devon and Cornwall, areas he helped evangelize.

The most repeated story about Nectan concerns the end of his life. He had helped a local farmer locate some lost pigs, and in gratitude the man presented Nectan with two cows. However, the cows were stolen. Nectan found the bandits and attempted to convert them to Christianity. They responded to his gesture by beheading him. According to the story, Nectan then picked up his head, carried it back to the spring, and then brought it back to the church he had built. This event is said to have occurred on June 17, 510. Other stories suggest King Arthur as the one who slew Nectan. Following his death, two women settled at the spring (some believe them to have been his sisters). They buried him and diverted the water so it flowed over his grave.

In the years after his death, miracles were reported to have occurred where Nectan was buried, and there were annual gatherings of those who venerated the saint. Today there are five chapels dedicated to Saint Nectan in Cornwall and Devon, and his name is attached to holy wells at Ladywell and Welcombe. The chapel fell into disuse and only ruins remain, but pilgrims still find their way to the spring, a spot prized for its natural beauty.

Sources:

Chope, R. Pearse. *The Story of Hartland.* Torquay, UK: Devonshire Press, 1940.

Doble, Gilbert H. *The Life of Saint Nectan.* Bideford, UK: Polypress, 1964.

———. *St. Nectan, St. Keyne and the Children of Brychan in Cornwall.* Penzance, UK: Oakmagic Publications, 1998.

SAINT NICHOLAS' TOMB

Saint Nicholas is the person who has in modern times taken on the form of Santa Claus in North America. The real Saint Nicholas is believed to be buried in Bari, Italy. Tradition traces the story

This spring at Saint Nectan's Glen in England has become a pilgrimage site associated with miracles connected to the death of a faithful sixth-century Welsh nobleman. *Fortean Picture Library.*

THE ENCYCLOPEDIA OF RELIGIOUS PHENOMENA

of Santa Claus to Bishop Nicholas, who lived in the fourth century in Asia Minor. He is reputed to have been born in Patara in Asia Minor (modern-day Turkey), and rose through church ranks to became the bishop of Myra, a Mediterranean port in Lycia. He supposedly attended the Council of Nicea that condemned the errors of the heretic Arius, but no one by that name is listed as being among the attendees. He eventually fell victim to the suppression of the church during the reign of the Emperor Diocletian (r. 284–305). In this version of Saint Nicholas's life, he was buried at Myra. In the centuries that followed, his legend grew and his tomb became a PILGRIMAGE site.

Muslim forces overran Lycia in the eleventh century, and in 1087 sailors from Italy stole the bones buried in the tomb at Myra and transported them to Bari in southern Italy. In subsequent years, the saint became so identified with Bari that his Turkish past was somewhat obscured. A crypt to house the saint was erected within a few months of his burial, and no less a personage than the pope came to Bari to place the relics in their new resting place. The crypt soon became one of the most popular pilgrimage sites in Europe, and over the next decade a new church was built over the crypt. In the twelfth century, Pope Urban II (r. 1088–1099) laid the relics of Saint Nicholas beneath the crypt's altar, consecrating a shrine that became one of medieval Europe's great pilgrimage centers. The main church was built within ten years, but it wasn't until the middle of the twelfth century that the imposing and majestic Basilica di San Nicola was completed. Its Romanesque architecture served as an inspiration for a number of other church buildings over the next centuries.

Adding to the mystical nature of the shrine were reports of a sweet-smelling, myrrh-like substance, the so-called "manna of Saint Nicholas," that exuded from his corpse. This substance also had been reported when Saint Nicholas rested in Myra. Believers sought some of the manna to prevent or heal sicknesses. The substance was gathered at an annual ceremony led by the priest in charge of the cathedral, and it was made available

to pilgrims in small decorated bottles. In recent years, the manna has been formally retrieved in ceremonies held annually on May 9, the day commemorating the movement of the relics from Myra to Bari. The local priest, accompanied by a delegate of the pope, the archbishop of Bari, an Eastern Orthodox bishop, and other local notables, presides over the ceremony.

In the mid 1950s, because of a renovation of Saint Nicholas's crypt, the nature of the manna was reconsidered. In 1954 the tomb was reopened and the saint's bones were placed inside an urn, where they remained for three years. During this time, it was observed that the bones "perspired." This perspiration, or manna, turned out to be water, which, by means not as yet fully explained, condenses inside the crypt. Believers continue to value the water, since it has been in contact with the bones of the saint.

Today, there is doubt that such a person as Saint Nicholas actually existed, a position that obviously casts doubts upon the identity of the person whose bones are venerated today in Bari. Nevertheless, Saint Nicholas has come to be known as the patron saint of children, as well as of various European countries.

Sources:

Cioffari, P. Gerardo. *Saint Nicholas: His Life, the Translation of His Relics and His Basilica in Bari*. Trans. Philip L. Barnes. Bari, Italy: Centro Studi Nicolaiani, 1994.

DeChant, Dell. *The Scared Santa: Religious Dimensions of Consumer Culture*. Cleveland, OH: Pilgrim Press, 2002.

Ebon, Martin. *Saint Nicholas: Life and Legend*. New York: Harper & Row, 1975.

Jones, Charles W. *Saint Nicholas of Myra, Bari, and Manhattan: Biography of a Legend*. Chicago: University of Chicago Press, 1978.

SALEM VILLAGE (DANVERS, MASSACHUSETTS)

At the end of the seventeenth century, Salem Village, Massachusetts, became the scene of one of the more important incidents in American history. Throughout the spring and summer of 1692, 19 people were tried, convicted, and executed for practicing witchcraft, including one who was killed after refusing to plead. More than fifty others were awaiting trial when the governor moved to stop the trials in October.

The trials grew out of the widespread belief among the members of the Congregational Church, which dominated Massachusetts at the time, that Satan was an active force in the human community who often lured people into practicing malevolent magic or witchcraft. Over the half century prior to the incidents at Salem Village, there had been a number of individual trials of accused witches in the New England colonies. The problem in Salem appears to have begun when Tituba, a servant working in the home of Salem Village's parish minister, Samuel Parris, introduced some folk magic practices to Parris's nine-year-old daughter, Elizabeth, and her friend Abigail Williams. The girls subsequently began to exhibit some bizarre behavior patterns and, when examined by a physician, were considered possible victims of witchcraft.

Tituba tried to counter these effects by working a magic spell. When the girls' behavior continued, they were pressured to name who was causing it. They accused Tituba, but then also pointed their fingers at village residents Sarah Good and Sarah Osborne, two women known to have bad relations with some of their neighbors. Following their arrest, Tituba confessed to practicing witchcraft and named Good and Osborne as co-conspirators. People searching the homes of the women found some items that seemed to confirm that the two did in fact practice magic.

Over the next month, four other young girls began to exhibit the same bizarre behaviors as Elizabeth and Abigail. They joined the first two in denouncing village residents as the source of the spells that afflicted them. Slowly, evidence of a possible hidden coven emerged. When the trials began in June, in many cases the only evidence against the accused was the testimony of the girls

who said they were victims of witchcraft. Boston minister Cotton Mather (1663–1728), himself a strong believer in witchcraft's existence, was nevertheless among the first to decry the use of such "spectral evidence." However, the court disagreed with this view, and as the trials proceeded the majority of those convicted were found guilty exclusively on the basis of spectral evidence.

The first executions occurred late in July. Nineteen died before Governor William Phipps (1651–1695) stopped the use of spectral evidence and then ended the trials. After a period of reflection on what had happened, the people of Massachusetts largely concluded that a great tragedy had occurred. Most of those directly responsible for the deaths publicly recanted their actions. The trials had a significant role in convincing the general public that no such thing as malevolent magic existed. The event at Salem Village was attributed to "hysteria," which remains a popular explanation to the present day. After the events that occurred at Salem Village were reinterpreted in a negative light, in 1711 the colony of Massachusetts passed a legislative measure that restored the rights and good names of those found guilty by the trials and granted a large sum to their heirs. In 1752 the town changed its name to Danvers, which resulted in the public's coming to see an adjacent community, Salem, Massachusetts, as the site of the trials.

In recent years a considerable amount of time has been devoted to reexamining the Salem Village event from historical, psychological, and sociological perspectives. A much more comprehensive understanding of the forces operating behind the trials and their supporters has therefore emerged. Interestingly, a neo-pagan witchcraft movement has arisen from all this that has adopted the history of the deaths at Salem Village as part of its lost past. In an uncritical appropriation of the story of the trials, modern Wiccans have moved to Salem, where they have become a vital element in the town's tourist industry. They treat the victims of the trials as martyrs of the Wiccan faith. At various times, government officials have responded positively to the Wiccan

Mass hysteria in 1692 colonial Massachusetts led to the execution of 19 innocent people for witchcraft. The tragedy occurred in Salem Village (now called Danvers), which has since been incorrectly identified with present-day Salem. *Time Life Pictures/Getty Images.*

community, such as in 1977, when then-Governor Michael Dukakis named Laurie Cabot (b. 1933), who was the first of the modern Wiccans to open a business in Salem, as the town's official witch. In 1992 the town erected a memorial to the victims of the trials.

Sources:

Boyer, Paul S., and Stephen Nissenbaum. *Salem Possessed: The Social Origins of Witchcraft.* Cambridge, MA: Harvard University Press, 1976.

Godbeer, Richard. *The Devil's Dominion: Magic and Religion in Early New England.* New York: Cambridge University Press, 1994.

Hansen, Chadwick. *Witchcraft at Salem.* New York: George Braziller, 1969.

Rosenthal, Bernard. *Salem Story: Reading the Witch Trials of 1692.* New York: Cambridge University Press, 1995.

SAMADHI

In modern-day Hinduism, Samadhi, which is essentially the goal of all yogic activity, has taken on a variety of connotations relative to sainthood. The term became established in Hindu thought through the Yoga Sutras of Patanjali (second century BCE). Patanjali described an eight-step process by which a practitioner can detach him- or herself from the mundane world and attain enlightenment. These steps include abstinence from the harming of others, as well as from lying, stealing, sex, and greed (*yama*); the practice of cleanliness, contentment, asceticism, study and meditation (*niyama*); the practice of the yoga postures (*asana*); breath control (*anga*); mastering the senses (*pratyahara*); concentration (*dharana*); and meditation (*dhyana*). These seven steps lead to the last step, the experience of the mystical oneness called *samadhi*. Samadhi is analogous to the higher mystical states found in most religions.

Many revered religious leaders in India are believed by followers to have entered into samadhi and to more or less permanently reside there. In attaining samadhi, most people have initial and sporadic experiences of unity that may become extended; this is followed, finally, by a permanent alteration of consciousness. The fact that they have entered this highest state of consciousness is a major source of their authority to act as gurus (teachers).

Since its entrance into the larger milieu of Indian religions, samadhi's meaning has been expanded. For example, the sanyasin, a popular Indian religious figure, has taken a vow of renunciation from worldly pursuits, possessions, and attachments to concentrate on personal religious pursuits. The act of taking the vows to become a sanyas in is seen as a kind of death. Thus, when a sanyasin ends his mortal life, since he has already died he is now seen as entering samadhi. The tomb of the deceased sanyasin may also be referred to as his samadhi. Such tombs may also become places of PILGRIMAGE. The idea of entering samadhi has been extended to also mean the burial site of many people considered saints or holy people (whether or not they have taken their renouncing vows).

Sources:

Feuerstein, Georg. *The Philosophy of Classical Yoga.* Rochester, VT: Inner Traditions International, 1996.

Jackson, Robert, and Dermot Killingley. *Approaches to Hinduism.* London: John Murray, 1988.

Organ, Troy Wilson. *Hinduism: Its Historical Development.* Woodbury, NY: Barron's Educational System, 1974.

SANTIAGO DE COMPOSTELA (SPAIN)

Santiago de Compostela, a town in the northwestern part of Spain, is reputedly the burial site of the Apostle James (or Santiago). According to legend, James went to this remote corner of the world and then he returned to Palestine, where in 42 CE he was taken prisoner and beheaded. King Herod refused to allow him to be buried, so some of his companions stole the body and put it on a ship. Various accounts suggest the ship was without a crew, or that it was manned by angels. After a swift voyage, the ship landed at the mouth of the river Ulla in Galicia (Spain). The group that accompanied the body then encountered another obstacle: the local rulers, King Duyo and Queen Lupa, were hostile to Christianity. However, the apostle was eventually buried secretly on an isolated mountainside.

Some eight centuries latter, a hermit named Pelayo had an angelic vision while traveling near the burial site. He heard music and saw a shining light in the woods near the town. He called the place he saw the shining "Campus Stellae," which is Latin for "field of the star." This was later shortened to Compostela. The occurrence was eventually reported to the bishop in the town of Iria Flavia, the closest community of any size. He began an investigation. As a result, the site of the apostle's tomb was reportedly discovered, which was seen as confirmation that the site was in fact where James was buried.

The story was then reported to King Alphonse II (765–842), who responded by declaring Saint James the patron of his empire. He ordered the building of a chapel dedicated to Saint James, and two others were subsequently dedicated to Jesus Christ and to saints Peter and Paul. He also commanded that a monastery of Augustinian monks be located in the area. From this beginning, the community of Santiago de Compostela emerged.

Word of the discovery and the building of the church spread quickly through the Christian west. The news that one of the twelve Apostles was buried in Spain immediately turned it into a popular pilgrimage site. As pilgrims came to the site, traveling along what became known as the Camino de Santiago (the way of Saint James), a miniscule community emerged to become the city of Santiago de Compostela. There, the original chapel was replaced with a cathedral. The cathedral came to rival those in Rome and Jerusalem, and Pope Calixtus II (d. 1124) declared a Jubilee grace (i.e., a plenary indulgence) to those who visited the site during those years when July 25 (Saint James's Day) occurs on a Sunday. His successor, Alexander III (1159–1181), designated Santiago a "holy town."

Beginning in the fourteenth century, pilgrimages to Santiago slowed markedly, as did pilgrimages in general, because of the Black Plague ravaging Europe. Pilgrimages to Santiago had almost stopped completely when, in 1878, Pope Leo XIII issued a bull that reiterated the belief that the Apostle James's remains were in fact at Santiago. Since that time the number of pilgrims has steadily grown, and today the city is once again a major site for Roman Catholics to visit. In addition, a renewed interest in Saint James emerged. This has led to the naming of many sites in his honor, especially in Spanish-speaking cities such as Santiago, Chile.

Sources:

Davies, Horton, and Marie-Hélène Davies. *Holy Days and Holidays: The Medieval Pilgrimage to Santiago de Compostela*. London: Associated University Presses, 1982.

Dunn, Maryjane, and Linda Kay Davidson. *The Pilgrimage to Santiago de Compostela: A Comprehensive Annotated Bibliography*. New York: Garland Publishing, 1994.

Gitlitz, David M., and Linda Kay Anderson. *The Pilgrim Road to Santiago: The Complete Cultural Handbook*. New York: St. Martin's Griffin, 2000.

Jacobs, Michael. *The Road to Santiago de Compostela*. London: Viking, 1991.

SANTO, AUDREY (1983–2007)

Audrey Santo was a young woman who resided in Worcester, Massachusetts. Since the age of three, she existed in a state known as akinetic mutism, meaning that she was unable to move and could not speak. In spite of her condition, she became the center of a movement of mainly Roman Catholic believers who claimed that she was the source of a number of miraculous occurrences.

On August 9, 1987, following an accident at a swimming pool, the three-year-old Audrey was taken to a hospital for an examination. The pool incident proved superficial, but the doctor mistakenly prescribed what amounted to an overdose of Phenobarbital. Audrey fell into a coma, and when she woke up three weeks later she was unable to speak or move. After several months in the hospital she was brought home.

As her story became publicly known, people gathered to pray for Audrey. Then, unexpectedly, the STIGMATA (wounds similar to those that the Bible describes Jesus having at his crucifixion) began to appear on Audrey's body. Next, various holy objects in and around the Santo home began to exude oil or bleed. On several occasions a Eucharist host manifested blood.

In 1998 the Most Reverend Daniel P. Reilly, the Roman Catholic bishop of Worcester, appointed a small group of scholars to investigate the situation. A guarded preliminary report was made the following year in light of which the bishop neither confirmed nor denied the presence of miraculous events at the Santos' home. The bishop promised more studies, but he was no longer among the detractors who had claimed that the oils and blood were fraudulently produced. The bishop said merely that they remained inexplicable, and called upon the faithful to refrain from visits to the home because they would interfere with the family's care of the young girl. The investigators then focused their efforts on the alleged ability of Audrey to communicate with people, because this matter was central to the belief in Audrey's role as an intercessor between people and God.

While waiting for further word from the diocesan chancery office, Audrey became the center of a growing devotional movement. The oil that emerges from the holy objects in her home is given away to those who ask for it. Two videos, a book, and various objects with Audrey's picture have been produced and are available from the Apostolate of a Silent Soul, the organization formed to facilitate the devotional activity.

The emergence of devotion around Audrey Santo provoked responses from skeptics. Investigations of similar bleeding statues and miraculous oils, many of which have turned out to be hoaxes, suggest that a more rigorous inspection of the miraculous claims surrounding this new devotional activity would be appropriate.

Sources:

Apostolate of a Silent Soul, Inc. http://www.littleaudreysanto.org/. Accessed March 28, 2007.

"Diocese Issues Interim Findings on Miraculous Claims." Posted at http://www.worcesterdiocese.org/news/communications/releases/audrey.html. Accessed March 28, 2007.

Nickell, Joe. "Miracles or Deception? The Pathetic Case of Audrey Santo." *Skeptical Inquirer* (September/October 1999). Posted at http://www.csicop.org/si/9909/santo.html. Accessed March 28, 2007.

SARNATH (INDIA)

Located approximately 135 miles from Bodhgaya, where Gautama Buddha sat under the BODHI TREE and found enlightenment, Sarnath is where he gave his first presentations concerning what would become Buddhism. It is now considered the birthplace of the Buddhist religion. In addition, Sarnath, also called Deer Park, was the site of the gathering of the first group of Buddhist monks and the formation of the initial Buddhist monastic community. Sarnath is just a few miles from the Hindu holy city of BENARES, also known as Varanasi and Kashi.

Asoka, the third century BCE emperor who converted to Buddhism, helped expand the monastic life at Sarnath. The community, which grew to include more than a thousand monks, flourished through the ninth century, but declined after the establishment of Muslim rule in the area. Eventually, everything Buddhist would be destroyed. In the late-nineteenth century, the British launched archeological work in the area. They uncovered a number of the old Buddhist sites. Control of the Buddhist ruins has since been placed in the hands of the Maha Bodhi Society, which has expanded its initial concern with recovering Bodhgaya and returning it to Buddhist hands.

Primary ruins identified at Sarnath include the Dharmarajika Stupa built by Asoka to hold some RELICS of Gautama Buddha, though the location of the casket that contained the relics is unknown, if it even still exists. The carvings on the STUPA's lower parts have survived and may be seen. Only the base of the Nulghandhakuti Shrine, an elaborate building used by the Buddha

The ruins of Sarnath, India, remain a holy place for Buddhists, who consider this the site where Gautama Buddha first began to share his philosophy with others. *Fortean Picture Library.*

for meditation, remains. At the beginning of the 1930s, the Maha Bodhi Society erected a modern temple, the Mulagandhakuti Vihara. It is decorated with scenes of the Buddha's life, but its main attraction is a silver casket found in Punjab in 1913. On it an inscription dated to 79 CE claims the casket holds some relics of the Buddha. Presented to the Society in 1935, it was subsequently taken to Sarnath.

Sources:

Majupuria, Trilok Chandra. *Holy Places of Buddhism in Nepal and India: A Guide to Sacred Places in Buddha's Lands.* Columbia, MO: South Asia Books, 1987.

Panabokke, Gunaratne. *History of the Buddhist Sangha in India and Sri Lanka.* Dalugama, Kelaniya, Sri Lanka: Postgraduate Institute of Pali and Buddhist Studies, University of Kelaniya, 1993.

Tulku, Tarthang, ed. *Holy Places of the Buddha.* Vol. 9. *Crystal Mirror.* Berkeley, CA: Dharma Publishing, 1994.

SCAPULARS

The scapular emerged as part of the dress of monks in the early Middle Ages. Simply a narrow cloth with an opening for the head that hangs down a person's front and back, the monk's scapular evolved from the aprons worn by agricultural laborers over their clothes. Over the centuries, the scapular began to be thought of as the identifying mark of monastic garb. As such, they were adopted for wear by laypeople who wished to show their support for a particular order.

As a lay garment, the scapular lost its functional role and evolved into a purely devotional item. It was cut down in size from a large piece of cloth to just two small squares of cloth connected by two strips of ribbon. These small stylized devotional scapulars tended to be worn under the clothing, as a matter of personal practice.

The wearing of the small scapulars was greatly influenced by knowledge of their association with the apparitions of Mary and Jesus. For example, the oldest of the devotional scapulars, the white

scapular, dates to the twelfth century. In 1198 Pope Innocent III, who sanctioned the new Order of the Trinitarians, had an angelic visitation. The angel wore a flowing white garment on the breast of which was the symbol of a cross with a blue horizontal bar and red vertical shaft. This cross became the symbol of the Trinitarians. The white scapular was then passed on to the laypeople who identified with the order.

Then, in 1251, the Blessed Virgin appeared to Simon Stock, who was the Superior General of the Carmelite Order. As part of the encounter, she gave him the brown scapular, promising that wearing it would preserve individuals from eternal damnation and that on the first Saturday after their death they would be taken to heaven. The scapular took on added significance as a sign of the dedication of the Carmelites to Mary and their desire to be committed to Christ.

The blue scapular originated with Saint Beatrice da Silva Meneses (1426–1492), the founder of the Order of Franciscan Sisters of the Immaculate Conception of the Most Blessed Virgin Mary (Conceptionists). It was included as part of the order's standard garb, and through them passed on to lay supporters. Not initially related to a particular supernatural event, the blue scapular would later receive a blessing in the seventeenth century. In 1617, toward the end of her life, Ursula Benincasa (1547–1618), founder of the Congregation of the Oblates of the Immaculate Conception of the Blessed Virgin Mary, had a vision of the Blessed Virgin dressed in white with an azure outer garment. As part of the lengthy vision, Mary showed sister Ursula a multitude of angels distributing the blue scapulars around the globe. After Ursula's death, the women of the order made the promotion of the scapular a special mission of their order.

With the expansion of the means of personal devotion in the last two centuries, additional scapulars appeared. In 1840 Sister Justine Bisqueyburu of the Daughters of Charity had one of her many encounters with Mary. On this occasion she carried a green scapular and told Sister Justine,

Worn by nuns or monks, scapulars can indicate the religious order to which one belongs. Each scapular has its own history, often associated with visions of Jesus, Mary, or angels. *Fortean Picture Library.*

"This holy badge of my Immaculate Heart is to be the means of conversion of souls." Over the next years subsequent visitations by Mary added to the meanings and usage of the green scapular.

In 1846 Sister Appoline Andriveau, of the Sisters of Charity of Saint Vincent de Paul, experienced an apparition of Jesus Christ, who showed her a red scapular. He promised an increase of faith, hope, and charity to any who would wear it on Fridays. This apparition occurred several times and was finally reported to the church authorities. In 1847 Pope Pius IX assigned the Lazarist Fathers the duty of blessing the scapulars and passing them on to the faithful. The red scapular has pictures of Jesus on the cross and the SACRED HEARTS OF JESUS AND MARY.

The scapulars further illustrate the supernatural origins of most forms of popular devotion in the Catholic Church (including, for example, the ROSARY, the MIRACULOUS MEDAL, the Sacred Hearts of Jesus and Mary, etc.), almost all of which were initiated by an apparition of Mary or Jesus. This tradition has continued to the present day. Most recently, a laywoman named Judith Elaine Melendez of Redford, Michigan, experienced a number of apparitions, as reported in a 1995 story of the encounters. While she was writing a poem, Mary appeared to Melendez as Our Lady of the Sun, a particular form of the Blessed Virgin indicating her disapproval of abortions.

Melendez described this appearance of Mary, noting several details: "In Her left hand is a yellow scapular. This scapular should be worn by women who are pregnant and all teenage girls. This scapular is a symbol of stopping abortion. On one side of the yellow scapular is a small rose bud with a drop of blood. This represents Our Lord Jesus as a child when He was circumcised and shed His first blood for all of mankind. On the other side of the yellow scapular is the Risen Christ on His Cross, represented by a full-blown rose. On each side of Our Lady's Mantle are three roses. On the left side of Her mantle, the three roses stand for the Holy Family: Jesus, Mary and Joseph. On the right side of Our Lady's Mantle, the three roses stand for The Holy Trinity: Father, Son and Holy Spirit."

Sources:

Callely, H. *The Blue Scapular of the Immaculate Conception*. Dublin: Catholic Truth Society of Ireland, 1936.

Haffert, John M. *Sign of Her Heart (Formerly Mary in Her Scapular Promise)*. Washington, NJ: Ave Maria Institute, 1971.

Lynch, E. K. *The Scapular of Carmel*. Washington, NJ: AMI (Ave Maria Institute) Press, 1996.

Magennis, P. E. *The Scapular Devotion, Origin, Legislation and Indulgences Attached to the Scapulars*. Dublin: M. H. Gill and Son, 1923.

SEDONA (ARIZONA)

A town in northwest Arizona, Sedona sits under the rim of the Colorado Plateau and provides residents a less extreme climate than the large deserts to the south and east. It was founded in 1901 by Carl and Sedona Schnebly. It developed into a retirement center and artists colony, and more recently emerged as a tourist draw.

The largely secular nature of the community stands in contrast to its prehistory. The area around Sedona had once been the subject of religious stories by the Hopi, Apache, and Havasupai tribes. Some of these native peoples associate their creation myths with the spectacular geography of the region. In the decades after World War II, various individuals began to tout the area as being a place where spiritual forces were particularly active.

The metaphysical side of Sedona can be traced back to 1957, when Mary Lou Keller moved there and opened the Sedona Church of Light. She sponsored weekly meetings at which the tapes made by Los Angeles metaphysical teacher Manly Palmer Hall were played. Keller was joined in the 1960s by Evangeline and Carmen Van Pollen, who headed a group in the "I AM" Ascended Masters tradition called the Ruby Focus of Magnificent Consummation, which regularly published messages received from the Ascended Masters. They were then joined by Spiritualist minister Judy Fisher, who opened what she called the New Age Center. The center evolved into the Church of the Living God, which held weekly Spiritualist services.

Throughout the 1960s and 1970s, Sedona grew, as did both its traditional and alternative religious communities. However, things began to change in the 1980s. Around this time, psychic Page Bryant claimed to have discovered several vortexes of psychic energy in the hills around Sedona. This claim integrated well with accepted understandings of sacred sites in the New Age Movement. Many New Age enthusiasts were consequently attracted to Sedona, where they encountered both the beautiful scenery and a welcoming spiritual community. Bryant's observations were elaborated upon by a number of New Age writers, such as Dick Sutphen, Tom Dongo, and Richard Dannelley.

Given the permeation of the idea of Sedona as a site alive with spiritual energy, it was not surprising that in 1987 it was singled out by José Arguelles as one of the major locations to celebrate the "Harmonic Convergence," a moment of peaking by cosmic forces derived from Arguelles' reading of Mayan prophecies. On August 16 and 17, 1987, thousands of New Age believers gathered together in the hope that the energy released through the cosmos on that day would facilitate a major shift in human consciousness. For Sedona, the event served to further its reputation as a place particularly favorable to New Age enterprises. It has become especially identified with channeling, the practice formerly called

New Ager Jody Glittenberg tries to capture spiritual energies in Sedona, Arizona. In the later half of the twentieth century, the tourist town began to be associated with supernatural forces. *Getty Images*.

mediumship in which gifted individuals contact and allow various spiritually evolved entities to speak through them.

Today, in the relatively small community one can find a significant array of channelers, metaphysical centers, spiritual retreats, and occult bookstores. One major national newsstand periodical, built around the material produced by channelers, the *Sedona Journal of Emergence,* is published there monthly. The associated Light Technology Publications also annually releases a number of books about channeling.

Sources:

Dannelley, Richard. *The Sedona Guide of Channeled Wisdom*. Sedona, AZ: Light Technology Pub., 1991.

Dongo, Tom. *Everything You Wanted to Know about Sedona in a Nutshell*. Sedona, AZ: Light Technology Pub., 1998.

Ruland-Thorne, Kate. *Experience Sedona: Legends and Legacies*. Phoenix, AZ: Many Feathers, 1989.

Sutphen, Dick. *Sedona: Psychic Energy Vortexes*. Malibu, CA.: Valley of the Sun Publishing, 1986.

SERPENT HANDLING

A regular part of some religious practices, serpent handling has emerged at odd times and places throughout human history. It reappeared early in the twentieth century in rural eastern Tennessee, and within a few decades spread throughout the Appalachian mountains from Georgia to Pennsylvania. The origins of this practice are often traced back to 1909 and the handling of rattlesnakes in services by Pentecostal minister George Went Hensley (d. 1955), who was preaching in Grasshopper Valley not far from Cleveland, Tennessee. In 1914, Hensley was invited by Ambrose J. Tomlinson (1865–1943), the leader of the Church of God (Cleveland, Tennessee), to introduce the practice into the fledgling denomination that was spearheading the introduction of Pentecostalism throughout the American South. During the 1920s the Church of God withdrew its support from the practice, but by this time it had developed a following. These people have continued snake handling, often under the name of the Church of God with Signs Following.

Pentecostalism is built around the biblical passages concerning the baptism of the Holy Spirit and the gifts of the Spirit. The movement teaches that Christians may be empowered by the Holy Spirit and will subsequently manifest one or more gifts of the Holy Spirit (SPEAKING IN TONGUES, HEALING, working miracles, etc.). Hensley and those who followed him extended their attention to the early church by noting that signs were said to follow those who believed in the Bible. One biblical passage states that "they shall cast out devils; they shall speak with new tongues; They shall take up serpents; and if they drink any deadly thing, it shall not hurt them; they shall lay hands on the sick, and they shall recover" (Mark 16:17–18). Pentecostals spoke in tongues and prayed for the healing of others, but many seemed to have forgotten the middle part of the passage concerning handling serpents and drinking poisons.

To biblical literalists, the arguments by the serpent handlers were perfectly logical, though many refused to add their support because of their discomfort with the actual practice. Then, in the mid-1920s, snake handler Garland Defries almost died from a snakebite. This incident led to the Church of God withdrawing its support from the practice.

In spite of the Defries incident, the movement continued to spread and went largely unnoticed by the larger world until 1945, when Lewis Ford, a member of a church near Chattanooga, Tennessee, died from a snake bite. The state of Tennessee responded to the public outrage and outlawed the practice. Over the years, other states banned snake handling. Incidents of fatal or near-fatal snake bites have been so rare, however, that law enforcement officials have rarely charged churches or their ministers because of this practice. One exception occurred in Alabama in 1991, when a minister was convicted of attempted murder after being charged with pushing the hand of his wife into a box of rattlesnakes.

Since the 1960s, snake-handling churches have been the subject of a variety of scholarly studies and journalistic features. Many remain puzzled by the rationale that would lead people to adopt such a dangerous practice, while others find the rarity of negative effects from handling snakes an enigma.

Sources:

Brown, Fred, and Jeanne McDonald. *The Serpent Handlers: Three Families and Their Faith.* Winston-Salem, NC: John F. Blair, 2000.

Burton, Thomas. *Serpent Handling Believers.* Knoxville: University of Tennessee Press, 1993.

Covington, Dennis. *Salvation on Sand Mountain: Snake Handling and Religion in Southern Appalachia.* New York: Penguin Books, 1995.

Kimborough, David L. *Taking Up the Serpents: Snake Handling Believers of Eastern Kentucky.* Chapel Hill: University of North Carolina Press, 1995.

LaBarre, Weston. *They Take Up Serpents.* New York: Schocken Books, 1969.

SHAH FAISAL MOSQUE (PAKISTAN)

The Shah Faisal Mosque, located near Islamabad, Pakistan, is the largest mosque in the world. The idea of building the mosque emerged as the new nation of Pakistan (founded in 1947) settled down after the turmoil of its independence movement. A site near the city was selected and the proposal presented to King Faisal of Saudi Arabia

Located in Islamabad, Pakistan, the Shah Faisal Mosque, named after a Saudi king, was completed in 1988 and can accommodate 100,000 Muslim worshipers. *AFP/Getty Images*.

(1906–1975) when he visited Pakistan in 1966. Enthusiastic about the proposed mosque, he offered to underwrite it financially. In gratitude, the Pakistanis named the mosque in his honor, as well as the main road from the mosque to the city. The design by a Turkish architect, Vedat Dalokay, was selected.

The cornerstone of the mosque was laid in October 1976 by King Khalid (who had succeeded to the throne of Saudi Arabia following the assassination of Faisal in 1975). The building was completed in 1988. The finished complex covers 47.87 acres. The covered area of the prayer hall encompasses 1.19 acres. It can accommodate approximately 100,000 worshipers at any given time.

Rivaling the Pakistani mosque is the Hassan II Mosque, constructed in Casablanca, Morocco, to honor the Moroccan king on the occasion of his sixtieth birthday. It boasts enough space for 25,000 worshipers inside and another 80,000 outside. Attached is a 210-meter minaret, the tallest in the world. The Hassan II Mosque was constructed totally from local materials, including granite, marble, and wood.

As with some other modern expensive religious structures, the Hassan II Mosque was not built without controversy. Many questioned the use of the half billion dollars expended in its construction, as well as protesting the destruction of a large, poor section of Casablanca to make way for it. None of the displaced residents received any compensation for the loss of their homes.

Sources:

Serageldin, Ismail, with James Steele, eds. *Architecture of the Contemporary Mosque*. London: Academy Editions, 1996.

Shaw, Isobel. *Pakistan*. Lincolnwood: Passport Books, 1996.

SHAKTIPAT

Shaktipat is an experience available to devotees of those Hindu groups that focus their attention on *kundalini*, the innate divine power that, it is believed, lies latent at the base of the spine. Once awakened, this power travels up the spine to the crown of the head. Enlightenment is not possible without the awakening of the kundalini. Shaktipat (literally the "transfer of power") occurs in the presence of a guru (teacher), who is believed to have the ability to awaken the kundalini of his or her follower. Shaktipat is believed to be the easiest of several methods in activating kundalini. In stimulating the devotee's kundalini, the guru also creates a subtle link between him/herself and the devotee that allows further stimulation of the kundalini at future dates. This thus allows the devotee to overcome obstacles while moving toward full enlightenment.

Shaktipat may occur in one of several ways. Most often it is by simple touch. The energy is allowed to flow from body to body. At other times, the teacher may simply gaze upon the devotee and allow the energy to move out from him or her. When the kundalini is awakened, the devotee may have one of a number of experiences, though actually feeling the flow of energy along the lower spine is the typical sensation.

Among the more notable gurus who have offered shaktipat in the west in the last generation are Swami Muktananda (1908–1982), Yogi Amrit Desai (b. 1937), and Dhyanyogi Madhusudandasji Mahant Maharaj (1878–1994).

Sources:

Kripananda, Swami. *The Sacred Power*. Oakland, CA: Siddha Yoga Dham of America Foundation, 1995.

Madhusudandasji, Shri Dhyanyogi. *Shakti: Hidden Treasure of Power*. Vol. 1. Pasadena, CA: Dhyanyoga Centers Inc., 1979.

Muktananda, Swami. *Kundalini: The Secret of Life*. South Fallsburg, NY: Siddha Yoga Dham of America Foundation, 1979.

Muni, Swami Rajarshi. *Awakening the Life Force*. St. Paul, MN: Llewellyn Publications, 1994.

Scott, Sarah. *Darshan 67: Baba Muktananda and the Glory of Shaktipat*. South Fallsburg, NY: Siddha Yoga Dham of America Foundation, 1992.

SHIPTON, MOTHER

Religious phenomena include numerous examples of false phenomena. Many of the most persistent of these have involved Mother Shipton. This legendary prophetess was introduced to many people in the English-speaking world in 1862, when book dealer Charles Hindley published a small chapbook about her. The booklet stated that Mother Shipton seemed to have accurately predicted a number of inventions, such as horseless carriages, the telegraph, and ironclad ships. Those who happened to encounter the chapbook over the next years were at first awed by the apparent accuracy of the predictions; then they were frightened by the last prediction: the world would end in 1881.

The public concern over Mother Shipton led to attempts to verify Hindley's claims. In the pamphlet, he cited a 1684 publication by Richard Head titled *The Life and Death of Mother Shipton*. Although the 1684 pamphlet does exist, it does not contain the prophecies Hindley quoted. In fact, he first confessed to having made up the end of the world prophecy, and then to having made up all the prophecies. His confessions did not circulate to anywhere near the same extent that his original book did, however, and so many continued to be anxious about the end of the world prophecy. Church attendance rose, and people panicked in other ways, as well.

Who was this Mother Shipton to whom Hindley had attached his fake prophecies? The first mention of her appears to have been made in 1641, when Richard Head published a work titled *The Prophecies of Mother Shipton, in the Reigne of King Henry the Eight. Foretelling the Death of Cardinal Wolsey, the Lord Percy and Others, as Also What Should Happen in Ensuing Times*. The later 1684 pamphlet was an edited and expanded version of this earlier publication. Head circulated a biography of Shipton, who was supposedly the product of a union between her mother and the Devil, thus suggesting that Satan was the source of her seemingly accurate prophecies. In 1645, the famous astrologer William Lilly (1602–1681) published a booklet on Mother Shipton, too, which elaborated upon Head's original publication.

In the end, the earliest accounts of Mother Shipton occurred more than a hundred years after her reputed prophecies were supposedly made. In fact, there is no evidence that a Mother Shipton ever lived. She appears to be a product of the imagination of Richard Head. As with many such mythical characters, Mother Shipton subsequently became part of the popular culture. In the 1660s she was even the subject of several stage plays (all comedies).

A full biographical account of Mother Shipton was compiled from the various books. She was born Ursula Sontheil in 1488 in a cave along the shore of the Nidd River outside Knaresborough, North Yorkshire, England. Nearby was a well with alleged mystical powers. Today, one may travel to Knaresborough and visit the cave and well. There are also a number of Internet sites and books that treat Mother Shipton as if she were a real historical personage.

Sources:

Easton, Jon, ed. *Mother Shipton: The Prophecies of Ursula Sontheil*. Chester, UK: Fenris Press, 1998.

Harrison, William H. *Mother Shipton Investigated*. London: privately printed, 1881. Posted at http://www.sacred-texts.com/pro/msi/. Accessed March 31, 2007.

Simpson, J. C. *The Life and Prophecies of Ursula Sontheil, Better Known as Mother Shipton*. Leeds, UK: Waverly Press, n.d.

SHROUD OF TURIN

The Shroud of Turin has emerged as one of the most important relics of Christendom. It is believed by many to be the burial cloth of Jesus. The Shroud is a woven linen cloth about 14 inches by 3.5 inches. Most extraordinary is the human image on it. There are actually two images, one of the front of the body and one of the backside, as if a person was lain to rest on one end of the Shroud and the other end was wrapped over the top of the body. The image pictures a person who seems to have been crucified. Some believe that the image was implanted on the cloth by some mysterious means at the moment of Christ's resurrection.

The Shroud first enters historical accounts in the middle of the fourteenth century. In 1355, its owner, Geoffrey de Charney, displayed it at a church in Lirey, France. He claimed that it was Christ's Shroud. As pilgrims made their way to see the Shroud, in 1357 a pilgrimage medal was struck to commemorate their journey. The Shroud soon came under attack from a local bishop who questioned its authenticity and launched an investigation. It would remain a controversial object until one of de Charney's descendants passed the cloth on to the Savoy family, who would later go on to become rulers of Italy. In 1532 a fire in the chapel where the Shroud was housed left burn marks on it (as well as water marks from attempts to douse the fire). In 1578 the Shroud was relocated to Turin, where it remains to this day. It is now housed in the royal chapel of the Cathedral of Saint John the Baptist. Ordinarily, the Shroud rests within a reliquary in the Shroud chapel, and only on special occasions is it taken out for viewing.

A new era for the Shroud began in 1898, when Seconda Pia was allowed to photograph the cloth. In developing the pictures, he discovered that the Shroud's image was a negative image, very much like a photographic negative. This discovery opened an ongoing debate about the Shroud as to its scientific credentials. The first question posed was, essentially, how a negative image could have been created if, as many of the Shroud's critics had long believed, the cloth was a product of the medieval traffic in relics?

Over the next decades, a variety of theories were discussed as to how the unusual image was created. Then, at the beginning of the 1970s, an American physicist named John Jackson called together a group of scientists who formed the Shroud of Turin Research Project (STURP). After four years of preparation, in 1978 the STURP team traveled to Turin, where in October they were given a total of 120 hours of access to the Shroud and were allowed to take new pictures

and conduct a series of experiments. The STURP group made its formal report in 1981. While inconclusive, the investigators offered a variety of findings that were basically favorable to its supernatural origins. Most importantly, they concluded that the image on the cloth had been produced in a moment of intense heat that emanated from a body that was, at that moment, weightless.

For skeptics, the most definitive experiments were conducted in 1988, when small samples of the Shroud cloth were removed and subjected to carbon dating analysis at three different laboratories. All three reported a date of origin between 1260 and 1390, which was consistent with the cloth having been produced shortly before Geoffrey de Charney first displayed it.

The 1981 STURP report and the 1988 carbon dating report are merely two highlights from a generation of continued study of and speculations about the Shroud that are by no means concluded. Additional testing has examined the Shroud from every angle imaginable, including the search for the remains of plant life from the Holy Land that might suggest the Shroud had at one time been there. Skeptics have been held at bay by their inability to reproduce an image similar to the Shroud. Proponents of the first century origin of the Shroud have countered the 1988 findings with suggestions that distortion occurred because of the 1532 fire, while simultaneously pointing to the many unique aspects of the cloth and image. They have also constructed various histories to fill the important gap between Jesus' burial and the first historical mention of the Shroud. It does not appear that any consensus about the Shroud will be reached in the near future.

In 1994, Lynn Picknett and Clive Prince published a book built on their theory that the Shroud was, in fact, an elaborate and creative product of the genius of Leonardo da Vinci. The account, largely built upon circumstantial evidence, satisfied neither skeptics nor believers, but received new life in the wake of the success of the publication of *THE DA VINCI CODE.* Their book reappeared in a revised edition in 2007.

Many consider this image on the Shroud of Turin to be that of Jesus. The nature of this preserved likeness of Christ has stumped many experts, though theories abound as to whether or not it is genuine evidence of Jesus' resurrection. *National Geographic/Getty Images*.

Sources:

Antonacci, Mark. *The Resurrection of the Shroud*. New York: M. Evans & Co., 2000.

Guerrera, Vittorio. *The Shroud of Turin: A Case for Authenticity*. Rockford, IL: Tan Publishers, 2000.

Guscin, Mark. *The Burial Cloths of Christ*. London: Catholic Truth Society, 2000.

Nickell, Joe. *Inquest on the Shroud of Turin: Latest Scientific Findings*. Prometheus Books, 1998.

Picknett, Lynn, and Clive Prince. *Turin Shroud: In Whose Image? The Truth behind the Centuries-long Conspiracy of Silence*. New York: HarperCollins, 1994. Rev. ed. *The Turin Shroud: How Da Vinci Fooled History*. New York: Touchstone, 2007.

Wilson, Ian. *The Mysterious Shroud*. Garden City, NY: Doubleday & Company, 1986.

SHWEDAGON PAGODA (MYANMAR)

Shwedagon Pagoda is the most sacred Buddhist site in Myanmar. It is a **STUPA** whose golden dome rises 98 meters (321.5 feet) high, and is plated with 53 tons of gold. On its tope are 5,400 diamonds, together measuring some 2,000 carats. The pagoda is located in Yangon, Myanmar's capital. Prior to the middle of the eighteenth century, Yangon was a small fishing village named Bagan. The British turned it into the capital of the country (then called Burma), in 1885. During the British era, which ended in 1948, it was known as Rangoon.

According to legend, Shwedagon Pagoda predates even the fishing village. In the fifth century BCE, just as the land was emerging out of prehistory, two Burmese merchants visited Gautama Buddha in India. They found him sitting under the **BODHI TREE**, just 49 days after he attained Enlightenment. Buddha gave them eight strands of his hair, which the two men brought back with them to their homeland. In conjunction with the local ruler, they enshrined the hairs in a casket on Singuttara hill. Reportedly, there was already a shrine housing relics of three earlier enlightened ones. Over the shrine a stupa was erected. The whole complex of stupas and the monastic building have been greatly expanded since 1769.

Surrounding the central structure of the pagoda are four shrines for the principal Buddhas, and eight smaller shrines based on the signs of the Burmese zodiac. Surrounding these are numerous additional shrines and gold-covered towers. The pagoda complex is built in the typical Burmese Mon style, which includes four entrances facing the four compass points.

Also built in a similar style is Sule Paya, located in the city's center. It is reputed to contain one of the original hairs of the Buddha brought back from India 2,500 years ago.

Sources:

Aung, Myint, Thaung Wai, and U Kyi Win, eds. *Shwedagon: Symbol of Strength and Serenity*. Yangon,

The Shwedagon Pagoda is a stupa in Yangon, Myanmar, that contains several hairs from Gautama Buddha, according to legend. It is one of the holiest and most beautiful of religious sites in the country. *AFP/Getty Images.*

Myanmar: Yangon City Development Committee, 1997.

Moore, Elizabeth, Win Pe U, and Hansjörg Mayer. *Shwedagon. Golden Pagoda of Myanmar*. London: Thames & Hudson, 1999.

U, A. Than. *Shwedagon*. Rangoon: Government of Burma, 1957.

SILBURY HILL (ENGLAND)

The prehistoric Silbury Hill, located in Wiltshire, England, is not far from STONEHENGE and AVEBURY. It is the largest manmade mound in Europe. The base of the hill covers some five and a half acres, and the hill is about 130 feet high. Built in the third millennium BCE, it took between twenty and fifty years to complete. A Neolithic site, it might have something to do with the same culture that built the many stone monuments across the British Isles. The hill's purpose, however, remains a mystery.

Investigations of the hill indicate it was constructed in three parts. In the middle of the hill is a mound approximately 20 feet high. This mound was then covered with a layer of chalk. Finally, a ditch was excavated around the hill and its material used to further build up the hill. The internal structure of the hill is hidden under the dirt that covers the chalk.

Some have suggested that the hill was a burial mound; however, no sign of any human remains have been detected inside the hill. Others believe that at one time a pole might have been erected on the hill, thus turning it into a large sundial. It might also have been a center for various worship activities that was later abandoned in favor of other nearby sites.

Silbury Hill is unimposing and can easily be missed by passing travelers who fail to see the sign that identifies it.

Sources:

Atkinson, Richard. *Silbury Hill*. London: BBC Publications, 1968.

Cunnington, M. E. *An Introduction to the Archaeology of Wiltshire, from the Earliest Times to the Pagan Saxons,* with Chapters on Stonehenge, Avebury, Silbury Hill, Woodhenge, Barrows, Earthwords, Etc. n.p.: privately printed, 1938.

Dames, Michael. *The Silbury Treasure*. London: Thames & Hudson, 1976.

SIRIUS MYSTERY

Sirius is the brightest star in the sky over North Africa, and as such was known and venerated by different ancient nations. In Egypt, for example, it appeared in the dawn sky shortly before the annual flooding of the Nile and was thus seen as a warning. Its appearance marked the beginning of the year in the Egyptian calendar.

In 1972 British author Robert K. G. Temple put forth a most intriguing claim. He asserted that the Dogon people, who reside in the African countries of Mali and Burkina Faso, had been aware for many centuries that the star Sirius was being orbited by a second star. This was a fact discovered by western astronomers only in the nineteenth century. Dogon legends about Sirius were said to have originated long before any astronomer could have figured out the existence of the second star (now called Sirius B), calculated its 50-year orbit, or discerned its status as a small white dwarf. The Dogon reputedly knew all of these facts. The discussion of the Sirius Mystery became an integral part of what was termed the "ancient astronaut" hypothesis, the idea that in ancient times earth was visited by extraterrestrials who seeded it with knowledge and left remnants of their presence in various ancient drawings and artifacts.

The Dogon's knowledge of Sirius and its dwarf twin was discovered by two French anthropologists, Marcel Griaule and Germaine Dieterlen, who worked among them in the years immediately after World War II. To this data, Temple added his own reflections on a Dogon legend that speaks of an ark descending to the ground amid a great wind. Temple interpreted this to be an old account of a spacecraft landing. The ark brought an amphibious group of beings known as the Nommo. Temple then suggested that the knowledge brought from Sirius some 5,000 years ago was passed on to Egypt and accounted for Egypt's fixation on Sirius. As consideration of the ancient astronaut theory lost support through the 1990s, the Dogon Sirius story remained a mystery to many and an idea that still inspires speculations about ancient astronauts.

Skeptics of the Sirius Mystery have offered a variety of explanations to counter Temple's hypothesis. Significantly, they have charged him with significantly misrepresenting Dogon belief. They point out that the Dogon believed that Sirius had two companion stars, not one, and that they understood the two stars symbolically, rather than literally. The two stars, one male and one female, are fertility symbols. Temple, furthermore, presents in his book an expurgated drawing of the Dogon understanding of Sirius that omits the image of the second orbiting star. Investigations of the Sirius Mystery have done much to dispel Temple's major claims and suggest alternate explanations of those elements that remain as yet unexplained.

Sources:

Ridpath, Ian. "Investigating the Sirius 'Mystery.'" *Skeptical Inquirer* 3, 1 (Fall 1978). Posted at http://www.csicop.org/si/7809/sirius.html. Accessed March 31, 2007.

Temple, Robert. *The Sirius Mystery*. Folkstone, Kent, UK: Bailey Brothers & Swinfen, 1972.

SKEPTICS SOCIETY

In 1991 a second organization devoted to the scientific refutation of miraculous and paranormal claims joined the Committee for the Scientific Investigation of the Claims of the Paranormal (CSICOP) in a program of public education. The Los Angeles-based Skeptics Society was founded by scholar/writer Michael Shermer, who was assisted by Pat Linse and Kim Ziel Shermer. Much of the rationale behind locating the new society at its west coast base was to be close to the many media outlets there; this complemented the resources available to the upstate New York base

from which CSICOP had been operating. Shermer has effectively and aggressively used radio and television as a major component in the Skeptics Society's educational efforts. The society's magazine, *Skeptic*, has over 40,000 subscribers.

The society sponsors an annual conference and a variety of programs throughout the year. For several years it had a weekly national cable television show, and Shermer is a frequent guest on shows that deal with psychic and supernatural issues and events. As a building block of the skeptics' pseudoscience debunking movement, the Skeptics Society operates from a position that assumes that most, if not all, supernatural and paranormal claims may be reduced to either baseless speculations on matters beyond the realm of science, or that they are fraudulent or simply misunderstandings of extraordinary but mundane phenomena.

Sources:

Carroll, Robert Todd. *The Skeptic's Dictionary: A Collection of Strange Beliefs, Amusing Deceptions, and Dangerous Delusions*. New York: Wiley, 2003.

Shermer, Michael. *Science Friction: Where the Known Meets the Unknown*. New York: Times Books, 2005.

———. *Why People Believe Weird Things: Pseudoscience, Superstition, and Other Confusions of Our Time*. New York: W. H. Freeman & Company, 1998.

SLATE WRITING

Slate writing is an activity that in the late-nineteenth and early twentieth centuries was a popular form of spirit contact in Spiritualist circles. A medium would begin with a blank writing slate (a small blackboard once used by children in elementary school). The slate was then placed in a position that appeared to prevent any normal access to it, and in a brief time a message seemed to be written on the slate by a spirit. Mediums William Eglinton (1858–1933), Fred P. Evans (b. 1862), and Henry Slade (d. 1905) were prominent early proponents of the slate's usage.

To the average, untutored person, slate writing can appear quite impressive. Beginning with

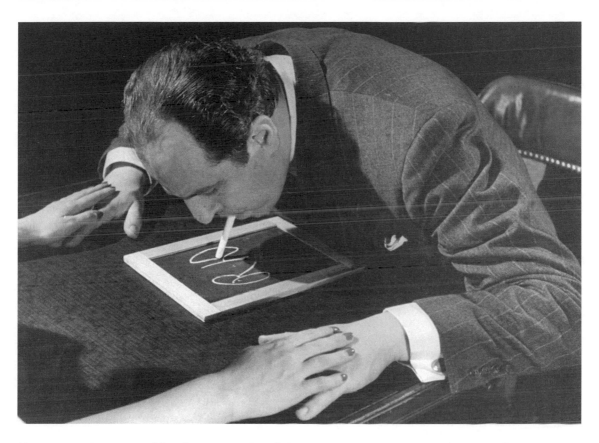

Slate writing, demonstrated here by magician Joseph Dunninger, is one way that spirits supposedly communicate with Spiritualists during seances. *Time Life Pictures/Getty Images.*

a blank slate placed so that neither the medium nor any assistants appears to have access to it, meaningful responses to questions posed by the sitter appear. These are often followed by sounds that seem to be coming from someone writing on the slate.

The practice largely disappeared in the early twentieth century, when the nature of the phenomenon as a conjuring trick was revealed and discredited by organizations such as the Society for Psychical Research. The trick involved either the substitution of prepared slates for the original black slate or the use of two-sided slates that could be turned around, revealing a message written on the back that everyone thought was the front.

Sources:

Abbott, David P. *Behind the Scenes with the Mediums.* Chicago: Open Court/London: Kegan Paul, 1909.

Robinson, William E. *Spirit Slate Writing and Kindred Phenomena.* New York: Munn & Company/Scientific American Office, 1898.

SLAYING IN THE SPIRIT

Among the more interesting of modern spiritual experiences occasionally seen in Pentecostal services is the loss of motor control by believers that causes them to fall on the floor. Such experiences are attributed to the action of the Holy Spirit. They were sporadically reported in revival meetings in the eighteenth and nineteenth centuries, but first became common at meetings held at the end of the nineteenth century by Maria Beulah Woodworth-Etter (1844–1924), a Pentecostal evangelist-healer. However, it was not a notable phenomenon within Pentecostalism through the mid-twentieth century.

The experience came to the fore during the ministry of healer KATHRYN KUHLMAN (1907–1976). During her healing services, Kuhlman would point to people and they would appear to fall back as if pushed. Some people reported an invisible force hitting their chest area, others simply felt a loss of balance and control of their leg muscles. The experience rarely lasted for more than a minute or two. During the height of Kuhlman's career in the 1960s and 1970s, other evangelists such as Kenneth Hagin Sr. and Charles and Frances Hunter also introduced the phenomenon into their meetings. In these cases, the slaying in the Spirit was not spontaneous as in previous centuries, but was controlled to a large extent by the minister in charge of the meeting.

In the years since Kathryn Kuhlman's death, being slain in the Spirit has been most frequently identified with the ministry of BENNY HINN (b. 1952), who has assumed Kuhlman's mantle. In his services people who have been healed are frequently called to the front of the congregation, where Hinn then lays hands on them and they appear to fall. Hinn usually designates assistants to catch anyone who falls, lest they hit the floor and are hurt, and others stand ready with cloths in case a female's skirt should inadvertently ride upward in an immodest manner.

Most recently, the phenomenon was associated with the Toronto Blessing, a revival movement centered on a single congregation located near the Toronto Airport in Ontario, Canada. The movement was most known for the so-called Holy Laughter, in which people broke into fits of uncontrollable laughing when affected by the Spirit. However, it soon became known for other phenomena as well, such as the slaying in the Spirit.

Slaying in the Spirit was criticized as soon as it became well known. Non-Pentecostals, especially conservative Baptists, attacked it as an unbiblical occurrence. This was a particularly stinging indictment, since Pentecostals had built their movement around an unquestionably biblical event, SPEAKING IN TONGUES, which they complained had been abandoned by other churches. Though no biblical passage details an experience that duplicates the contemporary phenomenon of slaying in the Spirit, its supporters point to passages in which people were knocked down during an encounter with God (Numbers 24:4; Matthew 17:6). Others have suggested that slaying in the Spirit is a sign of psychological disorder (not unlike possession or obsession), while supporters have seen it as an event that marks a new level of intimacy with God by those who experience it.

Sources:

MacNutt, Francis. *Overcome by the Spirit.* Tarrytown, NY: Revell, 1990.

Nader, Mikhaiel. *Slaying in the Spirit: The Telling Wonder.* Punchbowl, NSW, Australia: Bruised Reed, 1992.

Warner, Wayne E. *Kathryn Kuhlman: The Woman behind the Miracles.* Ann Arbor: Servant Publications, 1993.

SMITH, HÉLÈNE (1861–1929)

Hélène Smith was a relatively young, attractive Swiss medium who, in the 1890s, offered her psychic visions of the planet Mars to Professor Theodore Flournoy (1854–1920). Flournoy's subsequent investigation of the material produced by Smith has become a classic of psychic research and stands as a warning to all who would investigate mediums and channelers.

Flournoy was initially impressed by Smith. She described events from his childhood, and he dutifully recorded her descriptions of her previous incarnations and her dramatic reenactments of historical events. At one point, for example, she announced that she was the reincarnation of Marie Antoinette. He was more impressed, however, with what he termed the "Oriental Cycle." In these sessions Smith claimed to be Simandini, the daughter of an Arab shiek from the sixth century, as well as the wife of Prince Sivrouka Nayaka of Tchandraguiri, Kanara, Hindustani, from the fifteenth century. During these sessions she occasionally spoke Hindustani or wrote in Arabic. She even used a few Sanskrit words. Only after a lengthy search was Flournoy able to find a book that related the basic facts of the story Smith was elaborating upon. He concluded that the material Smith produced was very difficult to explain by normal means.

However, the events of 1894 were to prove decisive. In her trance state, Smith claimed that she astrally traveled to Mars and subsequently offered both verbal descriptions and sketches of what she saw. Her descriptions of Mars built on the 1877 announcement of Milan astronomer Giovanni Virginio Schiaparelli (1835–1910) that he had seen "canali" on the surface of Mars. He saw what in English would be accurately rendered as channels, but which were understood at the time to be canals. The Martian canals were interpreted to be similar to the recently completed Suez Canal, and were thus believed artificial. Other astronomers, including French astronomer/psychical researcher Camille Flammarion (1842–1925), expressed their agreement with Schiaparelli's views. However, in the mid-1890s a new advocate of the idea had appeared. American astronomer Percival Lowell (1855–1916) initiated the construction of a new observatory in 1894. The observatory, which now bears his name, was designed primarily for the further observation of the structures on Mars.

The world Smith described, as Nandor Fodor (1895–1964) observed in the book *These Mysterious People*, was very similar to 1890s Europe, with some minor variations. There were horseless and wheel-less vehicles, unisex clothing, and a Martian alphabet. As the séances continued, Smith began to speak Martian and offered translations of the Martian language.

The very interesting material being produced by Smith did not stand up well under scrutiny, however. Flournoy began to examine the reputed Martian language, only to discover that it was entirely based on French. This revelation offended Smith and led to the two parting company. Smith continued to produce material related to Mars and to other celestial objects, primarily Uranus and the Moon.

Flournoy finally published his study of Smith in 1900 (released in English as *From India to the Planet Mars*). It turned out to be a classic study of the use of mundane sources by a creative mind to produce an elaborate body of material that, upon first examination, seemed to be of paranormal origin. While Flournoy and Smith had parted company, the book did not damage her reputation the way that some exposés had destroyed careers of Spiritualists. Smith continued to operate as a medium, and at her death in 1929 she left a voluminous collection of materials behind. She never again allowed herself to be scrutinized by a scholar, but following her death her papers were examined by Professor Waldemar Deonna (1880–1959) of Geneva. He produced a study of her later work, including material from a religious phase through which she passed in which there were many Christian references. Deonna noted the unusual quality of paintings done of religious themes during this time, but Smith's legacy failed to present any outstanding evidence of the paranormal.

Sources:

Deonna, Waldemar. *De la planète Mars en Terre Sainte. Art et subconscient—Un Médium peintre: Hélène Smith*. Paris: E. De Boccard éditeur, 1932.

Flournoy, Theodore. *From India to the Planet Mars*. New York: Harper, 1901.

Fodor, Nandor. *These Mysterious People*. London: Rider & Co., 1934.

SPEAKING IN TONGUES (GLOSSOLALIA)

Speaking in tongues (glossolalia is the technical term) is a form of religious utterance that to the outsider is meaningless and is often confused with gibberish. To the believer, however, it is a form of sacred language spoken under the influence of the Holy Spirit. Speaking in tongues appears prominently in the New Testament, and it became an integral part of Christian worship in the first century. The practice largely disappeared as a significant part of Christian worship by the second century, though it occasionally reemerged during times of spontaneous religious revivals. Records indicate a number of outbreaks in the English-speaking world in the nineteenth century.

The modern attention to speaking in tongues began in 1900 in a small Bible school in Wichita, Kansas. The founder of the school was a former Methodist heavily influenced by the Holiness Movement, a late-nineteenth century belief that advocated a Second Blessing for Christians that brought them into a holy state and which they identified with the "baptism of the Holy Spirit." The school founder thus began to think about the idea of the baptism of the Holy Spirit, an experience that Holiness people valued. He asked his students to investigate the idea in conjunction with their Bible study. The students concluded that the experience of speaking in tongues was intimately connected with the baptism of the Spirit. Thus, the school's teacher, Charles F. Parham (1873–1929), led his students in prayer for the baptism of the Holy Spirit and its accompanying sign, the experience of speaking in tongues. That experience first came to Agnes Ozman (1870–1937) on January 1, 1901, and soon spread to Parham and the other students.

Parham began to spread the word of the baptism and tongues. Among the people who accepted the message was African American minister William J. Seymour (1870–1922). In 1906, Seymour took his knowledge of the experience with him to Los Angeles, where he was to pastor a church. His ministry resulted in a three-year revival that brought people from across North America to the small mission on Azusa Street. Over the next decade, those who received the baptism of the Holy Spirit at the mission then spread the message around the world.

At Azusa, those who spoke in tongues questioned exactly what was happening to them. One early explanation was that they were speaking a different language. As they saw when they read the account of the first Pentecost (Acts 2), some believed that they had been gifted by God with the ability to speak another language. One of these, Lillian Garr, the wife of Reverend A. G. Garr (1874–1944), believed that she could now speak Chinese. Based upon that belief, she and her husband moved to Hong Kong in 1907, only to be sadly disappointed that no one could understand any words that she spoke. Reverend Garr concluded that speaking in tongues was purely for devotional use, not for communicating information.

Others at Azusa concluded that they were speaking the languages of the angelic world and that speaking in tongues requires the associated gift of interpretation. Thus, although speaking in tongues had a value in itself, especially when exercised in private, in worship, after someone spoke in tongues, it became common to wait for someone to interpret the message in English (or whatever language the congregation used). While this explanation satisfied many, it led to further questions. For example, observers frequently noted the seeming lack of relationship between the length of the tongues message and the interpretation.

In spite of such questions, a variety of new theologies emerged that affirmed speaking in tongues as a normative experience of the Christian life. These theologies were adopted by the different churches of the Pentecostal movement.

In the 1960s, the Pentecostal movement experienced a significant growth when the practice of speaking in tongues spread into older Protestant denominations and to Catholicism. The new Charismatic movement, as it was called, did not happen without significant opposition, though. Church leaders denounced speaking in tongues as a false form of piety, while other equally sophisticated leaders defended the experience. In the 1970s, the interest aroused by the Charismatics also generated a number of significant new studies. For example, Charismatic fellowships were studied to see if, as psychologists of previous generations had charged, experiences such as speaking in tongues were evidence that the speaker was suffering from mental problems. Some prominent psychologists working early in the twentieth century suggested that involvement in Pentecostalism and speaking in tongues were signs of psychological pathology. In the 1970s, studies of Pentecostal/Charismatic groups were conducted that laid the earlier suggestions to rest. Charismatic believers actually scored higher on mental health scales than the general public.

Most important to the understanding of speaking in tongues was the work of linguists who had developed very sophisticated tools for understanding the structure of languages, even those they had never previously heard. Such people as William Samarin quickly disposed of two hypotheses. First, speaking in tongues was not XENOGLOSSY, the speaking of a second language that was not learned in any ordinary manner. Second, speaking in tongues was not simple gibberish or nonsense. The sounds that were articulated by the speakers did indeed have structures and patterns. Speaking in tongues, is something different; it is a proto-language, a means of verbalizing religious experience. It differs from real language by its limited number of vowels (only two or three) and consonants (approximately 12 to 15). There are not enough sounds available to construct a real language. Samarin also noted that the tongues spoken by any individual Pentecostal believer will be based on the language she or he speaks under normal circumstance.

After a number of studies through the 1970s, scientists felt that they had reached a consensus on the nature of glossolalia, and the leadership in the movement came to terms with the work of various social scientists who have researched the phenomenon. The admission of this scientific data has been difficult for the movement to swallow, since speaking in tongues was considered a way in which God interacted directly with His congregations.

Sources:

Burgess, Stanley M., ed. *The New International Dictionary of Pentecostal and Charismatic Movements.* Grand Rapids, MI: Zondervan, 2002.

Goodman, Felicitas D. *Speaking in Tongues: A Cross-Cultural Study in Glossolalia.* Chicago: University of Chicago Press, 1972.

Kildahl, John P. *The Psychology of Speaking in Tongues.* New York: Harper & Row, 1972.

Samarin, William J. *Tongues of Men and Angels. The Religious Language of Pentecostalism.* New York: Macmillan Company, 1972.

SPEAR OF LONGINUS

On March 12, 1938, Hitler annexed Austria, and upon his arrival in Vienna he made a stop at the Hofmuseum to take possession of an obscure artifact: an ancient spear. He had the spear sent to Germany, and it resided in the Church of Saint Catherine in Nuremberg throughout World War II.

This obscure artifact was known as the Spear of Longinus, or, more dramatically, the Spear of Destiny. Legend said that it was the very spear used to pierce Jesus' side as he hung on the cross (John 19:31–37). The soldier with the spear is unnamed, but he later came to be known as Longinus. The use of that name is traced to a Syriac manuscript from the sixth century found in the Laurentian Library in Florence, Italy, which includes an illustration of the incident. On that illustration, above the head of the soldier who held the spear, the word *Longinus* is written in Greek. Legends had accumulated around this spear, suggesting that it has passed through the hands of a number of prominent world leaders—Constantine, Charlemagne, Otto the Great, the Habsburg Emperors, and finally, Adolf Hitler.

It must be noted that several spears claim to be the spear mentioned in the Bible. For example, one was said to have been buried in the cathedral church in Antioch. It was unearthed by a crusader in 1098. It eventually found its way to Etschmiadzin, Armenia, where it remains to the present day. Another claimant traces its history to 570, when it was supposed to have been displayed in Jerusalem. When Jerusalem fell to the Muslims in 615, the spear point was snapped off. The point was subsequently integrated into an icon and made its way to Constantinople, and then to Paris, France. It disappeared during the French Revolution. The lower part of the spear also went to Constantinople, but in 1492 it was sent to Rome as a gift to Pope Innocent VIII by Sultan Beyazid II. Innocent then had it placed inside a pillar at the then-new Saint Peter's Cathedral, where it remains today.

The spear that Hitler claimed in 1938 seems to be the one that first appeared in 1273. Current observations suggest that it was actually made in the seventh century. It came into the possession of the Holy Roman emperors, belonging initially to Otto I (912–973). Eventually, it found its way to the museum in Vienna as part of a collection of the royal insignia of the Empire.

Hitler's belief in the spear seems not to reside in its connections to the Holy Roman Empire, but rather from its having entered into the King Arthur legends. Part of the legend associated with the spear, which Hitler and some of his chief lieutenants literally believed, was that the possessor of the spear would have the power to conquer the world. However, if they lost it they would instantly die. This belief gave credence to a modern version of the story. It was rumored that the spear, which came into possession of a U.S. Army general (namely, General George Patton) at the end of World War II, had actually been captured on April 30, 1945 (the day of Hitler's suicide). In fact, it was some months after the war that the spear was recovered from the church in Nuremburg. It was later returned to the Hofmuseum, where it currently resides. More recent research on Hitler's involvement with the spear has also called into question many of the details of the story.

Sources:

Anderson, Ken. *Hitler and the Occult.* Amherst, NY: Prometheus Books, 1995.

Buechner, Howard A., and Wilhelm Bernhart. *Adolf Hitler and the Holy Lance.* Metairie, LA: Thunderbird Press, 1989.

MacLellan, Alec. *The Secret of the Spear: The Mystery of the Spear of Longinus.* London: Souvenir Press, 2005.

Ravenscroft, Trevor. *The Spear of Destiny: The Occult Power behind the Spear which Pierced the Side of Christ.* New York: Putnam, 1973.

SPIRIT PHOTOGRAPHY

In the late nineteenth and early twentieth centuries, Spiritualists frequently made use of the relatively new technology of photography to create pictures of what they alleged were spirits of the dead. Usually, a picture would be taken of a medium's client, and when it was developed one or more images of deceased people—typically, relatives or acquaintances of the client—would also appear on the print. The photo would then be offered as further evidence of the afterlife.

Spirit photography was introduced in the 1860s by Boston photographer William H. Mumler, though within a short time his work was exposed as fake. However, New York photographer Frederick A. Hudson picked up the practice in the next decade, and before the end of the century the practice of producing spirit photographs became popular in England. The appearance of the spirits as somewhat vague figures, often wrapped in ectoplasm-like drapery, led to a belief in their authenticity.

Following up on the periodic discrediting of spirit photographers, in the 1920s and 1930s the Society for Psychical Research (SPR), based in London, sponsored a broad examination of the whole phenomenon under the guidance of Fred Barlow (d. 1964) and W. Rampling Rose. In 1933 they reported that they had been unable to find any genuine spirit photographs. This report was soon accepted by those who study psychic phenomena, and no serious attempt to present spirit photographs has subsequently been made. It should be noted that the SPR study of spirit pho-

With the invention of photography, Spiritualists became convinced that it was possible to take pictures of ghosts and other paranormal phenomena. Such photographs as these have not survived scientific scrutiny, though many people still believe they are real. *Fortean Picture Library.*

tographs followed the widespread controversy concerning the photograph of the **COTTINGLEY FAIRIES**, but it did not include the photos widely heralded by Arthur Conan Doyle in its survey. Doyle had been an ardent proponent of spirit photography.

The dismissal of spirit photography did not end the use of photography as a tool by various people who believed in paranormal phenomena. In the late-twentieth century, two psychics, American Ted Serios (b. 1918) and Tomobichi Fukurai of Japan, claimed to be able to psychically project images onto undeveloped film. While their claims were accepted by a few people, the phenomenon was difficult to study and the major-ity of researchers were unconvinced. Unlike spirit photography, such "thoughtography," as it was called, had little religious value.

Of more importance in religious circles were a variety of odd effects that showed up on snap-shots. Most often appearing as swirls of light, they were not visible to the person taking the picture. Such snapshots were passed around gatherings of New Age followers and informally used to bolster belief in various unseen forces. They were, how-ever, rarely taken seriously by psychic researchers. A very few such photographs, such as one of Pen-tecostal healer **WILLIAM MARION BRANHAM** in which the light effect appears as a halo over his head, have been more widely circulated.

Sources:

Doyle, Arthur Conan. *The Case for Spirit Photography.* New York: George H. Doran Company, 1925.

Eisenbud, Jules. *The World of Ted Serios.* New York: Paperback Library, 1967.

Gettings, Fred. *Ghosts in Photographs.* New York: Harmony Books, 1978.

Permutt, Cyril. *Photographing the Spirit World.* Wellingbourough, UK: Aquarian Press, 1988.

SPIRITUALIST CAMPS

In the decades after the American Civil War, the Spiritualist movement, drawing on the Methodists and other revivalist churches, adopted a format of holding summer camp meetings. These were usually held in late summer after crops had been planted but before the harvest season, when farming families had more free time. Held during the hottest part of the year, the camp gatherings were located at sites that typically included shade trees and often a lake. As with the revivalist centers, these campsites began more-or-less informally and then grew into more permanent establishments with cottages, hotels, restaurants, businesses, and a variety of other buildings to house a spectrum of extracurricular activities.

Those attending a camp in the nineteenth century could stay in the hotel, rent a cottage, or pitch a tent. Daily schedules would allow for time to attend lectures, sit in at séances, or receive the ministrations of a healer. There would always be plenty of time left for a variety of recreational opportunities, from shopping to sailing on the lake to dance parties in the evening. Officials and leaders in the movement could gather at the campgrounds to conduct their regular business. Most importantly, the camps supplied a welcoming and friendly atmosphere in which people who felt that contacting the spirit world through mediumship was possible could practice their faith and meet with like-minded believers.

By 1880 Spiritualist camps had spread from New York, where the movement began, throughout New England and across the Midwest. Significant expansion of the movement over the next two decades saw the first camps in California. Summerland, south of Santa Barbara, was founded in 1889, and Harmony Grove, near Escondido, opened in 1896. The South was the least hospitable to the movement, but one of the most famous camps, located at Cassadaga, Florida, opened in 1894.

The camps remained for many years among the most stable institutions of Spiritualism, which continually suffered ups and downs, especially with the occasional exposure of fraudulent medium practices. Then, in the last half of the twentieth century, many of the camps were closed when the movement as a whole declined.

Among the Spiritualist camps that have survived are the ones at Cassadaga, Florida, and Lily Dale, New York. Both are associated with the National Spiritualist Association of Churches, the oldest national Spiritualist body in America. Others include Harmony Grove in California; Pine Grove Spiritualist Camp in Niantic, Connecticut; Temple Heights Spiritual Camp in Maine; and Camp Chesterfield near Anderson, Indiana.

Camp Chesterfield became the site of one of the most recent major revelations concerning mediumistic fraud. In 1960 two young parapsychologists were allowed to film several séances where spirits supposedly regularly materialized. Although the séances took place in the dark, they were using infrared cameras. The manifestations occurred, but when the film was developed it was clearly revealed that confederates were using phosphor-covered cheesecloth to imitate the mysterious substance known as ectoplasm. Besides the medium in charge, several other Chesterfield mediums were clearly identified in the resulting pictures. Interestingly enough, when the Spiritualist periodical *Psychic Observer*, ran the pictures it lost so many subscribers and advertisers that it went out of business. Chesterfield, however, survived the scandal. It has also survived subsequent exposés by former medium Lamar Keene (1976) and paranormal debunker Joe Nickell (2002).

Spiritualist camps, which first became popular in late-nineteenth-century America, are secluded places where people of similar religious conviction can gather in private to attend meetings and focus on nurturing their faith. *Fortean Picture Library.*

Sources:

Brittan, Emma Hardinge. *Nineteenth Century Miracles; or, Spirits and Their Work in Every Country of the Earth: A Complete Historical Compendium of the Great Movement Known as "Modern Spiritualism"*. New York: William Britten, 1884.

Guthrie, John J. *Cassadaga: The South's Oldest Spiritualist Community*. Gainesville, FL: University of Florida Press, 2000.

Keene, M. Lamar. *The Psychic Mafia*. New York: St. Martin's Press, 1976. Reprint, Amherst, NY: Prometheus Books, 1997.

Nickell, Joe. "Undercover among the Spirits: Investigating Camp Chesterfield—Investigative Files." *Skeptical Inquirer* (March 2002). Posted at http://www.findarticles.com/p/articles/mi_m2843/is_2_26/ai_83585955. Accessed March 31, 2007.

Wicker, Christine. *Lily Dale: The True Story of the Town that Talks to the Dead*. San Francisco: HarperSanFrancisco, 2003.

STIGMATA

The stigmata are wounds that appear on the body that resemble the wounds received by Christ during his crucifixion. The basic wounds are traditionally in the palms of the hands, while others may also occur on the feet, the brow of the head (where the crown of thorns was placed), the side (where Christ was stabbed with a spear), and the back (where he was whipped).

The first appearance of the stigmata is usually traced back to the last years of the life of Saint

Francis of Assisi (1182–1226). It initially manifested following a forty-day fast that culminated on Holy Cross Day (September 14), when he had a vision of the crucified Christ. The vision culminated in the appearance of the wounds appearing on his body. The wounds were quite spectacular, and many have suggested that he might have unconsciously inflicted them upon himself while lost in his vision.

Over the next century no less than 30 cases of the stigmata were reported, and hundreds of cases have appeared in subsequent centuries. Included in the list of stigmatists are Catherine Emmerich (1774–1821), whose visionary experience would become the basis for the movie produced by Mel Gibson, *The Passion* (2004), and modern Italian mystic **PADRE PIO** (1887–1968).

A variety of explanations have been offered for the appearance of the stigmata. It has been noted that they came at a time during which contemplation of the sufferings of Christ for the world was being emphasized as a form of Christian piety. It has also been noted that on occasion people caught up in their contemplation of the sufferings of Christ would unconsciously inflict wounds upon themselves; the wounds on the palm, for example, may result from digging fingernails into one's hand.

The stigmata generally seem more closely tied to hypnosis, resulting in many body changes accomplished through the power of suggestion during a trance. When such wounds have been produced under hypnosis they usually clear up very quickly. However, the stigmata as demonstrated by Catholic mystics may linger for years. Furthermore, they will often appear at specific holy times of the year. Those seeking something other than supernatural explanations for the stigmata have often concluded that, in addition to the power of self-suggestion, the marks may have some correlation with the person's propensity for self-punishment. A number of stigmatists have been shown to indulge in self-mutilation, for instance. Catholic scholar Herbert Thurston, who had become an accomplished student of the paranor-

mal, considers the stigmata to be a "pious obsession" stemming from very suggestible people who manifest what he termed a "crucifixion complex."

One of the problems with the stigmata concerns the placement of the wounds. Thurston noted, for example, that wounds in the side would vary from person to person as to their being located on the right or left side. In recent years it has become common knowledge that during Roman times the crucified had nails driven through their wrists, not the palms of their hands, because the bones in the hand would not support a person's weight. However, throughout the Church's history, Christ is depicted in artworks as having the nails driven through His palms. The stigmata, therefore, do not so much reproduce the wounds of Christ as they reproduce the medieval version of the wounds of Christ.

Sources:

Freze, Michael. *They Bore the Wounds of Christ: The Mystery of the Sacred Stigmata*. Huntington, IN: Our Sunday Visitor, 1989.

Harrison, Ted. *Stigmata: A Medieval Mystery in a Modern Age*. New York: Penguin, 1996.

Nickell, Joe. *Looking for a Miracle*. Amherst, NY: Prometheus Books, 1998.

Thurston, Herbert. *The Physical Phenomena of Mysticism*. Chicago: Henry Regnery, 1952.

STONEHENGE (ENGLAND)

Stonehenge is a large, prehistoric monument located in Wiltshire, England. The British Isles are covered with stone buildings and monuments that range from the small and simple to the large and complex. Many of these, such as **AVEBURY** and **SILBURY HILL**, are also located in Wiltshire. Stonehenge is best understood as the culmination of the culture that produced these many stone monuments.

Stonehenge was constructed in several distinct stages. It began as a large, circular earthwork construction consisting of a ditch, a bank, and holes dug in the chalk. This initial construction dates

Probably the most famous ancient archeological site in England, Stonehenge dates back to 2100 BCE and may have been used by Druids or Neolithic people to observe the motion of the sun and other stars. *National Geographic/Getty Images.*

to the third millennium BCE. Around 2100 BCE a set of stones was brought in from the Preseli Mountains in Wales. Termed "blue stones," they weighed as much as four tons each and were brought by a circuitous route (covering almost 250 miles) over land and via two rivers. Once at the site, the 82 stones were arranged upright in a semicircle. At the same time, the entranceway to the site through the outer earthworks was widened, and two Heel Stones were placed outside the central site.

Possibly a century later, the largest stones (weighing as much as 50 tons each) on the site were brought in from the northern part of Wiltshire. They were placed upright in a circle around the blue stones from Wales and topped with lintels. As part of this construction phase, five stones were placed in the center of the site in a horseshoe shape. A final construction phase was completed approximately around 1500 BCE, when the blue stones were rearranged into a circle and horseshoe.

The people who constructed Stonehenge, as with the other stone monuments across Great Britain, left no written record of their life and little representational artwork. Over the centuries the many sites across Great Britain were abandoned, and the memory of their purpose was lost. Later residents often raided the older sites for building materials. Archeologists have more recently tried to reconstruct a picture of the ancient society that built Stonehenge, while theories both scientific and otherwise about its exact purpose have varied from the bizarre to the mundane.

Interest in the abandoned Wiltshire sites, especially Stonehenge, revived in the eighteenth century, and in the nineteenth century speculation included the ancient Druids. However, little progress was made until the latter half of the twentieth century, when more systematic archeological work was concentrated on the megalithic culture. That work pushed the dating of Stonehenge to the Neolithic peoples who inhabited the British Isles prior to the Druids, Romans, and Danish folk, when written documents first appear.

A significant advance in understanding Stonehenge occurred in the 1960s, when it was discovered that the placement of the stones, both those in the center and the Heel Stones outside, were aligned in such a way as to predict various astronomical phenomena, especially the movement of the sun in the sky between the summer and winter solstices. Knowledge of such phenomena probably dictated planting and harvesting schedules, as well as providing a calendar for religious celebrations.

Modern Neo-Druids used the discovery of the astronomical alignments to bolster their claims for having access to Stonehenge for religious services. For many years, the Druids and a limited number of worshiper-spectators have been admitted to the site for celebrations at the beginning of the day on the summer solstice. The establishment of the worshiping rights of the Druids has become all the more important in recent decades, since, due to the damage done by tourists, the site itself has been fenced off.

Sources:

Burl, Aubrey. *The Stone Circles of the British Isles*. New Haven, CT: Yale University Press, 1976.

Hawkins, Gerald S., and John B. White. *Stonehenge Decoded*. New York: Barnes & Noble, 1993.

Mohen, Jean-Pierre. *The World of Megaliths*. New York: Facts on File, 1990.

Newham, C. A. *The Astronomical Significance of Stonehenge*. Leeds, UK: John Blackburn, 1972.

Souden, David. *Stonehenge Revealed*. London: Collins & Brown, 1997.

STUPA

In Buddhist culture, a stupa (in Tibetan, a chorten) is a shrine to the dead. Their origins can be traced to prehistoric times, when they were simple mounds where important people were buried. As Gautama Buddha (the founding figure in Buddhism) approached the end of his earthly life, he requested that his remains (cremation being the common mode of disposing of bodies at the time) be placed in a stupa. At the same time, he

Stupas such as the famous **Pha That Luang (or Pha Chedi Lokajulamani) in Laos, contain relics of buddhas and serve as important holy sites in Buddhist cultures.** *AFP/Getty Images.*

requested that people change their thinking about stupas. Rather than being merely a place to remember the dead, a stupa should be seen as a symbol of the enlightened mind. From that time on, the stupa evolved into its present complexity. Traditionally, the stupa is a hemisphere topped with a square shape. Above the square is an umbrella-shaped cone with a pointed top.

The stupa represents the body of a buddha (an enlightened individual, but not necessarily Gautama Buddha) and should call to mind the buddha's presence in physical form. The base represents his throne; the four steps symbolize his legs crossed in the lotus position; the dome signifies his torso, with the square specifically standing for his eyes (and in some cultures they have eyes

drawn on them); and the spire is his crown. Contemplating stupas over the years has allowed for the development of a rather elaborate correspondence between different parts of the stupa and Buddhist teachings.

Within it, every stupa contains a life tree and holy relics. The central pillar in the midst of the stupa corresponds with the world tree, which in Indian mythology united heaven and earth. As the stupa evolved, the monument became a pivotal place, an axis around which believers moved like the planets traveling through the universe. It is also likened to the human spinal cord.

The relics placed inside a stupa may be as simple as a few bones that survive a cremation or items that belonged to the person, or as elaborate as the mummified body of an especially important person. (The earliest Buddhist stupas were built to house relics of Gautama Buddha.) For example, the mummified remains of many of the Dalai Lamas were placed within stupas that rest inside the **POTALA**, in Llasa, Tibet. Also inside the stupa one might place copies of Buddhist scriptures, prayers or mantras, statues of Buddha, or clay tablets called *tsha-tsha,* which have various symbols on them.

Stupas are widespread throughout southern Asia. In Sri Lanka they are known as dagobas. In China and Japan, they evolved into the pagoda. The largest stupa in the world is **BOROBUDUR**, an Indonesian temple complex near Yogyakarta, Java, that incorporates many small stupas surrounding a large main stupa at the temple's highest point.

Stupas reached the epitome of their development in Tibet, and in the last generation the scattered Tibetan community has erected stupas around the world. In the West, the construction and dedication of a stupa has often become a significant event in the development of a Buddhist center, signifying its having attained a certain level of stability. Such stupas may be erected upon the death of a movement's founder (and hence contain his or her relics); however, they may be constructed in a more general context and contain relics related to famous Buddhists contributed by older centers. A believer generally shows respect when visiting a stupa/chorten by walking around it clockwise so that the right arm is closest to it.

Sources:

Cummings, Joe, and Bill Wassman. *Buddhist Stupas in Asia: The Shape of Perfection.* Oakland, CA: Lonely Planet Publications, 2001.

Pant, Sushila. *Origin and Development of Stupa Architecture in India.* Columbia, MO: South Asia Books, 1977.

Snodgrass, Adrian. *Symbolism of the Stupa.* Delhi: Motilal Banarsidass, 1992.

TAI SHAN (CHINA)

China has five traditionally sacred mountains of which Tai Shan is the most famous, largely due to its location between the large cities of Beijing and Shanghai. It is the subject of many stories that tie it to traditional Chinese wisdom. For example, some describe it as the head of a dragon whose body consists of other mountain chains that snake across the country.

Tai Shan is also the home of the Jade Emperor, the Ruler of Heaven and Creator of the Universe who is the primary deity in traditional Chinese religion. Earthly emperors receive their authority to rule by the Mandate of Heaven passed to them by the Emperor of Heaven. Earthly emperors were required to annually present themselves before the heavenly emperor, validate their right to rule, and offer a ritual sacrifice.

From the second century BCE until the eighteenth century, emperors traveled to Tai Shan. They offered a sacrifice at the base of the mountain. They then climbed the mountain, which was a sign of their continuing favor with the Jade Emperor, and offered a second sacrifice. Like others who visited the mountain, they left behind personal items. In many cases this was a stone monument commemorating their accomplishments.

A staircase of 7,000 steps is the primary avenue to the mountain's top. At the summit is the Jade Emperor Temple, where believers will find a bronze statue of the deity. Many pilgrims make the trip up the stairs in the night so as to be on top in time for the spectacular sunrise. In addition to the emperor, many Chinese elites and millions of common people have visited the mountain. As with other modern sites, a variety of support facilities were developed to service the needs of the pilgrims, too. With so many pilgrims, it is not surprising that almost every spot on the mountain has been assigned some kind of religious significance and that a number of secondary temples have been constructed there.

When the People's Republic of China was formed in 1949, Tai Shan was still visited by upwards of three million pilgrims a year, even though it had been several centuries since the last visit by a Chinese ruler. Travel to the mountain dropped dramatically after the Communists took over, and it almost ceased entirely during the Cultural Revolution that began in 1966. With the end of the Cultural Revolution and the renewed acceptance of "traditional culture" in China that began in the early 1980s, pilgrimages have resurged. The government has taken steps to improve transportation to Tai Shan and has added a cable car for those not up to climbing the 7,000 steps. The government now views the mountain in terms of Chinese history and culture rather than as posing any kind of religious threat.

Sources:

Geil, William Edgar. *The Sacred 5 of China*. London: John Nurray, 1926.

Mt. Tai Shan Landscape. House of Shandong Province: People's Publishing, 1982.

Mullikin, Mary Augusta, and Anna Hotchkis. *The Nine Sacred Mountains of China*. Hong Kong: Vetch & Lee, 1973.

TALISMANS

Talismans are one of two common varieties of magical objects, the other being amulets. The two are often confused. Amulets are magical objects that are designed to protect the owner/wearer. Talismans are much more active items, usually designed to assist a transformation or cause something to happen. Thus one might obtain an amulet to protect him- or herself from an enemy, a curse, or a disease. On the other hand, one might use a talisman to find a love, obtain a better job, or acquire wealth.

Like amulets, talismans may be made of different materials and come in a wide variety of shapes and sizes. Some common talismans draw on astrological symbolism, while others use the names of angelic or deific figures or words of power. A soldier, for example, might wear a talisman based upon the symbol of the planet Mars so as to bring success on the battlefield, while a talisman with an angelic name could be used to bring healing. One of the most unusual talismans was one utilizing the severed hand of a thief, which would then be used by other thieves as a magical aid in their work.

Textbooks on magic often contain detailed rules for the production and empowerment of talismans. Talismans could not just be drawn; they had to be produced correctly at the proper time, and be energized by a magical ritual. The most difficult talisman to produce was the so-called Philosopher's Stone, which, among other powers, could assist the alchemist in the transformation of base metals into silver or gold. The use of talismans begins in prehistoric times and continues to the present. They have become very popular in the West as magical religions (ceremonial magic, Wicca, Neo-paganism) have experienced significant renewal. They continue to be used by a variety of older indigenous religions that include magic in their practice and that perpetuate the belief in malevolent magic.

Sources:

Budge, E. A. Wallis. *Amulets and Talismans*. New Hyde Park, NY: University Books, 1968.

Ferrell, Nick. *Making Talismans, Living Entities of Power*. St. Paul, MN: Llewellyn Publications, 2001.

Gonzalez-Wippler, Migene. *Complete Book of Amulets and Talismans*. St. Paul, MN: Llewellyn Publications, 1991.

Waite, Arthur Edward. *The Book of Ceremonial Magic*. 1911. Reprint, New York: Barnes & Noble, 1999.

TAROT

What today we know as Tarot cards, a popular tool for divination and self-understanding in the Esoteric community, first emerged in the late-eighteenth century as Esotericists began to interpret playing cards within an occult context. As developed in the nineteenth century, the common Tarot deck has 78 cards. There are four suits with fourteen cards each, ten numbers, and four court cards. There are also 22 trump cards.

The first to publicly advocate a symbolic interpretation of playing cards was Antoine Count de Gébelin (1719–1784), a French Protestant minister who had been attracted to Martinism, the teachings of Esoteric thinker Louis Claude de Saint-Martin (1743–1803). In 1781, de Gébelin published *Le Monde primitif*, which includes his speculations on the Italian *tarocchi* playing cards. He traced the cards' origins to ancient Egypt. Some who read his book began to use the cards for divination.

Not to be confused with an amulet, a talisman can take many forms to serve as a means of actively aiding its bearer in some kind of task. *Getty Images.*

The use of the Tarot took a giant step forward in the middle of the nineteenth century, when Eliphas Levi (1810–1875), a former Roman Catholic priest, developed his comprehensive magical system and presented it to the public in a series of books on what he termed "transcendental magic." He continued the identification of the Tarot with ancient Egypt, especially with the magical teachings ascribed to the ancient teacher Hermes Trimegistus. More importantly, however, he associated the deck with the mystical branch of Judaism known as the **KABBALAH**. The Kabbalah pictures the cosmos in terms of ten realms (*sephiroth*) that are tied together by a number of pathways. The ten numbered cards were thus identified with the ten sephiroth; the four suits with the four letters in the Hebrew name for God (the so-called tetragrammaton); and the twenty-two trump cards with the twenty-two letters of the Hebrew alphabet. By identifying the cards with the content of the Kabbalah, the reputation of Tarot as a tool for divination greatly increased.

Both Levi and those who came after him were dissatisfied with the main Tarot deck then in use, the so-called Marseilles deck. It would only be after the founding of the Hermetic Order of the Golden Dawn (HOGD) in the 1880s that a new deck was produced. This deck, which was intended for the exclusive use of the HOGD's members, was developed by Moina (1865–1928) and S. L. MacGregor Mathers (1854–1918). One of the order's members, Aleister Crowley (1875–1947), in collaboration with Freda Harris, would later develop his own version, which he called the Book of Thoth, again suggesting an Egyptian origin.

It was a third Golden Dawn member, Arthur Edward Waite (1857–1942), who, working with Pamela Coleman-Smith, developed the most popular version of the Tarot deck. The Waite-Smith deck was released in 1910, along with a book explaining the Esoteric meaning of each card, and the Waite deck would subsequently dominate Tarot card reading until the late-twentieth century. During the period of the New Age movement in the 1970s and 1980s, a host of new Tarot decks, each with a different twist or developed for a specific audience, appeared. Together, they pushed the Waite-Smith deck from the center of the Tarot world. As the twenty-first century began, several hundred versions of these decks became available for purchase.

Various ways of reading Tarot cards have been suggested, but most involve shuffling the deck and then laying out the cards in one of several patterns (spreads). Generally, the person reading the cards sits facing the person receiving the reading. A small table is placed between them. Each card is then read in terms of its own symbolism, its position in the pattern, and its orientation.

Sources:

Almond, Jocelyn, and Keith Seddon. *Understanding Tarot*. St. Paul, MN: Llewellyn Publications, 1991.

Cortellesi, Linda. *The User-Friendly Tarot Guidebook*. Worthington, OH: Chalice Moon Publications, 1996.

Kaplan, Stuart R. *The Encyclopedia of Tarot*. Vols. 1–3. New York: U. S. Game Systems, 1978, 1986, 1990.

Woudhuysen, Jan. *Tarot Therapy: A New Approach to Self Exploration*. Los Angeles: Jeremy P. Tarcher, 1979.

TEMPLARS

The Templars, a medieval order of knights, emerged in the wake of the first crusade. During the last quarter of the eleventh century, pilgrimages to the Holy Land from Europe had been largely blocked by a change of hands in the Muslim leadership in Jerusalem. In response, a crusade to retake Jerusalem was initiated, and by the end of the century Jerusalem had been returned to Christian control. However, many hazards remained for pilgrims attempting to travel to the Holy Land. Thus, in 1118 a group of nine young men, including Hugh de Payens and André de Montbard, presented to the king of Jerusalem their plan to create an order of warrior monks. Their intention was to secure the lands gained from the crusade, so that pilgrims could be better protected. Several of the men were already Cistercian monks, and all took (or reaffirmed) the standard monastic vows of poverty, chastity, and obedience.

In Jerusalem, the order was given land that included the **AL-AQSA MOSQUE**. The mosque had been misidentified as the former Temple of

Solomon, resulting in the group becoming known as the Knights of the Temple. This led to their later nickname, the Knights Templar, or simply Templars.

Subsequently, Hugh de Payens journeyed to the West to obtain the Church's blessing for the new order. At a council held at Troyes in 1128, there was an agreement to adopt the Rule of Saint Benedict, as revised by the Cistercians. The Templars also adopted the Cistercians' white habit on which they placed a red cross. As the order developed, members assumed one of four primary duties—knight, sergeant, farmer, or chaplain.

With the Catholic Church's blessing, and a growing reputation as ferocious warriors, the order soon found itself the recipient of numerous recruits, a great deal of financial support, and many gifts of land. The order grew large and wealthy. On their estates they erected fortified castles and laid out farms. They tended to select the most militarily strategic sites, even if these added significantly to the difficulty of constructing their fortified centers. They also developed a reputation for adding water gates to their castles along coasts or rivers. The Templars usually built distinctive round churches that utilized an octagonal pattern modeled on the Church of the Holy Sepulcher in Jerusalem. This structure can be seen today in the Temple Church in London, formerly the Templars' British headquarters.

The order prospered for almost two centuries, but their success came to a sudden halt in 1307. On October 13 of that year, representatives of King Philip IV of France (r. 1285–1314) moved against the order. Insofar as it was within their ability to reach, they arrested all members of the order and took possession of Templar properties. It appears that Philip was attempting to swell his budget, and other European powers, including the pope, allowed him to act. European rulers had come to fear the powerful organization that was showing signs of rivaling their governments in strength and political clout.

The suppression that culminated in the burning death of the order's grand master, Jacques de Molay (c. 1243–1314), ended the order's presence in Europe for all practical purposes. However, for many the death of the grand master merely completed the public phase of the order's life while initiating what has since been a hidden operation of the order. This concealed existence has been credited with ending the temporal power of the papacy in the nineteenth century. At the time of de Molay's death, the papacy controlled much of northern and central Italy. Groups such as the Bavarian Illuminati and the Freemasons have also been seen by some as revived versions of the Templars.

With the downfall of the monarchy in France at the time of the French Revolution, a new Templar movement came to the fore. In 1805, two French Freemasons, Philippe Ledru (1754–1832) and Bernard-Raymond Fabré-Palaprat (1775–1838) founded a new Order of the Temple, with the latter being named the new grand master. They were able to carry on a spectrum of public activities, including processions through the streets of Paris, since they were seen as similar to Freemasonry. In fact, Ledru and Fabré-Palaprat did understand their work to be within the larger Esoteric community, and they organized a Gnostic church to compete with Roman Catholicism. These two organizations became the source of a number of later Neo-Templar organizations and Esoteric churches. One of these Neo-Templar groups, popularly known as the Solar Temple, made headlines in 1994, when nearly 50 of its members, including almost all of its leadership, died in an act of mass murder/suicide.

The emergence of the Gnostic Neo-Templar groups implied an acceptance of a particular idea of the nature of the Templar's life before 1307. For many years prior to King Philip's moving against it, rumors had been circulated by its critics that the members held heretical ideas and practices that were also blasphemous and immoral. Fabré-Palaprat concluded that the secret of the order was its following of Gnostic beliefs and practices. Others have, especially in the last generation, reached very different ideas about the Templar's inner life.

One new idea about the Templars was floated in the 1960s by Pierre Plantard (1920–2000), a minor figure in France's Esoteric community who founded an Esoteric society called the Priory of Sion. He also identified the priory with the Abbey of Our Lady of Mount Zion that had been founded in 1099 in Jerusalem by Godefroy de Bouillon (1060–1100), who later became King of Jerusalem after the First Crusade. Plantard, and a number of writers who would pick up on his initial ideas, suggested that the Templars were not founded so much to protect pilgrims as to conduct excavations in Jerusalem in search of a set of documents that verify the place of the Merovingians as the rightful rulers of France. Later, people extrapolated Plantard's ideas to suggest that the documents recorded a different history of Christianity's early years. These documents suggested that Jesus had charged Mary Magdalene, his consort, with founding the Christian church, not Peter and the other Apostles. Upon finding these documents, they brought them to Europe and eventually secreted them in their center at a small French town, **RENNES LE CHÂTEAU**. Until their destruction, the Templars thus operated under the Priory of Sion to protect the documents and keep the secret of Jesus' bloodline.

Sources:

Baigent, Michael, Richard Leigh, and Henry Lincoln. *Holy Blood/Holy Grail.* London: Jonathan Cape, 1982.

Brown, Dan. *The Da Vinci Code.* New York: Doubleday & Company, 2003.

Gardner, Laurence. *Bloodline of the Holy Grail.* Gloucester, MA: Fair Winds Press, 2002.

Introvigne, Massimo. "Beyond *The Da Vinci Code:* History and Myth of the Priory of Sion." Posted at http://www.cesnur.org/2005/pa_introvigne.htm. Accessed March 31, 2007.

TEMPLES OF THE LATTER-DAY SAINTS

A semi-secret element of the life of the Church of Jesus Christ of Latter-day Saints is centered on their temples. The basic structure of the church is the ward, which is comparable to a protestant congregation or Catholic parish. Each ward has a meetinghouse where members gather for weekly worship and other educational, social, recreational, and cultural activities.

In contrast to the ward, the temple serves a widespread constituency and is used for a limited number of rites, all involving fully accredited and credentialed members. Those attending any event at the temple must be baptized and confirmed members, with males ordained into the lower level of the priesthood (termed the Melchizedek priesthood). They must also have a meeting with the bishop, who determines whether they are living by the precepts of the church, including the law of tithing. Being assured of a member's worthiness, the bishop issues a temple recommend, a document that allows the person to enter the temple. The interview also prepares the person to participate in the temple ordinances.

Several basic ordinances are enacted within the temple. Some are based upon the Latter-day Saints' understanding of heaven. According to them, the afterlife will find people in one of three levels of glory according to the laws they obeyed on earth. The great majority of people will go to the Terrestrial Kingdom. This is for good people who did not come to the truth of God and Jesus during their earthly lives. The highest, or Celestial Kingdom, is for those who believe the Gospel and follow its basic ordinances of baptism by immersion and receive the Holy Spirit by the laying on of hands (that is, they have become members of the Church of Jesus Christ of Latter-day Saints). Within the Celestial Kingdom, there are also levels. The highest level is for those who fully participated in the temple ceremonies.

The basic ordinance performed in the temples is termed the receiving of one's endowments. In specific rooms in the temple that are decorated with pictures depicting the Latter-day Saints' understanding of the cosmos and creation, members participate in a ritual that includes an explanation of the requirements for living in God's presence in the celestial world. Integral to the ritual is the making and receiving of a set of promises. The reception of one's endowment is believed to empower the Christian to overcome all circumstances in life.

Mormons take marriage very seriously and believe that marital relationships will continue in the life to come. One is initially married for this life, but in the temple couples are sealed together for all eternity. In the nineteenth century, sealing was intimately tied to teachings about polygamy, but under pressure from the outside world these teachings have been dropped. The Mormon Church, however, does continue to teach that a couple's sealing in the temple is a necessary requirement for entrance into the highest levels of the Celestial Kingdom. Finally, the Church also believes in the baptism for the dead.

The Church of Jesus Christ of Latter-day Saints was formed in 1830 as a recovery of the apostolic church. Over the centuries the essence of the true church was lost, and people who lived at that time would not be eligible for the higher levels of heavenly glory. In each temple is a large baptismal fount at which such baptisms may be conducted by proxy. Periodically, the Church has been cited in the news for the baptism of some famous historical character or had to deal with controversies such as when the Jewish community decried the baptism of the Jewish dead.

The first Latter-day Saint temple was constructed in the mid 1830s in Kirkland, Ohio. Even before this temple was begun, church-founder Joseph Smith, Jr. (1805–1844) laid a cornerstone for a future temple in Independence, Missouri. Both the Kirkland temple and the Temple Lot in Independence passed from the church's hands, however. A third temple was constructed in Nauvoo, Illinois, in the mid 1840s, but had to be abandoned following Joseph Smith's assassination and the relocation of the Church to Utah. In Salt Lake City a permanent temple was constructed. Additional temples were also constructed in St. George, Manti, and Logan, Utah.

Early in the twentieth century, as the Mormon movement expanded beyond Utah, the first tem-

ples were constructed in neighboring states such as Arizona, California, and Idaho. The first temple outside of the United States was completed in Bern, Switzerland, in 1955. The Swiss temple signaled a new emphasis in temple construction responding to the global mission program of the Church and its worldwide growth. By 2004, there were 117 temples in operation and a dozen more under construction. They were by then established around the world on every continent.

After construction, temples go through an elaborate consecration ceremony. It has been the Church's practice to delay the consecration ceremony and allow people who are not Church members to visit and see the inside of a Latter-day Saint temple. This practice has done much to reduce the level of secrecy surrounding Mormon temples. The level of secrecy has been further reduced by the revelations of former Church members who have chosen to explain the meaning (including the ritual texts) behind temple ceremonies. The discussion of temple rituals has centered upon their relationship to those of traditional Freemasonry. The Mormon Church, though, has been adamantly opposed to any revelations concerning temple ritual secrets.

Sources:

Cowan, Richard O. *Temples that Dot the Earth*. Salt Lake City, UT: Bookcraft, 1989.

Homer, Michael W. "'Similarity of Priesthood in Masonry': The Relationship between Freemasonry and Mormonism." *Dialogue* 27, 3 (Fall 1994): 1–113.

Packer, Boyd K. *The Holy Temple*. Salt Lake City, UT: Bookcraft, 1980.

Talmage, James E. *The House of the Lord*. Salt Lake City, UT: Deseret Book Company, 1971.

TENRI CITY (JAPAN)

Tenri City is the official headquarters of Tentikyo, one of Japan's most successful new religions. It is located at what in 1838 was a small village called Shoyashiki, about ten miles from the great Buddhist temples at Nara. Here, on October 26, 1838, Miki Nakayama (1798–1887) began to teach, sharing the revelatory experiences she had had and would continue to have over the next half century.

Nakayama believed that she had been shown a plot of land near the village of Jiba, which was the center of the universe. Here she saw to the erection of Oyasato, the Parental House, the residing place of Tenri-O-no Mikoto, God the Parent, who created the universe. Here, He awaits humanity's return. As Nakayama's teachings spread, and believers found their way to Shoyashiki, new building arose and eventually a city emerged. The movement was recognized by the government and survived the Meiji era as a part of sectarian Shinto.

In the main temple at Tenri City, there is an area where believers reenact the creation story as related by Nakayama in a musical dance-rite called *mi-kagura-uta*. This ritual is performed with the expectation of the transformation of this present world and social order into the Joyous Life World. At the main temple's center is the *kanro-dai*, a sacred pillar-like structure that marks the exact place of the Nakayama's revelation at the origins of human creation.

Following World War II, with the arrival of religious freedoms, Tenrikyo separated from the other Shinto groups. It began a process of purifying its teachings, which many felt had become distorted by the close association with sectarian Shinto. The movement expanded rapidly for several decades, during which time followers constructed a university, an orphanage, a hospital, a museum, a library, and a publishing house at Tenri city.

Among the many buildings in the city, one is designated as the Foundress' Sanctuary, where it is believed that Nakayama (also known as Oyasama) continues to live and work. In recognition of her presence, its residents prepare her three meals and hot baths every day. The door of the sanctuary is guarded by priests who rotate shifts every half-hour. These same priests also perform rituals of "perpetual veneration." Here, too, blessings are presented to the people. As a sign of their visit, they are given an **AMULET** that con-

tains a piece of clothing worn by Oyasama. Believers may present this amulet as proof of their "return." The amulet functions as a protective device for those who wear it.

Sources:

The Doctrine of Tenrikyo. Tenri, Nara, Japan: Tenrikyo Church Headquarters, 1995.

Ellwood, Robert S. *Tenrikyo: A Pilgrimage Faith*. Tenri: Oyasato Research Institute, 1982.

The Teachings and History of Tenrikyo. Tenri, Nara, Japan: Tenrikyo Overseas Mission Department, 1986.

van Straelen, Henry. *The Religion of Divine Wisdom, Japan's Most Powerful Religious Movement*. Kyoto, Japan: Veritas Shoin, 1957.

TEOTIHUACAN (MEXICO)

Teotihuacan was an ancient city in Mexico located some 18 miles from modern Mexico City. It was founded at the beginning of the Common Era, and by around 500 CE had a population in excess of 125,000. It was, in fact, the sixth largest city in the world at the time. The city was located in the Valley of Mexico between the surrounding mountains and Lake Texcoco. Because Lake Texcoco is a salt lake, the residents developed a sophisticated system for collecting rainwater.

Religion was an integral, even dominating, aspect of life in ancient Teotihuacan. A broad street that was named the Avenue of the Dead ran through the center of town and connected the major buildings. The Sun Pyramid was situated on the eastern edge of the Avenue of the Dead in the northern part of the city. In its final form, each side was more than 700 feet long at the base. The pyramid was a major ritual center, especially the cave under it. The cave was sacred to the god Tláloc, who was the god of rain. The Pyramid of the Sun was balanced by the Pyramid of the Moon found at the northern end of the Avenue of the Dead. It faced south toward the rest of the city, and at the plaza immediately in front of it was a space for religious gatherings. At the very center of the city was a large enclosed space that is called

During the spring equinox, the ancient city of Teotihuacan draws Mexican pilgrims who believe they can receive spiritual energies here. The ancient Aztecs considered the city to be the home of their gods. *Getty Images*.

the Ciudadela and is approximately 1,300 feet square. The plaza could easily accommodate about 100,000 people. In the center of the city is the Feathered Serpent (Quetzalcóatl) Temple, the most well-known structure at Teotihuacan.

The exact nature of the religion practiced by the first inhabitants of the city is not well understood. They left no written records. What is known is that the city was abandoned around 750 CE, possibly after being overrun and sacked by invaders from the mountains. The city remained uninhabited for some five centuries after that. Then, around 1300, it was rediscovered by the Aztecs, who were in the process of settling the large valley. Though they did not repopulate the city, they were impressed by the structures and des-

ignated Teotihuacan as the home of their deities. Thus, the city became their sacred place to which they journeyed for various ritual occasions.

With the coming of the Spanish in the sixteenth century, Aztec culture was destroyed and Teotihuacan was again abandoned. While never really forgotten, it was neglected for centuries. Only at the beginning of the twentieth century did archeologists turn their attention to the site. As its importance was recognized, it was gradually excavated and brought back to some degree of its former splendor. It is now a tourist site rather than a religious center.

In recent years Teotihuacan has been reinvested with sacredness by leaders in the New Age movement, who, having been alerted to its existence by author Peter Tompkins, have designated it an important spiritual site. They believe that the former residents recognized the natural flow of energies and that the city was located at its present site in recognition of those energies. Today, large gatherings of New Agers visit Teotihuacan during the equinox.

Sources:

Berrin, Kathleen, ed. *Feathered Serpents and Flowering Trees*. San Francisco: Fine Arts Museum of San Francisco, 1988.

Diehl, Richard A., and Janet Catherine Berlo. *Mesoamerica after the Decline of Teotihuacan AD 700–900*. Washington, DC: Dumbarton Oaks, 1989.

Miller, Mary, and Karl Taube. *The Gods and Symbols of Ancient Mexico and the Maya*. London: Thames and Hudson, 1993.

Pasztory, Esther. *Teotihuacan: An Experiment in Living*. Norman, OK: University of Oklahoma, 1997.

Tompkins, Peter. *Mysteries of the Mexican Pyramids*. New York: Harper & Row, 1976.

THAIPUSAM

Thaipusam is an annual South Indian festival primarily celebrated by the Tamil-speaking Saivite Hindus of Tamil Nadu. The festival gets its name from its occurrence at the full moon during Thai, the tenth month of the Tamil calendar that runs from the end of January to the beginning of February. Thaipusam is the birthday of Lord Subramaniam (Lord Muruga), who in Hindu mythology is the younger son of Lord Shiva.

Interestingly enough, the event includes some acts of devotion and austerities that many westerners have found offensive; for a while the celebration was even banned in India. However, by the nineteenth century many Tamils had moved to Malaysia, Singapore, and other parts of the world, where the British needed laborers. Today, while one may still find celebrations of Thaipusam at the Periyanayaki temple in Palani, India, the most well-known celebrations are held in Penang, Malaysia, and in Singapore.

The festival may extend over a week or more and culminates in an all-day procession. In Singapore it starts at one temple and passes every Tamil temple in the city. In Malaysia, it begins at the Sri Mahamariaman Temple in Chinatown and ends at the Batu Caves. While most in the community take part in the processional, a few, mostly young adult males, engage in the more memorable part of the procession. Their actions are the result of a belief that the way to salvation is best found by enduring a time of penance and pain. They spend a month of preparation before the day of the procession. This preparation begins with a ritual bath and entrance into a trancelike state. Then, still early in the day, they have their bodies pierced with a number of fishhooks. Once in place, a large platform, the *kavadi*, is lifted onto each person's shoulders; lines are attached to it with hooks. A young man undergoing this ritual then carries the *kavadi* along the processional route. This event, now widely known around the world, attracts many observers.

Upon reaching the end of the route, which in Malaysia is a set of steps leading to the main temple in the caves at the top, the men lay down the *kavadi* and some experienced assistants help with the removal of the hooks while a priest chants. The wounds are treated with hot ash, and those who participate in the ritual surprisingly suffer no scarring from their ordeal.

Sources:

Collins, Elizabeth Fuller. *Pierced by Murugan's Lance: Ritual, Power, and Moral Redemption among Malaysian Hindus*. De Kalb, IL: Southeast Asia Publications, 1997.

Hullet, Arthur. "Thaipusam and the Cult of Subramaniam," *Orientations* 9 (1978): 27–31.

Ward, Colleen. "Thaipusam in Malaysia: A Psychoanthropological Analysis of Ritual Trance, Ceremonial Possession and Self-mortification Practices," *Ethos* 12 (1984): 4.

THERAPEUTIC TOUCH

Therapeutic touch is a modern variation on time-honored techniques of the LAYING ON OF HANDS,

A young woman carries ritualistic milk in a procession during the Thaipusam festival in Kuala Lumpur. Hindus in India, Malaysia, and Singapore celebrate to mark the birth of Lord Subramaniam, a son of Lord Shiva. *AFP/Getty Images.*

a healing method that is present in many cultures and religious traditions. Therapeutic touch was developed and named in 1972 by Dolores Krieger, a nursing professor at New York University. Krieger, a theosophist, had been inspired by the therapist and clairvoyant Dora Kunz (d. 1999), the former president of the Theosophical Society who had been studying the laying on of hands. Kunz introduced renowned Hungarian psychic healer OSKAR ESTABANY to Krieger.

As a nursing professor, Krieger sought a means of introducing paranormal healing into nursing care in such a way that the scientific credentials of the nurses would not be compromised nor would a particular religious form of healing be introduced. Estabany, who had worked with researchers Bernard Grad and Justa Smith, was the healer utilized in what were the best experiments on psychic healing to date. At the same time, Krieger had herself run experiments on patients that indicated that such healing could have remarkable effects on patients. Her primary claims for her healing technique included its abilities to reduce pain and anxiety, promote relaxation, and stimulate the body's natural healing process.

Krieger suggested that therapeutic touch worked on the theory of a flow of life energy in the healthy body, much as is suggested in Oriental understandings of the human body. In a healthy body, the life energy flows freely along established pathways. If the energy is blocked, illness is the result. Many healers claim to "feel" the energy flow. Therapeutic touch practitioners work with the energy field and inject new energy into people with stifled energy flows. Practitioners generally include in their sessions an attempt to feel the energy flow of the patient and direct their healing activity to bring it back to normal. Krieger suggests that the body's energy field is a form of electromagnetic phenomena.

Once announced to the public and her colleagues, therapeutic touch underwent considerable criticism. Krieger's own experiments suffered because of the complexity introduced by using human subjects in the healing incidents. Any

healing effects of the kind claimed may have been due to other unreported factors, critics held. The suggestion of Oriental energy systems at work further distanced her ideas from accepted experimental methods. On the other hand, Krieger has referred to the work previously done by Estabany as setting the precedent for her own methods.

Sources:

Krieger, Dolores. *Therapeutic Touch: How to Use Your Hands to Help or Heal*. Englewood Cliffs, NJ: Prentice-Hall, 1986.

————. *Therapeutic Touch Inner Workbook*. Santa Fe, NM: Bear & Company Publishing, 1996.

Macrae, Janet. *Therapeutic Touch: A Practical Guide*. New York: Alfred A. Knopf, 1988.

Sayre-Adams, Jean, and Steve Wright. *The Theory and Practice of Therapeutic Touch*. New York: Churchill Livingstone, Inc., 1995.

THREE MAGI (RELICS)

One of the most beloved stories in Christendom is the account of the three Zoroastrian astrologers (also called magi or kings) who observe a new star and travel from their homeland to find the child whose birth has been heralded by the stellar phenomenon. In 326, SAINT HELENA (c. 248–c. 329), the mother of the Emperor Constantine (c. 272–337) and recent Christian convert, made a trip to the Holy Land to find any artifacts directly connected with Jesus. While the TRUE CROSS upon which Jesus was crucified was her greatest find, she also found numerous additional items, among them the RELICS (bones) of the Three Magi.

The relics of the Three Magi were taken to Constantinople and subsequently sent to Milan, Italy. (Alternate sources indicate that the relics were brought from ancient Persia to Constantinople by the Emperor Zeno in 490 CE.) Then, in 1164, they were taken by Holy Roman Emperor Frederick Barbarosa (1152–1190) to Cologne, where they would be housed in the city's cathedral. An artist named Nicholas of Verdun was commissioned to design a proper reliquary for the

Three Magi (as well as several notable saints). The box he designed, measuring 86 inches by 60 inches by 43 inches, was made out of gold and numerous pearls and precious stones. The gold was fashioned to depict scenes from the Bible, and the jewels were clustered to show the location of the heads of the Three Magi. It is the single most valuable manifestation of the medieval art of goldsmithery in existence today.

In Cologne, the legend of the three wise men spread. Names were associated with the wise men in the seventh century, and new details of their lives emerged. According to a calendar printed in Cologne at the time, the three men met in Armenia in 54 CE to celebrate Christmas, which was not yet a Christian holiday. A few days later, all three died—Melchior on January 1 at age 116; Balthasar on January 6 at age 112; and Caspar on January 11 at age 109. After they were named saints, the Magi were honored with feast days associated with these death dates.

Sources:

Abou-El-Haj, Barbara. *The Medieval Cult of Saints: Formations and Transformations.* Cambridge: Cambridge University Press, 1997.

Cruz, Joan Carroll. *Relics.* Huntington, IN: Our Sunday Visitor, 1984.

Saunders, William. "The Magi." *Arlington Catholic Herald* (January 8, 2004). Posted at http://www.catholicherald.com/saunders/04ws/ws040108.htm. Accessed March 31, 2007.

Whatley, Gordon. "Constantine the Great, the Empress Helena, and the Relics of the Holy Cross." In Thomas Head, ed. *Medieval Hagiography: An Anthology.* New York: Garland, 2000: 77–95.

TIRUMALA/TIRUPATI (INDIA)

Though few westerners have heard of the Tirumala Mountains or the nearby town of Tirupati, together these places are more frequently visited by pilgrims than any other site in the world, including Jerusalem, Rome, and Mecca. The mountain range is believed by many to be Adisesha, the serpent upon which the Hindu deity Vishnu reclines. Its seven peaks are the serpent's seven heads. Here, Vishnu appeared as Lord Venkateswara.

According to the story, at one point Vishnu's mate, Lakshmi, incarnated as Princess Padmavati. Vishnu took the form of Venkateswara and came to earth to search for her. Her earthly father agreed to allow his daughter to marry Venkateswara after the god provided proof that he was a man of great wealth.

Today, pilgrims are attracted to three major sites: Sri Venkateswara's temple on Tirumala, one of the seven peaks; the shrine of Padmavati, located at Tiruchanur about three miles south of Tirupati; and the shrine of Govindaraja in the town of Tirupati. These are, however, by no means the only noteworthy temples in the area. Because of the number of pilgrims who arrive annually and the patronage of royalty through the years, Sri Venkateswara's temple is reportedly the richest temple in the world. It is the home of a significant collection of rare and precious ornaments and receives many gifts from people who attribute their healing or good fortune to Lord Balaji (another name for Sri Venkateswara). It has been noted that about 150 kilograms of pure gold was used to cover the granite canopy over the most holy part of the main temple.

Sri Venkateswara's temple dates to the ninth century CE, but it did not emerge as a major center for pilgrimages until the fifteenth-century Vijayanagara dynasty. Pilgrims believe that they can attain *mukti* (bliss) by worshiping Sri Venkateswara. Because of the story of Venkateswara's search for his mate, the temple is popular with couples about to be married.

Since 1933 the administrative activities of the temples in Tirupati and environs have been administered as an autonomous body established by the government in Madras: the Tirumala-Tirupati Devasthanam (TTD) Committee. In the last half of the twentieth century, tens of thousands of South Indians have moved to North America. Here they have built several replicas of Sri Venkateswara's temples in different locations, including Pittsburgh, Pennsylvania; Bridgewater,

New Jersey; Cary, North Carolina; Aurora, Illinois; and Agoura, California. There is also a large Sri Venkateswara Temple in Tividale (West Midlands), England.

Sources:

Chetty, P. M. Muniswamy. *Tirumala-Tirupathi: Sri Venkateswara's Story and Mahatyam*. Tiruapti, India: Chukkala Singaiah Chetty, n.d.

Sitapati, Pidatala. *Sri Venkateswara: The Lord of the Seven Hills-Tirupati*. Mumbai, India: BVB, 2001.

TOMB OF CHRIST

Following Jesus' crucifixion, according to the Bible, his body was turned over to Joseph of Arimathea and wrapped in a linen cloth. Joseph saw to its burial in a sepulcher hewn out of rock. From this spot, the most important event in the Christian faith would occur: Jesus' resurrection.

By the time that the mother of the Emperor Constantine, HELENA (c. 248–c. 329), visited the Holy Land in 326, a site in what is now the northwest quarter of the Old City of Jerusalem had already been designated as the sepulcher in which Jesus' body was lain. Ten years later, Church leaders dedicated a new church that Constantine had ordered for the site. In the intervening years, a Pagan temple had been built over the sepulcher. The remaining part of the sepulcher that was not razed was incorporated into the church. Given that the crucifixion site was located nearby, the Church of the Holy Sepulcher was designed to encompass both Jesus' tomb and Golgotha, the place where Jesus was crucified and where Helena found the TRUE CROSS.

Over the next centuries, the church was destroyed and rebuilt several times. It was destroyed by the Persians in 614, and again in 1009 by the Egyptian Muslims. The crusades were launched, ostensibly, to regain control of the Church of the Holy Sepulcher from the Muslims. Once Christians recaptured Jerusalem in 1099, the crusaders rebuilt the church. It is this church that remains standing today, though it was charred by a major fire in 1808.

Through the centuries of the post-Crusade era, when Jerusalem was part of the Ottoman Empire, the various factions of the ancient church petitioned the authorities for the right to control it and the tomb. In 1852 the Ottomans decreed that six Christian communions would share the space within the church. The Greek Orthodox, Roman Catholic (represented by the Franciscan order), and Armenian Orthodox Churches control the main floor of the church, including the space in front of the sepulcher. Three other churches also have space at the church: the Coptic Orthodox Church (Egypt), the Syrian-Jacobite Orthodox Church, and the Ethiopian Orthodox Church.

The sepulcher might be thought of as a church within a church. A building called the edicule was constructed over the tomb, which is now located in the center of the main rotunda. The Franciscan chapel at the north end of the church marks the spot where Mary Magdalene encountered the post-resurrection Christ.

Most Christians look toward Jerusalem as the site of Christ's burial and resurrection. Muslims offer a very different perspective, though. Most Muslims believe that Jesus did not die on the cross but was instead raised by Allah into heaven, where He continues to live, and that He will return during the end times. That view has been challenged in the modern world by groups of Pakistani and Indian Muslims known as the Ahmadiyyas. They emerged in the nineteenth century as a result of the preaching mission of Mirza Ghulam Ahmad (1839–1908).

In his book *Jesus in India* (1899), Ahmad suggested that Jesus did not die on the cross, but rather escaped his enemies. He then left Palestine for India and Afghanistan. He eventually settled in Kashmir, where He lived out a long life and then died. His tomb has been traced and found in Khanyar Street, Srinagar. This tradition, though attributed to some visions given to Ahmad, is based in no small part on the rather questionable writings of Nicholas Notovich, whose *The*

Unknown Life of Jesus Christ (1894) claims that Jesus traveled to India and Tibet as a young man. Ahmad specifically repudiated Notovich on Jesus' early travels to India, but claimed that Jesus did go there late in His life.

The structure identified by Ahmad as Jesus' resting place is known locally as the Roza Bal (or Rauza Bal). It stands in front of a Muslim cemetery in the Kan Yar district of Srinagar, the capital of Kashmir. Inside is a wooden sepulcher surrounded by four recently installed glass walls. The sepulcher is empty, though, and the entombed personage lies instead in an underground crypt. A sign in front names the occupant Yuz Asaf (Leader of the Healed).

The theses articulated by Notovich and Ahmad have generated a variety of writings through the twentieth century, including one relatively famous text, the *Aquarian Gospel of Jesus Christ,* by Levi Dowling. The idea of the Srinagar site being the grave of Jesus has been severely hindered by antagonism toward the Ahmadiyya movement by mainstream Islam, which has declared the movement heretical. Its most recent exponent is German writer Holger Kersten, who has collected supporting data on Jesus' presence in Kashmir.

Sources:

Ahmad, Mirza Ghulam. *Jesus in India.* 1899. Reprint, London: The London Mosque, 1978.

Biddle, Martin, et al. *The Church of the Holy Sepulchre.* New York: Rizzoli, 2000.

Duckworth, H. T. F. *The Church of the Holy Sepulchre.* London: Hodder & Stoughton, 1922.

Kersten, Holger. *Jesus Lived in India: His Unknown Life before and after the Crucifixion.* London: Element Books, 1994.

Pappas, Paul C. *Jesus' Tomb in India: The Debate on His Death and Resurrection.* Fremont, CA: Asian Humanities Press, 1991.

TOPKAPI PALACE (TURKEY)

Topkapi Palace in **ISTANBUL** was erected by Sultan Mehmet II (1432–1481) after his army took Constantinople in 1453 and turned the city into the headquarters of the new Ottoman Empire. Along with building a palace, he converted the large Orthodox church, the **HAGIA SOPHIA**, into a mosque.

Mehmed II spent much of his reign establishing and further extending Ottoman territory, and his successors would turn Istanbul—as Constantinople was renamed—into a significant center for the Muslim world. The empire encompassed most of the land associated with the origins of Islam, and beginning early in the sixteenth century successive sultans used their position to turn their capital into the leading Muslim city. One way they did this was by accumulating many relics of Muhammad, which were gradually collected at the palace. The first relics appear to have been given to the Sultan Selim, who assumed the title caliph after his conquest of Egypt. On that occasion, his representative in Mecca sent him some of Muhammad's relics.

The items that came to be included in the collection reputedly include some hair from Muhammad's beard, a chip off one of his teeth, and his footprint preserved in porphyry. Among items he is believed to have used are his cloak, his seal, a bow, and a letter he wrote. In addition, there is the oldest known copy of the Qur'an, which was written on gazelle leather, two pieces of cloth from the cover of the Kaaba in **MECCA**, and a sword used by the first four caliphs, who have a special place in secular and sacred Muslim history. The cloak, called Hirka-i Saadet, is one of the most valuable items in the collection, and so it is kept in a box made of solid gold. Maintained in a single room, this extensive collection of relics, the largest of its kind in existence, turned Topkapi into a pilgrimage site.

By the middle of the nineteenth century, the Ottoman Empire was in rapid decline. It chose the wrong allies in World War I, and after the revolution led by the Young Turks, the empire was dismantled and the central lands turned into the secular state that is now modern Turkey. By 1924 the sultans had abandoned the palace as a residence. It has subsequently been turned into a museum.

The relics of Muhammad and the four caliphs are now housed in the Chamber of the Sacred Relics at Topkapi Palace. It was first opened to the public in 1962. An imam (Muslim teacher) is on duty at the chamber and reads verses from the Qur'an as part of an attempt to insure the solemnity of the spot for believers. It is interesting that the larger palace has also been decorated to convey a certain ambiance as a Muslim holy place. For example, the front doorway was brought to Istanbul from Mecca, where it had previously served as the doorway to the Great Mosque.

Sources:

Cimok, Fatih. *Topkapi Palace*. Istanbul: A Turizm, 1990.

Davis, Fanny. *The Palace of Topkapi in Istanbul*. New York: Charles Scribner's Sons, 1970.

Rogers, J. M. *The Topkapi Saray Museum: The Treasury*. London/Boston: Thames & Hudson/Little, Brown, 1987.

TOURO SYNAGOGUE (RHODE ISLAND)

Touro Synagogue is the oldest Jewish center of worship in the United States. The original congregation was formally organized in 1658, and the building was dedicated in 1763. The original congregation traced its history to the fabled Jewish community of the Iberian Peninsula (Spain and Portugal) who in 1492 and 1493 were expelled from their homes by Christian rulers. Forced to convert to Christianity or leave, many Iberian Jews professed Christianity while secretly remaining adherents of Judaism. Such converts became known as *marranos*, a derogatory term meaning swine that is a reference to their refusal to eat pork.

Suspected of remaining loyal to their former faith, the marranos lived under the threat of the Spanish Inquisition. Many moved to Brazil, where a large population existed in Recife by the seventeenth century. In 1624, Holland, then the most religiously tolerant country in Europe, seized land from the Portuguese in northern Brazil, including Recife. Shortly thereafter, Dutch poli-

cies resulted in the marranos casting off their Christian facade; immigration of other Iberian Jews who had previously settled in Holland also increased. In 1636, Recife Jews built the Kahal Zur synagogue, and the Jewish population peaked at about 1,500 around that time.

Then, in 1654, the Portuguese retaliated and drove the Dutch out of Brazil. They left with their Jewish citizens, who settled Dutch territory on the island of Curaçao and in New York (then New Amsterdam). Curaçao, off the coast of Venezuela, is now home to the oldest synagogue in the western hemisphere, and New York became the site of the first Jewish congregation. The primary relic of this congregation is their cemetery.

In 1658 fifteen Iberian Jewish families who had earlier settled in Barbados moved to Newport, Rhode Island. Here they were able to take advantage of the guarantees of religious freedom promulgated by Roger Williams, the colony's governor. In 1658 Congregation Jesuit Israel, the second American Jewish congregation, was established. This congregation, joined by fellow Jews from Recife and Curaçao, survived over the next century, and in 1758 Isaac de Touro of Amsterdam became its rabbi. He led the construction of the synagogue building that now bears his name. It survives as the oldest synagogue standing in America. It was built by Peter Harrison, an outstanding architect who happened to live in Newport.

The original congregation was not able to enjoy the building for long, however, because the establishment of British control of the city during the American Revolution led to the scattering of the congregation. Yet, the building survived and eventually a few families returned to the city and reopened the synagogue. Concerned about their status in the new country, in 1790 Moses Seixas, the congregation's warden, wrote George Washington concerning the American government's policies. Washington's reply, written a year before the ratification of the Bill of Rights, is one of the earliest statements of the religious freedoms soon to become the law of the land.

Over the years, the Sephardic element in the Newport congregation died out. The present congregation consists of Jews not of Iberian background. Visitors to Newport may see Washington's letter on display, as well as the oldest Torah scroll in America.

Sources:

Fisher, Leonard Everett. *To Bigotry, No Sanction: The Story of the Oldest Synagogue in America.* New York: Holiday House, 1998.

Foster, Geraldine S. *The Jews in Rhode Island: A Brief History.* Providence, RI: Rhode Island Heritage Commission/Rhode Island Publications Society, 1985.

Gutstein, Morris Aaron. *The Story of the Jews of Newport: Two and a Half Centuries of Judaism.* New York: Bloch Publishing Co., 1936.

Touro Synagogue of Congregation Jeshuat Israel, Newport, Rhode Island. Founded 1658, Dedicated 1763, Designated as a National Historic Site, 1946. Newport, RI: Society of Friends of Touro Synagogue National Historic Shrine, 1948.

TOWER OF BABEL

One of the most well known biblical stories is related in Genesis 11. It tells of an ancient people who built a city with a tower that reached to the heavens. In the face of such hubris, God confused their language so that the people spoke many different tongues and could not understand one another. They thus scattered to the corners of the earth. The site of this tower, Babel, recalls the ancient city of Babylon and is the origin of the modern word "babbling."

In the nineteenth century, many questioned the story, dismissing it as a baseless fable. However, archeologists exploring ancient Babylon, located in modern Iraq, uncovered the ruins of a ziggurat, a temple in the form of a stepped pyramid. It was soon discovered that for several thousand years the people of the Tigris and Euphrates Valleys had centered their town on one or more ziggurats. The Babylonian ziggurat had a square base, each side being some 300 feet in dimension.

It honored the deity Marduk and is believed to be the source of the biblical story.

Ziggurats were made of mud bricks, and even in the dry climate they have not fared well over time. Babylon, as an urban center, disintegrated after the fifth-century Persian conquest. Only the base of the Tower of Babel now exists, though a few other small examples of ziggurats have survived. The largest surviving ziggurat is found at Elam in southwestern Iran. The best preserved is at Ur, in modern Iraq, a ziggurat dedicated to the the moon god Nanna.

In the contemporary world, the discovery of ziggurats has been used as evidence for the historical accuracy of the biblical text. However, critics have pointed out that while the Tower of Babel story probably refers to a real historical building, the myth itself is not a believable explanation for the origins of the world's languages. Not to be outdone, a small group of conservative Christians has attempted to argue that ancient Hebrew was the original human language and other languages descend from it. Such arguments have met with little positive response from linguists.

The Tower of Babel story might also have derived from an ancient Sumerian belief in a distant age during which everyone worshiped Enlil, the main Sumerian deity, until Enki, the god of wisdom, confused the people's speech.

Sources:

George, Andrew R. *House Most High: The Temples of Ancient Mesopotamia.* Winona Lake, IN: Eisenbrauns, 1993.

Kramer, Samuel N. *The Sumerians: Their History, Culture, and Character.* Chicago: University of Chicago Press, 1963.

Oppenheim, A. Leo. *Ancient Mesopotamia: Portrait of a Dead Civilization.* Chicago: University of Chicago Press, 1964.

Pennock, Robert T. *The Tower of Babel: The Evidence against the New Creationism.* Cambridge, MA: MIT Press, 1999.

Walton, John H. "The Mesopotamian Background of the Tower of Babel Account and Its Implications." *Bulletin of Biblical Research* 5 (1995): 155–175.

The book of Genesis tells how a king built the Tower of Babel—depicted here in an illustration from a circa 1300 German publication—in an attempt to reach heaven. Some believe the legend is based on the construction of an actual Babylonian ziggurat. *Getty Images*.

TRIER (GERMANY)

Trier (or Treves) is one of Germany's oldest cities. The Roman Emperor Augustus founded it during the first century BCE. It later became the capital of the Roman province of Belgica and, in the third century, of the prefecture of Gaul. It was the site of a sacred healing spring associated with the god Mars, as well as a healing center dedicated to the deity Aesclapius.

Trier was also an early Christian center, and a church was constructed there during the reign of Constantine (c. 272–337). In 326 Constantine's mother, HELENA (c. 248–c. 329), made her famous trip to the Holy Land looking for relics of Jesus.

Among the items she is said to have brought back to Constantinople was the seamless garment that Jesus was said to have worn and for which the soldiers overseeing his crucifixion gambled (Matthew 27:35). Two stories conflict as to how the coat—whose authenticity has been widely questioned—reached Trier. One story suggests Helena contributed the coat herself. Others suggest that it was obtained at a later date by Charlemagne (c. 752–814) and then presented to the church.

The coat was regularly shown to the public, beginning in 1512, when the Diet of the Holy Roman Empire met at Trier. Shortly thereafter, Pope Leo X granted a plenary indulgence to pilgrims who went to Trier when the coat was being

THE ENCYCLOPEDIA OF RELIGIOUS PHENOMENA

shown. The showing of the coat followed a seven-year schedule of public viewing. The building of Trier as a pilgrimage site, unfortunately for the city, ran counter to the Protestant Reformation, which had its origin in Germany and had made indulgences a central issue. Trier therefore discontinued the public displays of the coat in 1545. The church was destroyed by French soldiers in 1674 and not rebuilt until 1757.

A campaign to show the coat again began again in the nineteenth century. By the end of the century, some two million pilgrims were making the trek to Trier. During this time people began to believe that it was also a source for healings.

Sources:

Heinen, H. "Helena, Konstantin und die überlieferung der Kreuzauffindung im 4. Jahrhundert." In Erich Aretz, et al. *Der Heilige Rock zu Trier: Studien zur Geschichte und Verehrung der Tunika Christi*. Trier, Germany: Paulinus Verlag, 1995.

Kann, Hans-Joachim. *Pilgrims' Guide to Trier and Area*. Trier, Germany: Michael Weymand, 1994.

TRONDHEIM CATHEDRAL (NORWAY)

In 1016 CE, Olav II Haraldsson was selected as the new king of Norway. A Christian, he was determined to bring the country into the Christian world. He mandated the conversion of Norway to his religion. However, he met with strong opposition, and in 1028 was dethroned. Leaving Norway for two years, Haraldsson returned in 1030 to fight for his crown and Christianity. He was slain in battle, and his body taken to Trondheim on the bank of the Nid River. Four years later, his son assumed the throne and proceeded with his father's original plans.

In 1031 Olav's grave was opened, and it was discovered that his body had not decayed but looked much as it had at the moment of death. The bishop present at the exhumation declared Olav a saint. His body was taken to the local church. A chapel was then erected over the spot where Olav

had been buried. That chapel was then replaced by a cathedral, which was erected at the end of the eleventh century. In the middle of the twelfth century, Trondheim was chosen as the center of Norway's first archbishopric, partly because the cathedral had become a major pilgrimage site. Pilgrims came to view the shrine above the high altar of the church in which the former king's preserved remains were now located. The naming of the archbishopric became an occasion for the significant enlargement of the building.

Through a variety of ups and downs to both the cathedral and the country, the church survived as a symbol of Norwegian nationalism. Not the least of these events was the movement of Norway toward the Lutheran Church in the 1530s. Two fires ravaged the cathedral in the early 1700s. In 1869, the decision was made to completely rebuild the cathedral and bring it back to its original state. This project took over a century, but was officially completed in 2001. In spite of the center of Norway's life moving to Oslo, the Trondheim Cathedral remains the center of its religious expression.

Sources:

Long C. *Trondheim: One Thousand Years in the City of St Olav*. Trondheim, Norway: Tapir Academic Press, 1992.

Mittet, Per. *Trondheim and Trondelag*. Trondheim, Norway: F. Bruns, 1948.

Raso, Alison. *Pilgrim Road to Nidaros: Oslo to Trondheim*. Milnthorpe, Cumbria, UK: Cicerone Press, 2002.

TRUE CROSS

The True Cross is the cross upon which Jesus Christ was crucified around 30 CE. For many reasons, the artifact disappeared from discussions within the Christian Church over the next centuries. During this time Christians operated as an underground movement and periodically experienced severe persecution. Their status changed radically early in the fourth century, when the Emperor Constantine assumed the throne of the

Roman Empire. Constantine, over a period of several decades, first decriminalized and then legitimized Christianity within the empire.

Constantine's mother, **HELENA** (c. 248–c. 329), became a devout and enthusiastic Christian, and with the support of her son founded a number of churches and assisted in the process of Christianity becoming a public religion. Following the visit of Macarius, the bishop of Jerusalem to Constantinople in 326, and his lamentations over the neglect of the Christian holy sites located there, she journeyed to Jerusalem and personally surveyed the locations described in the Gospels. Macarius assisted her in finding the exact locations mentioned in the four biblical books about Jesus' life and ministry.

Among the places she visited was a rocky outcropping that was pointed out to her as the place where Jesus was crucified. This site was outside the ancient city but close to one of its gates. Nearby was a cave identified as the place where Jesus' body was placed and from which he was resurrected. The Roman Emperor Hadrian (r. 117–138) had a large earthen foundation erected there that covered both sites. Upon this foundation a temple to Venus was constructed. Helena's visit, however, followed Constantine's conversion of the empire to Christianity, and the temple to Venus had been dismantled by the time she arrived.

Helena began excavations of the rubble of the former pagan temple site. According to the stories that circulated several generations later, she discovered three crosses. They looked very much alike and gave no indication as to which might be the True Cross, though the board that Pilate had placed on Jesus' cross, the *titulus*, was also found. The means of distinguishing Jesus' cross from the other two was provided by a dying woman who resided nearby. The three crosses were taken to her, and she was asked to touch each one. When she touched the True Cross, she was immediately healed. The earliest account of the discovery of the crosses and the healing of the unnamed lady is recorded in the historical work of Rufinus (c. 345–410), which was written some seventy years

later. Constantine would later see to the building of the Church of the Holy Sepulcher on this site.

Through the fifth century, variations on Rufinus's account of Helena's discovery emerged. They offered very different details about the finding of the cross. For example, Sozomen (c. 375–c. 447) suggested that Helena found the cross as a result of some dreams she had. He also said that the Roma Sybil (prophetess) had predicted the finding of the cross.

By the end of the fourth century, a number of writers mention the cross and suggest that the wood had been divided and distributed to churches and church leaders in a variety of locations. Cyril of Jerusalem (c. 315–c. 386) suggested that relics of the wood from the cross could be found throughout the whole inhabited earth (i.e., around the Mediterranean Basin). There are also a variety of documents from this period that were accompanied by gifts of pieces of the cross; usually, these were letters from one prominent church leader to another. The main part of the cross left in Jerusalem seems to have survived until the time Saladin defeated Christian forces at the Battle of Hattin in 1187. Soon afterward Saladin took the True Cross away and it has not been seen since.

The belief that the True Cross had been found and was in the hands of the Church would affect the Church's liturgy. The Church of the Holy Sepulcher was dedicated in September 335, and by the seventh century a feast of the Exaltation of the Cross was being celebrated as far east as Rome on September 14 in memory of that event. About the same time, a similar feast that recalled the date of Helena's founding of the True Cross was celebrated in various places on May 3. Both days were later added to the calendar of the western church, though the May 3 celebration was dropped in 1970.

In his attack on the use of relics, Protestant reformer John Calvin (1509–1564) remarked, "There is no abbey so poor as not to have a specimen. In some places there are large fragments, as at the Holy Chapel in Paris, at Poictiers, and at Rome, where a good-sized crucifix is said to

The cross upon which Jesus was crucified has long been called the True Cross. Supposedly rediscovered by Saint Helena in 326 CE, fragments of the cross are now purportedly scattered around the world, where they are revered as holy relics. *Fortean Picture Library.*

have been made of it. In brief, if all the pieces that could be found were collected together, they would make a big ship-load. Yet the Gospel testifies that a single man was able to carry it." This is an exaggeration, to say the least, but the quote does carry the emotional reaction to an overemphasis on relics in many parts of the Catholic Church in the sixteenth century. The Protestant aversion to relics in general would be superseded by the historical and scientific attack upon the authenticity of those objects held by the Church as genuine relics. That attack has highlighted the gaps in the records of all of the relics that are believed to relate directly to Jesus and events in the Gospels. In the face of the

attacks on the True Cross relics, in 1870 French Catholic scholar Rohault de Fleury published a study of all the known relics that supposedly included part of the True Cross. He concluded that, if brought together, they would contain considerably less wood than would have been in the cross used to crucify Jesus.

Pieces of the True Cross can be seen at many locations around the world. The majority of these can be traced to a piece that appeared during the era of the crusades, when so many relics were brought back from Jerusalem. The largest single piece appears to be located at Santo Toribio de Liébana in Spain. Heiligenkreuz, a Cistercian abbey in Austria, claims to house the second largest collection of fragments of the True Cross. There are at least four pieces of the True Cross in the United States. They are located at Saint Helena Catholic Church, the Bronx, New York; Holy Angels Catholic Church, Mt. Airy, North Carolina; Cathedral of the Holy Cross, Boston, Massachusetts; and the Shrine of the North American Martyrs, Auriesville, New York City. The *titumus* is on display at the Church of Santa Croce in Jerusalem.

Sources:

Borgehammar, Stephen. *How the Holy Cross Was Found: From Event to Medieval Legend*. Stockholm: Almqvist & Wiksell, 1991.

Pohlsander, Hans A. *Helena: Empress and Saint*. Chicago: Ares Publishers, 1995.

Thiede, Carsten Peter, and Matthew d'Ancona. *The Quest for the True Cross*. New York: Palgrave, 2002.

TULKU

In Tibetan Buddhism, a variety of interrelated names have been adopted to describe religious leaders. The basic term is *lama*, which is equivalent to the Hindu term *guru*, or teacher. In most religious traditions, however, teachers are not simply knowledgeable persons who spend their days sharing information; they are people who have special cosmic attributes who speak from a state of spiritual attainment.

Most lamas are also tulkus. A tulku exists as the physical manifestation of a deity or other enlightened being, such as a buddha. In Mahayana Buddhism, the Buddha had three bodies: the higher dharma-kaya, the bhoga-kaya (enjoyment body), and the nirmana-kaya or transformation body. The last of these is seen as a projection of dharma qualities into physical being. Bodhisattvas, enlightened beings who assist in the liberation of humanity, are seen as having an abundance of dharma qualities to the extent that they can be manifested as a physical body.

Identified with a deity figure, lamas are regarded by believers as semi-divine beings. Such beings, once incarnated, are destined to reincarnate, and the search for the next incarnation is a vital part of maintaining the lineage of leadership within Tibetan Buddhism. By far the most famous tulku is the Dalai Lama, who is believed to be the emanation of Chenresi (know elsewhere as Kuan Yin, Avilokiteshvara, Kannon, etc.)

Following the death of a lama/tulku, Tibetan leaders believe in the necessity of engaging in a search for the tulku's reincarnation. Most commonly, they would create a list of candidates, usually children born a short-time after the death of the former tulku. Such children would be put through a series of tests, including being asked to pick out objects that belonged to the deceased lama from among other equally possible objects. At the same time, those who had known the former lama would look for signs of recognition.

Over the centuries, the recognition of tulkus has largely been a Tibetan and Mongolian practice. All tulkus resided in either Tibet or Mongolia, and the search for their successors was carried out among the children of those lands. However, the incorporation of Tibet into China in the 1950s, the subsequent suppression of religion in China, and the voluntary exile of many of the tulkus to other countries has had a profound effect upon traditions in Tibetan Buddhism.

In the years following the religious persecution of the Cultural Revolution in China (1966–1976), tolerance of Buddhism has returned. The result, though, has been the rise of competing authorities who debate the naming of successive tulkus both inside and outside China. The most famous case concerns the Panchen Lama, who is considered the second highest-ranking lama in Tibetan Buddhism. The Tenth Tibetan Panchen Lama died in 1989. Subsequently, two distinct searches began for his successor. One occurred within Tibet and was sanctioned by the Chinese government; the second was conducted among exiled Tibetans. The Dalai Lama announced the result of the latter search in May 1995. In December of that same year, Chinese officials announced their own candidate for the office. It was that lama who was formally enthroned in Tibet. These two candidates continue to vie for the support of the Tibetan community, however.

Through the last decades of the twentieth century, Tibetan Buddhism has spread to most western countries, where it has attained a large following. The question has since been posed as to whether tulkus could incarnate among western followers. As early as 1976, O. K. MacLise, the son of rock drummer Angus MacLise, was recognized as the reincarnation of Sangye Nyenpa Rinpoche, an emanation of Manjushri, who was a leader of the Kaygu Karma School of Tibetan Buddhism. In succeeding years, a variety of western children, mostly the sons of Buddhist parents, have also been recognized.

Possibly the most interesting of the western tulkus is Alyce Zeoli (b. 1949). Zeoli was not only a female but also an adult at the time she was recognized as a lama. She grew up in Brooklyn, married, and bore several children. She also became the head of a New Age group, the Center for Discovery and New Life. She met the head of the Nyingma school of Tibetan Buddhism in 1985, H. H. Penor Rinpoche, when he came to the United States. Following their meeting, he declared that, even without being familiar with eastern beliefs, Zeoli was nevertheless teaching Tibetan Buddhism. He came to believe that she was a tulku, and thus instigated a formal effort to determine if that was so. Two years later Zeoli was recognized as the reincarnation of Ahkon Norbu Lhamo, a tulku who had not reincarnated for three centuries. She was formally installed in 1988.

In general, the leaders of the various Tibetan Buddhist schools and sub-schools are seen as tulkus. An uncounted number of others, possibly as many as two hundred who now lead western Buddhist organizations, are also considered tulkus.

Sources:

Coleman, Graham. *A Handbook of Tibetan Culture*. Boston, MA: Shambhala, 1994.

Hilton, Isabel. *The Search for the Panchen Lama*. New York: W. W. Norton & Company, 2001.

Mackenzie, Vicki. *Reborn in the West: The Reincarnation Masters*. London: Marlowe & Company, 1996.

Rawlinson, Andrew. *The Book of Enlightened Masters: Western Teachers in Eastern Traditions*. La Salle, IL: Open Court, 1997.

TUMMO

Tummo (i.e., "inner fire" or "psychic heat") is a Tibetan yoga practice that involves various body exercises. These include the control of the breath and intense concentration on or visualization of various metaphysical goals (inner peace). Tummo, however, has become best known for a very practical goal practiced in frigid Tibet. It is used to generate enough body heat to survive overnight in the mountains without the benefit of any outside sources of warmth.

This practice was initially made known in the West through the writings of a French woman, Alexandra David-Neel (1868–1969), who explored India and Tibet in 1911 as her way of escaping an unbearable marriage. Gaining some acceptance in a land that was unusually hostile to outsiders, she was able to master many of the Tibetan meditative practices, including tummo. She not only claimed to be able to raise her body temperature, but in her book *Magic and Mystery in Tibet* (1931) she explained the method to her readers.

In the last half of the twentieth century, various Western groups, mostly of an esoteric nature, also drew on Tibetan traditions and incorporated tummo into their course of study. More recently, as Tibetan teachers have spread throughout the West, they have begun to offer training in the meditation practices associated with tummo. Their practice includes yoga asanas (postures), visualization, the use of mantras (words that are intoned in a manner as to resonate with the body), and breathing techniques. Such techniques have generally been taught in a retreat setting so they can be practiced a number of times in the presence of an experienced teacher.

Rabbi Yaakov Ifargan, a tzaddik, offers help to a blind Jewish man. Many believe tzaddiks have supernatural abilities to look into people's lives and show them the right path to follow. *Time Life Pictures/Getty Images.*

Sources:

David-Neel, Alexandria. *Magic and Mystery in Tibet.* London: John Lane, 1931.

Ray, Reginald A. *Secret of the Vajra World: The Tantric Buddhism of Tibet.* Boston: Shambhala, 2001.

Yeshe, Thubten, et al. *The Bliss of Inner Fire: Heart Practice of the Six Yogas of Naropa.* Somerville, MA: Wisdom Publications, 1998.

TZADDIK

A tzaddik (or zaddik; literally, "a righteous man") is a title usually given to the leader of one of the various Hassidic Jewish groups. The tzaddik is generally considered to be a person who has conquered his (or occasionally her) evil inclinations,

such as pride, to live a life of humility. They strongly identify with the oppressed. Righteous people are often also believed to have extraordinary spiritual or mystical powers.

Many consider Noah to have been the first tzaddik. He is described in Genesis 6:9 as a "just man and perfect in his generations, and Noah walked with God." The idea of a just person has been discussed throughout Jewish history. Scholars have argued over how many there were at any given moment, noting that many would be ordinary people whose goodness would go unacknowledged by their own local community. These people form a class known in the Jewish tradition as the hidden tzaddikim. However, in the eighteenth century the term began to be applied especially to the leaders of the emerging Hassidic movement, an orthodox mystical sect that arose in eastern Europe.

As the leader of a Hassidic community, however, the tzaddik is a public person to whom is ascribed supernatural abilities. People bring to the tzaddik a spectrum of spiritual and mundane problems with the hope of receiving miracles or some kind of extraordinary insights. Many believe that the tzaddik has special knowledge of the purpose for an individual's life, and that they can thus draw information by accessing the deepest levels of a soul. Thus, members of the community tend to listen carefully to the admonitions and words of guidance from these *rebbe* (holy men).

Among the most famous tzaddiks of the last century were Aryeh Levin (1889–1969), Joel Teitelbaum (d. 1979), and Menachem Mendel Schneersohn (1904–1996). Rav Aryeh, as Aryeh Levin was popularly called, lived in Jerusalem in the days both prior to and just after the formation of Israel. He became particularly well known for his compassion and concern for the sick and those in prison. He regularly visited the local lepers' hospital and worked to refurbish its facilities. He also visited the central Jerusalem jail, which housed many political prisoners, and held prayer services there on the Sabbath.

Teitelbaum, the head of the Satmar Hassidic community, was best known for his opposition to Zionism and the secular state of Israel. He believed that the establishment of a religious state in Palestine would be accomplished by God and that the Jews should wait for God to accomplish that end. He saw the founders of the present state of Israel as wrongfully assuming God's prerogative.

Schneersohn was the leader of the Lubavitcher community, which under his leadership became the largest and most geographically widespread of the several Hassidic groups. It became the focus of Jewish messianic expectations toward the end of his life. As the level of devotion grew, many came to see him in unique terms. They believed he had supernatural powers of insight and that he could even alter the course of world events. Miracle stories were collected and circulated about Schneersohn. When he died, many believed that he would return, and the Lubavitcher community decided to wait for him before taking any further actions. In the years since his death, his followers have yet to name a new leader.

Sources:

Dresner, Samuel H. *The Zaddik*. New York: Schocken Books, 1974.

Jacobson, Simon. *Toward a Meaningful Life: The Wisdom of the Rebbe Menachem Mendel Schneerson*. New York: William Morrow, 1995.

Raz, Simcha. *A Tzaddik in Our Time: The Life of Rabbi Aryeh Levin*. Nanuet, NY: Feldheim, 1978.

V, W

VERONICA'S VEIL

According to a story included in the sixth-century apocryphal book the Acts of Pilate, as Christ was carrying the cross to his crucifixion a woman showed kindness to Him by wiping His face with a veil. As a result, an image of His face was impressed upon the cloth, much as it is on the SHROUD OF TURIN. Centuries later the woman came to be known as Veronica, a name that appears to derive from the Greek term "vera icona," or "true icon."

The story of Veronica and the veil entered into popular culture, and in 1300, on the occasion of the proclamation of the Holy Year, the reputed veil was placed on display in Rome and joined the list of the wonders of the city to be seen by pilgrims. Over the next centuries a variety of accounts were written about the veil. They reported that is was made of fine material and that the image was on both sides of the veil. In the image, Christ's eyes are open, and there is evidence of blood spots on His face.

A problem with the history of the veil arises during the reign of Pope Paul V (r. 1605–1621). In 1608, the chapel in Saint Peter's Basilica, where the veil was kept, was demolished as part of an extensive renovation. According to historical accounts, the veil was eventually placed inside a statue of Veronica that stands beside the main altar in Saint Peter's. Apart from this official history, however, several European churches claim to house the true veil. An interesting twist to the story was put forth in the summer of 2001 by Heinrich Pfeiffer, a professor of Christian art history at the Pontifical Gregorian University in Rome and an official advisor to the Papal Commission for the Cultural Heritage of the Church. Pfeiffer claimed that the veil that had been displayed for so many years in Rome had actually been stolen in 1608. Afterwards, it had found its way to the Sanctuary of the Sacred Face, a Capuchin friary in Manoppello about 150 miles from Rome.

The Manoppello cloth is approximately 6.5 by 9.5 inches and is kept in a silver ostensory. The cloth is quite thin, almost transparent. On it there is an image of a man with his eyes open and bearing signs of suffering, such as bruises, cuts, and blood on the face. According to one mid-seventeenth century account, the cloth at Manoppello came into the hands of a woman named Marzia Leonelli, who sold it to Donato Antonio de Fabritiis, who then donated it to the friary. Pfeiffer cited a variety of evidence that the veil had disappeared from Rome, including the action

In this 1955 photo of a reenactment, a child holds Veronica's Veil, which reveals Christ's image that was imprinted on the cloth when a woman kindly wiped Jesus' face before His crucifixion. *Getty Images*.

of Urban VIII (r. 1623–1644), who both prohibited further reproductions of Veronica's Veil and ordered the destruction of all existing copies.

Quite apart from Pfeiffer's work, the veil at Manoppello has been the subject of observations by scholars and scientists. Optical tests by Donato

Vittori, a professor at the University of Bari, pointed to the unusual nature of the image on the cloth, and subsequent tests have compared it to the Shroud of Turin. Many questions remain concerning both the object in Saint Peter's, which is not available for observation, and the veil at Manoppello. As answers to these questions are sought, both are venerated by devout Roman Catholics.

Sources:

Kuryluk, E. *Veronica and Her Veil: History, Symbolism and Structure of a "True" Image.* Oxford: Blackwell, 1991.

Nickell, Joe. *Looking for a Miracle.* Amherst, NY: Prometheus Books, 1998.

VIRGIN OF LAS LAJAS (COLOMBIA)

One of the most extraordinary stories involving the APPARITIONS OF THE VIRGIN MARY occurred in Colombia in the eighteenth century. A native woman named Maria Meneses de Quifiones was walking between the villages of Potosi and Ipiales one day in 1754. She took refuge from a storm in a cave at a place known as Las Lajas ("the rock slabs"). Some time later she again traversed the route, this time with her daughter Rosa, who could neither speak nor hear. While resting from the walk, Rosa pointed to the cave and spoke her first words, calling attention to a woman with a boy in her arms standing in the cave. A similar experience occurred the next time the two passed the cave sometime afterward. In each case, Maria saw nothing. Maria's neighbors heard her relate the story with some skepticism.

A few days later, Rosa disappeared. Unable to find her in the village, Maria went to the cave and found her in front of the lady and playing with the child, who had left his mother's arms. After seeing the woman, she and Rosa came to the cave on a number of occasions, adding candles and flowers. This activity continued sporadically until one day when the girl fell ill and died. In her anguish, Maria took the body of Rosa to the cave and pleaded with the Virgin to return her life. To her mother's astonishment, the girl was resurrected.

When the villagers went to the cave the next day, they found it decorated with the picture of the Lady. In the picture, Jesus is in Mary's arms. To either side is Saint Francis and Saint Dominic. Devotion to the location would develop slowly over the next two centuries, but eventually a good road was made to the area. A chapel was built in 1803, and later replaced by a larger church erected around the cave between 1916 and 1948.

As Maria's story became better known to the outside world, skeptics rightly noted that there was opportunity for Maria, or perhaps some of the Dominican priests who had been evangelizing the region in the eighteenth century, to paint the figures. Questions about the picture led to tests on the rocks during the construction of the church. Several bore holes were drilled into the rock to remove small bits of the picture. Geologists who examined the rock noted that there was no paint or other pigment on the surface. The colors making the picture are the natural colors of the rock. No other tests have since been conducted on the rock.

Sources:

Coral, Bravo, and Luis Alberto. *Historia de Nuestra Señora de Las Lajas.* Pasto, Colombia: Tipografía y Litografía Cabrera, 1980.

VISHNU'S FOOTPRINTS

Several places in India have become pilgrimage sites where reputed footprints of the god Vishnu are located. In Hindu mythology, the universe unfolds from Vishnu's dream, and whenever disorder enters the universe, the god, or one of his many incarnations, battles the forces of chaos. In these battles, he often steps on the earth, leaving his imprint.

Among the best known of these footprints is one found stamped on a rock called Dharmasila in a Vaishnava temple in Gaya, Bihar State. Gaya is an ancient pilgrimage site. The origin of the footprint is lost to history. Surrounded by a silver frame, it is commonly provided with offerings of food and flowers. Vishnu's footprint is regarded by believers as an axis mundi (world axis) for the region, and the temple as the meeting point of heaven, earth, and hell. Non-Hindus and, until the founding of the modern Indian state, people of lower castes, were barred from entering into the temple.

Another of Vishnu's footprints is found in Guwahati, the capital of the Indian state of Assam that is just south of Bhutan. According to the legend, Lord Vishnu was in the area to battle a demon king named Narakasur. In the midst of the battle, he left his footprint behind in a stone. As with other similar honored places, one day each year pilgrims flock to the site to make offerings to their ancestors; such offerings are meant to free the soul from the cycle of reincarnation.

In recent years, shifts in the course of the Brahmaputra River have created a problem. Vishnu's footprint, located on the eastern section of the Aswakranta temple in North Guwahati, is now under water for a period of time each year during the monsoon season. The wall is already showing signs of erosion, and temple officials fear that the river might soon obliterate the footprint.

Another footprint can be found in **HARDWAR** in northern India. It is found on the Hari-ki-Pairi ghat, which is one of the bathing steps used by pilgrims to make their way to the Ganges River. The ghat is located on the western bank of the Upper Ganges Canal. Yet another place cited as having a footprint of the deity is the Humayun Tomb in New Delhi.

Sources:

Singh, Rana P. B., John McKim Malville, and Anne L. Marshall. "Sacredscape and Manescape: A Study of Gaya, India." Posted at http://www.colorado.edu/ Conferences/pilgrimage/papers/Singh-3.html. Accessed March 31, 2007.

Wilson, H. H. *The Vishnu Purana: A System of Hindu Mythology and Tradition.* London: Trubner & Co., 1864.

WAILING WALL (ISRAEL)

The Wailing Wall is a 190-foot portion of the western retaining wall of the Temple Mount in Jerusalem. It is a traditional site used by Jews for prayer. The significance of both the Wailing Wall, and the larger Western Wall of which it is a part, requires some explanation.

In 70 CE, the Romans destroyed the Jewish Temple on the Temple Mount in Jerusalem that had been the center of Jewish ritual activity. From that time until 1967, Jews were denied access to the Temple Mount by a succession of Roman, Christian, and Muslim rulers. At the same time it was believed by many that the Shekinanh (Divine Presence) that had been focused in the holy of holies (the innermost part of the Temple) had not departed from the temple site. The only part of the temple that remained, and that was still accessible, was the Wailing Wall. It took on a new significance as Jews, who had been scattered throughout Europe and Asia after the temple's destruction, began to resettle Jerusalem in the sixteenth century.

The name "Wailing Wall" derives from the content of the prayers of those Jews who came to the Temple Wall and lamented the destruction of the temple. The term "Wailing Wall" is actually quite new, having come into use only in the twentieth century during the time of British rule of Palestine.

In the nineteenth century, the wall began to symbolize Jewish hopes for the reestablishment of a Jewish state that would include Jerusalem. In the preceding millennium, Muslims had established themselves on the Temple Mount. Then, in 1947, as the fighting that led to the founding of the state of Israel proceeded, Muslims were able to maintain their control of the Old City of Jerusalem. Following the cease-fire in 1948, Muslims denied Jews access to even the Wailing Wall. The situation did not change until 1967, when, during the Six-Day War the Old City was incorporated into modern Israel.

In the aftermath of the Six-Day War, the open space in front of the Wailing Wall was cleared and large numbers of Jews gathered daily at the

Also known simply as the Western Wall, the Wailing Wall is a ruin of the Jewish Temple in Jerusalem that was destroyed by the Roman Empire. In modern times it has become an important pilgrimage site, as well as a point of political contention between Jews and Palestinian Muslims. *Getty Images*.

site. Focus shifted from just the Wailing Wall to the entire retaining wall, now called the Western Wall. This entire wall has become the object of contention in the continued negotiations between Palestinians and Jews since 1967. Jewish believers gradually dropped the term "Wailing" Wall, saying that after 1967 the access to the site, not to mention the very existence of Israel, is a matter of celebration.

Today, the wall has become a major destination for travelers to Jerusalem. People may be found there almost 24 hours a day. It is especially crowded on the anniversary of the destruction of the temple (Tisha B'Av in the Jewish calendar) and on the several festival days mentioned in the

Torah and tied to pilgrimages to Jerusalem. It has also become a matter of contention between Orthodox Jews, who largely control religious matters in Israel, and the growing number of Reform and Conservative (and even secular) Jews. Orthodox Jews favor giving privileges to male believers so that only they have access to the wall. The dissenting groups want it open to all.

Those who do make it to the Western Wall will often leave written prayers in the openings in the wall, a symbol of their belief in the continuing Divine Presence localized in this spot.

Sources:

Kasher, Menahem. *The Western Wall*. New York: Judaica Press, 1975.

Ross, Mandy. *The Western Wall and Other Jewish Holy Places*. London: Heineman, 2003.

Urnstien, Shmuel. *Diary of the Wailing Wall*. Jerusalem: Urnstein Publushing House, 1968.

WEEPING STATUES AND ICONS

While accounts of statues and other representations of holy figures oozing blood or dripping tears have been reported throughout history, the number of cases has increased markedly since the twentieth century. These occur almost exclusively within Roman Catholic or Eastern Orthodox contexts in which believers value the importance of statues (Roman Catholic) and Icons (Eastern Orthodox).

One traditional account relates to the Icon of the Holy Virgin located at the Orthodox monastery at Nicula, Romania. Painted in 1681, it was given to the church in Nicula a few years later. Then, in February of 1694, a few visiting soldiers from Austria noticed the icon weeping tears that seemed to originate from the icon's eyes. They called attention to the phenomenon, and as the faithful gathered the icon continued to weep for 26 days. Accompanying the weeping was the healing of some sick people who came to the church and touched the icon. Eventually, the icon was placed in a new church built by the Austrian emperor in a nearby monastery. The icon remained on display there until 1948, when the suppression of religion by the Romanian Communist government led to its being hidden. It was finally located by authorities who kept it until after the Romanian Revolution. Returned to the monastery in 1992, the icon has not wept in recent years, but it is the subject of an annual special veneration every August 15.

More recent is the report of a bleeding picture of the Sacred Heart of Jesus owned by a Hispanic family in Austin, Texas. The picture they owned initially bled from the area around the heart in 1991. With the cooperation of their priest, copies of the picture were reproduced and circulated. Several days before the fifth anniversary of the blood's first appearance, a local visionary predicted that it would bleed again and that those who displayed copies of the picture in their homes would be protected and blessed.

In January 2003 reports surfaced of a statue of the Virgin Mary at a church in Caracas, Venezuela, that began to weep blood. The statue depicted Mary as she had appeared in apparitions at Montichiari-Fontanelle, Italy. A few weeks later, another statue of the Virgin at the same church (depicting Mary as she had appeared to the chief of the Coromoto people) began exuding delightful-smelling oils. This latter event was associated with the death of a woman who had been baptized a few days before. The statue has made the church a pilgrimage site where people may take away a piece of cloth that has been dipped in the oil from the statue.

In the modern world, such incidents cry out for scientific analysis of the substances that appear to come from these statues and pictures. Not only are the blood and tears subject to analysis, but the circumstances under which the weeping or bleeding began deserve investigation. In the cases of those pictures and statues that have been critically observed and tested, a significant number have been debunked. Substances other than blood and tears have been found to produce the phenomena, and mundane causes for the substances have been located.

Most cases have been ascribed to pious frauds. One relatively well-known case concerned the Abbé Vachère, a French Roman Catholic priest who resided at Mirebeau-en-Poitou early in the twentieth century. After he reported that blood had appeared on a picture he owned, as well as on a statue that sweated blood and on Eucharist wafers he had distributed, psychic researcher Everard Fielding investigated the situation. Fielding first had the "blood" analyzed and discovered that it was not blood at all. Several years later, after an investigation by the local bishop, the priest was excommunicated. Fielding conducted one further investigation of the bleeding picture, placing it in a sealed box. The next day he found

Weeping statues, such as this one of the Virgin Mary, have been reported at various times in churches all over the world. Most such incidents are not officially recognized by the Roman Catholic or Eastern Orthodox Churches, however. *Fortean Picture Library.*

that the box had been tampered with. In spite of repeated questioning of the "miracles" claimed by the priest, he continued to report additional phenomena throughout his life.

In recent years, church authorities have tended to withhold official recognition of bleeding statues, weeping icons, and the like because too many have proven to be either fraudulent or mundane. One exception concerns the bleeding statue in the convent at Akita, Japan. Here, in 1973, the Virgin Mary gave messages to Sister Agnes Katsuko Sasagawa. The wooden statue of Mary associated with the miracle was noted to have wept some 100 times over the next few years. It also perspired sweet-smelling substance,

and its right palm dripped blood. A medical professor analyzed the substances exuded by the statue and found them to be real blood, sweat, and tears. After several rather spectacular HEALING MIRACLES occurred, the local bishop investigated, and in 1984 he concluded the occurrences were, indeed, supernatural. That opinion was seconded four years later by Cardinal Joseph Ratzinger, who is now Pope Benedict XVI.

Sources:

Nickell, Joe. *Looking for a Miracle*. Amherst, NY: Prometheus Books, 1998.

"Weeping Statues." Posted at http://www.mcn.org/1/ Miracles/weeping.html. Accessed March 22, 2007.

"Weeping Statues and Icons." Posted at http://www. visionsofjesuschrist.com/weepingstatuesandicons.ht m. Accessed March 22, 2007.

Yashuda, Teigi. *Akita: The Tears and Message of Mary*. Trans. John Haffert. Ashbury, NJ: 101 Foundation, 1991.

WHIRLING DERVISHES

As Western travelers published accounts of the Ottoman Empire in the eighteenth and nineteenth centuries, among the most prominent images were of the Whirling Dervishes. Their ecstatic dance seemed unusual and novel to Western eyes, yet the dervishes contributed an important element to the development of Muslim culture, especially in Turkey, the center of the Ottoman Empire.

Those who did a little research learned that the dervishes were members of a semi-secret Sufi mystical religious community, the Mevlevi, founded by Mevlana Celaleddin (also known as Jelaluddin al-Rumi) in the thirteenth century. Rumi was born in what is now Tajikistan in 1207. His family left their homeland to escape the invading Mongols. Settling in what is present-day Turkey, he followed his father in becoming a scholar. Here he was also introduced to Sufism, the mystical branch of Islam. The key event in Rumi's life was the death of his teacher. He expressed his grief through poetry, music, and

Spinning rapidly in place, these Whirling Dervishes perform in Istanbul, Turkey. Dervishes achieve a higher state of conciousness in this fascinating Sufi tradition practiced by the Mevlevi. *Getty Images.*

dance. As he continued to write, the major theme of both his poetry and prose was the love of God. His death on December 17, 1273, is commemorated annually by members of the order.

Within the order, the whirling dance, and its accompanying music, is designed to induce a trancelike state in which the love of God becomes personal reality. Music is provided by a flute and various string and percussion instruments. Rumi's poetry is recited to the music. The chief drummer serves as the ceremonial conductor. The most obvious feature of the dance is the twirling. It is done in a precise manner around an imaginary axis that runs from the head to the stationary left foot. The right hand is lifted upward to receive God's love, which is transmitted down-

ward through the heart and to the earth via the left arm. The circular movement is prompted by the steady rise and fall of the right foot, which follows the beat of the music. Significant deviation in the method of spinning quickly produces mere dizziness rather than a heightened consciousness.

One of the order's sheikhs, Jelaluddin Loras (d. 1985), introduced the mystical teachings and practices of the Mevlevi to the West in the 1970s. An initial following was brought together in the Threshold Society, which in the 1990s relocated from Vermont to California. In 1990 the head of the society, Dr. Kabir Edmund Helminski, was the order's representative in North America. Among the activities of the society has been the sponsoring of events at which visiting members of the

THE ENCYCLOPEDIA OF RELIGIOUS PHENOMENA

order from Turkey allow the public to see and experience the dervish dance and music. The Mevlevi Order is headed today by a descendant of Rumi, Frank Hemdem Celebi, who succeeded his father in 1996.

Sources:

Friedlander, Shems. *The Whirling Dervishes*. Albany: SUNY Press, 1992.

Hatman, Talat Sait. *Mevlana Celaleddin Rumi and the Whirling Dervishes: Sufi Philosophy, Whirling Rituals, Poems of Ecstasy, Miniature Paintings*. Istanbul: Dost Yayinlari, 1983.

Helminski, Camille, and Kabir Edmund Helminski. *The Rumi Collection: An Anthology of Translations of Mevlana Jelaluddin Rumi*. Boston: Shambhala Classics, 2000.

Rumi, Jelaluddin Mevlana. *The Essential Rumi*. Trans. Coleman Barks with John Moyne. San Francisco: HarperSanFrancisco, 1995.

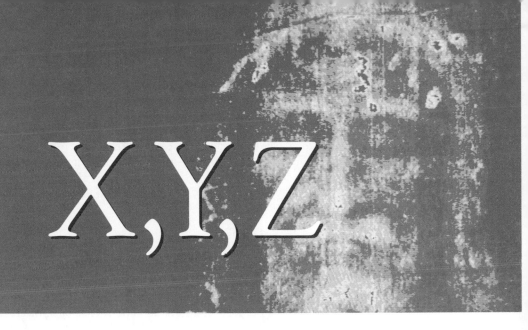

X, Y, Z

XENOGLOSSY

Xenoglossy, a term coined in the nineteenth century by French parapsychologist Charles Richet (1850–1935), is the ability to speak in a foreign language not previously learned by any normal process. This rare phenomenon is often confused with glossolalia, or SPEAKING IN TONGUES, the ecstatic language spoken by Pentecostals and Charismatics as they pray. Glossolalia is most commonly concerned with speaking a kind of proto-language derived from the language already spoken by individuals.

There are a variety of reports of xenoglossy throughout history. For example, the possessed nuns at the famous convent at Loudon were said to speak several languages, which was seen as an indication of their dealings with Satan. Then, during the nineteenth century, accounts of Spiritualist mediums speaking in foreign tongues while in a trance led researchers of the paranormal to investigate. John W. Edmonds (1799–1874), a prominent judge and early convert to Spiritualism, claimed in the 1850s that his daughter could converse with spirits in a variety of languages. The most well-documented case of xenoglossy, however, concerned Swiss medium HÉLÈNE SMITH (1861–1929), who falsely claimed to speak the Martian language.

The Spiritualists' paranormal claims relative to xenoglossy did not bear up well under the scrutiny of scientific researchers, however. Some cases were shown to actually be incidents of forgotten memory (e.g., a person spoke a forgotten language heard and stored in his or her early childhood memories), and other cases were found to be merely glossolalia. The claims of Spiritualists were supplemented early in the twentieth century by those of the Pentecostals, but these claims fared little better in proving xenoglossy was a real phenomenon.

In the twentieth century, many claims involving xenoglossy stemmed from studies into reincarnation in which a person supposedly recalled a language spoken in a previous life. The most impressive evidence for such cases was compiled by University of Virginia psychiatrist Ian Stevenson (b. 1918). Typical of Stevenson's cases is that of Uttara (b. 1941), a Marathi-speaking woman from India. In 1974 she began to speak Bengali after her personality was taken over by someone who called herself Sharada. Bengali was unknown to Uttara or to members of her family. Sharada claimed to have lived early in the nineteenth century. Besides speaking Bengali, Sharada could also write it.

Stevenson's research remains the most substantial body of evidence in support of xenoglossy to date. He has offered his research as further evidence of reincarnation, which is an important facet of many alternative religions. Critics assume that xenoglossy must have a more mundane explanation, though no one has yet produced a convincing refutation of Stevenson's work.

Sources:

Bozzano, Ernesto. *Polyglot Mediumship (Xenoglossy).* London: Rider, 1932.

Griffiths, John Gwyn. *Some Claims of Xenoglossy in the Ancient Languages.* Leiden: Brill, 1986.

Samarin, William J. *Tongues of Men and Angels: The Religious Language of Pentecostalism.* New York, The Macmillan Company, 1972.

Stevenson, Ian. *Unlearned Language: New Studies in Xenoglossy.* Charlottesville, VA: University Press of Virginia, 1984.

YANTRA

The yantra is a meditation/contemplation tool used by Shaktaite Hindus (those who follow Tantric teachings), who have passed their use to Vajrayana Buddhists, primarily in Tibet. A yantra is a geometric design whose elements carry specific meanings that can be multiplied by juxtaposition. The yantra is seen as helpful to the individual in focusing upon spiritual realities. Yantras may be identified with a specific deity and a contact point with the powers of that deity. After they are drawn, they may be memorized so that they can be recalled when needed.

Every yantra has a border that separates the design from its surrounding environment. The border thus functions as a magical circle to contain and focus cosmic energies. The geometric design is then made up of a combination of selected elements. Often in the center there is a dot (*bindu*), which represents the center of one's concentration. The dot is identified with the deity Shiva. Triangles symbolize Shakti, the female deity and her energy. The triangle (*trikona*) may point downward as a symbol of the female sexual organ (*yoni*), and hence the source of creation. It may point upward, too, as a symbol of the energy seen in fire.

Two triangles, one pointed upward and one downward, may be imposed on each other to form another symbol (*shatkona*), which looks like the Jewish Star of David or Solomon's Seal (Western Esotericism). In yantra symbolism, however, it represents the union of Shakta and Shiva in the act of creation. There are obvious sexual connotations here that may be taken literally or spiritually.

Circles (*chakras*) are reminiscent of the whirling energy of the chakras, the points of concentration of the subtle energy body, which Tantric Hindus and Vajrayana Buddhists believe mirrors the physical body. The square (*bhapura*) is a symbol of earth, just as the circle is a symbol of air. The square most often appears as the border of the yantra. More complex yantras may also include a Lotus (*padma*), which is a symbol of purity.

The most famous yantra (and among the most complicated) is the Shri Yantra. It consists of nine intersecting triangles, six concentric circles, and several lotus petals, all within a complex border pattern that represents four doors to the outside world. It is seen as a model of the cosmos, with a *bindu* in the center representing the Absolute from which the manifest world derives. The Shri Yantra is one connection between the yantras and the more complicated MANDALAS, which are used to represent the universe and often employ yantras as part of their design.

Believers will use yantras as part of their development toward higher states of consciousness, as well as for objects of worship (since they often symbolized and carry the power of a deity). They can be seen decorating the temples of Hindus and Buddhists (in the Tantric Vajrayana tradition).

Sources:

Bolton, N. J., and D. N. Macleod. "The Geometry of the Sri-Yantra." *Religion* 7, 1 (Spring 1977): 66–85.

Kulaichev, K. P. "Sriyantra and Its Mathematical Properties." *Indian Journal of History of Science* 19, 3 (1984): 279–292.

Mookerjee, Ajit. *Tantra Art: Its Philosophy and Physics.* New York: Ravi Kumar, 1971.

Rawson, Philip, *The Art of Tantra*. Greenwich, CT: New York Graphic Society, 1973.

YAZD (IRAN)

Yazd, a city in central Iran, has become the last stronghold of Zoroastrianism in the world. Once the dominant religion of ancient Persia, it was pushed aside by Islam in the seventh century. The faith started by Zoroaster (660–583 BCE) affirmed belief in the supreme creator god, Ahura Mazda, who gave the prophet teachings in the form of seventeen hymns, the Gathas, which constitute the Avesta scripture. Zoroastrians observe three central commands—Good Thoughts, Good Words, and Good Deeds.

In Yazd, some remnants of Zoroastrian life remain for the 30,000 believers who reside there. There are six holy shrines (called pirs or pirangah) in the Yazd region, most of which are located outside the city on the edge of the adjacent mountains. In the center of town is a temple that houses a sacred fire that purportedly has been burning since the fourth century CE. The temple stands in the midst of a garden and has a large half-eagle, half-man symbol on its roof. Fravahar is the representation of Ahura Mazda. (The primary mosque in the city now stands where there was once a Zoroastrian temple.)

For pilgrims to Yazd, the most important of the six pirs is Pir-e Sabz. This temple is also called Chek Chek after the sound of dripping water from the mountain stream that allows people to exist in the desert area. Each year, from June 14 to 18, this temple is the sight of the annual festival that attracts Zoroastrians from across the country (over 100,000 still reside in Iran). Generally, pilgrims journeying to Pir-e Sabz will abandon their automobiles as soon as they see the shrine and continue from that point by foot.

Zoroastrians have unique funerary practices that stem from a belief in the purity of the four basic elements—earth, air, fire, and water. They do not bury their dead because this would contaminate the earth, and they do not practice cre-mation so as not to pollute the air. In the past, they erected "towers of silence," where the flesh of the dead was consumed by vultures. This practice continued at Yazd until 1970, when it was outlawed in reaction to complaints from the city's inhabitants that bits and pieces of human bodies were falling from the sky as vultures dropped them. Two towers of silence still exist near Chek Chek, but they are no longer in use.

As a result of the legal changes, the species of vultures that inhabited the towers of silence have become extinct, and Zoroastrians now bury their dead in cement-lined graves to prevent contamination of the earth.

Sources:

Boyce, Mary. *A Persian Stronghold of Zoroastriansim*. Oxford: Clarendon Press, 1977.

Mehrshahi, Daryoush. "Zoroastrian Sacred Sites." *FEZANA Journal* (Fall 1999): 55–57. Posted at http://www.sacredsites.com/middle_east/iran/zoroastrian.htm. Accessed March 31, 2007.

YOGANANDA, PARAMAHANSA (1893–1952)

Paramahansa Yogananda, the most prominent of the early Hindu teachers to reside in America, was born Mukunda Lal Ghosh on January 5, 1893, in Gorakhpur, India. While still a teenager, he became the disciple of Swami Sri Yukteswar Giri. He also attended Calcutta University from which he graduated in 1915. He afterward took the vows of a sanyassin (the renounced life) and emerged as Swami Yogananda ("the bliss of yoga").

His rather mundane life changed radically in 1920, when he was invited to attend an interfaith gathering sponsored by the American Unitarian Association in Boston, Massachusetts. Following the conference, he decided to remain in America, where he founded what was soon to be known as the Self-Realization Fellowship (SRF). At the time only one other Hindu organization with a national outreach, the Vedanta Society, was operating in North America.

A Zoroastrian woman prays at the Chek Chek temple in the city of Yazd, Iran, the last stronghold of people of this ancient monotheistic faith. *AFP/Getty Images*.

THE ENCYCLOPEDIA OF RELIGIOUS PHENOMENA

In 1925 he settled in Los Angeles, which would remain his base of operations for the next segment of his life. For those who sought his guidance, he created a mail-order course teaching that was called kriya yoga. The disciplines of kriya yoga, the secrets of which are restricted to initiated disciples, were designed to bring followers into an enlightened spiritual state.

Through the mid-1930s, Yogananda concentrated on travel, lecturing, and personal contact with members and potential members. However, in the late 1930s he withdrew from most of his public activities and concentrated on writing. The most notable book from these later years was *Autobiography of a Yogi,* which was released in 1946. Unique in its day as the story of an American spiritual teacher, it also introduced the world to the enigmatic figure known as **BABAJI**, who has subsequently become the primary focus of several newer spiritual groups.

Yogananda died on March 7, 1952, but he had one remaining surprise left for his disciples. His body apparently refused to exhibit any signs of decay. In a statement issued by Harry Rowe, the director of Forest Lawn Memorial-Park: "The absence of any visual signs of decay in the dead body of Paramahansa Yogananda offers the most extraordinary case in our experience.... No physical disintegration was visible even twenty days after death.... No indication of mould was visible on his skin, and no visible desiccation (drying up) took place in the bodily tissues. This state of perfect preservation of a body is, so far as we know from mortuary annals, an unparalleled one.... At the time of receiving Yogananda's body, the mortuary personnel expected to observe, through the glass lid of the casket, the usual progressive signs of bodily decay. Our astonishment increased day after day without bringing any visible change in the body under observation. Yogananda's body was apparently in a phenomenal state of immutability.... No odour of decay emanated from his body at any time.... The physical appearance of Yogananda on March 27th, just before the bronze cover of the casket was put into position,

was the same as it had been on March 7th." Yogananda was subsequently buried at Forest Lawn in the Los Angeles suburb of Glendale.

Critics of Yogananda's followers point out that on March 8 the swami was embalmed and that it is not unusual for a body to remain preserved for several months after such treatment. There is, of course, no indication as to how long Yogananda's body might have remained in its incorruptible state.

Regardless of the controversy concerning his body, Yogananda assumed a special role in the latter decades of the twentieth century as Hinduism established itself more substantively in the United States. Along with Swami Vivekananda (1863–1902), the founder of the Vedanta Society, he is revered by American Hindus as a pioneer of their faith in the West. In addition, several groups have emerged from the SRF that also teach kriya yoga. Within this context, vigorous controversy has arisen over the particular claims of the SRF as opposed to the general claims of the larger Hindu community over Yogananda's legacy.

Sources:

Lal Ghosh, Sananda. *Mejda: The Family and the Early Life of Paramahansa Yogananda.* Los Angeles, CA: Self Realization Fellowship, 1980.

Paramahansa Yogananda in Memoriam, Personal Accounts of the Masters Final Days. Los Angeles: Self-Realization Fellowship, 1997.

Yogananda, Paramahansa. *Autobiography of a Yogi.* Los Angeles: Self Realization Fellowship, 1946.

ZIMBABWE

When Europeans began to theorize about the origin of Great Zimbabwe, the large medieval city they first discovered in 1871, racist presumptions prevented them from ascribing its construction to the ancestors of the local inhabitants. It was not until the 1930s that more thorough archeological investigation proved that the Shona, a Bantu people whose presence in the area dated back to fifth century CE, had constructed the complex of buildings spread over some 1,800 acres. Construction of the city appears to have begun around 1100 CE, and its expansion and habitation continued through the mid-fifteenth century.

Great Zimbabwe, located on the plains between the Limpopo and Zambezi rivers, constitutes the largest prehistoric stone structures in sub-Saharan Africa. Its site, which is relatively distant from a major river, was constructed because of its proximity to substantial gold deposits and along preexisting trade routes. Though water was a concern, grasslands for cattle and wildlife were abundant. The city flourished for more than three centuries. Artifacts from as far away as China and Persia have been unearthed there, as well as jewelry and products from its iron forge, which was part of its contribution to the regional economy.

At its height, Great Zimbabwe would have been home to about 20,000 people, most of whom lived in the upper and lower parts of the site now called the Hill Complex and the Valley Complex. Those of higher status, including the religious functionaries, lived on the hillside, while the workers and herdsmen lived in the valley. However, much of the interest in Great Zimbabwe is directed toward its third component, the Great Enclosure. The 32-foot-high wall of the enclosure is all the more impressive because it was constructed without mortar. It has a circumference of more than 800 feet. Inside one can find brick altar-like structures, interior walls, pillars, and stone monoliths.

Research into the religious and other uses of the Great Enclosure has been hampered by modern alterations of various features, including some of the pillars, which have been moved by vandals, people using the stones for their own buildings, and careless visitors. In spite of these problems, it can be seen by the architecture that the builders had some knowledge of astronomy. For example, a pattern on the southeast corner of the outer wall appears to be a marker of the summer solstice, and a large interior passageway seems positioned to align with the Milky Way during the summer sol-stice. (The Milky Way played a prominent role in the worldview of the local people.) Other markers were placed in such a way as to measure the coming of the spring and fall equinoxes.

Great Zimbabwe was abandoned in the middle of the fifteenth century, probably because the inhabitants exhausted the local grassland and timber resources. Without written records, the real reasons may never be known. Further archeological work in the region nevertheless holds promise for future revelations. In 1986, UNESCO named Great Zimbabwe a world heritage site.

Sources:

Barnes-Svarney, Patricia. *Zimbabwe*. Philadelphia: Chelsea House Publishers, 1999.

Garlake, Peter S. *Kingdoms of Africa*. Oxford: Elsevier Publishing, 1978.

Vogel, Joseph O. *Great Zimbabwe: The Iron Age in South Central Africa*. New York: Garland Publishing, 1994.

ZION (ILLINOIS)

Zion, Illinois, a town located just south of the Wisconsin-Illinois border, was the brain child of John Alexander Dowie (1847–1907). Born in Scotland, he moved with his parents to Australia when he was 13. A spiritual healing when he was 16 helped shape his life. He felt himself called to the ministry and spent three years studying at the seminary of the free Church of Scotland. In 1872 he became a Congregational minister. Six years later he left his pastorate in Scotland to become an itinerant evangelist.

Dowie settled in Melbourne in 1882 and built a large tabernacle. He also organized the International Divine Healing Association, which was indicative of the central role healing had taken in his ministry. In 1988 he left Australia to settle in Chicago. To accommodate those who came to him for healing, he opened a set of Healing Homes in the city. In 1894 he founded the periodical *Leaves of Healing*.

In 1895 he organized a new denomination, the Christian Catholic Apostolic Church, and for the next few years he operated out of a large tabernacle in Chicago. Dowie also nurtured a dream of a place where he could be free of criticism from his fellow ministers concerning his healing practices. He wanted to encourage people to lead healthful Christian lives that included refraining from eating pork; he also objected to memberships in secret societies. Thus it was that on New Year's Eve 1899 members of his church gathered for an all-night service during which he announced plans for the city of Zion. The city was formally dedicated in the summer of 1901. Dowie hired a professional city planner named Burton J. Ashley to design Zion.

Dominating the new city was Zion Tabernacle, which had seating for 8,000 people. Visitors could find accommodations at the 300-room Elijah Hospice. The streets were given names drawn from the Bible, with the exception of two, Caledonia and Edina, which were named for places in Dowie's native Scotland. The Tabernacle stood adjacent to a 200-acre park

Residents of Zion were overwhelmingly associated with Dowie's church. The community, though numbering only in the thousands, would have a dramatic effect on the development of free-church Protestantism. Missionaries were sent out from Zion to travel around the world. The Zionites, in fact, were responsible for establishing a strong Pentecostal movement in South Africa.

A crisis came to Zion in 1906, when an ill Dowie turned over the church and community to his successor, Wilbur Glenn Voliva (1870–1942). Voliva found the community in complete financial disorder. The church had to file for bankruptcy and was held in receivership for the next 15 years. Voliva is credited for its recovery. However, outside of Zion, Voliva is most remembered as an exponent of flat-earth theories. In 1931 he made a trip around the world in an effort to convince others of his theories. Toward the end of his leadership Voliva lost power and influence; in 1935 all of his candidates for city offices were defeated in the Zion elections. Then, in 1937, the Tabernacle and the church's radio station were both lost in a fire. The community rebuilt and carried on.

Though the city of Zion never approached the 200,000 residents its founder wanted, it has continued as a viable community through the years. It gradually secularized and became more religiously diverse, though considerable evidence of its early character remains. The Christian Catholic Apostolic Church went through several name changes, too, and is now known as the Christ Community Church. Visitors may still soak up some of the flavor of the town's unique heritage, and it has become a popular stop for those travelers between Chicago and Milwaukee.

Sources:

Cook, Philip L. *Zion City, Illinois: Twentieth-Century Utopia.* Syracuse, NY: Syracuse University Press, 1996.

Dowie, John Alexander. *The Sermons of John Alexander Dowie, Champion of the Faith.* Comp. Gordon Lindsay. Dallas, TX: Christ for the Nations, Inc., 1987.

Lindsay, Gordon. *The Life of John Alexander Dowie: A Story of Trial Tragedies and Triumphs.* Dallas, TX: The Voice of Healing Publishing Company, 1951.

INDEX

Notes: **Boldface** type indicates the page numbers of main entries; (ill.) indicates photos and illustrations.

A

Abadir, Shaykh, 140
Abbas, 181
Abbey, Heiligenkreuz (Austria), 144
Abbey of Our Lady of Mount Zion, 328
Abbey of Zion, 76
Abdu'l-Baha, 26, 27
Abgar, King, 159
Abhishiktananda, 16
Abraham, 1, 26, 138, 171, 220
Adam, 6
Adefunmi I, 248
Aderemi, Ooni Adesoji, 248
Adi Granth, 4
Adisesha, 335
Aesclapius, 340
African Americans, 248
African Theological Archministry, 248
Agapoa, Tony, 259
Agritius, Bishop, 149
Ahkon Norbu Lhamo, 345
Ahmad Gran, 140
Ahmad, Mirza Ghulam, 336–37
Ahmad, Seyyed, 182
Ahmadiyyas, 336
Ahura Mazda, 361
Aidan, Saint, 161
Airaudi, Oberto, 79
Ajatsatni, 263
Akal Takht, 4
Akiva, Rabbi, 147
Alacoque, Margaret Mary, 281
Alamo, 60

Alamo Christian Foundation, 63
Al-Aqsa Mosque (Jerusalem), 1–2, 2
  (ill.), 326–27
Alba, 161
Albertus, Frater, 3
Alchemy, 2–3
Alexander III, Pope, 293
Alfonso I, King, 105
Alfonso II, King, 105
Alfonso VI, King, 105
Ali ibn Abi Talib, 5, 181
Ali Mohammad, 26
Al-Isra wa Al-Mirah, 1
Allah, 1, 139, 219
Allen, A. A., 42
Alleyne, 19
Alper, Frank, 69
Alphonse II, King, 293
Altman, Rochelle, 168
Altyn Khan, 77
Amar Das, Guru, 3–4
Ambrose, Saint, 145
Ameda Buddha, 186
American Humanist Association
  (AHA), 60
American International Reiki Associa-
  tion, 266
American Reiki Association, 266
Amica Master Institute of Color Aware-
  ness (AMICA), 58
Amida Buddha, 180
Amrita, 189, 272
Amritsar (India), 3–4
Amulets, 4–5, 324

An Najaf (Iraq), 4–5
Ananda, 257
Ananias, 199
Ancient and Mystical Order Rosae Cru-
  cis (AMORC), 76, 234–35
Ancient astronaut, 307–8
André, Brother, 286–87
Andrea, Valentin, 76
Andriveau, Sister Appoline, 297
Angad Devju, Guru, 4
Angel of Mons, 6–7, 7 (ill.)
Angels, 6–7, 7 (ill.), 117
Angels, guardian, 133–35, 134 (ill.)
Anne of Austria, 9
Anne, Saint, 7–9, 8 (ill.), 55
Anthony (hermit), 287
Apollo, 84, 85, 86
Apparitions, 88, 185, 280
Apparitions of the Virgin Mary, 9–12,
  10 (ill.). *See also* Apparitions
    Beauraing/Banneux (Belgium),
      27–28
    Cartago (Costa Rica), 50
    Conyers, Georgia, 63–64
    ecstasy, 93–94
    Ecuador, 241
    Fatima (Portugal), 107–9
    Garabandal (Spain), 117
    La Salette (France), 196–98, 197 (ill.)
    Lourdes (France), 204–5, 205 (ill.)
    Mary's House (England), 214–15
    Medjugorje (Bosnia-Herzegovina),
      221–22, 223 (ill.)
    Miraculous Medal, 227–28

THE ENCYCLOPEDIA OF RELIGIOUS PHENOMENA

THE ENCYCLOPEDIA OF RELIGIOUS PHENOMENA

THE ENCYCLOPEDIA OF RELIGIOUS PHENOMENA